CITY of the GREAT KING

Fair in situation, the joy of the whole earth . . .
the city of the great King.

PSALM 48:3

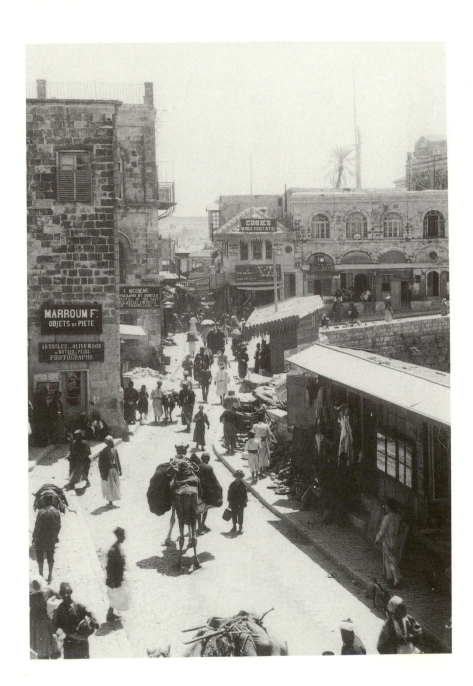

CITY of the GREAT KING

Jerusalem from David to the Present

Edited by NITZA ROSOVSKY

HARVARD UNIVERSITY PRESS · Cambridge, Massachusetts, and London, England · 1996

Copyright © 1996 by the President and Fellows of Harvard College
All rights reserved
Printed in the United States of America

Design by Marianne Perlak

Library of Congress Cataloging-in-Publication Data

City of the great king : Jerusalem from David to the present / edited
by Nitza Rosovsky.
    p. cm.
  Includes bibliographical references and index.
  ISBN 0-674-13190-8 (alk. paper)
   1. Jerusalem—History. 2. Jerusalem—Description and travel.
 3. Jerusalem in Judaism. 4. Jerusalem in Christianity.
 5. Jerusalem in Islam. I. Rosovsky, Nitza.
  DS109.9.C58 1996
956.94'42—dc20

95-20941
CIP

Contents

THE EARTHLY CITY

THE CITY IN LITERATURE, ART, AND ARCHITECTURE

Chronology

The First Commonwealth — ca. 1004–586 BCE

- King David captures Jerusalem from the Jebusites and makes the city his capital — ca. 1004
- King Solomon begins to build the Temple — ca. 960
- The kingdom is divided between Israel in the north and Judah in the south — 928
- The northern kingdom falls to the Assyrians — 722
- Sennacherib besieges Jerusalem during the reign of King Hezekia — 701
- Nebuchadnezzar destroys the city and the Temple and exiles the inhabitants to Babylon — 586

The Second Commonwealth — 538 BCE–70 CE

- Cyrus allows the Jews to return to Jerusalem and rebuild the Temple — 538
- The Second Temple is built under Zerubbabel — 520
- Following Ezra, Nehemiah goes to Jerusalem and repairs the city walls — 445
- Alexander the Great conquers the country — 332
- Ptolemy captures Jerusalem — 313

Early Arab Period

- Jerusalem surrenders to the armies of Caliph Umar   638
- Abd al-Malik builds the Dome of the Rock   691
- Al-Aqsa Mosque is completed by al-Walid al-Malik   715
- Power shifts from the Umayyads of Damascus to the
  Abbasids of Baghdad; Abbasids continue to enhance
  Jerusalem   750
- Fatimid conquest is soon followed by the destruction
  of churches and synagogues   969
- Seljuks devastate the city   1071

Crusader Period   1099–1187

- Crusaders conquer the city, slaughter Muslims and
  Jews   1099
- The Church of the Holy Sepulchre is rebuilt   1149

Ayyubid and Mamluk Period   1187–1517

- Saladin captures the city   1187
- Treaty returns Jerusalem to the Crusaders   1229
- City is again in Muslim hands   1244
- Mamluks rule Jerusalem from Cairo   1260
- The Ramban (Nachmanides) establish the Ramban
  Synagogue   1267
- Acre, the last Crusader stronghold in the Holy Land,
  is captured by the Mamluks   1291
- Jews arrive in Jerusalem following the Spanish Exile   1492

Ottoman Period   1517–1917

- Palestine and Jerusalem become part of the Ottoman
  Empire   1517
- Suleiman the Magnificent rebuilds the city wall   1538

- Napoleon invades Palestine but does not try to
  conquer Jerusalem — 1799
- Mohammed Ali of Egypt rules the country for nine
  years — 1831
- Consecration of Christ Church, the first Protestant
  church in the Near East — 1849
- After the Crimean War, Turkey starts to liberalize
  policies regarding aliens — 1856
- Jerusalem begins to expand beyond the Old City — 1860
- Road from Jaffa to Jerusalem is improved; several
  royal dignitaries visit the city in connection with the
  opening of the Suez Canal — 1869
- Railroad connects the city to the coast — 1892

British Mandate Period 1917–1948

- Jerusalem surrenders to General Allenby — 1917
- The Mandate for Palestine is conferred on Britain — 1920
- Arab-Jewish disturbances — 1921–1929 and 1936–1939
- Lord Peel's commission proposes the partition of
  Palestine and limiting Jewish immigration — 1937
- The United Nations votes to create a Jewish and an
  Arab state in Palestine — 1947
- The British withdraw from Palestine; the country is
  invaded by armies from neighboring states; the State
  of Israel is declared on May 14 — 1948

The Divided City 1948–1967

- Cease-fire finds the city divided; Jerusalem is
  proclaimed the capital of Israel; East Jerusalem is
  ruled by Jordan — 1949
- The Sinai Campaign — 1956

Since 1967

Introduction

NITZA ROSOVSKY

Some three thousand years ago King David captured Jerusalem from the Jebusites and made the city his capital. A few years later, when Solomon built the Temple there, Jerusalem became the spiritual center of the Jewish people as well as their seat of government. In the following three millennia, many battles were fought over Jerusalem, some because of the country's strategic location as a bridge between continents, most others because Judaism, Christianity, and Islam claimed the Holy City as their own.

While *City of the Great King: Jerusalem from David to the Present* celebrates the city and not the king, their names remain forever entwined. Like the world's most complex city, David's character was multifaceted as well. The man Dante called "Israel's sweet harpist" and Byron, "the loved of heaven" was a tender of sheep, yet a brave warrior. A leader of men, he was also a poet, a musician whose harp assuaged King Saul's black despair. He was a man with many wives, yet he coveted Bathsheba and sent her husband to a certain death. He brought the Ark of the Lord to Jerusalem and purchased the threshing-floor from Arawnah the Jebusite, the site of the Temple to be. Yet God withheld from the king the privilege of building the Temple and the honor fell to Solomon, David and Bathsheba's son.

David's name still appears in the headlines. In the summer of 1993, a segment of a ninth-century BCE stela was found in Tel Dan, in the northern Galilee, with an inscription which included the words *"beit david,"* "the house of David," the earliest known mention of the king

1

outside the Bible (see Chapter 1, Figure 1). (While *beit david* could also be read as a place name, the stela commemorates a military victory over a "king of Israel." Thus a reference to "the House of David" seems logical, as scholars Avraham Biran and Joseph Naveh have suggested.)

In December 1994 the Israeli government barely avoided a no-confidence motion after Foreign Minister Shimon Peres remarked in the Knesset that he did not approve of everything David had done either "on the ground or on the roof," referring to the king's military conquests and the Bathsheba affair. Chaos ensued as the Orthodox accused the minister of insulting not only "the sweet singer of Israel" but also the entire Jewish people in all generations, and only an apology from Peres averted the motion. (One rabbinic justification of the king's rash behavior is the claim that in biblical times, before leaving for battle, it was customary for men to give their wives a conditional divorce, and that therefore Bathsheba technically was not married to Uriah when she conceived David's child.) Some members of Jerusalem's City Council expressed opposition to the upcoming trimillennial celebrations of "Jerusalem 3000," fearing lest a planned musical misinterpret David's lament when Jonathan was killed by the Philistines: "Wonderful was thy love to me, passing the love of women."

Just as the life of David, a king handpicked by God, was filled with light and shadows, so is the history of Jerusalem, "the joy of the whole world." As the City of David is about to enter its fourth millennium, the cynics among us might recognize the Lord's sense of irony as He seems to create another major millennial crisis. A thousand years after David, a new religion was born in Jerusalem, and soon the city itself was destroyed by the Romans. One thousand years later, the world shook again as the mighty forces of Christianity and Islam fought over the Holy City in a battle that is as yet unresolved. And now, three thousand years after David established his royal city, the tender shoots of peace are periodically threatened as Israelis and Palestinians struggle over the future of Jerusalem.

What makes Jerusalem's soil so desirable? To begin with, it is a beautiful city. "Mountains are about Jerusalem," wrote the psalmist, rock-strewn mountains from which the city emerges, a city built of stone—reddish, gray, white. Winter rains briefly color the mountains green, and, year round, manmade parks soften the harsh cityscape.

When the sun rises over the Mount of Olives, it first touches the city's easternmost monument, the Dome of the Rock with its white marble and blue-tiled walls and its gold-covered dome. Other domes, stone cupolas, red tile roofs, steeples, turrets, and minarets soon stand out against the stark blue sky, creating deep shadows. In the evening the sun's last rays are reflected on the city walls and in a thousand window panes. Jerusalem turns golden.

In the heart of Jerusalem lies the Old City, surrounded by a sixteenth-century crenelated wall built by the Turks over ancient foundations from the days of the Hasmoneans and Herod the Great. Seven gates lead into the Old City; the eighth, the Golden Gate, is sealed, awaiting—according to Jewish tradition—the arrival of the Messiah. The Old City retains the quadrilateral shape and road network of a Roman colony, dating back to 135 CE, when Emperor Hadrian rebuilt the city after the futile Bar Kochba revolt. The north-to-south axis, the *cardo*, and the west-to-east thoroughfare, the *decumanus*, bisect the city and create four quarters of unequal size—Muslim, Christian, Armenian, and Jewish. The Temple Mount—the Haram al-Sharif—occupies a sixth of the Old City. The circumference of the Old City Wall is 4,018 meters, or about two and a half miles. The city stands 725 to 790 meters (2,415 to 2,630 feet) above sea level.

The narrow stone-paved alleys of the Old City wind their way between tall, blank walls. Windows face inner courtyards to provide privacy and protection. In a city where water has always been in short supply, flowerpots—often mere tin cans—provide a spot of color: jasmine, marigolds, the ubiquitous geranium. Covered bazaars lie at the center of the Old City, where goods spill over into the narrow lanes, goods delivered by handcarts and donkeys in the carless inner city. The sacred and the profane intermingle in the four quarters, ordinary houses with holy places. Churches, monasteries, hospices, and the residences of the patriarchs in the Christian and Armenian quarters; synagogues and yeshivahs in the Jewish Quarter; mosques and madrasas (religious schools) in the Muslim Quarter. The sound of church bells and *muazzins'* calls to prayer from the minarets intermingle with the voices pouring out of synagogue windows.

One dimension of the dense urban fabric of the Old City is most clearly pronounced in the Jewish Quarter, because of the circumstances created by two wars. While it was assumed for centuries that ancient archaeological treasures lay beneath the streets and houses of the Old City, it was not possible to excavate a living city. But the Jewish Quarter was badly damaged in 1948 during Israel's War of Independence, and when the Israelis returned in 1967 and began to reconstruct the quarter, building sites first had to be examined by archaeologists, to comply with a law protecting antiquities. And thus began Jerusalem's golden age of archaeology.

Now, within a few hundred square feet, the ancient architectural texture of the Holy City blends in with old and new construction, and Jerusalem's history can be read through layers of archaeological remains. There is King Hezekiah's Broad Wall, built in 701 BCE, and an Israelite tower that failed to protect the city from the Babylonians in 586 BCE, with traces of the the soot and ashes from the fire which consumed the city still in evidence. Walls of Hasmonean fortifications from the second century BCE lie directly underneath the Byzantine *cardo*. Once a broad arcaded street lined with shops, the *cardo* was excavated and partially restored, and now it features modern stores that, like the ancient ones, cater to pilgrims and tourists alike.

A rebuilt arch of the Hurvah Synagogue, destroyed in 1948, stands next to the Ramban Synagogue, established by Nachmanides in 1267 and reconsecrated in 1967. Above it looms the minaret of the Sidi Umar Mosque, built in 1473. Nearby are the foundations and apses of the Crusader Church of St. Mary of the German Knights, which in turn abuts the Herodian Quarter, an underground site-museum which contains mosaic floors, fresco-covered walls, and numerous baths and other water installations of six opulent residences, including what was probably the mansion of the high priest in the days of the Second Temple. An apse and the barrel vaults of the Nea Church—the "New" Church built in honor of the Virgin Mary by Emperor Justinian in 543—and part of an Ayyubid tower from the thirteenth century are within the Garden of Redemption, planted in memory of the six million Jews exterminated by the Nazis.

East of the Jewish Quarter, around the western and southern walls of the Temple Mount platform—today the Haram al-Sharif—a monumental stairway that led to the Second Temple was uncovered, as was an early eighth-century Abbasid palace complex, a contemporary of al-Aqsa Mosque. South of the Temple Mount, by the Gihon Spring, lay the City of David. It clung to the steep slope, as does the village of Siloam across the Kedron, or Jehoshaphat Valley, where the roof of one house often serves as the terrace of the house above it.

Obviously, Jerusalem's true uniqueness does not stem from its beauty or its relics but rather from its spiritual meaning. Jews, Christians, and Muslims regard it as the threshold to heaven, or, in the words of Joseph Dan, "the touching point between the divine and the earthly, the place where heaven and earth meet." There, at the End of Days, the nations will be judged at the Valley of Jehoshaphat—"the Lord judges," in Hebrew—and "the Lord shall roar from Zion and utter His voice from Jerusalem" (Joel 4:16). And then peace shall reign: "And the wolf and the lamb shall feed together, And the lion shall eat straw like the ox" (Isaiah 65:25).

One may speak to God anywhere, but many think that He can hear them best from Jerusalem. The problem begins when each believer claims to hear a different answer, when each thinks God is speaking to him or her alone, when each claims to know best the desires of the Lord. (So certain are those who hear His voice that it is not surprising to learn of a recently identified condition known as the "Jerusalem syndrome." It seems to affect pilgrims—mostly American Protestants. These visitors develop messianic delusions and begin preaching, shouting, and behaving strangely, each believing him or herself to be John the Baptist, Mary, or even Jesus. After a few days of treatment in a quiet hospital, they usually return to normal.)

According to theologian Krister Stendahl, holiness cannot be divided, and therefore one cannot say that the city is "holiest" to any one group. Yet the city has played different roles in the spiritual development and the history of the three monotheistic religions.

For Christianity, the holiness of the city derives from the events in the life of Jesus that took place there. Had the Crucifixion and Resurrection occurred in Jericho, it would have become a city holy to Christianity. In fact, in its early days, Christianity held conflicting views about the city condemned by Jesus, cursed because of the circumstances that led to his death. As far as the Church fathers were concerned, the earthly Jerusalem was doomed and was to be replaced by the heavenly Jerusalem. Yet for the simple people, physical contact with the places where Jesus walked, what Robert Wilken calls "the need to touch," made Jerusalem a city of pilgrimage, a Holy City to Christianity. It was only a millennium after the Crucifixion, when a deranged caliph attacked the Holy Sepulchre, that the issue of physical repossession of the city arose. Eventually, "liberating Jerusalem from the Muhammadan yoke" became the rallying call to battle of the Crusaders. Now, since access to and ownership of their holy places remain secure, Christians are out of the political contest for Jerusalem.

Islam's spiritual attachment to the city stems from Sura 17 in the Koran which describes the Prophet Muhammad's Night Journey from Mecca to al-Masjid al-Aqsa, the "furthest shrine," whence he ascended to heaven. Was Jerusalem, which is not mentioned by name in the Koran, the Prophet's destination? Was it the "furthest shrine"? The answer is yes, since the same sura refers to Moses, to whom God had given "the Book" to guide the Israelites; but twice they committed "evil in the land," and twice they were punished by armies that destroyed al-Masjid, obviously the Israelites' Temple. Jerusalem was also the first kibla, the first direction of prayer Prophet Muhammad faced, before the Kaaba in Mecca became Islam's final kibla.

After the Muslims lost Jerusalem to the Crusaders, the need to physically possess it again became very important. When, nearly a century later, Saladin recaptured Jerusalem, he was seen as restoring the dignity of Islam. Yet Jerusalem never served as a Muslim capital, either between 638 and 1099, or between 1187 and 1917. Early on, the Abbasids founded Ramla and designated it the capital of the district of Palestine. Over the centuries, various Muslim empires ruled the country and the city from Damascus, Baghdad, Cairo, and Constantinople. More recently, when East Jerusalem and the West Bank were under the Jordanians, Amman remained the Hashamite capital while the Holy City stagnated.

Jews were barred from Jerusalem for nearly six centuries after the end of the Second Commonwealth and the destruction of the Temple in 70 CE. They were forbidden first by the Romans and then by the Christians to live in the city, and were rarely allowed to visit. Yet for two millennia, the certainty that some day they would return to the Holy City bound them together with silken cords as one people, one nation. Even when they were dispersed to the four corners of the earth, they longed for Jerusalem. Pilgrimage to the city never really stopped, and as soon as life became somewhat more bearable, they began to return to live there. And while they fared better under Islam than under Christianity, they remained second-class citizens whose life and livelihood were never really secure, depending on the mood of the greater populace and the whims of the ruler.

In 1800, the city's population numbered 9,000. Today more than half a million people live in Jerusalem. It is hard to believe that before 1860 only a few buildings stood outside the Old City Wall. Yet despite Jerusalem's phenomenal growth, and with few outstanding violations, construction around the city maintained a low profile, and to this day the city maintains a feeling of closeness to the rocky Judean hills that surround the sprawling metropolis. Since 1967 expansion has taken on an added political dimension, and new Jewish housing projects now form a ring around the city to insure that it stays undivided. In the process, land has often been expropriated from Muslim owners against their will, while new Arab construction has come to a near halt.

Jews have been the majority in the city since the 1860s, and the city has now been Israel's capital for nearly half a century. With the exception of the Crusader period, the only time when kings ruled from Jerusalem—when the city was the capital of a nation—was during the First and Second Jewish Commonwealths.

A personal note. Although I live elsewhere now, I will always think of myself as a Jerusalemite. I share the sentiments of Sir Ronald Storrs after he left the city, where he had served as the British military governor (1918–1926): "I cannot pretend to describe or analyse my love for Jerusalem . . . For me Jerusalem stood and stands alone among the cities of the world . . . in a sense I cannot explain there is no promotion after Jerusalem."

I was born in a house built by my grandfather in the 1880s outside the Old City. I grew up in the shadow of the conflict between Arabs and Jews. On the night of November 29, 1948, when the United Nations voted to partition the land and create a Jewish and a Palestinian state, I danced in the streets with fellow Jews. I lived through the long siege and constant shelling of West Jerusalem that, like the invasion of the country by the armies of neighboring Arab states, followed the UN resolution. Politics and ideology seemed simpler in those days, when the world appeared in black and white: Jerusalem was the once and future capital of the Jewish people alone. Nearly half a century later, three of my cousins having fallen in the Arab-Israeli wars, among so many others, both Jews and Muslims, the question of Jerusalem is still unresolved, as is the conflict between Israelis and

Palestinians. The question of right and wrong is no longer so simple, and wise leaders are needed to find a lasting solution.

Thousands of books have been written about the city, and one volume alone cannot cover all its astonishments. In *City of the Great King: Jerusalem from David to the Present,* we try to capture the excitement and wonder of that ancient and multifaceted city and present some of its aspects to the reader: Who lived there? How did it become holy to three religions? What makes it both an earthly and a heavenly city? In addition to spiritual depictions, the book gives portraits of the city as seen in art and literature, and conveys some of its unusual architectural features. Only two chapters deal with politics. A short, contemporary bibliography offers additional sources for further reading in English.

The authors who contributed to this volume come from different backgrounds and often have differing views. In his chapter in this book, Muhammad Muslih quotes an Armenian Jerusalemite who wrote that in the Holy City each person carries a mirror, but each holds it in only one direction. We hope that this book will bring other reflections into the mirror, and that through it the reader will gain a better understanding of the city, its citizens, and its meaning to millions around the world, whether they are Jewish, Christian, or Muslim. We were guided by respect for the right of other people to have different opinions, as that is the basis for civilized discourse. We are mindful that for years Teddy Kollek, Jerusalem's fabled mayor, stamped his official stationery with the word "Tolerance."

To the citizens of the Holy City and to all the millions who seek her well-being, we end with the words of the psalmist: "Pray for the peace of Jerusalem."

The Inhabitants of Jerusalem

MAGEN BROSHI

The two main sources of information for the history of Jerusalem are literary and archaeological. In spite of a century and a half of intensive archaeological research, Jerusalem is almost the only city in the Holy Land where the written data are richer than the mute archaeological finds.

The earliest sources are the Egyptian Execration Texts from the twentieth to the eighteenth century BCE. Thus the literary evidence concerning Jerusalem stretches over four millennia. The next source, again coming from Egypt, but whose language is Accadian, are the Amarna Letters from the fourteenth century BCE.

From ca. 1000 BCE to the mid-second century BCE—that is, from the time David conquered Jerusalem until the time when the last verses of the Book of Daniel were written—we have a wealth of information in the Old Testament. This anthology is by and large a Jerusalemite book in which the word "Jerusalem" is mentioned more than 600 times and, with its other appellation—Salem, Zion, the City—almost 2,000 times.

Several of the Second Commonwealth books, that is, the intertestamental Jewish literature such as the Letter of Aristeas and the Books of the Maccabees, provide us with important data about the city, but the most important source is Flavius Josephus (36/37 CE–after 100 CE), the prolific and gifted author who was a native of the city and an eyewitness to its fall and destruction. His information about the topography and archaeology of Jerusalem, especially the description of the city on the eve of the Roman siege of the year 66 CE (*Jewish War* V, 136–247), is almost unparalleled in ancient history.

The New Testament affords us certain glimpses of the city, while the talmudic data, with the noteworthy exception of the detailed descriptions of the Temple, are often of a legendary nature.

The first in a long line of pilgrims—Christian, Jewish, and Muslim—who left us their impressions of the Holy City in writing is the Bordeaux pilgrim in 333 CE. The first map of the city is the sixth-century Madaba mosaic map (see Plate 2).[1] The first realistic plans of some of its buildings were done after the oral description of Arculf, who visited Jerusalem toward the end of the seventh century. Arculf was a bishop of Gaul who was on his way home when his boat was carried off by a storm to the tiny island of Iona, off the western coast of Scotland. There he told the story of his pilgrimage to Abbot Adomnan (670–704), who wrote down his account and drew the plans. Pilgrim accounts and maps have been our main sources for the history of Jerusalem for a millennium and a half, and, until it was overtaken by Paris in the seventeenth century, no other city in the world loomed so large in travelers' accounts.

Modern archaeological research in Jerusalem, as in the rest of the country, began in 1838 with the pioneering work of Edward Robinson. This erudite and sharp-eyed American scholar made two brilliant discoveries—remains of a "fly-over" leading to the Temple precinct, now called Robinson's Arch, and the Third Wall, the last of the Second Commonwealth city walls. The first scientific excavations were carried out in 1867 by Captain Charles Warren of the British Royal Engineers. This officer found the shaft leading to the Gihon, the Spring of Siloam, that bears his name, and conducted a meticulous study of Temple Mount walls and their environs. Since then, archaeologists of many nations have excavated in Jerusalem almost uninterruptedly, although mostly on a small scale.

However, beginning in 1961 with Kathleen Kenyon and ending a quarter of a century later with Yigal Shiloh, the archaeological exploration of the city experienced a period of unprecedented expansion. The intensive activity of that generation is unequaled, and it is doubtful that it will ever be surpassed. This period was distinguished not only by the number of excavations and their large scale but also by extensive excavations within the walls of the Old City. (In the first century of archaeological activity, almost all the work had been done outside the walls.) Significantly, the excavators unearthed samples of all the periods since the city was founded some 5,000 years ago. Few cities can boast such a long and ancient lineage.

Canaanite and Jebusite Jerusalem

In the twentieth century BCE, Palestine was nominally under Egyptian hegemony, but Egypt was too weak to enforce its rule, and therefore it had to resort to magic in order to obtain its goals. This was done with the Execration Texts—clay figurines and pottery vessels on which the names of disobedient rulers in foreign provinces were inscribed and then smashed, so as to bring a curse upon the pharaoh's enemies. The first occurrence of the name Jerusalem (Urusalimum) and the names of two of its rulers appear in these Execration Texts. Jerusalem carries a North Semitic name, meaning "the city founded by the god Salem," and so too must its inhabitants, Levant Canaanites. The city occupied the elongated hill that was later to be known as the City of David. It was about five hectares (12.5 acres) in size, was naturally well defended, and had at its base one of the mightiest springs in the area. There is also some Jerusalemite correspondence in the Egyptian El-Amarna royal archive, which contains letters written on clay tablets dating back to the fourteenth century BCE. Jerusalem at that time, and probably in earlier and later centuries as well, was a city-state ruling over a sizable part of the central mountainous region.

Sometime at the end of the second millennium, probably about 1000 BCE, the city underwent a sharp ethnic change: it became Jebusite. This name is unknown to us from other sources, but several details—such as the name, or rather title, of its ruler Arawnah, meaning lord—suggest that these people were akin to the Hittites whose homeland was Anatolia and northern Syria. To this ethnic group must have belonged Uriah the Hittite, an officer in David's army and Bathsheba's first husband. A vague memory of those times is preserved in the prophet's dictum: "Thus saith the Lord God unto Jerusalem: Thine origin and thy nativity is the land of the Canaanite; the Amorite was thy father and thy mother was a Hittite" (Ezekiel 16:3).

Israelite Jerusalem—The First Commonwealth (1004–586 BCE)

In 1004 or thereabout, David conquered Jerusalem. Unlike so many conquerors in world history, and certainly contrary to the divine injunction, "Thou shalt smite them; then thou shalt utterly destroy them" (Deuteronomy 7:2 and *passim*), David treated the local population most leniently. Not only were they not deported, but they were allowed to keep their property and become full-fledged citizens. The threshing floor, on which David erected an altar and on which Solomon later built the Temple, was purchased by David at full price from Arawnah the Jebusite, the former king of Jerusalem (2 Samuel 21:21–24).

The young Israelite kingdom lacked political and administrative experience, so several non-Israelite officials were appointed. These included Shisha, whose name seems to be of Anatolian, that is, Jebusite, origin and who was succeeded by his sons during Solomon's reign, and Adoniram, who was in charge of collecting taxes and also bore a foreign name. Non-Israelites held some other economic posts.

Several army officers were also non-Israelites, including the above-mentioned Uriah the Hittite. His widow, Bathsheba, later King David's favorite wife, was probably also of foreign, or autochthonous, extraction, since her father Eliam was the son of Ahitophel, whose pagan name indicates that it was an aboriginal family. When her son was born, his father, David, wanted to call him by the Jahvistic name Jedidiah, but Bathsheba preferred the pagan name Solomon, after the city's patron god Shalem.

David was not the first to marry a non-Israelite wife. Many of the key biblical figures had done so, including Judah, Simeon, Joseph, Moses, Gideon, and Samson. Some of the kings in the Davidic dynasty were born of foreign mothers: Rehoboam was the son of Naamah and the grandchild of Hanun, king of Amon. The mother of Rehoboam's successor, Abiam, was the granddaughter of the Aramean king of Geshur, and Ahaziah, son of Athliah, was the grandchild of Ethbaal, king of Sidon.

All through the First Commonwealth, the Bible does not take a dim view of "intermarriages," as later ages will. This can be gathered explicitly from the law of "the captive beautiful woman" (Deutero-

Figure 1. A fragment with the inscription "house of David" (ca. 885 BCE). Discovered at Tel Dan in 1993, the monument celebrates a victory by a king of Aram. The incomplete inscription, in ancient Aramaic, contains the words "king of Israel" and "house of David" (the latter, *beit David*, read from right to left, begins on line five from the bottom, second to seventh letter; see Introduction).

nomy 21:10–15), and implicitly from the fact that none of the prophets ever condemned intermarriage while dwelling on what they took to be crimes and misdemeanors. The polemics against such marriages were started by Ezra and Nehemiah in the fifth century BCE, at the very beginning of the Second Commonwealth. It was a time when the Jewish people were a minority in the land and they faced the danger of turning from an assimilating to an assimilated people.

During the First Commonwealth the city underwent two phases of growth, under Solomon and Hezekiah. While David's city was confined to the walls of the Jebusite city (see Figure 2, page 39), Solomon (965–928 BCE) added a sizable area, to the north, on which were built both the Temple and his palace—the building of the former lasting seven years and the latter thirteen. Thus the city grew from five hectares to about sixteen hectares (forty acres). Under Hezekiah (727–698 BCE), the city grew 400 percent, to about sixty hectares (150 acres), or ten times the size of the City of David. This was due not to normal demographic growth but to an influx of refugees from the northern kingdom of Israel, which had been conquered by Assyria in 721 BCE, and later to an influx of those fleeing the western provinces of Judah, which had been ceded by the Assyrians to the Philistine city-states in 701 BCE. Naturally, the refugees preferred to live with the brethren in the south rather than remain under cruel foreign rule.[2]

In 586 BCE rebellious Jerusalem was conquered by the Babylonian king Nebuchadnezzar, who "burnt the house of the Lord, and the king's house and all the houses of Jerusalem, even every great man's house, burnt he with fire" (2 Kings 25:9).

Jewish Jerusalem—The Second Commonwealth (538 BCE–70 CE)

In 538 BCE Cyrus, the magnanimous Persian king, issued an edict ordering the restoration of the Jewish community in Palestine, and in 516 BCE the newly built Temple was inaugurated. By the middle of the fifth century, after many years of "days of small things" (cf. Zechariah 4:10), two outstanding leaders came to Jerusalem, Ezra and Nehemiah, who tried to restore the city to its former glory. The latter reconstructed the city walls, but even after that, "only a few people lived there, and the houses were not built" (Nehemiah 7:4). As a matter of fact, Jerusalem was even smaller than it was in David's time, and it grew to become a metropolitan city only under the Hasmonean dynasty (in Jerusalem 164–37 BCE). Under this dynasty the city expanded once again to its former size during the heyday of the First

Commonwealth; in many places the builders used the remains of the older walls. As befits an expanding kingdom, the capital took on a metropolitan look as the Hasmonean kings built a palace, a number of public buildings such as the boule (town hall) and a gymnasium, and carried on large-scale building on the Temple Mount (buildings later obliterated by Herod's gigantic renovations). The first aqueduct bringing water to the city from springs to its south was also a Hasmonean contribution.

But the unprecedented colossal development of Jerusalem took place under Herod the Great (37–4 BCE), his son Archelaus (4 BCE– 6 CE), and the Roman procurators (6–66 CE). Herod was undoubtedly the greatest builder in the history of the country, obsessed by an "edifice" complex. Though he built extensively in Palestine and abroad, his greatest efforts were directed toward Jerusalem, and his greatest projects there were the Temple (the old one was dismantled and a new one built instead) and the huge podium, or platform, on which the Temple stood. The platform, which has survived to our day, was the largest of its kind in the ancient world.[3] Other projects included the enormous palace, two citadels, water installations, and the elegant network of well-paved streets, and the excellent sewage system. By the end of the period the area of the city, excluding the Temple Mount, was four times larger than that of the Hasmoneans. Recent excavation in the Upper City (today's Jewish Quarter) have shown that at least part of the population enjoyed a very high standard of living in spacious, well-built, lavishly furnished mansions, decorated with wall frescoes and mosaic floors.[4]

The city was not large by our standards (just 170 hectares, or 425 acres, twice the size of today's Old City), but it was very elegant (see Map 1). Its population must have numbered some 60,000.[5]

During the Hasmonean and Herodian periods the country witnessed great economic development, and the principal cause of the prosperity of Jerusalem was the revenue related to the Temple—from pilgrimage and the "half-shekel" due. There is no way to estimate the number of pilgrims, but undoubtedly it was large and brought the city considerable income and active trade. The half-shekel due, raised from every Jewish male above the age of thirteen, both in the Land of Israel and in the Diaspora (by that time the majority of Jews already lived abroad), together with additional, voluntary gifts, must have

Map 1. Jerusalem through
the ages.

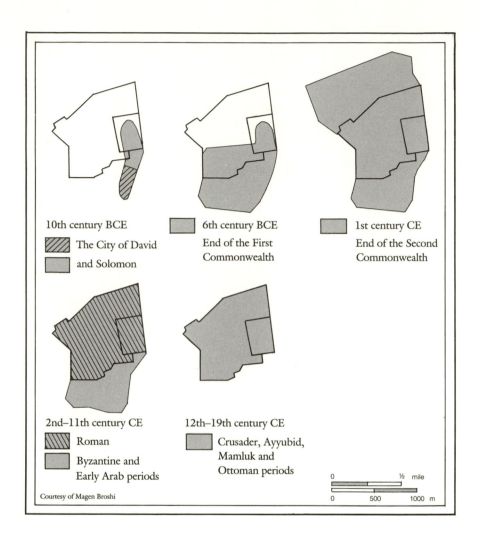

10th century BCE

The City of David
and Solomon

6th century BCE
End of the First
Commonwealth

1st century CE
End of the Second
Commonwealth

2nd–11th century CE

Roman

Byzantine and
Early Arab periods

12th–19th century CE

Crusader, Ayyubid,
Mamluk and
Ottoman periods

Courtesy of Magen Broshi

0   ½ mile

0   500   1000 m

brought in huge sums of money. The money was used not only
for Temple expenses but also for "the [upkeep of] the aqueduct, the
city wall and its towers and all the needs of the city" (Mishnah,
Shekalim 4, 2).

The city was predominantly Jewish, although at certain periods the
citadels were occupied by foreign garrisons. Side by side with native
Jews there were quite a number of Diaspora Jews who settled in
Jerusalem. A list of synagogues "of Libertines [probably freedmen],
and the Cyrenians, and Alexandrians, and them of Cilicia and those

CITY OF THE GREAT KING

of Asia" (Acts 6:9) indicates this. The prevalent language was Aramaic—a dialect called Jerusalem Aramaic—but Hebrew was spoken, or at least understood, by most. In addition to Greek and Latin, many other languages were heard in the streets of Jerusalem, especially during the pilgrimage holidays.

In 70 CE the city was conquered by Titus and totally destroyed.

Roman and Byzantine Jerusalem (70–638 CE)

Over the ruins of the city the camp of the Tenth Roman Legion was established—the legion that had conquered and ruined it. The extensive camp was situated in the northwestern part of the city and seemed to have numbered some 2,500, about one-half of the legion's strength. In addition, camp followers—those who rendered service to and lived off the army—as well as common law wives (only at the end of the second century CE would legionnaires be allowed to marry, but illegal cohabitation existed long before that) joined the legionnaires. Many of the veterans probably settled in the city after the termination of their service. The rest of the inhabitants were mostly Greek-speaking pagans who were naturally, unlike the inhabitants of other Palestinian cities, first-generation settlers. The small Christian community that left for Pella during the war returned to Jerusalem. Some Jews may have returned as well.

In 130 the emperor Hadrian decided to establish a Roman colony where Jerusalem stood, to be called Aelia Capitolina after the monarch's family, Aelius, and the Capitoline triad, Jupiter, Juno, and Minerva. The decision to establish a new city on the ruins of holy Jerusalem and the plan to build a pagan shrine on the Temple Mount were among the principal reasons for the outbreak of the Bar Kochba revolt (132–135), which ended disastrously with the extermination of the Jewish population in most of Judea and turned the Jews into a minority in their own land. Most probably, Jerusalem was not conquered by the rebels. From then on, for the next five centuries, Jews would not be allowed to dwell in the city.

Aelia was designed as a Roman legionary camp, in a quadrilateral shape with two main streets bisecting it: the *cardo* from north to south, and the *decumanus* from west to east. This network has been preserved for the last eighteen centuries.

In 324 Jerusalem came under the rule of Emperor Constantine the

Great and thus began its Byzantine, Christian era. From a provincial town it turned into one of the most celebrated cities in the empire, studded with numerous splendid buildings of a religious nature and overflowing with crowds of local residents and pilgrims. Constantine's mother, Helena, who was a devout Christian (her son converted only on his deathbed), is said to have discovered the True Cross and other relics of the Passion. A temple to Aphrodite, which stood on the site, was torn down and a Christian temple was erected in its stead—the Holy Sepulchre complex. This was the first of many religious buildings constructed in the city by various powers and monarchs whose seat was outside Jerusalem, and it continues to our time.

The population of Jerusalem in the early fourth century was largely pagan, but by the beginning of the fifth century Christians constituted the majority. There was hardly a Christian denomination that was not represented in the Holy City, although most were Eastern, with some Western representation. The dividing lines were primarily theological. The Monophysites, for example, held that in the person of Jesus there was only a single, divine nature, while the Orthodox believed that Christ had two natures, divine and human. To those differentiating distinctions were added others of great significance—ethnic, cultural, and political.

The main language was Syriac—that is, Christian, Palestinian Aramaic—but Greek was quite prominent, and other languages such as Latin, Georgian, and Armenian were also spoken, although mostly by monks.

The ban on Jewish residence imposed by Hadrian was in force throughout this period, but there is evidence that a small Jewish community might have existed in the city, illegally, in the early fourth century.

Aelia Capitolina—which originally resembled today's Old City in size—was sparsely populated. But as of the fifth century the city spread out, its population became denser, and it was surrounded by populous suburbs. In its heyday, probably under Justinian, ca. 540, the population must have numbered between 40,000 and 45,000.

The Early Arab Period (638–1099)

The Arabs conquered Jerusalem about 638. The date is uncertain[6] because the Muslims did not attach great importance to Jerusalem at that time. The city still retained its Roman name, Aelia, until the tenth century, when it was superseded by the Arabic al-Quds (the Holy) or Bayt al-Maqdis (the Shrine). When a capital was appointed for the southern part of the country, it was the newly founded Ramla, in 716, lying amid a fertile region on the main road connecting Egypt and Syria, halfway between Jerusalem and the port of Jaffa.

The first century of Arab rule was a prosperous one. The ascending empire of the Umayyads, stretching over vast areas from the borders of France to the borders of India, had its capital in Damascus. The proximity of the capital to Jerusalem was one of the reasons that the Damascus caliphs paid special attention to the city. In 762, after the Umayyads were replaced by the Abbasids, the capital moved to Baghdad, and that marked the beginning of a steady decline of the country and of Jerusalem. In 841 an uprising of peasants and Beduins against harsh taxation signaled the start of a long series of internecine uprisings, conquests, and reconquests by different Muslim powers that decimated the population and considerably weakened the country. A long list of attritional wars was capped by the Turkish Seljuk occupation of 1071 (or 1073) and the Egyptian Fatimid reconquest in 1098, both events paving the way for the Crusader capture of the land in 1099.

During the first four centuries of the Early Arab period, the city remained the size it was during the Byzantine era, but in 1033 a severe earthquake toppled the city walls, and when the southern part of the wall was rebuilt—a wall still serving today—it left Mount Zion and its slopes and the City of David outside the walled area. In the first hundred years of this period, the number of inhabitants seems to have been similar to the number in the previous period, probably around 40,000, but from the mid-eighth century on, the population receded. In 1047 the Persian traveler Nasir-i Khusraw estimated the population to be 20,000, most probably an exaggeration.[7]

In the first part of this period and possibly even to its end, the majority of the population was Christian. The erection of the Dome of the Rock in 691—not only the first Muslim shrine and the first major Islamic public building but also one of the greatest achievements in world architecture—was meant to counterbalance the Church of the Holy Sepulchre. Both have concentric plans, and their diameters are identical, but the Dome of the Rock is decorated with antitrinitarian koranic quotations.

The makeup of the denominational Christian mosaic was very similar to the one existing in the Byzantine period. The largest denomination was the Greek Orthodox, and the most common language was Syriac—that is, Christian Palestinian Aramaic. However, as of the eighth century the Greek Orthodox community underwent a marked process of Arabization. Arabic gradually replaced Syriac as the common vernacular and was used more and more, as the language of cult and Greek religious texts were translated into Arabic. Religious literature written in Arabic during the ninth to the eleventh century was not meant for Muslims converting to Christianity—something Islamic law prohibits under the pain of death—but for the Greek Orthodox community. Other Eastern churches also adopted Arabic gradually, but in the Coptic and Jacobite (Syrian) communities Arabic became a written language only between the twelfth and the fourteenth century. In the course of time, partly due to conversion, the Muslims became the largest contingent in Jerusalem's population.

In the seventh century, as Jerusalem came into Muslim hands, the ban on Jewish residence was lifted. After 500 years of being Judenrein, Jerusalem again included a Jewish community.

At an unknown date, the central Jewish academy (the Palestine Yeshiva) moved from Tiberias to Jerusalem. The head of the academy and its principal scholars divided their time between Jerusalem and Ramla, the capital. The Jewish quarter was situated in the City of David, close to the Temple Mount, but after the earthquake of 1033 when that part of the city remained outside the new city wall, a Jewish quarter was founded in the northwestern part of the city. The Karaites, the Jewish sect which came into being in the eighth century, made Jerusalem their spiritual center in the last two centuries of the Early Arab period. Here would all its literature be composed and its principal characteristics shaped. Unlike the Jewish immigration to Jerusalem—motivated by practical reasons—the Karaites' immigration was predominantly ideological and was aided materially by Diaspora Karaite communities.

The Crusader Period (1099–1187)

When Jerusalem was conquered by the Crusaders in 1099, virtually all its Muslim and Jewish populations were butchered, while a few survivors were sold into slavery. The local Christians who sought refuge in the Anastasis (Resurrection) basilica next to the Holy Sepulchre were the only survivors. During this period, residence of non-Christians was banned, and thus the city underwent a drastic demographic change. From a provincial town it became the capital of the independent Latin Kingdom of Jerusalem and one of the most important centers of Christendom. With minor changes, the intensive monumental building and the street grid gave the city the form preserved today. So much so that in the nineteenth century a French scholar claimed that he could tour Jerusalem with the aid of a book composed by a Crusader pilgrim.

Most of the construction activity was concerned with religious edifices such as churches, monasteries, pilgrims' hostels, and hospitals, but it also included a variety of other buildings, like the royal palace, covered markets, and various structures for the use of the religious orders. All through the period, Jerusalem was Christian— neither Muslims nor Jews were allowed to dwell there. Small numbers of infidels might have infiltrated illegally, like the four Jewish families encountered there by the traveler Benjamin of Tudela, but they carried no weight.[8] The same traveler was impressed by Jerusalem's ethnic and denominational variety: "Jacobites and Armenians and Greeks and Georgians and Franks and from all the Gentile tongues." Because the population of the city had been decimated by slaughter, the authorities devised all kinds of means to attract new residents, including reduction of taxes and commercial concessions (especially to Italian traders). Baldwin I, king of the Crusader Kingdom of Jerusalem, brought Christian Arabs, probably Jacobites, from Transjordan, which was under Muslim rule. Most of the population belonged to Eastern denominations, which numbered at least eight, and was very similar to the Christian population of the former period. The new element consisted of European newcomers, the "Latins" or the "Franks," estimated to be—unlike in other Crusader cities—the majority of the population.

The Latins were composed of motley ethnic and linguistic groups. The largest component was French, and theirs was the principal language. A German traveler, John of Würzburg, complaining that the Germans were underrepresented in Jerusalem, tells us "that the city has fallen into the hands of other nations—Frenchmen, Lorrainers, Normans, Provençales, Auvergnats, Italians, Spaniards and Burgundians."[9] A short time after this complaint was made, in 1128, a street was named the Street of the Germans, after the church, hospital, and hospice known as St. Mary of the German Knights. This was the cradle, somewhat legendary, of the German, or Teutonic, Order. It was natural that people sharing a common origin preferred to live together, and thus we have a Beaucaire Quarter after a Provençal town, Spanish Street, and a Hungarian hospice.

Jerusalem remained Crusader for only eighty-eight years.

The Ayyubid (1187–1516) Periods

In 1187 Saladin conquered the city, although part of the country stayed in Crusader hands for over a century (until the fall of Acre in 1291). For the next seven centuries, except for a short interlude, Jerusalem remained under Muslim rule. The Latin Christian population was allowed safe conduct out of the city in return for payment of personal ransom. Those who could not afford it—and it is reported that their numbers reached 15,000—were sold into slavery. The Eastern Christians were allowed to stay and even to keep their property, but they were required to pay an annual head tax. Great efforts were taken to obliterate any signs of the Crusader occupation: not only were the mosques which had been turned into churches now reverted to their original function, but quite a number of Crusader buildings were made into Muslim institutions.

Under the threat of the Third Crusade, Saladin and his successors reconstructed the walls of Jerusalem, walls that had fallen into disrepair because of the Crusaders' false sense of security. Hardly had the reconstruction of the city's defenses been completed when Saladin's nephew, al-Malik al-Mu'azzam 'Isa, who had carried out most of the building operations, gave the order to dismantle the walls (Figure 2).[10] During that year, 1219, the Crusaders were fighting the Muslims on Egyptian soil, and there was a high probability that they would reconquer Jerusalem or receive it in a settlement in exchange for a retreat from Egypt. Hence the Ayyubid ruler applied his uncle Saladin's principle of scorched earth. Most of the population of Jerusalem left the unwalled, ill-defended city.

From that point until the Ottoman reconstruction 320 years later, the city remained unwalled. During the ephemeral and ineffective rule of Jerusalem by the Hohenstaufen emperor Frederick II (1229–1244), a second exodus followed. The Turkish Khawarism conquest exterminated the entire Christian population of Jerusalem of 7,000, except for 300 who survived by fleeing to Jaffa. Additional attacks, this time by Mongols, further decimated the population, and the survivors fled to safe places.

In 1260 the Mamluks defeated the Mongols in the Battle of Ein Jalut in the Jezreel Valley, and for the next two and a half centuries Palestine remained under their rule. After the massacre perpetrated by the Khawarism hordes and the Mongol onslaughts, the city was virtually empty, but when the Mamluks established law and order, the city was gradually inhabited again. Law and order prevailed throughout most of the Mamluk period, a state which enabled the city to function without defensive walls.

The Jewish scholar Nachmanides, who came to Jerusalem from Catalonia in 1267, tells that some 2,000 people returned to the city, 300 of them (Eastern) Christians. Anyone could get a house for free, "for the city is lawless, and whoever wishes to benefit from the ruins can do so," since so many perished, leaving no one to claim their property.[11]

The capital of the Mamluk kingdom was Cairo, but Jerusalem belonged to a province governed from Damascus. The authorities did little to develop Jerusalem's economy or to enhance it in order to draw new citizens, other than clergymen and theologians. At the same time, substantial contributions were made toward the erection and maintenance of religious institutions—mosques, madrasas (theological colleges), *zawia*s (convents), *khanakah*s (Sufi mystics' centers), hospitals, and hospices. On the eve of the Ottoman conquest, the city numbered forty-four madrasas and twenty *zawias,* according to Mujir al-Din.[12] Jerusalem served the Cairo Mamluks as a place of exile for high-ranking military personnel and other officials, a mild version of recent-times Siberia. Some of the exiles founded and endowed religious institutions, partly out of piety and partly out of financial considerations, since their heirs were to manage the endowments. Slave traders who supplied young Mamluks[13] also donated their share of religious buildings and foundations. Since Muslim clergy and theologians played such an important role in the city, it was only natural that

Figure 2. A fragment of a wall inscription commemorating the reconstruction of Jerusalem's walls by Saladin's nephew, al-Mu'azzam 'Isa.

non-Muslims were frequently persecuted. Representatives from all parts of the Islamic world were among the religious personnel. From Spain came refugees fleeing the Christian reconquest and the persecutions under the fanatic Muwahhidun (Almohades) dynasty; the North Africans founded their own quarter near the Temple Mount, while Egypt contributed most of the state-appointed religious offices. However, most of the scholars and laymen came from Iraq, Iran, Afghanistan, and even Azerbaijan.

The Christians remained a small minority throughout this period, 300 out of 2,000 in 1267, according to Nachmanides, and 1,000 out of an estimated 10,000 in 1484, according to Father Felix Fabri.[14] The local Eastern Christian communities were joined by Franciscan friars, who erected a monastery on Mount Zion in 1344 and whose zealous activities made them a butt of constant harassment.

The Jews were even a smaller minority. In 1267 Nachmanides discovered only two Jewish brothers in the semideserted city. He founded a synagogue but left the city for Acre, where he established a yeshivah. Harsh taxation, the generally poor economic conditions, and Muslim intolerance restricted the size of the community. Fabri estimated that only 300 Jews lived in Jerusalem in 1484, and the figure is corroborated by Rabbi Obadiah of Bertinoro in 1488, who reported that about seventy families were there, and many widows.[15] The Jewish Quarter was where it is at present.

The Ottoman Period (1516–1917)

The first half-century under the Ottomans was an epoch of prosperity for Jerusalem, as it was for the rest of the Turkish empire. Under Suleiman the Magnificent the realm reached its cultural, economic, and military zenith. In 1532 the aqueducts were repaired and started supplying water to the city once again, and between 1538 and 1541, after 320 years, the badly needed city wall was rebuilt, the same wall that still surrounds the Old City today. Old bazaars were reconstructed and new ones were added. But under Suleiman's successors the city, again like the rest of the empire, underwent a sharp decline that lasted for about three centuries, until the middle of the nineteenth century.

The big change began during the nine years, 1831–1840, of the Egyptian occupation of Jerusalem and Palestine by Muhammad Ali and his son Ibrahim Pasha. A large disciplined army and a relatively efficient administration enforced far-reaching changes in the socioeconomic regime and in the status of the non-Muslim communities, and the city was opened to the influence of Europe and the United States. The strong central government, which enforced law and order, enabled foreign diplomatic representatives to defend the civil rights of their subjects and other clients residing in Jerusalem. This and other privileges—known as capitulations—were granted by the Ottomans after they regained control over Syria and Palestine with the help of European powers. From then on France looked after the interests of the Catholics, Russia kept an eye on the interests of the Greek Orthodox, Britain and Prussia protected Protestant interests, and Prussia, Austria, and especially Britain did much to save the Jews from the customary injustice and constant persecution.

From the Egyptian to the British conquest, in less than a century, Jerusalem's population multiplied eightfold, while the Jewish contingent grew twentyfold. The city experienced unprecedented building activity, private as well as public—the latter mainly of religious institutions, and both mostly with foreign funding.

In the twelve centuries since the city came under Muslim rule (indeed, with the exception of the Crusader period) the erection of non-Muslim houses of worship, even the restoration of ruined ones, was forbidden. Various steps, most involving bribery, were taken through the ages to circumvent the prohibitions, usually with little success. Under the Egyptian rule the restrictions were abolished. The first religious buildings to be reconstructed were the Four Sephardi Synagogues, in 1835–1836. The first church to be built was the Protestant Christ Church, opposite the Citadel, in 1841–1848, which was also the first modern building in Jerusalem. By the end of the century the city, intramural and extramural, was filled with a multitude of religious edifices, each designed in the style of its sponsoring country, such as Russian, British, German, or Italian.

The crowded Old City and its unhygienic conditions encouraged construction outside the walls, and the first building was the Bishop Gobat School (1856), named for the Protestant clergyman. Thirteen years later the first modern road connected Jerusalem with its port city of Jaffa; a railroad followed only in 1892. In 1860 the first residential quarters were built outside the wall, Mishkenot Sha'ananim (Figure 3), and it did not take long before the population of the new city outside the walls outweighed that of the Old City.

In the heyday of the Ottoman rule, between 1525–1526 and 1562–1563, four censuses were conducted, the last three with a high degree of reliability. The last one counted about 15,000 citizens, 82 percent of them Muslims. The proportions thereafter vary, but the Muslims maintained their majority until the late 1850s, when the Jewish community reached 50 percent of the population.[16]

In the early nineteenth century the Christian communities were the same ones that existed in Jerusalem throughout most of the Middle Ages, the three major groups being the Greek Orthodox, the Armenians, and the Latins or European Catholics, and the three minor

Figure 3. Mishkenot Sha'ananim. The Jewish housing project, one of the earliest buildings outside the Old City, is seen during construction in a rare photograph from 1859.

ones being the Egyptian Copts, the Ethiopians, and the Syrians. At the beginning of the century the Christians numbered about 3,000, one-third of the total population. Like the Jews, they had to pay a poll tax (abrogated in 1855) and were forbidden to serve in the army (until 1908). In the nineteenth century a Protestant community was established in the city, and within a short period it became the most dynamic Christian denomination. The first bishop was appointed in 1841, and the parishioners were both German Protestants and English Anglicans, but political tensions made the parish split along national lines in 1887.

Until the beginning of the nineteenth century, the Jews constituted less than one-fifth of the population. Under a regime that did not care particularly about human rights, the status of the Jews was the lowest. In 1839, well into the century, William. T. Young, the first British consul in Jerusalem, told his foreign minister, Lord Palmerston, that a Jew in Jerusalem was considered not much more than a dog. A constant trickle of immigration and financial aid from the Diaspora kept the community in existence. As the Ottoman rule became more lenient, immigration intensified, and by the second half of the century Jews constituted a majority of the population. From 1860 on, most of the construction outside the Old City was Jewish.

On December 9, 1917, Jerusalem surrendered to the British, and four centuries of Ottoman rule came to an end.

Jerusalem under the British Mandate (1917–1948)

In historical perspective, the thirty years of British rule in Palestine were relatively a very short period, but this was arguably Palestine's most revolutionary and intensive era. After long periods of Oriental misrule, the country was governed by a Western, democratic, enlightened power. During this period the population of Palestine tripled—the Arab sector doubled in number while the Jewish sector, due to intensive immigration, grew tenfold.

The number of inhabitants of Jerusalem also trebled, and the built-up area reached four times its former size. The phenomenal growth took place despite terrible suffering during World War I, when hunger, plagues, forced emigration, and voluntary flight decimated the city's population. The whole country underwent a difficult time during the war, but the agrarian settlements fared much better than the largest city, which was cut off from foreign aid and from a normal food supply. The Jewish population of the city, which numbered 45,000 out of a total population of 75,000, was reduced in the aftermath of the war to less than half, or 21,000, in 1918.[17] The British made Jerusalem the capital of the country, a status the city had lost in the twelfth century, with the defeat of the Crusaders. Due to efficient administration, large-scale immigration of European Jews (many of whom were well educated), and the help of massive investments, the city underwent an accelerated process of modernization. The water supply, which up to that time depended on rainwater stored in cisterns—a source of various illnesses, including endemic malaria—was augmented by water pumped in pipelines from springs in the south, east, and west.

A sewage system and electricity, both total innovations, established European standards in the city. Numerous public buildings were added, not only of a religious nature, as in the nineteenth century, but also the High Commissioner Residence, the Hebrew University campus on Mount Scopus, the Palestine Archaeological (or Rockefeller) Museum, the Hadassah Hospital, and the King David Hotel. By 1931, 23 percent of the city's work force was occupied in administration or belonged to the liberal professions.

Between 1922 and 1946 the total number of inhabitants increased from 62,700 to 164,000; the number of Jews from 34,000 to 99,300. The growth of the Jewish community was partly due to natural increase and partly to immigration, mostly from Europe but also from Asia—Iraq, Iran, and Yemen.[18] In 1931 as well as in 1939, half the Jewish residents were the city's natives. The Arabs' population growth was due to a large extent to natural increase and to a smaller measure to local immigration, mostly from Hebron and nearby villages. This growth called for a very intensive building operation. Traditionally in Jerusalem, members of different religious communities tended to live together, as far as was possible. The new Jewish neighborhoods were built west of the Old City, the Muslims lived to its north and south, and the Christians mostly to the southwest.

This phenomenal growth was achieved with armed clashes in the background. In 1920, 1921, 1929, and especially in 1936–1939, Arab attacks on Jews, with moderate Jewish reprisals, resulted not only in heavy casualties on both sides but also in intensified separatist tendencies; mixed neighborhoods were deserted by minorities. The Old City, where 5,200 Jews lived in 1931, was left with only 2,100 in 1939.[19]

When the 1948 war broke out, Jerusalem was practically a divided city.

The Divided City (1948–1967)

The hostilities which heralded the 1948 war—called by the Israelis the War of Liberation or War of Independence and by the Arabs, usually,

Al-Nakbah; that is, the Defeat, the Catastrophe—started on November 30, 1947, the morning after the United Nations' decision on the partition of the country into two states—Arab and Jewish. This resolution also called for the internationalization of Jerusalem. The war lasted exactly one year: on November 30, 1948, a cease-fire agreement was signed between Israel and Jordan, the country which annexed the West Bank and East Jerusalem. For the next nineteen years the city remained divided with a vast track of no-man's-land separating the two halves, a sordid landscape of barbed wire, minefields, and dilapidated ruins. The cease-fire borders surrounded Jewish Jerusalem on three sides, with only the west being open—a narrow corridor that connected the city to the rest of Israel.

A short time after the end of hostilities, West Jerusalem was proclaimed the capital of Israel, and the nascent state made great efforts to make the city worthy of its title. The government offices and the Knesset (the parliament) were moved to Jerusalem, many immigrants were settled there from 1949 to 1951, and large-scale building projects took place, partly for public but mostly for private usage. Jerusalem's being the seat of the government and numerous institutions and organizations—Hebrew University, the Jewish Agency, religious academies—accounts for the fact that by 1961, 47 percent of its labor force was employed in public service, in comparison with 26 percent of the total number of Israeli Jews in the country.

The population of West Jerusalem, practically all Jewish, doubled in the thirteen years between 1948 and 1961—from 83,000 to 165,000. Most of the growth was due to mass immigration, a trend that started in the nineteenth century but gained momentum after World War I. In 1961 only 17.2 percent of the residents of Jerusalem were second-generation natives, 44.7 percent were from Muslim countries in Asia—mainly Iraq and Iran—and Africa, mostly Morocco, while 38.1 percent were from Europe, mainly the satellite states of the Soviet Union, and America. The fecundity of Jewish women in Jerusalem was considerably higher than in Tel Aviv and Haifa, and slightly higher than the country's average. (In 1964–1966 in Jerusalem there were 25.6 births per thousand people, whereas in Tel Aviv there were 17.7, and in Haifa 16.7. The average birthrate for the country as a whole was 22.5 births per thousand people.) This difference stemmed principally from the high percentage of Orthodox and ultra-Orthodox persons living in the Holy City who did not practice birth control.

Although Jerusalem in this period was ethnically homogeneous, 99 percent Jewish, it was marked by outstanding cleavages: between Orthodox and secular; poor and better off; the various political, ideological camps—left, right, and center—and the Orthodox and splintered ultra-Orthodox.

East Jerusalem, which was in Jordanian hands, was the principal city of the West Bank. Jordan oversaw its life, as it did the rest of the West Bank to a lesser degree than it did the East Bank, that is, Jordan itself. The greatest efforts of the Jordanians were directed toward the capital, Amman. In spite of the influx of thousands of refugees during the 1948 war—20,000 Arabs from West Jerusalem alone went eastward—the Eastern part of Jerusalem hardly grew. In 1946 there were 46,000 Arabs in Jerusalem, and fifteen years later only 51,000. Not only did the refugees move onward, mostly to the East Bank but to other Arab countries as well, but the local Jerusalemite population also migrated in large numbers.

The Christian communities, being better educated and thus better candidates for immigration, dwindled from 32,000 in 1946 to a mere 12,000 in 1961. The outflow of immigrants was significantly compensated by refugees who settled in Jerusalem. About one-fifth of the inhabitants in 1967 were formally refugees—or the head of the family at least was born in an area conquered by Israel in 1948. A salient component of the population came from Hebron and its environs. A small cigarette factory constituted almost all the industry in Jerusalem, and, being dethroned from the status of a capital, the city had very few jobs to offer, except services and commerce to its impoverished rural hinterland and to a rather small number of Christian pilgrims and other tourists.

Jerusalem since 1967

On June 7, 1967, the third day of the Six-Day War, Jerusalem was reunited under Israeli rule. In the following quarter century it became the largest city in Israel—in the number of inhabitants and in its municipal area. From 266,000 in 1967 it grew into a city of 545,000

Map 2. Jerusalem,
municipal area.

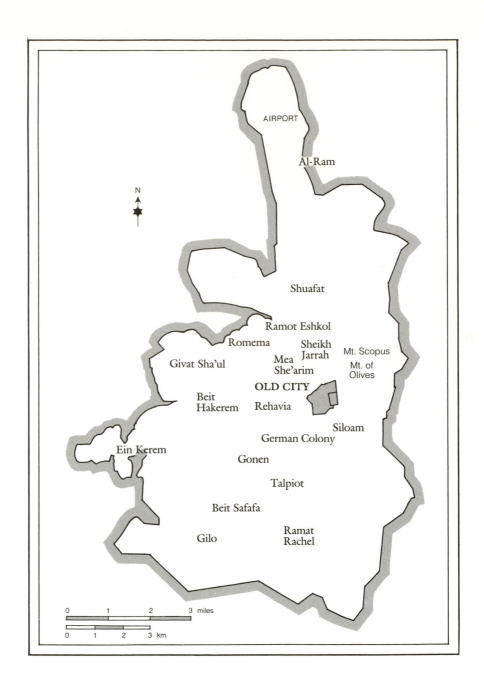

AIRPORT

Al-Ram

N

Shuafat

Ramot Eshkol

Romema

Sheikh
Jarrah

Mt. Scopus

Givat Sha'ul

Mea
She'arim

Mt. of
Olives

OLD CITY

Beit
Hakerem

Rehavia

Siloam

German Colony

Ein Kerem

Gonen

Talpiot

Beit Safafa

Gilo

Ramat
Rachel

0   1   2   3 miles

0   1   2   3 km

inhabitants in 1991—a growth of 105 percent, 90 percent for the Jewish population and 106 percent for the Arab. The share of Arab population increased there because of high fertility rates and the settlement of a great number of "internal" immigrants from rural areas.

The municipal area grew from 44 square kilometers—38 in West Jerusalem, 6 in East Jerusalem—to 123 square kilometers. Of the 70 kilometers in the east, some 23 square kilometers were expropriated from former Arab owners for what was termed public use (see Map 2).

In its long history Jerusalem was a homogeneous city for only short periods, but in its most contemporary epoch it has reached the height of its heterogeneity. It is a multinational, multiethnic, and multireligious city. The ratio of Jews to Arabs has remained constant during this time—in 1967 it was 74.2 to 25.8, and in 1991, 72 to 28.

About 80 percent of Arabs in Jerusalem are Muslim. The other 20 percent are predominantly Christian, and make up about 70 percent of the total Christian population in the city. The birthrate among all the Arabs is considerably higher than among the Jews, but the gap is getting narrower; in 1972–1975 it was 36 per thousand for the Arabs and 22 per thousand for the Jews, whereas in 1983–1985 the figures were, respectively, 28 and 22.

The population growth has brought massive building operations and new neighborhoods. In 1990, about one-third of the Jewish population lived in one of the ten new neighborhoods, built mostly to the north and the south. While some 75,000 new apartments were built in Jerusalem, the Arab sector got less than its share—only 12 percent of building permits for almost 26 percent of the population.

The standard of living rose fivefold and can be seen, inter alia, in the consumption of electricity, which increased fivefold in domestic use and eightfold in public-commercial use. Water consumption increased by 80 percent.

Marked differences between Jews and Arabs can be seen in occupation characteristics. Of the Jews, 17 percent are employed in academic and high-skilled occupations, while 3 percent of the Arabs hold such positions. In manual labor the proportions are 15 percent among the Jews and 32 percent among Arabs. In unskilled labor the ratio is 3.5 percent versus 12.7 percent.

Of the last period's four cleavages in Jewish Jerusalem, only two remain: the cleavage between Orthodox and nonreligious, and the one between the so-called Left and Right (actually having little to do with the original, historical-political designations). The political situation being what it is, the latter is very significant, but the real, formidable cleavage is, of course, between Jews and Arabs.

In 1995 Jerusalem is far from being an integrated city. The old 1948 borderline does not exist anymore, but Jerusalem behaves in many ways, especially since the Intifada, as a divided city.

THE HEAVENLY CITY

The Holy Places   2

F. E. PETERS

When Jerusalem first appears in biblical history, it is a town without a past, a newly conquered Jebusite settlement that David had made the capital of his still insecure Israelite kingdom. Today it is once again the capital of a Jewish state; but in the three millennia that separate the modern city from David's cramped settlement on the southeastern spur of Mount Moriah, Jerusalem has become as well the Holy City of three of the world's most important religious communities: Judaism, Christianity, and Islam. What unites the three is their claimed descent, by nature, grace, or providential plan, from Abraham.

The later Jewish tradition delighted in putting Abraham at the site of Jerusalem, chiefly in connection with the binding of Isaac, but the sanctity of the city, and of most of the holy places within it, has little to do with the Hebrew patriarch. According to the Bible, it was the Israelite people, "a kingdom of priests, a holy nation" (Exodus 19:5) and the land of Canaan itself (Leviticus 18:1–5) that were pronounced holy long before Jerusalem was possessed by David. In these texts, holiness is not defined in terms of place or time but in practices: the purity code set up in opposition to the defiling and abhorrent practices "of the people who were in the land before you."

But the early books of the Bible recognize quite another form of holiness that is, in fact, tied to place. Before Moses ascended Sinai, he was instructed by the Lord to issue a warning: "You must set bounds for the people, saying, 'Take care not to go up to the mountain or even touch its base.' Anyone who touches the mountain shall be put to death" (Exodus 19:12). Here we are clearly in the presence of the holy, a dangerous enterprise for the people in case "the Lord shall break out against them" (Exodus 19:22, 24). Moses is permitted to approach the presence, though with visible and not entirely reassuring alterations in his appearance (Exodus 34:29–35).

At one point Moses is accompanied by the newly constituted priests, and it is here that the two norms of sanctity, the presence of God in a specific place and behavioral holiness, come into play: adherence to the purity code, and particularly to the stringent one required of the priests, is the only acceptable preparation for entering into the presence of the holy.

In the Torah, the presence of the Holy One is random and arbitrary. Even His departure from the Tent of Presence (the Tabernacle), His chosen abode among the Israelites, is sudden and unexpected, a signal for the people to move on (Exodus 40:36). Once in the Promised Land, the emphasis on the presence of the Lord shifts from the Tent to the Ark housed within it. The Ark is noted in passing to be located at another holy place, Shiloh, where "the Lord continued to appear" (1 Samuel 3:3, 21), presumably in and around the Ark, where "He is enthroned upon the cherubim" (4:4). When the Ark is captured by the Philistines, "the glory of God departed from Israel" with it (4:22). Even when the Philistines return the Ark, seventy Israelites of Beth Shemesh are struck down by their contact with it. "No one is safe in the presence of the Lord," the Beth Shemeshites astutely observe (6:19–20).

The Ark, "which bore the name of the Lord of Hosts, who is enthroned upon the cherubim" (2 Samuel 6:2), next appears in the well-known story of David's transfer of it from Baalath-Judah to the new capital city of Jerusalem, and once again there is a mortal casualty from accidental contact with the Ark (2 Samuel 6–7). The Ark continued to be housed in a tent (7:17) until Solomon constructed a magnificent temple—almost as grandiose as his own palace—to serve as its home and began the process of converting Jerusalem into a holy city.

Was Jerusalem a holy city before the arrival of the Israelites? The Israelite-riveted Bible is not generous with such information, of course, and we can only speculate, though without any degree of certainty.[1] Where the ground beneath the speculation grows firmer,

Figure 4. City of David (diorama), from the Museum of the History of Jerusalem at the Tower of David.

though once again the biblical account does not concede it, is that David chose to build his altar to the Most High—Jerusalem's first certifiable Israelite holy place—at what is described as a "threshing floor," whose Jebusite owner himself urged David to make a sacrifice, and conveniently has at hand both the sacrificial animals and the fuel for a burnt offering.[2] Our suspicion that the threshing floor is a pre-Israelite holy place is supported, in part, by the conviction that holiness, and particularly the holiness associated with places, is endemic—that it survives changes of regimes, churches, and even gods. So it is not implausible that, if there was a Jebusite-recognized sanctity attached to sites in Jerusalem, at least some of those sites continued to be regarded as holy even under the far more jealous regime of the One True God.

By the seventh century BCE Jerusalem possessed in its Temple Israel's sole certified holy place, though it is difficult to believe that the earlier sacred locales,[3] high places,[4] and tomb cult sites,[5] like that of Abraham and his family at Hebron, lost either their cultus or their allure at Josiah's decision to centralize formal liturgical worship in the capital. Josiah's act was essentially political; it gave the Jerusalem Temple a monopoly on divine worship, which may have enhanced the prestige of the city but did not alter its status.

But there were other events at work. The northern kingdom fell to the Assyrians in 722 BCE, and the passage of substantial elements of both Israelite population and Israelite territory—and its minor cult centers—into the domains of pagan rulers, and then the eventual erection of a rival temple on Mount Gerizim in Samaria, brought the focus of Jewish piety even more closely upon Jerusalem. We can read it out of the prophets: it was Jerusalem that was the symbol and center of their concerns for Israel; Yahweh would again choose Jerusalem (Zechariah 2:12), it is to Jerusalem and its Temple that "the glory of the Lord" will return at its restoration (Ezekiel 43:4–6).

The rise of the Pharisaic party and its program of ritual purity,[6] and above all the destruction of the Second Temple in 70 CE, finally shifted the emphasis away from the sanctifying presence of God to the holiness of ritual purity, even with respect to places. Mishnah, Kelim 1:6–9 provides us with a holiness map of Eretz Israel. There we learn that all of the land of Israel is holy, that the walled cities within it are more holy than the countryside, and that "within the wall [of Jerusalem] is more holy than they," that is, than the other walled cities of Israel (1:8). The only reason offered by the Mishnah for Jerusalem's special status vis-à-vis the other walled cities of Israel is that "they eat there the lesser holy things and the second tithe," which was not done elsewhere.

This is to describe but not to explain; it seems clear, nonetheless, that even on this type of evidence, two things may be said of the holiness of Jerusalem: First, whatever the metaphysics of later theories of the city as the navel of the earth,[7] Jerusalem's sanctity was due in the first instance to the presence of the Temple there, just as the holiness of the Israelite encampment—and the banishment of certain activities to without its perimeter—was due to the Tent of the Presence in its midst. And second, this temple-derived holiness was, unlike that of the Israelite encampment and the ancient Arabian taboo enclaves called *haram* or *hawta,* prescriptive rather than defensive. Jerusalem was not of limited access, as the inner courts of its Temple were, or as the environs of Mecca and Medina are to this day.

Nothing particular was forbidden to the resident in Jerusalem as such; but a number of things had to be done—could *only* be done—within its juridically defined limits. The Mishnah mentions two, as we have seen, but we may make our own additions. In Temple times, the central acts of the high holy days, the Bible's own prescribed *haggim,*[8] could be performed only in Jerusalem (Deuteronomy 16:16). According to the original legislation, the Passover lamb, for example, had both to be slaughtered and eaten within Temple precincts (16:7; 2 Chronicles 25:1–9); eventually the eating was permitted anywhere within the city of Jerusalem.[9] Thus Jesus might lodge in nearby Bethany, just as others camped in the fields around the city (Josephus, *Ant.* 17.217), but to celebrate the feast, it was necessary for his followers to go into the city and find a room *within* Jerusalem (Mark 14:3, 12–13). For this principle to operate, Jerusalem had obviously to be defined, perhaps simply by its walls,[10] just as Eretz Israel was juridically defined for purposes of the full observance of the law.[11]

The first Christian holy place in Jerusalem appears in the Gospels themselves, in the rather precise localization of Jesus' burial place. It was on the property of one Joseph of Arimathea, "near the place where he had been crucified . . . a garden, and in the garden a new tomb, not yet used for burial" (John 19:41). The topographical detail suggests that the place was remembered, and so almost certainly venerated, like other tombs in and about Jerusalem, from a very early date in the Christian era.[12] The Gospels are filled with similar details that would allow at least a general identification of the sites in which various events in the life of Jesus occurred, though with no suggestion that there might be a cult attached to the place. At least as early as the second century there was a historical interest in visiting such sites. Though doubtless religious motives were present, early travelers had history on their minds, Bible history, and not merely the life of Jesus.[13]

Whatever devotion the early Christians might have felt toward sites in Jerusalem and elsewhere connected with the earthly life of Jesus, the city itself had quite a different status for the new Christian community than it had for the Jews. Paul, in a famous passage in Galatians (4:21–27), drew a sharp distinction between Hagar and Sarah, two women who stood for two covenants: Hagar represented the Torah covenant and "the Jerusalem of today"; Sarah, on the other hand, was "our mother" and "the heavenly Jerusalem." A "heavenly Jerusalem" was not a new notion—it appears in the apocrypha (most graphically perhaps in 4 Ezra 10:40–55), but in Paul's use it is precisely the contrast, and the judgment, regarding the earthly and the heavenly city that had profound consequences in the Christian tradition. When Paul was writing, the city was intact and the Temple still stood, but after 70 CE Christian exegesis was confronted with a quite different state of affairs.

"This is an allegory," Paul had announced at the beginning of the Galatians passage, and the Christian exegetes understood it as such. Though there were other understandings of the text, Origen projected Paul's distinction back onto the Bible's, and particularly the prophets' references to Jerusalem, and forward to the Christians' own hope of a restoration: it was not the Jerusalem of Origen's day of which they were speaking, but of a new heavenly city, "a spiritual vision of heavenly bliss."[14] As Origen put it in *Against Celsus* (7.28): "Moses taught that God promised a holy land . . . to those who lived according to his law. And the good land was not, as some think, the earthly land of Judea." That much must have been clear to all of his Christian contemporaries. Rebellious Jerusalem was destroyed by the Romans not once but twice—the second time in 135 CE—and then quickly rebuilt by Hadrian as a spanking new, and ostentatiously pagan, metropolis of Roman Judea, a province from which the Jews were henceforth banned. Jerusalem once again had holy places, but they were now of the pagan variety. On the main forum in the Upper City there was a temple of Venus, and perhaps one dedicated to the tutelary deity of the new Jerusalem, Jupiter Capitolinus.[15] Though no Jews were permitted in the city, there was a small Christian community, now solely of the Gentile variety, that was acceptable to the Romans and was becoming increasingly dominant in the churches.[16]

The new Aelia Capitolina, as Hadrian called his city, must have been attractive, as we can infer from his contemporary project at nearby Gerasa/Jerash, but it could hardly have enjoyed any great prosperity beyond imperial subsidy. From David's day down to the Roman apocalypse, the chief industry, employer, and money-and-goods magnet of Jerusalem had been the Temple. Without it, and without the Jews who were banned from the city in the wake of the insurrection of 135, Jerusalem would doubtless soon have sunk to the status of an inglorious, and overdressed, provincial town (since the Romans preferred to rule from Caesarea on the coast), had it not attracted the pious attention of another emperor, the newly converted Christian Constantine. Through his agents—and his mother Helena, as tradition has it[17]—he sought out, identified, and enshrined at imperial expense the primary places in Jerusalem and elsewhere associated with the life of Jesus.[18]

The centerpiece of Constantine's intent was his progressive efforts around the sites of Jesus' execution and burial. The local Christian community in Jerusalem seems to have identified the places for him as being beneath a temple complex on the northern side of Hadrian's forum in the Upper City.[19] Jupiter Capitolinus and Venus were both worshiped there. Constantine's engineers excavated the area around the tomb site—the original tomb was carved into a rock or earth hillock—and surrounded the newly freed site with a domed martyrium of an already familiar type (Eusebius, *Life of Constantine*, 3.28, 40). Eastward lay an open courtyard, and there, in its southeastern corner, was the hillock Golgotha, the site of Jesus' crucifixion.[20] Abutting this and running eastward all the way out to the *cardo* or main north-south avenue of Jerusalem, Constantine constructed an enormous and sumptuously decorated aisled basilica,[21] whose atrium court and monumental entryway opened onto Hadrianic Jerusalem's main thoroughfare.[22] In Herod's day the site of Jesus' crucifixion was outside the city walls, but in fourth-century Jerusalem Constantine's complex of shrines stood at the busy commercial heart of the city.

There had been Christian shrines and cult stations before; the Christian cult of the martyrs, for example, long antedated Constantine's enshrinement of the Jesus sites in Palestine,[23] and when the Christians emerged from the catacombs, the public martyria they soon erected were in fact modeled on the imperial mausoleums of the day. But Constantine's activity had an almost immediate effect on Christian pilgrimage to what now became the Christian Holy Land, not in the covenantal sense understood by the Jews, nor even as an eschatological locus, as some early Christians believed, but a land hallowed by Jesus' *historical*, *physical* presence there, now certified by Constantine's identifications and enshrinements. One could now touch and see the *actual* places where Christ had done his redemptive work.

The newly adorned sites soon became public knowledge thanks to pilgrims' enthusiastic accounts of their visits to the holy places.[24] More, the glory that accrued to Constantine—much of it due to his historian and encomiast, Eusebius—marked only the beginning of a sustained burst of enshrinement of Christian holy places in Jerusalem and environs that lasted into the sixth century.[25]

Among Eusebius' other works is one written before Constantine's activity and entitled *Onomasticon,* or "On the Names and Places among the Hebrews." As the title indicates, the inspiration was biblical, the same desire for a more precise knowledge of the Jewish Holy Land that had motivated both Origen and Jerome. But Constantine's enshrinement of the holy places associated with Jesus turned the visitors' attention away from what was now called the "Old Testament" to a whole new range of sacred sites connected with New Testament figures and events. Christian pilgrims continued to visit Jewish holy places, but they were now chiefly those associated with the prophets or with a typological association for Christians.[26] And, equally important, the Jerusalem holy places were, very early on, knit together into a stational liturgy, Christian commemorative rituals celebrated publicly at specified times at specified places in and around Jerusalem.[27] The places were already sanctified by their historical identification; now their holiness was fortified and enhanced by Christian ritual.

We have a rare and precious picture of the enshrined Christian holy places in Jerusalem in the mosaic floor map in the sanctuary of a church in Madaba (see Plate 2) in Jordan.[28] The date is sometime about 580 CE, and the well-preserved Jerusalem cartouche on the map shows the walled city of the sixth century with its churches and shrines highlighted in gold; Constantine's church, called the Anastasis or Resurrection,[29] shines like a medallion from the midst of the city. Unhighlighted, unmarked, and almost unidentifiable, is the site of the Temple on the southeastern side of the city (the upper right, slightly distressed part of the cartouche). Judaism's holiest of holy places, "God's holy mountain," was, as evidenced by the map's ambiguous

THE HEAVENLY CITY

iconographical vacuum and the eyewitness testimony of Christian pilgrims who visited the site, nothing more than a field of ruins during the entire period from the Roman destruction down to the Muslim rebuilding projects in the seventh century.[30] And there were some few Jewish pilgrims, a few hardy souls—it must have been a dangerous enterprise under any circumstances, Roman or Christian—who bought or stole their way into the forbidden Jerusalem and up onto the Temple Mount. The observant and well-informed Jerome knew they came on the Ninth of Ab, the anniversary of the destruction of both temples, "a piteous crowd, woebegone women and old men weighed down in rags and years." Jerome was not only observant; he was also a theologian: "all of them showing forth in their clothes and bodies the wrath of God" (*On Zephaniah* 1.15–16).

The wrath of God, or perhaps simply the gods of war, descended upon Jerusalem in the form of Persian armies that in 614 CE finally broke through Byzantine provincial defenses they had been battering for centuries. Jerusalem was occupied and may have been briefly handed over to vindictive Jewish mobs, who burned churches but do not seem to have done any substantial damage to the chief of the Christian shrines, the Church of the Anastasis (Resurrection).[31] What the Persians did was considerably more shocking to Christian sensibilities: they carried off to Ctesiphon Christendom's primary relic, the remains of Jesus' Cross.

The discovery of the True Cross had by then entered into Christian legend. Constantine's mother Helena had discovered three crosses, and the indictment *(titulus)* nailed to Jesus' Cross, in the excavations for the basilica; the one on which Jesus was crucified was identified by a miraculous cure.[32] When the European nun Egeria visited Jerusalem in the late fourth century, she witnessed what had already become a ritual of veneration for this famous relic. On the Friday before Easter, the anniversary of Jesus' death, the remains of the Cross and the *titulus* were brought forth in a gold and silver box, removed from their container, and put on a table before the bishop of Jerusalem. He was seated at Golgotha in front of a silver replica of the Cross set up there; as the faithful filed by, each would bow to kiss the Cross and the *titulus*.[33]

After the Persians carried off the container and its precious contents to their capital in Iraq in 614 CE, the Christian emperor Heraclius devoted the next couple of years to mounting a counteroffensive against Persians, and late in the next decade his efforts were crowned with success. The Persian defenses collapsed as rapidly as had the Byzantine's a decade earlier. Heraclius entered Ctesiphon in triumph, and in 630, a full year after the end of the war, the emperor, with great solemnity, carried the remains of the Cross, still sealed in its container, to its accustomed place on Golgotha,[34] where it remained until the time of the Crusades.

Given the nature of the city and its importance in Christendom, the seventh-century fall of Jerusalem was a frightening and ominous event, redeemed only in part by the body of legend and cult that began to grow up around the True Cross in the wake of Heraclius' restoration.[35] News of the event may even have reached into the heart of Arabia; so, at least some read the obscure allusion in the opening lines of Sura 30 of the Koran: "The Romans have been defeated in the nearer land," followed by what appears to be prediction, "and after their defeat they will be victorious in a few years" (Koran 30:2–3). Whatever the reference, the lines reflect one of the Koran's few adversions to the larger world beyond Mecca and Medina. The point is of some importance since it speaks to Muhammad's knowledge of, and interest in, Jerusalem. Later biographical accounts connect the Prophet with Jerusalem in two important regards: first, he prayed toward Jerusalem before changing his practice and facing toward the Kaaba in Mecca during his early years in Medina;[36] and most traditional glosses on Koran 17:1 ("Glory be to Him, who carried His servant by night from the holy shrine [*al-masjid al-haram*] to the distant shrine [*al-masjid al-aqsa*]") identify the "distant shrine" with Jerusalem and construct out of it the famous story of Muhammad's Night Journey, whether in a dream or waking, to the Jews' and Christians' Holy City.[37]

In 638 CE the Muslims stood before Jerusalem. The city capitulated without a struggle, its surrender negotiated by its Christian bishop into the hands of (the Muslim tradition insists) no less than Caliph Umar.[38] The stories grow even denser in detail after the caliph's entry into the city. According to some versions, Umar requested to be taken to "the mihrab of David," that is, his place of prayer or, possibly, his palace,[39] and when shown the Church of the Resurrection, he refused the identification. Eventually he was taken up to the Temple Mount, still a ruin covered with refuse. Satisfied that this was in fact the holy place of Jerusalem, Umar ordered the site cleared and at its southern end built Jerusalem's first mosque, a somewhat makeshift building that could house 3,000 worshippers.[40]

So Jerusalem remained for about half a century a city with an overwhelmingly Christian population still in untroubled control of their holy places,[41] a Muslim occupying force of a few thousand that worshipped in their mosque atop the Temple Mount, and, once again after some five hundred years, Jewish inhabitants. As the Karaite Salman ibn Yeruham recalled it some three hundred years later, "When by the mercy of the God of Israel the Rum [the Byzantines] departed from us and the kingdom of Ishmael [the Arabs] appeared, Jews were permitted to enter and reside there. The courts of the [House of the] Lord were handed over to them, where they prayed for a number of years." If that meant that the returned Jews were permitted to pray atop the Temple Mount itself—or even at the entries leading into it—the privilege did not last very long. Because of their own intemperate behavior—Salman is doubtless laying the blame at the feet of the rival Rabbanite faction—they were restricted to one entry and then eventually banned from approaching any of the gateways to Herod's platform.[42]

The Christians were treated more formally. It was they who negotiated the surrender terms, which included, in the form reproduced by the Muslim historians,[43] a guarantee of their persons, their churches, and their freedom to practice their rituals. It was not very different, in fact, from the surrender terms given to most of the voluntarily surrendered cities.

The earliest Muslim inhabitants of the city may have been—*pace* the reports on Umar's enthusiasm for the Temple Mount—either ignorant or indifferent to their newly occupied holy city. But toward the last decade of the seventh century that attitude underwent a dramatic reversal. Up to that point there were only two holy places in Islam, the *temenos/haram* at Mecca around the Kaaba, the House of God, and a similar *haram* at Medina; set in its midst, though unconnected with the haramization of the city and hardly yet enshrined, was the tomb of Muhammad. But Caliph 'Abd al-Malik (r. 685–705) undertook the construction of a third. The Dome of the Rock atop Herod's platform, which bears 'Abd al-Malik's signature

Figure 5. Map of Jerusalem by
A. G. Wartensleben, 1870. While
the map stays within a realistic
scale of proportion, it still emphasizes the heavenly dimension
of the city through the difference between the built-up, compact city and the uninhabited
area around it.

and the dedication date of 692 CE,[44] is quite unlike any other building
in Islam. Umar's earlier mosque at the southern end of the platform
was simply that: a prayer and assembly hall functionally identical with
every other such edifice in Islam. But the Dome of the Rock (Qubbat
al-Sakhra) is unabashedly a shrine, an octagonal domed building constructed around and over an outcropping of the base rock from under
Herod's platform. There is as yet no satisfactory answer as to why the
caliph built such a shrine or what is the significance (or history) of the
Rock it so gloriously commemorates.[45] Was its purpose to divert
pilgrimage from Mecca, as some have maintained,[46] or, more plausibly,
to rival, and in some sense replace, the Church of the Anastasis, the

primary Christian holy place in full view westward across the valley in the Upper City?[47]

The problem of the Rock is more difficult to solve. Eventually the Muslim tradition was inclined to connect it with the touchdown of Muhammad's Night Journey of Sura 17:1, but that does not appear to have been the original impulse. Too many other indices point to a biblical inspiration, to the site of Abraham's sacrifice of Isaac, or to the mysterious "foundation stone" mentioned in the Mishnah, Yoma 5:2 in connection with the Temple. A Christian pilgrim from Bordeaux saw the Jews anointing a "pierced rock" on the Temple Mount in the fourth century,[48] and Jewish legend was eventually filled with stories about a rock on the Temple Mount,[49] though the chronology makes it difficult to say whether they were influencing the Muslim imagination or the other way around.

Whatever the Umayyads' plans for Jerusalem, religious or political, they ended when the dynasty fell in 750 and their successors, the Abbasids, chose to rule from Baghdad, where the only holy place was the caliph's *sacrum palatium*. Jerusalem's still small Muslim population was almost invisible, but Christian pilgrims continued to come to the city—and often remarked favorably on the Muslim administration. A valuable document, the anonymous *Memorandum on the Houses of God and Monasteries in the Holy City* written for Charlemagne about 800, describes the Christian holy places, and particularly the Anastasis, as well staffed with monks and nuns, many of them from outside Palestine and even from Europe. Christian affairs appear to have been normal under the new religious regime,[50] though two elements bear notice. The Patriarch of Jerusalem had to pay the Muslims for religious privileges—the Christian holy places were now part of the Muslim income in Jerusalem—and Charlemagne, a European Christian ruler, now had a decided and acknowledged stake in Jerusalem.[51]

Jews at that time had no holy place in Jerusalem save the site of the former Temple, to which they had only partial access. But Jewish interest in the city was growing, sometimes spontaneously, sometimes through outright efforts to draw other Jews to the Holy City. Aliya—immigration to Palestine—was an important issue for Jerusalem Jews in the ninth and tenth centuries, particularly in the light of the rivalry between the Karaite and Rabbanite communities there.[52]

Pilgrimage too was encouraged, and with some success. Many of the pilgrims—they were called, perhaps under the influence of the Arabic *hajji, hogegim*—were from the Arab lands, and they generally came to Jerusalem for the Succoth festival. They assembled, whether by preference or by necessity is not clear,[53] on the Mount of Olives, whence they descended and circumambulated the Temple Mount, praying aloud at each of the gates. The ceremony and the assembly on Olivet were done with the consent of the Muslim authorities, but only after payment of a fee.[54]

Jewish pilgrims, who were of modest means and traveled under modest circumstances, were not much marked by the Muslim inhabitants of either Jerusalem or Palestine. Not so the Christians. European Christians sometimes came with great pomp—and sometimes paid the price, as in the Beduin massacre of the pilgrimage *à la grande luxe* led by Bishop Arnold of Bamberg in 1065[55]—but Eastern Christians especially made little effort to conceal their sometimes ostentatious piety. The pilgrimage caravan that left Cairo for Holy Week in Jerusalem in the year 1064/5 "departed with great and expensive display, much in the fashion of pilgrims departing for Mecca," the historian Ibn al-Qalanisi reported.[56] One interested observer was the eccentric, and possibly deranged, ruler of Egypt, al-Hakim (r. 996–1021), who became so outraged at the display that in 1009 he ordered the destruction of the Church of the Holy Sepulchre.[57] So it was, or nearly so, and with important consequences: news of the atrocity soon reached Europe, where it further fueled a growing concern about the Christian holy places, and the church's reconstruction introduced, now on a significant scale, the principle of foreign intervention in the affairs of Muslim Jerusalem.

Al-Hakim's agents of destruction left a good part of the rotunda surrounding Jesus' tomb intact, though the tomb itself seems to have been destroyed as well as whatever construction there was at Golgotha. Entirely swept away was most of Constantine's great basilica stretching from the site of the crucifixion out to the *cardo,* the main Roman avenue of the city. It remained in ruins until 1030, when the local Christians petitioned the Byzantine ruler Constantine IX Monomachus (r. 1042–1055) for financial assistance in its reconstruction. He agreed, obviously with the approval of the Muslim authorities, and the new, truncated Anastasis was completed in 1048.[58] In 1063 the emperor once again came to the assistance of the Jerusalem Christians, but this time for a price, a price exacted from the Muslims. He would pay for the reconstruction of the city wall around the Christian Quarter, but only on condition that "none but Christians should be permitted to dwell within the circuit of the wall which they proposed to erect by means of the imperial donation." It was the beginning of a new era. "Up to that time the Saracens and Christians dwelt together indifferently," William of Tyre remarks. But the Muslims had now to vacate the quarter—in effect, the entire northwest quadrant of the city—leaving only the Christians to live there, and they, in turn, were governed in most matters by the Patriarch, the metropolitan bishop of Jerusalem,[59] who now had standing behind him a Christian emperor in Constantinople.

The Christian Quarter apart, Jerusalem was then ruled from Egypt by the Isma'ili Shi'ite dynasty of the Fatimids that had seized control there and in Palestine in the tenth century. In 1071 they were replaced by the Turkish Seljuks. We cannot be sure what actual difference that made in the city, but the change of regime did not improve the tales of Muslim atrocities reaching Europe.[60] It was the emotional response to such stories—the defilement of altars and churches, the forced circumcision of Christians, the expropriation of churches—compounded, to be sure, with many other motives both sacred and profane, that set in train the holy war against the infidel called the Crusade, or, as the Christians preferred to call it, "a pilgrimage in arms."[61]

The call for the Europeans' Crusade went forth at Clermont in November of 1095, to take the road to "the land which . . . was given by God into the possession of the Children of Israel," that is, the New Israel that is Christendom; to Jerusalem, "this royal city situated at the center of the world, now held captive by His enemies, and now in subjection to those who do not know God, to the worship of the heathen."[62] The pious mission of the Crusaders came to its cruel end in the summer of 1099, and the blood-drenched city they took must have appeared neither holy nor royal to its conquerors. Some Jews had fled, many others were ransomed, and the last Muslim defenders had been slaughtered.

The Crusaders set about the expropriation of the holy places: the Christian ones from the hands of the startled Greeks, Armenians, and

Eastern Christians who had neither summoned the Crusaders nor fought with them against the Muslims; and the Islamic shrine and mosque atop the Temple Mount.[63] The Dome of the Rock was converted into a church (Templum Domini); and the Aqsa Mosque, called by the Crusaders the Templum Solomonis, briefly became the dwelling of the new Latin ruler of the city and then, when the king moved his palace to the western gate where Herod had lived, the headquarters of the Knights Templars, a monastic order of knights pledged to the defense of the holy places.[64] They newly enshrined the place identified with Jesus' Last Supper on Mount Zion,[65] and the site of the home of Mary and her parents, Anna and Joachim, north of the Temple Mount and just inside St. Stephen's (or the Lions) Gate.[66] They were obviously in possession of the remains of the True Cross, since they carried it into their final battle against the Muslim forces of Saladin at Hattin in Galilee in July 1187. It worked no miracles on this occasion, however; the Crusaders were routed and the relic—"a prize without equal since it was the supreme object of their faith"—fell into the hands of the Muslims.[67]

Saladin retook Jerusalem in October 1187, but not until he had gathered up support from a largely indifferent Muslim world that either ignored the Crusaders or regarded them as a temporary affliction on an otherwise troubled landscape. Muslim consciousness about the sanctity of Jerusalem was raised by the appearance of a new literary genre—or rather, the application of an old genre, tracts in praise of a city, to Jerusalem. Works "On the Merits of Jerusalem," for the most part prophetic sayings praising the Holy City and attaching blessings to visits made or prayers said there, began to be recited in the mosques of Aleppo and Damascus.[68] The effects of this propaganda were long term.[69] For the first time Muslims began to look upon the city itself as holy. The Frankish attack appeared more than an act of war; it was a sacrilege. The Muslims, particularly those of Syria and Palestine, never forgot or forgave. Henceforward, Muslims were willing to die for what had now come to be regarded as the third holiest city in Islam.[70]

Once in possession of Jerusalem, Saladin immediately ordered re-appropriation of the Muslim holy places. The Dome of the Rock and the Aqsa Mosque were restored to their original form—the Crusaders had covered the Rock under the dome with marble[71] and adorned the walls with pictures, while the Templars had made a number of modifications in the Aqsa.[72] A more difficult issue was what to do with the principal Christian holy place, the Anastasis.[73] There was a lively debate. Some of the sultan's counselors were for razing it to the ground; but there were others who somewhat better understood the nature of holy places: "It is not the visible building but the home of the Cross and the Sepulcher that is the object of worship. The various Christian races would still be making pilgrimage here even if the earth had been dug up and thrown into the sky."[74]

Less noted by both the Christian and Muslim historians of the era was Saladin's creation of what would eventually turn out to be an entirely new set of holy places in Jerusalem. Both Saladin and his predecessor, Nur al-Din, were Sunnis, devoted to the cause of a holy war directed not only against the Christians, the nature of whose long-term danger to Islam was uncertain, but against the Isma'ili Fatimids whose radical view of Islam profoundly threatened the Sunni consensus. The response of both men was to vigorously take up arms against the Franjis but to confront the Shi'ites with aggressive intellectual warfare directed at producing an educated Sunni rabbinate, the ulema, formed on the principles of traditional, that is, Sunni, Islam. To achieve this end, the Sunni rulers used a new institution, the law school (madrasa). Thus, the convent next to the former Church of Saint Anne—the church itself was turned into a mosque—was converted into the Saladin Madrasa and was supported, like the Crusader institution that preceded it, from the income of shops in Jerusalem's principal market street.[75]

The grandeur, allure, and, in the end, extension of the Muslim holy places in Jerusalem were the result of an institution and a set of historical circumstances that turned the robber barons of their day— the Egyptian military fief holders called Mamluks, for whom Jerusalem was a favored place of exile[76]—into veritable Carnegies and Rockefellers of piety. Saladin's dynasty of the Ayyubids lasted until 1250, when they were replaced by their own former military slaves, the Mamluks, who ruled their domains, including Jerusalem, until 1517. The Mamluks were outsiders, Circassians captured or bought as boys outside the Abode of Islam, converted to Sunni Islam, and trained solely to be professional soldiers. Now they were rulers as well.

Piety may have been the motive, or a thirst for legitimacy, but the

Mamluks poured wealth collectively into the Hajj to Mecca and individually into the embellishment of their capital city of Cairo and their Holy City of Jerusalem (see Chapter 17).[77] In Jerusalem they lined the western and northern sides of the Haram al-Sharif, and the streets leading into it, with madrasas and with Sufi hostel-convents. And as they had done in Cairo,[78] they supported these with the institution of *waqf,* the sacralization of an income-producing property whose usufruct is dedicated in perpetuity to the building or to the support of some pious cause, in this case Jerusalem's growing number of law schools and convents, their staffs and residents.[79] It is not the economics of the endowment system that concern us here, but the sacralization in the first instance of the donated property—which might be anywhere in the Islamic world.[80] The endowed building became, in effect, a holy place, not because of either its site or its function but because it was rendered sanctified—and inalienable—by an act of the donor's will.

The Mamluks brought a new, quite artificial and short-lived, prosperity to Jerusalem, but something else is in evidence as well in the pilgrim reports of the period. A profound hostility had crept into Muslim-Christian relations, at least into the relations of the Palestinian Muslims (though it was probably broader than that) and those alien Christians from abroad who continued to visit the holy places,[81] as well as the Christian clergy that returned as permanent residents. In 1291 Pope Nicholas IV successfully petitioned the sultan that some Franciscans be permitted to return to Jerusalem. In 1300 St. Louis' brother, Rupert of Apulia, came to Jerusalem in person and begged Sultan al-Nasir to "give" him—the privilege cost Rupert 32,000 ducats—the Church of the Cenacle (Upper Room) on Mount Zion as well as the Virgin's chapel inside the Holy Sepulchre, the tomb of Mary in the Kedron Valley, and the Cave of the Nativity. Once again the local clergy were dispossessed and the Franciscans took their place; the Franciscan superior was confirmed by Rome as "Guardian of Mount Zion," later "Custodian of the Holy Land," a position that effectively gave him a Muslim-certified jurisdiction over, and responsibility for, every European pilgrim to the Holy Land, which later included some very irritated Protestant visitors.[82]

The Jews of Jerusalem, who had about 250 households in 1480, constituted a separate quarter in the southern part of the city, wedged

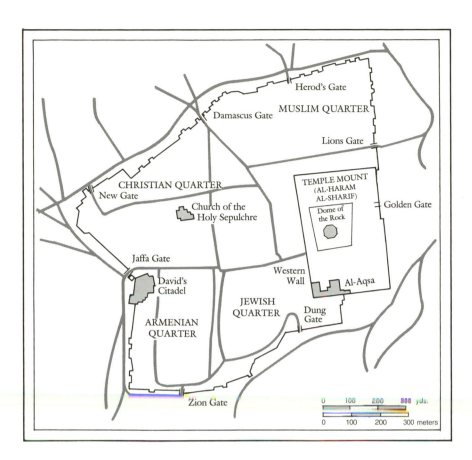

Map 3. The Old City.

between the Armenians on the west and the Muslims to the east.[83] Their life was not easy, but their poverty and near invisibility shielded them from the hostility generated by the Crusades and the Jerusalem Muslim regime's chronic need for money. It was chiefly the latter that caused the Muslim authorities to regulate—and charge for—access to the only income-bearing holy places in the city, the complex within the Holy Sepulchre. Meanwhile, inside the church there were ongoing problems with dissident Christian groups jockeying for territorial advantages that were sometimes calculated in inches. When the Ottomans replaced the Mamluks in Jerusalem in 1517, they soon learned to take profit from the competition and to play one group off against another in the heated struggle for possession of slivers of the Anastasis complex.[84] The chief players were now the Greeks, Armenians, and Latins, in that order of affluence and importance; lesser, or less affluent, communities like the Georgians, Copts, Nestorians, and Jacobites were pinched into the corners—the Abyssinians had to be content with the roof—or were forced to sell out under an accumulating load of debt. The Protestants arrived far too late to find any foothold at all—had they wished for one.[85]

Finally, even the Ottomans had had enough. First in 1757, and then more definitively in 1852, the Ottoman sultan issued a decree, "to serve constantly and forever as a permanent rule," defining everyone's place within the church—with pride of place going to the Greeks—with an adjuration that they should remain precisely there. It came to be called the "status quo ante."[86]

The "status quo" of 1852 is perhaps as close to a permanent rule as Jerusalem has ever had. It was affirmed by the succeeding British, Jordanian, and Israeli administrations of Jerusalem, but in their day the problem of the holy places was no longer that of the Christian ones—the Ottoman *diktat* had effectively solved that—but rather those of the Jews, whose claims challenged Muslim ones, and then of the Muslims, whose claims challenged Jewish ones.

Juridical bodies, whether individual like the Ottoman sultan or corporate like the League of Nations, often enter where no theologians, or even the notoriously more brazen anthropologists, would dare to tread. In November of 1949, for example, when it was still young and perhaps foolish, the United Nations took it upon itself to tote up—and thus, of course, implicitly define—the number of holy places in Jerusalem. It found that there were precisely thirty: fifteen Christian, eleven Jewish, and four Muslim.[87] It is not certain what exactly they were counting—churches? synagogues? mosques? There were scores of Muslim law schools and convents in Jerusalem whose *waqf* charters precisely separated them from the profane, and particularly from the profane hands of government, whether Muslim or Israeli. In 1967 all of these Muslim holy places fell into the profane hands of the Israeli conquerors of the Old City, including the two most inflammatory holy places of all, the Haram al-Sharif—the Noble Sanctuary— with the Dome of the Rock and the Aqsa Mosque atop it.

The earlier Ottoman decrees had effectively frozen the Christians in place—a very favorable place, from the Greek point of view. The

Jewish holy places were not included in those *firmans,* but during the Mandatory period the British found it expedient to freeze them as well under the same convenient rubric of status quo, "as you were."[88] The Muslim holy places, on the other hand, were obviously never an issue in Muslim Jerusalem, whether Ottoman or Jordanian, nor even under the Mandate, since no one was contesting them. The British had, however, constituted a Supreme Muslim Shari'a Council to administer the Muslim courts, the *waqf* properties, and the Haram. But in the summer of 1967 the Israelis held all of those elements in their own hands, and the Muslim administrative structure created by the British had disappeared. In the first flush of victory, some Israelis rushed up to the Temple Mount to pray, and soon thereafter Rabbi Shlomo Goren set up an office there and announced his intention to initiate regular prayer services.[89] A crisis was in the making. Then on June 17, 1967, Moshe Dayan, the Israeli minister of defense, formally handed over the Temple Mount to the Muslim authorities. The Israeli government and people eventually affirmed his decision, and history has so far shown that it was a wise one. Eventually, the chief rabbinate of Israel has, for its own halachic reasons, made the area taboo for Jews.

The principal Jewish holy place in Jerusalem in late medieval and early modern times is the Western Wall of the Temple platforms, and it provides a not atypical example of how a Jerusalem holy place begins with the presence of God and ends up in the hands of lawyers. At the destruction of the First Temple by the Babylonians in the sixth century BCE, many Israelites were convinced that God's enhoused presence, His Shechinah, had gone elsewhere. He would return, Ezekiel promised (44:1–4), and presumably so He did, to the Second Temple of Zerubbabel and Herod. But what occurred in 70 CE? in 135? Where was God's Shechinah, His sacred presence that gave sanctity to the precinct? We have seen that Jews defied the Roman ban and returned to the Temple Mount after the destruction, but it was not to sacrifice, nor perhaps even to pray, but to lament the misfortune that had fallen upon the place. The Midrashim of the seventh century CE maintained that the Presence of God had never left the Western Wall, but they were almost certainly referring to the western wall of the city and not, as understood in the sixteenth century, the western face of Herod's platform.[90] This is not to suggest that the Temple site ceased to be revered by Jews; they simply were not permitted to enter it. It was on the Mount of Olives that the Jews assembled for Succoth, and it was there, some suggested, that the Shechinah had come to rest.[91]

It is not easy to trace the subsequent growth of the tradition, but by the sixteenth century the Jerusalem Jews had found a new place to pray—with the appropriate adjustment of the earlier rabbinic exegesis—in the narrow open space between the towering western face of Herod's platform and the house of the nearby Muslim mosque and Moroccan quarter.[92] And squatters' rights had in effect been established. Squatters' rights are the stuff of dreams, however, not of reality. In the nineteenth century, after a progressive liberalization of the municipal administration of Jerusalem—Muhammad Ali had established the first city council there—and the growing backing of the Jerusalem Jews by some of their European co-religionists,[93] the tiny piece of ground called the Western Wall—1,290 square feet to be exact[94]—grew into a major source of contention between the Jews and the Ottoman authorities.

Under other circumstances the two sides might have taken up arms, but this was a Muslim time in a Muslim land and so the issue invariably ended up in court, a Muslim court, which equally invariably found against the Jews.[95] In the wake of World War I it was no longer a Muslim land, however, but a British one, at least in a mandatory sense. The British had their own courts, but they preferred, as we might today, an International Commission, whose findings, which continued to restrict Jewish access and usage, were incorporated into Palestinian law by an Order of Council in 1931.

The next change was a cataclysmic one, the Israeli conquest of the Old City; not only were the tables turned, but the entire city was as well. Quickly, the Moroccan quarter was bulldozed away and the space before the wall broadened out. The Muslims appealed to the 1931 Order of Council, but that was, quite obviously, a dead letter. What was vigorously alive, however, was the argument among Jews about whether the site was a holy one or a historical one. It was both, obviously, but the real question was who had jurisdiction, the Ministry of Religious Affairs, which wanted to convert it into a synagogue, the National Parks Authority, which wanted to preserve it as a landmark, or the archaeologists. To pray or to dig at the foundations of Herod's Temple? The answer was—as UNESCO sputtered ineffectively in the background—the usual pragmatic Israeli one, a little of both, with a strict, though imaginary, line of demarcation between the sacred Torah stands and the profane bulldozers.[96]

Despite the June 1967 Israeli Law of the Holy Places guaranteeing both protection and access,[97] the question of these Jerusalem sites hangs suspended like a sword over future negotiations regarding the city. Access is not possession, nor even control. During the Mandate, the Jews had pleaded that the Western Wall was a *res Dei,* the possession of God, and so not subject to barter, sale, or even control. In a sense, all of Jerusalem, and all the multiplying holy places within it, are *res Dei*. But in the past the designation has never protected these sites from the *lex Caesaris,* and there is little reason to think that it will in the future, whoever the Caesar may be.

3

Jerusalem in Jewish Spirituality

JOSEPH DAN

The components of the spiritual significance of Jerusalem are variegated and deeply embedded in the experience of Western man. Some of them are temporal: Jerusalem signifies the glories of the past, the moments in history in which Man and God have become closest. An example can be found in the *Akedah,* the Binding, when Abraham was declared God's Beloved and Isaac represented the ultimate human sacrifice, the prototype of all martyrs; another is in the building of the Temple, when God descended to earth to reside among men. Jerusalem also represents the future, the ultimate union between humanity and God, when the in-gathering of the exiles will bring the people to the divine fold, to be united forever. A vision of an eternal future utopia is identified with the name of the city, a vision which embodies a craving for eternal life, the overcoming of death, individual and national redemption, the reign of justice, the achievement of happiness, and religious fulfillment. And finally, Jerusalem expresses the present desire for spiritual uplifting—for a personal, religious, and mystical experience.

For Jews, in addition to its temporal component, Jerusalem's spatial configuration is also significant. Since creation began in Jerusalem, it is the center of the universe, the meeting point between chaos and creation. It is the name of God which blocks the deluge of chaos from engulfing the earth; it is both the core of the universe, and its point of emergence. It represents the ultimate evidence of God's gift to humanity—earthly existence. Celestial Jerusalem, by contrast, represents the indestructibility of perfection. The constant contrast between physical ruins and spiritual eternal structure, between earthly desolation and sublime perfection, expresses both the hardship and suffering and the opportunity of spiritual unity in the divine abode, into which the mystic is invited to share God's eternal residence. Jerusalem is the supreme expression of exile and destruction, of poverty and suffering, while it also represents eternal spiritual bliss.

The Place in which Heaven and Earth Meet

The *Sefer Yezira* (Book of Creation), written probably in the third century, described the cosmos as the infinite expansion of ten directions or dimensions,[1] which represent space, time, and ethics: North, South, West, East, Up, Down, Beginning, End, Good, and Evil. These are described as divine arms expanding and engulfing the universe. The center is "the holy Temple, which is suspended in the middle." This image obviously unites the spiritual and the worldly, the divine and the earthly, into the cosmic concept of Jerusalem as the center of human and divine existence.[2]

The image of Jerusalem as a spiritual symbol appeals to all human faculties. It includes the intellectual craving for knowledge, truth, and wisdom; at the same time, it represents the consummation of justice and purity. And, most of all, it represents the touching point between the divine and the earthly, the place in which heaven and earth meet, and where a person can stretch his hand and touch the divine. Unlike the concept of afterlife, which became so dominant in religion in the Middle Ages and modern times—a concept which puts death at the center of human life, by making it the touching point between temporality and eternity, between suffering and perfection—Jerusalem represents the achievement of eternity and immortality without the intervention of death. Jerusalem is the place where present and future merge without the traumatic destruction of one's body. Jerusalem negates the separation between soul and limbs that was a major component of the Neoplatonic spirituality that imbues religious concepts but is contrary to both human experience and cravings. In Jerusalem, redemption and perfection are offered as a direct transition into numinous bliss.

The very beginning of Jewish mysticism—and, possibly of mystical expression in any religion[3]—is deeply connected, as recent studies demonstrate, with the pilgrimage to Jerusalem. The earliest descriptions of a spiritual ascent to God, found in the Hekhalot mystical literature (third to seventh centuries),[4] are among the most intense expressions in religious literature of the uplifting of the mystic's soul stage by stage until, overcoming difficulties and threats, it confronts the Throne of Glory and faces the King in His Glory in an ancient expression of numinous perfection. It has been suggested that the mystical ascent is a pilgrimage, a substitute for the earthly three-times-a-year trip to Jerusalem.[5] Ezekiel's vision of the holy chariot, which travels from earth to the celestial and divine world, has been identified with the Jerusalem Temple, transformed into intense mystical symbolism.[6] It seems, if these conclusions are correct, that the very concept of mystical ascension emerged in scriptural religion as a counterpart of the pilgrimage to Jerusalem, and that the celestial worlds envisioned by the mystic are reflections of the idealized images of Jerusalem and the Temple. Jerusalem is then identified with the Godhead Itself, the purpose of the mystical ascent.

Jerusalem as not just a religious and ritualistic entity but also as a political entity—the ideal "king's city,"[7] the city of King Solomon's palace and government—is central to the image of the mystical visions of Jerusalem.[8] The most important complex of symbols and pictures, which was fused with that of the Temple and became one of the most potent sources of spiritual and mystical drives in Judaism and Christianity, is the Song of Songs. The allegoristic depictions of this work did not erase its literal, monarchic, and sexual descriptions, which became basic metaphors for individual and communal union with God.[9] A mystical text of that period identifies Solomon's throne with that of God Himself.[10] R. Elior emphasized the priestly characteristics of the Hekhalot terminology;[11] Rabbi Ishmael ben Elisha, for example, the central figure in several Hekhalot texts, is described as a high priest who is the son of a high priest, and a mystical paragraph describing his meeting with God when officiating in the Temple is found in the Talmud.[12] Another example is a group of Hekhalot mystics described as meeting in Jerusalem, in the "third entrance" to the Temple, even though the mystics named in this narrative lived two generations after the destruction of Jerusalem and the Temple.[13] Thus, the first picture of a congregation of mystics, which was destined to play a major role in medieval Jewish mysticism—in the depictions of the *idras* ("sacred conventions") in the medieval *Zohar*—is seen in the destroyed yet mystically alive Jerusalem. One of the most influential Hebrew mystical texts describes in detail the revelation of God in Jerusalem while the Second Temple was being built.[14] Thus, the earliest texts of Jewish mysticism established a vast panorama of symbols, metaphors, and terminology that associated Jerusalem with every vision of God, adding new dimensions to the biblical and talmudic traditions which described the political, ritualistic, and cosmic significance of the city.

The Jerusalem of these early mystics is both destroyed and alive, in ruins and in full splendor. This dual nature of Jerusalem was regarded as expressing the dual state of the human soul, residing in a body and in a world of matter, evil and exiled, yet at the same time a resident of utmost beauty and perfection in the divine city. Two different elements were interwoven in this concept: the utopian-apocalyptic and the individual-mystical. When Rabbi Akibah is depicted in a talmudic story as walking over the ruins of Jerusalem laughing while his colleagues were weeping, because the promise of the rebuilding of Jerusalem is going to be fulfilled in the same way that the promise of its destruction was,[15] he was expressing the utopian belief in the imminent, worldly salvation of the city. The same Rabbi Akibah is described in the mystical treatise *Hekhalot Zutarti* as ascending to the divine palaces and achieving the supreme spiritual proximity to God as an individual.[16] Hebrew apocalypses of late antiquity, like the *Sefer Zerubavel,* describe the beginning of cosmic redemption in Jerusalem, which will be destroyed again during the wars of that era, but from one corner of the city the victorious messiah will emerge and overcome the hosts of the devil.[17] These two aspects of the visionary Jerusalem combine with the duality of dead-yet-alive Jerusalem: it represents the way the individual can escape his imprisonment in the world of matter and suffering within the framework of the present phase in history, and it represents the future, utopian eschatology of the people and the community, in which there will be no more exile and oppression, and in which the two Jerusalems, the ideal and the earthly, will be reunited. The future building of Jerusalem thus becomes the descent of the celestial city to earth (or the elevation of everything earthly to the level of the spiritual entity).[18] The basic duality of eschatology, that of individual fulfillment and national redemption, is clearly reflected in the vision of the spiritual Jerusalem.[19]

We do not know the origins and early development of the concept of a celestial Jerusalem which exists parallel to the earthly one.[20] There is very little doubt, however, that this concept was not the result of the destruction of the city but developed during the Second Commonwealth period. It thus served both talmudic Judaism and early Christianity as a traditional belief, deeply inherent in the concept of Jerusalem; the destruction in 70 CE only gave it a new impetus and a new importance. Indeed, it seems that the rabbinic sources emphasize that the celestial Temple was created before the creation of the world, and that the earthly Jerusalem and its Temple were built in correspondence to the celestial ideal.[21] Philo of Alexandria, who wrote before the destruction of Jerusalem, seems to have been uncomfortable with the national aspect of this tradition, and reinterpreted it in a cosmic, universal manner.[22] According to him, the logos can be conceived as offering homage to the supreme God like a priest praying in the temple.[23]

The Messianic Role of Jerusalem

Jerusalem's messianic role is interwoven of earthly and spiritual elements. The earthly Jerusalem is the constant guardian of the universe from the primeval chaos; and the rock on which God's name is engraved, deep inside the Temple Mount, is the barrier between the waters of a new deluge and the inhabited world. When King David found it and tried to lift it, the waters surged and endangered the whole universe.[24] This legend is repeated constantly in ancient and medieval Hebrew sources, making geographical Jerusalem no less significant than the celestial one.

In apocalyptic visions and speculations, both aspects of Jerusalem play a central role. The concept of the messiah and Jerusalem are inseparable in Hebrew texts for nearly two millennia. Throughout the Middle Ages and early modern times Jews were constantly drawn to Jerusalem as the place from which redemption will start and where the Messiah is destined to make his first appearance. This is the place where resurrection will occur, and people who are buried in this city will not have to wander under the earth until they reach the resurrection-point.[25] In this way, Jerusalem was not just an abstract ideal but a constant option in the life of every individual. Each person had to decide whether he is able to immigrate to Jerusalem and be buried there.

Figure 6. The Western Wall, ca. 1870.

Another concept of Jerusalem, of the city as a feminine entity, began to emerge in antiquity, long before it was integrated in kabbalistic symbolism. The apocryphal work, the Fourth Ezra, includes a detailed parable in which Jerusalem is depicted as a grieving woman;[26] this picture is repeated dozens of times in Jewish mystical literature as well as in folklore.[27] But in none of these motifs has the celestial Jerusalem replaced the earthly one. The concept rested completely on these two legs of the earthly and the divine cities, which only together constitute a whole. While Jerusalem is an intensely significant historical entity, and its fate reflects the vagaries of historical change, the duality itself is not subject to history: Jerusalem is equally meaningful in the creation of heaven and of earth, and continues to retain its dual character in each phase of the universal past, present, and future.

The High Middle Ages

In the early centuries of the Middle Ages we find a decline in the centrality of speculations concerning Jerusalem in Jewish culture. The emergence of rationalism and science, and the theologies which emphasized the religious bond between every individual and God, rather than those of the people or the nation, limited the scope of such speculations.[28] For several centuries the mystical dimension in Jewish culture was diminished. Even messianic speculations, like those of Maimonides, were formulated in a rational, political mode, minimizing the place of the city. This despite the fact that at the same time Jerusalem acquired new dimensions of meaning in Christian theology and history (during the period of the Crusades), and its important place in Islamic thought and practice was enhanced. Nevertheless, Nachmanides, the great mystic of the first half of the thirteenth century, pointed out that no non-Jewish entity could be established in Jerusalem; even when Jews were absent from the city, nobody else could claim it as his.[29] Yet many other mystics of the thirteenth century did not develop Nachmanides' theme beyond the traditions received from late antiquity.[30] It was the new mystical school which emerged in the second half of the twelfth century and dominated Jewish mysticism for eight hundred years, the Kabbalah, that reformulated the concept of the spiritual Jerusalem within the framework of a new system of symbols and myths, and reinvigorated the centrality of the celestial Jerusalem in Jewish spirituality.

Jerusalem and the Kabbalah

In the earliest work of the Kabbalah, *Sefer ha-Bahir*, written in Provence or northern Spain around 1185, the celestial Eretz Israel is identified with the supreme divine Wisdom, the second divine emanation in the system of the ten divine hypostases, or *sefirot*, which is the core of kabbalistic symbolism.[31] This work is attributed to various sages of the mishnaic period, and was modeled, to some extent, after

Hekhalot mystical literature. Rabbi Nehunia ben ha-Kana, the head of the mystical circle in *Hekhalot Rabbati*, is the speaker in the first paragraph of this work, and the whole book was often attributed to him; Rabbi Akibah is described as the speaker in several key sections of this pseudepigraphical treatise. The same tendency is evident in the most important work of the Kabbalah, *Sefer ha-Zohar*, which was written in northern Spain at the end of the thirteenth century.[32] The author of the *Zohar*, Rabbi Moses de Leon, followed the Hekhalot and the Bahir's literary tradition and described a circle of mystics of the mishnaic period, led by Rabbi Shimeon bar Yohai and his son, Rabbi Eleazar. The deliberations of this circle included celestial ascensions and meetings with emissaries from the divine world, as well as homiletical and hermeneutic discussions of biblical verses. The *Zohar* presented a new integration of the concept of the spiritual Jerusalem within Jewish thought and Jewish ritual.

The vast myths and mystical speculations of the *Zohar* employed all the old motifs concerning Jerusalem, but gave them a new meaning and a new complexity. Thus, the *Zohar* states, when discussing the term "Zion":

> When the world was created, it was created from that place which is the perfection and completion of the world, for it is the single point of the world and the center of all, and what is it? Zion . . . as it is written [Psalms 50:2] "Out of Zion, the perfection and the beauty, God has shined forth," from the place that is the limit of the perfection of complete faith, as it should be. Zion is the strength and the point of the whole world, and from that place the whole world was made and completed, and from it the whole world is nourished.[33]

This is a restatement of the ancient concept of Jerusalem or Zion as the center and source of creation. The two names of the city represent a duality within the divine realm, the separation between divine judgment, embodied by the fifth *sefirah*, *Din* or *Gevurah* (Judgment, Power), and by the tenth, *Shechinah* or *Malchut* (Presence, Kingdom), and divine mercy, embodied by the fourth *sefirah*, *Hesed* (Mercy), and the ninth, *Yesod* (Foundation). These two aspects of the Godhead are connected by the sixth *sefirah*, *Tiferet* (Glory, here referred by another frequent symbol, Voice). Zion is regarded as the representation of divine mercy, while Jerusalem is identified with divine judgment, with the Shechinah, which is also the divine presence in the universe.[34]

The two aspects of the physical city, the source and foundation of the universe, and the destroyed capital, the expression of God's punishment, are hypostasized in the *Zohar* as the two aspects of the unfolding of divine power into the universe, as the power of creation and the power of destruction and punishment. Thus divine duality and historical, physical duality are united into one set of symbols, which are the central aspects of the Godhead itself. The relationships between God and the universe have been transformed, in kabbalistic symbolism and experience, into the internal divisions and dynamics within the Godhead itself. On the other hand, universal phenomena and events have been transformed into the dynamics of the unfolding of the divine aspects and their cosmic manifestations.[35] Jerusalem thus became an expression of the union with God, without departure from the physical city; rather, physical union with the city was identified with the spiritual union with God. Whereas in Hekhalot mysticism the ascent of God's palaces entailed a departure from the material world, in the zoharic system the physical contact was identified with the spiritual journey.

This is evident in another central theme of the *Zohar*, expressed in the many passages dedicated to the interpretation of the sacrifices and the rituals in the ancient Temple.[36] The new dynamic concept of the inner life within the Godhead which characterizes the *Zohar* has been expressed in the detailed unity depicted in this work between the rituals in the Temple and the process of unification among the divine hypostases of God.[37] In this context, the feminine character of Jerusalem was again enhanced and developed into an intense erotic symbolism. The identification of Jerusalem with the Shechinah, which is regarded by the kabbalists as the feminine element within the Godhead, gave an erotic dimension to the relationship between God and His abode in Jerusalem and in the Temple. Several passages in the *Zohar* describe in detail the sexual union experienced there:

> At midnight [the Shechinah] enters through the point of Zion, the place of the Holy of Holies and she sees it destroyed, and the place of her dwelling and her couch defiled . . . She cries bitterly, raises her voice, and says: "My couch, my couch, the place where I used to dwell

. . . My husband would come to me and lie in my arms and all that I asked him, and all my requests he would fulfill, when he came to me and made his home with me and took delight between my breasts . . . Do you not remember the days of our love, when I would lie in your arms . . . Do you not remember how you stretched out your left hand beneath my head, and how I rejoiced in the flow of peace, and your right hand embraced [me] with love and kisses . . . ?"[38]

In the passages dedicated to this subject, such descriptions abound not only concerning the lost past but also as pictures of the future redemption and reestablishment of the Temple ritual. The mystical meaning of the Song of Songs, which played a prominent part in Hekhalot mysticism, has reemerged in the zoharic myth; the erotic element in this biblical text, which was largely ignored in the ancient mystical texts, has become now the central theme, representing the dynamic aspects of the relationships within the Godhead.

Another aspect of the zoharic myths concerning Jerusalem and Zion, God and the Shechinah, is its integration with present-day rituals. Jerusalem and the Temple are not only distant memories, paradigms of the creation and the sacrifices at the Temple; they are also represented by the daily prayers, the rituals of the Sabbath and the festivals, and the vast body of Jewish precepts and commandments. When performing the everyday commandments and rituals, the same dynamism is evoked within the divine realms, and the union between the divine male and female may occur, instigated by human religious activity. The identification between the rituals of the ancient Temple and the commandments of present-day Judaism has turned every person into a participant in the dramatic myth described in the *Zohar.* The erotic symbolism is thus related also to the worshipper, and not only to the divine powers.[39]

This extension of the symbolism concerning Jerusalem had its spiritual price. The identification of Jerusalem with the Shechinah and the various myths connected with her in the *Zohar,* which was developed further in subsequent kabbalistic works, made "Jerusalem" one of the hundreds of religious terms, rituals, and concepts which are associated with this central feminine aspect of the divine world, losing its uniqueness. When "Jerusalem" became one of a series of symbols, which included the Sabbath, *Kneset Yisrael* (the Congregation of

Israel), "earth," "night," and dozens of others, the eschatological and utopian element became diminished. The connection between the spiritual concept and the physical, geographic designation was blurred; large segments of the prayers and the rituals were associated with the Shechinah, and the specific meaning of "Jerusalem" was merged with the general, mystical craving for union with the divine world. Yet, throughout the Middle Ages we do not find a definite substitution of the spiritual concept of Jerusalem instead of its unique physical essence. On the contrary, in the late medieval period and the beginnings of modern times, the messianic element in the Kabbalah increased, and with it the centrality of the symbol of Jerusalem representing a union between its earthly and divine aspects. The intensely messianic works of Rabbi Abraham berabi Eliezer ha-Levi,[40] who immigrated to Jerusalem in the beginning of the sixteenth century, are a clear example of this reintensification.

During the sixteenth century the physical focus of kabbalistic ritual became centered in another place in the Land of Israel, in the small town of Safed in the Upper Galilee, where a group of kabbalists established a major spiritual center, close to the legendary tomb of the hero of the zoharic legends, Rabbi Shimeon bar Yohai.[41] These kabbalists, however, did not see Safed as replacing Jerusalem in any way; it was part of the combination of the spiritual and material Land of Israel, the subject of mystical adherence and physical connection.

The messianic movement of Sabbatianism in the last third of the seventeenth century, which flourished in various ways during the eighteenth century as well, reinforced the union between the spiritual symbolism and the actual messianic endeavor of returning to Jerusalem. The two leaders of the movement, Shabbatai Sevi and his "prophet" Nathan of Gaza, frequently visited the city, where they had many adherents from the earliest stages of the development of the movement.[42] In the year 1700 a large group of Sabbatians from Eastern Europe, led by Rabbi Judah the Pious and Rabbi Hayyim Malakh, immigrated to Jerusalem to await the return of the Messiah,[43] this being the largest among many groups who settled in the city motivated by messianic expectations. Similarly, several of the leaders of the early Hasidic movement in the second half of the eighteenth century immigrated, or tried to immigrate, to Jerusalem and the Galilee.[44] In this movement, however, we find the clearest separation between spiritual and physical Jerusalem in the history of Jewish mysticism. Some of the Hasidic leaders who remained in Eastern Europe and established communities of adherents there developed, for the first time, a distinction between Jerusalem as a spiritual symbol and the physical-geographic entity. The subject has been discussed in detail by Rivkah Shatz,[45] who presented the important Hasidic texts relating to this phenomenon, most of them from the school of Rabbi Elimelekh of Lizensk in the late eighteenth century. Several statements of these Hasidic leaders express the view that the spiritual Land of Israel and Jerusalem are to be found in the proximity to the Zaddik, the divinely endowed mystical leader of a Hasidic sect, rather than in a physical pilgrimage to the earthly city. These authors made use of the kabbalistic identification of Jerusalem with Zion as the ninth divine *sefirah* or the Shechinah, the tenth, to deny the spiritual significance of the earthly city and generalize its meaning in a way which could be included in the rituals carried out in exile.[46] Rabbi Nachman of Bratslav formulated this concept in the ambiguous statement: "Everywhere I go, I go to the Land of Israel," which actually means that geography is meaningless; spiritual significance is to be found only in the internal intention.[47] This attitude, which was based on some scattered statements in medieval and early modern kabbalistic writings, acquired political significance in the last hundred years, supplying a theological dimension to the fierce opposition of most of the Hasidic leaders to the Zionist movement.

This change in the attitude toward Jerusalem can be explained as the result of a change in the concept of the city as the actual and spiritual center of the universe. The two aspects of the city, the physical and the spiritual, remain united as long as this belief persists. Once a different *axis mundi* replaces Jerusalem, the bond between the two aspects can be broken. The formulation of the Hasidic concept of the Zaddik as the center of the world and the source of present and future redemption created a physical and spiritual substitute for the Holy City: clinging to the Zaddik, geographically and spiritually, became the main purpose of religious life. The pilgrimage to the Zaddik's court replaced the pilgrimage to Jerusalem. In the medieval Kabbalah both Zion and Zaddik serve as symbols for the ninth *sefirah*, which is also called *axis mundi*.[48] The ancient Hekhalot mystics substituted a mystical journey to the celestial temples for the pilgrimage to Jerusalem; modern Hasidim found such a substitute in the mystical adherence to the Zaddik and the physical visits to his court. In contemporary Jerusalem, followers of the Habad (Lubavitch) Hasidic sect used to travel on the holidays to the court of the late Menachem Mendel Shneersohn in Brooklyn, and when they returned to the city they described their experiences there in terms reminiscent of the pilgrimage to Jerusalem and the Temple in ancient times. They thus expressed the full paradoxical turnabout; in order to be united with the spiritual Jerusalem one has to leave the physical city and travel to the Zaddik's dwelling across the ocean, at 770 Eastern Parkway, Brooklyn.[49]

The intensity of Hasidic mysticism, which was renewed in the last few decades, despite the catastrophic results of the Holocaust among the Hasidic communities of Eastern Europe, marginalized other contemporary Jewish mystical traditions and directions. Yet within the vast picture of the history of Jewish spirituality, this separation between earthly Jerusalem and mystical salvation is an exception. The dominant elements described above are present today, even among many Hasidic sects like Belz and Gur, which made Jerusalem their worldly center.

Jerusalem has become, in the last eighty years, the center of fierce political conflict, which marginalized to some extent the contemporary meaningfulness of the heavenly city. Its physical presence has been, and is, so overwhelming that pure spiritual concentration on its numinous significance was relegated to a secondary place. But for the first time in its long history the city has become in this century the meeting place of the three religions which worship it, even though this meeting has been characterized more by conflict than by mutual understanding.

I belong to a generation of Jews, Muslims, and Christians who grew up in this city when it was divided between Jews and Arabs and governed by a Christian empire, Britain. During the long decades of intense Arab-Israeli conflict, the realization of the deep interest of the Christian world in everything that happened in this city has become evident. In this century, more and more people of the three religions have become aware—for the first time—that narrow streets, synagogues, churches, and mosques in the city represent three spiritual geographies, superimposed one above the other in the tiny area of the Old City. The spiritual significance of the Holy Sepulchre and al-Aqsa can no more be ignored by Jews; Muslims and Christians cannot ignore the meaning of the Western Wall and the excavations of the City of David. A process of mutual recognition of the sanctity of the city is going on, even though it is still characterized mainly by hatred and struggle.

In previous generations, the spiritual and mystical literatures of each of the three religions completely ignored the very existence of the "spiritual geography" of the other two. History is relentlessly pushing the faithful of all three into recognizing the basic similarities in their attitudes toward the city. This is a new experience in the three thousand years of history of spiritual and earthly Jerusalem; the hope that it will culminate in peaceful mutual acceptance may not be completely futile.

4

The Holy City in Christian Thought

PAULA FREDRIKSEN

The importance of the city of Jerusalem within Christianity is the measure of the younger community's attachment to the traditions and scriptures of Israel. By tracing the history of the church's views on Jerusalem, we trace as well an intellectual and social history both of the religion itself and of its relation to other religions, most especially Judaism. During the formative period of Christianity, roughly from the first to the fifth century, the new Christian community forged its own identity, composed its foundational texts—which, by the second century, began to appear collected as a specifically Christian canon, the New Testament—and constructed its fundamental theology. To better understand why the early Christian texts and traditions about Jerusalem were what they were, we must place them within their historical context.

From Jesus to Paul

Jerusalem became holy to Christians because it was holy to Jesus. The founder of a messianic movement within Judaism, Jesus had preached the coming Kingdom of God from the beginning of his public activity.[1] His journey to Jerusalem for Passover was the crescendo of this preaching: perhaps he expected the Kingdom to arrive, beginning in Jerusalem, at or as the climax of his mission. We do not know whether he regarded himself as the messiah or whether any of his followers claimed that title for him during his lifetime (the evidence is extremely ambiguous);[2] but, once in Jerusalem, he certainly died as if he had, crucified by Rome for sedition ("Jesus of Nazareth, King of the Jews," John 19:19). In subsequent Christian tradition, Jerusalem's messianic status was enhanced by the miracle of Jesus' Resurrection. The Risen Lord stayed in Jerusalem for forty days to instruct his disciples further about the Kingdom of God (Acts 1:3); just outside the city, he ascended into heaven from the Mount of Olives (1:9, 12).

This early postresurrection community was thus doubly bound to Jerusalem. As Jews, they cherished Jerusalem as David's holy city, the site of God's temple, and, in apocalyptic perspective, the city of the coming messiah (cf. Zechariah 9:9). As followers of Jesus, they esteemed the city as the site of the great redemptive miracle of his Resurrection, and as the place of his promised return in glory. The movement gave up its Galilean roots and adopted Jerusalem as its center, and it was from Jerusalem that the first apostles proclaimed the *evangelion*, the "good news" of the impending Kingdom of God, to be ushered in with the return of his Son, the crucified and risen messiah.[3]

Their gospel eventually moved out from Judea and the Galilee to the cities of the Mediterranean Diaspora, but Jerusalem retained its special authority and prestige. Even Paul, who was not part of the original group and who resented its challenge to his own authority (Galatians 1:12–2:9, 12–14; 1 Corinthians 15:1–10), attempted to coordinate his mission with the mother church (Galatians 2:1ff.; cf. Acts 15). And he saw his work among his own communities as "priestly service," bringing their donations, like a sanctified offering to the altar, to "the poor among the saints in Jerusalem" (Romans 15).

But against the expectations of the first apostles, time stretched on between the Resurrection of Jesus and his anticipated return, the *Parousia* (a Greek word for "presence" or "arrival"). The movement grew, but fewer and fewer Jews received their message. By the 50s, on the evidence of Paul's letters, the trend was clear: most believers were Gentiles. What, then, was to be these Gentiles' relation to the sacred obligations encoded in Torah, observed by Jesus of Nazareth and the apostolic community, and embedded in those Scriptures through which his followers increasingly expressed their postresurrection faith? Should they assume responsibility for the covenant—circumcision, food laws, Sabbath, behavior codes? And if not, how then were they to distinguish themselves from their pagan world and express their new allegiance to Christ and thus to his father, the God of Israel?

Paul's letters provide our first view of this early controversy, and of his own part in it. Christ, he held, was the end-point or culmination *(telos)* of the Torah (Romans 10:4). Since God's spirit, through baptism, had passed to his Gentiles in Christ, it enabled them to fulfill the Law's requirements through their faith (3:31, and frequently). No need, then, for them to be circumcised, that is, convert to Judaism and so "be obligated to the whole Law" (Galatians 5:3). Gentiles had been saved through grace, as a gift.

The community in Jerusalem concurred with Paul: Gentiles in Christ need not convert to Judaism in order to participate in Israel's redemption (2:2–10; cf. Acts 15).[4] So too did those apostles, whoever they were, who in advance of Paul established the *ekklesia* at Rome (Romans 1:10). But other Christians disagreed, urging these Gentiles, in the age before the end, to normalize their relationship to Israel and so convert to Judaism—for men, to receive circumcision.

Their position infuriated Paul. In letter after letter, he railed against "false brothers," "so-called apostles," and "circumcising dogs"—that is, these rival Christian missionaries. In his most intemperate epistle, Galatians, in full voice against his competition, Paul argued by evoking Jerusalem:

> Tell me, you who desire to be under the Law, do you not hear the Law? For it is written that Abraham had two sons, one by a slave and one by a free woman. But the son of the slave was born according to the flesh, and the son of the free woman through promise. *Now this is an allegory. These women are two covenants. One is from Mount Sinai, bearing children for slavery: she is Hagar. Now Hagar is Mount Sinai in Arabia. She corresponds to the present Jerusalem, for she is in slavery with her children. But the Jerusalem above is free, and she is our mother.* For it is written,
>
> > Rejoice O barren one who does not bear;
> > Break forth and shout, you who are not in travail;
> > For the children of the desolate one are many more
> >   than the children of her that is married. [Isaiah 54:1]

> Now we, brethren, like Isaac, are children of promise. But as at that time he who was born according to the flesh persecuted him who was born according to the Spirit, so it is now. But what does the scripture say? "Cast out the slave and her son; for the son of the slave shall not inherit with the son of the free woman." So, brethren, we are children not of the slave but of the free woman.

Clearly Paul meant to insult and demean his opponents through this double allegory. Hagar, the first woman, stood for both the Sinai covenant and the earthly Jerusalem. Her children (by implication, Paul's rivals), who persecute the child of the free woman, are slaves: they shall be cast out. But the free woman (Sarah) represents not the flesh or slavery—Paul's code words for Gentile circumcision—but freedom and promise. She is Jerusalem above, the mother of Paul's community. These children, like her son Isaac, though persecuted by Hagar's children, are born of spirit and promise. They shall inherit; they, in Christ, are free (5:1).

Later generations of Christians, of course, did not read Galatians in this way—that is, as a moment of high polemic, embedded in a precise social context within the formative years of the movement. They read it instead as Paul's blanket condemnation of Judaism itself.[5] All Jews, they held, not just Paul's Judaizing rivals, were the children of enslaved, earthly Jerusalem. They, the Gentile church, were born of a celestial mother, the free city, Jerusalem above.

Something more persuasive than Paul's rhetoric stood behind this later reading, however. The facts of history reinforced it. For in the year 66 CE, after decades of uneasy relations between the Jews and Rome, Judea erupted in open revolt. A long and bloody campaign ended when Titus' troops captured Jerusalem in the summer of 70. They slaughtered her inhabitants and leveled her buildings. The great Temple crowning Jerusalem was utterly destroyed.

Jerusalem Below

With the exception of Paul's letters, all the other writings eventually collected into the New Testament canon were composed sometime after the devastation of Jerusalem. Their authors regarded the destruction of the city in religious perspective: Why would God have permitted the destruction of his Temple, unless he was displeased with the Jews and their cult? They knew, further, the reason for God's displeasure: the Jews had failed to heed his Son. Worse: his death had been their work.

This conviction shaped the evangelists' presentation of Jesus' life and—even more—his death. We know that Jesus of Nazareth, around the year 30, died by crucifixion. From this fact we may infer two others: he was executed by Rome, and he was accused of sedition. But the gospels, composed sometime between 70 and 100, present a Jesus who died for religious, not political, reasons. Inheriting traditions of Roman fiat, the evangelists elaborate on Jewish initiative.[6] The real agent in Jesus' death, in their view, was the High Priest (Mark, Matthew, and John), or the priestly court, the Sanhedrin (Luke). By comparison, and contrary to contemporary witness, Pilate, the Roman prefect, emerges as a sympathetic figure.[7]

The reader is prepared for this reversal of agency through the evangelists' device of the passion predictions. These inculpate not only the priests but also the city, which throws the sinister shadow of the cross over Jesus' Galilean ministry. "From that time Jesus began to show his disciples that he must go to Jerusalem and suffer many things from the elders and chief priests and scribes, and be killed" (Matthew 16:21). Jerusalem is a place of death.

Knowing that the Jews will reject him, Jesus weeps over the city, "foreseeing" her desolation: "O Jerusalem, Jerusalem, killing the prophets and stoning those who are sent to you! How often would I have gathered your children together as a hen gathers her brood under her wings, and you would not! Behold, your house is forsaken and desolate" (Matthew 23:37–38; Luke 13:34–35). Condemning Jewish worship in the Temple as an offense to true piety (Matthew 21:13; Mark 11:17; Luke 19:46), Jesus subsequently "prophesies" its destruction: "Do you see these great buildings? There will not be left here one stone upon another, that will not be thrown down" (Mark 13:2). Luke, writing a generation after Mark, is yet more precise: "But when you see Jerusalem surrounded by armies, then you know that its desolation has come near . . . Alas for those who are pregnant or nursing in those days! For . . . they will fall by the edge of the sword, and be led captive among all nations; and Jerusalem will be trodden down by the Gentiles" (21:20, 23–24).

Finally, when through the machinations of the Jerusalem religious elite Jesus dies on the cross, the curtain of the Temple itself tears in two (Mark 15:38). The rending of garments, of course, was an ancient sign of mourning; and this is the meaning that some early Christians gave to this tradition. Jesus' death sealed the fate of the Temple: it too had to die. And so the curtain tore "as though mourning the impending destruction of that place" (*Clementine Recognitions* 1.41). Thus, concluded evangelical tradition, in attempting to destroy Jesus the Jews actually became the agents of their own destruction.

In the course of the following century, Jews fought, and lost, two more wars against Rome: one in 115–117 in the Diaspora, one under Bar Kochba in Judea, in 132–135. With this last defeat, Hadrian forbade Jews even to enter Jerusalem. He raised a new city, Aelia Capitolina, on its ruins, and dedicated a statue to Jupiter on the site of the former Temple.[8] These events, for Gentile Christians, only confirmed the Gospels' claims.

Reading Jewish scriptures as their own, these Christians understood the prophecies concerning the destruction of the First Temple in light of recent history. "For the circumcision of the flesh," explained Justin Martyr shortly after the Bar Kochba revolt, "was given for a sign . . . that you [Jews] alone might suffer what you now suffer: that your land be desolate, your cities burned . . . and no one of you may go up to Jerusalem" (*Dialogue with Trypho* 16). Jews had compounded their guilt in killing Jesus by continuing to reject him, refusing the call of his church. And so, Justin continued, quoting Isaiah, "The city of your Holiness has become desolate; Zion has become a wilderness; Jerusalem a curse" (24).

As time passed and the period since the destruction of the city and the Temple lengthened, this empirical argument grew ever more central to Christian apologetics. A century after Justin, the great Alexandrian theologian Origen pointed to the same rough synchrony—the death of Jesus; the destruction of Jerusalem and the Temple; and the end of Jewish national sovereignty—as proof of Christian claims: "What nation but the Jews alone has been banished from its own capital city and the native place of its ancestral worship?"

(*Against Celsus* 2.6). And in the early 300s, Eusebius began his *Ecclesiastical History,* on the growth of the church, by evoking the now-familiar theme of Jewish disaster, "to describe the calamities that overtook them . . . in consequence of their plots against our Savior."

But empirical arguments are vulnerable to empirical disconfirmation. An unexpected turn in fourth-century imperial politics almost brought this tradition extreme embarrassment. In 361, Constantine's nephew, Julian, became emperor. Julian had been raised Christian. Free, as emperor, to make his own choices, he converted from Christianity to traditional Graeco-Roman paganism. And with his insider's knowledge, he resolved to lay to rest the Church's historical argument that Jewish desuetude proved Christian claims. Julian began to rebuild the Temple in Jerusalem.[9]

Ultimately, his plan came to nothing: fires plagued the building site on the Temple Mount, and Julian himself died in battle shortly thereafter, in 363. The purple reverted to the church, and any hope of an independent Jewish religious presence in Jerusalem, let alone a third Temple, receded over the horizon of possibility.

A millennium and a half later, the Roman Catholic Church responded to the convening of the first Zionist Congress with an argument that would have been familiar to the Christians of antiquity: "One thousand eight hundred and twenty-seven years have passed since the prediction of Jesus of Nazareth was fulfilled, namely that Jerusalem would be destroyed . . . A rebuilt Jerusalem, which would become the center of a reconstituted state of Israel . . . is contrary to the prediction of Christ Himself" (*Cività Cattolica* 1897). The Balfour Declaration called forth similar reactions from secular governments. "Many Christian sects and individuals," wrote U.S. secretary of state Robert Lansing to President Wilson in 1917, "would undoubtably resent turning the Holy Land over to the absolute control of the race credited with the death of Christ."[10]

Paul's image of "Jerusalem below" as Hagar in slavery with her children had begun as a polemical allegory. Years after his death, the actual city's confrontation with Rome turned allegory into reality. The idea of a vestigially Jewish Jerusalem would have a very long life in the symbolic universe of Western culture as a potent confirmation of Christian identity.

Jerusalem Above

Christian theology was born of the marriage of hellenistic philosophy and biblical narrative.[11] From hellenistic philosophy it inherited its sense not so much of the other-worldly but of the upper-worldly. For many thinking Christians, as for their educated pagan and Jewish counterparts, this physical world only imperfectly expressed the spiritual realities that were its true source: The material universe was a passing shadow cast by the world above. But from biblical narrative—the scriptures of Israel, which the church would adopt as its Old Testament—Christianity inherited its esteem of this world as the willed creation of God, and of history as the medium of God's will. More specifically, it inherited these traditions as expressed in the historical drama of Israel: the promise of redemption; the Exodus from Egypt; the Exile and Return; God's love of David and his house; the holiness of the Land of Israel, of Jerusalem, and of the Temple.

These traditions combine variously in later Christian thought. The author of the Epistle to the Hebrews, for example, gave positive meaning to the Jewish practices and beliefs familiar to him from Scripture by transposing them into the key of popular hellenistic philosophy. Thus, for this author, the Temple in Jerusalem and the Levitical priesthood that served it had been good in their way; but they were only imperfect earthly copies of their heavenly prototypes. The many priests of the earthly tabernacle, merely mortal, had to repeat their sacrifices daily (7:8, 23, 27). But Christ, the unique and eternal priest, offered himself once for all as the perfect, enduring sacrifice for sin (7:24–10:12). "When Christ appeared as high priest . . . , then through the greater and more perfect tabernacle (not made with hands, that is, not of this creation), he entered once for all into the Holy Place, taking not the blood of goats and calves but his own blood, thus securing an eternal redemption" (9:11–12).

Israel's worship had engaged only inferior copies of the heavenly realities now available to the believer through Christ. But those now in Christ must hold fast to their faith, like the witnesses whom the author proceeds to cull from the narratives of the Old Testament. He thus deftly renders the heroes of Jewish tradition into Christians *avant la lettre* who had been sustained by their faith—"the assurance of things hoped for, the conviction of things not seen" (11:1). "By faith Abraham obeyed . . . By faith Isaac invoked future blessings . . . By faith Jacob blessed the sons of Joseph" (11:8–21). "By faith Moses . . . refused to be called the son of Pharaoh's daughter . . . He considered abuse suffered for the Christ greater than the wealth and treasures of Egypt, for he looked to the [eternal] reward" (11:24–26). The history of Israel thus becomes the prehistory of the church.

For the homeland of the church, as Abraham knew, is a heavenly country and a heavenly city, "the city which has foundations whose builder and maker is God" (11:10, 16). This promised homeland the Christian now inherits: "You have come to Mount Zion, to the city of the living God, the heavenly Jerusalem" (12:2). In this lower world the Christian is a sojourner. "Here we have no lasting city, but we seek the city which is to come" (13:14), the Jerusalem above.

An other-worldly Jerusalem is a nonpolitical Jerusalem, removed from considerations of earthly power. But Christianity was built on the substratum of Jewish messianic hopes in a kingdom of righteousness established upon the ruins of current unjust authorities. The powers of earthly unrighteousness—"Babylon" in apocalyptic parlance—would cede to the power of God, encoded as "Jerusalem." Thus some Christians, stirred by evangelical and Pauline descriptions of the Second Coming, retaining the temporal sense of the Gospels' proclamation of the Kingdom, and encouraged by their reading of the prophetic books of Jewish tradition—Isaiah, Ezekiel, Daniel—continued to look forward to a Kingdom of God on earth. The descent of the heavenly Jerusalem would signal the completion of redemption.

This is the vision of the final things recorded by John of Patmos in the Book of Revelation. After terrible travails—celestial disturbances, plagues, and huge carnage; the persecution of the righteous by the apocalyptic Whore—John saw that Babylon, suddenly, would be no more (17–18). Those martyred for Christ would wake at the First Resurrection and reign with him for a thousand years (20:1–5). Fire from heaven would consume evil Gog and Magog, and the rest of the dead would be judged at the Second Resurrection (20:7–15). "And then," wrote John, "I saw a new heaven and a new earth; for the first heaven and the first earth had passed away, and the sea was no more. *And I saw the holy city, new Jerusalem, coming down out of heaven from*

God, prepared as a bride adorned for her husband" (21:1–2). "The walls of the city were jasper, her buildings gold, her foundations crowned with jewels" (21:15–21). But unlike the heavenly Jerusalem of Hebrews, which enclosed the eternal tabernacle served by Jesus as High Priest, and unlike the restored Jerusalem of Isaiah (54), Ezekiel (40), and Tobit (13), whose visions our author echoes, this Jerusalem would have no temple, "for its temple is the Lord God Almighty and the Lamb" (John 21:22). Their presence will illumine the entire city. And when will these things happen? "Surely," concludes the Lord Jesus, "I am coming soon" (22:20).

John's vision proved fundamental to a paradoxically long-lived tradition of millenarian expectation: the belief that Christ was about to return soon to establish his Kingdom on earth. Embedded in this belief were doctrinal positions definitive of that stream of Christianity that history would deem "orthodox." Against more radical churches that, in rejecting Judaism, likewise rejected the scriptures of the Jews and the God they spoke of,[12] the orthodox insisted that these scriptures, though superseded by recent revelation, were sacred, too, to the church. And against the radicals' position that no divine being could or would assume a lowly body of flesh, and thus that resurrection was a matter solely of the spirit, the orthodox insisted that this world was good; that God had sent his Son in the flesh to redeem it; the saints would be raised corporeal at the end, to enjoy the fruits of redemption here, in the world that God had made.

Hence Justin Martyr—no friend, as we have seen, of Jewish hopes of restoration—nonetheless proclaimed a vision of Christian redemption drawn directly from the restorationist prophecies of the Old Testament. When his Jewish interlocutor asks, "Do you really admit that this place, Jerusalem, shall be rebuilt; and do you expect your people to be gathered together and made joyful with Christ [the messiah] and the patriarchs?" (*Dialogue* 80), Justin readily concurs. The saints can look forward to "a resurrection of the dead, and a thousand year reign in Jerusalem" (80–81), the renewed center of God's eternal kingdom (117). The roll call of second- and third-century fathers—Irenaeus, Tertullian, Victorinus, Lactantius—affirms this belief. Jerusalem below, the Jewish Jerusalem, might rightly lie in ruin; but Jerusalem above, once descended in Judea, would signal the bodily redemption of the saints and the final establishment of God's kingdom.[13]

City of Christ, City of God

Intellectuals among the orthodox were sometimes embarrassed by the literalness of millenarian expectation. They preferred to understand prophetic passages allegorically, as witness to timeless spiritual truths rather than future historical events.[14] Thus Origen, in the early third century, dismissed those who believed in the resurrection of the body and a restored Jerusalem in Judea as carnal, unintelligent men "who reject the labor of hard thinking" (*On First Principles* 2.2, 3). "The sceptre of Judah" (Genesis 49:10), he observed, has passed to Jesus, the king not of fleshly Israel, the Jews, but spiritual Israel, the church. Quoting Paul and Hebrews, Origen concluded, "Israel is a race of souls, and Jerusalem a city in heaven" (4.3, 8). Such spiritual realities were not meant to "appear" physically on earth.

Origen's students were happy to continue his program of allegorizing scripture. But they were overtaken by events which forever altered the political context of Christianity. In 312, as the result of a victory, prompted by a vision, Constantine became the imperial patron of the church. The earthly Jerusalem, as a result, was very much back on the map.[15]

Emperors had always endorsed large projects of public building, and in this sense Constantine was little different from his pagan predecessors. To the earlier imperial repertoire of temples, theaters, and circuses, however, Constantine added grand churches, basilicas built to house the swelling numbers of new, perhaps opportune worshipers. First in Rome, then later, after conquering the eastern empire, in Byzantium, he poured his new religious allegiance into the forms of monumental architecture. Sometime in the 320s, he turned his attention to Jerusalem.

Since the early second century, Jerusalem had continued to serve as a magnet for Jewish pilgrims, who would come to mourn their ruined city. Christians, too, would sometimes journey to see the places mentioned in Scripture. But the new imperial patronage, accompanied by a lavish building program that reshaped the city according to sites sanctified by the passion of Jesus, encouraged the growth of a specifically Christian pilgrim piety. No longer valued primarily as the object of Christian *Schadenfreude* or the terrestrial counterpart to a more glorious heavenly city, Jerusalem now was venerated as itself a place holy to Christians. Devotion to Jerusalem was an expression of devotion to the humanity of Christ, and to the redemption worked by his Passion.

Christian Jerusalem sparkled with beautiful new basilicas built over sites hallowed by saving events—Golgotha, Christ's tomb, the place of his ascension. The new city centered not around the Temple Mount, as Jewish Jerusalem had, but around the glorious Church of the Resurrection (Anastasis), established over Christ's empty tomb—a new, Christian temple of prayer, as Eusebius called it (Figure 7). This language of a restored and resplendent city with a new temple in her midst drew upon the biblical prophets of Jewish restoration, as Eusebius intended. For the restored Jerusalem cohered theologically and politically with Eusebius' presentation of Constantine himself, the first Christian emperor and thus, as God's chosen one, a non-apocalyptic messiah. Isaiah's praises of the eschatological peace divinely established at the end of days thus transmute in Eusebius' rhetoric to descriptions of Constantine's government: the Kingdom of God had arrived on earth in the form of the *Pax Romana Christiana*.

By so closely identifying earthly politics and heavenly intent, Eusebius was mounting an empirical argument—and empirical arguments, as we have seen, are vulnerable to empirical disconfirmation. Alliance with the government brought the church some rude surprises, however. Constantine's sons, redividing the Empire, backed different contestants in the debate between Athanasius and Arius; then Constantine's nephew Julian traumatized ecclesiastical culture by reinstituting paganism and attempting to rebuild the Temple in Jerusalem. But nothing was more traumatic than the fall of Rome to Gothic invaders in the year 410.

Rome's fall released a torrent of apocalyptic speculation.[16] Earlier millenarians had been hostile to the Empire. Thus John of Patmos' apocalyptic Babylon, seated on seven hills, was clearly Rome (Revelation 17:9): at her fall the saints shout Hallelujah! (19). Ireneaus identified the fourth beast in Daniel's vision as the Empire (Daniel 7:7ff.), and the name of John's beast, encoded in the mystical number 666, as "Latinus" (Revelation 13:18). Victorinus, commenting on Revelation, awaited "the destruction of Babylon, that is, of the city of Rome." But even before Constantine, and certainly since, more prudent bishops had identified the fate of Rome with that of the church. The fall of Rome, accordingly, changed from something to be longed for to something to be dreaded: its collapse would occasion the appearance of Antichrist, and the terrors before the end.[17]

Jerusalem was the epicenter in these scenarios of Antichrist. According to interpretations of Daniel and 2 Thessalonians, he would set himself up in the Temple to be adored as a god. Of the tribe of Dan, that is, a Jew, he would inflict circumcision on those under his dominion. In this nightmare form of apocalyptic, the ruined Jewish Jerusalem would rise up to take its vengeance on the Christians of the Empire.

Julian had given the church a *mauvais quart d'heure*. But the invading Goths plunged the entire Mediterranean world, pagan and Christian, into deep shock. Christians calculated the times; pagans, meanwhile, observed that since the Empire had deserted the gods, the gods had deserted the Empire.

It was in and to these circumstances that Augustine, bishop of Hippo, responded with his masterwork, *The City of God*.[18] Against the pagans he argued that Rome's fortunes had fluctuated even when the gods had been worshiped; where Rome had succeeded, it was due to ambition for glory and love of power. Morally and religiously, then, classical culture had been a failure. Against Christian triumphalism, he argued that history was inscrutable: the hand of God could not be discerned in any extrascriptural occurrence, even if that occurrence happened to benefit the Church. And finally, against the millenarians, he insisted that the arrival of the end could in no way be known: it was futile, then, to attempt to calculate the times by matching scriptural prophecies to current events.

Augustine spread out his argument over a huge canvas—twenty-two books, written over thirteen years. The whole was united by his pursuit of a single theme: an analysis of the history of love. Ever since

Figure 7. Greek ceremony of washing the feet in the outside court of the Holy Sepulchre, ca. 1880.

Cain and Abel, all humanity has been divided up between two great cities according to the orientation of their love. Those who love carnal, lower things—and most insidiously of all, themselves—belong to Babylon, the earthly city, the *civitas terrena;* those who love God, to the heavenly city, Jerusalem above, the *civitas Dei.*

Imperial Christianity, as we have seen, had tended to appropriate that stream of Jewish Scripture that spoke of territory, triumph, homecoming. When Constantine built up Jerusalem, it was as if "the glory of the God of Israel" had returned to its ancient seat: "Perhaps," wrote Eusebius, "this is the new and second Jerusalem announced in the prophetic oracles" (*Life of Constantine* 3.33).

Augustine, rather, recalled the psalmists' and prophets' language of exile, loss, and longing. His Jerusalem was a distant, heavenly homeland, glimpsed in this life only from afar. Humanity was separated from her by the first sin of the first man, Adam; by the weight of original sin afflicting each generation thereafter, disordering human love and hence human society; by the vast river of time, flowing on toward a future of unknowable duration.

Thus man in this world is *peregrinus;* his present life a *peregrinatio.* The English equivalents of these words are "pilgrim" and "pilgrimage," but truer to Augustine's tone is "exile." Like the Jews of old unwillingly resident in Babylon, the citizens of the heavenly city sigh for their homeland, hearts heavy with "yearning" or "longing." When will this exile end? Only when time itself ends, Augustine argued, asserting, against his millenarian co-religionists, that none can know the hour nor envisage the place. Raised bodily, the saints will ascend to "a place of eternal peace and security, 'the mother, the Jerusalem which is free,'" Jerusalem above (*City* 17.13, a reference to Paul's allegory in Galatians).

Against this evocation of distance and yearning, then, Augustine, again like the ancient Jewish seers he drew on, counterposed the certainty of God's love and the divine promise of salvation. His huge work closed with a meditation on Jerusalem as the *visio pacis,* the vision of eternal peace. "Blessed are those who dwell in your house; they will praise you for ever and ever!" (Psalms 84:5; *City* 22.30). Redeemed and renewed, the community of saints will celebrate an everlasting Sabbath in the presence of God in his holy city.

The Kingdoms of the Earth

Both Rome and the earthly Jerusalem would face further shocks in the centuries after Augustine. In the West, successive waves of Germanic invaders broke over the remnants of empire, plunging Europe and North Africa into a cultural twilight zone. In the East, Christian Jerusalem fell to infidel invaders twice within a generation: once in 614, to the Persians; and again in 638, to Islam.[19] Inexorably, the Christian East and the whole rim of Africa came under Muslim hegemony, while competing Arians, Catholics, and Teutonic pagans fractured the old Roman unity of Europe. The Empire, however, continued at the level of symbol, or fantasy: just before his coronation as "emperor" in 800, the Frankish chieftain Charlemagne received from the patriarch the keys to the city of Jerusalem.

With much greater difficulty than in centuries before, pilgrims from the West continued to make their way to Jerusalem. But as the year 1000 approached—a traditional date for the expected return of Christ—pagan Hungary converted to Christianity. This sudden opening of a cheap land route from Europe to Palestine, combined with the apocalyptic hopes stimulated by the date, swelled the volume of pilgrims journeying to the anticipated site of the Parousia. The sudden flood of foreigners provoked Fatimid Isma'ili, also known as Al-Hakim, the caliph of Cairo. In 1009 he demolished the Christian shrines in the city, including Jerusalem's premier pilgrimage site, the Church of the Holy Sepulchre.

The convulsion of Christendom lasted generations. Chronographers described Al-Hakim in terms reminiscent of Antichrist. Jews, blamed for having encouraged Al-Hakim's action, became the local target of Christian rage: in 1009 and again in 1095, Jewish communities were slaughtered when they refused to convert.[20] Apocalyptic convictions and long traditions of penitential discipline combined to turn Europeans eastward. A succession of pilgrimages, popular and elite, clerical and lay—1027, 1033, 1065—departed for Jerusalem; by 1095 these had transmuted to Crusades, led by armed warriors bent on liberating the Holy Land.[21]

The Crusader rule over Jerusalem endured from 1099 to 1187, when it fell in turn to Muslim forces under Saladin. Various waves of Western military initiatives continued to batter the Levant in the succeeding centuries; most succumbed to internecine struggles among the Europeans, and between Roman and Greek Orthodox Christians. By the beginning of the fourteenth century, Mamluks and Muslim Mongols reabsorbed the last of the Crusader kingdoms. Painfully, even grudgingly, Europe relinquished the dream of reestablishing a Christian Jerusalem.

Powerful as Jerusalem was as a holy place, it was even more powerful as a religious idea. As such, it expressed in biblical idiom the hope of moral transformation, whether social or individual. Thus the oaths to peace sworn by Aquitainian warriors over the relics of saints before clerics and peasants put one eleventh-century chronicler in mind of Isaiah's vision of the end of days: "Come ye, and let us go up to the mountain of the Lord, to the house of the God of Jacob . . . for out of Zion will go forth the Law, and the word of the Lord from Jerusalem" (2:2–4; Ademar, First Sermon, *Patrologia Latina* 141 col. 118). Medieval monasteries, efforts concentrated on sustaining harmonious community, saw in themselves a small reflection of the *visio pacis*. The monk, said Bernard, was a citizen of Jerusalem; the Cistercian order at Clairvaux, "ipsa est Hierosolym" (Epistle 64). But the perfected soul, too, was to be understood by "Jerusalem," wrote his younger contemporary, Aelred of Rivaulx, "the Jerusalem which the Lord Jesus . . . builds out of living stones."

The heavenly Jerusalem was brought to earth in a new kind of realized eschatology with the dazzling invention of Gothic architecture. Cathedrals, oriented on a west-east axis, propelled the approaching faithful in the direction of the altar, which faced toward the earthly Jerusalem. Entering through the main portal, the believer would pass under a tymphaenum whose sculpture announced the Second Coming of Christ and the Last Judgment. And with the Judgment behind him, the believer would come into a space bejewelled by the play of light through ten thousand panes of stained glass: an earthly vision of the heavenly Jerusalem, adorned like a bride for her husband, "having the glory of God, its radiance like a most rare jewel" (Revelations 21:11).

Finally, the prophetic vision of Jerusalem as the center of a morally renewed society eventually floated free of its ecclesiastical referents. The very name conjured the biblical images of justice and peace. Thus late renaissance Florence became Jerusalem to Savanarola; thus too the bare coast of seventeenth-century Massachusetts, where John Winthrop looked forward to founding "a City upon a Hill, God's new Israel."[22] And against the dark satanic mills of industrializing England, Blake summoned his chariots of fire:

> I will not cease from mental fight
> Nor will my sword sleep in my hand,
> Till I have built Jerusalem
> In England's green and pleasant land.

Throughout the centuries and on into our own period, these multiple meanings of Jerusalem—historical, messianic, celestial, moral—have resonated in Christian tradition. But the systole and diastole of modern empires—the Ottoman after World War I, the British after World War II—and the subsequent reestablishment of Jewish sovereignty over the land and, especially since 1967, over the city, have combined to present Christian churches with a social reality unanticipated in New Testament texts and ecclesiastical commentary. A renewed Jewish Jerusalem is now a fact of history.

With the Second Vatican Council, Catholic Christianity began the difficult work of critically addressing its continuous and centuries-long traditions of theological and liturgical anti-Judaism. In 1964 the Church pronounced the Jewish people free of criminal responsibility for the death of Jesus, and moved to drop the prayer for the conversion of "the perfidious Jews" from its liturgy. Protestant churches, especially in the wake of the Nazi-sponsored destruction of European Jewry, have also worked to redefine their relationships to Jews and Judaism. All three communities—Catholic, Protestant, and Jewish—currently pursue vigorous and vital interfaith dialogue. Other traditions, meanwhile, continue ever new: as fundamentalist millenarian churches grow and spread with the approaching end both of the century and of the millennium, we see that the combination of current events and biblical apocalypses (presupposing, as they do, a Jewish presence in Judea, Samaria, and the Galilee) continues to exert its old appeal.[23] (Augustine would be annoyed, but doubtless not surprised.)

The historical and the theological roots of Christianity run deep in the matrix of Judaism. This fundamental connection between the two communities is nowhere more concretely expressed than in their mutual attachment to the city of Jerusalem: holy to Jews for what it is, holy to Christians for what it witnessed; holy to both for the vision of peace it represents. Perhaps now, in the changed political circumstances at century's end and with the churches' repudiation of their ancient angers, the fundamental things both share—a love for Jerusalem and for the Scriptures that praise her—can serve, finally, to foster peace and goodwill between Christians and Jews.

The Spiritual Meaning of Jerusalem in Islam

5

ANGELIKA NEUWIRTH

Any new attempt by a religion to define its particular relation to Jerusalem builds on the bedrock of a famous ancient text:

> If I forget thee, O Jerusalem,
> Let my right hand forget her cunning.
> Let my tongue cleave to the roof of my mouth,
> If I remember thee not;
> If I set not Jerusalem
> Above my chief joy!   (Psalms 137:5–6)

Jerusalem, as evoked in these lines is the very guarantor of the psalmist's personal integrity, of his legal capacity.[1] Jerusalem, it appears, has never lost this aura of a divine token. In Judaism, it has remained a unique place of memory, a spiritual focus in diverse contexts, the most suggestive being the motto, "Next year in Jerusalem!" In neither Christianity nor Islam, it seems, does the believer face Jerusalem in a comparably personal way. Christianity, it is true, has accepted the Hebrew Bible into the canon of its Holy Scriptures, yet it holds—regarding the site of the central sanctuary of biblical history—a rather ambiguous position. For Islam the opposite is true: though censuring the Jewish and Christian Scriptures as not fit—at least in their preserved textual forms—to become part of the Islamic canon, Islam has taken over the *topographia sacra* that underlies those Scriptures, in particular the sanctuary of Jerusalem, which it considers a central symbol of the monotheist cultus inherited from the older religions and thus worthy to rank as an Islamic sanctuary.

The Three Honorary Titles of Jerusalem in Islam

For the Muslim, Jerusalem marks an important station under the itinerary to holy places. In Islam, Jerusalem is a place of pilgrimage, to be visited together with the two other sanctuaries that alone enjoy a comparable rank, Mecca and Medina. The three together constitute—if a metaphor may be borrowed from physics—an "electric field." The triple honorary name[2] that has been bestowed on Jerusalem in Islam, dating back at least to Saladin's time[3] and still regarded by the believer to encompass the significance of the place for his religious community, therefore refers to the city not as an isolated phenomenon but in its changing relation to the other two sanctuaries:

> First of the two directions of prayer,
> Second of the two sanctuaries,
> Third after the two places of pilgrimage.

In its traditional function, as an honorary title, the three attributes will appear surprising. Obviously they do not simply constitute an accumulation of panegyric expressions of the particular "merits of Jerusalem" (*fada'il al-Quds*);[4] rather they also appear as a striking abbreviation of the inconsistent historical process of attraction and repulsion. Thus the rhetorically suggestive increase of the numerical values in the beginnings of the three honorary titles should not obscure the actual decrease in terms of official recognition and the process of the successive ousting of Jerusalem from its inherited first rank as a central place of monotheistic worship.

Read as a mnemonic device, the titles are apt to serve as guideposts to the changing recognition Jerusalem received during the formative period of Islam, which allows for a division into three subsequent phases. The first epitheton, "First of the two directions of prayer," recalls a ritual custom—the physical orientation of the praying person toward Jerusalem, which was practiced by the Muslim community during the earliest period of the genesis of Islam, in the Meccan phase of the activities of the Prophet.

The middle epitheton, "Second of the two sanctuaries," also recalls a development from the time of the Prophet; it refers to the tension that the believers in Medina sensed soon after the Hijra (the emigration of Muhammad from Mecca to Medina in 622) between the two foundation places of monotheist Islamic worship. Mecca, with the

Kaaba, was recognized as the place from which the Abrahamian worship—primarily the rites of pilgrimage, the Hajj—had originated; opposite it, Jerusalem, *al-masjid al-aqsa*, the "further sanctuary," appeared as the center of the "Blessed Land" of those koranic prophets whose message has survived primarily in verbal—not in ritual—forms: Moses and Jesus. Since the Abrahamian foundation[5] must be more ancient than the sanctuary of the Banu Isra'il, the people of Moses, known to be built by Solomon in Jerusalem, the city falls to second place, after Mecca.

The last honorary name, "Third after the two places of pilgrimage,"[6] reflects a later compromise, the ultimate concession some religious scholars thought tenable to be granted to those growing circles within Islam who, in orthodox view, exaggerated their esteem of Jerusalem.[7] The epitheton expresses restriction[8] rather than appraisal: now Jerusalem ranks only third, after Mecca and—once the Prophet's tomb had become a place of pilgrimage—after Medina as well.[9]

It is obvious that this set of titles would hardly have survived into modern times as honorary names had they actually been understood merely as describing a successive loss of significance. They should, therefore, be read in a quite different way, as each apparently implies a perspective of its own, with particular relations to the time and space in which Jerusalem is viewed. What are the complexes of collective memory hidden behind the three epithets? Which are the particular Jerusalem experiences deemed worth keeping by the Muslim community because they have contributed to the emergence and preservation of an Islamic identity? The following observations are an attempt at approaching this complex problem, which has not yet received its due consideration in research.[10]

The First Kibla as Symbol of a New Coherence

What does Jerusalem mean to Islam as its first kibla, its first direction of prayer?[11] It is not self-evident that Islamic tradition preserved an honoring memory of the once practiced ritual custom of facing Jerusalem in prayer,[12] since it was upheld for only a few years and is not explicitly attested in the Koran.[13] Already during Muhammad's lifetime, because of sharpening conflict with Jewish groups at Medina, the orientation toward Jerusalem had begun to present a burden in politico-religious terms, as a symbol no longer fully convincing.[14] It was abolished through a koranic revelation datable to 623, year two of the Hijra, and thus "abrogated" in later theological terms.[15] The commentaries on this passage,[16] which go back to the early third-century Hijra, betray the tendency to minimize the duration of the custom, viewed as an undesired expression of affinity toward Judaism. It is sometimes even presented as a mere interim solution between the ritual custom of facing the Kaaba in prayer—claimed to have been practiced by Muhammad at the beginning of his career in Mecca—and the reinauguration of this custom through a koranic passage authorizing it as a binding religious duty.[17] Still, this polemic has not succeeded in disclaiming Jerusalem's honorary place in the genesis of Islam.

There must be a strong reason for this. In other words: the first honorary title must have soon become the vehicle for a significant remembrance, strong enough to secure for the first kibla a venerable memory even over the politico-religious changes occurring at Medina. This should be the remembrance of a particularly eventful phase in the development of the Meccan community, when the ritual orientation in prayer toward Jerusalem was newly introduced into worship as a clear recognition of its symbolic value.

It is difficult to determine what particular consciousness found its expression in this gesture so long as one relies solely on the historical sources—including those concerning the Prophet's biography—controversial as their accounts of the genesis of Islam are. Therefore only the text that chronologically and substantially accompanies the development of earliest Islamic worship, the Koran itself, can guide us. One particular verse is of special interest, since it singularly associates the person of the Prophet with the Jerusalem sanctuary[18] and at the same time fits into the chronologic framework established by some of the exegetes for the introduction of the kibla:[19]

> Glory be to Him, who carried His servant by night
> from the Holy Sanctuary [*al-masjid al-haram*]
> to the Further Sanctuary [*al-masjid al-aqsa*]
> the precincts of which We have blessed,
> that We might show him some of Our signs.
> He is the All-hearing, the All-seeing.   (Sura 17:1)

This somewhat cryptic verse mentions a nocturnal journey, or rather flight, conceived as an experience of liberation—even viewed in analogy to the Exodus led by Moses and the escape of Lot,[20] leading the Prophet out of Mecca toward "the other sanctuary," which in the context of the religiogeographical horizons of the early community can hardly be located elsewhere than on the Temple Mount of Jerusalem, the "*masjid* of the Banu Isra'il," the Jews.[21] The simplest explanation of the event alluded to in this verse would be to assume it to be a dream, an explanation upheld in Islam only by a minority of the exegetes. Still, it has been incorporated into the most renowned tenth-century commentary on the Koran by al-Tabari, who quotes a cousin of the Prophet, Umm Hani':

> As to the nocturnal journey [Isra] of the Messenger of God the following took place: He had been staying in my house over night. After performing the last evening prayer he retired and so did all of us. At dawn the Messenger of God woke us up for morning prayer, and when we had performed it together, he said to me: "Umm Hani', you remember that I performed with you in this very place the evening prayer. Thereupon, however, I was in Bayt al-Maqdis and have prayed there. And now I have been praying again with you the morning prayer in this place."[22]

According to this account, nothing supernatural had happened: the miraculous element immanent in the experience that is echoed so distinctly in the allusive style of the koranic verse is reflected exclusively through the phenomenon of a standstill of time, as well as a "compression" of a vast spacial distance into a few hours' journey—both familiar features in dreams. It should not detract from the convincing force of this simple and sober account that the same Sura 17:1 a short time later was to become the *locus probans* for the elevation of the Prophet to the rank of an ecstatic. In later traditions this verse is usually understood as an allusion at a unique nocturnal ride, miraculous as to time and space but also in other respects: the Prophet is imagined to be riding a fairy-tale, Pegasus-like beast, the Buraq, from Mecca to Jerusalem, passing by diverse stations of salvation-historical significance.[23] At the end of the exegetic development, the journey goes beyond Jerusalem, through the seven celestial spheres[24] to heaven itself. According to the tradition of the Prophet's scribe, Ibn Mas'ud, his ascent reaches its climax in Muhammad's being given the institution of the five Islamic prayers by God himself.[25]

Two images of the Prophet underlie these two interpretations of verse 17:1. On the one hand, the person of the Prophet as we know him from the Koran, unaffected by any miraculous powers, called to be a messenger of verbal transmission only, and on the other, the ecstatic endowed with supernatural faculties[26]—contrarily different images.[27] Still, the sober descriptive version and the mythifying interpretation do have one trait in common, namely the realization that the aim of this journey—the "revelation of the signs" announced in the koranic verse—is nothing less than the unique closeness to God granted to the Prophet through prayer. In both accounts the event is put in relation to prayer, the Prophet himself performing or even leading the prayer, *salat,* in the midst of the older prophets in the Jerusalem sanctuary in the one version, and in the other, being granted the very institution of prayer by his divine Lord. One may be tempted to identify this constant, the relation to prayer, as the "historical nucleus," perhaps the trace of a spontaneous comment on the miraculous experience given by the Prophet in private, before communicating the experience to the community through the somewhat enigmatic verse. The nocturnal journey, the exodus to the *masjid* Bani Isra'il, would then appear associated with the "last evening prayer" in the account of Umm Hani'. It could be interpreted as a spiritual movement continuing the journey already started in the imagination of the Prophet by his facing the kibla toward the "further sanctuary" in Jerusalem, which, newly introduced as the orientation for prayer, must still have been deeply engraved in the worshippers' minds. The orientation toward a kibla and prayer itself are elements of one and the same cultic practice.

How is it that taking up the kibla could appear to be so significant a departure as to be conceived as an exodus to the space of the memory of the Banu Isra'il? It is noticeable that the entire Sura 17 is dominated by a longing for release from the situation of "exile" experienced in Mecca, pointing to a spiritual need that would suffice as the motive for the imaginary exodus to the House of the One God.[28] (The situation is not unlike the one presupposed in 1 Kings 8, where a comparable longing underlies Solomon's prayer at the Temple inauguration, a text that promises the worshipper a similar mode of spiritual return.[29]) The remembrance of the only freely accessible great "other sanctuary"—since the Meccan Kaaba had become difficult for the increasingly isolated group of believers to get access to—is apt to guarantee the closeness to God sought by the worshipper, the "envisaging the Face of God" that he strives for by "turning his own face toward" His house, facing Jerusalem as the direction of prayer.[30] The close association of Jerusalem with prayer that is manifest here, that would become a fixed topos in Islam through the short historical episode of the Jerusalem kibla, will remain very lively in later times. Again and again in Sufism, religious poetry, and edification literature,[31] Jerusalem appears as the ideal place of prayer. It affirms itself as an Islamic sanctuary through this wealth in meaning, although it lacks any physically real association with the biography of the Prophet.

Again this development is not self-evident. On the contrary, it seems surprising that the Islamic tradition in general, beyond the limits of local Syrian circles, should have preserved the remembrance of the particular affinity of Jerusalem to prayer.[32] After all, the Koran, and in accordance with it, the *sira*—the traditions pertaining to the life of the Prophet—attest unequivocally to the fact that the rites performed at the Kaaba at Mecca should have been at the origin of Islamic ritual prayer.[33] Moreover, the Kaaba is celebrated explicitly in a koranic passage as the place where the prayer rites were implemented through a divine decree.[34] We find here two separate "memories" confronting each other, with the memory of the long-lasting appreciation of the *masjid* Bani Isra'il being the older one. The Koran, it is true, relates several significant events of salvation history to Jerusalem, such as the annunciation of a son gifted with prophecy to the aged Zacharias,[35] the sojourn of young Mary in the Temple in the care of Zacharias,[36] David's judgment, viewed in the Koran as a divine trial,[37] and finally the catastrophe of the destruction of the sanctuary, the Temple, by foreign conquerors, understood to be a punishment imposed on the Banu Isra'il.[38] These koranic references to Jerusalem, though often unexplicit, may have contributed to Jerusalem's esteem in Islam, but they hardly explain how Jerusalem could retain its high position even after its "aura" as the central monotheistic sanctuary had been transferred to Mecca. It is worth noticing that another significant monotheistic sanctuary evoked several times in the Koran, namely Mount Sinai,[39] has not retained much importance in later Islam. Therefore, in the case of Jerusalem, additional factors promoting memory should be assumed.

In fact, the Jerusalem sanctuary in its function as a ritual orientation—as the focus of an imaginary space becoming accessible in prayer—did not develop in the consciousness of the Islamic community at a haphazard time. Rather, it appeared during a phase of development when, thanks to a complex process of new orientation, a remarkable widening of the young community's horizons was taking place, in terms of time as well as space. Thus the "further sanctuary," so suggestive in its topographical and historical setting, could become a forceful symbol. One might dare to hypothesize that the Jerusalem kibla came about as a gestic expression of the deeply felt experience of having gained new spiritual horizons.

One must remember that during the Prophet's Meccan career, the young community was driven to segregate itself, at least as to its locale of worship, from the traditional Meccan rites. The process is clearly reflected in the evolution of new Islamic forms of worship, less dependent on the worship presence at holy places and concentrating on verbal expression rather than ritual gestures. This process is not simply a change in forms; its full dimensions reach much deeper. It is a radical break of a community with its inherited tradition, caused by the intrusion of writing into the space of memory. For the first time in Arabic literature, the medium of writing is consistently integrated into the composition of texts and the techniques of their preservation—though the wording may not yet be fixed for an envisaged reader but for a second mediator, a reciter of the texts.[40]

Two essential novelties, the newly reached convergence of the koranic revelations with the Scriptures of the two other monotheistic religions, considered to be represented primarily by the Torah, the Scripture of the Banu Isra'il, and the adoption at the same time of the *topographia sacra* of that very group, together created a new self-consciousness for the young Islamic community that was based no longer on the rites practiced at the Kaaba but on a new awareness of being among the receivers and bearers of a Scripture and thus having a share in the memory of salvation history, transported by the medium of writing. (Jan Assmann has coined a phrase for this type of change in orientation, the "transition of a society from ritual coherence to textual coherence."[41]) By its very gesture, the kibla oriented toward Jerusalem points to this new connection between the emerging Islamic community and the older religions. It is not surprising, then, that the koranic allusions to the Meccan sanctuary and its rites,[42] as the previous guarantors of societal coherence—allusions so numerous

THE HEAVENLY CITY

until then in the introductory sections of the Meccan suras—were soon replaced by a stereotypical introductory evocation of the Book, *kitab,* now recognized as the most significant common spiritual possession. The images now appearing in the beginning sections of the suras, the Book and its requisites,[43] unequivocally point to the awareness that a stream of tradition had come to a standstill and now was accessible through the means of writing. It was a new form of remembrance that found expression there and would soon penetrate the daily ritual practices: the strong attachment to place, which was characteristic of the worship at the Kaaba, gave way to a new situation of the Muslim worshipper in space—in a spiritual space, that is, reaching far beyond the horizons of the inherited rites into the world and history of "the others," of the Banu Isra'il.[44]

Whereas there had been in the earliest suras few places considered worth mentioning except for Mecca, now, with the sole exception of Sura 17, one does not find any further references to Mecca. Instead the "Blessed Land"[45] is introduced as a space in which the oppressed believer may take refuge and where most of the prophets had worked. Accordingly, there is a substantial change in orientation in terms of time as well. Instead of the numerous allusions to ritually relevant times of the day that appear in the beginnings of the early suras,[46] the ones originating in the new phase of development display a new setting in time. They culminate in an oft-repeated appeal to the examples reaching far back into the history of the spiritual forebears, the Banu Isra'il, formally introduced with a simple referential "at the time when," *idh.*[47] Jerusalem is the central sanctuary of the space marked by this Scripture and thus by writing. All prayers gravitate in the direction of Jerusalem as their natural destination; to Jerusalem the worshipper turns his face in prayer.

Two substantial changes have thus taken place. On the one hand, in the middle Meccan period of the koranic development, when tales about prophets emerging from the memory of the older monotheistic religions become frequent, time is widened to encompass the salvation history of the Banu Isra'il. On the other hand, the space of the communication between God and man is expanded as well. This becomes clear through the new form of worship, which has grown more complex through the incorporation of an essentially novel element into the already existing parts, the fixed ensemble of gestures demanded by the traditional ritual prayer, such as prostration *(sajda)* and bowing *(ruku')*, and the variable element of Koran recitation, the text of which is chosen individually by the worshipper with every single prayer. For the first time there appears a verbally fixed part of the ritual that complements the recitation of the word of God and the ritual gestures of self-humiliation: the community prayer, or *fatiha*.[48] This prayer is spoken by the worshippers in an upright position *(qiyam)* and enounced in the grammatical form of the first person, with the worshippers acting as autonomous partners in the communication process. Together with the recitation of the Koran selection, which is also performed in an upright position by the worshippers, who thus create further space above themselves, the *fatiha* constitutes a ceremony that may be rightfully considered a religious service *in nuce*. It is entirely oriented toward the sanctuary of Jerusalem—the site of divine-human communication; the focus in space toward which, at certain cosmically determined times of the day, a movement from the profane "now" to the extratemporal vicinity of God becomes possible.[49] Thus, even if the temporal determinant for the rite of prayer has remained Meccan, following the periods of the day taken from the rites at the Kaaba,[50] the temporal and spacial horizons of the consciousness of the community have expanded substantially with the recognition of Jerusalem as the center of the imaginary space accessible in liturgy.

Jerusalem as the Second Sanctuary

What is to remain of Jerusalem's rank after the transfer of the direction of prayer to Mecca? The Muslim community at Medina dissociated itself from Jerusalem in view of the growing precariousness of its relation to the Medinan Jews. This dissociation was also the reversal out of a recollection: the rediscovery of Mecca as the essential destination of the longing of the exiles at Medina. Hardly two years after the Hijra, in 624, there is a change of orientation, this time attested by a koranic passage.

> The fools among the people will say,
> "What has turned them from the direction
> they were facing in their prayers aforetime?"

Say:
"To God belong the East and the West.
He guides whomever He will to a straight path."
Thus We appointed you a midmost nation
that you might be witnesses to the people,
and that the Messenger might be a witness
to you; and We did not appoint the direction
thou werst facing, except that We might know
who followed the Messenger from him
who turned on his heels—though it were a grave thing
save for those whom God has guided; but
God would never leave your faith to waste—
Truly God is All-gentle with the people;
                    All-compassionate.
We have seen thou turning thy face about
in the heaven, now We will surely turn thee
to a direction that shall satisfy thee.
Turn thy face toward the Holy Mosque [*al-masjid al-haram*];
and wherever you are, turn your faces toward it.   (Sura 2:143–145)

The spiritual return of the worshippers to the Kaaba at Mecca heralded in these verses dislocates Jerusalem from the center. Yet as a prototype of a center to be visited in the believer's imagination, the Jerusalem direction of prayer remains in force, even though the first kibla is viewed in the retrospect of the Koran as a mere touchstone for the obedience of the believers. In the exegetical literature it even appears disdained as an institution, obsolete since the community's dissociation from the Medinan Jews. The replacing of the Jerusalem kibla should not, however, be viewed merely from a negative point of view, as a solely pragmatic politico-religious step. A ritual reorientation in space, expressed by so dominant a gesture in worship, reflects the reality of a genuine change of spiritual longing. Mecca was able to replace Jerusalem because the memory shared with the Banu Isra'il by the Medinan community had been eroded to some degree by the novel experience of exile, within which the Meccan central sanctuary had increased substantially in symbolic value. Not only had the community become—thanks to decisive political successes—sufficiently detached from the Meccan experience that it could view Mecca positively as the genuine place of their own tradition, but additionally, although there had been a leap in development there had not been a total break with the Meccan ritual practices. Substantial elements of the Meccan worship, such as the ritual gestures and the three cosmically determined times of prayer, had been retained in the Medinan Islamic worship.[51] Once the evocation of a central sanctuary through ritual gesture had been realized as a precondition for prayer, after the symbols shared with the Banu Isra'il had become problematic, there could hardly have been any orientation other than to the Meccan Kaaba, whose sacred time periods had remained in force. But more important, the ideal Mecca as conceived in exile had itself gone through a substantial change. It had become integrated into that particular form of memory that is transported by the vehicle of writing—which we might identify with the biblical tradition—and this bestowed on it the rank of a place honored by a significant episode of salvation history. It had become the central place of the career of a biblical hero, Abraham himself.

Abraham's inauguration prayer of the Kaaba[52] has been rightfully associated with the Solomonic inauguration prayer of the Temple.[53] In both prayers, the sanctuary is conceived not only as a place of pilgrimage for a peculiar group but also as a sign set up for all humankind. In Abraham's prayer, the Kaaba appears as the monument of a new divine foundation. It has become the first monotheistic temple, as we read in the Koran:

> . . . "My Lord, make this
> a land secure, and provide its people
> with fruits, such of them as believe in
> God and the Last Day."
> . . . And when Abraham and Ishmael with him
> raised up the foundation of the House:
> "Our Lord, receive this from us; Thou art
> the All-hearing, the All-knowing;
> and, our Lord, make us submissive to Thee,
> and of our seed a nation submissive [*umma muslima*]
> to Thee; and show us our holy rites, and
> turn toward us; surely Thou turnest, and art

<blockquote>
All-compassionate;
and, our Lord, do Thou send among them
a Messenger, one of them, who shall recite
to them Thy signs, and teach them the Book
and the Wisdom, and purify them; Thou art
the Almighty, the All-wise."   (Sura 2:126f.)
</blockquote>

The part played by Abraham at the Kaaba—the account of which had probably circulated in the peninsula long before[54]—is perhaps to be interpreted in terms of a mere restoration of a sanctuary that went back to Adam as a founder. The Koran admits a cosmologically based origin of the Kaaba without ever confirming it explicitly.

This text implies that the pilgrimage, being the most significant among the rites associated with the Meccan Haram, was introduced by Abraham. The fact that admission to these rituals—which originally marked seasonal change[55] but had developed into a symbol of common bonds celebrated since time immemorial by participants from all over the peninsula—had come under the discretion of the most obstinate enemies of Islam and was denied to the exiles, must have been extremely offending, particularly after the new orientation toward Mecca was introduced. The situation was made more grave by the fact that the Hajj itself, in the new theology of exile, was gaining spiritual significance. It is only logical, once the Meccan Kaaba was conceived as a monotheistic foundation consecrated by Abraham, that the ceremonies of the Hajj should have taken on the aura of a feast going back to Abraham as well. In any event, the Hajj in Islamic context—as will become manifest even in the Koran at a later time through Muhammad's reform of the calendar[56]—is devoid of any association with seasonal change. It has received a totally new meaning, having become—insofar as it is performed in response to a call for pilgrimage that Abraham uttered on divine order—an obligatory rite incumbent on all further generations of believers. It has become a feast in commemoration of an episode of salvation history, comparable to the situation in 1 Kings, where temple and pilgrimage appear interlinked as well.[57]

Through this new etiology, the Hajj of Islam underwent a change comparable to the development of the Israelite feasts in Deuteronomy: from a ritual celebrating seasonal change to a ceremony commemorating an episode of salvation history.[58] This holds true even though—according to the explicit koranic text—the association of the Hajj with salvation history remains limited to the mere obedience to be paid by the worshippers to the call of Abraham.[59] Mecca thus has become the locus of a monotheistic pilgrimage of remembrance.

Contrary to the pre-Islamic situation, the local destination of the Hajj in Islam is no longer primarily Mount ‘Arafat.[60] In first place is Mecca itself with its Kaaba, and in this sanctuary—according to the prayer of inauguration—there shall take place, besides the rites so constitutive for the ancient cultus verbal worship and reading of Scriptures as well: Abraham's inauguration prayer ends up with the plea that a prophet should arise, to read the Book to the participants in the rites at the Kaaba, conceived to be Arabian monotheists already familiar with ritual prayer and pilgrimage. The prayer reaches its fulfillment with the appearance of the Prophet Muhammad, whose mission it is to complete the complex structure of Islam as a religion whose cultus is based equally on ritual and verbal elements.

Through this new increase in meaning, for the second time a part of the previous aura of Jerusalem is transferred to Mecca. What had been a prerogative of Jerusalem attested by the prophet Isaiah—"The Law will go out from Zion and the word of the Lord from Jerusalem" (Isaiah 2:3)—was conferred on Mecca by the koranic verse relating to Abraham's prayer. In its newly conceived function as a foundation of Abraham, Mecca not only shares most significant merits with Jerusalem, but it can also boast of holding a monotheistic sanctuary older than Solomon's Temple. Jerusalem, reduced to a mere prototype, recedes into the background behind the Islamic Mecca. Mecca, depicted in the Koran as a place without vegetation, having to rely for fruit on supplies from outside,[61] thus appears physically as an obvious antipode to Jerusalem, situated in a land blessed all around. Mecca enters, moreover, into a spiritual rivalry with Jerusalem, since—in fulfillment of the prayer of Abraham, the first propagator of the worship of the One God—it has become a place of theophany for a second time. This new theophany, rising to new expectations, is inspired by the examples of the salvation history of the two other religions, which demand that a genuine theophany, a divine revelation, should take the shape of a book, a writing.

Mecca thus is associated with the remembrance of the times of prayer always in force in Islam and originating from the Kaaba, a remembrance that is from this point on reinforced continuously through the spacial orientation toward Mecca. Mecca also remains the destination of the Hajj—the place of the most significant event in the cultic year—a ritual that may be viewed as reproducing, on a larger scale in terms of time and space, the rite of prayer as the most significant caesura in the profane time of the day. The Hajj indeed constitutes a unique communal exit out of profane time and profane space.[62] For the duration of the cosmically determined sacred time of the Hajj and for this duration alone, the Meccan Haram—conceived as bearing cosmical associations of its own[63]—becomes sacred space.[64] The uniqueness of the rites originating in Mecca and sanctioned by the Koran[65] are perceived as preceding in time the phenomenon of revelation through Scripture, associated so closely with Jerusalem. Thus we find at the end of the koranic development, after Mecca had been won back and its sanctuary had found a last further anchoring in Islam, the final statement: "The first House established for mankind was that at Bekka [Mecca], a place holy, and a guidance to all beings" (Sura 3:96).

Salvation History in 'Abd al-Malik's Jerusalem

What is Jerusalem's destiny after being thus reembodied by Mecca? No later than at the end of the first Islamic century, it is recognized as a legitimate place of Islamic pilgrimage, a holy place. A *hadith*, an uttering attributed to the Prophet—which may serve as the *locus classicus* for the new appreciation of Jerusalem—says, "You shall only set out for three mosques: The Sacred mosque [in Mecca], my mosque [in Medina], and al-Aqsa mosque [in Jerusalem]."[66] M. J. Kister has illuminated the further context of this uttering and stressed the restrictive character of the *hadith*, which must be interpreted as opposing the admission of further sanctuaries into Islam.[67] Jerusalem is granted the third place as a concession, since it is too strong a symbol to be repressed. It becomes the destination of a *ziyara*, a pious visit without a particular time fixed to it.[68]

Meanwhile, Jerusalem has long been determined, in space and time, by the two other sanctuaries. It is integrated, in terms of real time, into the framework of the new era, originating from and introduced at Medina, the place of the worldly self-affirmation of ancient Islam. In terms of space, its sacred buildings are oriented toward Mecca. By perceiving the holy places of Islam as being three in number—including Medina—the community has taken a most significant fact into account, a fact that manifests itself even more perspicuously in the new dating system relating to the Hijra of the Prophet: that is, the entrance of Islam as a historical phenomenon in its own right into real time and real space. The significance of this novel reality becomes enhanced through Muhammad's reform of the calendar. The resulting incongruity between the new Islamic dating system and all the older ones—those practiced by neighboring societies as well as those of the Arabian forebears—made an easy association with the historical past of any of the surrounding societies impossible. With the breakthrough of Islam as a new, politically dominant identity, its particular memory is canonized, and other memory is censured. Thus with the final redaction of the Koran under the third caliph, 'Uthman, around the year 653, canonical Scripture is limited once and for all to the revelation received by Muhammad, whereas the Torah and the Gospels are excluded from this closer concept of Scripture. Against these limitations, the central symbol of the Banu Isra'il, the monotheistic Temple of Jerusalem, which had already been integrated into Islamic memory by the Koran, further asserts itself as an Islamic sanctuary.[69]

In 692, about sixty years after the death of the Prophet, this central symbol—the Temple Mount of Jerusalem—was adorned by a unique Islamic monument, the Dome of the Rock, Qubbat al-Sakhra. It is obvious that the Dome of the Rock, maintaining a central position within the whole area of the Haram al-Sharif, is intended to be an answer to the most prominent Christian churches[70] dominating the city since the times of Constantine and Justinian. This intention becomes manifest through the peculiar structure and decoration of the building. The octagon, crowned by a cupola, reflects—even in terms of its precise scale—the rotunda above the tomb built by Justinian at the Church of the Holy Sepulchre.[71] Furthermore, the Dome of the Rock was originally adorned by mosaics not only on its interior walls but on the exterior ones as well. Finally, not only is the site as such distinguished by being the Jewish Temple site,[72] but the building is also erected over a most significant requisite of cult history, the Rock. To this Rock are attached—as is attested by the rich Jewish haggadic tradition, which in turn is reflected by *hadith* literature codified somewhat later[73]—a multitude of cosmologic and ethico-historical traditions that were probably in circulation locally at the time of the Umayyad building activities.[74] Josef van Ess has lately evolved the thesis that a particular detail of the Rock that had already attracted the haggadic imagination and become associated with the creation of the world should have been the very nucleus of the venerability of the Rock and thus the motive for the erection of the Dome above it: a cavity in the surface of the Rock that had been interpreted as the imprint left by God's own foot when, after completing His six days of creation, He departed from His worldly throne—the Rock on the Temple Mount of Jerusalem—to return to His throne in heaven.[75]

With the presupposition of such mythical beliefs as the motive for the erection of the Dome, it is surprising that the verbal self-portrayal left by the builder, Umayyad caliph 'Abd al-Malik ibn Marwan, in the Dome's long building inscription (dated 692) is devoid of any anthropomorphic or figurative representation of the holy.[76] The inscription, consisting mainly of koranic quotations, twice mentions the beginning of the so-called Throne verse (Sura 2:225f.),[77] the imagery of which might remind one of the haggadic throne tradition in question. Still, the full text of the inscription—apart from two polemic passages addressed to the Christians[78]—is mainly a testimony of the two basic articles of the Islamic catechism: the unity of God[79] and the dignity of Muhammad as His messenger.[80] (Both are affirmed in a similar way in contemporary coinage.[81]) As is to be expected in an imperial building, the issue of self-legitimation is also prominently reflected.[82] It finds expression in the repeated recourse to the reign as belonging to God alone and granted by Him to whomever He wishes.

If there is one comprehensive main message to be read from the inscription, it is the following: the Prophet Muhammad, mentioned in the text more than ten times, is, like Jesus, a servant and a messenger of God.[83] He is—as is upheld by the Christians for Jesus—highly esteemed in heaven and on earth. He even transcends—as a koranic verse quoted or alluded to several times in the inscription (Sura 33:56) makes us understand[84]—the borderline between heaven and earth, and is expected to be the intercessor for his community at the Day of

Judgment. A unique prayer, which culminates in this very plea for Muhammad's eschatological intercession,[85] is the longest and most pathetical passage in the inscription, except for the verses directed against the Christians. The association with the world of the angels, established for Muhammad through the quotation of the theologically outstanding verse (33:56), bestows on him the aura of a mediator par excellence, comparable only to Jesus as conceived in the Christian context.

In view of the eschatological role of Muhammad reflected here, it is hardly astonishing that the footprint in the Rock, ascribed by the Jewish Haggadah to God himself, was found fitting for the Prophet Muhammad. He who is of high standing in heaven as on earth, and over whom God and the angels utter benedictions, had himself been touched by the aura of Jerusalem, as the koranic allusion to his nocturnal journey, Sura 17:1, attests. As to his closeness to God, he is in no way inferior to the revered person par excellence in Jerusalem, namely Jesus, whose own ascension to heaven is recalled through a special building in the very same neighborhood. Thus it is only plausible that Islam elevates Muhammad to a figure closely related to the founder of the monotheistic Jerusalem, David, and to the person deemed to be the restorer of creation through his salvation work in Jerusalem, Jesus. Tradition—as presented by a scribe of the Prophet, Ibn Mas'ud—has Muhammad entering Jerusalem in Davidian guise, riding on a beast closely associated with the messianic ass, and ascending from there to heaven to meet God himself. The account culminates in the following scene, a miraculous etiology for the introduction of the Islamic institution of prayer. The Prophet, accompanied by the angel Gabriel, as Ibn Mas'ud relates,

finally reached the seventh heaven and his Lord. There, the duty of fifty prayers was laid upon him. The apostle said: "On my return I passed by Moses and what a fine friend of yours he was! He asked me how many prayers had been laid upon me and when I told him fifty he said, 'Prayer is a weighty matter and your people are weak, so go back to your Lord and ask him to reduce the number for you and your community.' I did so and He took off ten. Again I passed by Moses and he said the same again; and so it went on until only five prayers for the whole day and night were left. Moses again gave me the same advice. I replied that I had been back to my Lord and asked him to reduce the number until I was ashamed, and I would not do it again. He of you who performs them in faith and trust will have the reward of fifty prayers."[86]

This narration about Muhammad's ascent (Miraj) starting from Jerusalem, related in Ibn Hisham's "official" biography of the Prophet, gives new, prophetological meaning to Islam's otherwise cosmically determined worship. This account, which also gave rise to the fixation of a particular feast in honor of the Prophet, was to become the main etiology for the holiness of Jerusalem in Islam and was finally established as the definite explanation for the erection of the Dome of the Rock, which is therefore conceived by the Muslim believer first and foremost as a memorial of the Prophet. The idea of Muhammad's transcending the border between heaven and earth, only alluded to in 'Abd al-Malik's inscription, thus becomes materialized in a narrative, figurative way.[87] Jerusalem, the place of pilgrimage, ranking in only the third place within the canon of sanctuaries, thus retains a wealth of meaning hardly inferior to that of the two other sanctuaries.

Although God's work of creation in Jewish haggadic tradition, and thus in Islamic popular piety, is closely associated with the Rock, so that this cosmologic association might even have contributed as a motive for the erection of the Dome over the Rock, still, in the inscription, there is no allusion whatsoever to the beginning of creation. There is, however, many a reference to the reestablishment of creation on the Last Day, when the Islamic prophet will act as a mediator—in analogy to the role played by Jesus as the restorer of creation in the Christian context. And even if the interior decoration of the Dome of the Rock—as has been convincingly argued by Miriam Rosen-Ayalon—evokes a paradisical landscape,[88] or perhaps an earthly paradise, in accord with the symbolism of sacred buildings already familiar to the observer from the iconography of the contemporary Christian churches, still, the idea of paradise in the Dome of the Rock is primarily related to the situation after the Last Judgment, not that of the beginning of creation. Not only does the inscription explicitly refer to the day of resurrection and repeatedly to God's power to resuscitate the dead, but in addition there are emblems of the Last

Judgment in the mosaic decoration that are echoed in the names of some of the Dome of the Rock's gates.[89]

The architecture of the Dome of the Rock,[90] and even more so of the whole building complex of the Haram al-Sharif, marked at the intersection of its axes with the Dome of the Chain—the sole function of which is to indicate the *omphalos mundi*—attests to a strong awareness of the centrality of the sanctuary.[91] This awareness is, however, not expressed verbally: the epigraphic articulation, relying heavily on the Koran, speaks a different language, its basic objective being ethico-historical. The only detail of the inscription that allows for a cosmologic interpretation is the koranic quotation of God's creational imperative, "Be" *(kun)*, which is adduced as a guarantee of His unity, since being able to create, He is not in need of procreation.[92] The believers may appeal to Him to bless Muhammad and accept his intercession for his community.[93] Thus the inscription—thanks to the often repeated benediction of the Prophet, *tasliya;* the confession of God's unity, *shahada;* and the evocation formula, "In the name of God the Merciful, the Compassionate," *basmala*—reflects some of the most substantial elements of Islamic prayer. It makes the Dome a unique space for the articulation of prayer, where prayer is already echoed by the scriptural adornment of its architectural forms. Missing, however, is the verbalization of the parallel between the Prophet and Abraham, so outstanding in the wording of ritual prayer; the inscription rather creates a parallel between the Prophet and Jesus. This could be due to a catalytic effect of the genius loci, which is reflected as well in the prominence given to the eschatological functions attributed to Muhammad in the text. Cosmologic traditions associated with the site thus appear, in the seventh century, marginal as against the epigraphic testimony of the Dome of the Rock, which sounds restrained and accommodated to the sober koranic way of thinking. Such traditions were later further overshadowed by a wealth of liturgic and eschatologic meanings connected with the remembrance of the Prophet.

The Haram and the "Pilgrimage of the Nations"

The Haram al-Sharif and its neighborhood are the destination of the eschatological pilgrimage. Such an affinity to symbolic meaning is

Figure 8. Al-Haram al-Sharif, ca. 1870. From the left: the Dome of the Chain next to the Dome of the Rock; al-Aqsa Mosque *(far center);* the western portico with Bab al-Silsila Minaret. (See Chapter 17.)

hardly surprising in a place where the border between heaven and earth, between time and eternity, is permeable. The entire Temple Mount was found by the Muslims, when they captured Jerusalem, to be *topographia eschatologica* that needed only to be identified as to its single elements. Thus, one of the gates of the Dome of the Rock is called after the angel of death, Israfil, who is also recognized in a mosaic through his emblem, the trumpet. What is announced only at the Dome of the Rock, itself a worldly image of paradise, takes place in its very surroundings: the Day of Judgment, *yawm al-din*. At that time, the small dome whose original function was to mark the axial center of the Haram, will reveal its true eschatological function as the Dome of the Chain, Qubbat al-Silsila, the place where the chain holding the scales of Judgment will be hung. It indicates the very center of a vast scenario of Judgment. Behind it, to the northeast, the Gate of Mercy, Bab al-Rahma, will open to receive the Blessed.[94] To the east, just below the Haram, is Wadi Jahannam,[95] the destiny of the Damned. Even further outside the Haram, on the slope of the Mount of Olives, is the area where all humankind will be summoned for Judgment, the *sahira*,[96] to which the name of a later a city gate, the Gate of the Place of Judgment, or Bab al-Sahira, alludes.

The eschatological scenario imagined to be located here is stressed not only in the literature in praise of Jerusalem, *fada'il al-Quds* as codified from the ninth century onward,[97] and in a number of travelogues written in the medieval period,[98] but also in the post-Umayyad epigraphic testimonies inside the Dome of the Rock. Whereas the Haram inscriptions added by Saladin still concentrate on the miraculous metamorphosis of the Dome of the Rock from a Crusader Christian shrine back into a Muslim sanctuary,[99] the Ottoman inscriptions unequivocally take recourse to eschatology. Besides the Throne verse, which obviously has remained closely associated with the Rock, the whole text of Sura 32, marked by its eschatological character, is adduced.[100] In addition, the unique koranic verse associating the Prophet with the site (Sura 17:1) is understood at this later period as alluding exclusively to the Prophet's ascent to heaven, the Miraj.

The awareness of the transitory quality of the site—where space is felt to turn into time[101]—and the resulting meritoriousness of the believer's approaching the sanctuary reach their climax in the Mamluk period. It is remarkable that the very neighborhood of the place of the future dissolution of creation and the resurrection of the dead to another life should have aroused the desire to eternalize earthly lives by building mausoleums[102] and other structures that may be considered memorials at least in their secondary intention.[103] This is most conspicuous in the luxuriously adorned main access road to the Haram,[104] described in M. H. Burgoyne's *Mamluk Jerusalem* as an architectonic complex in itself, with its superelevated and expressive facades adorned with monumental epigraphic and heraldic emblems of imperial, or at least knightly, self-legitimation.[105] The facades conceal a multitude of institutions charged with the preservation of memory:

religious foundations with fixed prescriptions to maintain liturgic, meditative, and theological activities.[106] These institutions are apt to preserve the memory of their founder long beyond his death, not only through the continuous uttering of his name in prayer, but even more so through another auditory device, the "remembrance of God"—ceremonial Koran recitation—that resounds into the street[107] and is heard and received as a blessing by worshippers passing through Bab al-Silsila Road on their way to the Haram.

The Haram al-Sharif is not only a place of pilgrimage for the living who come to enjoy the blessing of the neighborhood of the sanctuary.[108] The Haram is also the final destination of the eschatological pilgrimage of mankind as well, where, on the Day of Judgment, all will be standing in front of their Lord—similar to the situation of the Hajj ceremony of *wuquf*—when the pilgrims stand still beneath Mount 'Arafat. This destination has been approached already by all those who were able to create for themselves a memory in Jerusalem through commissioning in their will the appointment of a professional Koran reader and through erecting a monument whose inscription contains koranic verses. The continuous blessings, coming back to the founders of such monuments from the passersby, who may be expected to utter a pious formula when reading an inscription or on hearing the koranic cantilena resounding from a mausoleum, create a singular communication between the dead and the living and help to bridge the time that still remains until they are allowed to take part in the Judgment scenario on the Haram, to which their tombs are already so close.

The significance of Jerusalem in Islam becomes fully conspicuous only in the ensemble of the three sanctuaries. It is perhaps best communicated through a drawing, a picture that is—according to local Jerusalemite custom—drawn in a naive popular technique on the wall or the door of the house of a pilgrim returning from the Hajj. The three sanctuaries are arranged to form a triangle: the Kaaba of Mecca and the Prophet's mosque of Medina mark the endpoints below, with the Dome of the Rock above. Both Mecca, place of the establishment of the rites through Abraham and their restoration through Muhammad, and Medina, place of the remembrance of the worldly, political self-assertion of Islam, could become the holy places of a universal religion only because Islam conceives itself as a new rendering of those older Book religions—Judaism and Christianity—whose bedrock is the Rock of Jerusalem. The experience of Muhammad, of having been himself touched by the particular aura of Jerusalem, has found in the forceful image of the Prophet's nocturnal journey and his ascent to heaven an easily remembered and evocative expression for every Muslim. The inextinguishable aura of the place as an opening to "the other world," to heaven, is matched in architectural terms by the form of the cupola of the Dome of the Rock, the Qubbat al-Sakhra, which still today asserts itself as the most suggestive icon of Islamic spirituality.

Christian Pilgrimage to the Holy Land

6

ROBERT L. WILKEN

Every year thousands of Christians make the journey to Jerusalem and the Holy Land to visit the sites of biblical history or the "holy places" associated with the life of Jesus: Bethlehem, Nazareth, the Church of the Resurrection, the Mount of Olives. Most of these visitors are pilgrims, not tourists. Unlike tourists, they carry not archaeological guides but Bibles and prayer books; they come not to be instructed but to pray. Recently I saw a group of Italian pilgrims visiting the shrine of the Visitation, where Mary, pregnant with Jesus, visited Elizabeth, who was pregnant with John (Luke 1:39–56) in Ein Karem, a tiny village south west of Jerusalem. As I passed by they were reciting the Hail Mary.

There is no command in the Christian Bible that Christians make pilgrimage to the Holy Land. Yet from the third century at least, Christians began to make the journey to Jerusalem "for prayer and investigation of the places" (Eusebius, h.e. 6.11.2). But it was not until the uncovering of the tomb of Christ in the fourth century and the construction of churches at the holy places that pilgrimage to the Holy Land began in earnest. By the end of the fourth century the practice was so widespread that some Christian leaders reminded the faithful that Christ had not commanded pilgrimage and that God was no less present in other parts of the world.[1]

Like other religious people, Christians were not exempt from the lure of holy places. Once pilgrimage emerged as a form of devotion among Christians, it became an enduring feature of Christian piety.

In the early Middle Ages when Muslims first observed Christians journeying to Christian sites under Muslim hegemony, it appeared to them that the command to make pilgrimage was a directive of Christian law. "Many times I have seen people coming here [Syria] . . . from those parts of the world [the west]. They mean no harm. All they want to do is to fulfill their *law*" (emphasis mine).[2]

A consideration of the early evidence of pilgrimage can help us understand how and why pilgrimage, though not commanded of Christians in the Bible, came to play such a preeminent role in Christian piety.[3] Certain features of Christian tradition appear inimical to the sacralization of space that is the mark of the piety of pilgrims. One of the most famous sayings of Jesus are his words to the Samaritan woman at the well. "Woman, believe me, the hour is coming when neither on this mountain nor in Jerusalem will you worship the father . . . God is spirit, and those who worship him worship in spirit and truth" (John 4:21–24). John Calvin, the reformer, called pilgrimage a form of "counterfeit worship."[4] Yet pilgrimage has outlasted its critics.

Pilgrimage in Antiquity

In antiquity pilgrims were a familiar sight.[5] At shrines and cult centers throughout the Mediterranean world they could be seen bringing their offerings, joining in sacrifices, fulfilling vows made in times of distress, seeking relief from pain or healing, giving thanks for benefits, participating in processions and banquets. At least two hundred sacred shrines were dedicated to the healing god Asclepius. His chief pilgrimage centers, Epidauros and Pergamon, were not unlike a sanatorium or spa where the infirm went to bathe, to drink mineral water, and to place themselves under the care of a physician. Often these centers included temples, fountains, and baths, as well as a gymnasium, theater, hostel for pilgrims, rooms for incubation. Visitors would stay for several days, sometimes for weeks.

At these and other well-known shrines—for example, Hierapolis in Syria, Delphi in Greece, the island of Philae in Egypt—pilgrims could be seen from all over the Mediterranean world. To Hierapolis, the cult center of the goddess of Syria, came people from Phoenicia, Babylonia, Cappadocia, and Cilicia, says Lucian.[6] He described the ritual of a pilgrim who was setting out to the shrine of the goddess of Syria at Hierapolis as follows:

> Whenever someone is about to go to the Holy City, he shaves his head and his eyebrows. Then after sacrificing a sheep, he carves it in pieces and dines on it. The fleece, however, he lays on the ground to kneel on, and the feet and the head of the animal he puts on his own head. As he prays he asks that the present sacrifice be accepted and promises a greater one the next time. When he has finished, he puts a garland on his head and on the heads of those who are making the same pilgrimage. Then he sets out from his own country to make the journey, using cold water both for bathing as well as drinking, and he always sleeps on the ground, for it is a sacrilege for him to touch a bed before he completes the journey and returns to his own country.[7]

For this pilgrim, the journey to Hierapolis required that he leave his home city and country to travel to another place. There were temples closer to home, but "none was greater than that in the holy city" of Hierapolis, for it was there that the gods are "readily manifest to the inhabitants."[8] Pilgrimage was rooted in a fundamental religious fact: the gods appeared at particular places and locales. In a way that is difficult for moderns to grasp, religion in the ancient world was wedded to place, as Walter Burkert reminds us: "The cult of the Greeks is almost always defined locally; the places of worship are fixed in ancient tradition and cannot be moved lightly."[9] Unlike the sacred space defined by a synagogue or a church or mosque, that is, religious space that was "chosen" or created by the construction of a building, the sacredness of a mountain or a grove or a cave was "discovered" or found. Its sacrality was given, and the building of an altar or a temple simply marked the location.[10]

Holy places not only drew people to them to pray, to fulfill a vow, to offer sacrifices, or to seek healing, but also provided a point of orientation, an axis or fulcrum, a center around which other points are located. At the shrine at Delphi, the pilgrim could view a smooth rounded stone, the *omphalos,* the navel of the world. Likewise at Claros, the site of an oracle in Asia Minor, there was a room in which had been placed a stone of deep blue marble. Around it were placed stone benches, and as the pilgrims stared at it they seemed to be sitting at the center of the earth. These sacred places created a zone or precinct extending out beyond the shrine itself. This land of Epidauros was "sacred to Asclepius," wrote Pausanias, the Greek geographer, and the "sacred grove of Asclepius was surrounded on all sides by boundary marks."[11] No death or birth was allowed to take place within the enclosure, and all offerings had to be consumed within its bounds. Usually only one entrance was allowed, and in some cases it was marked by a ceremonial gate that set apart the sacred territory from the common or profane space that surrounded it. In most cases the zone was limited to the immediate vicinity, a grove or a temple precinct, but in places it was extended to include a town or city, or even a group of villages in the surrounding region.[12]

At the pilgrimage shrines, piety was nurtured not only by seeing and touching, by the proximity to holy places and holy things, but also by history, myth, and memory. "I will relate," writes Lucian, "the stories that are told about the 'holy place' and how the temple was built."[13] At the shrines could be found guides or "hosts"[14] whose task it was to recount the stories and myths associated with the site, to point out significant details, and to explain their meaning to the pilgrims and visitors.[15] In his *Description of Greece,* Pausanias, the geographer and traveler, provides many examples of the stories that were told at the pilgrimage centers, as well as at other sites of historical interest.[16] In antiquity, no less than today, pilgrimage and tourism existed side by side, and for much the same reasons. Without memory, without historical (or mythical) associations, trees and stones and rivers and temples are dormant and inert.

Early Jewish Pilgrimage

For the Jew, pilgrimage centered on Jerusalem, the city that stood "in the center of the nations" (Ezekiel 5:5). In ancient Israel there had been other pilgrimage sites—Shiloh, for example, the setting for an annual pilgrimage—but in the period of the Second Commonwealth, when the Temple was standing, Jerusalem was the chief goal of Jewish pilgrims. "Three times a year shall all thy males appear before the Lord thy God at the place which he will choose [Jerusalem]; on the feast of unleavened bread, and on the feast of weeks, and at the feast of tabernacles" (Deuteronomy 16:16). Besides these pilgrimage festivals, pious Israelites traveled to the city to fulfill other ritual obligations, for example, marking the birth of a child.

Pilgrimage to Jerusalem was a communal undertaking, a joyous and happy occasion as people from the same town or village traveled to the Holy City in company with fellow Jews.[17] The historian Josephus says it fostered "mutual affection" among Jews: "For it is good that they should not be ignorant of one another, being members of the same race and partners in the same institutions."[18] Anthropologists have observed that the journey to the holy place and fellowship with other pilgrims is as important as the goal.[19] Often pilgrims would remain in Jerusalem for weeks and months, and hostels were built for that purpose. During their stay in the Holy City, they not only offered sacrifices in the Temple but they also fulfilled other ritual obligations, such as purification, and during their stay some engaged in study of the Torah. An inscription found on a building in Jerusalem reads: "For the reading of the Torah and the study of the commandments, and the hostel and the rooms and the water installations, for needy travelers from foreign lands."[20] Pilgrimage was much more than a visit to holy places; it was an occasion to renew friendship, to study, to forge and strengthen bonds of loyalty to Jerusalem and the Land of Israel.

With the destruction of the Second Temple in 70 CE, the ancient laws on pilgrimage could no longer be observed. Pilgrimage for the Jew had been a ritual act whose purpose was to offer prescribed sacrifices in the Holy City. The loss of the Temple, and the occupation of the city by non-Jews, did not, however, put a stop to pilgrimage. Though the traditional ritual obligations could no longer be fulfilled, Jews continued to return to the city. At first they may have continued to observe those laws that still seemed applicable, for example, the offering of the second tithe, the *Maaser Sheni*. This was an offering of produce that was supposed to be eaten in Jerusalem or "redeemed" by putting aside coins of the same value. For a time this practice was continued by Jews living in the vicinity of Jerusalem.

Later, Jews came to Jerusalem, or at least to the outskirts of the city, for another reason: to mourn the destruction of the Temple. This practice, visible even today at the Western Wall (the remains of the Second Temple platform from the time of Herod), had its origins in the generations after the Bar Kochba revolt. Attested by Christian as well as Jewish sources from the Roman and Byzantine periods, it became the most visible expression of Jewish devotion to the fallen city. A description of the practice is found in the works of Jerome, the fourth-century Christian scholar, who lived in Bethlehem. He often had occasion to view, in his words, the "pitiful crowd" of Jews who came each year on the Ninth of Ab, the anniversary of the destruction of Jerusalem, to mourn the lost city. When they reached the summit of the Mount of Olives they wailed and lamented as they gazed at the ruins of the Temple and remembered its altar.[21]

This lugubrious band of pilgrims presents quite another face when the observer is a Jew. To the Jews, they were not a pitiful mob but a company of the pious engaged in a purposeful religious act with its own ceremony and formalities. Mourning the destruction of the Temple was not simply the by-product of an occasional journey to Jerusalem; it was becoming a regular practice. A text from the Cairo Genizah, a storeroom in the Cairo synagogue, discovered early in this century, describes the ritual to be observed on arriving in sight of the Holy City:

> If you are worthy to go up to Jerusalem, when you look at the city from Mount Scopus [you should observe the following procedure]. If you are riding on a donkey step down; if you are on foot, take off your sandals, then rending your garment say: "This [our] sanctuary was destroyed" . . . When you arrive in the city continue to rend your garments for the temple and the people and the house of Israel. Then pray saying: "May the Lord our God be exalted" and "Let us worship at his footstool . . . We give you thanks, O Lord our God, that you have given us life, brought us to this point, and made us worthy to enter your house" . . . Then return and circle all the gates of the city and go round all its corners, make a circuit and count its towers.[22]

From these fragments in the Cairo Genizah as well as several passages in the Talmud, it is apparent that pilgrimage to the fallen city had become a distinct ritual. The rabbis debated, for example, what specific rites one should perform, and at what places. Should one rend one's garments when one actually sees the Holy City or not until one is able to see the ruins of the Temple? Some said that there were two distinct "rendings," one for the city and a second for the Temple. "As soon as one reaches Mount Scopus he rends. Does he rend for the

Holy Temple separately and for Jerusalem separately? The former ruling [he rends for the Holy Temple] obtains where one first encounters the site of the sanctuary and the latter [he enlarges it for Jerusalem] where one first encounters Jerusalem." The rabbis, ever practical, even discussed how one repairs the garment that has been rent![23]

Jews also venerated places that marked the sites of significant events in the life of the people. An early example within the Scriptures is the account in the Book of Joshua of the fording of the Jordan River by the Israelites before the conquest of Canaan. After the Israelites had passed through the river to dry ground and were safely on its opposite bank, Joshua ordered representatives of the twelve tribes to take stones out of the river and construct a monument in the river and in Gilgal, the place where the Israelites camped after crossing the Jordan. These stones were to be a "sign" to the people, a "memorial" so that when "in time to come" their children asked: "What do these stones mean?" their parents could tell them that here God cut off the waters of the river before the Ark of the Covenant. "So these stones shall be to the people of Israel a memorial for ever" (Joshua 4:4–7).

According to the book of Joshua, a cairn marked the place where God had performed this marvelous deed on behalf of his people. At a later period in Jewish history, places where God had intervened in history were remembered with special prayers and blessings. In the treatise on blessings (m. Berakoth 9.1) in the Mishnah, the question arose as to where and when one should speak a blessing. "If one sees a place where miracles have been wrought for Israel, he should say, blessed be He who wrought miracles for our ancestors in this place."

In the discussion of this passage in the Talmud, the rabbis distinguished blessings that were incumbent on the people of Israel as a whole and blessings that were spoken only by individuals. If, for example, someone were attacked by a lion or a wild camel and were "miraculously saved," whenever that person passed that place again he was to say: "Blessed be He who wrought for me a miracle in this place." Because the deliverance concerned only an individual, only the person for whom the miracle was done was required to say a blessing.

The other type of blessing applied to all Israel. "If one sees the place of the crossing of the Red Sea, or the fords of the Jordan, . . . or the stone which Og king of Bashan wanted to throw at Israel . . . or the pillar of salt of Lot's wife, or the place where the wall of Jericho sank into the ground, for all these one should give thanksgiving and praise to the Almighty" (b. Berakoth 54a). These miracles God had done for Israel, and they were to be remembered with a blessing by any Jew when he or she viewed the place where the miracle took place.

Whether the deliverance was individual or corporate, the holiness of the place was "created" by the event that happened there; unlike a sacred grove, it was not "discovered." At such places, the appropriate ritual action was not only prayer or vows or petitions for healing; the place required retelling the story of what happened there. In reciting the story, however, the pilgrim did not simply recall what happened to others in the past; the prayer acknowledged God's mercy in the present. By the ritual act of offering a blessing, blowing a ram's horn at Rosh Hashannah, or eating bitter herbs at Pesach, faithful Jews made the past part of their own present. Invoking God's marvelous deeds at the very place where the events had taken place intensified and heightened the sense of participation in the marvelous deeds of old.

In the Footsteps of Jesus

Marcel Proust wrote, "The past is hidden in some material object (in the sensation which that material object will give us) which we do not suspect."[24] Memory is linked inescapably to tangible things that can been seen (or tasted or smelled), and it was to recollect and remember that Christians first set out "to trace the footsteps of Jesus," in the words of Origen.[25] It is, however, misleading, indeed anachronistic, to call Origen a pilgrim, if by pilgrim one means someone who prays or engages in a ritual at a holy place. Origen's interest was as much historical and exegetical as it was religious. Several generations earlier, another Christian thinker, a bishop from western Asia Minor, Melito of Sardis, had made a journey to the "east," presumably Palestine, to the "place where these things had been proclaimed and accomplished." His purpose in going there was to obtain "precise information" about the books of the "Old Testament." He wanted to know the number as well as the order of the books that Christians shared with the Jews.[26] Like Origen, he was interested in Palestine because it was the land of the Bible and it could provide information that was not available elsewhere.

Already in the third century, pilgrims had begun to visit Palestine "for prayer" and "investigation of the holy places."[27] But we have no firsthand account of an actual journey until the fourth century. This is the *Itinerarium Burgidalense*, the record of a Latin-speaking "pilgrim" from Bordeaux in Gaul, who arrived in the East in 333, four years before the death of Constantine.[28] He made the long and arduous journey to Palestine by land, passing through northern Italy, down the coast of modern Yugoslavia, across northern Greece and Macedonia, south to the Bosporus, which he crossed at Chalcedon, traveling across the spine of Asia Minor to Ancyra, then through the Taurus Mountains to Tarsus, finally reaching Antioch in Syria. From there he traveled along the coast through Laodicea, Beirut, and Sidon to Palestine.

The record of this anonymous pilgrim's journey is a brief, almost stenographic account, noting where he went, what he saw, where he changed horses, distances from one place to another. His pilgrimage took him all over Palestine, not simply to Jerusalem and the scenes of Jesus' life but also to obscure places, sometimes where little-known biblical events had taken place. His comments take this form: "Mount Carmel is there. There Elijah did his sacrifice." "City of Jezreel; it was there that King Ahab lived and Elijah prophesied; there also is the plain where David killed Goliath." "A mile from there is the place called Sychar, where the Samaritan woman went down to draw water, at the very place where Jacob dug the well, and our Lord Jesus Christ spoke with her."[29]

Jerusalem is presented in the same terse style. The pilgrim from Bordeaux mentions the pools built by Solomon; the pools of Bethsaida; the place on the Temple Mount where the Lord was tempted; the site of the Temple; the statues of Hadrian; the column where Christ was scourged; Mount Zion, where, according to his report, seven synagogues stood; Golgotha, "where the Lord was crucified and about a stone's throw from it the vault where they laid his body and he rose again on the third day." Here, he observes, without further comment, the emperor had built a "basilica," a "place for the Lord." He also mentions the new basilicas constructed on the Mount of Olives and at Bethlehem and also the basilica at Mamre, which he says was "exceptionally beautiful."[30] He went to Jericho and saw the tree Zacchaeus climbed to see Christ, the spring of the prophet Elisha, the

Figure 9. Illustrated in Mainz (983–991), this *maiestas* from a royal prayer book in Pommersfelden shows the figure of Christ in a clipeus shaped by concentric lines, with two angels. (See Chapter 13.)

house of Rahab the harlot, the spot where the Israelites placed the twelve stones, the place in the Jordan where the Lord was baptized by John.

It is tempting to smile at this pilgrim's credulity. The house of Rahab standing in Jericho 1,500 years later! Zaccheus's tree 300 years old! Pilgrims were shown the water pots used at the wedding of Cana, and in Arabia they could see the dung hill on which Job sat.[31] Yet even modern pilgrims are shown "Jacob's well" and the inn used by the good Samaritan on the road to Jericho. Like pilgrims of old, they often make the same circuit that this pious pilgrim traced, peering curiously at the scenes of biblical history to evoke images of the mighty heroes of ancient times. There is more here than credulity; these sights were narrow beams of light that penetrated the soul.[32] In the aphorism of Cynthia Ozick: "A visitor passes through a place; the place passes through the pilgrim."

What stands out in the account of the pilgrim from Bordeaux is not his credulity but his juxtaposing of minor biblical events and the places of the central "mysteries" of the Christian faith. The book exhibits almost no "theological" interest. It moves indiscriminately from one place to another. When he came to the Mount of Olives he wrote: "On the left is a vineyard where is also the rock where Judas Isacariot betrayed Christ; and on the right is the palm-tree from which the children took branches and strewed them in Christ's path. Nearby, about a stone's throw away, are two memorial tombs of beautiful workmanship. One of them, formed from a single rock, is where the prophet Isaiah was laid, and in the other lies Hezekiah, king of the Jews."[33] The pilgrim of Bordeaux has no hierarchy of place. If a site is mentioned in the Bible, and it can be located, it is worthy of a visit.

Patterns of Pilgrimage

A much fuller account of pilgrimage to Palestine was written by an aristocratic woman from Spain named Egeria.[34] By the time Egeria visited the land in the late fourth century, Jerusalem was a bustling Christian city, filled with pilgrims, monks and nuns, clerics and adventurers. Its new monuments at the holy places dazzled pilgrims from all over the world, and the elaborate liturgies celebrated in the chief churches thrilled visitors. Nevertheless, her pilgrimage, like that of the pilgrim of Bordeaux, was as much a quest to satisfy her own intense curiosity about the land of the Bible as it was to worship at the holy places in Jerusalem and elsewhere. "You know how inquisitive I am," she wrote of her visit to the valley of Cherith (1 Kings 17:3–6). She wanted to know from the monk who lived there why he had built his cell in that place (*Itinerarium Egeriae* 16.3).

Egeria wished to see with her own eyes the places where the great events of biblical history took place. She visited the "holy mount of God," Mount Sinai, deep in the desert and difficult of access even today; Mount Horeb, where the prophet Elijah fled from the presence of King Ahab; the land of Goshen; and Mount Nebo, the place where Lot's wife was turned into a pillar of salt. She had hoped to see the "actual pillar," but what she saw was only the place where it had stood. Disappointed, she wrote home to her sisters: "The pillar itself, they say, has been submerged in the Dead Sea—at any rate we did not see it, and I cannot pretend that we did" (12.7). She saw the tomb of "holy Job," Tishbe, the village from which the prophet Elijah got his name, and many other places before arriving in Jerusalem itself. Like other pilgrims, her "first desire" was to see, and the verbs "see" and "was shown" run throughout her account as well as those of other pilgrims.[35]

In part Egeria's journey was a grand adventure, a sightseeing tour of bibical history, the breathless journey of one of the idle rich. As she moved from place to place, she dreamed of the time when she could recount her exploits to her sisters back home, very much like the modern pilgrim who is thinking of gathering friends and neighbors for a slide show in the very act of taking pictures of the trip. But she always carried a Bible with her, and when she came to a "holy place," that is, a biblical or historical site, she read the account of what had happened there. "Whenever we arrived [at any place] I always wanted the Bible passage to be read to us" (4.3). At another site she wrote: "So there too we had a passage read from the Book of Moses" (4.5). The Bible was read not simply to remind the pilgrim of the details of the event that happened at the place; it was also part of a ritual involving prayer and a reading from the psalms. "When we reached this plain [where Moses blessed the Israelites before his death] we went on to the very spot, and there we had a prayer, and from Deuteronomy we read not only the song, but also the blessings he pronounced over the children of Israel. At the end of the reading we had another prayer, and set off again, with thanksgiving to God" (10.7). The parallels to Jewish pilgrimage are close. Egeria read the biblical account of what had taken place at the site; her company also offered a prayer and sometimes celebrated Holy Communion. "All there is on the actual summit of the central mountain (Sinai) is the church and the cave of holy Moses. No one lives there. So when the whole passage had been read to us from the Book of Moses (on the very spot!) we made the Offering [Eucharist] in the usual way and received Communion" (3.6). The phrase "in ipso loco" ("on the very spot" in John Wilkinson's felicitous translation) captures the thrill and excitement of the moment.[36] The experience was without parallel and nothing could prepare people for it.

Of all the places in Palestine where Egeria the pilgrim paused to read the Bible, pray, and offer the Eucharist, Jerusalem stood apart. There the central events in Christ's life had taken place. By far the longest section of Egeria's book is devoted to the city of Jerusalem and the holy places contiguous to the city. When Egeria reaches Jerusalem, her narrative changes character; her interest shifts away from "seeing" places to participating in the rituals that took place in the city and describing them to her sisters back home. "Loving sisters, I am sure it will interest you to know about the *daily services* they have in the holy places, and I must tell you about them" (24.1).

By the time Egeria arrived in Jerusalem, late in the fourth century, Christian worship in the city had begun to settle into distinctive patterns dictated by the presence of the holy places. That Christians could gather for worship at the "very spot" where the saving events had taken place made a deep impression on the Christians living there as well as on pilgrims. Egeria writes: "What I admire and value most is that all the hymns and antiphons and readings they have, and all the prayers the bishop says, are always relevant to the day which is being observed *and* to the place in which they are used" (47.5). A few details illustrate the practice. On Thursday of the "great week" (Holy Week), after services in the Martyrium (the great basilica), the congregation would return home for a short meal and then gather at the Eleona on the Mount of Olives. After psalms and readings and prayers, they would process to the Imbomon, the hillock of the Ascension on the Mount. Early in the morning they moved to the place where Jesus had been arrested on Gethsemane, returning to the atrium of the chapel adjacent to Golgotha. On Friday the faithful came to this chapel to venerate the wood of the Cross and to listen to the accounts of his Passion. This was followed by services of prayer in the Martyrium and the Anastasis. On Saturday the paschal vigil took place in the great church, the Martyrium, and afterward the newly baptized were led to the Anastasis (tomb). The bishop went inside the screen of the aedicule and said a prayer for them. Then they returned to the church, where the congregation had continued its vigil.

The development of stational liturgies—rituals celebrated at particular places or stations—is the most visible evidence of the way pilgrimage attained a privileged place in Christian piety. From the beginning, Christian worship had been oriented to time, to the "end time," the eschatological hope that was foreshadowed in the liturgy, and to "ritual time," the representing of the historical events of Christ's life, the suffering, death, resurrection within the context of liturgical celebration. The narrative character of the Gospels (recording Jesus' life from birth through death) indelibly imprinted on the minds of Christians the sanctity of time. For Christians in Jerusalem, however, the proximity of the holy places made possible a sanctification of space. The liturgy could now be celebrated not only according to the rhythm of Christ's birth, life, suffering, death, and resurrection, but also at the Eleona (Mount of Olives), or the Imbomon ("little hillock," place of the Ascension), Golgotha, or the Anastasis—that is, at the places where the events had taken place.

"There Is Something about Touching It"

When the Vietnam Veterans' Memorial in Washington was dedicated several years ago, I recall that men and women came from all over the United States, some traveling hundreds, even thousands, of miles by car or bus to be present at the site. When they arrived, all they found was a low wall with long lists of names of those who died in the Vietnam War engraved in the black marble. Yet they came, and continue to come, to indulge in the simplest sort of human memorial, seeking out the name of a friend or loved one and running their fingers over the cold stony texture of the engraved letters. "I don't know what it is," said one veteran who stood for two hours at the wall. "You have to touch it. There's something about touching it."

"There's something about touching it." Without the images and impressions of touch and sight and smell, memory is formless and vacuous. Memory that is purely mental, that is not anchored in things, will not endure.[37] This elementary truth was understood by the peasant who came to Jerusalem to kiss the wood of the Cross, by Egeria, who celebrated the Eucharist at the holy places, and by learned theologians who had never seen Jerusalem. When the faithful came to receive the wine in the Eucharist, Cyril of Jerusalem urged them to touch their fingers to their lips while they were still wet with wine and then touch the brow and eyes and other organs of sense.[38] No one expressed it more clearly in this period than Paulinus, a bishop from the city of Nola in Campania in southern Italy. "No other sentiment draws people to Jerusalem than the desire to *see* and *touch* the places where Christ was physically present, and to be able to say from their own experience, 'We have gone into his tabernacle, and have worshipped in the places where his feet stood'" (*Epistola* 49.14). Paulinus reasoned that if one wished to recall someone or represent an event, there was no better way than to "see the place" or to touch a fragment of something that person touched, for example, a fragment of the Cross.

Paulinus' sentiments were echoed by Christians living all over the Mediterranean world, in North Africa, in Palestine, in Asia Minor, and not only in reference to the holy places in Jerusalem. By the end of the fourth century the tombs of martyrs and saints had become places of veneration, drawing Christians to see and touch the remains (relics) of holy men and women buried in their own regions. One bishop wrote: "When one touches the bones of a martyr, one shares in the holiness which is present in the grace inhering in the body."[39] Gregory of Nyssa said that he had buried some of the bones of a group of martyrs alongside his parents. Normally, he said, one does not like to go to a tomb, but at the tomb of a martyr one receives a "sanctifying blessing." "To touch the corpse itself, if ever good fortune would allow such an opportunity," is like touching the "living and blooming body itself, bringing in the eyes, mouth, ears and all the senses . . . as though [the martyr] were fully present."[40]

As these statements suggest, devotion to the holy places in Palestine did not stand apart from other forms of veneration practiced at this time. A new tactile piety that attached itself to things, to bones and relics, to places and shrines, to sacred books, even to liturgical implements such as chalices and veils, was evident all over the Christian world. In a letter to Theophilus, pope (patriarch) of Alexandria, Jerome urged that all who minister at the altars in the church show proper reverence for the "accessories" used in the liturgy. These things, he writes, are not "lifeless and senseless things devoid of holiness; from their association with the body and blood of the Lord they are to be venerated with the same awe as the body and the blood themselves." Elsewhere, Jerome defends the veneration of the bones of martyrs. In kissing and adoring "ashes wrapped in a cloth" (the remains of a saint), he said, it is as though one "beheld a living prophet" in one's midst.[41]

This tactile piety, worship with the lips or the fingertips, took many forms, depending on the place or object that was venerated. Some pilgrims journeyed from Jerusalem down through the Judean desert to the Jordan River to bathe at the place where Christ was baptized. Others took home objects that bore a tangible relation to the place they had seen and touched—oil, water, earth, wood, bones. These objects, called "blessings," allowed the pilgrim to maintain physical contact with the holy place or thing. Holiness was transmitted through touching. The "blessing," writes the art historian Gary Vikan, was "not a memento to evoke pleasant memories, as is a modern tourist trinket, but rather a piece of portable, palpable sanctity which possessed and could convey spiritual power to its owner."[42] Others, dissatisifed with ersatz relics, tried to get the real thing. When the bishop of Jerusalem exposed a piece of the "holy Cross" for veneration, he had to hold it firmly and his deacons had to keep their eyes on the pilgrims, lest, while kissing the Cross, someone tried to bite off a piece.[43]

For the pilgrim, the "holy places" were not simply historical sites that invoked a memory of the past. Seeing was more than seeing, it was a metaphor for participation. Theodoret of Cyrus tells the story of Peter Galatia, who went down to Palestine (from Syria) "in order that by *seeing* the places where the *saving sufferings* had taken place he might worship *in them* the God who saved us." Peter, Theodoret reminds us, did not believe that God was "confined to a place." He knew that God's nature was without limit. Nevertheless, he went to Palestine to "treat his eyes with the sight of his desire." It was not enough that the eye of the soul enjoyed God through faith. Peter's delight in the holy places was like the pleasure a lover receives from gazing on the clothing or the shoes of the beloved. Wounded with love for God, and longing to see God's "shadow," Peter "took himself to those *saving places* where he could *see* the founts that gushed forth."[44]

In Christian discourse, the terms "sign" and "symbol" designated things that could be seen and touched that pointed beyond themselves. They were tiny windows that opened on another world. Among signs, the most important were, of course, water in Baptism, and bread and wine in the Eucharist, but also oil for blessing, relics, and gestures such as the making of the sign of the Cross. Signs were not simply pointers; they also shared in the reality they signified. "With the inner eye one sees the whole power of the Cross in this tiny fragment," wrote Paulinus of Nola (*Epistola* 31.1). Hence they deserved honor and veneration.[45]

At several places in his writings Gregory of Nyssa calls the holy places "signs." On a visit to Jerusalem made, in his words, "according to a vow," he rejoiced to be able to see the "*signs* of the Lord's sojourn in the flesh." In one place he calls the "holy places" [his phrase!] "saving symbols."[46] Now Gregory was a subtle and sophisticated thinker, the most rigorously intellectual of all the early Christian writers, and he chose his words with care. In a dispute over the Christian doctrine of God, Gregory had protested against the uncompromising intellectualism of a fellow bishop, Eunomius. One of his arguments against Eunomius rested on an appeal to the necessity of "signs" for Christian faith. According to Gregory, Eunomius transformed Christianity into a philosophical system in which "dogmatic exactness" was prized over all else. What Eunomius overlooked, said Gregory, was that Christianity was not solely a matter of the mind; it also invited "participation in sacramental practices and symbols."[47]

What did he mean by calling the holy places signs? These places, writes Gregory, had "received the footprints of Life itself,"[48] and for this reason they are palpable reminders that God once walked this earth. Just as perfume leaves an odor in the jar after it has been poured out, so God has left traces of his presence in Palestine. As we are able to savor the fragrance that was once in the jar, so, through the traces Christ left on earth, can human beings glimpse the living reality that was once visible in this land. By visiting those places that bear the imprint of "Life itself," the pilgrim was able to perceive the transcendent God who was beyond human comprehension.

There was, however, another side to Gregory. He was also an articulate critic of pilgrimage, a fact that has caused embarrassment to later advocates of the practice. In the letter in which Gregory had observed that the Lord gave no command to go up to Jerusalem, he also presented several other arguments against pilgrimage. There he states with exemplary brevity the classical theological case against sacralization of place: God is no more present in one place than in another. Even writers who praise and defend pilgrimage—for example, Theodoret of Cyrus in the passage on Peter of Galatia—always qualify their approval with a remark such as, "not as though God is confined to a place." In his letter on pilgrimage, however, Gregory develops the argument at greater length. What advantage, he asks, is there in being present at the "places themselves"? Can the Spirit not journey to Cappadocia (where Gregory lived)? He is just as present on the altars of Cappadocia as in Jerusalem. There may be a smidgeon of Cappadocian chauvinism here, but the point is clear: change of place does not bring one closer to God.[49]

Gregory's letter is puzzling in the light of his other statements about pilgrimage and holy places. There can be no question that he had reservations about pilgrimage, especially for monks and nuns. And he also states with his usual lucidity the theological and spiritual perils of a piety that is attached to place. Gregory was a disciple of Origen, the great Platonist theologian, and among Greek Christian thinkers from this period he is the most philosophical. More than any Christian thinker from antiquity, he gave philosophical expression to the belief that God is wholly transcendent, that by definition God is boundless, without extension in space, beyond measure.

Gregory was, however, as much a theologian of the Incarnation as he was of transcendence. As the eighteenth-century patriarch of Jerusalem, Chrysanthus, recognized, the key to understanding Gregory's devotion to the holy places was not only that God had become flesh but also that God had appeared at particular places. Consequently those places are unlike "other common places."[50] If God had once been present on earth in Jesus of Nazareth, the soil on which he walked, the cave in which he was born, the stones of the tomb in which he was buried bear the imprints of God's presence and are, in the words of John of Damascus several centuries later, "receptacles of divine energy."[51]

Christian pilgrimage has had its critics. With its many subsidiary forms of devotion, its commericalism, its vulgar reliance on touch and sight, pilgrimage seems to appeal only to the credulous and superstitious. It has been malevolently branded a form of "natural piety" that has little or no place in the higher spiritual religion of Christianity. But as Samuel Johnson observed:

> [Although] long journeys in search of truth are not commanded, to visit the place of great actions moves the mind in uncommon ways; curiosity of the same kind may naturally dispose us to view that country whence our religion had its beginning; and I believe no one surveys those aweful scenes without some confirmation of holy resolutions. That the Supreme Being may be more easily propitiated in one place than in another, it is the dream of idle superstition; but that some places may operate upon our own minds in an uncommon manner, is an opinion which hourly experience will justify.[52]

The spirit of Christian pilgrimage is caught in a beautiful book written by Stephen Graham, *With the Russian Pilgrims to Jerusalem*. Graham, an Englishman fluent in Russian, made the pilgrimage with a group of Russian peasants, walking across southern Russia, sailing in steerage across the Black Sea and into the Mediterranean. After observing the intense piety of these pilgrims, he described the difference between a pilgrim and a tourist. "The road from the Jerusalem of the tourist to the Jerusalem of the pilgrim is long indeed. The difference between the man surveying the Church of the Sepulchre with a handbook and the poor peasant who creeps into the inmost chamber of the Tomb to kiss the stone where he believes the dead body of his savior was laid, is something overwhelming to the mind."[53]

7 Jewish Pilgrimage after the Destruction of the Second Temple

MARK FRIEDMAN

The Roman destruction of Jerusalem in 70 CE brought to an end the city's reign as the center of the Jewish world. No longer would the biblical commandment to assemble in the city three times a year be observed or sacrifices be offered there. No longer would pilgrims arrive from all over the world bringing the half-shekel tax to the Temple or benefit from the wisdom of the city's sages. For long periods Jews would be prevented from visiting, much less settling in, Jerusalem. Even when a Jewish community was re-established in the city, it would generally remain secondary to other such communities in Eretz Israel—Tiberias, Acre, or Safed. The country itself, in turn, became secondary to the major communities of the Diaspora—Babylonia, Egypt, Spain, and northern Europe. Nonetheless, Jerusalem always remained at the crossroads of the major trends in Jewish history. It never lost its sacred and secular importance.

For Jews, pilgrimage meant travel to the Holy Land for religious reasons. Some stayed for a short visit, others permanently. After the destruction of the Temple, no rabbinic law ever established a commandment to visit Jerusalem or Eretz Israel, and while some rabbinic authorities encouraged pilgrimage, others mistrusted the motive and value of travel. The main question had been whether Jews were required to settle in Eretz Israel, since many commandments can only be performed there, and in rabbinic Judaism it was the opportunity to observe those commandments which represented the acceptable rationale for aliya—the term for "going up" to live there. The Tannaim of the Mishnah issued laws to prevent Jews from leaving the country but did not require Diaspora Jews to settle there. Even Maimonides, the medieval codifier of Jewish law, did not include settlement in Eretz Israel in his list of 613 commandments. Nachmanides, in thirteenth-century Spain, was the first codifier to do so, but the question of aliya continued to be debated through the centuries, and the battle among rabbinic authorities is still being fought.[1]

Jewish pilgrimage to Jerusalem, although often interrupted, never ceased. It changed significantly over time, reflecting developments in Jewish social and religious life. A major factor influencing pilgrimage was the existence and nature of a permanent Jewish community in Jerusalem, and that depended on the rulers of the city—Rome and Byzantium, the early Muslims, the Crusaders, Mamluks, and the Ottomans.

Under Rome and Byzantium (70–638)

After the destruction of Jerusalem, Yavneh became the nation's spiritual center, and the history of the Jewish community in Jerusalem came to a halt. Yet Jews did not lose hope of regaining control over the city and rebuilding the Temple. In the second, fourth, and probably the seventh century as well, they tried to re-establish ritual sacrifice in Jerusalem (and perhaps even succeeded), although these attempts were little more than short-lived aberrations in the course of history.

Since there was as yet no ban on Jewish presence in the city, and there is some evidence that a small permanent settlement existed there as well, we may assume that pilgrimage continued between 70 and the Bar Kochba revolt (132–135), but records are scarce.[2] The futile revolt claimed an enormous number of dead and captives and was followed by severe restrictions imposed by Rome. Emperor Hadrian built a new Roman city over the ruins of Jerusalem and forbade Jews to enter it. He changed the name of the city to Aelia Capitolina, and the name of the province to Syria-Palestina.[3] The center of Jewish life gradually shifted to the Galilee and the city Tiberias, and there would be no permanent Jewish community in Jerusalem for 500 years. Although few records exist of Jews visiting the city between the Bar Kochba revolt and the fourth century, they benefited from a de facto easing of Hadrian's edicts in the latter part of the third century.[4]

After Constantine recognized the Christian religion, his mother,

Helena, came to Jerusalem in 324 and began the construction of churches in an effort to christianize the Holy City and the Holy Land. The position of the Jews then worsened. Until Helena's intrusions, Judaism's battles with pagan Rome—which accepted the existence of many religions—were political. The battles with the Church—which saw itself as the "true" Israel—were religious. Constantine enacted many anti-Jewish decrees, among them the renewal of the ban against pilgrimage to Jerusalem, except on the Ninth of Ab, when Jews were permitted to mourn the loss of the city on the anniversary of the destruction of the Temple—an annual testimony to the triumph of the Church.[5] In 333, as the Bordeaux Pilgrim reported, not far from the statues of Hadrian—that is, on the Temple Mount—"there is a perforated stone, to which the Jews come every year and anoint it, bewail themselves with groans, rend their garments, and so depart."[6]

Constantine's laws remained in place for the balance of the Byzantine era, with a short-lived respite during the reign of Emperor Julian (360–363), who opposed Christianity and sought to rebuild the Temple in Jerusalem. Jews were admitted back into the city and even established a synagogue near the site of the Temple. They may even have begun the construction of a temple, but an earthquake on May 27, 363 (some sources cite a suspicious fire), destroyed the building materials; all hope disappeared when Julian was killed shortly thereafter.[7]

Jewish pilgrimage to Jerusalem during the Roman and Byzantine eras was an individual act, although Jews may have occasionally gathered there in numbers. While there is no detailed description of the pilgrimage in Jewish sources, it was essentially a looking backward to the past, mourning the loss of the Temple. There are references in the Palestinian Talmud, compiled in the second half of the fourth century, and in the Babylonian Talmud, compiled one hundred years later, regarding pilgrimages to Jerusalem, about how many times one should rend one's garment—a sign of mourning—and pray on seeing the different levels of destruction of Judea, Jerusalem, and the Temple.[8]

The Early Arab Period (638–1099)

Soon after Jerusalem fell to the Muslims, the site of the Temple Mount was cleaned, apparently by the order of Caliph Umar. Jews were said to be involved in the project,[9] and, according to tenth-century Jewish sources, Umar allowed seventy Jewish families to settle in Jerusalem.[10] Shortly thereafter the talmudic academy moved from Tiberias, and it became known as the Jerusalem Yeshivah or the Great Council. It was composed of learned men who made decisions regarding law, religious beliefs, and rituals such as the annual calendar and synagogue liturgy. Yet the Jerusalem community could not wrest away from the Babylonians the leadership role for world Jewry.[11] Several waves of aliya occurred during the Early Arab period, frequently motivated by economic and political hardships in other lands, rather than by faith.[12]

In the first half of the ninth century, Karaites began to arrive in Jerusalem. A Jewish sect which developed in Persia in the eighth century, the Karaites posed a serious challenge to rabbinic Judaism during the Middle Ages as they rejected the Talmud and its interpretations of the Torah. They identified themselves with the Mourners of Zion—a group which existed in Jerusalem between the seventh and eleventh century—and took on many of their ascetic practices, such as mourning the destruction of the city, fasting and praying, and refraining from eating meat and drinking wine while anticipating the arrival of the Messiah.[13] The Karaites frequently appealed to their brethren in the Diaspora to come and join them. One of their leaders, Daniel al-Kumisi, called for at least five men from every city to come to Jerusalem, and the tenth-century missionary Saul ben Masliah invoked the language of Jeremiah to call for "one from every city and two from a family" to return to Zion.[14] The Karaites established a new quarter outside the city wall, apart from the ongoing community of the Rabbanite Jews. Karaite students from Byzantium would come to study at the Bakhtawi academy in Jerusalem, and their stay in the city would strengthen the Karaite center there and train scholars who would assume positions of leadership upon their return to their communities. The correspondence of Tobias ben Moses, a Karaite of Constantinople, reflects the life of one who came to Jerusalem in the mid-eleventh century to study Karaite law, biblical exegesis, and philosophy, and who may have stayed for as long as a decade among the Mourners of Zion.[15]

There is ample evidence of pilgrimages to Jerusalem made by Jews from many countries during the Early Arab period, even though the journey was hazardous—whether by land or by sea. Pilgrims arrived for the annual assembly which took place on the seventh day of the

Feast of Tabernacles, Hoshanah Rabah, when a procession would go through the city, around the gates of the Temple Mount, and up the Mount of Olives.[16] The pilgrims circled the Mount of Olives seven times, in song and prayer, centering around a stone from which the Divine Presence is supposed to have ascended to heaven. The assembly was conducted by the Jerusalem Yeshivah as an exercise of communal authority and leadership. In a sense the assembly was a re-enactment of Temple rituals, including a special role for the priests. Jews paid the rulers handsomely for the privilege of holding the assembly on the Mount of Olives.[17]

The assembly was a joyous assertion of community and of living in the present, different from past rituals which centered around mourning the destruction of the city, and also from the eschatological nature of future pilgrimage rituals. The many "fellows of the Academy" from Syria, Egypt, and other Mediterranean lands arrived in Jerusalem early, to decide on religious and communal issues.[18] Ibn Daud writes in *Sefer ha-Qabbalah* that "when the Jews used to celebrate at the Festival of Tabernacles on the Mount of Olives, they would encamp on the mountain in groups and greet each other warmly."[19] The head of the Yeshivah would announce the fixing of the festival calendar for the coming year, appoint new members to the religious courts, and bestow honors upon those who had contributed to the Yeshivah.[20] Ibn Daud continues: "The heretics would encamp before them like little flocks of goats. Then the rabbis would take out a scroll of the Torah and pronounce a ban on the heretics right in their faces, while the latter remained silent like dumb dogs."[21] The "heretics" were the Karaites with whom the Rabbanites continued to feud. Both communities enjoyed a special status in the eyes of their brethren in the Diaspora because of the virtue attached to living in the city, even though they were poor and often had to appeal to the Diaspora for support.[22]

After the 970 Fatimid conquest, Jerusalem and the rest of the country entered a period of slow decline brought on by the upheavals which recurred during the tumultuous eleventh century. The Jews of Fustat in Egypt, the seat of government, assumed the role of leadership in the area which lasted until the sixteenth century. The last evidence of the annual Hoshanah Rabah pilgrimage is from 1062, by which time it had lost much of its relevance as a religious and political event, and as a mode of pilgrimage. The Yeshivah moved to Tyre in 1073, as did many of the Rabbanites, leaving behind a Jewish Jerusalem that was just a shell of its former self. Indeed, in 1081 the Hoshanah Rabah assembly was held in Tyre.[23]

The Crusader and Mamluk Periods (1099–1517)

On Friday, July 15, 1099, the victorious Crusaders massacred the Muslim and Jewish population of Jerusalem. Many Jews were burnt in their synagogue, while others were sold into slavery.[24] As in Byzantine times, Jews were forbidden to live in the Holy City, although it appears that they were allowed once again to mourn the destruction of the city on the Ninth of Ab, perhaps to satisfy Christian triumphalism. Unlike the Rabbanites, most Karaites, who emphasized the importance of living in Jerusalem, had not left the city in the 1070s and were there until the Crusaders' arrival. A document from the Genizah records the redemption of 350 Karaite holy books from the hands of the Crusaders.[25] An inscription found on a Karaite Torah scroll mentions that holy Karaite books were redeemed in Jerusalem on the tenth of Ab in the year 1105, so it is possible that the Karaites had been allowed back into the city to observe the day of mourning there.[26]

One consequence of the Crusaders' rule was the discontinuation of easy access to Eretz Israel by Jews who lived in countries under Islam, and, at the same time, better maritime connections for Jews in European countries. Pilgrims began to arrive from the lands of the Crusaders—France, Spain, and Germany. For some the goal was pilgrimage to Eretz Israel alone, while others combined it with travel to other lands. Since Jews were not allowed to live in Jerusalem, Acre, the flourishing Crusader port with its small community of Jewish merchants, became their main stop.

While pilgrims visited tombs of sages throughout the country, the main purpose of pilgrimage was to pray in Jerusalem. But, in the absence of a Jewish community there, compact itineraries were established which individuals could follow in a short time. As in earlier days, upon seeing the "ruined city" pilgrims rent their garments and said special prayers for the city and for the destroyed Temple, pleading that both be rebuilt. Prayers were apparently said near one of the Temple Mount's gates, or on the Mount of Olives.[27]

Pilgrims' accounts contribute to our knowledge about life under the Crusaders. One distinguished pilgrim was Maimonides, in 1165, who stayed in Acre for five months, and in Jerusalem for five days only. Two other travelers in the second half of the twelfth century left detailed accounts: Benjamin of Tudela and Petahiah of Regensburg. Benjamin recorded that only four Jews lived in Jerusalem, and they were dyers, a Jewish craft. A decade later Petahiah noted only one dyer.[28]

After Saladin's victory over the Crusaders in 1187, Jews were again permitted, in fact encouraged, to settle in Jerusalem, as reported by Yehuda al-Harizi, a pilgrim from Spain who stayed in the city for a month in 1218. In *Sefer Tahkemoni,* written in rhyming prose, he expressed the ambivalence of the pilgrim: the joy experienced upon reaching the goal of Zion and the mourning evoked by its destruction.[29] Al-Harizi also mentioned a group of French Jews who settled in Jerusalem. This is the earliest known case of a group of scholars following their teacher with the goal of settling in the Holy Land.[30] In the first half of the thirteenth century, several other groups arrived from France, when life for Jews there became nearly impossible; other Jews came from Europe, Yemen, and North Africa.

The clash between giants—between Islam and Christianity—focused the world's attention on the Holy Land, wrote Joshua Prawer. Jews saw a deeper, hidden meaning in the destruction of the land, believing that no one could settle there except Jews, and that brought a surge of pilgrims and settlers after the Crusaders were defeated.[31]

One of the events which influenced pilgrimage during the thirteenth century was the return of Jerusalem to the Crusaders, from 1229 to 1244, followed by a renewed ban on Jews' entering the city.[32] Another was the invasion of the country by Mongol hordes in 1260, which caused the inhabitants of Jerusalem to flee the city. When Nachmanides—the Spanish codifier of Jewish law who included settlement of Eretz Israel as one of the 613 commandments—arrived in 1267, he visited Jerusalem and found only 2,000 people in it, including 300 Christians and 2 Jewish dyers. Nachmanides helped the dyers establish a synagogue in the city, to which pilgrims from Damascus and other places in the East would come as well. He left Jerusalem after about one month and settled in Acre.[33]

In the thirteenth century there was a re-evaluation of religious laws concerning living in Eretz Israel, since more people were settling there, not waiting for the arrival of the Messiah. In midcentury, for example, the Maharam of Rutenberg ruled that a wife must accompany a husband going to settle permanently in Eretz Israel, while a wife of someone just planning to visit could refuse to accompany her husband without defaulting on her obligations under the marriage contract. The rabbinic concept of an ideal pilgrim was of a mature scholar who would go to Eretz Israel to settle with his family and his wealth (since the country was poor and it was difficult to make a living there), and lead a life of learning. This ideal was the opposite of the spiritualist view of pilgrimage for the sake of penance, which involved poverty and asceticism—a view related to trends of pietism among Jews and to the mendicant spiritualists in Europe. In general, Western aliya in the Mamluk period was essentially elitist, as those who came were mostly scholars and intellectuals.[34] The end of Crusader rule also meant that fewer ships arrived from Europe, making it harder for Western Jews to make a pilgrimage.

A different pattern was common among Jews from Muslim lands during the Mamluk era, a pattern known as *ziyara,* an Arabic word used to describe visits to holy shrines.[35] It was a communal pattern with roots in popular religion, and perhaps folklore, but nonetheless one in which all levels of Eastern Jewish society participated. They would come to holy sites—mostly tombs of sages—at particular times, usually on one of the three festivals when pilgrimages had been performed while the Temple stood. At first, sources describe pilgrimages to Jerusalem during the Feast of the Tabernacles, as in the earlier Muslim era; but in the fifteenth century, Passover and Pentecost appear as the time of the *ziyara,* influenced perhaps by Christians from the East and by Muslim pilgrims coming in the spring to celebrate Easter and the Feast of Nebi Musa, the "Prophet Moses." In the fifteenth century, the *ziyara* involved a circuit which included Meron, the site of the tombs of the Tannaim Hillel and Shammai, and Ramah, where the Prophet Samuel is said to be buried. It culminated in Jerusalem in time for Pentecost.[36] (The *ziyara* had a later European version among the Hasidim of Eastern Europe, and may be said to continue in the Lag ba-Omer celebrations at Meron in our time.)

In contrast, the Western pattern of pilgrimage to Jerusalem was not based on participation in communal events at specific sites at

Figure 10. A family on their way
to the Western Wall.

appointed times. Even when the Western pilgrim traveled as part of a
group, the experience was an individual one, not tied to any date or
season. The ritual did not look to the past, to invoke the power of an
ancient sage or saint, but toward the ultimate messianic future. This
future was to be represented by the rebuilt Temple, the return of the
Divine Presence, and the re-establishment of Jewish sovereignty. In
the thirteenth century we find the first mention of the tombs of David
and Solomon as part of the pilgrim's path.[37]

Under the Mamluks, many Islamic schools and other religious
institutions were built in Jerusalem, and in an increasingly orthodox
atmosphere Jews were frequently harassed. Yet in the fourteenth and
fifteenth century, several waves of refugees from Europe came there

nevertheless: Jews from Germany arrived in 1349 as a result of the Black Plague, followed by Jews from the Iberian Peninsula, escaping the harsh measures issued in Spain in 1391, followed by the Expulsion in 1492 and the forced conversions in Portugal in 1497. The European Jews were not always accepted by the local Jews, who were known as Musta'rabs—non-Arabs who took on the language and manners of the Arabs. Jews from Germany complained that the local Jerusalem Jews were "wicked" and bothered the Western Jews, who were pious and "kept the Torah." On the other hand, the local Jews were suspicious of the arrivals from Spain, some of whom had been forced to live as Christians prior to the Expulsion. The elders of the Musta'rabs, who represented the Jewish community to the Mamluk authorities and were responsible for collecting taxes, were often blamed for making life miserable for other Jews living in Jerusalem.[38] Rabbi Ovadiah of Bertinoro (Italy), for example, who immigrated to Jerusalem in 1488, stated that out of the 4,000 families in Jerusalem, only 70 were Jewish, down from 300, because of the high taxes and the high-handedness of the elders.[39] By 1521, four years after the Turks conquered Jerusalem, Moshe Basola, an Italian Jew, reported that of the 300 Jewish families in the city, Spanish Jews were the majority—as a result of the Expulsion; only 15 families were Ashkenazim, or Western Jews, and the rest were local and North African Jews. He also noted that many widows lived in Jerusalem.[40]

The Spanish exiles brought with them mysticism and messianism. Safed, which enjoyed better economic conditions than Jerusalem, emerged as the center of kabbalistic study, led by Rabbi Moses Cordovero and Rabbi Isaac Luria. (Gershom Scholem has described the Lurianic Kabbalah of Safed as the last great religious trend in Judaism to spread throughout the entire Jewish world.)

Pilgrimage was thus overshadowed as the primary motivation for Jews going to Eretz Israel, and Jerusalem was overshadowed as the primary destination. The primary motivation had become to escape from persecution. Both the refugees and those drawn to the Kabbalah went to the Galilee, and especially to Safed.

As we have seen, the forms of Jewish pilgrimage changed over time, reflecting trends in Jewish life and depending on the existence and nature of the permanent community in the Holy City. Pilgrimages could be individual or communal, elitist or popular, within the religious mainstream or outside it. Until the Enlightenment and the emergence of Reform Judaism in the nineteenth century, there was no trend in Jewish religious life that bypassed Jerusalem, or its pilgrims.

Jewish pilgrimage has been influenced by Christian and Muslim forms of pilgrimage, but it differs from them in a very fundamental way. The Christian pilgrim to Jerusalem seeks to retrace the final footsteps of Jesus, formalized as the stations of the Cross. The Muslim on the Hajj reenacts the historical journey of the Prophet to Mecca. Jewish pilgrimage is not tied to historical events, nor does the pilgrim follow a set path. Instead, the pilgrim looks back at the remains of the past in order to strengthen his faith in the redemption to come. From the Temple Mount he goes across the Valley of Jehoshaphat to the Mount of Olives, a symbol of eschatological import both for individual resurrection and national rebirth. The Jewish pilgrim ultimately believes in the words written by Nachmanides to his son in 1267, that "he who merits to see Jerusalem in her ruins will merit to see her rebuilt and repaired when the Divine Presence returns to her."[41]

THE EARTHLY CITY

Jerusalem and Zionism

8

ARTHUR HERTZBERG

Both the Orthodox Jewish faith and modern Zionism assert that the Jew is in exile, but their explanations of this exile are radically different. The religious explanation is summarized in the liturgy: "Because of our sins we were exiled from the land."[1] This phrase, occupying a central place in the prayers of all the festivals, carries forward the prophetic assertion that ancient Assyria, the destroyer of the kingdom of Israel and the scourge of the kingdom of Judah, was the rod of God's anger.[2] The Jews suffered for many centuries because God was punishing them for sins for which others were forgiven, and He would restore them at the End of Days to unique glory. The exile will end when the sins have been expiated, through some combination of suffering and increased piety, and God will then return the Jews to the Holy Land. The center of this drama would be in Jerusalem. In the Bible, it is the essential capital of God's people; its destruction was His ultimate act of punishment of the Jews for their sins, and its miraculous restoration is to be the indispensable event of their redemption.

The Zionist drama of the restoration of the Jews to Palestine is radically different. Modern Zionism began as a secular movement. Its central problem was not the alienation of Jews from God but their suffering on the margin of society. This suffering was not explained as a sign of God's special involvement in His chosen people. On the contrary, Theodor Herzl, and Leon Pinsker before him, explained anti-Semitism, past and present, as the inevitable response by the majority to the abnormality of the Jews. They had long been a minority society: "We are everywhere guests and nowhere the hosts," in Pinsker's formulation. Modern Zionism proposed to make the Jews normal, by making them into a nation among the nations. In the effort to become "normal," Pinsker never mentioned Palestine in his *Auto-Emancipation*. He wanted to find a "land that would be productive and well-located and of an area sufficient to allow the settlement of several millions." He thought that this "land might form a small territory in North America or a sovereign pashalik in Asiatic Turkey recognized by the Porte and the other Powers as neutral."[3] Herzl was more ambivalent. In *The Jewish State*, the pamphlet in which he announced his solution for the "Jewish question," Herzl suggested that a commission should investigate the comparative merits of Argentina, where there was much empty land, and Palestine, the land to which Jews were linked by religion and memory. Obviously, the regaining of Jerusalem was not at the center of Herzl's outlook at the beginning of his Zionist career.[4]

Religious Dream, Zionist Quest

To be sure, the religious dream of restoration and the Zionist quest for normalcy in the modern age were not, and could not be, kept separate. Herzl was correct, in theory, that the Jews could create a modern state anywhere, but the overwhelming majority of his followers, including many of those who were most vehemently secular, insisted that only Palestine could be the magnet of modern Jewish nationalist aspirations. But the Zionists had no thought of joining the existing Jewish community; they were coming to build a new contemporary Jewish society in Palestine. The Zionists had little sympathy for the Jews who were already in the land, because the community had long been supported by alms from abroad: its members were waiting for the glories that God had promised for the end of days. For the older community, Jerusalem was the center; they prayed, like all the believers everywhere, "that their eyes might see His merciful return to Zion," which, in the liturgy, means Jerusalem.

For the new settlers, who were founding a modern nation, the

Figure 11. Jewish tinsmith in Jerusalem, ca. 1880.

emotional center was the farming settlements they were creating. This clash in outlook came to an early climax in 1902, when the British government offered the Zionists a tract in Uganda (it was actually a region of what is now Kenya) for Jews who were fleeing from Eastern Europe. Herzl wanted to accept the offer, as an "asylum for the night" for those who were in immediate need. He suggested that the refugees be resettled immediately in Uganda, while the Zionist movement continued to work toward the creation of their ultimate home in Palestine.

At the Zionist Congress of 1903, when this offer was debated, there was a large reversal of roles. Herzl was supported by many of the more religious-minded, and he was opposed overtly by such secular Zionists as Chaim Weizmann and by the bulk of the delegation from tsarist Russia. The believers seemed to think that it did not matter where Jews in trouble established themselves, because God had guaranteed that all Jews would ultimately be returned to the Promised Land. The secular Zionists opposed any diversion from Palestine. They wanted to use the established Jewish feelings about the Holy Land to give energy to their program for establishing a modern nation. This battle helped to define a paradox: modern, secular Zionism showed clear signs of its roots in the Jewish religion, which it thought it had transcended, or even denied. Many of the Zionists no longer believed in God, but they refused to give up the notion that He—or His avatar, history—had given the Jews an unbreakable claim to the land of their ancestors. The very name they had given their movement—Zionism— derived from the name of the mountain in Jerusalem on which the Temple had stood. The literal restoration of the glories of ancient Zion was not on their agenda, but they could not dispense with the older mystique.

The interplay between religion and secularity is, thus, one of the central themes of the history of Zionism. It has undergone many permutations. The overt battles have been fought over the question of the role of Jewish religion in the new society. At the beginning, Theodor Herzl imagined the synagogues as places where the ceremonies of the new state would take place, but he denied the Jewish religion any role in deciding the policies of the new society. In *The Jewish State*, he wrote:

Shall we end by having a theocracy? No, indeed. Faith unites us, knowledge gives us freedom. We shall therefore prevent any theocratic tendencies from coming to the fore on the part of our priesthood. We shall keep our priests within the confines of their temples in the same way as we shall keep our professional army within the confines of their barracks. Army and priesthood shall receive honors high as their valuable functions deserve. But they must not interfere in the administration of the State which confers distinction upon them, else they will conjure up difficulties without and within.[5]

Herzl's opinions did not stop religious believers, either inside or outside the Zionist movement. They soon began to fight with the secularists for some control over the nature of the new society, and the battle has never ended.

A more complicated battle has been fought over Jerusalem. The varying attitudes toward Jerusalem is a central theme of Jewish history in the last century. Some of the believers, especially those who were not Zionists, made no immediate claim to Jerusalem because they believed that its Jewish future was guaranteed by God. Some of the secularists continued to hope that Jerusalem, despite the long connection to it for Muslims and Christians, would eventually belong to the Jews. The believers, of all varieties, insist that a legitimate Jewish state which does not possess Jerusalem is unthinkable; many, perhaps even most, secular nationalists can imagine sharing Jerusalem, in some manner, with Muslims and Christians. Much of the evidence is in silence, in those Zionist theories which do not put Jerusalem at their center, or which do not even mention the Holy City. But theory and ideology are not sufficient evidence. The changing and embattled realities of the Jewish-Arab conflict, which is now a century old, must be added to the account, and, especially, the deep feelings about Jerusalem that exist very widely among Jews—and among Muslims. It would be wrong to paint with too broad a brush. On the question of Jerusalem, the truth can be found only through attention to details.

In his own short career, Herzl had conceived of an orderly process toward building a new state which, he was certain, would attract the majority of the Jews of the world. The effort would begin with international recognition of the claim of the Jews to the land. The settlement of many hundreds of thousands would be organized through a company empowered by this formal international act. Herzl himself spent his time seeking the assent of the European powers and organizing the institutions of the new Zionist movement as the germ of a future government. What Herzl wrote in his diaries remained consistent with what he said in the very beginning of his career, in *The Jewish State*. With some solemnity he promised that if the Jews would be given Palestine, "the sanctuaries of Christendom would be safeguarded by assigning to them an extra-territorial status such as is well known to the law of nations."[6]

He did, indeed, make one trip to Palestine, in 1898. Herzl came to the Holy City not to pray, or to lay claim to it as the future capital of a Jewish state, but to keep an appointment with the German kaiser, Wilhelm II. That potentate had come to Jerusalem to help consecrate the new Lutheran Church of the Redeemer, and to extend the influence of Germany in the Turkish empire. According to the account in his diaries of this meeting, Herzl avoided the issue of Jerusalem. At the end of the formal address to the kaiser which Herzl had prepared, he talked in lofty language about the importance of Jerusalem to all mankind. He clearly knew that the Lutheran emperor would be outraged to be asked to support the Jews in reclaiming the city which contained the Holy Sepulchre. Earlier, in June 1896 in a conversation in Istanbul with officials of the Turkish court, Herzl had been more precise: "The holy cities of human civilization must belong to everyone. I believe that we will ultimately have to consent that Jerusalem remain in its present status." In his audience with Pope Pius X in January 1904, Herzl, while arguing for the return of the Jews to the land of their ancestors, agreed with the uncompromising Catholic leader that Jerusalem should remain *"extra commercium."* On the other hand, when talking to himself, at his most private, Herzl did dream of possessing Jerusalem. He knew that the Jews were already a majority in the city, and he hoped that their efforts would make a jewel of the new Jerusalem.[7] Herzl hoped that Jerusalem might eventually be the Vienna of a Jewish state, but he thought that Jewish possession of Jerusalem was a far-off possibility—and he well knew that there were deep and abiding Christian and Muslim connections.

Breaking with the Past

The attitude of the Halutzim, the pioneers who began the Jewish agricultural settlements, is less ambiguous. Their effort to create a self-sustaining community had begun before Herzl became a Zionist in 1895, and, for that matter, even before Leon Pinsker had appeared in 1882. In the middle years of the nineteenth century a few older settlers, from the traditionalist Yishuv, began to move away from depending on alms. Sir Moses Montefiore, the Anglo-Jewish public figure, had come to Palestine seven times to help this Jewish community. In 1857 he ordered the building of a windmill so that Jews might thresh their own wheat, and in 1860, with money from the bequest of the American philanthropist Judah Touro, Montefiore financed the creation of Mishkenot Sha'ananim, the first Jewish settlement outside the walls of the Old City. In 1870 the Alliance Israelite Universelle founded an agricultural school called Mikveh Israel to train Jewish farmers. These initial efforts did not transform the older Jewish community, but they did point away from relying on alms. When the Hibbath Zion (Love of Zion) movement arose in Eastern Europe, after the pogroms of 1881–1882 in Russia, its purpose was to help settle Jews on farms in Palestine. In these "colonies" Jews who had been peddlers or petty traders would transform themselves into peasants. The first arrivals did not insist that they had to do the farming themselves; they were willing to employ Arab laborers, for they had no ideological commitment to working with their hands.

This soon changed. When Theodor Herzl established the World Zionist Organization in 1897, he wanted it to be free of parties. Until the Jews established their own commonwealth, the movement was to remain united in the task which all Jews shared, the building of the state. This hope could not be realized, because everyone knew that the character of the new community would be determined by the shape of its earliest institutions. The socialists fought early, and hard, to control the nascent society. In *The Jewish State,* Herzl had suggested a shortened seven-hour work day, a very advanced idea for the last decade of the nineteenth century. The socialists added an even more radical idea, which they derived from Karl Marx, who had appropriated this notion from the physiocrats of the eighteenth century: physical labor on the farm or in fashioning raw materials into usable forms was good; commerce was bad because it exploited the value that the true producers, the farmers and the artisans, had created. It followed that the Jews, who had long mostly engaged in commerce, had been living in "unproductive" occupations. They needed to be "productivized."[8] The socialists conceived the Zionist venture as the great historic opportunity to create a normal economy in which Jews would return to labor.

This negative estimate of middlemen occupations was much more than a comment on the economy. It contained a strong moral element: those who worked with their hands were healthier people, spiritually, than those who did not. Physical labor, especially in farming, put man in touch with his primal self. Those who would come to Palestine to work would be transformed by their labor into new men and women. This was the doctrine of Aaron David Gordon, the major spiritual mentor of the pioneers who founded Daganya, the earliest Jewish collective farm in Palestine in the first two decades of the twentieth century. Near the beginning of this effort, in 1911, Gordon wrote:

> There is only one way that can lead to our renaissance—the way of manual labor, of mobilizing all our national energies, of absolute and sacrificial devotion to our ideal and our task. Not even by thousands of title deeds can national assets be acquired, for whatever title deeds we do possess to land in Palestine have so far not given us real title to our country. Truth to tell, we have as yet no national assets because our people has not yet paid the price for them. A people can acquire its land only by its own effort, by realizing the potentialities of its two-sided transaction, but the people comes first—the people comes before the land.[9]

The programs of the Halutzim, no matter how much they differed in politics and social vision, all contained a pronounced and profound desire to break with the Jewish past in exile, with its economy, culture, and memories. Those who were leaving Europe to find a new life in Palestine were also leaving the religious culture of the East European ghettos. In the early years of the twentieth century, Jewish Jerusalem was a transplanted shtetl. The socialist pioneers did not want to connect with the older Jewish community in Palestine, and especially not with the strong and very Orthodox group in Jerusalem—the "Old

Yishuv"—for it was an extension of the society which they were abandoning.

Tel Aviv versus Jerusalem

Not all those who came to Palestine in the formative years of modern Zionism were socialists. A majority of the new arrivals had no intention of transforming themselves into farmers. They were city people who wanted to make their living in commerce or manufacturing. Some of these newcomers came to Jerusalem, or to the other older Jewish centers of Tiberias and Safed, but in all three cities the pressure of religious and social conformity was very heavy. Many among the resolutely middle-class newcomers had become secular or semisecular in their religious outlook and practice. They could best express their post-Orthodox Jewishness in a city of their own. The first all-Jewish city to be created in many centuries, Tel Aviv, was founded in 1909 on a sand dune north of the ancient city of Jaffa. From its beginning to this day, the city has represented the new Israel. Tel Aviv is contemporary and secular, while Jerusalem has remained profoundly marked by the many centuries of Jewish religious life which predate modern Zionism.

Jerusalem, even though it was not central to the earliest ideologues of political Zionism and of Zionist socialism, did play a much more significant role in the thinking of the cultural Zionists. The leading figure, Asher Ginsberg (Ahad Ha'am), was put off by his very first encounter with the Jews in the Holy City. In the spring of 1891, on the eve of Passover, he stood at the Western Wall watching "a large number of Jerusalem Jews standing and praying aloud." These were people of the older settlement. Ahad Ha'am reacted to them with distance and anger: "As I stand and look at them, a single thought fills my mind. These stones bear witness to the destruction of our land, and these men to the destruction of our people. Which of the two catastrophes is the worse? Which gives greater cause for mourning?"[10] In the thirty years that followed, the Jewish population of Jerusalem changed, with the addition of more secular elements who lived in newer neighborhoods. Nonetheless, when Ahad Ha'am finally moved to Palestine early in 1922, he chose to live in Tel Aviv and not in Jerusalem, even though his son was moving there because he had been appointed to a job in the education department of the British government under the mandate. The major reason for Ahad Ha'am's choice was that more of his personal friends were in Tel Aviv, but he also felt that he would be less comfortable in Jerusalem because it remained under the dominance of the older, Orthodox community.[11]

But despite his dislike of the older Jewish settlement, Ahad Ha'am was a moderate and a traditionalist. He was vehemently opposed to the most radical Zionists who wanted to create a totally new Jewish culture that would break completely with the past. On the contrary, he wanted to fashion the Zionist community in Palestine as the secular equivalent of the older religious community. In the last years of his life, Ahad Ha'am was deeply interested in the effort to create the central cultural institution of Zionism in Jerusalem. A Russian Jewish mathematician, Hermann Shapira, had first suggested the establishment of a Jewish university in 1884, at the founding meeting in Kattowitz of Hibbat Zion, the immediate precursor of Herzl's Zionist movement. This was part of a larger suggestion by Shapira that a modern Jewish settlement should be created outside of Jerusalem, in contrast to the life largely dependent on alms of the Old Yishuv, and that a university should be at the center of this new life. After Herzl founded the World Zionist Organization, this idea was soon taken up by the young Chaim Weizmann, who had just gotten a doctorate in chemistry in Fribourg, Switzerland, and had gone on to an academic appointment in Manchester, England.

Weizmann and those who supported him had no doubt that such a Jewish university could be created only in Jerusalem. The support for the idea was sufficiently powerful that a cornerstone for the university was laid in July 1918 on Mount Scopus, in the near outskirts of Jerusalem, seven months after the city was captured by the British Army. The Hebrew University was formally opened in 1925 with a dramatic ceremony in which Lord Balfour participated. Ahad Ha'am was not at the celebration, because he was too ill to come to Jerusalem, but his old and close friend Chaim Nachman Bialik, the acknowledged "national poet" of the Zionists, gave one of the main addresses at that meeting. In Bialik's speech at this great occasion, he spoke eloquently of the role that the great academies for the study of the Talmud had played throughout the centuries of the Jewish exile. He hoped that the lecture halls and laboratories of the new university would play a comparable role in the creation of a Jewish culture appropriate to this age.[12] Bialik clearly agreed that the Hebrew University was rightly being established in Jerusalem. This city would endow a secular university with ancient mystique. A location in Jerusalem would help make a university into a contemporary "holy place." At the very least, the Zionists were saying that they, too, had a direct stake, through a newly established spiritual institution of their own, in the ancient city.

After World War I

The authority and legitimacy conferred by Jerusalem was equally important to the more practical institutions which the Zionist movement established in Palestine. To be sure, before World War I the main representative of the World Zionist Organization was its Palestine office, which was engaged in purchasing land and helping the new farming settlements establish themselves. This bureau was located in Jaffa, the major port city in Palestine where most of the immigrants arrived. The change came after the war, when the British government had agreed to a special role for "a Jewish agency," to represent the interests of the Jewish people in Palestine. The offices of this entity (which was, de facto, the World Zionist Organization) were established in Jerusalem. This action was a necessary reaction to the changed situation in Palestine. Jerusalem had been the administrative center of much of Palestine under the Turks,[13] but after the British took over at the end of 1917, they governed all of the country from the Holy City. The Zionists knew that placing their offices in Jerusalem helped to confer authority on the Zionist institutions. On the other hand, the most powerful indigenous organization, the collection of labor unions which became known as the Histadrut, established, and has kept, its central office in Tel Aviv. The headquarters of the labor unions did not need to be in Jerusalem; the unions represented those Zionists who actually lived in Palestine, and relatively few of their members were in the Holy City. The World Zionist Organization and the Jewish Agency had to establish their base in Jerusalem, because they spoke for the interest and involvement of world Jewry in the Zionist venture.

The modern Zionist movement could not really choose to play

down its connection to Jerusalem and concentrate only on "constructive Zionism" by creating farming settlements alone. The plurality of Jerusalem's population had been Jewish since the middle of the nineteenth century, and all the world knew that this was so. *The Encyclopedia Britannica* stated this fact in its 1844 edition. The next year, in 1845, the Prussian consul gave a somewhat lower estimate of the Jewish proportion of the population of Jerusalem: he put it at 7,000 out of a total of 15,000. Somewhat larger estimates were given in 1854 by Karl Marx in an article which he wrote for the *New York Daily Tribune*. By 1890 there were 43,000 inhabitants in Jerusalem, of whom 28,000 were Jews. The numbers rose in 1912 to an estimate of more than 70,000, of whom 45,000 were Jews. In 1931 the total population, according to the British census, was 90,000, containing a Jewish majority of 52,000. In 1948 when the battle was fought for the establishment of Israel, 65,000 Jews were almost a two-thirds majority in a total population of 100,000.[14] Jews had long been gravitating to Jerusalem, motivated more by historic connection than by secular Zionist ideology, and making it their major center in Palestine.

Under the British Mandate

In the 1920s and 1930s, Jerusalem became ever more important to the Zionist movement because it was the seat of British government in Palestine under the League of Nations mandate. The high commissioner, who was, effectively, London's viceroy in Palestine, ruled from Jerusalem. Almost every issue that the Zionist bodies had to address required negotiation with the British authorities, at their headquarters. The Zionists could bring in people legally only by persuading the high commissioner to allocate certificates which allowed new settlers to enter the country. Jerusalem was also a major arena of confrontation with the Arabs. There were riots and murders elsewhere in the 1920s and the 1930s, but the Western Wall of the ancient temple enclosure in Jerusalem, which stood within the Old City, was a unique flashpoint. During the riots in 1929, the largest number of murders were perpetrated on Jews in Hebron, but the exact definition of the right of Jews to pray at the Western Wall, which the Arabs contested by violence, was the one issue that had to be adjudicated by the League of Nations. The majority of those who prayed regularly in this holy place were from the older, pre-Zionist community. Some insisted that their religious rights should not be represented by the Zionists or even by the non-Zionists who had become associated with the World Zionist Organization in fundraising and political efforts to help the newer settlers. But the World Zionist Organization needed to be the prime representative of Jewish religious interests in Palestine. It had to shore up its role, under the League of Nations mandate, as "the Jewish agency" which represented all the Jews in the land. The Zionists led the fight for the right of Jews to pray undisturbed at the Western Wall.[15]

Earlier, in 1921, the new British government in Palestine had created a chief rabbinate of the Land of Israel. Two chief rabbis were chosen, an Ashkenazi, Rabbi Abraham Isaac Kook, and a Sephardi, Rabbi Yaakov Meir, in an electoral process controlled by the Zionists. The Ashkenazi office was new; the Sephardi chief rabbi was the successor to the *ha'cham bashi,* who had been the head of the Jewish religious community in Palestine after 1841, when the office was created by the Ottoman Turks. Despite the opposition of the older community, especially in Jerusalem, the new chief rabbinate was recognized by the government as the religious authority, in law, of the Jews in Palestine. This institution had final jurisdiction in matters of personal status, and especially in all matters which concerned marriage among Jews. The opponents of the Zionists did succeed in achieving some exceptions for their own groups, but the new, Zionist chief rabbinate was widely accepted as the religious authority for most Jews. As a matter of course, this institution was located in Jerusalem. The Zionist movement had thus found Jerusalem to be indispensable to its political agenda with the British, and to establishing its leadership among all the Jews in the country.

Religious and Ultra-Nationalistic Zionists

The significance of Jerusalem for the Zionists was changing, for even deeper reasons. The founders of the movement had consciously tilted toward secularism, in order to transform the Jewish people as a whole into a modern secular national society. Nonetheless, even in contemporary heretical and agnostic times, the Jewish commitment of the large majority all over the world remained essentially religious. Much of the support of Zionism came from Jews—and some Gentiles—who paid little attention to the new Zionist ideologies. They helped the Zionist endeavor because it seemed to have some connection to the religious dream of the restoration of the Jews. This was especially true for some Orthodox believers, who had joined the World Zionist Organization at the very beginning. Within a few years, in 1902, the religious Zionists organized themselves into a distinct faction. This group could not deal in undefined emotion. It had to face the question that had already appeared some sixty years earlier, in the 1830s and 1840s, among a handful of rabbis who had thought, then, that the time was ripe for the return of the Jews to the Holy Land. These authorities knew that human activity to bring the End of Days nearer had long been forbidden by the law of the Talmud. They agreed that the total restoration of the Jewish commonwealth could not take place by unaided human effort, but they proposed, on the basis of kabbalistic teaching, that active immediate stirrings toward the redemption would be useful. They ruled that such efforts would be permitted and even a necessary first step toward arousing stirrings in heaven.[16] The religious Zionists in Herzl's movement adopted this view: they declared the new Zionist effort to be a preamble to the great day of the Lord.

Rabbi Abraham Isaac Kook, the greatest theologian to espouse this view (he was chief rabbi of the Holy Land from 1921 until his death in 1935), went even further. He could not help knowing that the Zionist pioneers, who were reviving Hebrew as a modern language and re-creating Jewish farming in Palestine, were self-consciously secular. Kook insisted that, despite themselves, these men and women were instruments in God's hands. They thought that they were secularizing Hebrew, but they were really reviving the holy language. They thought that they were creating a new, unprecedented Jewish community in Palestine, but they were really preparing the way for the miracles to come.[17] For such religious thinking, Jerusalem was what it had always been, the Zion which was central to Jewish messianic hopes. This outlook built a bridge, early in Zionist history, between the ideological nonbelievers and at least a significant element among the believers. The nonbelievers did not agree with Rabbi Kook, but here was a rabbi who did not excommunicate them. The believers among the Zionists were assured that, even though the founders of the kibbutzim were disobeying Jewish religious law, the future of the Holy Land belonged to God.

Jerusalem also rose in importance even among some of the secular Zionists. An important fraction had moved, very early in the history of the movement, toward very pronounced nationalist doctrines. These men and women had accepted Theodor Herzl's basic contention that the Jews were a nation and that they were now engaged in becoming "normal." The ultra-nationalists insisted that normalcy required the Jews to establish a nation-state within borders that resembled those in ancient times. The League of Nations mandate for Palestine had, in fact, included the land between the Mediterranean Sea and Jordan River and a large tract of land east of the Jordan. These two territories were severed by British decision in 1921; the promises made in the mandate, to foster the Jewish national home in Palestine, were limited to the territory west of the Jordan River. The ultra-nationalist Zionists refused to accept this act. The hymn of their party asserted that the land which belonged to the Jews was "on both banks of the Jordan." This song was intoned with increasing passion after the Emirate of Transjordan was created by the British government. The hymn was a reminder that Palestine had already been partitioned in 1921. The most nationalist faction among the Zionists insisted, as they sang the song of their party, that, at the very least, the land west of the Jordan River had to belong entirely to the Jews.

The acknowledged leader of the ultra-nationalist faction was Vladimir Jabotinsky. Except for two brief periods in the 1920s, the British had not allowed Jabotinsky to live in Palestine, but that did not prevent him from developing a very large following throughout the Jewish world, and especially in Eastern Europe. In 1935 he broke with the World Zionist Organization and transformed the Revisionist Party, which he led into the independent New Zionist Organization. Jabotinsky and his followers had no doubt that the capital of the restored Jewish state would be Jerusalem. Their claim to Jerusalem was not based on the promises in the Bible. In the mind of these nationalists, Jerusalem had been fashioned by long history as the Jewish capital. Jerusalem could no more be taken away from the Jews than Rome could be kept from the Italians.

In 1936, in the face of ever more violent tensions between Arabs and Jews, the British government appointed a commission to investigate the conflict and to recommend a solution. This group was known as the Peel Commission, after its chairman, Lord Robert Peel. It behaved as a judicial body, holding hearings both in Palestine and in London. Among the many Jewish leaders who testified, the most important were Chaim Weizmann, who was then president of the World Zionist Organization, and Vladimir Jabotinsky, the leader of the New Zionist Organization. In 1936 the Jews were a minority in the land, no more than 400,000 within a population of nearly 1.5 million, and they were in actual possession of less than 4 percent of the territory of Palestine. Before the Peel Commission, Weizmann defended the right of Jews to continue to come to Palestine in substantial numbers and to develop their own institutions. He proposed leaving for the future the question of the ultimate political destiny of Palestine, because he did not think that the Zionists were strong enough yet to lay claim to all of the land.[18] Jabotinsky had no such qualms. He testified in London in the House of Lords in the spring of 1937 and openly claimed all of Western Palestine, the land between the Mediterranean Sea and the Jordan River, for the Jews. He denied that this was an injustice to the Arabs; they were expressing their identity through a half dozen existing states, while the Jews had not a single nation-state of their own. Western Palestine in Jewish hands would soon be peopled by a Jewish majority, because the doors of the state would be open to millions of Jews who needed to flee oppression in Europe or who wanted to be part of a nation of their own. The Arabs who wished to remain in the Jewish state would be treated with every consideration, but they would have to accept the status of a minority. Those who would want to live as part of an Arab majority would have the option, with help, to move across one of the borders to a neighboring Arab state.[19] The same logic applied to Jerusalem. It would undoubtedly be the capital of the Jewish state. The religious shrines and rites of worship of Muslims and Christians would be safeguarded, but political control would be exercised by the Jewish authorities.

The uncompromising secular nationalism of Jabotinsky and his followers was attractive to some of the religious believers. These nationalists were fighting to regain all of the soil of Israel as the Jewish patrimony, and they refused to think of sharing power in Jerusalem with other religious traditions. Those who dreamt that the messianic era was near—that God was about to restore the twice-destroyed Holy

Temple—found Jabotinsky's nationalism to be particularly congenial. In fact, some of Jabotinsky's followers were Orthodox Jews. The young man who was elected head of the youth movement in Poland of the New Zionist Organization, Menachem Begin, was not absolutely Orthodox, but he was a religious believer. Some of Jabotinsky's disciples in Palestine, who organized the Irgun Z'vai Leumi (National Military Organization), which engaged in armed struggle with the British authorities to force them to yield all of Palestine, including Jerusalem, to the Jews, were Orthodox Jews.

In the critical decade between 1937 and 1947, the ultra-nationalist school of thought, and the organizations which represented such opinions, were very much in the minority among the Zionists. Everywhere, the World Zionist Organization, and especially the leaders of the Labor Zionist Party which dominated in Jewish Palestine, fought the ultra-nationalists, even to the degree of cooperating, on occasion, with the British authorities who were hunting down members of the Irgun and its offshoot, the Lohamei Herut Yisrael (Fighters for the Freedom of Israel), as terrorists. In 1937 the World Zionist Organization had agreed to accept the basic principle of the report tendered by the Peel Commission, that Western Palestine should be partitioned into a Jewish and an Arab state. The central region, which included Jerusalem, would be administered by the British. The World Zionist Organization wanted to negotiate larger boundaries for the Jewish enclave, but it accepted the notion that Jerusalem would have special status and would not be included in the Jewish state. This concession was made with a particularly heavy heart, because Jewish opinion preferred that the city should be divided with largely modern West Jerusalem included in a Jewish state. When the idea of partition appeared in the deliberations of the Peel Commission, David Ben-Gurion, who was then already the acknowledged leader of the Yishuv in Palestine, had first agreed in January 1937 that Jerusalem and Bethlehem had a special, separate status under British administration, but by April he had joined the overwhelming majority of Jewish opinion that at least part of the city had to be allocated to a Jewish state.[20]

Jerusalem Divided

Ten years later, after the horrors of World War II, the pressure for the creation of a Jewish state became irresistible. In November 1947 the

United Nations came to the same basic conclusion that had been reached by the Peel Commission a decade earlier: Western Palestine should be partitioned between Jews and Arabs, with a special status for Jerusalem. The World Zionist Organization–Jewish Agency accepted the United Nations proposal: the Jewish authorities were willing to live with a Jewish state without Jerusalem.[21] When the Arabs, both inside Palestine and in the surrounding Arab states, made war to destroy the embryo of a Jewish state, the Zionist military forces won the fight. The new state of Israel succeeded in holding on to the Jewish areas in Western Jerusalem, but the Jewish forces could not conquer the Old City, the seat of the shrines holy to Judaism, Christianity, and Islam. The state of Israel had been proclaimed in Tel Aviv on May 14, 1948, because Jerusalem was already under siege and encircled by the Jordanian army and Palestinian irregulars. The Jewish Quarter in the Old City could not be defended, and it eventually surrendered to Jordan's Arab Legion.

The siege of Jerusalem, and the heroism of its defenders, immediately became one of the great patriotic tales of the new state of Israel. In war, Jerusalem became an even more precious and indissoluble part of the new Israeli reality. The United Nations kept ruling that the status of Jerusalem, including mostly Jewish West Jerusalem, should remain separate. On December 9, 1949, the General Assembly of the United Nations passed a resolution, almost unanimously, requiring the internationalization of Jerusalem. Ben-Gurion decided to defy this vote because he feared that if he took no action the United Nations might soon try to implement the decision. He was particularly fierce in asserting that the world community had no moral right to determine the future of Jewish West Jerusalem, because it had been silent when the city had been under siege by the Arabs. On December 13, 1949, the Knesset, the parliament of the new state, voted to move from Tel Aviv to Jerusalem. This action set the seal on the status of the city as Israel's capital.

In the early years of the state of Israel, Jerusalem remained divided but its central role in the new state had become a fact. Jerusalem was then a sleepy town in comparison to bustling Tel Aviv, but it was the seat of government. By 1952 almost all of the ministries, including Foreign Affairs, had moved to Jerusalem. The only one that remained in Tel Aviv was the Ministry of Defense. The premier academic institution in the country was the Hebrew University in Jerusalem, but the newspapers, and most of the cultural journals, were all published in Tel Aviv. The government of Israel, and many Jewish voluntary bodies, instituted many programs to place new institutions in the capital and to add some industry to provide jobs. A government building and a new campus for the Hebrew University, at Givat Ram, were built in the 1950s, as well as the central Holocaust memorial, Yad Vashem, and the seat of the chief rabbinate, Hechal Shlomo. In August 1951 the World Zionist Organization, which had never convened in Palestine, held its International Congress in Israel, in Binyanei Haumah, the then unfinished convention center which was being built near the entrance to Jerusalem.

The intangible factors were even more important in making Jerusalem into the capital of Israel. For the first time in many centuries, Jews had been separated by war from their own holiest shrines, and especially from the Western Wall of the Second Temple. The Jordanian authorities who ruled the Old City refused to permit any Jewish access, even for prayer. The buildings of the Hebrew University and the Hadassah Hospital, two of the crown jewels of contemporary Jewish effort in Jerusalem, were behind the Jordanian lines. Worse still, everyone knew that all of the synagogues in the Jewish Quarter of the Old City had been destroyed by the Jordanians. Jews could only stare from afar, with longing, at their ancient shrines and at the modern buildings on Mount Scopus which still stood empty behind enemy lines. In 1937, and again in 1947, Jewish majority opinion had been ready to accept a regime in Jerusalem which they would not control but which would not exclude them from access to their shrines. The loss of access after 1948, and the destruction of many sacred buildings, made Jerusalem more precious to all the elements of the Jews of Israel.

The pervasive popular feeling was expressed in the spring of 1967, before the outbreak of the Six-Day War, in a song which swept the country, "Jerusalem the Golden." The lyrics spoke of the longing of Jews for all of Jerusalem. In those very weeks, one of the leading figures in the Orthodox community, Rabbi Zvi Yehuda Kook, the head of the Yeshivah which had been founded by his father, Rabbi Abraham Isaac Kook, told his students that the miraculous day was approaching when Jews would regain all of Jerusalem.

The Unified City

War broke out at the beginning of June 1967 between Israel and all of its Arab neighbors. In less than a week, the Israeli Army captured the Sinai Peninsula from the Egyptians and the Golan Heights from the Syrians, but the most important prize was the Old City of Jerusalem and all of the territory west of the Jordan River. The triumphs of Israel's Army astonished the world. Most of the believing Jews were ecstatic, and even many of the secularists thought that they had witnessed a miracle. Within hours of the conquest of the Old City, generals who had seldom, if ever, been to synagogue were disregarding snipers' bullets and walking toward the Western Wall. They were not embarrassed to follow the time-honored custom of writing prayers on chits of paper and pushing them into the crevices of the Western Wall or of kissing its stones.

Israel had suddenly become the political and civil authority which set the rules not only for the Jewish shrines but also for the Muslim religious authorities and for the Christian churches. The defense minister, General Moshe Dayan, was in charge of the newly occupied territories. He immediately decided on June 7, 1967, that no Israeli flag would fly over any of the Muslim or Christian places, and ten days later he restored the responsibility for the Temple Mount to the local Muslim authorities. On the other hand, the warren of narrow streets populated by Arabs, known as the Moroccan Quarter (which had included a passageway in front of the Western Wall, where worshipers had been disturbed before 1948 by hostile traffic), were dynamited a very few days after the Jewish conquest. A great open space was cleared for the many thousands of Jewish pilgrims and visitors who were rushing to visit the holy places. On June 26, 1967, the Knesset passed a law uniting Jerusalem. The next day the minister of the interior extended the city limits and the jurisdiction of Israeli law to East Jerusalem, and one day later the barriers between East and West Jerusalem were removed.

The people of Israel, in all of its parties and factions, no longer felt constricted and hemmed in by the narrowness of Israel's boundaries after 1948. The Israelis were now no longer dealing with the quiescent Arab minority within its pre-1967 borders. Major Arab cities, such as Nablus, Hebron, and, most important, East Jerusalem, had come under Israel's control. In the early months and years after the war, the newly acquired Arab population had not yet become restless. Visiting the Arab towns and shopping in them, and especially in East Jerusalem, became the preferred outing for many Israeli Jews, especially on the Sabbath. While the believers were going to the Western Wall to pray, the nonbelievers found the open stores of Eastern Jerusalem a relief from the austerity of the Sabbath in the Jewish sector. One could walk into the *suq* in the Old City of Jerusalem, from Jewish West Jerusalem a few yards away, and find a restaurant in which to order lunch even on the most solemn of fast days, Yom Kippur. The newly united Jerusalem gave the believers hope that they were living at the beginning of messianic time; it gave the nonbelievers a heady sense of increased space and personal freedom.

Almost immediately after the end of the war in June 1967, the Israeli government and public opinion made a critical distinction between all of the other territories that Israel now governed and Jerusalem. At the beginning, most Israelis were willing, and even eager, to give back the territories in return for peace with the surrounding Arab states. There was early talk of the need for some border rectifications, and even of the military need for Israel to control some points beyond its pre-1967 borders, but there was an early consensus that Israel should not keep, indefinitely, the land mass which it had won. Jerusalem was exempt from this consensus because even those, such as David Ben-Gurion, who were eager to return the territories—with some minor rectification—to Arab sovereignty would not hear of redividing Jerusalem.

It was soon evident that there was no possibility of peace, because the Arab League meeting in Khartoum in August 1967 utterly rejected any compromise, or even discussion, with Israel. At that session Arab policy was defined in three "no's": no negotiation or peace with Israel; no recognition of Israel; and "no compromise at the expense of the rights of the Palestinian people." In the absence of any movement toward peace, currents of opinion, both secular and religious, which preached that Jews must now hold on to the "undivided land of Israel" began to gain visibility and influence. The number of Jewish settlements in the West Bank and on the Golan Heights has kept growing through the years, through the initiatives of small groups of zealots and the changing policies of Israel's various governments.

These settlements have made a profound difference in the history and politics of Jewish-Arab conflict, but they have remained objects of controversy among Israel's parties and schools of thought.

Jerusalem has always been different. No leader of consequence, from Left to Right, has ever been willing to return the Old City to Arab sovereignty, and only a few have contemplated ceding East Jerusalem, in which no Jews were living in 1967. The integration of the Old City and of East Jerusalem into the Jewish state has been settled policy under all Israeli governments, of whatever party, since June 1967. In 1980 the Knesset formally annexed East Jerusalem, along with substantial surrounding areas, to the territory of the state of Israel. The Knesset declared that all of the inhabitants of the area were no longer subject to Jordanian law or to the rules of occupation. That part of the Old City which had once been the Jewish Quarter already had been rebuilt; it had again become the home of many Jewish families and of a substantial number of institutions. The government of Israel, which had come into the control of the ultra-nationalist Likud Party, hastened to place some government offices, including the central command of the national police, in East Jerusalem. Most important, a number of new neighborhoods were being built and peopled by Jews, placed to ring East Jerusalem. The enlarged city was thus being made indivisible, with East Jerusalem physically separated from the West Bank. The ever-increasing Jewish population in the new neighborhoods set the seal on a Jewish majority in the enlarged Jerusalem.

During all these changes, the municipality of Jerusalem, headed by Mayor Teddy Kollek, eagerly extended its authority to the newly annexed areas. Kollek insisted, over and over again, that the Arabs of East Jerusalem should not be driven out by harsh treatment or by denial of municipal services, but even under Kollek's benign rule much less money per capita was spent on the sections of the unified city that were inhabited by Arabs. The overwhelming majority of the Arab population refused to accept Israeli citizenship or to vote in municipal elections. The Palestinians continued to insist that East Jerusalem could not be annexed by the Jews and that they would not make peace with Israeli rule over the Old City. Jerusalem thus became, in the 1970s and 1980s, the rock on which all the plans for negotiating a settlement in the area foundered and broke. Neither the Jews nor the Arabs would budge. For a number of years only one comforting cliché was available, that the question of Jerusalem should be left to the very end of peace discussions, after all the other issues had been settled and confidence had been built between Israelis and Arabs by prolonged, amicable association.

Two ideas about the future of Jerusalem, nonetheless, kept surfacing. Teddy Kollek proposed that Jerusalem should be divided into boroughs, with East Jerusalem as a separate, largely autonomous, Arab municipal entity. He thought that such an arrangement would make it more palatable for the Arabs to remain part of a unified city under Jewish control. A second idea was to give control of the Christian and Muslim holy places to an international authority or to the individual concessions. These ideas came from the Jewish side. The Arabs responded by repeating the demand for a Palestinian state in the West Bank and Gaza with its capital in East Jerusalem. The Arabs did not insist on the sealing off of the two parts of Jerusalem from each other. They suggested that the city remain open, and that the Israeli and Palestinian authorities should arrange, together, to keep peace and order in all of Jerusalem. The most accommodating ideas from the Jewish and the Arab sides, thus, did not bridge the chasm between Jewish insistence on retaining all of Jerusalem under Israeli sovereignty and the continuing Arab demand that East Jerusalem had to be returned to Arab sovereignty. The Arab position hardened after December 1987, when active resistance in the territories, the Intifada, became ever more violent, not only in Gaza and the West Bank but also in Jerusalem.

The continuing battle over the future of Jerusalem played a major role in municipal elections in the city. After the formal annexation, the Arabs of East Jerusalem had the right to vote in the city elections, even if they had refused to register themselves as citizens of Israel. Very few ever exercised that vote, because such action might be understood as making peace with Israeli sovereignty. In 1993, when Teddy Kollek ran for reelection, his prospects were dim, because the large and growing Orthodox element in Jerusalem, which had risen to more than one-third of the Jewish population, was disaffected by his support of the rights of the secular elements of the population. He had been particularly annoying to the Orthodox because of his impassioned support for the building of a new soccer stadium in the outskirts of the city, where games would be played on the Sabbath and thousands would drive to watch the sport, contrary to the prescriptions of the religious laws of Sabbath observance. Kollek could not be reelected unless the Arabs in East Jerusalem turned out to vote for him. Even though the other candidate, Ehud Olmert of the Likud, was much less acceptable to the Arabs, they chose not to vote. Their mass abstention made certain Kollek's defeat—but it reemphasized the insistence of the Arabs of East Jerusalem that they would not recognize the act of Knesset in 1967 declaring all of the city to be part of Israel.

Negotiating for Peace

The clash between Jews and Arabs over Jerusalem could not be papered over. Negotiations began in Madrid in December 1990 in which Israel and the Palestinians of the West Bank and Gaza, along with all of the Arab states on Israel's borders, took part. Israel, then led by Prime Minister Itzhak Shamir of the Likud Party, announced that it would not negotiate with the Palestinian Liberation Organization, but it tacitly agreed that Palestinians from the West Bank and Gaza could coordinate with and even receive their instructions from Yasser Arafat in Tunis. The point on which Israel would not budge was Jerusalem. The Israeli delegation would not sit at the same table with any Palestinian who was a resident of East Jerusalem, because the Israelis regarded all of the inhabitants of the areas that they had annexed as citizens of Israel. An exception could be made only for such Arab Jerusalemites who also had homes in the West Bank or Gaza. Israel succeeded in barring any Arab who lived in Jerusalem from the meetings.

In the national elections of 1992 the Labor Party, under the leadership of Itzhak Rabin, returned to power, and the temper of the peace negotiations changed. On the surface, the discussions which had begun in Madrid had stalled. The most immediate problem, for Israel, was to bring an end to the Intifada, but that hope was not realized. The Palestinians from the West Bank and Gaza did not have the power, or the will, to make a political deal with Israel. A back channel to the PLO was opened in the fall of 1992, with the help of the Norwegian government and under the auspices of Israel's foreign minister, Shimon Peres. When these contacts began to bear some promise, Itzhak Rabin, who had long been less flexible than Shimon Peres, changed position and encouraged the secret negotiations. The astonishing result surfaced in late August of 1993: an agreement with the PLO to hand over Gaza and the city of Jericho to its control, looking toward Palestinian self-rule, before long, in all of the West Bank. This agreement, which was proclaimed in a ceremony on the lawn of the White House in Washington on September 13, 1993, left many issues unsettled, including matters as sensitive as the future status of the 120,000 Jews who had established themselves in various places on the West Bank. The Israeli government made it clear that it had not agreed to the creation of a Palestinian state in Gaza and in the West Bank. The PLO made it equally clear that it had accepted the agreement that had been made in Oslo only because it would lead to a Palestinian state.

The question of the future of Jerusalem was avoided by both sides, even in the informal statements by leading personalities. Many Israelis could imagine accepting a Palestinian state if the PLO demonstrated its intention and ability to rule in peace in the West Bank and Gaza and to quell acts of terrorism against Israel, but Jerusalem was another matter. The large majority of Israelis could not think of agreeing to redivide the city. A few suggestions were being made, in the aftermath of the agreement with the PLO, about the future of Jerusalem. In that document, the discussion of all the divisive issues about the city was postponed for later negotiation, by the middle of 1996, when the final arrangements between Israel and the PLO were to be negotiated. Nonetheless, there was some growing acceptance of a distinction between the Arab areas of East Jerusalem and the Old City. De facto, the Intifada had succeeded in dividing the city, because most Jews, for their safety, avoided the Arab areas. Various opposition spokesmen complained that the government was turning a blind eye to the existence of central agencies of Palestinian self-government in East Jerusalem, but Prime Minister Rabin did little to stop these activities.

The first public change of Israel's policy toward Jerusalem came not in the interim negotiations with the Palestinians but in its agreement with Jordan in the summer of 1994. This document included a sentence in which Israel accepted the special relationship of the Jordanians to the Muslim holy places in the Old City. The formal treaty, signed in October 1994, repeated this promise to King Hussein and his government. A comparable agreement was made the same year with the Vatican. The seed had been planted in December 1968 when Pope Paul VI dropped the longstanding demand of the Church that Jerusalem be internationalized. He issued a declaration asking for international supervision of the holy places. In December 1993, after Israel's agreement with the PLO had cleared the way, the Vatican joined Israel in announcing formal diplomatic relations. In a personal statement, Pope John Paul II reiterated the view that the holy places be put under some international authority. In the agreement itself, Israel affirmed its continuing commitment to respect the rights of the Christian communities in their holy places as they had existed for the past hundred and fifty years.

Israel will, no doubt, eventually accept a broadened role for Christian religious authorities in supervising their shrines in the Old City. It is even possible that Israel will allow the Arabs in East Jerusalem to claim Palestinian citizenship in return for Israeli control of the Jewish settlements in the West Bank. What is completely unlikely is the severance of the Old City, or of the new Jewish neighborhoods in East Jerusalem, from the state of Israel. On the contrary, the policy of the government of Israel after 1967, regardless of which party was in power, was to build new neighborhoods ringing Jerusalem, and most of the growth was on land beyond Israel's borders in 1967. At the end of 1991, one-third of the more than 400,000 Jews who lived in the enlarged Jerusalem were housed in these neighborhoods, in new blocks of apartments in the half circle ringing the city.

The essence of the matter is that Jerusalem became central to the Zionist state because life prevailed over ideology. In the organized beginnings, in the 1880s and 1890s, the normalization of the Jews was the prime objective of the Zionist movement, and the fate of Jerusalem was a secondary concern; but in the course of a hundred years, Jewish nationalism has changed. Most of the Jews who came to the land did not arrive according to early Zionist plans. A few thousand of the Second Aliyah, who arrived between 1905 and 1914, were marked by secular and socialist ideological fervor. They, and their followers, did dominate the Zionist institutions for many decades, but they were not a majority even in those early, fabled days. After World War I, the Zionist authorities allocated "certificates of immigration" which were allowed to them by the British authorities, but these were for Jewish immigrants whose support was guaranteed by the institutions of the World Zionist Organization. The majority of the new arrivals, even then, were middle-class people who came on their own to Palestine, and most were rooted in traditionalist Jewish emotions. After Hitler came to power in 1933, until war broke out in 1939, some 200,000 Jews arrived in the country, about half of them from Germany. In their large majority, these newcomers were not ideological Zionists. They came as refugees to the land about which they had heard all their lives in Jewish prayers. Some refugees escaped to Palestine during World War II. Few were Zionist ideologues. Among the arrivals were such figures as Rabbi Aaron Rokeach, the Hasidic leader from Belz in southeastern Poland, who had been vehemently opposed to Zionism; until the war he had discouraged his followers from emigrating to the Holy Land before the Messiah appeared to lead them.

The largest transformation of Israel's population happened in the very earliest years of the state. Some survivors of the Holocaust, more than 200,000, came to Israel from Poland, Bulgaria, and Romania between 1948 and 1951. They were a random sample of Eastern European Jewry, not a collection of ideologues. The largest immigration was of Jews who had lived among the Muslims. From Iraq and Yemen to Morocco, the Jews of the Arab world moved to Israel. This was a mass of a million people who had been largely untouched by Zionist ideology. Most were Orthodox in religion, after the more relaxed fashion of most of their communities. Some even believed that David Ben-Gurion was really a contemporary incarnation of the biblical King David from whom the Messiah is descended. This new population had a passion for Jerusalem rooted in its living ties to the religion of their ancestors. This process of the transformation of Israel away from early Zionist secularism continued as the state grew.

Soon after Israel's independence was proclaimed, it had enacted, in 1950, "the law of return" which entitled every Jew to come to Israel without hindrance and to claim immediate citizenship. This open door was particularly attractive to large numbers of Orthodox Jews, most of whom opposed the secular Zionist state even after it had been created. These believers came to Israel because it was easier for them to live their religious lives in an all-Jewish environment than anywhere else. The numbers of religious inhabitants kept increasing, especially after the victory in 1967. By 1990 Orthodox Jews were more than a third of the entire Jewish population, by far the highest proportion in any of Israel's major cities. Among the Orthodox, the Haredim, the ultra-Orthodox, were the majority. The most extreme element of this community refused to accept the legitimacy of the government of Israel, though the majority of the Haredim did vote in Israeli elections, through their own religious parties. Despite the differences among the various Orthodox factions, the growing size of this population and its political power—its parties were essential to several coalition governments—meant it was an increasing force for making the Jewish connection to Jerusalem stronger, and nonnegotiable. Both the Zionists and the non-Zionists among the Orthodox held fast to Jerusalem. A handful did adhere to the opinion that Jewish control of the Old City and its holy places had been achieved by the armies of the heretical Zionists. They refused to visit the Western Wall under such auspices, but most of the Orthodox rejoiced in the new freedom of access to the sacred places in the Old City. For many of the believers, the words that Zvi Yehuda Kook had uttered a few weeks before the war, that all of Jerusalem would belong to the Jews, seemed confirmed.

The National Religious Party, to which the Zionists among the Orthodox belonged, underwent radical change. It had always been politically moderate, in long alliance with the Labor Party, which had taken the lead in accepting the compromises offered by the Peel Commission in 1937 and the partition plan of the United Nations in 1947. The younger elements in the National Religious Party moved rapidly to adopt the passion and fervor of the new, messianic feeling. Many had been students in the yeshivah which Rabbi Kook headed. In 1969 some of these enthusiasts formed Gush Emunim, "the Bloc of the Faithful," to restore Jewish presence in the Old City of Jerusalem and everywhere else in the occupied territories, which they refused to call by any other name than the biblical ones, Judea and Samaria. Offshoots of this current of opinion soon engaged in making garments for the priests and sacred vessels, according to biblical specifications, for the future service in the Third Temple, which they were sure would soon be built, with divine help, in Jerusalem. The restoration, so they proclaimed, was near. A handful even wanted to dynamite the two Muslim shrines that had been built on the Temple Mount, to clear the way for rebuilding the Temple and perhaps even to force God to intervene. Adherents of Gush Emunim led the fights to establish and sustain a Jewish presence in Hebron and in Nablus (the ancient Shechem). Jerusalem was, and has remained, at the very center of their fervor.

Nearly a hundred years ago, Rabbi Abraham Isaac Kook, the father of Zvi Yehuda, predicted that Zionism could not succeed in secularizing the Jewish people. He was certainly right about Jerusalem. It may have been a peripheral issue to the socialist Zionists who built the kibbutzim, but Jerusalem has become the seat of government of the Jewish state. It is irreversibly the capital of the modern state of Israel. Spiritually and emotionally it is even more central now, at the end of the twentieth century, than it was a hundred years ago, as the eternal capital of the Jews of the world. All Jewish religious believers, wherever they live and no matter what passport they carry, continue to turn their hearts toward Jerusalem. Secular Israelis such as the writers Amos Oz and Hayim Guri,[22] even as they still feel the counterpull of Tel Aviv, know that Jerusalem is unique; it is the indispensable link with all the ages of Jewish history; it is the "earthly Jerusalem" over which the "heavenly Jerusalem" continues to hover. The very success of modern Zionism in establishing the third Jewish commonwealth, after a lapse of almost twenty centuries, has given new vigor to the age-old passion for the eternal city of the Jews.

9

Palestinian Images of Jerusalem

MUHAMMAD MUSLIH

Love of Palestine and its cities is constantly reaffirmed in Palestinian writings. The theme of particularism, or love of a particular Palestinian city, is powerfully expressed in art, prose, and poetry, and this love is reflected from the city onto Palestine itself. There are specific Palestinian images of Jerusalem, images in which the cosmic and the particular, the religious and the nonreligious merge. No city evokes in the Palestinian the passion, history, and ideas that Jerusalem evokes. In the case of the Christian Palestinians, the process is connected with the life and death of Jesus Christ; for the Muslim Palestinians, it is connected with their long and intimate affiliation with the city. Said a fourteenth-century scholar, "The choice of Allah of all his lands is Jerusalem . . . the dew which descends upon Jerusalem is a remedy from every sickness, because it is from the gardens of Paradise."[1]

The Place of Jerusalem in Islam

The Arab-Muslim special connection with Jerusalem began with Prophet Muhammad's nocturnal journey from al-Masjid al-Haram in Mecca to al-Masjid al-Aqsa in Jerusalem (Isra) and his ascension to heaven and return to Medina (Miraj): "Glory to [God] who did take His Servant for a journey by night from the Sacred Mosque [al-Masjid al-Haram] to the Farthest Mosque [al-Masjid al-Aqsa], whose precincts we did bless,—in order that we might show him some of Our Signs: for He is the One who heareth and seeth [all things]."[2] Tradition has it that before his ascension to heaven, Muhammad, accompanied by the angel Gabriel, met Abraham, Moses, Jesus, and other prophets and led them in prayer in a cave beneath the Cave of the Prophets, where the Dome of the Rock stands.

The Night Journey and the ascension and return to Medina created a special connection between the adherents of Islam and the city of Jerusalem. This connection has been reinforced by Islam's recognition of biblical prophets as God's messengers and by the intimate links between Jerusalem and important events in the lives of these prophets, including Solomon, Abraham, Lot, David, Moses, and Jesus.

Since the rise of Islam, then, veneration for Jerusalem has manifested itself in the Isra and Miraj and in the traditions of the Prophet and his Companions. An especially famous *hadith* of the Prophet ordained that "the saddles [of the riding animals] shall not be fastened [for setting out for pilgrimage] except for three mosques, the Haram mosque [in Mecca], my mosque [in Medina], and al-Aqsa Mosque [in Jerusalem]." The prayers and practices of ordinary Muslims also contributed to the elevated position of Jerusalem. Another *hadith* says, "It is the land of the ingathering and aggregation, go to it and worship in it, for one act of worship there is like a thousand acts of worship elsewhere."[3] One can mention in this regard the "eulogies of Jerusalem" literature *(fada'il al-Quds)* which emerged between the eighth and eleventh centuries. As shown by Abdul Aziz Duri, the literature of the *fada'il* "reached its outer limits in scope and emphasis."[4] This was reflected in *hadith* collections, *tafsir* (interpretation), and in many works on the *fada'il* written mostly by Jerusalemites.

Similar ideas continued to find expression through the work of Islamic writers: Judge Amin al-Din Ahmad ibn Muhammad al-Hasan ibn Hibatullah al-Shafi'i wrote a history of the landmarks of Jerusalem and their significance *(al-Uns fi Fada'il al-Quds)* around 1206; al-Shaykh Burhanuddin Ibrahim ibn Ishaq ibn Tajiddin Abdullah ibn 'Abdul-Rahman al-Shafi'i al-Fazzari (d. 1328) wrote a book on the uniqueness of Jerusalem *(Ba'ith al-Nufus ila Ziyarat al-Quds al-Mahrus);* Imam Abu Mahmud Ahmad ibn Surur al-Maqdisi al-Shafi'i (1314–1363) prepared a book on the distinctive attributes of Jerusalem and al-Sham around 1356 *(Muthir al-Gharam bi Fada'il al-Quds wal-Sham);* and Nasiruddin al-Rumi al-Halabi (d. 1541) wrote a detailed description of al-Aqsa Mosque *(al-Mustaqsa fi Fada'il al-Masjid al-Aqsa)*.

The *fada'il* works drew mainly on the *hadith* and on *qisas al-anbiya'* (stories about the prophets), and they described the sanctity of Jerusalem sites, provided biographies of the Companions who settled in Palestine, and narrated the history of the city. In addition, the *fada'il* literature gave details about the virtues of visiting Jerusalem and the blessings of living there.[5]

Saladin's success in regaining Jerusalem for Islam in 1187 during the Third Crusade was seen throughout the Islamic world as an event of monumental religious and historical significance. As Saladin himself so forcefully put it to Richard the Lion Hearted when the latter demanded that the city be divided between Christians and Muslims: "Al-Quds is to us as it is to you. It is even more important for us, for it is the site of our Prophet's nocturnal departure and the place where people will assemble on Judgement Day. Therefore do not imagine that we can waver in this regard."[6]

The regaining of Jerusalem from the Crusaders also fostered a new kind of unity between the city and the rest of the Islamic world, a unity expressed in the acceptance of *ziyarat* (pilgrimages) to Jerusalem as well as in the restoration of Muslim shrines and the establishment of new religious and educational institutions.[7]

The tradition of according a special status to Jerusalem persisted after the defeat of the Ayyubids in the thirteenth century. The successors, the Mamluks, tried their best to enhance the Muslim character of the city. Mamluk sultans and emirs extended their patronage to Jerusalem, restoring al-Aqsa Mosque, building madrasas (academies), setting up a system for bringing water into the city, and supplying revenue for the maintenance of buildings in the Haram.[8]

A similar role of honoring the special status of Jerusalem was played by the Ottoman sultans, after the decisive victory of Sultan Selim I in northern Syria at Marj Dabiq, in August 1516, and his special visit to the Holy City in December of the same year. Jerusalem was held in special reverence by the Ottoman sultans, many of whom undertook major reconstruction works in the city, established hospices and kitchens *(takiyya* or *'imara),* and founded new endowments *(awqaf)* for the upkeep of mosques, schools, hospitals, and other public utilities.[9] But it is also true that there were periods during which endowment property and other institutions were allowed to deteriorate, due to neglect or the dishonesty of Ottoman and local administrators.

Indeed the Ottomans did not always bestow great care on the city, and the traces of neglect could be seen in the poor condition of the city by the end of the eighteenth and the beginning of the nineteenth century. The schools were in decay, mainly because of the disappearance of their endowments, either due to a lack of maintenance or because the endowments of many schools were sold for cash or leased for long periods of time in exchange for repair work. Other reasons for the decay were the social and political crises that afflicted the empire, as well as successive military setbacks throughout the eighteenth century and the rise to power of sultans who spent large sums of money on their personal luxury and pleasure.[10] Even in the nineteenth century, when the city witnessed an improvement in its economic and communications structures, that improvement was primarily due to outside support, including foreign funds channeled to the Christian and Jewish communities of the city.[11]

However, Palestine in general, and Jerusalem in particular, were always high on the list of Ottoman priorities. The same applied to Syria and the Hijaz. Several factors accounted for the critical significance of these territories. On the one hand, the legitimacy of Ottoman authority was, in Muslim eyes, bound up with the sultan's control of the Islamic holy cities and the routes of the annual pilgrimage to Mecca. Moreover, precisely because these territories were of paramount—though not equal—importance from a religious point of view, exercising political control over them meant exercising control over the nerve centers of the Muslim world. No Ottoman sultan would have legitimacy in Muslim eyes if he did not exercise authority over Mecca, Jerusalem, and Damascus. It was primarily for these reasons that the Ottoman government had to impose real and decisive authority on Palestine, Syria, and the Hijaz, while it relaxed its control over Egypt and North Africa.[12]

The Palestinian Connection with Jerusalem

In addition to its occupying a special place in the Arab-Muslim tradition, four factors added to Jerusalem's political significance in the eyes of the Palestinians before the dismemberment of Palestine in 1948. First, the annual religious celebrations, most notably the yearly Nabi Musa pilgrimage by delegations from different parts of Palestine, created a common political bond between the various parts of the country. The many pilgrimages to the tombs of saints and sanctuaries made by Christian and Muslim Palestinians from the various sections of the country undoubtedly strengthened this bond.[13] Second, some of the notables of Jerusalem played a leading role in expressing their opposition to Zionism, thus helping to crystallize the political ideology of Palestinian nationalism. Yusuf Diya' al-Din al-Khalidi, elected from Jerusalem to the first Ottoman Parliament of 1877, wrote a letter around 1899 to Zadok Kahn, the chief rabbi of France, asking him to "let Palestine be left alone."[14]

Third, among the politically active Palestinian elites, the notables of Jerusalem wielded the most power in the political process of Palestine for reasons that had to do with the sanctity of the city, the fact that its aristocratic families had lived there for many centuries, and also the fact that those families were more heavily involved in the economy and administration of the city.[15] Fourth, Jerusalem almost acted as a capital for Palestine in late Ottoman times. It housed, for example, the consulates of Britain, France, Prussia, Austria, and Spain. The city was also the residence of a Greek Orthodox patriarchate, a Latin patriarchate, and an Anglican bishopric.[16]

By the onset of the British occupation, then, three characteristics of Jerusalem's special status were already in evidence: the sanctity of the city, its uniqueness in Arab eyes, and its particular role as an indispensable source of political legitimacy. A fourth was also coming into existence: Palestinian nationalism was becoming the dominant political ideology after the final defeat of the Ottoman state, and Jerusalem was consolidating its position as the center of Palestinian political activity. This was a process that took place from within, with the rise of one of the notable urban families, the Husayni family, to supremacy over the others. To ensure widespread support throughout Palestine, the Husaynis articulated the goals of Palestinian nationalism and forged political alliances with other families throughout the country.

Al-Hajj Amin al-Husanyi, the political leader of the Palestinians from 1929 until 1948, was a founder of Palestinian nationalism. He did not, it is true, confront the British until after 1936. However, by striking a balance between Palestinian and Arab-Muslim interests, he helped to create the political environment in which Palestinian nationalism took shape.[17] In addition, the organizational framework of the Palestinian nationalist movement—the Arab Club (al-Nadi al-'Arabi), the various Muslim-Christian associations, the Arab Executives, the Supreme Muslim Council, and the Arab Higher Committee—was based in Jerusalem.[18] The city was also the locale in which the General Islamic Congress was convened to create a united Arab-Muslim front against the Zionists.

What is certain, therefore, is that Jerusalem had more than just religious significance for the Palestinians. It also had unparalleled political significance. In a major work on Palestinian nationalism, the Israeli scholar Yehoshua Porath shows how the Palestinians highlighted the importance of Jerusalem to affirm their claim to the country. At the beginning of the British occupation, Porath tells us, the Palestinians emphasized that Jerusalem, and "in parentheses the whole country," was holy to all religions, and that therefore the religion of the few (meaning the Jews) should not take precedence over the religions of the many (meaning the Christians and Muslims). Later, however, the Palestinians insisted that the Jews had few ancient places of worship in Palestine, while the Muslim Arabs had al-Masjid al-Aqsa and the Christian Arabs had the Church of the Resurrection, or the Holy Sepulchre, in addition to the many other Muslim and Christian places in Jerusalem, Nazareth, Hebron, Bethlehem, Mount Carmel, and elsewhere in Palestine.[19] Hence Jerusalem served as a focal point for the political consciousness of the Palestinians during the British Mandate. It was also the nerve center of their body politic.

Following the 1948 Palestine war, when the Jordanian government shifted the locus of decision making from Jerusalem to Amman and chose the East Bank as the favored recipient of investment and development resources, Palestinians complained—even though many Jerusalem notables aligned themselves with the Jordanian government sitting in the Parliament in Amman and accepted senior political and administrative positions. Palestinian displeasure was rarely expressed in public. In general it was largely confined to private utterances. The Palestinians acquiesced to the fact that Amman was the capital. They may have calculated that the Jordanian government gave priority to the East Bank out of a fear that Israel would try to capture the rest of the city by force, posing in the process a lethal threat to the Hashemite monarchy. Other factors explain Palestinian acquiescence, most notably the lack of political and organizational resources, the stable administration of Jerusalem, the integration of the West Bank into the Jordanian state, and above all the fact that the Hashemite regime was an Arab government and that it respected endowment property, preserved the Arab character of the city, and kept its traditional society intact.

Of course, activism on behalf of Jerusalem and in support of its centrality to Palestinian national aspirations was not absent, even though the Palestinians chose not to challenge the status quo in the West Bank during the period from 1948 to 1967. The most telling example of this activism was the first meeting of the Palestine Liberation Organization (PLO) in East Jerusalem in 1964. At that meeting, the PLO drafted the National Charter, which outlined Palestinian national demands.[20]

Palestinian Images of Jerusalem

Palestinian images of Jerusalem since the fall of the Ottoman state in 1917–1918 may be examined through the writings of three periods: the period of British rule, 1917 to 1948; that of Jordanian rule, 1948 to 1967; and that of Israeli occupation, 1967 to the present. When discussing Palestinian works about the city, there are some main themes and subthemes worth noting.

The Period of British Rule, 1917–1948

The significance of Jerusalem formed, so to speak, the "intellectual" ideological basis of Palestinian writings on the city. Like the Jews, Muslim and Christian Palestinians believe that the uniqueness of Jerusalem was created by God. Jerusalem is blessed by God, and its sanctity reveals everything done by man, both good and bad. How the Palestinians thought and felt about the city after the emergence of political Zionism is reflected in books and articles written on the Palestine question in general, and on Jerusalem in particular. There are two reasons for this flowering of Palestinian historiography: the development of a literate class, and the existence of a unified subject matter, which gave writers not only a historical process to be explained but also a cause to be defended.

Among the histories of Jerusalem written by Christian and Muslim Palestinian Arabs during the Mandate period are 'Arif al-'Arif's *A History of the Haram of Jerusalem*,[21] Khalil Baydas's *A History of Jerusalem*,[22] Ahmad Samih al-Khalidi's edited collection, *Inciter to Love, Regarding the Virtues of Jerusalem and Syria*,[23] and Father A. S. Marmarji's *A Topographical Historical Dictionary of Arab Palestine*.[24]

The works of these scholars take us right into the history of Jerusalem, highlighting its political and religious significance to the Arabs. In such works, as well as in many others written on the history of Palestine, the subject matter is scholarly but the spirit is nationalist. They were written not only to narrate the history of Jerusalem but also to plead its case and record it for posterity. A large number of textbooks, newspaper and journal articles, lectures, and memoranda submitted to the British government also belong to the same tradition.[25]

What emerges in many of these works is the image of Palestine incorporated into the image of holy Jerusalem. The city was viewed not just as a part of Palestine but as the dominant part of the country. Indeed Jerusalem was viewed as the embodiment of Palestine, and from this conception came other ideas of what Jerusalem and Palestine should be. Implicitly or explicitly, the Palestinian image of Jerusalem was neither as an Arab city closed against the outside world nor as a one-dimensional city in which members of the Jewish community would be dissolved, but something between the two: a "plural" city in which communities, different on the level of inherited religious loyalties, would coexist within a common framework of mutual respect and tolerance.[26] This was the dominant Palestinian image of Jerusalem before the city was divided and before Palestine was dismembered.

The Period of Jordanian Rule, 1948–1967

The ideas about Jerusalem found in the writings of the Mandate period persisted after 1948. Under Jordanian rule, writing history was seen as primarily a national legacy used for supporting the cause of

Palestinian rights. For nearly two decades after 1948, the Palestinians wrote very little about themselves and about their country, including Jerusalem. This is not surprising, since the vast majority of them were caught up in the wave of Arab nationalist sentiment. Most Palestinians also accepted Arab tutelage and entrusted Arab governments with the responsibility of defending the cause of Palestine.

Of the Palestinian writers who wrote about Jerusalem after 1948, the following deserve special mention: 'Arif al-'Arif, a Palestinian historian from Jerusalem, published in 1961 a major book on the history of the city, *A Detailed History of Jerusalem*.[27] It is divided into seven parts: The history of the city in ancient times, Jerusalem in the early Islamic period, the Crusades and their impact on the city, Jerusalem under the Mamluks, Jerusalem under Ottoman rule, the geography and economy of the city, and its Christian, Jewish, and Islamic holy places. At the end of the book, the author gives a list of the sources he has used. They include earlier Arabic works; books in English, French, German, and Turkish; a few unpublished manuscripts; and his own memoranda, kept, we are told, since his early career as an official in the British administration and later as a mayor of the city in the early years of Jordanian rule.

In its coverage of history, the book adds little that is new, but for other topics—particularly the author's personal experiences in the city and his description of its political and daily life—the work is interesting. It gives a list of the libraries of the city and their acquisitions.[28] Moreover, the book presents a rather detailed description of the life of the inhabitants of the city at the time. The author's specific purpose is not to express a political point of view but to provide a historical narrative that depicts a whole structure of a city that is in many respects unique in terms of its religious significance and historical experiences. What gives importance to 'Arif's work is his mastery of his sources. His history of Jerusalem throws light on major historical development, but there is little in the book on the social history of the city and its political importance to the Palestinians, probably because it was published six years before Israel's occupation of the Old City, when the question of Jerusalem did not have its own dynamic.

The same could be said about other works written on the city. These books were started before or around the Six-Day War and completed after the war. They include *The Arab Character of Jerusalem*, by Ishaq Musa al-Husayni,[29] and A. L. Tibawi's monograph *Jerusalem: Its Place in Islam and Arab History*,[30] which is based on primary sources including British consular and diplomatic papers covering the period from 1839 to 1920. Each of these works presents a general description of Jerusalem in Arab and Muslim history and, in the case of Tibawi, a general description of the status of Jews in the city during thirteen centuries of Muslim rule.

Tibawi did not allocate any space to the Jews' association with the city, partly because he believed in the primacy of the Arab-Muslim association with Jerusalem, and partly because he simply wanted to describe the city's place in the hearts of the Arabs. In the concluding pages of his monograph, he tried to refute Israel's claim to Jerusalem, a city that is, from his perspective, overwhelmingly Christian and Muslim Arab in population and culture. The same cannot be said about 'Arif al-'Arif's history, because in his work one finds two images of Jerusalem—Jerusalem as the embodiment of Arab-Muslim history, and Jerusalem as a multidimensional city.

Israel's persistent efforts to drastically change the status quo in Arab East Jerusalem after its capture of the city in June 1967 gave rise to another genre of Palestinian writings. These writings not only underpinned already existing images of Jerusalem but also gave expression to new ones when it became clear to the Palestinians that Israel's occupation of the city would not end soon.

The Period of Israeli Occupation, 1967–Present

In political terms, the main emphasis of the Palestinians during this period has been on the Arab sector of the city, which was under Jordanian sovereignty between 1948 and 1967. There is little consensus on the demarcation of the boundaries of this part of the city. Certainly, however, the first and most important component of Arab East Jerusalem, indeed of Jerusalem in its entirety, is the Old City, a walled area of approximately one square kilometer that contains many of the places holy to Christians, Jews, and Muslims. The Palestinian population of the Old City, which is heavily Muslim, was estimated in 1993 at 25,900.[31]

Palestinian writings about Jerusalem during this period reflect four perspectives, all revolving around a core theme that highlights the centrality of Jerusalem to Palestinian self-definition. The main idea is that of a political community with a continuous historical tradition centered on Jerusalem as the locus of an independent state.

The first perspective is pluralist, and its advocates tend to view Jerusalem as a city whose significance transcends a single community or state. Thus it has a truly multidimensional character that calls for open-mindedness and creative solutions to the problems of a city cherished by Christians, Jews, and Muslims. The second perspective is exclusivist, and its adherents outline Jewish claims to the city with the goal of establishing the supremacy of Palestinian claims. The third perspective is legalistic; its advocates examine Israeli practices in the city since 1967 with a view to demonstrating the inconsistency of these practices with the principles of international law. And the fourth perspective, embraced mainly by opposition groups inside the Palestinian camp, stresses the priority of Palestinian claims, but its advocates try to use the question of Jerusalem as a political weapon with which to undermine the Israeli-PLO Declaration of Principles. This perspective does not represent a broad theme that underlies Palestinian thinking about Jerusalem. However, it is likely to come to represent such a theme if Israel and the PLO fail to hammer out a deal that recognizes Palestinian rights in the city.

The Pluralist Perspective. This perspective is expressed in numerous Palestinian writings, mostly in short essays, lectures, and public statements. The ideas adopted by the advocates of this perspective revolve around two images, one of Jerusalem having strictly Palestinian aspects, and the other of Jerusalem as the ecumenical city. Walid Khalidi, a Sunni Muslim who hails from a prominent Jerusalemite family, is among those who express their ideas about Jerusalem in the narrow Palestinian sense as well as in the broad ecumenical sense.

In Khalidi's view, the narrow or strictly Palestinian aspect of Jerusalem relates the viability of a Palestinian state in the West Bank and Gaza as a final, and permanent, settlement between the Palestinians and Israel. Khalidi argues that in geostrategic terms there cannot be a Palestinian state without East Jerusalem: "One forgets that if pre-1967 Israel has a narrow waist in the plains, so has the West Bank at Jerusalem. The waist of the West Bank at Jerusalem resembles the waist of the figure eight, or the waist of a 'B.' Remove East Jerusalem

Figure 12. Spice merchant on Bab al-Silsila Road.

from the Palestinian State and the districts of Nablus to the North and Hebron to the South [the two main districts of the West Bank] would be completely cut off from one another."[32] Other Palestinians would agree with him.

In articulating this perspective, Khalidi is motivated by the goals of Palestinian nationalism, but the ecumenism of the city induces him to look beyond the narrow confines of his nationalism. Khalidi argues that no party should have a monopoly on the religious aspects of the city, that the Hebrew prophets are the "marrow" of Islamic religious consciousness as much as they are the marrow of Christianity, that political Jewish biblicalism in Jerusalem will breed a chronic counter-crusade, and that the political formula most fitting for Jerusalem ecumenically is the one that allows for East Jerusalem to be the capital of a Palestinian state and West Jerusalem to be the capital of Israel.[33]

The ideas of Ibrahim Dakkak, a Palestinian development consultant living in Jerusalem and directly involved in a number of its many institutions, including the Arab Thought Forum and the Council for Higher Education, are also significant. Dakkak's conception of Jerusalem is shaped largely by his own beliefs, experience, and understanding of the life of a Palestinian city. Dakkak starts with the premise that Jerusalem is a multidimensional city whose human, cultural, and religious fabric has been molded by a long historical process. In his view, Jerusalem has a pluralistic value system that is absorptive and assimilative. It takes the outsider in, exposes its unique and multidimensional features, and blends into its indigenous fabric the diverse cultural elements of outsiders who come and go, day in and day out.

From this perspective, Jerusalem is seen as more than just a mosaic structure. Rather, it is seen as a cultural center whose values are organically enriched by interactions between cultures. Jerusalemites are seen as an integral part of this structure, indeed of an ongoing historical process that involves perpetual interaction between different cultural currents. Why this process exists and how it should be comprehended were questions that produced a new sort of Palestinian idea about Jerusalem, one with a specific purpose—not to defend an ongoing Arab legacy or glorify a distant past, but to give expression to a unifying force and create a driving sentiment to push the Palestinians toward Jerusalem.

Whereas Khalidi focused on the political dimensions of the two aspects of Jerusalem, Dakkak was more interested in expressing how Jerusalem shaped his personality as a Palestinian Arab and as a person. As a Palestinian, Dakkak feels that Jerusalem is a Palestinian city with a strong Islamic character. By virtue of its centrality to Palestinian self-definition, Jerusalem is the only city that can bind all Palestinian towns, geographically and spiritually. Moreover, by virtue of the Isra and Miraj, Jerusalem is the only city in the world, besides Medina, that has a powerful spiritual relationship to Mecca.

As a person, Dakkak feels that he has a multidimensional identity formed by his ethnicity and by his interaction with the various cultural elements, both local and foreign, that blend into the cultural and social fabric of the city. Because of its unique features, and because it has been an "eternal city" since time immemorial, Jerusalem was never considered to be the eternal political capital of any one people or state. Israel's attempt to make Jerusalem its political capital not only goes against historical precedent but also violates the eternity and ecumenism of the city. Above all, it threatens to turn Jerusalem into a one-dimensional city confined within a Jewish perspective.[34]

Dakkak's views are typical of ideas that have become current among Palestinians in recent times. Adnan Abu Odeh, a Palestinian diplomat who held senior positions in the Jordanian government, provides another example of these kinds of ideas and perspectives.[35] What unites their two perspectives is the multidimensional character of the city and its meaning to the Palestinians. Abu Odeh, however, goes a step further by focusing on what should be done to solve the problem of Jerusalem, both procedurally and substantively. The procedural aspect assumes that the problem of Jerusalem must be addressed now, and not later, because the ongoing Arab-Israeli peace negotiations offer a propitious and unprecedented opportunity to address the problem in a creative way.

The substantive aspect starts with an analysis for introducing constructive proposals for the drawing of a distinction between the walled Old City and the areas outside the walls. Abu Odeh starts from the simple fact that Jerusalem has both Arab and Jewish inhabitants, that the Arabs consist of Christian and Muslim Palestinians, and that all the inhabitants are equally bound to the city for religious, historical, and political reasons. A core assumption is that the holiness conferred by God on Jerusalem is confined to the walled Old City, more specifically to the main holy places of the three religions, namely the Church of the Holy Sepulchre, the Wailing or Western Wall, and the Dome of the Rock and Al-Aqsa Mosque. A further assumption is that the expansion of the city limits by man-made decisions does not expand the areas of God-given holiness.

On the basis of these assumptions, Abu Odeh constructs a conceptual framework for a settlement comprising two components. First, since the essential dispute over Jerusalem revolves around the walled Old City, which is the "true and holy Jerusalem," this part of the city would belong to no single religion or nation, but rather to the whole world, in conformity with the universal character of the city, and would be governed by a council representing the most senior Christian, Jewish, and Muslim authorities. Each religious authority would run the holy sites of its faith, and all would participate as equals in the administration of the Old City.

Second, the Palestinian flag would be raised in the Arab part of the city (Al-Quds)—that is, the urban areas that stretch beyond the walled Old City to the east, northeast, and southeast—while the Israeli flag would be raised in Yerushalayim, or the urban areas that stretch beyond the walled Old City to the west, northwest, and southwest. In this scheme of things, the Christian and Muslim Arabs would be Palestinian nationals entitled to participate on an equal footing in their national political institutions, and the Jews would be Israelis participating in the political system of their own state.

Christian Palestinians have expressed similar, though not necessarily identical, ideas about Jerusalem. Again, their stress has been on the multidimensional character of the city and on the need for Christians, Jews, and Muslims to live together in peace nationally, religiously, and culturally. Bernard Sabella, a Jerusalemite who teaches at the Department of Social Sciences at Bethlehem University, talks about a "Palestinian vision of heavenly Jerusalem." He highlights the importance of dealing immediately with the question of Jerusalem, but his stress is on the urgent need to overcome the communal friction in the city. Focusing on the problems that are peculiar to Jerusalem, Sabella talks in general terms about cultural and religious autonomy in the context of sharing resources and sovereignty among the various communities that inhabit the city. It is only through shared sovereignty and resources that communal peace can be achieved in Jerusalem and the ideal of "oneness with equality" in the city realized. According to Sabella, sharing sovereignty would enable the different communities to preserve their political, religious, and cultural identities. And sharing resources would address the inequalities between Arabs and Jews in the areas of economic opportunity, planning, quality of life, taxation, and human rights.[36]

Hanna Siniora, a Christian Palestinian from Jerusalem who was editor-in-chief of the newspaper *al-Fajr*, proposed with Moshe Amirav, a former member of the Jerusalem City Council, the model of Jerusalem as a metropolitan council. The model is based on the conception of Jerusalem as a multidimensional city whose problems are, in many respects, unique. Siniora and Amirav separate the issue of political sovereignty from the issue of municipal government. Using the 1947 Partition Plan divisions, they propose that West Jerusalem be the seat of the Israeli government and East Jerusalem the seat of the

Palestinian government. The model also proposes a "Jerusalem Charter," or an agreement between Israel and the Palestinians to suspend the question of sovereignty over the entire area of Greater Jerusalem. Although Israelis and Palestinians would be allowed to vote in their respective national elections, the government of Greater Jerusalem would exercise those powers related to the daily life of the city. To counterbalance Israeli settlements in and around Jerusalem, the Siniora-Amirav model calls for the creation of Palestinian neighborhoods in the area of West Jerusalem.

Siniora admits that this is a far-fetched solution, but at the same time he suggests that Israelis and Palestinians must think seriously about making preparations now for its implementation in the future.[37] The Siniora-Amirav model contains elements incorporated in the "scattered sovereignty" concept, which envisions the creation of Arab and Jewish zones of sovereignty that are not necessarily contiguous geographically, and some form of joint municipal supervision.[38]

Albert Aghazarian, an Armenian from East Jerusalem, presents a similar image of the city. In his view, Jerusalemites carry mirrors, but each holds the mirror in only one direction. Every community has a mirror of history and of the cultural identity of the city, and there is a dialectical relationship between the different communities that live in the city. At least three different modes of activity dynamically interact in Jerusalem. First, there is the cosmopolitan mode: that of a small Levantine city where people know each other, where foreigners are visible, and where religion and politics are practiced in churches, mosques, and synagogues, all in one package. Second, there is the Jerusalem community whose Palestinian component is the key to its pluralism. Aghazarian, himself a Christian, feels that his "umbrella" is Palestinian but that his "framework" is Arab-Islamic.[39] This is one aspect of the interaction between Christians and Muslims in the city, and many Christians would agree with Aghazarian on this point.[40] Third, there is the Israeli government's mode of activity. This is reflected in policies aimed at marginalizing the diversity of Jerusalem and turning it into a Jewish city.[41]

The Exclusivist Perspective. Writings that reflect this perspective lay special emphasis on the primacy of Arab claims to Jerusalem. Perhaps the most representative of this type of writing is that of A. L. Tibawi.

Tibawi's main interest is to portray the evocative and emotional associations of Jerusalem in the minds of Christian and Muslim Arabs. In the process of doing that, he tends to overlook Jewish claims to the city. Instead, he highlights what he calls the Israeli "assault" on the city, considering the Zionists to be modern crusaders who have earned the enmity of all Arabs and Muslims.[42]

The work of Henry Cattan also deals with Israel's violations of international law with respect to Jerusalem. An international lawyer with long experience in the international legal aspects of the Palestine question, Cattan relies heavily on UN resolutions, primarily to establish the case for Palestinian sovereignty in the context of international law. After cataloging what he considers to be Israel's offenses against moral and legal principles, Cattan concludes that the internationalization of Jerusalem, unlike certain aspects of the 1947 Partition Plan, is consistent with Palestinian sovereignty, and therefore is valid under the principles of international law as laid down in UN Resolution 181 of 1947 and subsequently reaffirmed by General Assembly Resolution 194(III) in 1948 and 303(IV) in 1949.[43]

The Legalistic Perspective. Palestinians who share this perspective have devoted their writings to the theme of Israeli practices in the city since 1967. Their writings project the image of a beleaguered city whose identity has been violated, whose unique architectural beauty has been compromised, and whose Muslim and Christian inhabitants have been subjected to repression, expropriation, and a dual system of law.

In this type of writing there is a tradition of placing Jerusalem in the larger context of Arab and Muslim history, but the focus is on human rights, the political identity of the city, and what is called Judaization of the city *(tahwid al-madina)*, like Muhammad Adib al-'Amiri's *Arab Jerusalem*,[44] which highlights the Arab identity of the city, tracing it to the ancient Canaanites, and Rawhi al-Khatib's *Israeli Conspiracies against Jerusalem, 1965–1975*[45] and *Memorandum on the Continued Attempts of the Israeli Military Authorities to Change the Conditions of the City of Jerusalem*,[46] which deal specifically with Israel's Judaization of the city and were written by an official who was the city's mayor at the time of its occupation. Among these, perhaps the most important are the studies written on the legal and human rights aspects of Israeli policies not only in Jerusalem but also in the rest of the Palestinian territories occupied since 1967.

Raja Shehadeh's work *Occupier's Law: Israel and the West Bank*[47] is the most complete and the most documented study written by a Palestinian Arab on this subject. The book deals primarily with the West Bank, but Shehadeh describes with full documentation the complex legal maneuvers by which Israel has massively appropriated land and violated human rights in the occupied Palestinian territories. What gives importance to Shehadeh's work is his complete mastery of the legal sources. He has sought out and studied the Israeli laws and military orders pertinent to the Palestinian territories, paying special attention to their theoretical basis and the procedures used to implement them. His study throws a flood of light on a process that violates human rights and builds up dangerous threats to peace between Israel and the Palestinians.

The tracts and monographs published by Palestinian associations and research groups, including the Arab Lawyers' Committee, the Institute for the Defense of Freedom, and the Palestinian Academic Society for the Study of International Affairs, focus to varying degrees on human rights, with special attention devoted to Jerusalem. That some Israelis are particularly sensitive about this issue has been shown by the emergence of numerous Israeli groups concerned with human rights, most notably B'Tselem, the Israeli Information Center for Human Rights in the Occupied Territories, the Committee for Israeli-Palestinian Dialogue, and Peace Now.

In Palestinian works written from a legalistic perspective, although much of the subject matter is documentary, the spirit is markedly nationalist. The ideas are expressed with a sense of urgency and an awareness that the character of the very soil of Jerusalem is about to change. It is as if the writers, each in his own way, are trying to capture a fleeting historical reality and to record it for future generations. But there is no forgetting Jerusalem, no way of giving up the struggle for its freedom. The following stanza from Yusuf Hamdan's poem "To Jerusalem" suggests the kind of freedom associated with Jerusalem:

> I want you to be a Kaaba for the people of the earth,
> A spacious house
> Without guards;

I love you . . . a voice from a minaret,
The sound of horns
Mingled with church bells.
I love you, a jasmine in the open air.[48]

The Opposition Perspective. This is a relatively new perspective that emerged with the appearance in the summer of 1993 of the first press reports about an impending Israeli-PLO agreement involving Gaza and Jericho. Advocates of this perspective share the underlying premise of the other perspectives in that they stress the centrality of Jerusalem to Palestinian nationalism and to the goal of establishing an independent state. The signing of the Declaration of Principles (DOP) brought to the fore internal Palestinian disagreements over the wisdom behind it. These disagreements gave rise to a new idea, the idea of using Jerusalem to undermine Yasir Arafat and delegitimize the DOP. Why Gaza and Jericho should come first before Jerusalem and how Jerusalem should be given priority are questions debated among Palestinians critical of the Israeli-PLO deal. Their purpose is not simply to glorify the city or defend Arab rights there, but also to mobilize Palestinians against the agreement.

An image of Jerusalem as the key to real peace in the region has now been projected with particular emphasis. Numerous speeches have been made about it, and numerous articles written in the local Palestinian press. There are at least two ideas connected with this image. The idea that is emphasized most is that Jerusalem is not simply a national Palestinian problem but is also an Arab-Muslim problem. To the extent to which it is an Arab-Muslim concern and responsibility, the Palestinians should use it as a weapon with which to fight Arab governments that try to strike deals with Israel before the question of Jerusalem is settled.[49] The second idea takes the form of an appeal made by the Palestinian opposition groups. Explicitly stated in this appeal is a strong criticism of the PLO leadership for not putting Jerusalem ahead of Gaza and Jericho—indeed ahead of everything else, because there can be no peace without Israel's withdrawal from Jerusalem. Again, the emphasis here is on the idea of Jerusalem as a focus of political loyalty and its centrality to the national aspirations of the Palestinians.

It is this image that has guided the Palestinian opposition more than anything else and given it the ammunition with which to attack the DOP. The events that took place after the signing of the agreement have shown how effective the question of Jerusalem can be in mobilizing support for the cause of the opposition. In the Bir Zeit University Student Council elections of November 24, 1993, the Jerusalem First coalition of the Popular Front for the Liberation of Palestine (PFLP), the Democratic Front, and Hamas got 52 percent of the votes, while the Jerusalem and the State coalition of Fatah and its supporters got 48 percent.[50] There is more than one way in which the results of this election can be explained. On the one hand, they indicate that support for the Arafat leadership was dropping at that time, because this was the first time that Fatah suffered a defeat in the student council elections. On the other hand, this was the first time that Hamas and the Palestinian Left had teamed up together, and if this indicates anything, it is that their ideological differences can only be patched up through a concept that can include both of them—that of the Jerusalem First formula, the embodiment of the special meaning of Jerusalem to the Palestinians.[51]

Other Jerusalem-Related Themes Raised by Palestinians

Within these perspectives there are many other ideas about Jerusalem, most of which revolve around the impact of Israeli policies on the Arab sector of the city. In addition to Israel's Judaization policies, two other related themes have been given special attention by Palestinians who express their views on the subject. One theme addresses Israel's attempts to transform the eastern part of the city into a satellite moving in the orbit of West Jerusalem. In this regard, the Palestinians highlight three sets of issues that are of major concern to them. The first relates to what they perceive to be an Israeli policy aimed at containing and limiting the city's Arab population, so that the Palestinians remain a minority not only in the Greater Jerusalem area but also in the Arab part of the city. The Palestinians point to Israel's expansion of the boundaries of East Jerusalem, its confiscation of Palestinian private property in the heart and outskirts of the city, its imposition of planning and building restrictions, the building of Jewish settlements or neighborhoods in and around the city, the deportation (ib'ad) of Arab residents through a complex web of rules and regulations, and the isolation of East Jerusalem by keeping it closed to other Palestinians from the West Bank and Gaza.[52]

Another set of issues deals with the inequitable distribution of economic opportunities, education, health, and social services, despite the fact that the Palestinians consider themselves to be overtaxed. This state of affairs has prompted the Palestinians to challenge Israel's claim that Jerusalem is united. They stress that Jerusalem is divided by political, economic, and psychological walls, that it is dualized, that it is strangled as a ghetto, and that its Arab inhabitants enjoy neither parity with Jewish citizens nor full civil rights.[53] Some have even gone as far as suggesting that the only cooperation between Arabs and Jews living in the city is in the underworld of crime and drugs.[54] Others suggest that a new ideology has emerged in Jerusalem as a result of Israel's Judaization measures and its one-sided distribution of economic opportunities and social services. This ideology has two components, one based on leftist principles and one on Islamic religious principles. According to this view, there is no conflict between the two components, since both assume an Arab dimension opposed to Judaization and occupation.[55]

A third set of issues relates to the complexities inherent in Israel's relations with its Arab neighbors, primarily Jordan in this case. The declaration concluded between Israel and Jordan in Washington in July 1994 contained a clause affirming Israel's acknowledgment of the special role of the Hashemite Kingdom of Jordan in Muslim holy shrines in Jerusalem, and its pledge to give high priority to the historical Jordanian role in the city. This clause caused a furor not only among the Palestinians but also in other Arab countries, primarily Saudi Arabia, which has a long history of rivalry with the Hashemites over the Muslim holy sites both in Jerusalem and in Saudi Arabia. The Palestinian anger over this clause highlighted the essence of the Jerusalem question: it showed that it is first and foremost a question of political control and sovereign rights. This is the fundamental reality in the Palestinian and Israeli positions with respect to Jerusalem. Because sovereignty and legitimacy are intertwined, no Palestinian leader can afford to leave himself open to the charge that he has relinquished Arab-Muslim rights in the city. "By God," Arafat declared in August 1991, "even if one put the sun in my right hand and the moon in my left, I would not do that."[56] His statements about Jerusalem after the signing of the DOP bear the same message.

The discussion in this chapter ranges over a variety of subjects and suggests a number of interrelated questions pertaining to East Jerusalem. It is therefore useful, in summarizing, to identify these different questions and to indicate the kinds of answers that have emerged from the discussion as a whole.

Three questions have been raised: What is the main theme of Palestinian discussions about Jerusalem? What are the Palestinian images or views of Jerusalem? What influence, if any, will these images have on negotiating an agreement regarding the status of Jerusalem?

First of all, what is the main theme? The main theme revolves around the indissoluble link between the city of Jerusalem and the Palestinian people. In this regard, when we talk about Jerusalem, we are talking about the eastern part of the city, which was occupied by Israel in June 1967. Deep in their hearts, the Palestinians believe that beyond a Palestinian's duty to his country lies his allegiance to Jerusalem and his loyalty to its Arab-Islamic heritage. In the view of the Palestinians, the city has a distinctive and multifaceted character. In the first place, it is strongly associated with Christianity and Islam. This makes it a focus of Christian and Islamic allegiance.

In the second place, the city is central to the political life of the Palestinians. In modern times, Jerusalem consolidated its position as a center of Palestinian political activity. After its fall to the British following the Ottoman defeat, Jerusalem served as the center of the Palestinian nationalist movement. It was also the locale in which the first Palestinian National Council met to draft the Palestine National Charter in May/June 1964. Today, Jerusalem houses some of the most important Palestinian institutions, including political institutions, newspapers, associations and unions, cultural centers, financial and trade organizations, and health centers, as well as educational and commercial establishments.

In the third place, Jerusalem is central to the viability of a future Gaza–West Bank Palestinian state. The exclusion of Jerusalem from the Palestinian state would mean that the northern and southern districts of the West Bank would be cut off from each other. Therefore there can be no Palestinian state without Jerusalem.

What are the Palestinian images of Jerusalem? This is an important question, because the answer is directly relevant to the Palestinian search for a solution to the problem of Jerusalem. The discussion in this chapter reveals a variety of perspectives, and it indicates how misleading it is to generalize about Palestinian thinking on this subject without carefully reviewing the available literature. Four perspectives have been distinguished, and they all deal, in one way or another, with the character and status of Jerusalem.

Advocates of the pluralist perspective recognize that Jerusalem has a special and unique meaning for adherents of the Christian, Jewish, and Islamic faiths. It is a multidimensional city whose significance transcends a single community or state. This pluralist vision forms the basis for open-minded ideas about the future of Jerusalem, and proponents try to strike a balance between the multidimensional character of the city on the one hand, and its specifically Palestinian aspects on the other. The pluralist view incorporates the essence of the living city of Jerusalem, a multiethnic and multicultural city that thrives when its different communities recognize each other's rights and each other's associations with its spirit.

For advocates of the exclusivist perspective, establishing the priority of Palestinian claims to the city seems to be the overriding goal. Although they recognize the uniqueness of this multiethnic city, they tend to give priority to the place of Jerusalem in Islam and in Arab history. From their perspective, the unique character of the city must be viewed within the context of the overarching principle of Palestinian national rights.

As regards the legalist perspective, its advocates are primarily concerned with showing that Israel has demonstrated no respect for religious or international law in the city. They appear to have two aims. On the one hand, they want to stress the illegality of Israeli practices in the city. On the other hand, they try to demonstrate that Israel has Judaized a city that they consider to be overwhelmingly Christian and Muslim-Arab in character and population.

The advocates of the opposition perspective condemn the settlement and expropriation activities of Israel in the city, not only because they find these activities objectionable on moral and nationalist grounds, but also because they want to use the emotional question of Jerusalem to undermine Arafat and the deal he struck with Israel.

What influence, if any, will these perspectives have on the process of negotiating a solution for the question of Jerusalem? Although the different Palestinian images of Jerusalem revolve around the theme of the city's special place in the hearts of all Palestinians, the very fact that there are differences in point of view and emphasis with regard to the character and status of the city should be a source of hope and optimism. It is worth noting that while both the Israeli-Jewish and the Palestinian camps have their messianics and crusaders, both also have their pragmatists. The more the pragmatists in the two camps work together to find a solution that befits this multidimensional city, the closer we will be able to move toward finding an answer to the question of Jerusalem. The cynics thrive when the prudent and compassionate ones weaken and lose hope. To a great degree, the future of the peace process hinges on the settlement of the problem of Jerusalem. Palestinian prudence has amply manifested itself in the pluralist perspective. Its impact should be felt at the conference table on the core issue of the status of the city of Jerusalem, which occupies a unique position in the national consciousness and values of two peoples, the people of Palestine and the people of Israel. In the collective consciousness of the Palestinians, Jerusalem is much more than a political, commercial, and cultural center. It is also more than a capital of a state which they so earnestly desire to establish. Above all, it is the embodiment of the Palestinian identity. If the goals of Palestinian nationalism can be fulfilled within the context of a Gaza–West Bank state, this state cannot be meaningful to the Palestinians except with Jerusalem.

THE CITY IN
LITERATURE, ART, AND
ARCHITECTURE

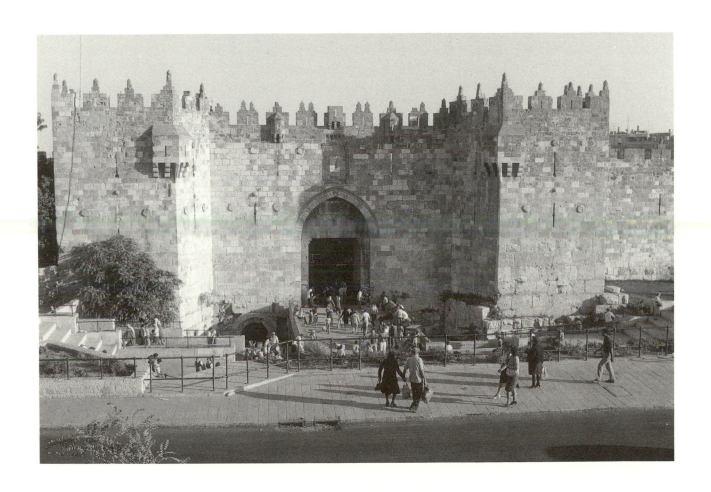

Jerusalem in Medieval Islamic Literature

10

JONATHAN M. BLOOM

Muslims consider Jerusalem to be the third holiest city in Islam. The holiest is, of course, Mecca—center of Islam and site of the Kaaba, its central shrine. It is also the place where, in the early seventh century, the Prophet Muhammad began to receive his revelations, later collected in the Koran. Medina, to which Muhammad was forced to emigrate in 622, is the second holiest city, containing the Prophet's mosque and tomb. Jerusalem, however, is neither mentioned explicitly in the Koran nor directly connected with events in the Prophet's life. It was only over the course of the centuries that Jerusalem acquired its eminent position among Islamic cities.

Some details of Jerusalem's history were certainly familiar to Muhammad, to judge from the Koran. The opening verses of the chapter "Bani Isra'il" ("Children of Israel," 17:2–8) relate to the destruction of the First and Second Temples, and in the first verse of this chapter—which may have been associated with verses 2–8 at a later date—the "furthest mosque" *(al-masjid al-aqsa)*, to which Muhammad was conducted from the Masjid al-Haram in Mecca in his miraculous Night Journey, has long been identified with the site of the Temple Mount in Jerusalem.[1] The Byzantine reconquest of the city in 630 from the Persians, who had taken it in 614, is alluded to in another passage (30:1–5), and koranic exegetes connect other expressions, such as *al-zaytun* ("the Olive," 95:1), *mubawwa sidq* ("the safe abode," 10:93), and *al-ard al-muqaddasa* ("the Holy Land," 5:21), with the city. Following the Jews, the first Muslims directed their prayers toward Jerusalem, until in 624, sixteen or seventeen months after Muhammad's emigration from Mecca, he received a revelation (Koran 2:136ff.) changing the kibla, or direction of prayer, from Jerusalem to the Kaaba in Mecca.

Jerusalem, known initially to the Arabs as Iliya' (from Aelia Capitolina, the name given it by Hadrian), Balat (from palatium), and Bayt al-Maqdis (a translation of the Aramaic for "temple"), did not have particular strategic or psychological importance in the earliest years of Islam. Although Muslim armies conquered southern Palestine in the summer of 634, two years after the Prophet's death, four years passed until Jerusalem was conquered. The earliest chroniclers of these events, such as the ninth-century historian Baladhuri, treat the conquest of Jerusalem rather casually, although later accounts embellish the event.[2] For example, it is often said that the reigning caliph, Umar (r. 634–644), toured the city and its holy places after conquering it, and his name is often connected to the Dome of the Rock, known to many tourists as the Mosque of Omar, although it is not a mosque, nor does it have anything to do with that caliph. The first Muslim inhabitants of Jerusalem, like new Muslim communities elsewhere, did build a mosque for their communal worship, and this building was seen ca. 680 by the Christian pilgrim Arculf, the first visitor to the city under Muslim rule to leave an account of his visit. Although Arculf was naturally more interested in the Christian monuments, he noted that "in the famous place where the Temple once stood . . . the Saracens now frequent an oblong house of prayer, which they pieced together with upright planks and large beams over some ruined remains. It is said that the building can hold three thousand people."[3]

Mu'awiya, governor of Syria and head of the Umayyad family, assumed the caliphate in 661 and made Damascus the capital, although under his successors, particularly the descendants of his cousin Marwan I (r. 684–685), a massive investment was made in rebuilding Jerusalem, which had been devastated by the brief Persian occupation earlier in the century. The Temple area was made level, the walls and gates to it repaired, a platform erected near the center, the Dome of the Rock and the adjacent congregational mosque constructed, and administrative and residential buildings built to the south of the Temple area, which eventually came to be known in Arabic as al-Haram al-Sharif (the Noble Sanctuary).[4] It is possible that Marwan's son and successor, the great caliph 'Abd al-Malik (r. 685–705), intended to make Jerusalem his new capital and thereby challenge Mecca, which along with many of the provinces had recognized the suzerainty of the countercaliph Ibn al-Zubayr, but the textual evidence is equivocal. The monumental evidence, however, shows this to have been the greatest public project of Umayyad times, with an undoubtedly political purpose.[5] In any event, this possibly unorthodox plan must have been abandoned by the pious caliph Suleiman (r. 715–717), who founded the city of Ramla, twenty-six miles northwest of Jerusalem on the coastal plain, as the new capital and economic center of the province of Filastin (Palestine).[6]

Despite the great efforts of the Umayyad caliphs to institutionalize the importance of Jerusalem, the economic and political fortunes of the city seem to have fallen on hard times with the dynasty's collapse in 750 and the rise to power of the Abbasids, who made their capitals in Iraq. A few Abbasid caliphs visited the city: after returning from the pilgrimage to Mecca in 758, the caliph al-Mansur (r. 754–775) set out for Jerusalem to fulfill a vow; accompanied by his army en route to quell an uprising in the Maghrib, he returned in 771. Al-Mansur's son al-Mahdi also came to pray in Jerusalem, but later caliphs did not make it part of their itineraries.[7] Nevertheless, after much of the Aqsa Mosque had been destroyed in the earthquake of 746, al-Mansur ordered its restoration, as did al-Mahdi and his son al-Ma'mun (r. 813–833). Al-Ma'mun's activities in Jerusalem are commemorated by the mosaic inscription on the octagonal arcade within the Dome of the Rock, where the name of the actual founder, 'Abd al-Malik, was obliterated and his own inserted in its place.

Although the Umayyad attempt to increase the political importance of Jerusalem may have failed and the surrounding land was too poor to make it much of an agricultural or commercial center, the spiritual importance of Jerusalem to Muslims seems to have grown during this very period, to judge from the evidence for the development of the *fada'il,* a literary genre in praise of the city. Arabic literature praising such cities as Mecca and Medina appeared as early as the eighth century,[8] and it seems likely that a similar literature concerning Jerusalem originated with the *ulema,* or religious scholars, of Jerusalem as early as the Umayyad period. A commentary on the Koran by Muqatil b. Sulayman (d. 768) contains many sayings that must have been current in his lifetime. For example, he reports that it is said that Jerusalem "is closer by 18 miles to heaven" than any other place and that "whosoever dies while he is dwelling in Bayt al-Maqdis for the sake of heaven is considered to have died in heaven."[9] Perhaps the most famous of these reports is the saying, "The saddles of the camels shall not be fastened for setting out for pilgrimage except for three mosques: the Mosque of Mecca, the Mosque of Medina, and the Aqsa Mosque," which was intended to prevent the creation of secondary places of worship in Islam.[10] The earliest treatises concerned specifically with Jerusalem are known to have appeared in the early tenth century, with the composition of books about the praises of the city, although the earliest surviving example of this genre is that of Abu Bakr al-Wasiti, a preacher *(khatib)* at the Aqsa Mosque of Jerusalem in the early eleventh century.[11]

A literature in praise of Jerusalem seems to have developed alongside an increased role of the city in the explanation of obscure passages in the Koran. The earliest commentators on the Koran believed that heaven was *al-masjid al-aqsa* ("the furthest place of prayer") to which Muhammad was carried from the Masjid al-Haram (surrounding the Kaaba in Mecca) on his Night Journey (Koran 17:1). The story of the Prophet's nocturnal ascension (Miraj) to heavenly spheres was elaborated by theologians and popularized by poets throughout the Islamic lands as a metaphor for the journey of the soul to the divine. Perhaps as early as the Umayyad period, the "furthest place of prayer" in the Koran came to be associated with Jerusalem, so that the Prophet was believed to have been transported miraculously from Mecca to Jerusalem. Muhammad's vision of a divine messenger, described in Koran 81:19–25 and 53:1–25 and presumably taking place on earth, was transformed into a miraculous ascension. Although some early hadith, or traditions of the Prophet, placed Muhammad's ascension from the Kaaba at Mecca, others placed it in Jerusalem, not very far from the site of Christ's ascension on the Mount of Olives. The various Islamic accounts and traditions were ultimately harmonized so that Muhammad was believed to have made a miraculous nocturnal journey from Mecca to Jerusalem on the steed Buraq and thence to heaven.[12]

The traditionalists of Medina, however, who made a profession of recording and transmitting the words and deeds of the Prophet Muhammad, were vehemently opposed to the elevation of the status of

Jerusalem, for they feared that the increased importance of the city would only continue to reduce the role of Medina, which had already been eclipsed as capital of the Islamic empire and relegated to the status of a provincial religious center. To this end, these scholars fabricated and disseminated traditions that ignored or denigrated the importance of Jerusalem. For example, they cited traditions stating that one should only visit two mosques, and a certain Hudhayfa related that "even if the distance between me and Jerusalem was reduced to one or two parasangs [3.5–7 miles], I would not proceed there nor would I wish to go [there and pray]."[13]

Despite the concerted efforts of its detractors, the religious significance of Jerusalem grew from its associations with the earlier religions that Islam had superseded. Considering that many early Muslims in Jerusalem must have been converts from Christianity and Judaism, it would not be surprising for them to have carried their feelings for the city when they changed their faith, particularly since Islam regarded itself as the successor to the earlier revelations. Thus, graves of biblical prophets and holy men continued to be venerated, particularly pious individuals sought to live an ascetic life near these venerated sites, and professional storytellers embellished the lives of these legendary and real figures.[14]

These various developments are confirmed by the reports of the Muslim geographers and travelers who from the beginning of the tenth century began to leave reports of their visits to the city. As elsewhere in medieval as well as modern times, there must have been a ready company of cicerones to guide the interested tourist around the attractions of the city, ending up, no doubt, in a favorite souvenir shop. These guides were probably responsible for the consistency, if not always the accuracy, of the information given in the Muslim sources. The speed with which the guides undoubtedly recited the information, the possibility that the tourists' notes got confused, and the lapses of memory when they composed their retrospective accounts probably explain much of the variation in the names and locations of gates and shrines.

The earliest geographer to have left an account is the Persian Ibn al-Faqih, writing ca. 903.[15] He noted the pre-Islamic associations of the city and identified many sites associated with such figures as Musa (Moses), Sulayman (Solomon), and 'Isa (Jesus), whom Muslims consider to have been prophets. Some of the gates of the Haram, notably Bab Hittah (Gate of Forgiveness) and Bab al-Rahma (Gate of Mercy), have names with koranic associations (Koran 2:55 and 57:13, respectively), and the Temple area had clearly become associated with the Prophet's miraculous Night Journey. In addition to the Aqsa Mosque at the south and the Dome of the Rock in the center, several smaller domes stood on the platform, including the Dome of the Prophet, the Station of Gabriel, and the Dome of (Muhammad's) Ascension. The association with the Miraj is emphasized by the name given to a gate, perhaps Barclay's Gate, near the southwest of the Haram complex, "the place of tying up Buraq." The cave in the Dome of the Rock is noted for the first time as a gathering place for prayer, and it is likely that the marble mihrab there, an arched panel set in the direction of Mecca, dates to this period.[16] The entire sanctuary complex was served by 140 slaves and lighted every night with 1,600 lamps. Sixteen chests contained magnificent manuscripts of the Koran set apart for public service, and four pulpits were maintained for voluntary preachers, as well as one for salaried preachers; within the mosque were three *maqsuras,* or enclosed areas, reserved for women.

It was popularly believed that on the day of the Last Judgment, a bridge would extend across the Kedron or Jehoshaphat Valley, known in Arabic as the Wadi Jahannum (Valley of Gehenna, or Hell), and all would have to cross it. Indeed, as Jerusalem would be the gate to Paradise, those who could afford it arranged for burial there, so as to be close when the time came. Following Jewish custom, it even became popular for Muslims to arrange to have their coffins carried to Jerusalem for burial. Among those who did so were several Egyptian figures, including an Abbasid governor, as well as Muhammad ibn Tughj, the founder of the Ikhshidid dynasty 'Ali ibn Ikhshid, and the regent Kafur. Indeed, the growing sanctity of the city induced the Ikhshidids, who governed Egypt in the early tenth century, to erect their family tomb outside the northeast corner of the Haram, an area beyond the city wall still used as a Muslim cemetery.

The Spanish traveler Ibn 'Abd Rabbih, writing a decade later (ca. 913), gives much the same impression of the city as Ibn al-Faqih. He notes the Dome of the Ascension, a dome where Muhammad prayed along with the former prophets, and the praying place of Gabriel. The Dome of the Chain, not mentioned by his predecessor, stood (and still stands) adjacent to the Dome of the Rock; Ibn 'Abd Rabbih explains that this was where, during the time of the Israelites, there hung a chain that could show whether one was truthful or lying. He was also shown a slab in the Dome of the Rock that lay directly over one of the gates of Paradise.

The most penetrating description of Jerusalem in the second half of the tenth century is given by Shams al-Din Abu 'Abdallah Muhammad al-Muqaddasi (or al-Maqdisi), who, as his name shows, was a native of the city.[17] The creator of a human geography that far surpassed his predecessors' "science of countries," al-Muqaddasi was one of a small group of contemporary Jerusalemites of Persian origin who had wide humanistic interests and demonstrated the high cultural level of the city at that time.[18] According to al-Muqaddasi, Jerusalem was close to Paradise: the climate was perfect and the people were chaste, the living agreeable and the markets clean, the fruit delicious and the men learned. The city had the advantages of both this world and the next.[19]

Despite this native son's chauvinism, al-Muqaddasi had to note that the city had some defects: Christians and Jews predominated, and no day passed without seeing foreigners, who came as pilgrims from all over. Indeed, the rhythm of the year was regulated by the Christian holidays. The mosque, by which he meant the entire Haram, was one of the largest in the Muslim lands; it was said that everywhere in the city one might find water and hear the call to prayer; and the Islamic holy places were numerous. Nevertheless, the city was not a great spiritual center, for "the Mosque is empty, there are no scholars and no savants, no disputations and no instruction." Furthermore, al-Muqaddasi had to admit that "nowhere are the baths filthier nor are the fees to use them higher." It is clear from his account that many associations had already been fixed to the city: it is the "land that God blessed for all nations" (Koran 21:71) and the plain of the Resurrection, where all men shall be brought together for the Last Judgment. Even Mecca and Medina will both be brought to Jerusalem on the Day of Judgment. And, he concluded, it must be the most spacious of cities, since all mankind would assemble there then!

Like his contemporaries, al-Muqaddasi notes how Jerusalem had little ground water but many cisterns and open tanks where rainwater was collected. Among the curiosities he noted was the heaviness of

Figure 13. The Dome of the Rock.

the dew in Palestine: when the south wind blows, dew falls every night in such quantities that it trickles down the gutters of the Aqsa Mosque. Unlike other Islamic cities, where mosques could be found throughout the settled area, Jerusalem was different, for it was clearly divided into quarters focused around its Christian and Muslim religious centers, and virtually all the Muslim religious activities focused around the Haram. Although al-Muqaddasi noted the major products and exports of the region, such as oil, cheese, cotton, and fruits, the town was too far away from the mainstream of international commerce to be a viable center. By the middle of the eleventh century, Jerusalem also began to become the main city of Palestine, for a large portion of Ramla was destroyed in the earthquake of December 1033.

Nasir-i Khusraw, the Persian traveler and probably also a spy for the Fatimid rulers of Egypt, stayed in Jerusalem from early March to the end of April 1047 and left an important account of his visit.[20] In May, after a visit to Hebron, he went to the Hijaz for the pilgrimage, returning to Jerusalem in early July before leaving again for Cairo. He noted that Syrians who were unable to make the pilgrimage to Mecca performed the requisite rituals of *wuquf* (the standing in the presence of God, which is the main ceremony of the pilgrimage at 'Arafat outside Mecca) in Jerusalem, with sometimes as many as 20,000 (probably an exaggeration) gathering during the first days of Dhu'l-Hijja, the pilgrimage month. Jerusalem, he wrote, was the third most holy place of God. Among those learned in religion, it was well known that prayers made in Jerusalem were worth 25,000 ordinary prayers, while those said in Medina were worth 50,000 and those said in Mecca, 100,000.

Nasir was struck by several peculiarities. The mountainous and stony terrain and lack of water meant that olives and wheat dominated the diet, although the bazaars were well stocked with goods. There were springs in the outlying villages, but none in Jerusalem, so rainwater was collected on lead-covered roofs and channeled into solid cisterns made of granite, supposedly by Solomon. Nevertheless, he wrote, the water in the city is the best and clearest imaginable, and rain washed the paved streets clean. 'Ayn Silwan, the Spring of Siloam, was half a stage south of the city; it was surrounded by buildings and its water irrigated nearby gardens. There was also a fine, heavily endowed hospital, with physicians who drew their salaries from endowment.

Nasir's description of the city enumerates many underground places and mosques complemented by passageways that lead up and down to them. The congregational mosque (the entire Haram enclosure) lay on the east of the city, attached to the wall. Beyond it was a large plain called Sahira, where it was said the Resurrection would take place; people came from all over to wait there and die, and there was a large cemetery at its edge. Between the mosque and plain was the Valley of Jahannum; the guides told Nasir that he should have been able to hear the voices of those in Hell crying out there, although

Nasir confessed that he heard nothing. On the other side of the Haram was a gate leading to *khanakah*s or convents, where Sufis resided and prayed, except on Fridays when they went to the mosque. Indeed, Jerusalem seems to have become quite the place for spiritual retirement, for in 1095 the great theologian al-Ghazali retired from his professorship in Baghdad to seek solitude in one of the *khanakah*s in the vicinity of the Dome of the Rock.[21]

Nasir's description of the Haram is largely similar to its present state, despite several important differences in the names of gates. God had commanded Moses to make the rock the direction of prayer. Solomon built the first mosque there, and people prayed toward it until God commanded that people pray toward the Kaaba in Mecca. Most remarkable is his description of the Bab Da'ud (Gate of David; now the Bab al-Silsila), which was a splendid gateway leading from the city to the mosque. Decorated with dazzling mosaics containing the titles of Fatimid caliphs of Egypt, it had a huge dome and two doors of Damascene workmanship faced with patterned brass. Great colonnades supported arcades on either side. Except for the arcades, no trace of this work survives, but this report indicates that the early Fatimid caliphs were active patrons in the city.

Commemorative structures or commemorative identifications to earlier structures on the Haram had proliferated by Nasir's time. They included Jacob's Dome on the north; the Dome of the Chain, where David had hung the chain that only the innocent could reach; Gabriel's Dome, where Buraq had been brought for the Prophet to mount; the Gate of Mercy; and the Gate of Repentance (probably the Golden Gate), where God had accepted David's repentance. Decorated with carpets and frequented by people who wanted to be forgiven of their sins, the structure was used as a mosque. Another mosque in the underground structures at the southeast of the Haram was known as Jesus' Cradle (Mahd 'Isa, after Koran 19:f.); the "cradle" was used as a mihrab, and other mihrabs were identified with Mary and Zachariah and inscribed with appropriate koranic verses. The mosque proper was firmly associated with Muhammad's miraculous journey, which its beautiful interior decoration and fittings described. Nasir was mightily impressed by the Double Gate under the Aqsa Mosque, the gate by which Muhammad entered the mosque. It was inconceivable to Nasir how humans had ever managed to move the enormous blocks of stone, and it was said that the structure had been made by Solomon. The cave in the Dome of the Rock had been created when the rock rose with the Prophet, trying to accompany him to heaven; the cave was left when the Prophet put his hand on the rock and froze it in midair. Unlike many other Muslim visitors, Nasir was also impressed by the Church of the Holy Sepulchre, which was large enough for 8,000 people and was where priests and monks read the Gospels and prayed all day and night. It was extremely ornate, with colored marble, brocades, designs, and pictures of Jesus and other prophets. He particularly noted many varnished icons, preserved under transparent glass; one, a painting of Heaven and Hell and their inhabitants, had nothing to equal it in all the world.

Jerusalem became a Christian city when the Crusaders arrived in 1099. Muslims and Jews were prohibited from practicing their religions or settling permanently, although eventually some were allowed to come to the city for business and prayer. A Syrian Arab gentleman with good Crusader connections, Usama ibn Munqidh, visited Jerusalem ca. 1140 and went into the Aqsa Mosque, by the side of which was a little mosque that the Franks had converted into a church. As the Aqsa Mosque was occupied by the Templars, who were Usama's friends, they assigned him this little mosque in which to say his prayers. A Frank, who had just arrived from Europe, tried to prevent Usama from praying south toward Mecca and force him to pray like a Christian toward the east, but the Templars restrained the Frank, saying that he did not understand the ways of the country. Usama also was able to visit the Dome of the Rock, where he saw one of the Templars go up to the emir Mu'in al-Din and offer to show him a picture of Mary with Christ on her lap.[22]

The Christian conquest brought new meanings to Jerusalem's buildings, the most famous example being, of course, the Dome of the Rock, which became the Templum Domini. Similarly, Christians thought the Dome of the Chain to be the church of the Holy of Holies, to judge from an account of the Muslim geographer al-Idrisi, who wrote for the Norman king Roger of Sicily in 1154. Although al-Idrisi never visited Palestine, his description was probably based on Christian sources. It has often been noted that the Crusader conquest of Jerusalem did not immediately arouse any strong Muslim reaction, suggesting that the city had not yet acquired the spiritual character it would later have. Strong propaganda for the reconquest of the city began under 'Imad al-Din Zanki and his son Nur al-Din (r. 1146–1174). In 1169 Nur al-Din ordered in Aleppo a splendid minbar, or pulpit, made for the Aqsa Mosque, which was still in Crusader hands. Propaganda reached its apogee under Saladin, who advanced toward Jerusalem after the decisive battle of Hattin in July 1187. By November the inhabitants had surrendered, and the city soon became predominantly Muslim in character, except after 1229, when the city was briefly ceded to the emperor Frederick II. By the middle of the thirteenth century the city had definitively reverted to Muslim control.

Saladin and his successors sought to repair, rebuild, and resanctify the holy places on the Haram, which had been in Christian hands, and this process again led to some misunderstanding and confusion as identities were reassigned to extant structures and new associations created. The celebrated ascetic and pilgrim 'Ali al-Harawi had visited the city in 1173, and this process is already visible in his account.[23] In the Dome of the Rock he noted the footmark of the Prophet on the Rock itself and the cave of the souls beneath it, with the grave of Zachariah. He also saw presumably Crusader pictures of Solomon and Christ encrusted with jewels. The subterranean structure at the southeast of the Haram was known as the Stables of Solomon, a conflation of Crusader usage and biblical associations, and the Dome of the Chain was now where David's son Solomon had administered justice.

Under the Mamluk sultans of Egypt and their governors in Damascus, the city was rebuilt. Jerusalem became a place of forced retirement in Mamluk times: it had long been a place of banishment for those with unorthodox views and ways of life, and its proximity to Egypt, combined with its relative isolation and lack of fortifications or great wealth, made it an ideal place whence to send recalcitrant emirs. After the defeat of the Crusaders, the city ceased to have military or political importance, but it became increasingly important as a religious center: over thirty works on the *fada'il* of Jerusalem are known from the period, and scores of madrasas, or theological colleges, and *khanakah*s were founded there, giving the city much of its present aspect, particularly in the area around the Haram.[24]

After the Crusades, the character of the city changed as it became predominantly one of Muslim divines temporarily stationed in Jerusalem and living on pious foundations and salaries. It became a city

LITERATURE, ART, AND ARCHITECTURE

of the poor and the pious, a likely spot for Sufis, who benefited from the endowments of the *khanakah*s. The many visitors and geographers often repeat earlier accounts: the geographer Abu'l-Fida, for example, in his description of Palestine written in 1321, copied the texts of the early geographers Istakhri and Ibn Hawqal verbatim. Nevertheless, travelers' reports show that the commemorative associations of the city continued to grow: Ibn Battuta, the great Moroccan traveler and freeloader who visited the city in 1355, states that he saw a great iron buckler, which he was told was that of Hamzah ibn 'Abd al-Mutallib, the Prophet's uncle.

In this period, pilgrimage guides began to lay out a pious itinerary for the visitor to the city: the pilgrim should first visit this place and pray here, then visit that place and recite a particular verse of the Koran, and so on. These liturgical prescriptions display a strong echo of the pilgrimage to Mecca, which disturbed some theologians who remembered that only Mecca and Medina had special status. The literature in defense of the holiness of Jerusalem, however, culminated in the work of the Arab historian Mujir al-Din (1456–1522). His principal work, a two-volume history of the holy places of Jerusalem and Hebron, placed Palestine—and particularly Jerusalem—on a par with the Hijaz and its holy cities, Mecca and Medina.[25] It was thus only after some eight centuries of Islam that the sanctity of Jerusalem for Muslims was assured. Oddly enough, it was the impetus of the Jewish and Christian veneration of the city that created its sanctity for Muslims.[26]

11 Nineteenth-Century Portraits through Western Eyes

NITZA ROSOVSKY

Napoleon's invasion of Egypt at the dawn of the nineteenth century underlined the strategic and commercial importance of the Near East and rekindled the interest of the Western powers in that part of the world. The fate of the "Sick Man on the Bosporus" would continue to preoccupy Europe until the collapse of the Ottoman Empire at the end of World War I.

There were other forces behind the renewed interest in the East. The Scientific and Artistic Commission that had accompanied Napoleon to Egypt continued to publish the multivolume *Description de L'Égypte,* capturing the popular imagination long after the emperor's retreat. At the same time, the Enlightenment, which had employed reason to combat ignorance, superstition, and the dogma of the Church, began to make way for Romanticism, as poets like Goethe, Blake, Coleridge, and Wordsworth rebelled against logic and science. Western society, shaken by new theories about creation and by other scientific discoveries, sought to return to a simple belief in God and the Bible.

A desire to reexamine the scenes of biblical events brought a growing number of visitors to the East, and as travel became safer—when steam replaced the sail on the Mediterranean in the late 1830s—Palestine became an integral part of the increasingly popular "Grand Tour." As Victor Hugo wrote in his introduction to *Les Orientals,* the "whole continent is leaning eastward." Scholars and adventurers, soldiers and missionaries, painters and photographers, and the literati journeyed to the Holy Land and the Holy City. Elated, puzzled, or disappointed, no visitor to the country—and especially to Jerusalem—was left indifferent, and many self-appointed scribes felt compelled to share their experiences. Hundreds of books rolled off the presses in Europe and the United States, chronicles of short or long sojourns. In his *Bibliotheca Geographica Palaestinae* (1890), Reinhold Röhricht listed 3,515 titles written between 333 and 1878, of which 2,000 were written by traveler-authors in the nineteenth century. Yehoshua Ben-Arieh, a foremost authority on the Holy Land in the nineteenth century, noted that about half the books in *Bibliotheca* were composed in the first 1,500 years, the other half in a mere 40 years, between 1838 and 1878![1] Considering that a journey to the East was still arduous and dangerous and that the actual number of people who made the trip was relatively small, 2,000 works by travelers alone is an astonishing number.[2]

Nineteenth-century writers were rarely "politically correct" by today's standards, and travel accounts of the East were full of ethnic slurs and derogatory remarks. Yet even within this genre, the negative comments about Jerusalem take on a particularly shrill pitch, heard most loudly in the remarks made by Protestants, who were responsible for many a portrait of the city. The impressions recorded in the diaries, journals, novels, and poetry of some well-known authors, such as Chateaubriand, Thackeray, and Melville, as well as the impressions of travelers whose books became best-sellers, shed some light on the writers' experiences and help explain the reasons behind the negative depictions.[3]

Long before the nineteenth century, Western literature was permeated with images of heroes and villains from the Scriptures and their exploits, and the name "Jerusalem" was familiar to every Christian since childhood. The "legacy of Israel" was preserved by the vernacular Bibles, especially in countries most responsive to the Reformation.[4] In addition to the Bible, depictions of Jerusalem and the Holy Land could be found in pilgrims' itineraries beginning in the fourth century and continuing to modern times. Yet, according to Howard Mumford Jones, Milton's *Paradise Lost* and *Paradise Regained* demonstrate that "the factual geography of Palestine had made virtually no impression upon the English imagination as late as the end of the 17th century."[5]

In the New World, where the Pilgrims arrived Bible in hand, America itself was considered to be the city upon the hill, the new

Zion,[6] and almost a thousand place names in the United States alone came from the Bible, from Ararat to Zion.[7] Negro spirituals were full of biblical allegories: crossing the River Jordan—like escaping across the Ohio River—symbolized freedom, and Jerusalem was the heavenly city, just as it was in the Christian hymnology of the eighteenth century. In the oft-repeated lines,

> I will not cease from mental fight
> Nor shall my sword sleep in my hand,
> Till we have built Jerusalem
> In England's green and pleasant land.

Blake's Jerusalem was not the real city, but Liberty, the inspiration of all mankind.[8]

The nineteenth century produced an enormous fiction library concerning the Holy Land, from Sir Walter Scott's *The Talisman* (1825) to Lew Wallace's *Ben Hur* (1880).[9] At the same time, a new literary form developed—descriptions of travel to exotic places, including the Holy Land, in which the British held first place.[10] Travel literature was extremely popular in the United States as well: William M. Thomson's *The Land and the Book* (1859) sold 200,000 copies and was surpassed only by *Uncle Tom's Cabin* in the nineteenth century, and Mark Twain's *The Innocents Abroad* (1869) outsold all his other books during the author's lifetime.[11]

Travelers who wrote about the Holy Land may be divided into three general categories. At one extreme were those who were so elated by being there, especially in Jerusalem, that they closed their eyes to reality and ignored the fact that by the end of three centuries of Ottoman rule, the country was barren and the Holy City—with a population of about 9,000 in the early 1800s—resembled a backward village. At the other extreme were travelers who arrived with high expectations and were bitterly disappointed by what they saw. In the middle were those who tried, at times with little success, to be objective.

Going up to Jerusalem

To this day hardly anyone arrives in Jerusalem, "a threshold to heaven," without some emotional baggage. In the nineteenth century, pilgrims and sinners alike—to borrow Mark Twain's designation—came full of preconceptions. Etched in travelers' minds were imaginary biblical landscapes, familiar since childhood. In the opening scene of *Souvenirs, impressions et paysages pendant un voyage en Orient,* Alphonse de Lamartine, politician, man of letters, and member of the French Academy, who visited Jerusalem in 1832, draws a picture of his mother teaching him to read from his grandmother's illustrated Bible. From age eight on he "burned with the desire of going to visit those mountains on which God descended . . . I was always dreaming of traveling in the East; I never ceased arranging in my mind a vast and religious epopee, of which these beautiful spots should be the principal scene."[12]

In addition to expecting beautiful spots, visitors could not distance themselves from religion. Even Harriet Martineau, a prominent Englishwoman who wrote about social and economic issues and was skeptical of religious dogmas, admitted that her main interest in Palestine was its being "the abode of Jesus." About to enter the Holy Land in 1847, she and her companions discussed "the impressions of our childhood about the story of Jesus, and the emotions and passions that history had excited in us."[13]

Disillusionment struck early on. Mark Twain quickly realized that he must "unlearn a great many things I have somehow absorbed concerning Palestine. I must begin a system of reduction . . . The word 'Palestine' always brought to my mind a vague suggestion of a country as large as the United States . . . I suppose it was because I could not conceive of a small country having so large a history." He found Jerusalem especially disappointing: "A fast walker could go outside the walls of Jerusalem in an hour. I do not know how else to make one understand how small it is."[14]

As we look at Jerusalem through the eyes of Westerners, we must remember not only their emotional state but also the physical discomforts they encountered daily: heat, dirt, dust, unpaved roads, poor accommodations, fleas, flies, and hostile natives. Most travelers disembarked at Jaffa, then followed the route well-trodden by Christians: a night in Ramla, four or five days in Jerusalem, and a two-day side trip to the Jordan River, the Dead Sea, and Bethlehem.

Travelers encountered hazards even before they set foot in the Holy Land. In 1844, William Makepeace Thackeray's steamer dropped anchor a mile out of Jaffa, where a "heap of black rocks" left only a narrow and dangerous passage. Small wooden boats carried passengers to shore, where "hideous brutes in brown skins and the briefest of shirts" waded to the boats, grinning and shouting in Arabic for everyone to mount their shoulders; "the ladies . . . were obliged to submit; and, trembling, were . . . carried through the shallows and flung up to a ledge before the city gate, where crowds more of dark people were swarming."[15]

Once on terra firma, the visitor had to hire a dragoman, as guide *cum* translator. Until the 1840s there were no hotels in Palestine, and, unless shelter was available at a nearby convent, the dragoman pitched his tents and supplied the vital necessities. Ross Browne, an Irish-born American Protestant who visited the Holy Land in 1851, named his book *Yusef* after his own dragoman, "the interpreter . . . [who] provides the provisions, horses, mules, tents, &c . . . speaks various languages, seldom less than five or six," and was responsible for the name of every town and village (although if he forgot a name, he would invent one), as well as for the weather, every fit of indigestion, the fleas, the unsatisfactory character of the scenery, the roughness of the road, and "the uncivilized appearance of the Arabs." He "must be dragoman, tutor, lexicon, valet, cook, caterer, comforter, warrior—all in one."[16]

Skirmishes with Beduins or other marauders were common. Witness the 1806 trip of Vicomte François-Auguste-René de Chateaubriand, the Romantic French writer, whose lively account, *Itinéraire de Paris à Jérusalem,* was published in 1811. The book, soon translated into English and German, became a best-seller on both sides of the Atlantic and was frequently cited by subsequent travelers. At the advice of a Catholic priest in Jaffa, Chateaubriand and his servants rode up to Jerusalem clad in "goatskin dress" such as was commonly worn by Beduins, in order to escape attacks and to avoid paying the multiple bribes and fees demanded by various pashas along the way, the result of the "pitch corruption, love of gold, anarchy, and barbarity" which prevailed in the "unhappy country."[17]

In Hebron, in 1857, Arab boys threw stones at William C. Prime—a Presbyterian minister traveling with his wife—shouting *"Nazara, kelb, kafir"* (Christian, dog, infidel).[18] A year later, Edward Lear, the landscape painter better known today for his nonsense verse and limericks, complained that "the country is in such a state that many places can only be visited at the risk of robbery." Some Americans, he wrote, were attacked near Nazareth by Arabs who "went off with all but one large blanket, of which Mr. & Mrs. T. made 2 garments, & therein rode to town." The Arabs even stole their books and a collection of Holy Land plants, probably "as diversions for their nasty little beastly black children."[19]

Cholera, typhoid, and dysentery were rampant. When Lamartine heard of a plague outbreak in Jerusalem, he proceeded nevertheless, but only after arranging for two horsemen to ride "about fifty paces in advance of the caravan, to drive off any Arabs or any Jewish pilgrims we might meet." And "we also anointed ourselves with oil and garlic" for it was well-known that "oil bearers and venders" rarely got sick![20] There was not one doctor in the country before the 1840s.

The forty-odd miles from Jaffa to Jerusalem could not be covered in a day, and most travelers stopped overnight at a convent in Ramla, some twelve miles southeast of Jaffa. In 1844 the Irishman Eliot Warburton stayed at the Franciscan convent, where in the "various cool cloisters and high-walled courts, shaded by the lemon, the orange, and the palm-tree, the air was delightfully refreshing." However, his "sleeping cell was less squalid than in the Jaffa convent, but still was such that no English felon would be obliged to occupy."[21]

After landing in Jaffa on January 6, 1857, Herman Melville noted in his journal: "Employed a Jew dragoman to take me to Jerusalem . . . Arrived at Ramla & put up at alleged (hotel). At supper over broken crockery & cold meat, pestered by moschitos [sic] & fleas, dragoman said, "Dese Arab no know how to keep hotel.""[22]

Complaints about fleas, bedbugs, cockroaches, and the occasional scorpion were universal. "How can a man think about Joshua or the valley of Jehoshaphat, when fifty indefatigable little bores are sharply reminding him of the actual and suffering present?" asked one traveler.[23]

First Impressions of the Holy City

"Above everything else, one's reaction to the first glimpse of Jerusalem, usually gained after the long climb on the hot dusty trail leading up from Jaffa, was a key to the modern pilgrim's reaction to the Holy Land," noted Franklin Walker in *Irreverent Pilgrims: Melville, Browne, and Mark Twain in the Holy Land*.[24]

Chateaubriand set the somber tone, frequently echoed by others. He left Ramla at midnight with his entourage and rode through a "dreary region," over a "naked plain bestrewed with loose stones," until he saw Jerusalem. Nothing had prepared him for the emotions he felt, not even the two hundred modern accounts, rabbinical compilations, and ancient texts he had read in advance of his visit. He paused to review "the recollections of history from Abraham to Godfrey de Bouillon, reflecting on the total change accomplished in the world by the mission of the Son of Man, and in vain seeking that Temple, not one stone of which is left upon another. Were I to live a thousand years, never should I forget that desert, which yet seems to be pervaded by the greatness of Jehovah and the terrors of death."[25] Chateaubriand certainly knew that the Temple he was "seeking" was destroyed long ago but probably wanted to remind his readers of the prediction Jesus had made.

At sunrise in the autumn of 1832, Lamartine first saw the city in a dazzling sheet of light like a vast ocean: "On the coast of this imaginary ocean . . . the sun shone upon a square tower, an elevated minaret, and the great yellow walls of some edifices which crowned the summit of a hill . . . This could only be Jerusalem . . . the Holy City: everything inspired the name of Jerusalem! It was herself! She sat detached by her yellow garb from the deep blue of the sky, and the black background of the Mount of Olives."[26]

John Lloyd Stephens, a young politician from New York, was the first American traveler to write about Palestine, which he visited in 1836. Coming up from Bethlehem, he first saw Jerusalem from the south: "It looked so small . . . I saw that it was walled all around, and that it stood alone . . . There were no domes, steeples, or turrets to break the monotony of its aspect, and even the mosques and minarets made no show . . . I was obliged to rouse myself by recalling to mind the long train of extraordinary incidents of which that little city had been the theatre, and which made it, in the eyes of the Christian at least, the most hallowed spot on earth."[27]

Thackeray wrote that the "feelings of almost terror with which, riding through the night, we approached this awful place, the centre of the world's past and future history, have no need to be noted down here."[28]

These four different reactions to the first glimpse of the Holy City were often repeated by other nineteenth-century travelers: Chateaubriand's somberness as he contemplated the "mission of the Son of Man"; the joy felt by a dazzled Lamartine; the disappointment voiced by Stephens; and the terror Thackeray would not even discuss evoked by "this awful place."

The Holy Places

Once inside the city walls, all Christians gravitated toward the Church of the Holy Sepulchre, shared—or rather fought over—by Greek Orthodox, Roman Catholics (Latins), Armenians, Syrians, Abyssinians, and Copts. By and large, Catholics and Protestants reacted differently to the holy places. Catholics were accustomed to ornate churches, but most Protestants were shocked: "For eighteen centuries avid and pious Christians of divergent sects had overlaid the simplicity of biblical scenes with tawdry symbolism, rude commercialism, and pious hokum."[29]

Chateaubriand assumed that Christian readers would want to know what he felt upon entering the church: "I really cannot tell. So many reflections rushed at once upon my mind . . . I continued near half an hour upon my knees in the little chamber of the Holy Sepulchre." A Catholic, he was not bothered by the church decor and had no doubts regarding "the authenticity of the Christian traditions concerning Jerusalem."[30]

Lamartine's heart was filled with "stupendous reflections," as he prayed long at the tomb: "All the pious emotions which have effected the souls in every period of life; all the prayers that have been breathed from our hearts and our lips in the name of Him who taught us to pray to his Father and ours . . . produce by their echoes . . . a bewildering of the understanding, and a melting of the heart, which seek not language, but transpire in moistened eyes, a heaving breast, a prostate forehead, and lips glued in silence to the sepulchre stone."[31]

"Lips glued to sepulchre" were not for Protestants, most of whom found the inside of the church "full of tawdriness and bad painting, redolent of vulgar superstition,"[32] as the following examples will demonstrate. Some even questioned the authenticity of the site.

Stephens, the New York politician, was swept by the crowd into the church during Holy Week, where a priest noticed that he was

Figure 14. Stephen Illes's large-scale model of Jerusalem from 1873 is very detailed and accurate. In the center foreground is Jaffa Gate with the Citadel, or Tower of David, on the right. (The Tower houses the Museum of the History of Jerusalem, where the model is on display.) Behind Jaffa Gate, to the left, is the dome of the Church of the Holy Sepulchre, between two minarets. In the center is the Dome of the Rock atop the Herodian Temple platform. The Mount of Olives is in the background, with the Russian Church of the Ascension. (See Chapter 16.)

better dressed than "the miserable, beggarly crowd . . . and expecting a better contribution from me . . . gave me a place at the head of the sepulchre." Shaken by the priest's behavior, Stephens fled to the house of an American missionary, Mr. Whiting. The only people in the Holy City praising Christ in "simplicity and truth," trying to reestablish the "pure faith and worship that were founded on this spot eighteen centuries ago," were an American (meaning Protestant) missionary and his wife, wrote Stephens, who then added: "If I can form any judgment from my own feelings, every man other than the blind and determined enthusiast, when he stands by the side of that marble sarcophagus, must be ready to exclaim, 'This is not the place where the Lord lay!'"[33]

Martineau, although alienated by what she called "Christian superstition," did not think that travelers should avoid "the Christian establishments in Palestine." She went to see everything "except the mummeries of Easter Week in the Church of the Holy Sepulchre," where the "pretended sepulchre" resembled "a heathen temple, but without its grace." It was advisable, she said, to look at the rituals there as if "one were looking at a Chinese or Indian ceremony."[34]

Thackeray was horrified by the swarms of peddlers and beggars outside the church, while inside he found that "deceits are too open and flagrant; the inconsistencies and contrivances too monstrous . . . The Greeks shew you the Tomb of Melchisedec, while the Armenians possess the Chapel of the Penitent Thief; the poor Copts . . . can yet boast the thicket in which Abraham caught the Ram . . . ; the Latins point out the pillar to which the Lord was bound. The place of the Invention of the Sacred Cross, the fissure in the Rock of Golgotha, the Tomb of Adam himself—all are here within a few yards' space." For the Englishman, said Thackeray, the Church of the Holy Sepulchre seemed to be "the least sacred place in Jerusalem."[35]

William Henry Bartlett, a well-known English painter and author whose *Walks about the City and Environs of Jerusalem* (1844) and *Jerusalem Revisited* (1854) remain classic guides to the city, was more tolerant. Though disheartened by the church, he still thought "of the thousands who have made this spot the centre of their hopes . . . have endured danger, and toil, and fever and want, to kneel with bursting heart upon the sacred rock; then, as regards the history of humanity, we feel this is holy ground."[36]

Twain ridiculed the relics so "conveniently" assembled under one roof and found the church "scandalized by trumpery, gewgaws, and tawdry ornamentation." Yet this great nonconformist for whom "nothing was holier than a joke," turned pious at Calvary: "And so I close my chapter on the Church of the Holy Sepulchre—the most sacred locality on earth . . . for a god died there . . . History is full of this old Church of the Holy Sepulchre—full of blood that was shed because of the respect and veneration in which men held the last resting place of the meek and lowly, the mild and gentle, Prince of Peace!"[37]

Nearly all Protestants expressed dismay at the "fanatical zeal" and "bigoted hatred" which existed among the different Christian sects at the Church of the Holy Sepulchre. "It is deplorable and melancholy to see how profaned are the precepts of Him who preached peace and good-will toward all men in this very spot; whose voice still lingers upon Zion and the Mount of Olives . . . Perhaps upon the whole face of the globe there could not be found a spot less holy than modern Jerusalem," wrote Ross Browne, author of *Yusef*.[38]

Travelers had nothing good to say about priests. With a monk as his guide, Eliot Warburton "impatiently traversed the squalid city." He ridiculed his "monkish cicerone" who showed him "where Lazarus lay, where the cock crowed . . . and even where the blessed Virgin used to wash her son's linen."[39] Thackeray derided the Armenian priests, "those Eastern quakers loom grave, and jolly, and sleek," with their "convent of St. James . . . ornamented by the most rich and hideous gifts ever devised by uncouth piety."[40] Even Lamartine found Catholic monks ignorant: "Not the slightest knowledge was displayed of sacred antiquity . . . or of the history of the places they inhabited." Monks know a few "popular and ridiculous traditions, which they transmit to each other without examination, and give to travellers as they have received them from the ignorance and credulity of the Christian Arabs of the country."[41] And Martineau, an Anglican, was offended by "the clergymen of the Church of England—getting leave from the Bishop of Jerusalem to carry wax candle in Passion Week in the processions in the Church of the Holy Sepulchre, and making obeisances to the priests, candles in hand."[42]

It appears that Catholics like Chateaubriand and Lamartine found little to object to in the decor or the rituals they encountered at the

Church of the Holy Sepulchre or at other Christian holy places, decor and rituals which dismayed or affronted most Protestants.

"The Muhammadan Yoke"

On the way to the Holy Land, all Westerners spent time in Egypt, Turkey, or Syria, where they encountered the realities of the Orient, dealt with Muslims, and voiced their nasty comments before arriving in Jerusalem. Yet Christians were indignant when they actually saw the Holy City—where Jesus died and rose again, where the Crusaders shed their blood—under the "Muhammadan yoke."

Stephens, the American early traveler, first mocked Empress Helena's fixing "the site of the Redeemer's burial place," but was still upset to see the Holy Sepulchre "in the hands of the infidels," with a "haughty Turk, with the air of a lord and master, standing sentinel at the door, and with his long mace beating and driving back the crowd of struggling Christians."[43] Prime, the Presbyterian minister, yearned for the day when the followers of Jesus would, "God grant it be soon!—sweep from the face of the earth every vistage of the religion of the Camel-driver from Mecca."[44] For Twain, "Rags, wretchedness, poverty, and dirt, those signs and symbols that indicate the presence of Muslim rule more surely than the crescent flag itself, abound . . . Jerusalem is mournful and dreary and lifeless. I would not desire to live here."[45]

Until the 1860s hardly any non-Muslims had been allowed to visit the shrines at the Haram al-Sharif—the Temple Mount—although some were able to view them from a house on the northern edge of the enclosure. In 1857 Prime received special permission to enter the Haram, but his comments were rather superficial.[46] Twain visited the Haram in 1867 and described it briefly: "I need not speak of the wonderful beauty and the exquisite grace and symmetry that have made this mosque [the Dome of the Rock] so celebrated—because I did not see them." His visit was too short, and by then he was "surfeited with sights."[47]

The Jewish Question

Christians' attitudes toward Jews and Jerusalem were far more complex than their feelings toward either Muslims or Christians of other sects. Contemporary Jews were seen as direct descendants of the ones blamed for the death of Jesus. Clinging blindly to their beliefs and refusing to convert, Jews were held responsible for the curse which hung over the Holy Land as well.

Most Christians went to visit the Jewish Quarter intrigued, perhaps, by Chateaubriand's exaggerated description: Between the "Temple [Mount] and the foot of Mount Sion, we entered the Jews' quarter . . . Here they appear covered with rags, seated in the dust of Sion, seeking the vermin which devoured them, and keeping their eyes fixed on the Temple."[48]

The holiest place for Jews is the Western Wall, a retaining wall of the Herodian platform on which the Second Temple stood. In 1827, when the Jewish philanthropist Sir Moses Montefiore and his wife, Judith, first visited Jerusalem, they went to see "the large stone [in the Western Wall], said to be the last relic of the Temple of Solomon. It is held in universal veneration, and is enclosed by a gate, the key of which is held by the Turks. The Jews . . . are obliged to pay every time it is unlocked for them." Friday was the day when it was customary for Jews "to view this only relic of former magnificence."[49]

Stephens, who called on the chief rabbi of Hebron and met with his Jerusalem counterpart, was sympathetic to the plight of the Jews. He visited "what they call a part of the wall of Solomon's temple . . . and I saw that day, as other travellers may still see every Friday in the year, all the Jews of Jerusalem clothed in their best raiment . . . under this hallowed wall, with the sacred volume in their hands, singing, in the language in which they were written, the Songs of Solomon and the Psalms of David. White-bearded old men and smooth-cheeked boys were leaning over the same book; and Jewish maidens, in their long white robes, were standing with their faces against the wall, and praying."[50]

Thackeray's was the standard description used throughout the 1800s: "On a Friday you may hear their wailings and lamentations for the lost glories of their city."[51] Non-Jews often mistook the daily prayers for special supplications said—or, according to them, wailed—only at what they called the Wailing Wall.[52]

The gathering of the Jews in their ancient land and their eventual conversion were seen by Christians as a necessary prelude to the Second Coming. Since 1820 the London Society for Promoting Christianity among the Jews worked diligently—if with little success—to convert Jerusalem's Jews. In the 1840s the Anglo-Prussian Bishopric was established in the Holy City, and Christ Church, the first Protestant church in the Ottoman Empire, was consecrated in 1849.

Not all Christians supported the efforts to convert the Jews. When Harriet Martineau saw the rising walls of Christ Church, she doubted "whether there will ever be Jewish converts enough to fill it," and added that those "who are intimate with the minds of educated and conscientious Jews are aware that such cannot be converted to Christianity . . . that there can be, to them, no reason why they should change."[53]

In his journal, Melville mentioned efforts by English and American missionaries "combining Agriculture & Religion . . . based upon the impression . . . that the time for the prophetic return of the Jews to Judea is at hand, and therefore the way must be prepared for them by Christians, both in settling them right in their faith & their farming." Yet at one such attempt not "a single Jew was converted either to Christianity or Agriculture." He noted that Montefiore, the "Croesus, visited Palestine last year [and] bought a large tract of the hill of Gihon . . . The idea of making farmers of Jews is vain. In the first place, Judea is a desert with few exceptions. In the second place, the Jews hate farming."[54]

Edward Lear also doubted that Jews would convert in Jerusalem, "at the very centre of that country they have been so long attached to." Protestants, he said, were "professing a better & simpler form of Christ's religion than their fellow Xtians—yet scandalizing the whole community by their monstrous quarrels: their Consuls & Bishops regarding each other with hatred . . . And this forsooth at a place of example for Turks & Jews . . . By Heaven!—if I wished to prevent a Turk, Hebrew, or Heathen from turning Christian, I would send him to Jerusalem!"[55]

Encountering Jews living and praying in Jerusalem stirred up old prejudices—modern Jews were identified with their biblical ancestors, blamed for the death of Jesus, resented for refusing to convert. Chateaubriand, for example, marveled at the Jews, still in Jerusalem after they had witnessed seventeen destructions of the city, still awaiting "a king who will deliver them," continuing their "deplorable infatuation."[56] Englishman Alexander William Kinglake, whose *Eöthen* was to become a Victorian classic, "could not help looking upon the Jews of Jerusalem as being in some sort the representatives, if not the actual descendants, of the men who crucified our Saviour."[57] Twain echoed the sentiment: "They say that the long-nosed, lanky, dyspeptic-looking body-snatchers, with the indescribable hats on and the long curl dangling down in front of each ear, are the old, familiar, self-righteous Pharisees we read of in the Scriptures. Verily, they look it."[58] Thackeray, after gazing upon the city from the Mount of Olives—"where the great yearning heart of the Saviour interceded for all our race; and whence the bigots and traitors of his day led Him away to kill him!"—saw a fellow boat passenger, an "old Polish Patriarch, venerable in filth, stalking among the stinking ruins of the Jewish quarter . . . in company of some red-bearded co-religionists, smartly attired in Eastern raiment; but their voice was the voice of the Jews of Berlin, and of course as we passed they were talking about so many hundert thaler [hundred thalers, German coins]. You may track one of the people, and be sure to hear mention of that silver calf that they worship."

For Thackeray the "unspeakably ghastly" landscape "seems quite adapted to the events which are recorded in the Hebrew histories . . . In the centre of this history of crime rises up the Great Murder of all."[59]

Christians saw the desolate state of the country as punishment, wrote Howard Mumford Jones: "That Palestine once flowed with milk and honey was readily believed, and the legend persists that, in losing this admirable economic abundance, Palestine, after the Crucifixion, labored under a special vengeance from the Almighty."[60] As a result of Ottoman rule, opined Warburton, the land once fertile became barren as the desert because the "dominion of the Porte is the form which the Curse denounced against Israel and his Land assumes at present."[61] Upon leaving the country Twain reflected: "Palestine is desolate and unlovely, And why should it be otherwise? Can the *curse* of the Deity beautify a land?"[62]

A Tale of Two Cities: Disraeli's and Melville's Jerusalem

Nowhere in nineteenth-century literature is there a greater contrast than between the Jerusalem of Benjamin Disraeli and that of Herman

Melville, as reflected in their private papers and in their published works. Such divergent attitudes merit a closer inspection.

Disraeli, the twenty-five-year-old novelist and future statesman, went on a Grand Tour to shake off a lingering depression, as well as to escape his creditors and collect material for future novels. His one-week stay in Jerusalem, in January 1831, had a profound and positive effect on his writing and his politics. Despite his conversion, he remained proud of his Jewish heritage, and his visit to the Holy City reinforced his sense of pride and strengthened his self-esteem.

In *Contarini Fleming* (1832), Disraeli lovingly describes contemporary Jerusalem from the Mount of Olives, his account markedly different from most others: "I beheld a city entirely surrounded by . . . an old feudal wall . . . In the front, was a magnificent mosque, with beautiful gardens, and many light and lofty gates of triumph; a variety of domes and towers rose in all directions from the buildings of bright stone. I was thunderstruck. I saw before me apparently a gorgeous city . . . Except Athens, I had never witnessed any scene more essentially impressive. I will not place this spectacle below the city of Minerva. Athens and the Holy City in their glory must have been the finest representations of the Beautiful and the Sublime."[63]

The Wondrous Tale of Alroy (1833) is known as "the first Jewish novel," written by a former Jew on a Jewish theme. It was first conceived by Disraeli in 1829, when England's Jews attempted to gain emancipation, and was loosely based on the story of a twelfth-century Jewish leader of a messianic movement in Kurdistan who dreamed of guiding his people back to Jerusalem. "The Prince of the Captivity [Alroy] at length beheld the lost capital of his fathers . . . garrisoned by the puissant warriors of Christendom, and threatened by the innumerable armies of the Crescent for the prize which he, a lonely wanderer, had crossed the desert to rescue."[64] Robert Blake, the author of *Disraeli*—a magisterial biography—wondered: Did Disraeli "half believe, or dream, that he might, like Alroy, be the man himself?"[65]

Tancred (1847) was set in the present. Young Tancred, the son of the Duke of Bellamont, was full of religious doubts and decided to go on pilgrimage and look for answers at the tomb of the Redeemer: "What is DUTY, and what is FAITH? What ought I to DO, and what ought I to BELIEVE?"[66] Once in the Holy City, Tancred fell in love with Eva, a beautiful Jerusalemite, the embodiment of Judaism. He wanted her to acknowledge his "Lord and Master" and be guided by the Christian Church.

"'Which?' inquires the lady; 'there are so many in Jerusalem.'"[67] Echoing Disraeli's sentiments, she admonished: "We agree that half Christendom worships a Jewess, and the other half a Jew. Now let me ask you one more question. Which do you think should be the superior race, the worshipped or the worshippers?"[68] The plot deteriorated into "an incoherent quasi-mystical oriental farrago"[69] and ended abruptly—the romance unresolved—with the arrival of the Bellamonts in Jerusalem. Yet Tancred's is a cheerful Jerusalem: "It was a delicious morn, wonderfully clear, and soft, and fresh. It seemed a happy and thriving city, that forlorn Jerusalem . . . Nature was fair, and the sense of existence was delightful."[70]

Tancred, said Disraeli's biographer Sarah Bradford, "evolved into an exposition of the debt of gratitude which European civilization, and the English Church in particular, owed to the Jewish people as the founders of their religious faith." Disraeli, "nervous, outwardly flashy, inwardly unsure of himself," was transformed into a young man "with enough inner confidence to face the world of fashion and politics." It was "the mystical joy of visiting the land of his forefathers and meditating on Jerusalem" which had the longest and most profound influence on him.[71]

Unlike the still unformed Disraeli, Melville was thirty-seven years old when he embarked on a six-month tour of Europe and the East, having published *Moby Dick* five years earlier. Working hard to support his growing family, he was suffering from bad eyesight and rheumatism, and it was hoped that the trip would restore his failing health and rescue his spirits "from a mood of profound skepticism, disillusion, and gloom."[72] Nearly twenty years later, Melville published *Clarel*, a massive narrative verse of 150 cantos set in Jerusalem and environs. He called it "a metrical affair, a pilgrimage or what not, of several thousand lines, eminently adapted for unpopularity."[73]

In January 1857, after landing in Jaffa and spending a sleepless night in Ramla, Melville proceeded "in saddle for Jerusalem . . . Hot and wearisome ride over the arid hills.—Got to Jerusalem about 2 p.m."[74] Melville did not comment on the approach to the city, possibly because he could not see it from afar. After a walk later that afternoon, he wrote in his journal that his eyes were "so affected by the long days ride in the glare of the light of arid hills, had to come back to hotel."[75] For a couple of days he was "roaming over the hills," then left to tour the Jordan, the Dead Sea, the Monastery of Mar Saba, and Bethlehem, sites which with Jerusalem were to form the skeleton for *Clarel*.[76]

Clarel, a young American divinity student, went to the Holy Land in search of answers to his doubts, like Disraeli's Tancred. (Disraeli was one of Melville's favorite authors.) Once in Jerusalem, he fell in love with Ruth, the daughter of an American Christian who immigrated to Palestine and an American Jewish woman. After Ruth's father was killed by Arab marauders, Clarel went on a pilgrimage with several acquaintances he had met in Jerusalem, "representative Men of the Contemporary Western world."[77] On his return he chanced upon a Jewish funeral—the funeral of Ruth and her mother. Bewildered, Clarel stayed in Jerusalem, his own future far from certain.

Melville's Jerusalem was full of lepers, dung heaps, and smelly rubbish, a "city besieged by an army of the dead.—cemeteries all around."[78] In *Clarel* he wrote:

> Like the ice-bastions around the Pole,
> Thy blank, blank towers, Jerusalem! (I.i.60)

Outside the Church of the Holy Sepulchre, he noted in his journal, "lies in open exposure an accumulation of the last & least nameable filth of a barbarous city." Inside, "wedged & half-dazzled, you stare for a moment on the ineloquence of the bedizened slab, and glad to come out . . . All is glitter & nothing is gold. A sickening cheat."[79] No wonder Clarel could not find peace there, as he listened to "the rival liturgies":

> If little of the words he knew,
> Might Clarel's fancy forge a clue?
> A malediction seemed each strain—
> Himself the mark: O heart profane,
> O pilgrim-infidel, begone! (I.vi.19) . . .
> We know thee, thou there standing mute.
> Out, Out—begone! (I.vi.26)

Clarel could not even pray. "Contentions for each Holy Place . . . Was feud the heritage He left?" (I.vi.42). When asked: "A pilgrim art thou?

pilgrim thou?" Clarel answered: "I am a traveler—no more" (I.ix.20, I.ix.28). This, most likely, is how Melville saw himself.

Clarel's Jerusalem is "no theater of miracles," wrote Walter Bezanson. "This Holy City is not the City of God, not even the City of Man . . . It is a Fallen City. It is the *Città Dolente,* the City of Dis."[80] Like Clarel, the gloomy Melville found no answers in the Holy City. His "experiences at the pyramids and around Jerusalem and the Dead Sea represent extreme depth of mental and spiritual depression, but that bleak tone is pervasively present throughout the journal."[81]

Different Visions of Jerusalem

How to reconcile Disraeli's, Melville's, and all the other visions of Jerusalem? Perhaps the answer lies in Ross Browne's remark at the Sea of Galilee, that "charm is greatly heightened by the predisposition to be enchanted in the eye of the beholder."[82] Because of religious prejudices, the very same sights evoked different responses among Jews, Catholics, and Protestants. In addition, individual circumstances which had little to do with the city often colored the visitor's outlook.

Among all the authors mentioned above, for example, the word "clean" is only mentioned twice in the same breath as Jerusalem: once by Lady Judith Montefiore, who, after passing through the bazaar "entered the Jewish quarter . . . which appeared the cleanest of any we had traversed,"[83] and again by Disraeli's hero, Contarini, who found "the interior of Jerusalem . . . hilly and clean."[84] Lady Montefiore was Jewish, Disraeli a convert to Christianity still proud of his Jewish origins.

Lamartine, a Catholic for whom "the radiant majesty of the East, its strange characters and romantic hues cover up unsavory reality,"[85] did not find Jerusalem "as it has been represented, an unshapely confused mass of ruins and ashes . . . [but] a city shining in light and color." It seemed waiting to rise "in dazzling glory from its seventeen successive ruins, and to be transformed into the New Jerusalem which is to come out of the blossom of the desert, radiant with brightness."[86] The enthusiasm of Prime, the Presbyterian minister, was typical of those Christians—Protestants or Catholics—who were elated just to walk "in the footsteps of Jesus." But Prime was also a man of means who traveled with his wife in relative luxury, and the combination of piety and comfort may account for his lyrical descriptions of Jerusalem.

Melville's negative reactions were largely the result of personal difficulties. He began his trip in "a morbid state of mind," as his friend Nathaniel Hawthorne wrote: "Melville . . . will never rest until he gets hold of a definite belief . . . He can neither believe, nor be comfortable in his unbelief."[87] Melville did not find "definite belief" during his week in Jerusalem and the desert: "No country will more quickly dissipate romantic expectations than Palestine—particularly Jerusalem. To some the disappointment is heart sickening."[88]

Twain had a different problem. His vitriolic attacks on the land and its people—Jews, Arabs, and Christians alike—went well beyond his specialty of exposing "sacred cows." In the Holy Land his humor turned sour, his prose inflated, his plagiarism knew no bounds.[89] Twain was in trouble, since his boat fare had been paid in advance by San Francisco's *Daily Alta California* in return for fifty letters he was to send back from the Grand Tour; upon reaching Alexandria, he discovered that fourteen of his letters from Europe (mostly from Italy) had never arrived. He had to stretch his Palestine notes, meant for four letters, into eighteen (or 40,000 words), which may account for his verbose and bitter prose.[90]

Harriet Martineau typified those who had no ax to grind. She found "a strange charm in the mere streets, from the picturesque characters of the walls and archways. The old walls of yellow stone are so beautifully tufted with weeds, that one longs to paint every angle and projection . . . And the shadowy archways, where the vaulted roofs intersect each other, till they are lost in a dazzle of the sunshine beyond, are like a noble dream."[91]

Another phenomenon related to the East is the fact that there are almost no images which portray the squalor—dirt, poverty, disease—which almost all travelers commented upon.[92] This is particularly true of Jerusalem, which, with a few exceptions, is depicted as romantic and serene by the many painters and photographers who flocked to the city, only to be denounced by the very same artists in their letters and diaries. Lear provides but one example. Commissioned by Lady Waldgrave, he painted "Jerusalem from the Mount of Olives," an enchanting view of a walled city afloat in golden sunlight against an azure sky and purple-hued hills, complete with shepherds and goats straight out of the Bible (see Plate 4). Yet in a letter to his patroness he moaned: "O my nose! o my eyes! o my feet! how you all suffered in that vile place!—For let me tell you, physically Jerusalem is the foulest & odiousest place on earth . . . & your memories of its interior are but horrid dreams of squalor & filth—clamour and uneasiness,— hatred & malice & all uncharitableness."[93]

It is interesting to compare the sharp contrast between Twain's remark, "I had only one pleasant reminiscence of this Palestine excursion—time I had the cholera in Damascus,"[94] and Disraeli's letter to his sister Sarah about his stay in Jerusalem: "I could write half a doz. sheets on this week, the most delightful of all our travels . . . Weather delicious—mild summer heat—made an immense sensation—received visits from the Vicar General of the Pope, the Spanish prior, etc. Never more delighted in my life."[95] Or compare Disraeli's terminology for Jerusalem—gorgeous, delightful, delicious—with Melville's—ghastly, melancholy, diabolical, lamentable, and barbarous.

To understand the different portraits, we need to consider not only the expectations and disillusionments, the hardships of the journey and religious prejudices. The reactions to the Holy City—far more intense than reactions to other places—often mirrored the emotions or conflicts within each writer. It was the particular "emotional baggage" carried by every individual who arrived that, more than anything else, colored that person's view of Jerusalem. Recalling that the average stay in Jerusalem was four to five days, it seems appropriate to quote Arthur P. Stanley, dean of Westminster and professor of ecclesiastical history at Oxford, who first visited the Holy City in 1852 and returned ten years later, accompanying the Prince of Wales: "Jerusalem is one of the few places of which the first impression is not the best."[96]

In 1860, when its population reached 18,000, double what it was at the beginning of the century, Jerusalem began to break out of the Old City walls.[97] In order to alleviate overcrowding in the Jewish Quarter (where the numbers increased from 2,250 to 8,000), numerous Jewish neighborhoods were established west and northwest of the Old City. The competition among foreign powers and their churches for the hearts and minds of Jerusalem's non-Muslim citizenry, and the special privileges, or capitulations, granted to the European powers by the Turks after the Crimean War, brought about major building

Figure 15. Jaffa Gate, exterior, ca. 1890.

activities, as consulates, schools, hospitals, and hospices were erected inside and outside the Old City. Jews and Christians alike had to purchase land from the Muslims who, in turn, began their own construction outside the Herod and Damascus Gates. Financial, commercial, postal, and municipal services opened, and new hotels, paved roads, and a railway all made for a better quality of life for residents and visitors alike. By the time Mark Twain arrived in Jerusalem in 1867, the nature of travel was changing as well. Visits to the Holy Land were no longer considered exotic, and Western markets were nearly saturated with travelogues. Reports by writers who followed Twain were neither as critical of the city nor as eagerly read as were earlier travel accounts.

Modernity had arrived in Jerusalem by the end of the nineteenth century, as the city the psalmist called "the joy of the whole earth" was about to enter a new era of challenges and conflicts as yet unresolved.

Depictions in Modern Hebrew Literature 12

DAN MIRON

Jerusalem pervades the so-called new, or modern, Hebrew literature of the past two centuries. Writers committed to a vision of a postrabbinic, humanistic Jewish culture and to the aesthetic ideals of contemporary European belles lettres have made the city all but ubiquitous, especially since the rise of Zionism in the last two decades of the nineteenth century. Jerusalem-Zion looms large as an emotional focus, a thematic center, or a significant descriptive backdrop in hundreds of Hebrew poems, dramas, novels, short stories, and essays. The exotic capital of ancient biblical Israel as well as the focus of the modern Zionist endeavor, Jerusalem is the Holy City of faith and ritual, temple and prophet, and also the emblem of Jewish sovereignty and worldly, political normality. It is the representative of Judaism as a civilization vis-à-vis other civilizations (hence such characteristic titles as *Rome and Jerusalem, Tyre and Jerusalem*) as well as a universal point of meeting for a variety of faiths, philosophies, and peoples.

In many literary works, Jerusalem functions primarily as a receptacle for swelling emotions, a lyrical focal point of intense national sentiment. In others, it is present as pictorial, epic space that calls for detailed mimesis. Often Jerusalem appears as a tragic memory of national and cosmic devastation; it is the core of the myth of *hurban* (destruction), all but a figment of a tearful imagination. Just as often, however, the city emerges as a harsh and blunt reality, an oppressive physical, social, and political entity on which all illusions are bound to founder. It suggests, alternatively, happiness and tragedy, harmony and discord, peace and war, health and sickness, even insanity, divine grace, and implacable divine wrath. In short, Jerusalem has become in modern Hebrew literature, and particularly in what has been written in the past hundred years, a core element of the Jewish psyche, the hub of its reality and the center of its dreams and visions.

It is easy to see why and how the ubiquity of literary Jerusalem was unavoidable. The city is situated at the very center of each of the various intellectual, ideological, and mythopoeic frameworks that most Hebrew writers shared and employed at one point or another during the past two centuries. The first and most important of these is the traditional Jewish myth of the covenant (symbolized by the ideal proximity to God through His temple), sin, punishment, destruction, and exile, and a future eschatological moment of return and reinstatement. Jerusalem is at the heart of this myth, which informs and controls the traditional Jewish sense of time and space, the traditional sense of being Jewish within a given historical and spatial continuum. It was there, on Mount Moriah, that the original act of Jewish faith, which initiated the covenant—Abraham's readiness to follow God's command and sacrifice his beloved son—took place. There the covenant reached its supreme moment of fulfillment and closeness to God with the founding of the Davidic kingdom and the building of the Temple by Solomon. The destruction of the city and of both the First and Second Temples on the Ninth of Ab—the first by the Chaldeans and the second by the Romans—indicated not only the downfall of the Jewish people but also a cosmic crisis caused by the separation between God and His chosen people. No holocaust in the history of the world could have been more tragic and destructive than the conflagration that consumed God's dwelling place on earth, His Temple in Jerusalem. Even after that holocaust, Jerusalem remained "the gate of heaven," that spot on earth where the earthly transcends itself and merges with the divine. For all these reasons, Jerusalem was bound to become the center of the great messianic drama, the site of the universal ingathering of the Jews, of the resurrection of the dead and the end of history as we know it.

Every Jewish boy born and raised in a traditional Jewish community imbibed this myth with his mother's milk. It informed the daily prayers he recited, the holiday rituals and the existential rites of passage, and his notions of life and death, of "now" and "then," of joy

PLATE 1. View of Jerusalem by A. M. Mallet, Frankfurt-am-Main, 1684–85. An interplay between
the realistic and apocalyptic visions of the city, which seems to be descending from the sky, while
a distant group of people gesticulates in adoration. (See Chapter 13.)

PLATE 2. The Madaba map *(detail shown here)*, in a Byzantine floor mosaic at the Church of Madaba, Jordan, was discovered in 1881 and is the earliest extant map of Jerusalem. It depicts the Holy Land with a walled Jerusalem in the center. Within the city, the map focuses on the Holy Sepulchre *(center front)*. It also shows the new colonnaded *cardo*, which begins at Damascus Gate, on the left, still known in Arabic as Bab al-Amud, Gate of the Column. The churches in the city are all marked in red. (See Chapter 16.)

PLATE 3. King David and his harp (detail), from a floor mosaic in a Gaza synagogue, ca. 508 CE, discovered in 1966 by the Egyptian Department of Antiquities. The face and one hand of David were destroyed a year later. The image was restored with the help of a 1966 photograph. The Hebrew inscription reads "David."

PLATE 4. Jerusalem from Mount of Olives, by Edward Lear (1858–59). Disappointed by the backwardness of the city, like so many other nineteenth-century Western visitors, Lear complained to the patroness who commissioned the painting that "physically Jerusalem is the foulest & odiousest place on earth." Yet he painted an enchanting walled city afloat in golden sunlight, with shepherds and goats straight out of the Bible. (See Chapter 11.)

PLATE 5. The *maiestas* from the Codex Amiatinus, now in the Laurentian Library, Florence, depicts a seated Christ flanked by two angels inside linear concentric circles. Pairs of evangelists and their symbols occupy the space between the circles and the frame. (See Chapter 13.)

PLATE 6. Jerusalem (?) shown to the Prophet Muhammad (detail). Dating to the first half of the fourteenth century, this Persian painting, now at the Topkapi Serai Museum in Istanbul, depicts the Prophet Muhammad on a rug in front of two personages. The detail here shows a flying angel bringing a city to the Prophet, probably Jerusalem. Seen as an idealized city, it contains mighty walls, fancy gates, and large sanctuaries set against a mountainous background. (See Chapter 14.)

PLATE 7. Dome of the Rock. The interior view looking west from the kibla door reveals the monument's marble paneled walls and rich mosaics. (See Chapter 17.)

PLATE 8. *Jerusalem*, by Nabil
Anani. In this 1984 painting,
the city is in a circle formed by
an outer row of people and an
inner row of buildings. Small
figures observe it from below.
The composition recalls medieval Apocalypse manuscripts.
(See Chapter 13.)

PLATE 9. *Jerusalem, the Holy City and Its Surroundings.* This 1704 painting, by an anonymous Greek artist within the Ottoman Empire, is now at the Musée du Château de Saumur. Representing holy sites from the Transfiguration *(on the left)* to Bethlehem and the cave of the Nativity *(on the right),* the city is dominated by the Holy Sepulchre complex. Towers and gates appear at regular intervals in the zigzagging, massive wall. (See Chapter 14.)

PLATE 10. A *ketubbah* (marriage contract) from Padua, 1732. A legal document protecting the rights of the woman, the text of the *ketubbah* has remained constant since the time of Maimonides. It is often surrounded by calligraphy and graphics, which in this Italian version include a depiction of the bride and groom, the zodiac signs, and various biblical scenes. Above the arch is a stylized Jerusalem with the Temple Mount in the center; the inscription reads "Mountains are about Jerusalem." (See Chapter 15.)

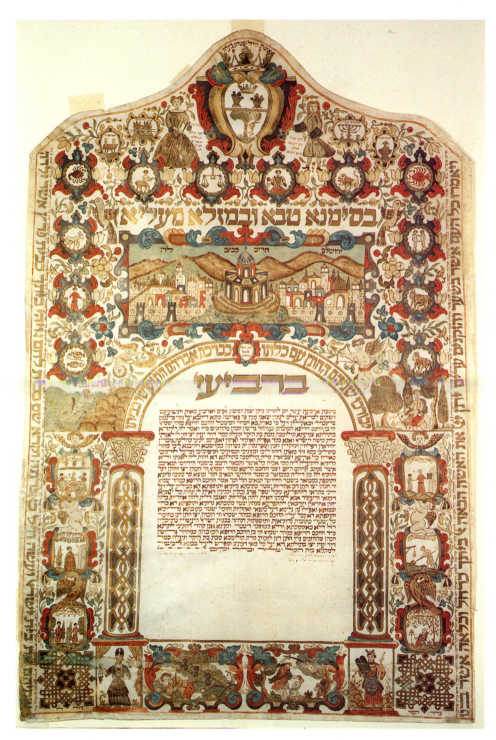

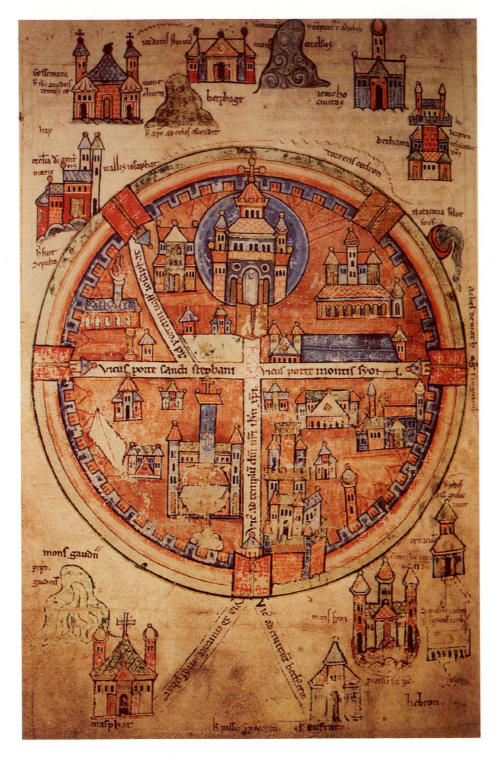

PLATE 11. The Uppsala manuscript map. In this twelfth-century map, one of fourteen extant Crusader maps, the city is surrounded by a circular wall. The main streets, the *cardo* and the *decumanus*, form a cross. In the foreground are the Church of the Holy Sepulchre *(left)* and the Citadel *(right)*. At the top is the Dome of the Rock—capped by a cross—which the Crusaders turned into a church they called Templum Salomonis. (See Chapter 16.)

and sorrow. Shalom Yaacov Abramovitsh (Mendele Mocher Sefarim), the prominent Hebrew and Yiddish novelist of the nineteenth century, described the mental universe of one of his protagonists in his childhood as being centered around the only two "real" places in an otherwise chaotic, demonic, and uninhabitable space: the child's own tiny Ukrainian hometown and Jerusalem, the latter envisioned as hovering in the air, above the earth, teeming with corpses, immune to corruption, and poised for resurrection.[1] One can safely assume that similar images filled the minds of many children born and raised in the shtetl, including, up until sixty or seventy years ago, the minds of those who were to become Hebrew writers. True, these children, like the protagonist of Abramovitsh, outgrew the mental world of their native, traditional society and adopted concepts and attitudes alien to it. However, no matter how far one distances oneself from a myth as potent and formative as the traditional Jerusalem myth, one can hardly eradicate it entirely, least of all could those writers whose creative imagination was rooted in their childhood fantasies. Hebrew writers of the nineteenth century, and at least of the first third of the twentieth, carried within themselves the mythological Jerusalem of the Bible, the Midrash, Kabbalah, and Jewish folklore.

The few outstanding writers of that period in whose work Jerusalem did *not* play an important role can be understood not as indicators of the marginalization and eventual obliteration of the child's image but rather as the result of hypersensitivity to its overwhelming and often unsettling suggestion. Such seems to be the case, for instance, for Chaim Nachman Bialik, the "national" Hebrew poet and the chief exponent of the so-called Hebrew Renaissance of the turn of the twentieth century. In all but one of his canonic poems, Bialik avoids the theme or the presence of Jerusalem. At the beginning of his career, in the 1890s, this avoidance might have had to do with his devastating critique of the currently popular "Love of Zion" poetry, in which Jerusalem was endlessly rhapsodized; as Bialik matured, however, his youthful recoil from the cloying sentimental hyperbole of Love of Zion gave way to other reasons, as indicated by the one significant exception in his work—the three opening chapters of Bialik's grand symbolist prose poem, *The Scroll of Fire* (1905). The poem focuses on an awesome description of the destruction of Jerusalem and the Temple by the Romans. Never before in modern Hebrew literature had

that chapter of the Jerusalem narrative found more tragic and poignant expression—nor has it since. The destruction is interpreted not as
the act of the enemy but rather as the result of the malevolent will of
a horrific God, a terrible divine terminator who, as much as He
Himself is devastated and undermined by the holocaust, is maliciously
keen on completing His project of destruction to the bitter end.
Obviously, in his mind, Bialik connected the downfall of Jerusalem
with an image of an unbearably harsh superego, an introject he could
barely encounter. The poet himself said that the holocaust scenes in
The Scroll of Fire were born out of a most frightening impression of a
fire he witnessed at the age of seven: "I thought half of the world, if
not the entire world, was being consumed."[2] The connection between
the conflagration and the midrashic and folkloric images of Jerusalem
in its death throes was most probably made right then and there, in
the mind of a seven-year-old who believed that God had decided to
destroy the whole world—including himself, the awestruck witness.
Jerusalem, it seems, was ever after tied in the poet's mind to images
of pain, fear, and desolation that were to find poetic expression, if at
all, via cryptic, indirect symbolic representations.[3] Jerusalem is, on the
whole, nonpresent in Bialik's poetry, not because its traditional myth
had become insignificant, but rather because it harbored too much
ominous significance.

However, the centrality of Jerusalem does not depend solely on
the religious tradition. The founding fathers of the "new" Hebrew
literature also turned to Jerusalem for purposes that seem to contradict at least some aspects of this tradition. They conceived of themselves not only as the harbingers of a new Hebraic culture but also as
the revivers of the ancient culture of biblical times. Like the artists and
thinkers of the European Renaissance, they took upon themselves the
task of bringing back to life an enlightened antiquity that needed to
be dug up from beneath the cumbersome debris of medievalism.
Jerusalem was to them what Athens in its days of glory had been to
the dabblers in classical Hellenism. They wanted to reinvent the world
of the Bible, with its "pristine" Hebrew language, its poetry and
stories, its colorful landscapes, and its allegedly "pure" religious feeling, untempered by rabbinic casuistry. As they set out to develop
biblical literature from the point at which it had ostensibly been cut
short by the bitter experience of exile and the concomitant advent of

the halachic tradition, they tried to become spiritual citizens of old Jerusalem. Time and again throughout the poetry and prose of the nineteenth century, we see them "dreaming" their way to that much sought-after haven, waking to its idyllic reality in its romantic streets and squares or in its elegant palaces and awe-inspiring Temple. There they mingle with the colorful crowd of free, Hebrew-speaking people and encounter the prophet Isaiah declaiming his sublime and stirring speeches as well as the king with his entourage, the priest in his shimmering, jewel-studded cloak, brave Israelite soldiers on horseback and on foot, poets, dignitaries, musicians, fair maidens, and handsome romantic youths.

Above all else, the "new" Hebrew writers craved the original sound of Hebrew as it was used in speech, song, and narrative. For instance, the early nineteenth-century poet Adam ha-Kohen (D. B. Lebensohn) falls asleep on the eve of Ninth of Ab and wakes up to the strains of the sweet Hebrew of antiquity:

> Thus desolate I sit until sleep takes over
> And my daytime thoughts turn into a dream
> Here I stand on Mount Moriah
> Watching with wonder, the ruins of the Holy Temple . . .
> I said to myself: "If anywhere, here I shall find her [the
>   "pure" Hebrew language]
> For this is her homeland and I shall see her at her best . . .
> We heard—in Hebrew—the songs of a palace,
> Sweet songs, songs of glory.
> Here Hebrew is crystal clear
> One can experience its pristine ancient taste."[4]

But the linguistic cult clearly points to an nonlinguistic desideratum: Jewish "normality"—that is, a Jewish life of freedom in both the political and the personal sense, a life in which a Hebrew poet can freely and naturally sing of the pleasures of living and of the beauty of nature as much as a Jewish young man can freely and naturally fall in love with a young woman or mount his horse and set out in the full bloom of youth to fight for his country. All of this freedom is incorporated into the image of the biblical Jerusalem conveyed, for example, in the first Hebrew novel, Abraham Mapu's *The Love of Zion* (1853), a historical romance of young lovers, set in the time of the kings

Ahaz and Hezekiah. The novel owes much of its extraordinary popularity with nineteenth-century and even early twentieth-century Hebrew readers to its vivid portrayal of Jerusalem as a free, bustling city in which the populace, accustomed to the pomp of the royal court and the splendid rituals of a functioning temple, vigorously and pleasurably goes about the business of daily existence. All this in the early and middle decades of the nineteenth century, when Hebrew literature, still under the influence of the Jewish Enlightenment movement (the Haskalah) was as yet very far from exploring and bringing out the political and ideological underpinnings of such visions of a linguistically and aesthetically idealized Jerusalem.

With Zionism emerging toward the end of the century and becoming for nearly a century the most influential ideological factor in the development of modern Hebrew literature, the stature of Jerusalem grew. The last two decades of the nineteenth century came to be known, in the history of Hebrew literature, as the Love of Zion period. Of course the concept of Zion covered not just Jerusalem but the Land of Israel as a whole. Still, Jerusalem dominated it. At first it evoked a special kind of troubadour-like love poetry characterized by its sentimentality and lilting choric quality. This was the poetry that Bialik rejected. Then, slowly, as the Zionist endeavor transcended mere sentiment and ideological abstraction, Hebrew writers arriving in Palestine in the beginning of the twentieth century flocked to Jerusalem and recorded in poems and stories their mood as they saw the city of their dreams for the first time. Positioning themselves at various vantage points, such as at the summit of Mount Scopus or on the road facing the city wall near Jaffa Gate and the so-called Tower of David, they knelt or stood, entranced, gazing at the medieval beauty of domes and towers, sharp Gothic rooftops and swaying palm trees through misty, tear-filled eyes. Thus, for instance, Yitskhak Kummer, the protagonist of Shmuel Yoseph Agnon's novel *Yesteryear*, arriving in Jerusalem in 1910, first viewed the walled city at sunset as he was carried in a carriage from the small Ottoman train station situated at the opening of a valley, Emek Rephaim, from whence this view was actually not immediately visible:

> He looked and his heart started beating like the beating of one's heart
> as one approaches one's destination—suddenly the wall of Jerusalem

was revealed to him, laced with red fire, plaited with gold, surrounded by gray clouds blended with blue ones etching and carving patterns in green gold and in the choicest of silvers and in burnished brass and purple tin. Yitskhak raised himself, wanting to say something, but his tongue was silent in his mouth as if it were held down by a silent song. So he lowered himself down in a squatting dance.[5]

The view, with its array of psychedelic, throbbing patterns of color, points to the level and intensity of excitement that seeing Jerusalem for the first time generated. Of course, what awaited the ecstatic viewers behind the dazzling first sight was a shocking encounter with the real contemporary Jerusalem. For Agnon's Kummer, for instance, this encounter would eventually mean a horrible, unspeakably obscene death.

The Demystification of Jerusalem

At this point, rather than proceed with what is starting to look like a unified, even dramatic narrative, I am compelled to raise a question that should, perhaps, have been raised earlier: With Jerusalem in the new Hebrew literature being as pervasive as the joint forces of religious tradition, the *maskilic* quest for Hebraic origins, and Zionism dictate, what kind of a statement or comment can the literary scholar make? At first glance, it seems that only two forums, diametrically opposed, are available: a bulky literary-historical monograph based on an extensive bibliography, focusing on various significant configurations of Jerusalem in as many literary works as possible, or a very short general text that would sum up the self-evident with the help of a few striking illustrations. The former, progressing along a slow developmental trail of periodization would offer analyses of as many literary "Jerusalems" as one would dare to call to the reader's attention. The latter would try to bestow as much elegance as one could muster on well-known, hackneyed generalizations, such as: Jerusalem represents the continuity of Jewish historical existence, the point in time at which the past meets the future and the point in space at which a stark and forbidding desert meets with the architecture of three civilizations; Jerusalem is the point on the scale of transcendence at which matter is rarefied into spirit or, conversely, spirit is reified into matter—hence its duality as both "heavenly" and "earthly"; and so on. But what should the scholar do if he or she deems the first of these impracticable and the other intellectually unacceptable? How should one go about looking for a third option?

One might start by taking into account the idea that Jerusalem, as much as it may have been idealized or even idolized by Hebrew writers, aroused in some—among them, writers of considerable prominence—very strong resentment. These writers frequently comment in a more or less cynical vein on the low—sometimes very low—artistic quality of much of the poetry and prose focusing on Jerusalem. As has been noted, Bialik viscerally loathed the "Mother Zion" love poetry written in the 1880s and 1890s, despite the fact that he himself wrote such poems in the days of his poetic apprenticeship. For years, in letters to his editor and to his literary friends, he sarcastically exposed the emotional and artistic emptiness of such poems. Yoseph Chaim Brenner, writing in the Land of Israel at the end of the first and throughout the second decade of the twentieth century, parodied and ridiculed the elevated treatment of the theme of Jerusalem in Hebrew prose fiction. In his novels, or rather antinovels as he presented them, the typical Jerusalem romance, stories about "the loves of the innocent and modest daughters of Zion and Jerusalem,"[6] will not be found. In the 1930s, the young, up-and-coming poet Nathan Alterman commented on the inundation of poems about Jerusalem that were mediocre, if not entirely worthless. Focusing on Jerusalem, Alterman maintained, was a poet's prescription for failure, precisely because the task seemed so easy: "Every poet knows the recipe: one-third prayer, one-third tears, one-quarter landscape, closure, and the poem is ready . . . Inscribe the title: Jerusalem!"[7] In another satirical lyric in which he deliberately catalogues empty Zionist phraseology and dead rhyme, Alterman placed Jerusalem at the very center of the deadliest of all Hebrew rhyming triads: *mayim* (water), *Yerushalayim* (Jerusalem), and *shamayim* (sky, heavens). To say that Jerusalem was "fair" or beautiful, Alterman hinted, was about as perceptive and original as saying that the sea was "blue" or that the sky at sunrise was full of light.[8]

However, this aesthetic or poetic critique was often a mere stratagem for indirectly conveying anti-Jerusalem messages that were far more radical and destructive. After all, mediocre and bad poems and stories were written on all popular topics and, on the other hand, quite a few of those centered on Jerusalem were, by all accounts, excellent. Within the anti-Jerusalem literary polemic, one can discern two separate, mutually independent, evolving "traditions." The first is the tradition of blunt, sometimes brutal, demystification. Writers who adhered to this tradition intentionally, almost gleefully, tore to pieces the soft, diaphanous haze that was characteristic of idealized descriptions of Jerusalem and pointed unabashedly to the provincialism, crudeness, stagnation, and social alienation that, they believed, were the hallmarks of the "true" Jerusalem of their times—a small uncivilized town inhabited by rival communities and characterized by endless internal strife. On top of all of its other shortcomings and deformities, the Holy City, the center of the monotheistic world, and so on, was tainted by unbearable hypocrisy, pompousness, and hyperbole. The second tradition emphasizes the *irrelevance* of Jerusalem. The proponents of this tradition, including Alterman, believed that, for all of its historical grandeur and symbolic significance, Jerusalem (at least until the 1967 war) played an insignificant role in the actual progress of Zionism in the Land of Israel, and that in the drama of shaping the modern Jewish polity that would eventually become the state of Israel, Jerusalem should be viewed as a mere backyard or back alley. The political, economic, organizational, cultural, and, eventually, military achievements that made modern Israel possible were fought for and realized in the agricultural communes of the Jordan and the Jezreel Valleys, in the mountains of the Galilee and in the steppes of the Negev, in the port and industrial compounds of Haifa, in the orange groves of the coastal plain, even in the bustling business sector, theaters, and literary cafés of Tel Aviv, but not in Jerusalem. (Of course, it was in the literary cafés of Tel Aviv that the "irrelevance" of Jerusalem was developed into a theory.) The difference between the two traditions and their respective literary agendas is considerable. The tradition of demystification did not, in the main, push for the eradication of Jerusalem as a central theme in Hebrew literature. Its adherents insisted on writing about Jerusalem, and indeed they produced some of the most memorable Jerusalem pieces, particularly in the field of prose fiction, in such novels as Brenner's *Breakdown and Bereavement* and Aharon Reuveni's Jerusalem trilogy, *In the Beginning of the Confusion, The Last Ships,* and *Devastation.* But they also insisted on writing "truthfully," demanding a shift in the literary treatment of the Jerusalem theme away from the ideal toward the real, away from the metaphorical to the metonymic. The tradition of marginalizing Jerusalem as irrelevant or unrepresentative of Zionist dynamism insisted on shrinking the volume of the Jerusalem theme in Hebrew literature, on cutting its presence down to size in terms of style and symbolic pretensions. Its adherents thought that Hebrew literature could be improved by paying as little attention to Jerusalem as possible.

The tradition of demystification first took root in the 1890s, in the heyday of the Love of Zion period. For instance, Ahad Ha'am (Asher Ginzberg), the most important Zionist philosopher and ideologue of the pre-Herzlian period, brought his very negative reports of his visits to Palestine in 1891 and 1893, both entitled *Truth from the Land of Israel* (I and II), to their gloomy climax and conclusion with short descriptions of his visits to Jerusalem and particularly to the Wailing Wall. In both cases, Jerusalem was left for the end of the article, as it epitomized national deformity and impotence. It reflected not only the miserable condition of the Jewish contingent in Palestine but also the historical deterioration of Judaism itself. Ahad Ha'am, pondering, on the one hand, the ancient misshapen wall and, on the other hand, the clamoring Jerusalemites shouting their prayers at it, could not decide which looked more miserable and bizarre, the "horrible" pile of stones or the supplicants with their "gaunt faces, queer movements, and outlandish garments." The two complemented each other. While the stones pointed to the devastation of the land, the people paraded the destruction of the nation itself.[9] Zionists and Hebraists everywhere were shocked and outraged by this image of Jerusalem, but similar ones continued to emerge throughout the 1890s, even as the adulation of Zion reached its shrill peak.

It was, however, only during the decade of the Second Aliya (1904 to 1914), when a trickle of determined pioneers had laid the foundations of both the ethos and the political constructs that eventually evolved into the ideological and organizational infrastructure of Israel, that the demystifiers of Jerusalem became fully aware of their intentions and developed a conceptual justification. The chief demystifier was Brenner, a writer whose status as a mentor and intellectual guide was at the time as firmly established as that of Ahad Ha'am a decade earlier. Brenner was determined to explode the romantic image of

Jerusalem, not only because he deeply mistrusted semi- or quasi-religious mystifications and believed that they were vitiating the new humanistic Jewish culture that Hebrew writers had been trying to create for more than a century, but also, more specifically, because he regarded that image as an essential part of the noxious illusions fostered by Zionist enthusiasts, particularly the notion that whatever was made or built in Israel was somehow "different," nonexilic by virtue of sheer location, because it existed in the Land of Israel rather than in some other Jewish center in Europe or America. To Brenner, this was a blatant fallacy. As far as he could see, even the modern Jewish community in Palestine, let alone the traditional one, the so-called Old Yishuv, was not noticeably different from similar groups of immigrants in London, New York, or South America. Emigration to Palestine in and of itself meant little. The only "true" revolution depended on a wide-scale national shift from a commerce-oriented to a labor-oriented economy and lifestyle. Until such a shift occurred, the Land of Israel amounted to only one of the two quantities that formed the equation of Jewish "parasitism," the other being the Diaspora.

This was the central idea that informed Brenner's most ambitious and complex work of fiction in those years, the experimental novel *Mikan u-Mikan* (From Here and from There [1911]), the very title of which declared its intention. The novel, structured kaleidoscopically in blatant disregard for temporal and spatial continuity, moves quickly through five or six Jewish "landscapes" in different parts of the world as well as in different parts of Palestine. Jerusalem, not accidentally, plays a central role as the backdrop for the middle (third) segment of the novel, the one in which the mood reaches a nightmarish nadir. This is because to Brenner, Jerusalem, as the "Holy City," was the center at which traditional Jews living on Halukah (charity from abroad) met Zionist functionaries who drew sustenance from and developed "activities" funded by modern "nationalist" charities. In other words, Jerusalem represented the quintessence of international Jewish parasitism and was therefore bound to swell like an abscess from which all of the various brands of Jewish moral corruption flowed like pus. This was exactly what Brenner was trying to illustrate in the third segment of *Mikan u-Mikan,* which he developed in the form of a symposium held by Jews from different parts of the world on the front steps of the Jerusalem Public Library. The protagonist of the novel finds his counterpart in a young yeshivah student whose wounds from a beating keep bleeding as the meandering colloquy develops the theme of the sameness of the Jewish condition everywhere. Jerusalem, represented by the bleeding scholar, appears as the ultimate Jewish hell. Brenner's other two Palestinian novels, *Between Water and Water* (1909) and *Breakdown and Bereavement* (1920), situated firmly within the framework of the Jerusalem complex, offer similar, although perhaps less horrific, views of the city and its "meaning." A harsh landscape—bare stones, bone-chilling winter damp, and suffocating summer dryness—social alienation and strife, sickness, madness, and all kinds of deformity function as the metonymies of "true" reality. Jerusalem, Brenner maintained, was "us" at our lowest point, in all of our despicable wretchedness.

Brenner's view of Jerusalem (and of course of the entire Palestinian Zionist experiment) had an impact on the work of a group of younger writers of the Second Aliya, where it was replicated but also diversified and further developed in variations of considerable interest. Among the latter, the work that most powerfully claims our attention is the aforementioned trilogy by Reuveni (published from 1920 to 1925), an epic that chronicles the downfall and devastation of Jewish Jerusalem during World War I. Within the vast social panorama created by the author, no one passes with moral distinction the tests of confusion, deprivation, and sheer horror inflicted on Jerusalem by the war and by the Ottoman authorities: neither the members of the Old Yishuv—simple folk whose only concern is their personal safety and well-being—nor the leaders of the pioneers nor even the writer Berenchuk, a fictionalized portrait of Brenner himself. The pioneer leaders are all quite ready to leave the community in the lurch and flee to safety; Berenchuk refrains from doing this only because he feels that it would undermine his literary work and prevent the completion of his new novel, which is his overriding concern. Reuveni, a social Darwinist in thought and a naturalist in art, bases his novel on a combination of meticulously accurate historical information, incisive psychological analysis, and relentlessly detailed mimetic portrayals of events, cityscapes, interiors and exteriors of old neglected houses, and the like. The result is a large-scale, realistic, credible, and extremely negative picture of moral, social, and physical decay. Furthermore, underneath the solid metonymic surface of the novel, a metaphorical net accentuates shadows of even deeper darkness, as does, for instance, the central metaphor of brutal sexual intercourse. On the one hand, Jerusalem is projected as a person—both female and male—who is subjected to rape by the Turkish masters. The only morally alive man in the novel commits suicide at its end because he is unable to live with the humiliation of having been homosexually assaulted by his commanders. (He is a soldier in the Turkish army.) On the other hand, the author also discovers the collaborationist whore in the soul of Jewish Jerusalem, which he projects in the figures of a brother and sister who crave the debasement of passive submission to violent sex as well as the enjoyment of an easy life of prostitution. Never has Jerusalem been portrayed more darkly than in Reuveni's masterpiece.

The debased or dark image of Jerusalem was further developed in works of prose fiction composed in the interwar period, such as Dov Kimkhi's powerful novel *The House of Chefets,* written in the 1930s but not published until 1951. The image also informed segments of Israeli fiction, as in such a representative novel as Amos Oz's *My Michael* (1968), in which the divided and sequestered Jerusalem of 1948 to 1967 and the schizophrenic Hanna Gonen mirror each other, thus taking up the Brenner tradition of identifying Jerusalem with psychosis and presenting it as quintessentially "sick," the epitome of national malaise. Of course, other significant Israeli novels, such as Shulamith Hareven's *City of Many Days* (1972) and particularly David Shahar's multivolume and still unfinished roman-fleuve *The Palace of Shattered Vessels* (the first part appeared in 1969), strongly contradict this image.

If the demystification, or rather the "unmasking," of Jerusalem occurs mainly in works of prose fiction (although it also had an impact on other genres) the emphasis on Jerusalem's "irrelevance" is tied to certain developments in Hebrew poetry. This emphasis, as has been pointed out, developed into a theory in the literary cafés of Tel Aviv during the 1930s. It was there that a group of modernist poets, led by Avraham Shlonski, set about the task of modernizing Hebrew culture. In the framework of their cultural-political polemics—in the course of which they challenged the "out-of-date" Zionist consensus—Jerusalem was branded as the representative of "classicism," "traditionalism," "philistinism," "academism" (Jerusalem was the only university town in the country for more than a quarter of a century), and sheer spiritual dullness. In addition, it was pronounced the source of bad poetry, of the *mayim-shamayim-Yerushalayim* banality. The rhetoric aimed at Jerusalem clearly echoed the impetus of the futuristic manifestos. Shlonski, the ideologue and mentor of the group, differentiated between two "styles" or "manners" in modern Hebrew culture, that of Jerusalem and that of Tel Aviv. The Tel Aviv manner emerged not only in Tel Aviv proper but also in other dynamic spots, such as the kibbutzim of the Jezreel Valley, while the voice of Jerusalem also expressed itself in other enclaves where the fervor of creativity and innovation had been extinguished long ago, such as the old *moshava* (settlement) of Petah Tikvah, the first agricultural settlement to be founded, even before the First Aliya, in 1878, by members of the Old Yishuv who had left Jerusalem. Shlonski succinctly defined the difference between "the young, unruly, secular" Tel Aviv and the old, gloomy Jerusalem, "burdened with holiness, petrified like its rocks." The latter projected the biblical dictum, "Wisdom shall die with us," while the former projected its opposite, "Wisdom shall be revived with us." Hence the conclusion: "Revival and innovation will not come from Jerusalem."[10]

Not surprisingly, Shlonski refrained from even mentioning Jerusalem in his poems. Alterman, his most gifted disciple and the poet who popularized the poetics of the group and ensured its dominant position in the development of Hebrew poetry for more than a decade, did the same in his "serious" poems. In his lighter satirical pieces, he poked fun at Jerusalem. In one of these, he explained why no "real" poem could be written about the Holy City: the discrepancy, the gap, between the prophetic aura of the city and the sluggish mundane reality of its daily existence paralyzes the muse. One cannot walk to one's office every morning and think creatively: "Jeremiah must have walked here."[11] While the poet Uri Tsvi Greenberg used the city as decoration for his histrionic display of nationalist moods, Alterman said, his poetic Jerusalem was like the city walls, a grandiose facade that sheltered only mice and silence. Jerusalem could elicit a yawn or a howl but never a poem.[12] Another member of the group, the leftist Mayakovskian Alexander Pen, wrote a "visionary" satire in the spirit of Soviet "constructive" futurism. In its title, he replaced the hackneyed combination *Yerushalayim ha-kdosha* (Jerusalem the holy) with the phonetically similar but in fact very opposite *Yerushalayim ha-*

kdesha (Jerusalem the whore). Pen, who donned the persona of the rowdy bohemian, portrayed himself in this poem as roaming the streets of Jerusalem in a pronounced alcoholic mood and being accosted by its feminine personification. The latter, sorely in need of the invigoration that only his youthful "prowess" can provide, demands his sexual attention. In return she promises to walk with him to Mount Scopus and there bestow upon him "a bit of [her] holiness." The speaker, however, is sober enough, or perhaps drunk enough, to tell her to her face what a wretched harlot she has always been, ever since the biblical days, and to send her to hell. She has always persecuted her prophets and flirted with her foreign rulers, with Sannecherib and Nebuchadnezzar in the past just as she does now (in the 1930s) with her "fuckers from Downing Street." Finally the poet leaves the old feminine city on his way to the "new masculine" one, that is, Tel Aviv. For people like himself, who have grown tall in their expectations of the morrow, Jerusalem, although perched on her high mountains, is "a little too short and low."[13]

Of course, not all of the members of the modernist Tel Aviv group of the 1930s and 1940s were swept away by such a scurrilous anti-Jerusalem mood. Some of them, such as the poets Yocheved Bat Miryam and Ezra Zusman, wrote delicate melodious poems in which the theme of Jerusalem was developed in a series of suggestions, analogies, associations, and stunning metaphors, according to the norms of symbolist poetics. As a matter of fact, there is a strange contradiction between the poetics of the group and its attitude toward Jerusalem. The poetics were by the 1930s essentially symbolist or neosymbolist, for Shlonski had started his career as a blatantly revolutionary postsymbolist influenced by Esenin's imaginism, Mayakovsky's futurism, and by the general drift of current European expressionism. All of these influences went well together with the debunking of the old and the spiritual. However, Shlonski gradually withdrew from his youthful poetic Sturm und Drang mood and went back to a turn-of-the-century symbolism in the manner of Alexander Blok. A parallel process occurred in the development of other contemporary Hebrew poets, pointing to a shift in the cultural and social orientation of Zionism, particularly labor Zionism, in the 1930s. Whatever the shift indicated, the neosymbolist stance that Shlonski now shared with his younger disciples did *not* seem to justify the anti-Jerusalem *ressentiment*. On the contrary, Jerusalem as a poetic theme offered all of the combinations and contradictions that symbolist poetics favor: the mundane and the sacrosanct; the concrete and the abstract; the clearly delineated and the open-ended; the literary and the allusive, metaphorical, suggestive, and so on. Alterman, for instance, focused in his best poems of the 1930s on the common denominator that united the old and the new, the moribund and the nascent. His major collection, *Stars Outside* (1938), includes glowing cycles of poems about old and new cities, in which the former were swept clean and revitalized by storms while the latter listened to the music of "an ancient violin" emerging from the clang of iron cranes and the hissing of locomotives. But while Alterman's new cities were clearly modeled after 1930s Tel Aviv, his old cities were modeled not on Jerusalem but on the Paris of his student years and the Warsaw of his childhood. With him, as with Shlonski and many others, Jerusalem was rejected not so much because it was "old," as the poets maintained in their futuristic rhetoric, but because it was inextricably identified with Jewishness—not just with the Jewish faith but with the very notion of a Jewish cultural particularity—while they, the modernist poets of the 1930s, wanted to modernize Hebrew culture and also to Europeanize it, to render it a part of the modernist milieu that then reigned supreme in the European centers. They wanted to urbanize or one might even say metropolize it—that is, to bring it closer to the sophisticated modern metropolitan ambiance of Paris, Berlin, and London. Thus they were bound to reject Jerusalem and, at the same time, project Tel Aviv, small and provincial as it was, as a budding Paris, a London in the making.

This explains the following paradox: Uri Tsvi Greenberg, the chief and most authentic exponent in Hebrew culture and literature of European, postsymbolist modernism, a staunch expressionist throughout his long career and also a fiery futurist in its early stages, was to become the great poet of the historical and transcendental Jerusalem and the vilifier of Tel Aviv, the symbol of burgeoning secularism and modernity, while Nathan Alterman, the symbolist par excellence, evolved into the great poet of Tel Aviv who could not bring himself even to mention the name of Jerusalem in any but a satirical tone.

The anti-Jerusalem cry of the Tel Aviv modernists of the 1930s and

1940s reverberated (and continues to reverberate) in Israeli culture, even as the poetic prominence and influence of the 1930s modernists petered out and disappeared. The anti-Jerusalem rhetoric resurfaced strongly after the war of 1967, when the reunified city became the darling of the euphoric Israeli public. Jerusalem photo albums and anthologies came pouring from the presses of publishers and cultural entrepreneurs. Even as the public was obsessively humming "Jerusalem of Gold," the lachrymose lyric by Naomi Shemer, the troubadour of greater Israel and its military prowess, Tel Aviv intellectuals of a generation much younger than that of Alterman and not at all favorably inclined toward its mental habits and political vocabulary, resumed the anti-Jerusalem campaign of the 1930s, occasionally soaring to climactic moments of vituperation as crude as those that were reached in Pen's "Jerusalem the Whore." Thus, for instance, a literary critic launched his attack on what he defined as the "Jerusalem poets"—the main target was Yehudah Amichai—by rejecting not only "all that sweet Jerusalem thing" but also the city itself: allegedly unreal, possessing "plenty of dimness and plenty of *decor* but nothing straightforward and immediate," a place where only "the literary snob" would choose to write poems.[14] This, at a time when Jerusalem was fast becoming the red-hot center of Israeli political and social reality, the place where every tension, every friction, every pain then plaguing Israeli society would soon explode in the face of Israeli smugness and swaggering self-confidence.

The Binary Condition of Literary Jerusalem

The anti-Jerusalem traditions in modern Hebrew literature produced important works of fiction. However, their claim to historical significance rests mainly not on their literary "results" as such but on their energizing role as a negative force within a complex cultural and aesthetic magnetic field charged with the tension of oppositions. Within such a field, a literary theme does not evolve along a linear, one-way developmental trail. Rather, it forms complex patterns determined by the tensions between opposites, their relative potencies, and the depth of their respective impact at any given moment and in each specific case. Locked in a tug-of-war, one does not simply "progress" in a certain direction. Instead, one carefully negotiates one's steps, shifting from side to side in a kind of dance. Thus the development of the theme at different times and under changing circumstances produces not merely an aggregate of similar or loosely associated variations but an ever growing corpus of closely and dialectically related configurations that are juxtaposed to each other or internally organized, each within its own boundaries, along the lines of bipolar patterns. Mere accumulation is necessarily replaced by structured interrelationships; the stasis of similarity gives way to the dynamics of recurring dramatic conflicts; continuity through change follows from the processes through which new experiences organize themselves within the bipolar format of a stable infrastructure.

Here, scholars and critics who look for that third methodological option for a critical delineation of the development of a ubiquitous theme, such as that of Jerusalem, can find their cue. The theme does not need to be pursued step by step in a magisterial monograph. (Such a monograph can be worthwhile, if its author can resist the temptation of sheer "bibliographism" and see not just the trees but the forest as a whole.) However, even such monographs, if they are not to drown in their own detail, require recognition and definition of a general principle that in itself could be concisely expressed in a relatively short essay. Such a recognition and definition might raise the critic above the shallow waters of truisms and vacuous phraseology, insofar as his or her general principle entails the discovery of the infrastructure itself. In the course of this process, the critic cannot afford to indulge in generalization, and must not only describe the infrastructure and the principles that determine its form but also illustrate—as summarily and as selectively as his scope allows—the way in which new experiences and new insights fit themselves into that infrastructure, thus conditioning and expanding it while being conditioned and delimited by it.

In the case of the Jerusalem theme in modern Hebrew literature, one must first recognize the fact that it has always evolved within a binary context. Every specific configuration of this theme finds its place along a scale, the two extremes of which point in different directions. Sometimes the locus is closer to one end and sometimes to its opposite, but in the most interesting cases, it is to be found in the middle of the scale. The nature of the two extremes and the content they represent varies. At certain moments, the polarity may be perceived as reality versus myth. But it may also be defined as a conflict between "life" and the religious code, between instinctual spontaneity and moral circumspection, between Judaism and Hellenism, or between nationalist particularism and humanistic universalism. Other possible oppositions include: old versus new, past versus present, past versus future, truth versus illusion, metaphor versus metonymy, and so on. What makes the structure stable are not the various appellations and their content—which of course form continuities of their own—rather, it is the duality itself, the presence of a position and its opposite.

Once one grasps the binary condition of literary Jerusalem, one may detect in most literary presentations of the Holy City some features of both the position and its opposite. Even when a specific presentation vehemently asserts one of two conflicting "truths," the perceptive reader—unless the presentation is intellectually and aesthetically flaccid—can find in it some rudiments of its opposite. In this way, one learns to appreciate the richness and complexity of the texts in which the two truths are genuinely juxtaposed, texts in which neither of the two is used as a mere foil for the other but rather both are projected as valid, albeit not on the same level. In other words, one gauges the greater depth of such a presentation of Jerusalem insofar as it presents a real conflict and produces in the reader a feeling of being "torn." The issue of synthesis—that is, whether the author manages to negotiate some compromise between the two truths, or even shows an interest in negotiating such a compromise—is of less significance. The paramount significance inheres in the reality and complexity of the struggle per se and in the author's ability to convey it forcefully. It is, in my opinion, in the texts where this reality and complexity are most convincingly conveyed that the development of the Jerusalem theme reaches its highest moments. There modern Hebrew literature succeeds in coping with the overwhelming presence of one of its main symbols. Within the scope of this chapter, this can be shown with very few illustrations, although many others may of course be adduced. My comments on the few texts that I have chosen as illustrations are short and general, despite the fact that the very reason for offering these texts over others—their complexity—calls for a detailed and subtle analysis. The purpose of my comments, however, lies in whetting the reader's appetite for a more extensive reading, both of the texts and of their interpretation and analysis.

From Mapu to Agnon

Superficially, Abraham Mapu's presentation of Jerusalem in his two historical romances, *The Love of Zion* (1853) and *The Sin of Samaria* (1865), seems idyllic, one-dimensional, naive. However, this view of Mapu's fictional world as a whole, upheld since the end of the nineteenth century by most critics and literary historians, has been proved wrong. While Mapu's numerous epigones, particularly those of the Love of Zion period (1880 to 1900), might have worked to flatten and trivialize his vision—Brenner's caustic parodies were in fact aimed at them rather than at Mapu himself—in its original literary-historical context, this vision was neither simplistic nor one-dimensional. True, in his novels Mapu concocted heady, sensational potions; as an artist he abided by the norms of the romance and not by those of the realistic psychological novel. The colorful and often fantastic fictional world that he created is populated by monolithic elemental characters who project "pure," intense feelings and attitudes (rather than psychologically credible but complicated and contradictory emotions), particularly erotic love in its straightforward or subverted form, but also greed, cunning, pompousness, and opportunism pitched against equally pure benevolence, innocence, humility, and loyalty. The soaring trajectories of these characters are made to intersect by means of convoluted and "artificial" plots that make for high dramas of love, misunderstanding, betrayal, changes of identity, unexpected reunions and recognitions, and, of course, grandly operatic happy endings in which all of the loving couples achieve erotic bliss and live happily ever after. Nevertheless, this did not hinder Mapu from conveying a serious, often complex, view of human behavior and of the Jewish predicament; a view that was realized by symbolic juxtaposition rather than realistic mimesis. Mapu's message involves a full and deeply internalized recognition, quite uncharacteristic of writers of the Age of Reason, of the ferociousness and vitality of instinctual urges and of the precarious position of forces, such as religious faith, reason, law, and common sense, that were supposed to overcome, control, and, when necessary, suppress them. Mapu firmly believed in the need for such controls, but he also suggested that the constant suppression of instinctual drives might lead either to the attenuation of all true vitality or to an anarchic explosion of the subverted libidinal forces after they had turned in destructive and evil directions. The former would produce wilting, lifeless people and a society like the contemporary Lithuanian Jewish community, in the midst of which Mapu had been born and raised. Libidinal anarchy, on the other hand, would create either a lawless society or a despotic one and would produce people completely controlled by irrational forces and engrossed in sensualism. Mapu believed that this had happened at least three times in Jewish history: in the northern kingdom of ancient Israel, which was therefore destined for destruction, in the spread of Sabbatianism in the seventeenth century, and in the contemporary upsurge of the Hasidic movement. The Jewish Enlightenment, Mapu maintained, should have been committed to a historical compromise; while speaking in the name of reason, it also had to assert the legitimacy of the erotic, the aesthetic, and the imaginative and to devise ways, both artistic and social, by means of which these contradictory forces would be introduced into Jewish life and culture in a controlled form. Thus, Mapu's life's work amounts to an insightful critique, not only of traditional Jewish rabbinic culture but also of the Jewish Enlightenment and of Hebrew Haskalah literature, both of which, he believed, were equally arid and rationalistic to the point that neither could make an impact on the mind and life of ordinary "simple" people.

This view found full expression in Mapu's suggestive image of biblical Jerusalem in its days of danger and triumph. Both novels are set against a stormy historical background: the northern kingdom of Israel falters and succumbs to the Assyrian armies; its population is exiled and its capital, Samaria, laid waste. At the same time, the southern kingdom of Judah survives; its capital, the Temple, and the ruling Davidic dynasty are miraculously saved by the supernatural removal of Sannacherib's armies as they are besieging Jerusalem. Only at its face value can this image be read as a panegyric to "the faithful city" of prophets and loyal kings. In fact, Mapu culled from the Bible everything that could be said against Jerusalem and its leaders and made full imaginative use of dark prophetic portrayals of the city. Thus, while he projected a wild and orgiastic Samaria, ripe for destruction, his Jerusalem was often smug, stupid, and unjust. The presence and prestige of the great prophet Isaiah notwithstanding, the kings and the nobility are portrayed as mediocre, self-serving, and not particularly perceptive. Both in the management of their family affairs and in their politics, Mapu's Jerusalem dignitaries make every possible mistake and are easy prey for impostors and charlatans, as they are controlled by petty envy and shortsighted self-interest. As for the rituals of the Temple, although they are maintained with rigid formalistic adherence to the letter of the priestly law, they have become as empty and meaningless as Isaiah proclaims. Furthermore, Mapu's Jerusalem suffers from a deficiency that the biblical sources do not illustrate and that the author projected from his own imagination: the city is weak and effeminate. It does not possess the kind of vitality that had run amok and waxed destructive in Samaria. As much as Mapu deplores the anarchy and sensualism of the northern capital, against his will he admires its flamboyant virility, its reckless joie de vivre, its military prowess, its wild beauty. Almost all of the "real" men in his two biblical romances hail from the north, and most of the passionate women, even when they function as the proverbial "daughters of Zion," are in one way or another related to it. The thin blood of Judah needs constant generous transfusions of the thicker, redder blood flowing in the arteries of the northern commonwealth.

To Mapu, Jerusalem represents the very center of the world. The plots of the two novels develop a jerky, pendular mobility that constantly enlarges the novels' spatial circumference. This violent mobility sends the protagonists ever greater distances, far away from their beloved Jerusalem. Of course, it also sweeps them back to the center, for only there can their fate be decided and the riddles of their existence solved. However, this spatial pattern, as much as it points to the centrality of Jerusalem, also suggests that Jerusalem is incomplete, that it does not possess something, which has to be brought from afar. For instance, a truly passionate love affair cannot be initiated in Jerusalem; it has to start in a location closer to nature, its beauty as well as its threatening wildness symbolized by wild beasts. The shapely, urbanized, mountainous landscape of Jerusalem is compared to the romantic openness of the wooded Carmel and, more impressively, to the wild, sublime, and dangerous summits of Lebanon. The comparison always suggests that to regain and maintain its vitality, Jerusalem has to incorporate into itself some of the wild beauty it forfeited and other places retained. The city has to import masculine men and the sense of freedom and simplicity that flourishes in the agricultural and uninhabited "natural" hinterlands. Of course, it also has to tame these imports, to refine and civilize them. This can be done through fulfilling marriages as well as through exposure, not just to the niceties of civilized society but, more important, to the spiritual influence of the prophets and the revitalized Temple services. In the novels, moments of such happy, harmonious balance occur particularly toward their happy endings. But although they do occur, the novels intimate that these moments are temporary and that the balance is precarious. Jerusalem could and should become its better self. It could achieve a harmonious stasis in which all of the necessary components of a perfectly balanced existence are not only present but also correctly organized, stratified within a benign hierarchy that reflects a justified order of priorities. However, such stasis is bound to founder and collapse on itself, and sooner rather than later. The dynamics of human life are irrepressible and unruly, and the "good" Jerusalem is therefore an ideal that can occasionally be realized but in the longer run will necessarily remain out of reach. That is why the image of Jerusalem in Mapu's novels had to alternate between a radiant, exuberant locus and a pale, shriveled city of intrigue, arrogance, and greed. This alternating current, which informs and energizes Mapu's Jerusalem, also renders it one of the most enduring Jerusalems of modern Hebrew literature.

More than ninety years and the entire aesthetic distance covered by the Hebrew novel in its development from romance-like beginnings to summits of modernist sophistication separate Shmuel Yoseph Agnon's *Temol Shilshom*, or *Yesteryear*, published in 1944–45, from Mapu's *Love of Zion*. The differences between the two novels and their respective Jerusalems are immense. Yet Agnon's vision, so superior to that of Mapu's in both its intellectual complexity and its artistic realization, is nevertheless connected in certain ways to that of the first Hebrew novelist. Like Mapu, Agnon could never accept an art of fiction completely cut off from myth, fantasy, and the tradition of the romance. Like his predecessor, he could not conceive of a Hebrew narrative not deeply rooted stylistically and associatively in the ancient Hebrew texts. Like him, he sought, in terms of plot and spatial and temporal mobility, maximal narrative variety: this, at a time when conventional poetic wisdom dictated a minimalist preference focusing on the consciousness of relatively few characters—mostly frustrated young intellectuals—within a relatively short time span. Agnon

crowded many of his stories, and such novels as *The Bridal Canopy,*
Yesteryear, and *Shira,* with a multitude of characters, events, and lively
vignettes that call to mind the color, density, and busyness of Mapu's
novels; and like Mapu, throughout his long career Agnon was fasci-
nated with Jerusalem, which he turned into one of the two centers of
his "world," the other being the provincial Eastern European town
of Shibush, modeled after Buczacz, his own hometown in Eastern
Galicia.

Agnon also realized, as had Mapu before him, that while no view
or image of Jerusalem ought to fail to take into account the city's
transcendental aspect—a quality that both Mapu and Agnon would
unabashedly term its "holiness"—this aspect was usually tarnished by
a thick layer of mundane pettiness, which often became extraordinarily
ugly. The radiance of Jerusalem flowed from a transcendental source
and was in this sense "eternal" and ever present; but the human eye
could perceive this only occasionally, in pathetically short and fleeting
moments of epiphany. As Agnon himself put it:

> Every city leaves its imprint upon its inhabitants; so much more so,
> God's city, which is superior to all others, for the Divine immanence
> has never abandoned it. Although the Divine immanence is hidden
> and covered, there are times that even the commonest among those
> Jews who are fortunate enough to have resided in Jerusalem can sense
> its presence according to his own sensibilities, virtues and the measure
> of grace that sheds its light upon his soul and also by virtue of
> having willingly and without complaint accepted the suffering which
> one experiences in the land of Israel . . . But this grace is never per-
> manent, for the condition of grace manifests itself only occasionally,
> let alone to a person who is not worthy of being continually illumi-
> nated by it.[15]

Hence, the radiance of Jerusalem in Agnon's works always possesses
a tragic quality, a bereaved, orphaned poignancy. It is reflected in the
pale light that shimmers from the crannies in the ancient stones of the
Wailing Wall when the darkness of evening already envelops everything else in sight, and in the "compassionate silence"[16] that descends
on the stones as the Wall is left alone by the departing crowds of
beggars, vendors, and tourists.

Agnon took up the theme of Jerusalem in "Agunoth," his very

first significant and successful work of fiction, published in 1908, a year after the nineteen-year-old author had arrived in Palestine. The story is written in the pseudo-naive tone of the traditional folksy narrator of a Jewish homiletic chapbook, a tone that the author would wield with masterful effectiveness for more than half of his career. "Agunoth," like all of Agnon's other pseudo-traditional narratives, is, however, far from a naïveté of any kind. It focuses on the incompatibility of the three "quests" that the young author perceived at the time as characteristic of a truly active spiritual existence: the quest for romantic-erotic self-fulfillment, the artist's quest for creativity and beauty, and the quest for faith, for transcendental reassurance. Each of these, young Agnon thought, invalidates the other two, thus rendering complete and harmonious spirituality unattainable and the human condition tragic by definition. The naive narration allows Agnon to treat the theme of Jerusalem in "Agunoth" in the conventional manner, and to make full use of the stylistic and narrative accessories that accompany this manner. But the story's essentially tragic modern implications, both psychological and philosophical, undermine the traditional stereotypes. Thus, even though the beginning of "Agunoth" presents Jerusalem as the archetypal Holy City, the story gradually reveals the city as the center of a modern malaise that assumes cosmic proportions. As if in spite of the narrator's intention, the Holy City he so reverently describes turns into a stage for devastating psychic failure, frustration, sickness, and insanity. Its holy radiance does not disappear completely, but it acquires the aforementioned "tragic quality." Jerusalem's lights glimmer rosily at sunrise and sunset on the tops of the hills like an elusive promise of harmony, which needs nothing short of a miracle in order to be fulfilled. Its pensive effulgence, however, acknowledges the impossibility of miracles. Quite a few of Agnon's many Jerusalems, from that of "Agunoth" to that of the novel *Shira*, left unfinished at the author's death in 1970, are suffused with a similar pensive luminosity of twilight.

According to some interpreters of "Agunoth," this story about failure and heartbreak in Jerusalem, where the best intentions often seem to produce the most disastrous results, exemplifies Agnon's criticism of Zionism and the Second Aliya, of which he himself was a member. The shortcomings of Zionism are reflected in the shortcomings of Zion, as it were. Without judging the merits of applying such

Figure 16. Jerusalem seen
from the east.

an interpretation to this particular story, one can accept it fully with respect to the Jerusalem of Agnon's great novel *Yesteryear,* written three decades after "Agunoth" and clearly representative of the writer's art and thought at the peak of full maturity. In *Yesteryear,* as in Agnon's other mature works, the earlier issues of erotic love, the artist's vocation, and the need for religious faith are not abandoned; on the contrary, the author's interest in them is sharpened and the exploration of their various facets and ramifications is significantly enlarged in the sociobehavioral sense, as well as deepened in the psychological and metaphysical sense. However, these and other important issues are now firmly rooted—even in the most fantastic tales—in the reality and immediacy of human pain and suffering as well as in history in general and in modern Jewish history, with all of its vicissitudes, in particular. Agnon distanced himself from the hazy legendary notion of history as "once upon a time," which had been characteristic of some of his early stories, to focus on a notion of history as a series of events that, from the perspective of those who experience them, always take place *now*. The root of this shift lies in Agnon's own sense of modern Jewish history as happening *now*. Modern Jewish history seemed to him to be essentially tragic, and this not only because of the destruction of his own Eastern European community and the genocide of European Jews. Even this overwhelming aspect of modern Jewish history aside, the spiritual and physical survival of the nation was at an impasse. As radical a Zionist as he was, Agnon did not believe that Zionism in and of itself could break through this impasse. On the contrary, even though Zionism was inevitable and its truths self-evident, it could also serve as a part of the obstacle in a way that could be summed up by the following formula: those elements in Judaism that actively sought after "redemption" had cut themselves off from the Redeemer. Conversely, those who were still "in touch" with the Redeemer had forgotten that redemption must be actively sought. In other words, those contemporary Jews who were ready to fight for a Jewish future had been torn away from the continuity of Jewish history and undermined the "Jewishness" of that future, while those who identified with the Jewish past could not realize that no Jewish future would be forthcoming unless Jews in the present would accept the pain and uncertainty of fighting for it.

The novel *Yesteryear* dramatizes this formula by suspending its protagonist, a naive Zionist pioneer of the Second Aliya, between two worlds, symbolized by two cities, Jewish Jaffa as the matrix of the soon-to-be-born Tel Aviv and Jewish Jerusalem as represented primarily by its ultra-Orthodox section, Me'a She'arim, meaning "a hundredfold" (after Genesis 26:12, "Then Isaac sowed in that land and received in the same year a hundredfold"). As the narrative pendulum swings to and fro with majestic epic slowness throughout the four parts of the novel (Agnon's longest), so unfolds the most memorable Jerusalem of modern Hebrew prose fiction. It is, in a way, a Jerusalem more terrible than that of both Brenner and Reuveni, if only by virtue of Agnon's artistic superiority in evoking impressions and moods. But it also possesses redeeming features of which the other novels of the Second Aliya were not yet aware. They had portrayed Jerusalem as sheer hell, but Agnon portrayed it as the tragically subverted heavenly city that, since it could not soar heavenward, descended into hellish depths without losing its sublime quality completely.

Agnon chose to focus on a Jerusalem plagued by protracted drought. He describes a small provincial town situated in a mountainous desert, swept by dust storms, hot as an oven, parched, dry, stinking, infested by stray dogs and swarms of angry wasps. Its Jewish community, poor, thirsty, and unwashed, is torn by endless strife between its Orthodox and "modern" contingents as well as within the contingents themselves. Only conflict, as petty as it is ferocious and vociferous, seems to flourish there. Like a contagious infection, it is carried by rabbis, intellectuals, scholars, newspapers, rival Hasidic groups, and above all else by the popular preacher Gronam, who holds Me'a She'arim in thrall with his fire-and-brimstone hell-and-damnation sermons. Into this Jerusalem the author sends his protagonists, the house painter Kummer and his counterpart, the stray dog Balak, whom Kummer unwittingly, through a silly prank—he paints the words "mad dog" on Balak's back—causes to be chased out of his native Jewish neighborhood by frightened Jews who believe that Balak is really sick. These two are the chief personages of the novel, which thus becomes double-tiered, with Kummer functioning on a realistic psychological level and Balak serving as the center of a grotesque allegory, chock-full of wit, puns, rhyme, and trumped-up scholastic erudition. The two characters are mirror images of each other, as well as each other's opposites. Kummer, a Zionist and a "modern," regresses to a childish naïveté as he attempts to find his place in Me'a She'arim among simple religious people whom he believes to be just like the parents he has left behind. Balak, a "common," simple-minded, naive dog, once chased out of his Me'a She'arim, waxes critical, philosophical, and "modern." Both become the victims of each other and of Jerusalem, as Balak finally contracts rabies and bites Kummer, who expires in excruciating pain and insane delirium.

Compared with this terrible Jerusalem, the Jaffa of *Yesteryear* appears to be an idyllic spot. It has its share of conflict and grievances, but these seem to mellow under the city's blue sky and among its green orchards. All troubles seem to wash away in the refreshing ripples of the Mediterranean. Jaffa is a town of "happy," optimistic people. Its Jewish community is essentially modern, active, Europeanized, and Zionist. Once Kummer comes to Jaffa, he can hardly tear himself away from its pleasant sensual ambiance. However, once he returns to Jerusalem he completely forgets Jaffa and his life there, as if they had been unreal. In Jerusalem Kummer's fate is sealed, tied inextricably to the city's tragic modus of being. The novel validates the primacy of this unpleasant, all but uninhabitable place; Jaffa, as pleasing as it could be, is a place where Jewish existence has no depth and no content. Jerusalem is projected, particularly through the subterranean vision of Balak the dog, as unfathomable, tricky, and dangerous, but "real" and fully historical in the Jewish sense of the word. It is, therefore, in Jerusalem that the tragic drama of modern Jewish history has to be staged. Naive, inarticulate, and undistinguished, Kummer intuitively recognizes not only that Jerusalem is the proper arena but that the battle that must be fought there involves, even in an erotic sense, a lethal embrace, which forces Jewish modernity into an unbearable intimacy with the religious tradition. Without fully understanding the implications of all this, Kummer gets caught up in this "embrace" and winds up paying for it with his sanity and with his life. As the novel ends, he is brought to burial and the drought is broken by torrential rain, as if a blood-thirsty Moloch has relented upon receiving his human sacrifice. Indeed, at the end of the novel, Jerusalem closely resembles the biblical Gehenna with its monstrous idols and child-craving Molochs. This horror, however, is not caused by evil per se. Rather, its source lies in the hazards of a life caught on the horns of the modern Jewish dilemma as Agnon saw it.

In *Yesteryear* Agnon cunningly hints that the Jerusalem of Me'a She'arim and the ultrasecular Tel Aviv, the founding of which is recounted in the third part of the novel, are in fact very similar to each other. Both are self-enclosed Jewish enclaves in which single-minded Jewish communities bar themselves from access to that middle ground on which a rapprochement between modernity and tradition can take place. They were both created with the best intentions. Me'a She'arim, as its name indicates, was meant to become an agricultural community, where God-fearing Jews escaping the overcrowding of the Jewish community in the Old City as well as its parasitic subsistence on Halukah (charity) funds could serve God and earn their living productively by the sweat of their brow. However, these agricultural plans were immediately abandoned because of the rabbinical ban on fertilizing the sacred soil of Jerusalem with manure. Succumbing to a prescriptive formalistic interpretation of a talmudic injunction, the little town is thus characterized by the meanness of its narrow alleys and by the barren fanaticism of its zealots. Tel Aviv was meant to become a garden city where Jaffa Zionists would be able not only to escape the discomfort and overcrowding of the Arab port city but also to develop freely a unique Jewish presence buttressed by education and art. But the gardens are quickly parceled out as construction lots and the Jewish presence is thinned by the intellectual poverty of art and education, cut off from their historical source. The end result, as indicated by the meanness and ugliness of Tel Aviv's narrow streets, leaves much to be desired. Together, Me'a She'arim and Tel Aviv present the same Jewish predicament that Kummer was trying to flee when he moved from Zionist Jaffa to Orthodox Jerusalem. However, Jerusalem is no haven for a person like Kummer. From time to time, he senses the potential of the city in which "not an hour passes which is totally devoid of the eternal life and the world to come."[17] But his death there is sufficient proof of Agnon's contention that such a lofty perception, if uncritically trusted, could spell mortal danger. The lure of heavenly Jerusalem has the power to kill.

Poets of the Third Aliya

If Agnon's epic Jerusalem is a moving and engrossing image of the Holy City as projected against the background of the Second Aliya, the hectic and ecstatic rhythms of the Third Aliya and of the entire interbellum period find their full and most authentic expression in the lyrical images of Jerusalem created by a host of poets. Unlike the trickle of pioneers who arrived in Palestine individually between 1904 and 1914, the pioneers of the Third Aliya, a much larger influx, arrived in bustling, nervous, and enthusiastic groups between 1919 and 1923. Inspired by the October Revolution in Russia, on the one hand, and by the Balfour Declaration on the other, these immigrants fled Eastern European communities devastated by World War I and by the ensuing chaos of civil war. In the barren hills and swampy valleys of Palestine, they hoped to find redemption—*ge'ulah*—personal, national, and universal. A revolutionary "new man" as well as a "new Jew" was to be born there in a communal framework. There people would overcome, at one and the same time, all barriers of social and psychological alienation, the difficulties of physical labor in a harsh climate, the unfriendliness of non-Jewish neighbors and eventually also that of the new British rulers, and the mental vestiges of their own bourgeois or traditional Jewish childhood. This was a Sturm und Drang period that found its main social expression in the kibbutzim of the Jezreel Valley and its main artistic voice in an expressionist-futuristic poetry that undermined the established poetic canon of the preceding Bialik era and swiftly changed the literary sensibilities of a new reading public. The new literary canon insisted on immediate, intense, overwhelming externalization of feelings, attitudes, and states of mind. It demanded expression rather than mimetic description, a delicate rendering of sensual impressions, a search for the ineffable beauty and truth of the metaphysical symbol, or the rigors of protracted psychological analysis. It favored forms that were not well rounded; a diction that was "mixed" and "ragged"; free rhythms, short and syncopated or long-winded, that cut themselves loose from formal, organizing, equalizing norms of meter.

The Jerusalem evoked by this new poetry is different from all of its literary counterparts. For one thing, it is conceptual, metaphoric, and never mimetic. The poets never really try to describe Jerusalem, allowing their impressions to settle slowly in differentiated patterns of shape and color. The poet Ezra Zusman, positioning himself, as did so many other poets, on the summit of Mount Scopus, confessed that he was looking at the city and at the country as a whole through the twin screens of "heat wave [*hamsin*] mist and the mist of tears."[18] What he saw was not a concrete landscape but rather the phantom of a beleaguered army—the defenders of a besieged Jerusalem in Roman days and the Zionist pioneers in the present—trying to ward off the attacks of an encroaching enemy and a crowd of merchants, money changers, and usurers who tend indifferently to their businesses today, just as they did in the time of Christ. Even when the eyes of the poet cleared, what they saw was not an empiric-mimetic Jerusalem but rather a city transfigured by the shorthand of an affective metaphor:

> Miserable tears on sallow cheeks
> drops dripped
> down the face of Jerusalem
> from crosses, turrets, domes,
> changing into slush.[19]

The poet Avigdor Hame'iri, whose lyric "From the Summit of Mount Scopus" evolved into a popular folk song, conveyed the excitement of Passover and spring in Jerusalem in this way:

> Lascivious angels chanted today in Jerusalem—
> Thousands of springs were compressed into me today
> And in its grave-hole every skeleton breathed sun . . .
> Jerusalem, Jerusalem, city of prayer and barrenness,
> Would you lay out for me today a warm bridal bed . . .
> To beget from under your heart the king, the Messiah?[20]

The first poet to develop this new nonmimetic, incandescent image of Jerusalem into a complex poetic locus was Yehuda Karni. When Karni arrived in Palestine in 1921, he was already thirty-seven years old and an established, albeit not highly respected, author of gloomy, musical, personal lyrics and wrathful, rhetorical national prophecies—in short, one of Bialik's many disciples. In the Land of Israel, however, Karni was reborn as a sinewy, tense expressionist who replaced lyrical melodiousness as well as prophetic rhetoric with a syncopated, jerky, enthusiastic—or, conversely, dirge-like—style that was public and intensely personal at one and the same time. He wrote short, compact odes bursting with contradictory emotions, as if energized by an alternating electric current. Jerusalem is the topic or the interlocutor to whom the best of these hectic apostrophes are addressed.

At first glance, these poems convey an overwhelming happiness and an overpowering need "to serve." To Karni, Jerusalem is still the gate to heaven, a bright crystalline palace, where one can touch the sky with one's hand and no cloud bars one's access to God. It is a temple lit by an enormous sun and illumined at different hours of the day with intense elemental colors. The mountains upon which it is perched glow like a polished altar, with the city itself burning like Isaiah's live coal, carried with tongs and placed there by the seraphim. All that the poet desires is to dwell in the courtyard of this temple and to serve, if not as a priest and a singer, then as a menial carrying the broom and the cleaning rag. The "service" clearly evokes both a personal religious association and a public nationalist one. However, one can detect dark undercurrents in Karni's ecstatic devotion to Jerusalem and in his celebration of its fairy tale–like beauty and multivalent radiance. The ecstasy is everywhere mingled with anger, violence, and cruelty aimed primarily at the poet himself. In one of his first and best-known Jerusalem poems, Karni wishes to be used as a stone covered with mortar, to be sunk into the city's wall. The wish is expressed in language reminiscent of the well-known midrashic tale about the ancient Hebrews who, in their bondage in Egypt, were forced to use the bodies of their own children as construction material, to bury them alive in the walls of the edifices that they were ordered to erect. In the Midrash, however, this burial of living children in the enemy's walls is presented as the ultimate atrocity to which the prophet referred in his accusation, "For the stone shall cry out of the wall, and the beam out of the timber shall answer it" (Habakkuk 2:11). In Karni's poem, this horrible death is vehemently sought after by the poet not only for the purpose of making a contribution to the strengthening of Jerusalem's walls but also as a means of elevating poetry to its highest sphere. In another poem, Karni calls on the bright sun of Jerusalem to dry out his eyes and blind him. In yet another, he alludes to Plutarch's story about the greedy Roman millionaire Crassus, who, as a military commander, steals the gold of the Middle Eastern temples until he is finally killed by zealots who pour molten gold into his insatiable throat. Similarly, the poet calls on the glowing midday sun of Jerusalem to pour its boiling gold into his insatiable soul and thereby gild "every remnant of a broken pillar in my temple."[21] All of these wishes are explained as the poet's response to the indifference and guilt of the Jewish people, who fail to realize the potential of Lord Balfour's promise of "a national Jewish home" in Palestine and flock to the devastated Holy City, which is in such dire need of their presence and energy. In their place the poet, as their representative, takes on himself the punishment that they deserve. But one suspects that Karni's violence emerges from sources that run deeper than mere Zionist reproof. Out of these sources other dark shadows emerge into the celebratory brightness of his Jerusalem odes. Suddenly, but not infrequently, Karni lashes out at the city that he so dearly loves and refers to it as a dusty graveyard perched on cadaverous mountains. Its famous radiance suddenly seems to him a mere theatrical lighting trick under which "the city of David" lies "dusty, exhausted, empty."[22] Jerusalem is branded with "a certain sin I cannot call by name."[23] The poet is quite ready to set it on fire "out of love and pain," to explode it and hurl its burnt debris at man and beast "in every country."[24] Quite unexpectedly the poet drops his elevated style, his hyperbole, and refers to the city in brutally coarse words, as if speaking of a place of ugliness and squalor. Karni's emotional and stylistic violence indicates a premonition or a suspicion that the ecstatic encounter with Jerusalem is potentially lethal and that the city he adulates as the epitome of realized personal and national yearnings might, after all, embody personal and national destruction. In the final analysis Karni's hymns, in their own lyrical, breathless, explosive manner, articulate an intuition not much different from the one that informs Agnon's epic portrayal of the city in *Yesteryear*.

For many, Karni became "the poet of Jerusalem." However, his Jerusalem poems were soon to be overshadowed by those of a younger poet, a pioneer of the Third Aliya who made Jerusalem the center of his vision. Uri Tsvi Greenberg came to Palestine in 1924 as a committed modernist, an expressionist, and a futurist in his poetic creed and in his political one, "a soldier of the Hebraic revolution" and a firm believer in the need for Zionism to define its goal as the immediate establishment of an extensive, powerful, industrialized, and militarized modern Jewish state. He had no interest whatsoever in Palestinian exotica, in the quaint deserted landscapes that he said could appeal only to "artists dreaming of profitable exhibitions in the West" and to tourists and pilgrims "in search of entertainment and titillation" and of views to "slip into the narrow mouth of their cameras and then board their countries' ships and sail back with Palestine tucked inside their valises."[25] The "poetry" of the sun-scorched landscape, the clear blue sky, the craggy mountains—which "did not contain oil wells and coal mines"—the antiquities, and the domes, and the arches all made him tired and depressed. What he wanted was "to desecrate this holy silence of historical desolation, / to run shrieking locomotives up to the valley of Jericho! / To wake up our Caesaria from its Edgar Allan Poe dream with siren calls from our ships and the singing of sailors."[26] When he referred to himself as a "Jerusalemite"—"How is it possible that this Jerusalemite body was born in Poland?" he asked himself[27]— or when he was talking about his "sealed interiority" as having been torn open and blitzed by the blaze of "the Jerusalemite vision,"[28] he was not referring to what most other poets were thinking of when they mentioned Jerusalem. Indeed, in the earliest poems he wrote in Palestine, the appellation *"Yerushalayim shel mata"* (the earthly Jeru-salem) clearly refers to the agricultural communities of the Jezreel Valley rather than to Jerusalem proper.

Jerusalem proper when he first encountered it shocked Greenberg and drove him to despair. It was a body "horribly pierced with a cross and a crescent," a "dissected corpse of a mother" whose "every member was torn apart,"[29] the head cut off and replaced by a mosque nailed to the truncated neck, the lifeblood still and always dripping. Walking in it was like trampling on human flesh. The poet, standing on the city wall, like "the last soldier of the House of David," prayed for an earthquake to destroy and eliminate the city and for a Beduin to come and "slaughter me in the moonlight on the wall." However, as the poet recoiled from the "disgraceful cadaver, the shattered spine, and the sand-filled kidneys" of a city that to him was more deadly than death itself, at the very same moment he also understood that he had to choose between only two roads: "One leads to the sea; the other—to the Wall," where one had to wait for the opening of "the last gate, for there was none other!"[30] The Jewish fate and the logic of Zionism dictated that Jerusalem, despite its horrible condition, despite the temptation to flee it, had to be "accepted" and acknow-ledged. Greenberg not only accepted it but also pressed it tightly to his heart, and eventually became its lover and its bard.

As Greenberg's Zionism progressed in a radical right-wing direc-tion, Jerusalem became the sine qua non of his poetry. Whoever— man, poet, Zionist leader—looked away from it, either in the direction of the socialist kibbutzim or in that of the lively and secular Tel Aviv, was accused of betrayal. A Zionist polity without Jerusalem as its center was not a Jewish entity but rather a kingdom of "Kozarim" (Khazars) who were also *"zarim"* (foreigners, aliens), and Tel Aviv as Jerusalem's rival was renamed by the poet "Tel-Khazar," its location on the sea coast *("shfela")* equated with baseness *("shiflut")*. Not that the poet really distanced himself from his initial vision of Jerusalem as deadly and horrific. In *"The Vision of One of the Legionnaires"* (1928), Greenberg's first full-fledged, prophetic political opus, Jerusalem figures not only as the citadel of the unvanquished enemy, at the ramparts of which the Zionist offensive was broken and its exhausted and demoralized pioneer soldiers defeated, but also as a vampire, "deeper than death in the vision of Titus, and still blood-thirsty, Jerusalem the killing one."[31] In this visionary poem, the quest for Jerusalem is projected as a descent into hell that could not end in any place other than at the banks of the Dead Sea, the lowest point on earth, where even the dead of the ancient cemetery of the Mount of Olives, once resurrected, were forced to undergo a second and even more horrible death. In the *House Dog* cycle (1929), the crucible in which both the poet's politics and his new prophetic political poetics takes shape at the highest emotional temperature, Jerusalem fluctuates among four very different images. One is that of an exotic Middle Eastern sun-scorched tourist attraction. Another is that of a hushed, depressed city, crouching under the heavy clouds of an approaching winter storm, tensely awaiting the decision being made in the secret cave where the military council of the "Hebrew rebellion" discussed the desperate situation and its equally desperate remedies. The third image is that of Christ's Jerusalem: the Temple and its courtyards, where Jesus (the poet) chased away the money changers and the usurers; the "new Jerusalem store," where the enemies of the Messiah ate pieces of his dissected flesh in a grotesque parody of the Last Supper; Golgotha, where Jesus was crucified, and so on. The fourth and most negative image is that of a deep well from which Jerusalem, a deadly Scylla-like temptress, beckons to all the unfortunate people who unknowingly come to the well for water. Even those who manage to flee the hypnotic feminine figure are inevitably drawn back to her and end up facedown, their skull broken and their arms in the well. The four images form a descending scale of negativity that starts with Jerusalem as a victim and proceeds to project her not only as the relentless enemy of the Messiah but also as the demonic, blood-thirsty female monster who craves the death of her most ardent lovers.

In spite of all this, Greenberg's identification with Jerusalem continually intensifies and expresses itself in attitudes and in a figurative vocabulary that belong at one and the same time in the realm of realpolitik, eschatological theology, and obsessive sexual attraction. On the level of realpolitik, whoever controls Jerusalem is the true master of the country as a whole, and whoever does not control it entirely—as was the case with the state of Israel before 1967—is bound to be defeated everywhere else. On the eschatological-theological level, only a return to the Temple Mount and a renewal of contact with the foundation stone—the rock in the Temple on which the Ark stood, and now the rock on which the Dome of the Rock stands—can trigger the full messianic renaissance of the Jewish spirit. On the erotic level, Jerusalem is both a mother and a lover whose sexual integrity and purity depend on the exclusion of any "foreign" presence. Such a presence amounts to rape, a violent phallic penetration of a consecrated vagina, a sexual contamination.

Greenberg was able to overcome his original loathing of Jerusalem partly as a result of the changing attitudes of the Jews, their growing readiness for self-assertion and the impact of their ever-growing presence in the city. Starting with the successful defense of the Jewish neighborhoods of Jerusalem in the Arab riots of 1929, which Greenberg celebrates in his "Defense Belt" (1930), the poet could afford an ever more positive and hopeful image, which was strengthened by the 1948 War of Independence and elevated to a temporary euphoria by the 1967 occupation of the Temple Mount. Greenberg could now envisage an eschatological Jerusalem united in Jewish military and political dominion, spiritual rebirth, and erotic bliss. However, these historical developments account only partially for the poet's change of heart, which was predicated mainly on Greenberg's ability to integrate Jerusalem as the centerpiece within the scheme of a personal myth. This myth, which controlled ever more pervasively both the content and the form of his poetry, is constructed as a sacred narrative based on the Bible, the New Testament, the messianic Midrashim, the Kabbalah, and a highly idiosyncratic interpretation of Jewish history. In this narrative, the poet figures as both the last and the first link in a chain of prophetic and messianic figures: last in the temporal sense, he is also the first in the sense that he is the prophet poet asserting the contemporary validity of the "mission" he shares with all other messianic figures. If Greenberg was the true follower of Abraham, King David, Jesus, Yehuda Halevi, Shlomo Molkho, Shabbetai Tsvi, and others, they were also his predecessors and forerunners. And since the dramas in which all of them had taken part had either been played out in Jerusalem or had pointed in its direction, he, the poet who was now reenacting them, also lived in and for Jerusalem. His very being was unified with that of the Holy City, no matter what the consequences might be.

Nevertheless, when all is said and done, Greenberg never completely suppressed his doubts and suspicions concerning Jerusalem. As late as the war of 1948, when his identification with the city had already been fully conceptualized and stabilized, he could with astounding sincerity adopt the hostile attitude of a bereaved mother viewing Jerusalem as a young and attractive woman who "stole" away her son and offered him a dry filthy hole for a grave rather than a blissful bridal bed, which the young man might have expected. Greenberg's poetry never transcends completely the bipolar arena in which modern Hebrew literature stages its Jerusalem spectacle.

Yehuda Amichai, the "Jerusalem Poet"

Israeli belles lettres are replete with such demonstrations of Jerusalem's duality. While the bulk of the Israeli "Jerusalem literature" was produced or at least published after 1967, when Jerusalem came to be perceived as the spatial, political, and social focal point of the "Israeli condition," the foundations of the Israeli image of Jerusalem were laid earlier, in the 1950s and early 1960s, when the characteristic physiognomy of Israeli culture emerged. However, most of the significant attempts to incorporate the Jerusalem landscape and "essence" into works of prose fiction, particularly novels, were made after 1967. Especially significant among these are the eight sequels of *The Palace of Shattered Vessels*, David Shahar's Proustian cycle of novels in which the meandering narrative, guided by memory and association, freely moves among different pasts and diverse groups of characters. Constantly practicing a technique that resembles a photographic "double exposure," Shahar attempts to present an integrated view of Jerusalem and of life in general that reconciles the sublime and the gross, pathos and bathos. Shahar's technique of integration, however, while often yielding fascinating results, also precipitates his narrative into the shallows of narcissism, sheer parochialism, and cloying "cuteness." (The last two characteristics, by the way, have become the hallmarks of much of the current trashy Jerusalem fiction.) Recurrent simplistic references to the doctrines and symbols of the Kabbalah also add to all this a troubling intellectual dimension.

In *Mr. Mani* (1991), A. B. Yehoshua presents a more vigorous, intellectually convincing, and serious juxtaposition of various historical and cultural Jerusalems, which quite intentionally do not add up to an integral whole. Israeli prose fiction, it seems, still has to cover a considerable distance before it reaches a contemporary version of the Jerusalem bipolarity that would be as daring and as engrossing as the one offered by Agnon in *Yesteryear.*

However, despite the fact that prose fiction has been for more than two decades the dominant genre in Israeli literature, it was initially a late bloomer that followed the lead of other genres, particularly poetry. It is in the works of the poets—once the "shock of statehood" had been absorbed, internalized, and developed into a self-conscious state of mind—that the Israeli literary idiom found its first articulation. Therefore it was the lyrical image of Jerusalem that became the model of the Israeli vision, rather than the epic one. From the early 1950s, a host of poets were hard at work, each in his own manner, on an Israeli redefinition of the "essence" of Jerusalem: a redefinition based on intuitions very different from and often contradictory to those that had informed the pre-Israeli poetic Jerusalems of Karni, Hame'iri, and Greenberg. It is impossible to mention more than a few of these poets here: Chayim Gouri, David Roke'ach, Avner Treynin, Harold Schimmel, Tsharni Carmi, and, of course, Yehuda Amichai, the most prominent among them. Naturally these are highly individualistic poets who differ from each other in many ways. However, in varying degrees and directions, they all dissociated their image of Jerusalem from those that had been most characteristic of the fervent pre-Israeli decades of the Zionist drive, particularly of those of Uri Tsvi Greenberg.

Indeed, at least at the beginning, many Israeli poems about Jerusalem could be read as answers to or refutations of Greenberg's vision. As a characteristic illustration, one may quote an early poem by Dan Pagis, written in 1956, that in terms of both content and style sets out to question the validity of such a vision.

"The Eternal City"

Wounded by songs of Praise
carved with daggers
on her thin shoulders, crowned with the halo
of the sacred fire. All the legions
swooped to seek their redeemer
In her arms, made her the heart of the world
For all seekers of miracles, bound
and crucified her for the glory of her name—
And never stopped to wonder why
She hid herself behind a wall within a wall.
The eternal city like a brown fist
Clenched in stone, and still expecting
In her fenced and circumscribed stubbornness
To live peacefully, her fingers interlocked.
But inside her all invokers of wonders,
All necromancers, pray for the omen
Which will descend on her from heaven
Turning her face upside down and hiding
Her soul in a bundle of clod, sanctifying her
for ever at their feet like in a graveyard.[32]

Here one detects antagonism to Greenberg not only in the poet's sarcastic comments on "seekers of miracles," "invokers of wonders," and the like, or even in the reference to "all the legions," which clearly targets Greenberg's "Vision of One of the Legionnaires," but also in the portrayal of Jerusalem as a sexual object, a woman whose self-proclaimed lovers seek redemption "in her arms." Unlike the seductive mother-bride of Greenberg's poems, however, Pagis's Jerusalem is an unattractive woman with thin shoulders who hides herself fearfully from these lovers behind walls and behind her "fenced and circumscribed stubbornness." Pagis also intuitively penetrates the suppressed aggressive resentment that often lurks at the bottom of Greenberg's overwhelming love for Jerusalem.

Pagis's Jerusalem was "eternal" not because of her transcendent qualities but because of her "stubbornness" and the stratagems that enabled her to hide herself from all those who would confer on her marvels, miracles, and omens. Spurning their dangerous love, she expected to live "peacefully" and within her circumscribed, small world of mundane daily affairs.

As a city of so-called normal everyday people, intent on living their daily life in relative security and with very humble expectations, Jerusalem made its most impressive appearance in early Israeli poetry in the work of Yehuda Amichai. Amichai, who has lived in Jerusalem for most of his life—he arrived there in 1936 at the age of twelve—and who has never tired of contemplating the city and comparing its life to his own, was to become the Israeli "Jerusalem poet" par excellence. As he himself comments,

> I am a Jerusalemite. Swimming pools with
> their voices and noises are no part of my soul.
> The dust is my conscious, the stone my subconscious
> And all my memories are closed courtyards
> at summer's high noon.[33]

Here then is Karni's and Greenberg's Israeli heir—as unlikely an heir as possible, since by temperament, weltanschauung, politics, and poetic practice alike, he is their quintessential opposite. Where they emphasize the primacy of the extraordinary, he is the poet of the ordinary; where they seek transcendental "redemption," he insists that the faint glow emanating from an opened refrigerator at night while a hungry woman fixes herself a meal is the only "otherworldly" light he knows; where they talk to the angels, the only rustle of angelic wings he recognizes is that of the pages of a newspaper, peacefully turned at night in bed after a hard day's work; where they command the Hebrew of all ages and styles—Greenberg actually compares himself to the prophet Ezekiel, bringing back to life the dry bones of a dead language—Amichai characterizes himself as a poet "who uses only a fraction of the words that can be found in the dictionary,"[34] and developed a poetic diction as close to the spoken idiom as had ever been used before in Hebrew poetry; where they resort to pathos, hyperbole, stunning metaphors, and heightened emotionalism, he prefers irony, wit, playful conceits, puns, humor, and calm elegiac contemplation; and, of course, whereas they stand at the forefront of Zionist maximalism, he is committed to minimalism, always putting the concerns of the individual before the national and collective goal.

In his early collections, *Now and in Other Days* (1955), *Two Hopes Away* (1958), and *In the Municipal Park* (1959), Amichai's Jerusalem amounts to nothing more than the city in which the poet lives, loves, and works, and from which he goes, more than once, to fight the wars of his generation. The arched windows characteristic of the city serve him as the basis for a conceit in which the poet and his lover bend toward each other until their foreheads touch and are supported by each other. Its tiny municipal park is to him the woman lover "in whom all beginnings become happy round endings,"[35] while the poet is the adjoining street that "tears the town" in two and in which "every peaceful end is a sign for a new sprint." The stratified stony earth, uncovered where the railway cuts the mountainside, projects the condition of the lovers, both in their living embrace and as buried one on top of the other after their death. The parched, cracking earth after the winter dampness has left it indicates the possible end of love, the ephemeral nature of happiness. Amichai, of course, does not suppress his awareness of the fact that Jerusalem has a tragic history, that it had been recently torn in two by war and is still scarred and divided, full of patches of no-man's-land and minefields that have not been completely "cleared." He remembers how, in 1948, all "of the beautiful buses of our city, lines 12, 8, and 5, led to the front,"[36] and how the soldiers would bivouac temporarily in empty municipal kindergartens, using the teddy-bears as pillows. His poem about the UN headquarters, situated between Jewish and Arab territories as if in limbo, compares it to the self, sequestered and yet connected to its environment "through winding pipes, through dark reins, like a fetus."[37] And yet, he does not allow "the open shouting mouth," the public voice that proclaims itself in poems, to speak for him. Rather, he wants "the terrible, shut up mouth" found under the debris of bombed houses to read for him "the proclamation of reality," in the Hebrew original, a pun on the proclamation of independence.[38] This is a proclamation that prescribes acceptance of things as they are, normal life even in an abnormal time and place.

In the poem "In Yemin Moshe" (referring to one of the early Jewish neighborhoods built outside of the walled city with the support of Moses Montefiore), Amichai re-creates a scene of lovemaking on scorched ground against the grand historical background of the Wall and the Tower of David:

Notwithstanding the prophecies
We lasted for a long time,
Vanquished and weak
And despite the insurance companies
Which refused to insure our happiness.[39]

And in "Poems for the New Year," he observes:

A house half torn down
Resembles a house yet unfinished
Jesus who spread his arms nailed to the cross,
Resembled Samson, who also
Stood with arms spread between the pillars
God, who only takes snapshots and then moves on
Cannot differentiate between the two.[40]

Thus the truncated Jerusalem and the circumscribed existence for which it stands are abnormal only in the eye of the beholder. Without hindsight and future projection, one could accept a house half torn down, live and love there for a long time. As Amichai was to say later and in a different context, even in the mouth of the lion one could make oneself a house as comfortable as circumstances allowed.

If this vision had crystallized into a fixed, unchanging attitude, Amichai could hardly have written the absorbing and complex Jerusalem poems of his later years. As much as the reductionist, minimalist interpretation of life in Jerusalem authentically expresses the mood of the 1950s, the emotional exhaustion of a generation sent too often into battle in the name of history, it could not accommodate the inherent bipolarity of the Jerusalem experience. But Amichai's attitude was changing. As early as the beginning of the 1960s, he recorded experiences of the city in temporal and spatial terms incommensurate with the dimensions of existence as a mere snapshot taken at a specific moment and accepted in the name of the reality of the here and now. The emphasis on the here and now remained at the very heart of Amichai's vision of life as it needs to be lived, even in the most historical of cities; but a growing awareness of the other dimensions of Jerusalem inevitably appeared as the poet matured. At first this awareness found expression indirectly, perhaps paradoxically, in what looked like an abandonment of Jerusalem. As if afraid of the complexity that could not be evaded anymore, the poet seemed to flee Jerusalem, which for some time ceased to be the self-evident "place" of his poetry. However, some short, poignant poems written at that stage reveal the true meaning of this "desertion." One of them is the well-known poem about the sadness of the mayor of Jerusalem: "How can a man be mayor of such a city? What can he do with it?" Amichai asked, adding that even as the mayor "builds and builds and builds"

> At night the stones of the mountain crawl down
> And surround the stone houses
> Like wolves coming to howl at dogs
> Who have become the slaves of men.[41]

In another poem, Amichai contemplates the laundry hanging on the roofs of the old Arab city and a kite flying there, connected by a taut line to the hand of an Arab boy he cannot see. Although Amichai said more than once that wherever laundry is hanging out to dry, people have a chance of surviving for a few days, because laundry and war do not go together, in this poem, the sight of the Arab laundry fills him with sadness and a sense of the complexity of life in a divided city, rather than with satisfaction. In both the poem about the mayor and the one about the laundry, Amichai has to face the fact that existence in his hometown cannot be reduced even to a temporary composure and will not countenance shallow consolation. Jerusalem is a city informed by pain. It is a "terrible" place, as its sad mayor knows. Both time and space are too big there, too divided between now and then, here and there, friend and foe, to derive any comfort even from the lively sight of new houses, or laundry, or flying kites. There are

> Too many olive trees in the valley,
> Too many stones on the slope.
> Too many dead, too little
> earth to cover them all . . .
> Too many memorial days, too little
> Remembering . . . Too many clocks,
> Too little time. Too many oaths
> On the Bible, too many highways, too few
> Ways where we can truly go . . .[42]

By the mid-1960s, Amichai was immersed in experimenting on a massive scale with integrating his experiences into ever larger and more comprehensive contexts. His early existentialist reductionism, although never completely abandoned, was now sufficiently expanded for a new "essentialist" intuition. The conceit, or non-"organic" metaphor, which until now had been the poet's chief tool in differentiating his "authentic" and "narrow" experiences from anything larger that might have resembled them but actually only falsified them, developed into an effective poetic means of detecting common denominators, even where no extrinsic resemblances seemed to exist. It was now put to use in large lyrical, prosaic, and poetic texts that could be read like personal Midrashim. In these, the poet negotiates—through metaphor, association, repetition, pun, allusion, cataloging, and collections of trivia—compromises between the various components of a heterogeneous reality. The first of these was the lyrical novel *Not of This Time, Not of This Place* (1963), in which two completely separate but parallel plot lines juxtapose the life of the protagonist, who, having been born in Germany, should have perished with his childhood love, Ruth, and the same protagonist as an Israeli scholar, who had fought in the 1948 war and was now immersed in a love affair in the Jerusalem of the 1950s. After the novel came a very long poem, "Travels of the Last Benjamin of Tudela," a comprehensive autobiographical compendium in which the poet, comparing himself to the famous Jewish medieval traveler, attempted to organize and interrelate, if not unify, not only the different parts of his own life but also large sequences of seemingly unrelated historical, military, liturgical, and literary associations.

Jerusalem is fully present in these large amalgams. However, characteristically, it was only after the Six-Day War that "Jerusalem 1967," the first extended midrashic cycle organized around the theme of Jerusalem, was written—just as the second large cycle, "Song of Zion the Beautiful," emerged in the wake of the 1973 war. In "Jerusalem 1967" (1968), Amichai's reaction to the new reality of the reunited and "redeemed" city, although fundamentally different from—indeed essentially hostile to—the then-current euphoric Jerusalem cult, complete with its accessories of instant historicism and kitsch metaphysics, amounted to an acknowledgment of the fact that the unification of the city paralleled the process of enlarging and better coordinating the poet's own being. Finally giving up any attempt to "understand" Jerusalem, and the self, in terms of the here and now only, Amichai accepted the unique reality of "the only city in the world where the right to vote was granted even to the dead."[43] As much as he knew that he had to travel a long way—in space—"to view the silence of my city," for a city "calms down from a distance" even as a baby calms down when you rock it, he also knew that distance in time was equally essential to an understanding of the dynamics of Jerusalem, its historic noise. For in this city, numbers indicate not bus routes but "70 after, 1917, 500 BC, '48. These are the lines you really travel on."[44] Nothing really disappears in Jerusalem, not even the barbed wire, which before the war used to separate the hostile Jewish and Arab contingents. History, with all of its pain, is ever present. The town, made of "houses with houses above them," and of "curved hooks holding air," "columns and arches supporting vain land," is constantly negotiating, bringing together "crusaders and guardian angels, a sultan and Rabbi Yehuda the Pious."[45] The here and now is a mere illusion. Above it, "the demons of the past" are meeting with "the demons of the future . . . in the high arches of shell-orbits above my head."[46] If the city looked static, it was only because our eyes could not see it as it really was: "a huge ship, a magnificent luxury liner" anchored for a while to let its passengers embark or board before it sailed away again out to the sea of "eternity." It was "always arriving, always sailing away."[47] It could stay put only because its vaulted foundation was formed by "a held-back scream." If the scream ceased, the city would collapse; if it emitted its "scream," Jerusalem would explode into heavens."[48] Because of this eternally tenuous stasis, Jerusalem could connect that which one deemed unconnectable. One could retrieve in it almost anything that one had lost. For instance, on Yom Kippur in 1967, the poet, entering the Old City, where he had not been in two decades, finds, not far from the Damascus Gate, an Arab "hole in the wall shop" of buttons, zippers, and spools of thread that is the exact replica of his own father's shop, burned down in his provincial German hometown. But in Jerusalem, one could reach back not only into one's own lost past but into all other lost pasts as well, for Jerusalem, unlike Sodom, its "sister city," does not allow the "merciful salt" to settle on it and cover it. It is "an unconsenting Pompeii," "an operation that is left open." One has to learn to live with Jerusalem as it is, although this is not easy, because the air over the city, as the poet said in a later poem, is saturated with prayers and dreams "like the air over industrial cities," and "from time to time a new shipment of history arrives."[49]

Necessarily, the city is full of "used Jews, worn out by history, second-hand Jews slightly damaged."[50] But Jerusalem is also a place where one genuinely experiences one's own continuous temporal reality. Here one touches one's existence by pressing one's fingers into the accumulated layers of desert dust, and here one can finally reach down to one's mental rock bottom, as to the rock that is "my subconscious."[51] In "Jerusalem 1967" and his subsequent Jerusalem poems, Yehuda Amichai masterfully articulates the Israeli version of the Jerusalem theme in all of its inherent binaries and oppositions.

13 Geography and Geometry of Jerusalem

BIANCA KÜHNEL

There is no city other than Jerusalem whose history is so intimately intertwined with its symbolism. No other city's history depends so much on its own symbolism. No other city's symbolism so dominates its very existence. No other city has been invested with so many identities by so many different peoples over such long periods of time. And no city has more consistently enjoyed the privilege of a double dimension, earthly and heavenly, or accomplished more swiftly the transition between one and the other, between earth and heaven, heaven and earth.

The unique destiny of Jerusalem, the real and the ideal, has inevitably left many imprints on its every aspect. However, in daily life as well as in the study of its history, politics, demography, and even archaeology and literature, the special dimension of Jerusalem, its complex personality, remains hidden behind trivial realities, numbers, dilapidated ruins and ugly reconstructions, particularistic fates, and even poetic dreams. The visualization of Jerusalem through art has an advantage over other forms, either scientific or literary, because of its ability to make clear in a single image, in a direct, condensed, but richly associative way, the whole range of Jerusalem's connotations at points in its long history. Visual representations can be syncretistic; they have the ability to capture in one glance physical appearances, religious connotations, and universal symbolism, without sacrificing historical parameters and artistic values. Visual representations of Jerusalem are, therefore, an immensely valuable source for the reconstruction of the city's multiple facets throughout its existence.

Following the paths taken by some of the visual formulas invented to depict or suggest Jerusalem in its earthly or heavenly dimension, at different times, locations, and religious contexts, allows us to understand Jerusalem's realities. Several aspects in particular best portray the character of the city and its history. They are representative of the impact of Jerusalem on the visual arts, of the kind of associative thought generated by Jerusalem, of the repetitive constancy and consistency (either intended or accidental) of some motifs, up to our own day, in Jewish, Christian, and Muslim art. In a word, this selection of topics and works of art sets out to illustrate the universal character of Jerusalem in art as a reflection of the universal character of the city.

Either because of historical vicissitudes or the Second Commandment, the first extant comprehensive visual depictions of Jerusalem are Christian, not Jewish, in spite of the fact that Jerusalem was chosen by King David to be the nation's capital, and in the following years also became the religious center of the people of Israel, and then, when lost, the national object of hope and the eschatological focus of every Diaspora community. Yet the first thousand years of Jerusalem's exclusively Jewish history did not remain completely devoid of visual expression. The Jewish beliefs and traditions concerning Jerusalem were formative in the Christian view of the Holy City, and as such they are implicit in almost any Christian visual representation.[1]

Ideograms of Early Christian Art

Because of the conceptual character of early Christian and medieval art, the first visual representations of Jerusalem are ideograms: pictures of a walled agglomeration of buildings, endowed with some special characteristics (prominent location, shining appearance, striking symmetry) of special connotation within an elaborate eschatological program. "Hierusalem" paired with "Bethleem" at the base of the triumphal arch of the fifth-century church of Santa Maria Maggiore in Rome is basically a neutral collection of buildings, distinguished by the vicinity of a combined circular and basilical building (a simplified rendering of the Constantinian Holy Sepulchre Church), the many precious stones on its walls, and the adoring sheep at its feet. The presence of Jerusalem on the arch in connection with its twin, Bethlehem, becomes comprehensible in view of their common correlation with Rome, represented by the apostles Peter and Paul, who are depicted on the apex of the arch and dominate the whole composition.[2] In Santa Maria Maggiore, Jerusalem is part of a political program created by a papacy anxious to assure Rome's primacy in the Christian world. The two founders of its own holiness, Peter and Paul, are placed along and above the two main places made holy by Christ's Nativity and Resurrection. The paired representation of Jerusalem and Bethlehem in Santa Maria Maggiore is the earliest in a series of similar wall mosaics usually associated with an apse composition showing Christ's Second Advent and found almost exclusively in Rome.[3] The ecclesiastical and political character of these depictions seems to be a constant feature of the Roman representations of Jerusalem, arising from church rivalries or as a means of ascribing additional strength to oneself through association with Christianity's holiest places or with heavenly Jerusalem.[4] The thirteenth-century mosaic by Jacopo Torriti in the apse of San Giovanni in Laterano, depicting heavenly Jerusalem watered by the Rivers of Paradise streaming from a *crux gemmata* in the center of the composition, has recently been interpreted as the embodiment of the aspirations cherished by the first Franciscan pope, Nicholas IV (1288–1292), to lead Rome to a spiritual revival.[5] The placement of Peter and Paul within the walls of the heavenly Jerusalem in this mosaic is a new expression of the same venerable aspiration of the early Christian papacy to associate itself with Jerusalem; the choice of heavenly Jerusalem, rather than earthly Jerusalem and Bethlehem, as the exponent of the Holy Land is better suited to the thirteenth century, at the peak of a two- or three-hundred-year-old tradition of Apocalypse illustration; in the early Christian period, interest in the holy places of Jerusalem and Bethlehem, only recently propagated by Constantine the Great and kept alive through continuous imperial interest and building, was more current.

The Jerusalem representations in sixth- and eighth-century floor mosaics in Jordan, although locally oriented, are by no means realistic renderings of the city: they served the local Church exactly as the Roman wall mosaics reflected the interests of the bishop of Rome. In the sixth-century Madaba floor mosaic, Jerusalem, enclosed in an oval wall, occupies the center of a pilgrimage map of the Holy Land.[6] The centrality of its location (with respect to the other places on the map, as well as to the church building); the closed geometrical shape; the inner symmetry, especially the location of the Church of the Holy

Sepulchre in relation to the *cardo*, the city's north to south axis—all these invest the representation of Jerusalem and the Holy Land with a pronounced eschatological character.[7] The eighth-century representation of Jerusalem in the Church of St. Stephen in Umm al-Rasas (Kastron Mefaa), inscribed "ΗΑΓΙΑ ΠΩΛΙϹ" (Hagiapolis, the Holy City), appears in a different context (Figure 17),[8] in a sequence of cities from the Holy Land and Jordan, depicted on the side borders of a large composition whose central field is occupied by populated scrolls framed by a maritime landscape. The representations of cities are divided into two tiers. The southern row is devoted to the local Jordanian cities and begins at the eastern end with Kastron Mefaa, while the northern row contains cities of the Holy Land and starts in the east with Jerusalem. The preeminence of Jerusalem is achieved by its location and by its pronounced symmetrical representation. Certainly the depiction of Kastron Mefaa, twice as big as that of any other city on the mosaic (the only one to cover two fields), competes with that of Jerusalem. Do we not see here the same tendency as in Rome, namely the desire to gain power for a local town from the vicinity of, parallelism to, and even competition with the Holy City? Is this not also a means to connect the historically limited geography of a region with eschatology, exactly as the biblical geography of the Madaba map turns out to be an itinerary for salvation?

In all these early Christian examples, in Rome as in the Middle East, Jerusalem is depicted according to a well-established late Roman formula of showing cities as a conglomerate of buildings surrounded by a wall and towers, in a combination of bird's-eye and side views. The uniqueness of Jerusalem is made clear by special features: precious stones, decided symmetry, or central location. Early Christian Jerusalem is an ambiguous visual creature: neither earthly nor heavenly, still bound to the formulas proper to any city but endowed with some unique features, definitely enjoying a special status but still comparable to Bethlehem, Rome, or even Kastron Mefaa.

The Geometry: Apocalyptic Jerusalem in Medieval Art

Only later, in medieval art, did the clear-cut apocalyptic context produce the first depictions of heavenly Jerusalem that no longer had anything in common with other cities, not even, or especially not,

Figure 17. The Holy City in a floor mosaic, Church of St. Stephen, Umm al-Rasas, Jordan.

LITERATURE, ART, AND ARCHITECTURE

with the city of Jerusalem in Judea. This is a natural development, since heavenly Jerusalem is presented by the New Testament (Revelation 21 and 22) as the only Jerusalem acceptable to the Christian, in contrast to the old, Jewish, historical Jerusalem rejected by Christ (Luke 19:41–44). It is still surprising, however, that Christian art took so long—until the ninth century—to create its own formulas for designating heavenly Jerusalem. This was the time of the first extant illuminated manuscripts of the Apocalypse, close to the writing of the Commentary to the Apocalypse by Beatus of Lièbana and probably also to the first illuminated manuscripts of it.[9] Some of the medieval illustrated Apocalypses may go back to sixth-century models, and it seems even more probable that some illustrations, but not all, were inspired or even borrowed from early Christian representations.[10]

Two Carolingian illuminated manuscripts of the Apocalypse have come down to us and are now in the Municipal Libraries of Trier (codex 31)[11] and Valenciennes (manuscript 99), respectively.[12] They evidently reflect two different pictorial traditions, exemplified in two illustrations of heavenly Jerusalem. The Trier illumination (folios 69, 70, and 71)[13] is entirely indebted to the early Christian mode, based on the antique tradition of illustrating cities through a neutral agglomeration of buildings and adding some special features to fit Jerusalem, in this case twelve towers, a compact, symmetrical appearance, and, on folio 71, the Lamb and a branching tree in the middle of the city. With all their differences, these illustrations still have a lot in common with the early Christian depictions of Jerusalem in Santa Maria Maggiore, Madaba, and Kastron Mefaa.

The Valenciennes Apocalypse contains an original representation of heavenly Jerusalem (Figure 18), very different from the late antique and early Christian patterns of visualizing cities, and well connected to medieval preoccupations with the structure of the universe. The illustration on folio 38 is a perfectly geometric, circular scheme formed by twelve concentric roundels of different colors, divided in cross form by four groups of three gates each (Revelation 21:12–13). The Lamb (Revelation 21:22–23) appears in the center of the round space enclosed by the concentric circles. Beneath the circular scheme, the Angel and John, both cut in half by the lower part of the page frame, point toward the heavenly apparition. This heavenly Jerusalem is clearly distinguished from earlier representations of the city by its abstract,

Figure 18. The Heavenly City, Valenciennes Apocalypse.

geometric form, in itself in accord with the Revelation text. The only significant difference between the geometric Jerusalem of Valenciennes and the Jerusalem of Revelation is that John speaks of a square (Revelation 21:16). The same circular representation appears again in the same context a hundred years later in a manuscript now in Paris, probably a copy of the manuscript in Valenciennes.[14]

The square of John's Revelation, disregarded by the illuminators of the Trier and Valenciennes Apocalypses as well as by the early Christian mosaicists, was first translated into a visual depiction of heavenly Jerusalem in manuscripts of the Beatus Commentary to the Apocalypse, written and probably also first illustrated in the second half of the eighth century. The earliest extant illustrated manuscript of a Beatus Commentary, that in the Pierpont Morgan Library in New York (Figure 19), dates from the second quarter of the tenth century.[15] The geometric scheme representing Jerusalem on folio 222v is formed by concentric squares enclosing a checkered square field for the Lamb, John, and the Angel. Like the circle of the Valenciennes Apocalypse, the square is divided in cross form by the twelve gates distributed in four groups. The triple gates are Mozarabic arch openings, each occupied by the figure of an apostle and a precious foundation stone (Revelation 21:14). Unlike the representation in Valenciennes, the square of the Pierpont Morgan manuscript, like that of other later Beatus copies, retains some resemblance to real city walls. The protruding towers and the outer contour have a jagged profile. As a result of these "realistic" elements and the relatively numerous personages incorporated in the scheme, as well as the rich palette of vivid colors and forms, the purity of the geometric scheme is somewhat veiled, especially when compared with the Valenciennes disk. Nevertheless, this scheme, too, initiated a long and solid tradition, as evinced not only by the later Beatus manuscripts, but also by monumental representations or liturgical objects that displace the square form from its immediate textual source and put it in totally different contexts. A good illustration is the three-dimensional copper and enamel Eucharistic Dove, manufactured in the thirteenth century in Limoges and now in the Rijksmuseum in Amsterdam (Figure 20).[16] The Dove stands in a citylike square enclosure with walls and towers that look as though they are made of brick. The object functioned as an altar vessel for the host and was shaped according to the call

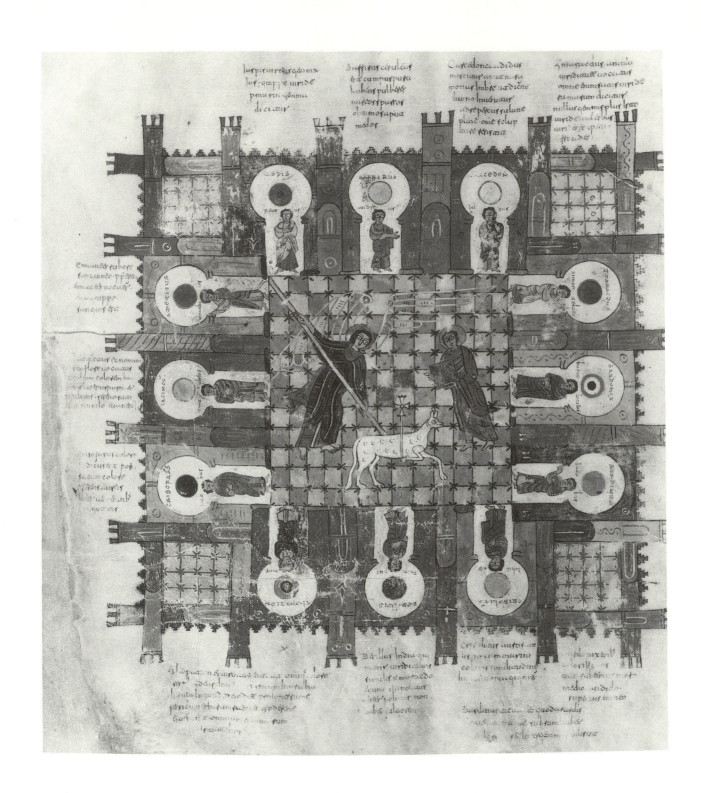

Figure 20. The Eucharistic Dove, Limoges.

Figure 19. Heavenly Jerusalem, Beatus of Liebana Commentary to the Apocalypse.

addressed by the priest to Christ during the Mass, to come down from heaven and allow the congregation the opportunity to experience his presence on earth.[17]

We may thus conclude that early medieval art produced two geometrical schemes to designate Jerusalem as the heavenly creature of Revelation, as against the ambiguous early Christian representations that floated somewhere between earth and heaven, between anonymous city depictions and special marks of the unique Holy City. The square scheme of the Beatus manuscripts is based on Revelation (21:16). However, the gap in time between the text and its translation into a matching visual depiction is puzzling, as is the round scheme of the Valenciennes and Paris Apocalypses, which is not even justified by a direct textual description. Of course, one may appeal to circumstantial evidence to explain the round Jerusalem or the late appearance of the square one in visual arts: there is the interchangeability of circle and square as two equally perfect geometrical shapes; the emphasizing of the square in the Beatus Commentary text; and, a more sophisticated reason, the resemblance between the plan of the Holy Sepulchre Church, as drawn by Arculf-Adamnan and copied several times in Carolingian manuscripts, and the round heavenly Jerusalem in the Apocalypse of Valenciennes.[18] These are all valid points. However, the main reason for the geometricity of heavenly Jerusalem in contexts where no other Jerusalem is involved, such as the Apocalypse or the Commentary, is still lacking, and is to be sought in areas not usually visited by art historians: astronomy and geography.

Medieval Schemes of the Universe

A geometric scheme was necessary to bring into focus the transcendental character of heavenly Jerusalem, its unearthly and antihistorical being. Not some arbitrary geometric design, but precisely that which was created to make visible the medieval concept of the universe, a concept based on antique knowledge, but collected, revised, and Christianized in the early Middle Ages in encyclopedias and treatises such as those of Isidor of Seville and the Venerable Bede, and largely propagated through massive copying and writing during the Carolingian renaissance. According to this concept, the universe, the world, *mundus,* consists of spheres, the planets, that revolve concentrically on preestablished orbits around the immovable earth. An outer sphere, that of the firmament of fixed stars, encloses the whole like a shell. This system was defined in the fourth century BCE by Eudoxus of Knidos, developed by Aristotle, and perfected and turned into an astronomical theory by Ptolemy in the second century BCE. The fathers of the early Church conferred Christian authority on this antique view of the world, although its first comprehensive Christian updating and formulation belong to Isidor of Seville's two major works, *Etymologiae* and *De natura rerum,* both written after he became an archbishop in 600. The corpus of Isidor's learning was cited, disseminated, enriched throughout the Middle Ages, and a dense chain of followers and commentators can be reconstructed between him and the late Middle Ages. The Carolingian period is especially well represented in this lineage: the Venerable Bede (672/3–735), Hrabanus Maurus (780–856), John Scotus Eriugena (ca. 810–877), Remigius of Auxerre (841–908).[19] Isidor of Seville has a special and direct importance for the history of art, since large parts of the scientific theories on nature that he reformulated were accompanied by graphics.

An encyclopedic Collectar manuscript compiled in the cathedral library of Cologne under Archbishop Hildebald (785–819) contains many excerpts from Isidor and Bede accompanied by plans illustrating not only the planetary system (Figure 21) but also the calendar with the twelve months, the seasons of the year, the winds and cardinal directions, the microcosmos with elements and temperaments, the world divided into four parts according to the elements and the cardinal directions, and so on.[20] All these schemes consist of concentric circles with the respective components specified through inscriptions and revolving around one more comprehensive component: the twelve months and the seasons around the year *(Annus),* the four elements and temperaments around the *Cosmos Homo,* the seven planets around the earth, and so on. Sometimes the addition of squares leads to more articulated schemes, as in the complex graphic of the world partitioned into four (Figure 22) that includes a square earth flanked by inscriptions specifying the four temperaments and elements, surrounded by the seven planets and the firmament in concentric circles; this disk is radially divided into twelve months and is placed in the center of a big square flanked by inscriptions indicating the four

Figure 21. The Planetary System, Collectar manuscript, Cologne.

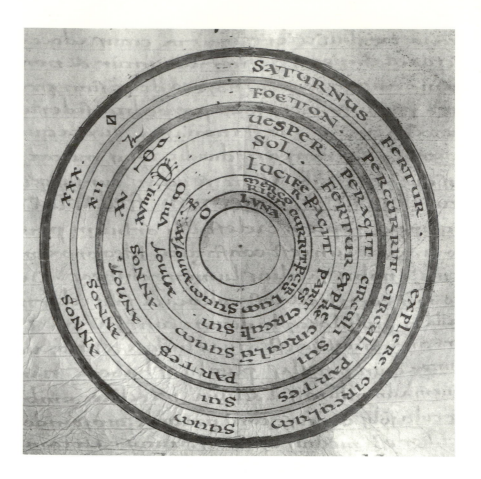

winds and cardinal directions. All these schemes are purely graphic and technically illustrative of a scientific text. They are accompanied only by explanatory inscriptions and have no claim to any artistic merit. It is perhaps this unintentional aspect that makes their impact on illustrations to various texts of a narrative, figurative, and symbolical character more convincing.

The illustration of heavenly Jerusalem on folio 38 of the Apocalypse in Valenciennes has exactly the same linear precision as the concentric circles indicating the seven planets and the firmament in the Collectar of Cologne. It also has explanatory inscriptions indicating the four cardinal directions (and explaining the presence of the Lamb). Of course, this is not automatic copying but a translation of the cosmos

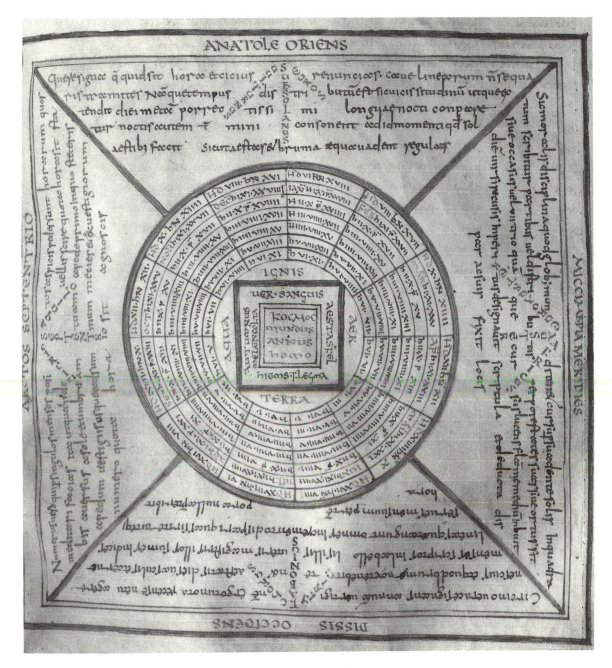

Figure 22. The Quadripartite World, Collectar manuscript, Cologne.

graphic of the Heavenly City of the Apocalypse: diverging from the technical designs of the encyclopedic treatises, the concentric circles of apocalyptic Jerusalem are twelve in number, and the central round field is occupied by the Lamb. In addition, the round scheme is divided in cross form by the symmetrical arrangement of the twelve gates, as the Revelation text requires. However, the interference with the cosmological scheme may also have a basis in the theological-cosmological field.

Gregory of Nyssa (309), as well as the Venerable Bede, Hrabanus Maurus, and Sedulius, introduced the cross into the scheme of the universe: the earth is determined by the cross, whose arms indicate the four cardinal directions.[21] The introduction of the cross in the well-known and universally accepted concept of the round universe led to a complementary emphasis on the square form of the world. The clearest written formulation of this link comes from Honorius of Autun, although it is evidently based on a long exegetical chain: in a dialogue between pupil and master, the pupil asks, "Why should Christ have wanted to die on the cross?" and the master answers: "He had to die on the quatrefoil cross, in order to bring Salvation to the world shaped in four [*quadrifidum mundum*]."[22] Encircled early medieval monumental crosses in the British Isles[23] are among the earliest visual outcomes of this connection between circle and cross, besides the Valenciennes illustration. The great emphasis, especially during the early medieval period, on the correlation between all factors of the universe that are four in number (cardinal directions, seasons, elements, material properties) is probably also related to the impact of the cross image on the shape of the world. A ninth-century manuscript in Munich of Bede's *De natura rerum* shows the graphic result of this correlation (Figure 23),[24] the square alternative to the circular diagrams in the almost contemporary Collectar manuscript in Cologne. The beginning of the use of the square scheme for heavenly Jerusalem in the Beatus manuscripts might be the direct result of an influence of diagrams based, like this one in Munich, on an interplay of squares.[25] We should remember that the Beatus representations of heavenly Jerusalem are consistently square (or rectangular) and that the first manuscripts of the Commentary were very probably illuminated during the Carolingian period. At all events, the linkage between the cross and the shape of the universe constitutes the main Christian contri-

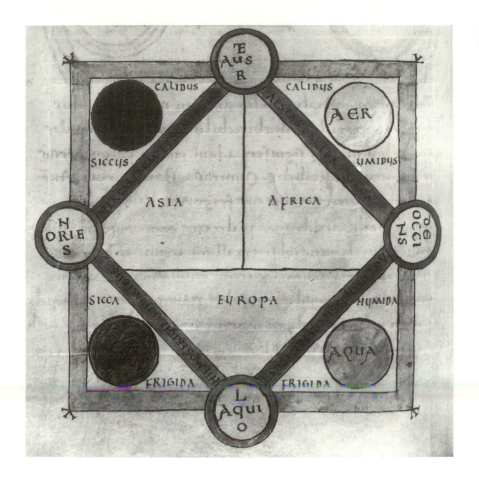

Figure 23. *De natura rerum*, Munich.

bution to the classical concept of the universe.[26] Justinus Martyr already identified the crossing between *Ecuator* and *Ekliptik* with the cross of Christ.[27]

A fourteenth-century representation of heavenly Jerusalem in the Welislaw Bible[28] is a clear exemplification of this associative system. A scheme of concentric circles revolves around the Lamb. The outer circle contains, radially disposed, twelve towers and gates. Eight of them are particularly emphasized through figures of angels, which thus single out the two crosses (an upright and an X-shaped cross) intersected by the concentric circles. Still in the outer circle, between the gates, personifications of the four winds, the four rivers, and the four cardinal directions alternate. Inscriptions identifying the figures in the representation and adding the missing figures, such as the apostles, are intercalated, thus increasing the similarity between this depiction of heavenly Jerusalem and the cosmographical schemes.

The supposition as to the influence exerted on geometric representations of apocalyptic heavenly Jerusalem by the graphic representations of the universe that antedated them and enjoyed a great distribution is substantially supported by additional evidence. The same early medieval cosmographical schemes had an obvious influence on other symbolic representations of heaven. During the Middle Ages, apocalyptic heavenly Jerusalem was the most common location of heaven in Christian art,[29] and it is not surprising, therefore, that the medieval repertoire includes some formulas indicative of heaven that are very similar in shape to the geometrical representations of Jerusalem, the resemblance being due to their common reliance on the same source: cosmographical diagrams connected with scientific treatises and encyclopaedias, very much in vogue at the beginning of the Middle Ages.

Maiestas Domini

A prominent group related to the geometric depictions of heavenly Jerusalem is that of Maiestas Domini representations.[30] At the border between late antiquity and the early Middle Ages, a type of *maiestas*, essentially geometric in composition, crystallized, dictated by a conceptual, hierarchical structuring of space. The *maiestas* at the opening of the New Testament in Codex Amiatinus (see Plate 5), a copy of the Bible manuscript *Codex Grandior* of Cassiodorus made in Northumbria around the year 700,[31] has a seated Christ flanked by two angels inside a clipeus formed by linear concentric circles in variegated bright colors. This disk dominates the rectangular page frame, while the spaces between it and the upper and lower margins of the frame are occupied by evangelists in pairs (each one standing on his own piece of ground) and their symbols (floating close to the clipeus). There can be no doubt that the heavenly space around Christ was delineated with the help of a scheme borrowed from more technical definitions of the cosmos, exactly as the compact and geometric heavenly Jerusalem of Valenciennes was depicted some one hundred years later.

Carolingian art further geometrized and elaborated the *maiestas* scenes. The figure-eight clipeus, the juxtaposition of clipei of different sizes, the combinations of oval mandorlas and round clipei, all these are Carolingian inventions that opened the way to even more complicated and colorful compositions in Ottonian and Romanesque art. Let us take, for example, the frontispiece to the Gospels in the Tours Vivian Bible, folio 329v.[32] The geometric structure of the page allows a hierarchical location of the figures: Christ's figure is enclosed in a figure-eight clipeus, which also contains the earth globe on which he is seated (Isaiah 66:1: "Thus saith the Lord, 'The heaven is My throne, and the earth is My footstool'"). Surrounded by the four *animalia,* the clipeus is set in a rhomb whose angles develop into circles, providing medallions for the busts of the four Old Testament prophets, who are identified by inscriptions: Esaias, Hezechiel, Hieremias, Daniel. In the spaces between the rhomb and the rectangular page frame, the four evangelists are seated, writing. All the inner frames have three concentric, linear, differently colored circles, strongly recalling cosmological diagrams.[33] The geometric structure of this page is basically the same as the diagram in the almost contemporary *De natura rerum* manuscript illustrations, a resemblance already stressed by Herbert Kessler.[34]

Maiestas compositions such as that in the Vivian Bible multiplied toward the end of the first millennium and became more and more geometric, strengthening their resemblance to diagrams of the universe. On folio 21r of a royal prayer book in Pommersfelden, illustrated in Mainz between the years 983 and 991, Christ is seated in a lightly pointed clipeus shaped by concentric color lines (see Figure 9, page 126).[35] The figure of Christ, the two angels holding the mandorla, and the purple ground show a strong Byzantine influence, while the shape of the cosmos ruled by Christ was either directly or indirectly inspired by early medieval illustrated treatises dealing with the shape of the world. Closer to the year 1000, a Gospel book from Trier, now in Berlin, shows Christ seated on a huge bright yellow globe, resting his feet on a smaller globe in earth colors, both similarly structured by concentric circles (Figure 24).[36] This *maiestas* is clearly related to Revelation 1:11–13, where the figure of Christ is surrounded by seven candelabra, thus providing an additional visual link between representations of heavenly Jerusalem and *maiestas* clipei and mandorlas.

Figure 24. *Maiestas* from a Trier Gospel book, Berlin.

The *maiestas* opening a Gospel book copied and illustrated in Cologne in the first half of the eleventh century shows three disks formed by concentric circles of different colors, two belonging to Christ's figure-eight mandorla, one, smaller, being the earth at his feet.[37] This *maiestas* from the manuscript in St. Maria ad Gradus in Cologne has the same iconographic components as the Carolingian Vivian *maiestas,* lacking only the figures of the writing evangelists. The stylistic differences are in the direction of the increased linearity and geometrical division of the page. The interplay of geometrical shapes expresses in an effective, direct, almost literal visual translation the idea contained in Jeremiah (23:24): "Do I not fill heaven and earth? saith the Lord." Here the cosmic spheres are more pronouncedly like flat wheels than in the Carolingian period, thus increasing their similarity to the scientific diagrams. These are also more linear and precise in the manuscript copies of the Ottonian, Romanesque, and later periods than in the early medieval manuscripts, as for example, in a copy of Plato's *Timaeus* with commentary by Calcidius in Cologne,[38] or in Lambert of Saint-Omer's *Liber Floridus* manuscript in Wolfenbüttel (Figure 25).[39] This last example, dated to the third quarter of the twelfth century, offers a unique visual solution to the question of the relation between God and the universe presented in medieval treatises on nature, as dictated by the prologue to the fourth Gospel (John 1:1–5). The illustration on folio 64v of the Wolfenbüttel *Liber Floridus* shows Christ in the mandorla dominating the circle of planets, thus deciding their movement. According to the Vision of John of Lüttich, from 1147, once arrived in heaven he saw among the spheres *("in illa coelestis orbis effigiatione apparebat")* a golden one *("coloris aurei"),* not round, but elongated *("longa et ductilis")* and twice as long as it was wide *("quae rotunditas licet duplo longior quam latior"),* which moved with great speed *("volvebatur celeritate grandi")*.[40] The popularity and reciprocity enjoyed by this composition show that this particular association between *maiestas* scenes in Bible manuscripts and representations of the heavens in the scientific literature of the medieval period was a *locus communis* on both the theoretical and the visual plane. A fifteenth-century copy of Walther of Metz's *Image du monde* (ca. 1245) in the British Library has the same composition on folio 149r,[41] but it is more organic and even closer to *maiestas* scenes. Christ resurrected is seated on an elaborate sarcophagus poised on top

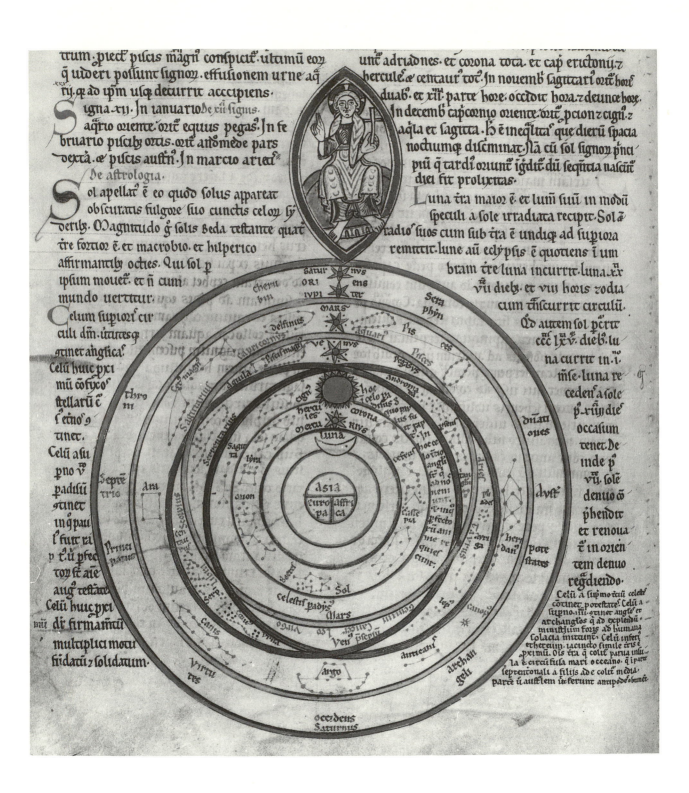

of the round world. He holds an orb with cross, while the evangelists' symbols are placed in the triangular spaces between the disk of colorful, concentric circles and the page frame. Thus "the image of the world" is organically integrated in a *maiestas* scene, fully identified as such by the four evangelists' symbols accompanying Christ.[42]

A unique combination of *maiestas* and circular heavenly Jerusalem, found on the dedication page of a royal Gospel book in The Hague,[43] demonstrates the viability of this system of visual associations in a most direct way (Figure 26): Christ, in a mandorla flanked by the apocalyptic letters A and ω, is placed in the upper part of an empty circle formed by a jagged motif suggesting city walls. Beneath the circle, Count Dietrich II of Holland and his wife, Hildegard, kneeling, are introduced to Christ by St. Adalbert, as is made clear by the expressive gestures of all the figures. The equivalence between heaven and heavenly Jerusalem is indicated through the relationship of the cosmic circle and the city walls, and the presence of the letters A and ω. The adoring gestures directed upward are also gestures of revelation, similar to those of John and the angel in Apocalypse illustrations. The dedication page in this Gospel book is dated to 975 and is thus very close in time to the Bamberg Apocalypse, made around the year 1000 (Figure 27). With all the stylistic differences between the Flemish[44] and the Reichenau[45] illuminations, they are evidence of the link established before the end of the first millennium between an encircling city wall and heavenly Jerusalem, a connection so strong that it could function in any iconographic context.

The Geography: Pictorial Maps

A second group of representations related to the geometrical depictions of heavenly Jerusalem, and similarly close to schemes of the universe, consists of pictorial maps (see also Chapter 16). The origins of circular geographical maps are actually intertwined with those of the cosmographical schemes, which necessarily included the earth. Homer, whom Strabo considered the founder and father of geographical science,[46] depicted in *The Iliad* (book 18, lines 480–610) what

---

Figure 25. *Maiestas, Liber Floridus*, Wolfenbüttel.

seems to be the oldest known *mappa mundi,* the shield of Achilles forged by Hephaestus.[47] Five metal disks, concentrically arranged, formed this shield, depicting scenes of various regions and human activities. A modern reconstruction of the shield of Achilles[48] shows its similarity to medieval cosmographical and circular representations of heavenly Jerusalem. The earth, sea, sun, moon, and stars form the center of the shield, while the two cities (one at peace and one at war) and the scenes from rural and urban life are arranged in three concentric circles. The whole is surrounded by the ocean. The ancient East already had a tradition of drawing circular *mappae mundi,* as demonstrated by the "Babylonian world map" on a stone tablet in the British Museum (probably ninth century BCE), a unique bird's-eye view of the earth's surface.[49] Two concentric circles form the contour of the map. Between the two circles is the cosmic ocean; inside the inner circle, the continental portion of the earth. On a sarcophagus cover from Saqqara, now in the Metropolitan Museum in New York and dated to the Thirteenth Dynasty (ca. 350 BCE), the land of Egypt is depicted with concentric circles in a disk protected by the arched figure of the goddess Nut, representing the sky (Figure 28).[50] This type of closed, geometric, idealized, and static image of the world was to remain viable, although not exclusively, throughout the Middle Ages, until Columbus and even later. The secret of its longevity lies in the purity of its form, in its elementary, associative power of expression, and, most important, in its extraordinary ability to adapt to Christianity. One of the most striking examples of Christian adaptation was the integration of Jerusalem and its multiple connotations into the pre-existing geometric, circular scheme.

The thirteenth-century maps in an English psalter in the British Library (Figure 29)[51] and in Hereford Cathedral in England[52] show a circular Jerusalem integrated in the round world system as its center. The Ebstorf world map, made around 1230 in the monastery of Ebstorf near Lüneburg in Germany, destroyed in 1943 but reconstructed from earlier reproductions,[53] shows an interplay of circle and square. A square Jerusalem with bricklike walls and towers, very much like

Figure 26. Christ with Count Dietrich II of Holland, his wife, Hildegard, and St. Adalbert, from a royal Gospel book, The Hague.

the heavenly Jerusalem in Beatus and like the city under the Eucharistic Dove's feet in Amsterdam, is placed in the center of the round world. The risen Christ appears within the walls of the city, as, for example, in the representations of heavenly Jerusalem in Civate[54] and in the Apocalypse manuscripts in Paris (nouv. acq. lat. 1366, folios 148v–149r)[55] and Toulouse (Bibliothèque municipale, ms. 815, folio 53).[56] The fourteenth-century copy of Ranulf Higden's map in the British Library shows the world in a rounded oval form.[57] Jerusalem at the center is round, with a tomblike building inside, indicating Christ's burial and the Resurrection.

These *mappae mundi* have much in common with the diagrams associated with scientific treatises: the closed geometric shape, the concentric circles, the winds. The Hereford map shows Christ standing at the top, as in the *Liber Floridus* illustration of the mandorla surmounting the planet system. In the British Library psalter map, the half figure of Christ is enthroned over the circular map, flanked by two angels. Christ holds in his left hand a very small disk of the tripartite world. (In the Maiestas Domini representation from the Beatus manuscript in Gerona, the same object in Christ's right hand is inscribed *"mundus"*).[58] In the Ebstorf map, Christ literally embraces the whole world: his head, framed in a square, is visible at the upper edge of the world's circle, his feet at the base, and his hands at the two lateral extremities. The four cardinal directions are thus indicated by the crosslike location of Christ's head and limbs. Already in the twelfth century, Christ was depicted clasping the cosmos in the same manner in the *Tractatus de Quaternario,* an English manuscript from the beginning of the century, in Gonville and Caius College, Cambridge.[59] Various representations of the mercy-seat Trinity offer good alternative illustrations of the same iconography as, for example, the interesting so-called *Vierge ouvrante* reliquary in the Metropolitan Museum of Art: a wooden, three-dimensional *Maria lactans* opens to reveal in her womb a seated figure of God holding a T-shaped cross whose intersection is marked by a circle in which a cross is inscribed, representing the orb, *mundus.*[60] The integration of cross and Crucifixion with the image of the world and the gesture of God or Christ

---

Figure 27. Heavenly Jerusalem, Bamberg Apocalypse.

Figure 28. Sarcophagus cover depicts Egypt in concentric circles and figure of the sky-goddess Nut, New York.

LITERATURE, ART, AND ARCHITECTURE

Figure 29.
World map
in an English
psalter, London.

embracing or holding the world in his lap bring us to additional associations: representations of the Creation, the old and the new, also belong to the now large family of medieval images based on geometrical schemes of the universe.

The Creation

On the Creation page of a missal from Hildesheim (ca. 1159) in the Fürstenberg-Stammheimsche Bibliothek, Christ holds a disk of concentric circles in which the seven days of Creation are depicted, with Adam and Eve in the central disk.[61] This composition found its way into thirteenth-century *Bible moralisée* manuscripts, as an opening illustration.[62] Here Christ is shown seated in a quatrefoil mandorla supported by four angels, creating the world, a disk lying in his lap, with the aid of a pair of compasses.[63] The quatrefoil mandorla evokes the cross, closely related to the Second Creation, made possible by Christ's sacrifice. Visual evidence of the Creation by Christ, meaning the Second Creation, destined to last forever, is provided in the Hildesheim missal on the Creation page itself: below the disk of Creation held by Christ, two scenes in a typologically inferior position remind one of the disastrous outcome of the first Creation, the expulsion from paradise and Cain's killing of his brother. As author of the new, second, perfect Creation, Christ is the creator *(conditor)* of the universe, the act of Creation representing only the beginning of his reign.[64] This role is assumed by Christ as a result of the Crucifixion.[65] The four arms of the cross embrace the four cardinal directions, the four elements, the four seasons, all in a better form: "Everything is recovered through the Cross, and is reborn and made better through Christ's passion."[66]

Thus the representations of Creation, where the newly created world is a disk formed by concentric circles and a square or a cross is implied, evoke in a most direct visual manner this whole system of exegetical associations, which is also tangential to the understanding of Jerusalem in Christianity. The representations in Valenciennes and Paris are only one kind of illustration of Jerusalem's association with the iconography of the universe. The same connection is also exemplified by later depictions, even those referring to earthly Jerusalem in a most concrete way, such as the Crusader maps.

Crusader Maps

Fourteen maps depicting Crusader Jerusalem are known to us, most of them drawn in the twelfth century.[67] All of them represent Jerusalem as a perfect geometrical form: in twelve of these maps the city is enclosed in a circular wall,[68] in the Montpellier map it is a square,[69] and in the Cambrai map (Figure 39, page 355), it is a rhomb.[70] The round maps show Jerusalem enclosed by a precisely drawn wall formed by several concentric circles, sometimes structured with a bricklike motif. All the walls have crenellations, directed outward or inward, with no claim to the suggestion of perspective as seen, for example, in the brick wall of heavenly Jerusalem in the Bamberg Apocalypse. The *cardo* and the *decumanus maximus* cross exactly in the middle of the city, either drawn continuously to form a full cross, or interrupted somewhere in the East and brought to a T shape. The five city gates are arranged symmetrically, suggesting the effect of the inscribed cross. Michael Avi-Yonah suggests that the circular Crusader maps of Jerusalem were influenced by the medieval *mappae mundi* of the T-O type. Milka Levy-Rubin also explains the circular maps of Jerusalem by the traditional and general connection between a cross inscribed in a circle and city (the cross symbolizing the crossroads meeting in the city, the circle its walls), a connection emphasized by Roberto Sabatino Lopez and Lewis Mumford.[71] However, the consistency with which the geometric scheme was applied to Jerusalem, rarely modified, and then only by a square or a rhomb, invites a more particular explanation. One would have to consider not only the resemblance between Jerusalem maps and T-O world maps, but also their similarity to diagrams of the universe and earlier representations of apocalyptic heavenly Jerusalem. Enlarging the group of visual associations evoked by the Crusader maps of Jerusalem may lead to a better understanding of their eschatological meaning. In spite of the detailed and sometimes even accurate location of places in and outside the walls, the Crusader views of Jerusalem are decidedly not realistic, scientific, geographical renderings with the intentions usually ascribed to modern maps. They use terrestrial Jerusalem and its geography to formulate a statement of Salvation, a message of hope for those left at home. These maps of Jerusalem are the faithful pictorial image of the Crusades, which were conducted not just for a piece of land in

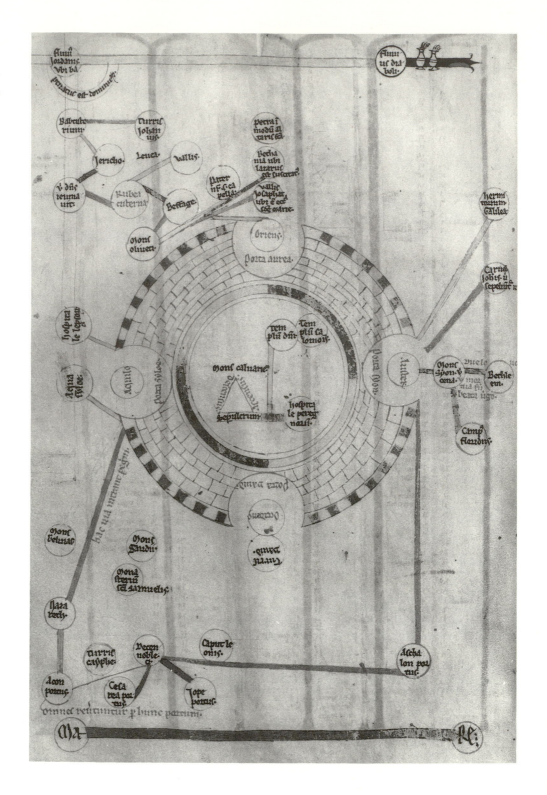

Figure 30. Thirteenth-century Crusader map of Jerusalem, London.

LITERATURE, ART, AND ARCHITECTURE

the Levant but for the eternal heavenly realm. They combine physical data with a universal and apocalyptic scheme, proper to Jerusalem and only to Jerusalem. Among the Crusader maps, those made in the thirteenth century, after the loss of the city, are comparatively more schematic and generalized from a geographical point of view, and closer to geometry and symbolism than the twelfth-century maps. The British Library map Harley 658, folio 39v (Figure 30) has more wall than inner space, formed of concentric circles with a bricklike motif. The gates are reduced to four, symmetrically arranged in crosslike form, inscribed not only with their names but also with the four cardinal directions. In the Copenhagen map, which has a perfect cross symmetrically dividing the round space, geometry clearly prevails over geography. This is also the period in which round or square Jerusalem takes its place in the center of circular *mappae mundi*. In a fifteenth-century Collectar in Berlin, we find a plan of Jerusalem (Figure 31)[72] shaped entirely of precise concentric circles and symmetrically arranged gates, very close to the Carolingian plan of heavenly Jerusalem in the Apocalypse of Valenciennes.

Jerusalem, indeed, holds a very special position in the history of geography. The uniqueness of this position is stressed by its persistence well beyond the boundaries of the essentially religious and conceptual mapmaking of the Middle Ages, beyond Columbus and Copernicus, notwithstanding the increasing tendency toward a realistic rendering of cities and landscapes in the Renaissance and the modern era. Not only in the history of geography but also in the history of visual representations in general, depictions of Jerusalem show an unusual degree of continuity, manifested mainly in the geometric and apocalyptic character of the representations. Geometry and Apocalypse are meant to express Jerusalem's appurtenance to heaven and earth alike, to the present and the future world. This concept and its matching visual expression were developed by medieval Christianity in a long process that reached its peak during the central Middle Ages. Once created and established through use in various connected contexts, the geometric and apocalyptic representation of Jerusalem made its way into unexpected contexts, including, for example, narrative scenes rendered in perspective during the Renaissance, and Jewish, Christian, and Muslim art in the modern period.

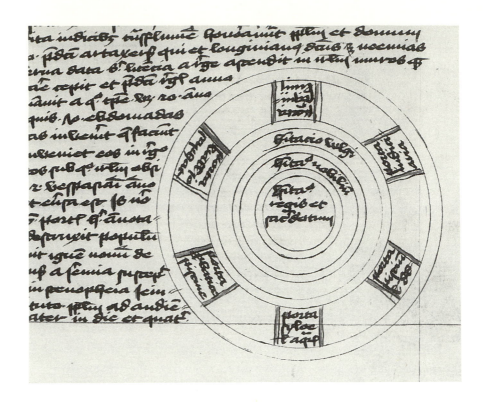

Figure 31. Plan of Jerusalem in a fifteenth-century Collectar, Berlin.

The City in Renaissance Art

Let us start our discussion of Renaissance and modern representations of Jerusalem with maps. The first printed map of Palestine, by Lucas Brandis in a German world chronicle of 1475, shows Jerusalem in the middle of a rectangle surrounded by water and the usual personifications of winds (Figure 32).[73] Jerusalem is unique among the cities depicted and identified on the map, not only because of its central location, but also through the compact rendering of its three concentric circular walls revolving around a prominent basilical building. The main difference between this map and the thirteenth-century maps in London, Hereford, and Ebsdorf is stylistic: the concentric walls are not flat, but seen in elevation, in a bird's-eye view, even though the perspective is distorted and the inner space unreasonably stretched. Very like Brandis's Jerusalem is the somewhat later and more famous

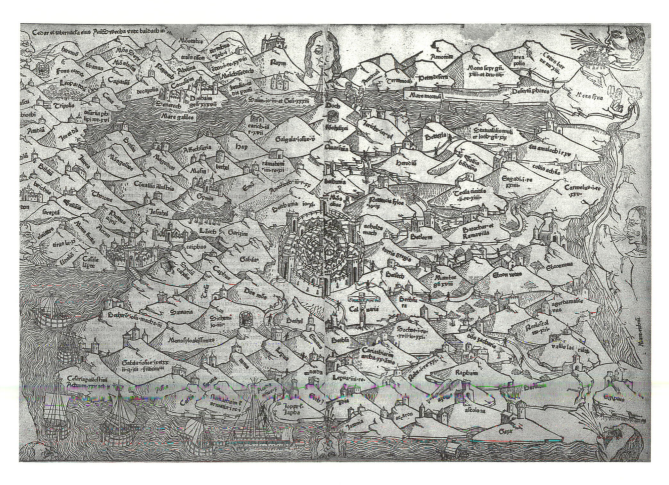

Figure 32. Map of Palestine by Lucas Brandis, 1475, Lübeck.

engraving by Michael Wolgemut for Hartmann Schedel's *Liber chroni-carum* (Nuremberg, 1493, folio XVII).[74] The same three concentric walls in the same exaggerated opening (though less distorted than in the Lucas Brandis) surround a circular building inscribed "Templum Salomonis," set on a platform. In spite of this reference to the Dome of the Rock, the view is strongly indebted to the ideal geometric medieval schemes. Not only the circle but also the square enjoyed perpetuation in later periods. The view of Jerusalem attached to the Bible commentary in guide form written by Heinrich Bünting in 1581 is square, and captioned *"Jerusalem die heilige viereckete* [square] *Stadt."*[75] This caption indicates that Bünting was aware of the eschatological implications of the square when applied to Jerusalem. The same is true for another square map in the Moldovan Collection, where the sun and the hill of Golgotha with three crosses appear prominently above the city.[76]

The interplay between real geohistorical data and ideal, cosmological, and, especially, apocalyptic connotations in the visual depictions of Jerusalem continued into periods in which the history of art was dominated by realistic aspirations, and geography and mapping took a scientific path. The map of Jerusalem by Frans Hogenberg and Georg Braun in a book on cities of the world *(Civitates Orbis Terrarum)* was drawn according to plans and sketches made on the spot by Peter Laicksteen.[77] The wall is not a perfect geometric form, and the buildings have some resemblance to the city's real architecture. However, the whole is tightly delineated by the wall and clearly separated from the surrounding landscape. Moreover, it is placed on the line of the horizon, and the stretching of its walls creates the illusion of a downhill movement. The effect of descent from the sky is emphasized by a group of figures standing close to the lower frame of the map, who, because of the exaggeratedly open angle of view, seem to be placed under the walls. The figures are gesturing in a lively way; one of them points upward. The relation between the figures and the city recalls John and the angel witnessing the revelation of heavenly Jerusalem in the Valenciennes Apocalypse. The French cartographer A. M. Mallet, who copied this view of Jerusalem into his *Beschreibung des gantzen Welt-Kreises* published in Frankfurt-am-Main more than a hundred years later, in 1684–85, put a still greater distance between the city and the group of people, and depicted the people as gesticulating in adoration toward the city (see Plate 1),[78] thus promoting its heavenly character. In the eighteenth century, the Chereau map exemplifies the same tradition.[79] Even maps that do not stretch the landscape unnaturally and stay within a realistic scale of proportion, like those of Cornelius de Bruyn, 1698,[80] or even A. G. Wartensleben in 1870 (see Figure 5, page 48),[81] still emphasize the heavenly dimension of Jerusalem through the pronounced difference between the built-up, compact, and walled city and the uninhabited area around it, by bringing the figures close to the spectator and making them point in admiration to the city, by suggesting an indefinite space between them and it, and by filtering the light and color in such a

Figure 33. Heavenly Jerusalem
in a lithograph by Matthäus
Merian, 1627, Worms.

way as to appear rarefied at the top of the picture and darker at the
base. The same methods are used in apocalyptic representations of
heavenly Jerusalem during the period. Matthäus Merian's lithograph
of 1627, one of a series of twelve illustrating the Apocalypse, represents
heavenly Jerusalem as a built-up square in a natural landscape, regarded in admiration from a hill in the front right side of the picture
(Figure 33).[82] The difference between Merian's apocalyptic Jerusalem and the geographical Jerusalem of the maps mentioned above

lies in the perfectly drawn square and the perfect inner symmetry of the heavenly city as against the tendency to impose symmetry and geometricity on an otherwise loose arrangement of wall and structures in the maps.[83]

The same methods of assigning a heavenly dimension to historical Jerusalem are also evident in the narrative art of the period. Jerusalem is the city in the background of most biblical and martyrdom scenes, as the place of Christ's act and sacrifice, the center of the history of Salvation. From the fifteenth century onward, the background city takes on a "realistically" detailed appearance. Usually this "realism" is that of a specific European city from the artist's and his public's immediate neighborhood (as, for example, the depiction of Xanten in the background of St. Victor's martyrdom by Bartholomäus Bruyn d.Ä.),[84] or that of a generalized amalgam of European architecture with Orientalizing elements (as in Jan Van Eyck's *Women at the Tomb* in Rotterdam, or Albrecht Dürer's *Lamentation* in Nuremberg).[85] The equivalence of any city and Jerusalem is expressed in Christian art not only through the substitution of more familiar cities for Jerusalem but also in the opposite way, through shaping European cities after the model of Jerusalem, in pictorial depictions[86] and also in their actual architectural construction; medieval Aix-la-Chapelle and Cologne were invested with walls and twelve towers to emulate the heavenly Jerusalem of the Apocalypse, *in imitatio,* as an act of faith and hope, and in recognition of the promise of Salvation.[87]

Islam invested Mecca with an importance similar to that of Jerusalem in Christianity, and Islamic artists' representations of Mecca are, accordingly, rather like Christian representations of Jerusalem.[88] In the pilgrimage itinerary of Maimunah dated 1433, now in London, the rectangular Kaaba is shown in an open circle framed by a square.[89] Also shown are oriented mihrabs (prayer niches) and various cultic utensils rendered in a combination of side view and planimetric flat depiction, which recalls the plans of the Temple and Tabernacle in Christian and Jewish art.[90] A much later topographical depiction of Mecca in an Indian manuscript of Badil's *Hamla-i-Haidari* from 1761, now in Berlin, strongly recalls the round, geometrical maps of the Crusader period.[91]

The fifteenth and sixteenth centuries offer examples of biblical scenes in Western art depicted against the background of a Jerusalem clearly inspired by the city in the land of Judea. Here, too, a distinction

should be made between representations based on direct observation or sketches done on the spot by the artist himself, and those based on plans, views, or drawings of Jerusalem made and distributed by travelers, pilgrims, or other artists.[92] A well-documented example of the first category is the work of Jan von Scorel, who visited the Holy Land in 1520 and painted a quite realistic *Entry of Christ into Jerusalem* in 1526, on a triptych commissioned by the Lochorst family (Figure 34).[93] The dissimulated and thus immeasurable distance between the figures in the foreground and Jerusalem at the back, the pronounced differences in color and light, the figures' dramatic gestures and expressions, all these underline the difference between the two worlds, the earthly and the heavenly, and introduce Jerusalem, in spite of the realistic exactitude of its depiction, as a heavenly apparition. The means and the scope are identical to those of the similar cartographic representations of Jerusalem. This identity between two such basically different media, cartography and pictorial narrative, demonstrates the strength and consistency of their common denominator—Jerusalem, with its dual location in heaven and on earth, and the long tradition of Christian visual representations that emphasize the iconographical implications of this dualism. Thanks to their wide distribution, the cartographic representations of Jerusalem conveyed the connections between themselves and the biblical narrative. A direct link between the *Lamentation* (1483) by the Master of the Hersbruck High Altar in Nuremberg[94] and a plan of Jerusalem drawn by a Nuremberg pilgrim in 1479[95] has been analyzed recently and shown to be based on similarities in the details of buildings and settings.[96] In our context, the position allotted to the view of Jerusalem in relation to the scene is significant. The composition is constructed vertically; the narrative drama of the *Lamentation* occupies the whole lower foreground, while Jerusalem spreads downward from the top of the hill, the skyline of which is close to the upper frame. Again we have the combination of a view inspired by the city of Jerusalem as it appeared to the Christian pilgrim at the end of the fifteenth century, and apocalyptic Jerusalem, descending at the End of Days from heaven, a promise understandably repeated here, first in connection with the dead Christ of the *Lamentation* and second with Adelheid Tucher, for whose tomb the epitaph was commissioned.

Jerusalem in Jewish Art

In Jewish Passover Haggadot of the seventeenth and eighteenth centuries, walled representations of Jerusalem occur in compositions similar to those discussed above: a symmetrical city wall stretched in a bird's-eye view, with only the Dome of the Rock appearing as the Temple, surrounded by tents inside the wall, is approached from the left by the Messiah on a donkey, preceded by Elijah with the shofar (Figure 35).[97] In later Jewish art and folklore, we still find pilgrimage maps of Jerusalem's holy places in which square, circle, and octagon[98] are combined to emphasize the centrality of the Western Wall (the Temple) in the Jewish hope of national revival.[99] These maps were often embroidered on the tablecloths for use on the Sabbath, made in the Diaspora at the end of the nineteenth and the beginning of the twentieth century.

The same period produced representations in which the apparition of distant Jerusalem, confounded with the sun, is revealed to Zionist Jews, represented either by a traditional Jew (Lilien, *Der Jüdische Mai,*

Figure 35. Jerusalem in the
Venice Haggadah (1740 edition),
Tel Aviv.

1902)[100] or by Theodore Herzl (on a wall carpet in the collection of
the Eretz Israel Museum in Tel Aviv).[101] The vision of Jerusalem in
the year 2006 proposed by Boris Schatz, the founder of the Bezalel
School of Arts, in a book prepared during the First World War when
the school had to close and its founder went into exile, belongs to the
same visual tradition. The illustration opening the 1924 edition of this
publication shows the author and Bezalel ben Uri, the first artist
mentioned in the Bible, looking at the panorama of Jerusalem from
the roof of the School of Arts. Bezalel ben Uri, with a broad, demon-
strative gesture, directs Schatz in his vision of Jerusalem, rather like
the angel directing John in his Revelation. Future Jerusalem is depicted diagonally on a hill, under a full, ideal light, contrasting with
the darker, solid appearance of the wall, the menorah, and the vision-
aries in the foreground.[102]

The Secularization of the Apocalypse
in Twentieth-Century Art

Notwithstanding this last example, we may generally assume that the
twentieth century brought about a radical change in the otherwise
conservative depictions of Jerusalem, the result of the secularization
and individualization in modern art in general, and, specifically, of
the secularization of the Apocalypse. Modern representations of the

Apocalypse are usually dominated by man, not God. They are free of tradition, personal, and flexible. A wealth of images called apocalyptic now appear, not related to the text of Revelation and with no interest in salvation in the religious sense of the term. The Apocalypse in the modern, larger sense has been consciously and largely used by artists as a way of responding to disasters of our century: the two world wars; the atomic bomb;[103] the sinking of the Titanic;[104] Prague 1968;[105] even solitude and estrangement in modern society.[106] Its very use could be interpreted as a message of hope, for calling on the Apocalypse in times of crisis and to depict destruction implies the belief that destruction is a necessary phase before renewal and redemption.

It is striking that no matter how personal, imaginative, and free of tradition modern renderings of apocalyptic themes may be, they still adhere to compositional principles and associative patterns invented in the Middle Ages. This is true not only of depictions of Jerusalem. For example, Kandinsky's *Apocalyptic Rider II* of 1914, in the Lehnbachhaus, Munich, is represented according to the usual medieval composition of the *maiestas*, with four animals.[107] Sometimes the general message is of despair, as in Felix Droese's trilogy *Man Leaves the Earth*, 1983–84.[108] The earth is a huge bleeding ball, and small human figures are depicted at the margins, abandoning it. Walther Dahn sees the universe as a gold-yellow ball with a bright red human heart at its center (*Weltherz*, 1985, in the Paul Menz Gallery in Cologne). The heart contains the continents of the earth, painted as irregular, black flecks, and strongly recalls the world map by Peter Apian of 1530.[109]

Man has taken the place of God in these images because of his destructive power. A. V. Lentulov's *A Victorious Battle*, also of 1914, in the Lentulova collection in Moscow, shows a rider in a huge clipeus of light, making the victorious gesture of Christ-Helios in the early Christian mosaic under St. Peter in Rome.[110] War is personified by a large personage obstructing the sun, trampling on naked, suffering figures at the base of the composition, in a posterlike lithograph made by Max Weber in 1918.[111] The personification of Peace, Celebration, and Liberation, in A. V. Lentulov's 1917 oil painting of the same name, shows a huge, youthful man in a mandorla, his belly and genitals enclosed in a scheme of concentric circles in the center of the composition.[112] The concentric circles still designate the center of the world, the center of eschatological hope, but they assume human shape, or give their shape to objects perceptible to man. Otto Dix's *Setting Sun (Ypres)*, 1918, depicts an enormous round sun enclosed in concentric circles formed by coarse, brightly colored brush strokes; it dominates the upper part of the composition and projects downward.[113] Below, two soldiers are distinguishable among many brush strokes in dark, earth colors. From a compositional point of view, the representation strongly calls to mind medieval Apocalypse manuscript depictions of the round heavenly Jerusalem revealed to John and the angel, or later map depictions of the city perceived from a distance by pilgrims and travelers. The mood, however, is completely different. The setting sun has a destructive power, the soldiers are shattered by it. In spite of the bright colors, this composition has nothing of the quiet, eternal, reassuring, heavenly revelation of medieval Apocalypses. The same is true for Ludwig Meidner's *Apocalyptic Landscapes* series, painted on the eve of the First World War. The city, both menacing and destructive, is in these paintings the metropolitan, industrial, and commercial city of modern Europe. However, the compositional context, as well as the evocation of the Apocalypse in Meidner's title, invites an analogy to heavenly Jerusalem. The cities on the hills, those depicted as the first recipients of bombardment from the sky, are, at the same time, closing in on the frightened or dead men depicted on the dark swath of earth below. This is true of Meidner's *Apocalyptic Landscapes* of 1912, now in a private collection and in Milwaukee; 1913, in the Nationalgalerie Berlin; and 1916, in Regensburg.[114] The negative connotations of the city in Meidner's landscapes are strengthened by the analogy and contrast with the heavenly city. The atrocity of war and the artist's fear of it translate the eschatological descent of the heavenly city into the tragic fall of city walls at the historical end of days caused by World War I. Meidner, as well as many other artists of the time, obviously used the symbols and images of the Apocalypse in a free and associative way to characterize World War I more effectively as the End of Days. The apocalyptic image of heavenly Jerusalem offered them a powerful contrast to the destructive, contemporary image of the big city. When medieval and Renaissance artists drew analogies between heavenly Jerusalem and their own cities, it was always in a positive sense, with the aspiration of "borrowing" sanctity. At the beginning of the twentieth century, God is absent from the Apocalypse, and heavenly Jerusalem is but an element of contrast.

Another striking illustration of the free use of Jerusalem in modern art is offered by Marc Chagall. Among the three tapestries made for the Knesset (the parliament building) in Jerusalem between 1964 and 1968, the one on the left, the *Entry into Jerusalem,* contains a closed, round image of the city in the central upper part of the composition, while the other two, *Exodus* and *Isaiah's Prophecy,* represent scenes that do not involve Jerusalem.[115] The *Entry into Jerusalem* principally depicts the procession, headed by King David, that brings the Ark of the Covenant into the capital of his United Kingdom, according to chapter 6 of the second book of Samuel. To this core image Chagall added several nonbiblical motifs, which extend the relevance of the biblical story up to the contemporary history of the people and the land of Israel: Hasidim in traditional kaftans, young women and men, some dressed as Russian peasants, working and rejoicing (the pioneers of the prestate period), a watchtower symbolizing the founding of a Jewish settlement,[116] a small agglomeration of tile-roofed houses standing for a kibbutz, pastoral scenes, and lovers. The whole historical procession in *Entry into Jerusalem,* echoed by the Succoth pilgrimage (Succoth is indicated by a figure close to the right frame, wearing a long kaftan and holding a *lulav* and an *ethrog*—a palm branch and a citrus fruit, which are two of the four plants used during Succoth), thus becomes a depiction of immigration to Israel and Jerusalem. To fit the levels of meaning conveyed by the tapestry, Jerusalem is represented with the aid of several visual conventions: first of all, it occupies the central upper part of the composition as a closed, round unit. It is the only component to be clearly separated from the others and linearly defined by a geometric shape, interrupted only by the married couple. The walled city of Jerusalem, with clear suggestions of its real architectural appearance, is placed diagonally inside the sphere, strongly lit by a dominant sun globe. Chagall's Jerusalem combines real geographical and ideal geometrical elements to show the meeting between the messianic hopes of the people of Israel and the national realization of the state of Israel, the identity between the future Jerusalem depicted by Isaiah 52:1–7 and 62:1–5 and the capital of the modern state.

Jerusalem in Palestinian Arab Art

It is on the common ground of Jerusalem that Jewish art meets Palestinian Arab art, not only because of direct influences, but also mainly because both make use of the long chain of associations and traditions connected with images of Jerusalem in Christian medieval and Renaissance art. After 1967 Jerusalem became a symbol of national redemption that is as important, as central, as longed for, and, at the same time, as distant and unattainable for the Palestinians as it always was in Judaism during periods of exile, and in Christianity as a symbol of Salvation. It is, therefore, in contemporary Palestinian art that we find representations of Jerusalem using—intentionally or by chance—the visual formulas found in Christian and Jewish art. The sun—a round, translucent, red, celestial body—contains a built-up city, centered around and identified by the Dome of the Rock, in Taleb Dweik's *Al-Quds* (The Holy, Jerusalem's Arabic name) of 1986.[117] The difference between this contemporary Palestinian representation of Jerusalem and that by Chagall in the Knesset contains the quintessence of the contemporary conflict between Jews and Arabs: in Chagall's tapestry, the sun is depicted inside the circle of Jerusalem, as an expression of fulfillment. Future Jerusalem is about to be built. Dweik's Jerusalem is as distant and unattainable as the sun rising above an empty land; the image is full of hope (the sun, the two doves, the flowers on the ground, are all symbols of hope), but it is directed toward the future, like Lilien's Jerusalem of 1902.[118]

Nabil Anani's *Jerusalem,* in an unpublished representation created in 1984, shows the city in a circle made of an outer row of figures and an inner row of buildings arranged concentrically around a central tree (see Plate 8).[119] Three stylized figures face the colorful disk from the right side, while a row of smaller figures observe the city from below the circle. This composition strongly recalls medieval Apocalypse manuscripts in which the angel and John witness the descent of heavenly Jerusalem, as, for example the Beatus manuscript in Paris and the Cambrai Apocalypse.[120]

Back to the Apocalypse: Jerusalem in Modern Christian Art

Modern art, by cultivating the link with venerable visual formulas in an artistic environment that is individualistic and free from religious constraints, demonstrates the viability, the universality, the extraordinary power of expression of the traditions created by the Christian art of the early medieval period. The secret of their longevity lies in their primary geometrical purity and the wide associative basis they allow, which can be, and indeed is, repeated without direct influence.

It seems appropriate to end our excursus across a period of more than a thousand years and three religions with the work of a modern German artist, Helmut Ammann, who without knowing it has created the modern parallel to the Valenciennes Apocalypse. Ammann, a Christian sculptor from Munich, has devoted three monumental compositions to heavenly Jerusalem, all of them decorating church apsides: two in stained glass—in the Luther Church in Munich and the St. Leonhard Church in Nuremberg—and one in brick mosaic revetment, wood, and glass, in the Erlöserkirche in Würzburg-Zellerau. The stained glass windows of the Luther Church in Munich, 1959, show a round heavenly Jerusalem, with concentric circles enclosing the Lamb in the center. Under the circle, the angel shows John the heavenly apparition. The stained glass window in Nuremberg, 1979–80, combines circle, square, and Crucifixion in one composition: the upper part of the cross and Christ's body to the waist are contained by a circle. Behind the lower part of the cross, square heavenly Jerusalem is depicted with bright yellow walls, crossed by the streets leading from its round kernel to four groups of three gates arranged symmetrically. The heavenly Jerusalem of Würzburg-Zellerau, 1962 to 1964, has a spatial dimension; it not only decorates the walls of the choir but also extends into its space. The walls are covered with colorful bricks, left over from the building, arranged so as to suggest different architectural details and ornaments: a whole city in two dimensions. Two groups of three angels each, carved in wood, stand in the space made by the two walls meeting at an angle. Between them hangs a glass roundel with a mosaic of the Lamb illuminating the city, as required by the Revelation text.[121] Ammann offers us three modern variants of heavenly Jerusalem visualized through combinations of circle and square. As a cultivated Western European and a believing Christian artist, he of course knows the previous representations of heavenly Jerusalem and the text of John's Revelation. However, he said his use of square and circle was motivated as follows: "The square has a strong geometrical form, and thus represents perfection, while the cross is always a sign of heavenly light. In my personal experience of these visions, square and circle of light are deeply associated."[122]

Jerusalem Elsewhere

OLEG GRABAR

Most investigations of Jerusalem have dealt with the city as a geographical entity, a city located at a specific place in the rather inhospitable and tortuous rocky landscape between the Dead Sea and the Mediterranean coastline. It is a city with a long and complicated history, from obscure walled settlements datable to the eighteenth century BCE to the contemporary capital of the state of Israel.[1] Fewer but often important investigations have dealt with what may be called a mythic or visionary Jerusalem, that is to say, the Jerusalem imagined as the city to come, from Ezekiel's architectural depiction (Ezekiel, chapters 40–43) to the "New Jerusalem, coming down from God out of heaven, prepared as a bride adorned for her husband" and covered with precious stones, found in the Christian Book of Revelations (Revelations 21:2, 10), or the medieval Jewish idea of a Jerusalem whose whole territory is covered with "precious stones and pearls," so that all conflicts disappear because wealth is available to all.[2]

But in addition to the physical and visionary Jerusalems, there may well be a third dimension worth investigating—a transformed Jerusalem.[3] It has clear connections with physical reality, yet it is never located in Palestine; it appears to be visionary, but does not deal with eschatology and the end of time, as it always maintains a concrete existence. It is not certain that a single name or attribute can be given to this "other" Jerusalem located "elsewhere."

First, it is worth mentioning briefly two areas related to a concrete Jerusalem that is not the city now seen by millions of tourists nor the one yet to come.

The first area consists of the uses of the words and concepts "Zion" and "Jerusalem" in the pious practices, liturgies, and prayers of Judaism, Christianity, and Islam seen together and comparatively rather than separately, as they usually are. Elaborate and unique uses are absent from Muslim practice, since Islam did not develop, to the same extent as the other two faiths, elaborate rituals with considerable variants or local liturgical habits and prayers. But it did develop one pious practice that is pertinent to Jerusalem and that is documented as early as the eleventh century. It is the *'umrah,* the local pilgrimage, often made in order to secure specific benefits, like divine blessings on the occasion of circumcisions, as mentioned in an eleventh-century source.[4] Even today, conversations with Muslims born and bred in or around Jerusalem elicit recollected stories and legends told by elderly relatives, about ritual practices that are not part of formal and official Islam, and are largely unrecorded. Within Christianity and Judaism, the liturgical uses of the words "Zion" or "Jerusalem" are more easily available. But a curious subsidiary topic emerges in the occurrence and symbolic significance of the two words in Protestant hymns from northern countries, quite different from the liturgical meanings of the words in rites created for the most part around the eastern Mediterranean. In approved ecclesiastical rituals or in the pious poetry of Anglo-Saxon divines, the prevalent vision of Jerusalem is not the image of the real city, nor is it always the eschatological Jerusalem of the end of time. It is, rather, a sacred shell, a faithful reflection, or a striking model for a great variety of human emotions and for the infinitely complex interaction between man and God.[5] The second area is the history of the representation of Jerusalem in the arts and the variations within these representations from period to period, artist to artist, and region to region.[6] Whether in Carpaccio's series dealing with St. George or in a large number of Flemish Crucifixion paintings after the publication of Breytenbach's travels to the Holy Land, images of Jerusalem appear that are not strictly fantasy, although fantasy does not really disappear from images before the second half of the nineteenth century. Most of these representations are focused on specific buildings, usually the Dome of the Rock as the Jewish Temple at the time of Christ or the Holy Sepulchre, but a more or less vague urban setting or a crowd of people in theatrical oriental clothes is included to remind the viewer that the monuments are in a city. The variations in the image of the city probably contain lessons about the perception of Jerusalem that existed in premodern Europe. Three groups of documents, different from each other in kind, complexity, and importance, illustrate the phenomenon of Jerusalem "elsewhere."

"Farthest" Jerusalem

A perusal of indexes of place names in atlases yields remarkably few results when one thinks of the consistency with which names with biblical connections were used in the Christian expansion over more or less empty territories. I found one Jerusalem in New Zealand and there is one Russian village near Moscow, not found on maps from Soviet times, called "New Jerusalem." It was actually a monastery, which grew into a larger settlement. A more interesting and more original case is that of Qudus in Indonesia, by now a sizable town in central Java with a fairly well known mosque complex developed around the tomb of a holy man. The complex goes back to at least 1533. The mosque is appropriately called al-Aqsa, as it was, when it was built (at least according to local tradition), the "farthest" from Mecca. The case is interesting in that the holiness involved in the root *qds* as used for the name of a city depends less on the intrinsic merits of that city than on its use in the name of the city in Palestine that contained a mosque identified by universal Muslim tradition as the place mentioned in the Koran, the *masjid al-Aqsa*—the "farthest" mosque to which God carried the Prophet during the mystical Night Journey or Isra.[7] Not much is available about the history of Qudus in Indonesia, even though photographs and plans of the mosque have often been published, especially because of its unusual minaret built in the nineteenth century.[8] But it is symbolically appropriate that the name of the Palestinian city has been reused and preserved in two lands, Indonesia and New Zealand, farthest away from the real Jerusalem.

Christian and Muslim Representations of the City

The museum located in the chateau of Saumur, a sleepy town on the Loire known for its old military school and heroic defense in 1940, possesses a large painting representing Palestine, or at least an approximate Palestine with many holy sites, from the Transfiguration to Bethlehem and the cave of the Nativity (see Plate 9). Its title, *Jerusalem, the Holy City and Its Surroundings,* is in Greek, and it is dated 1704. The painting, remarkable for its representation of Jerusalem in the center of the composition, belongs to a tradition of sacred cartography going back as far as the sixth century mosaic map from Madaba in Jordan (see Plate 2).[9] The complex of the Holy Sepulchre occupies most of the city, its major components are clearly recognizable, and an obvious and perfectly appropriate emphasis is given to the three sacred events of the Crucifixion, Burial, and Resurrection. The rest of the city is fitted inside walls zigzagging their way over formalized hills; one can easily recognize the citadel and especially the Haram al-Sharif with the Dome of the Rock and the Aqsa Mosque.[10] This image of Jerusalem in its Palestinian setting was probably made for Greek or other Orthodox Christians living away from Palestine and provided a view of the city which, though not visually accurate, contains all the striking elements of the actual city that would have been reported orally by pilgrims: massive walls, towers, impressive gates, sanctuaries, houses, and the Holy Sepulchre.

A century or more later, a Muslim pious popular painting now in the Aleppo Museum (Figure 36) also shows walls, houses, and sanctuaries, but *its* focus is the Dome of the Rock dominating an image of the city with the fullness of its urban setting, including even churches and synagogues but without the dramatic appearance of a walled city. How legitimate it is to draw any kind of conclusion about Jerusalem itself from the evidence of these images remains a debatable matter, inasmuch as no one has, to my knowledge, worked on folk representations of architecture in Ottoman times.[11]

A third representation takes us many centuries back. In an extraordinary painting from the rich collection of the Topkapi Serai Museum in Istanbul, the Prophet Muhammad is shown settled on a rug in front of two personages, with a crowd of other people arranged below in groups characteristic of Persian painting from the early fourteenth century (see Plate 6). A large angel flies in from the upper right carrying a piece of land with a city on it. The painting was first interpreted by the late Richard Ettinghausen as showing Constantinople brought to the Prophet as a gift yet to come.[12] But there are, as Ettinghausen sensed, many difficulties with this interpretation, the

Figure 36. *Jerusalem*. Anonymous, nineteenth century, Aleppo, Syria.

main one being that none of the accounts of the heavenly Journey of the Prophet ever relate the bringing of Constantinople to the Prophet. Furthermore, the arrangement of the personages did not make sense, and the cylindrical shape of the minaret, which he interpreted as Turkish, is an anachronism for the fourteenth century.

A solution to the problem of this miniature lies in the Arabic text of the *Mi'raj-nameh*, which was not known to Ettinghausen in 1957. It is Jamel Eddine Bencheikh who seems to have discovered the correct explanation, even though he does not say so. His publication of a French translation (in reality a literary adaptation) of the Arabic text has been designed in such a way that this particular miniature faces a very striking and appropriate passage at the end of the book. As it turned out, according to this version of the story, the inhabitants of Mecca refused to believe the Prophet's story about his journey to Jerusalem on the way to the heavens, and in order to test him, they asked him to describe the city. He could not do so, because he had visited it during a dark night. Then God ordered the archangel Gabriel to go to Jerusalem, to take it with "the mountains, hills, and valleys around it, with its streets and passageways, and with its sanctuaries," and to carry it to Muhammad in Mecca so that he could describe it to local skeptics.[13]

If this is indeed the correct interpretation of the city represented in the Persian miniature, Jerusalem is shown as a "type" city, with rivers, most un-Palestinian minarets and domes, and many other features clearly relating it to the visual memory of early Mongol Iran.[14] But the mountains, the mighty walls, the fancy gates, and the large sanctuaries are all there. Just as in the Madaba map, the Greek painting of 1704, the Aleppo folk painting, and probably scores of other images, Jerusalem is shown not as it was, but as a typical or idealized city of the culture for which the image was made, to which a few specific "signs" were added that had become associated with Jerusalem, mostly through oral transmission by travelers or by reciters of hagiographical accounts.

Russian Transformation

A third series of documents emerged during an investigation of the appearance of Georgian monks in Jerusalem. The search led me to the early medieval history of the monastery of the Holy Cross in Jerusalem, located just east of the present Israel Museum. The monastery is alleged to have been founded by Georgian monks in the sixth century, rebuilt in the eleventh, decorated in the twelfth, and passed on to Greek monks in the eighteenth century.[15] Finding that monastery, in turn, led to a monastery of Holy Zion built circa 1060 in Georgia itself.[16] And the monastery in Georgia, first published and discussed by Russian scholars before the revolution, revealed the existence of a considerable literature in Russian on what has recently been called the "many-layered holy model" of Jerusalem in medieval and, as it turns out, premodern Russia.[17] Following are a few observations pertaining to the image of Jerusalem in Russia.

Like the rest of Palestine and at times like Constantinople, Jerusalem became a text, almost a completed book, in the sense that the knowledge of its spaces was a lesson in sacred history and, therefore, a model for a moral life. It has even been argued that the urban structure of many settlements from old Rus' was meant to reproduce Jerusalem as it had been described by pilgrims. Such may have been the case for Novgorod and Arkhangelsk, and, as one scholar had pointed out, an imaginary specificity for Jerusalem appears as late as in Boris Pasternak's poetry when he writes about "a road [that] went around the Mount of Olives [while] below flowed the Kedron," a depiction of the Kedron only possible for someone who had never been there.

Much earlier and equally strangely, a legend about an early holy man from Novgorod called John included a story of his Night Flight to Jerusalem on a wild beast that transformed itself into a steed, while the holy man prayed in the Church of the Holy Sepulchre. There is obviously some connection here with the story of Muhammad's Miraj and possibly also with the Egyptian account of a Muslim converted to Christianity as he was transported on a winged horse from the Arabian desert to the monastery of St. Mercury in Egypt.[18] Instantaneous travel opportunities obviously existed for holy men everywhere, as they had been available to Solomon.

Curiously, Solomon is not mentioned in any of the stories I encountered in my brief foray into medieval Russian literature. But David does appear as the hero of a book of sacred legends entitled *Jerusalem Talks*. He is depicted interpreting the dream of the Russian legendary hero Voloto Volovich in the following way: "There will be in Rus' the main city of Jerusalem and in that city will be gathered the apostolic church of Sophia, the Divine Wisdom, with its seventy tops, that is to say the Holy of Holies." The Holy Land is in Holy Russia, and every city is a Jerusalem or acquires a direct connection with Jerusalem through miraculous events or through real or imaginary pilgrims.[19]

These myths, ideas, and fragments of concrete knowledge find their most original expression in several works of late-sixteenth- and seventeenth-century architecture, a time when the lands of Orthodox eastern Europe and especially the Muscovite realm underwent complex and fascinating transformations under the simultaneous impact of the fall of Constantinople in 1453, the spread of the Renaissance and the Reformation, and a variety of internal pressures. The most immediately pertinent example is the cathedral of the Resurrection built between 1658 and 1685 in the monastery near Moscow, which was specifically called New Jerusalem. But the most remarkable example is the celebrated Church of St. Basil on Red Square, which appears in all pictures of Moscow and is one of the most fascinating monuments in the history of architecture in general. It was founded in the second half of the sixteenth century and much redone in the seventeenth. It was a "Jerusalem," as it was even called by the Western traveler Olearius, because it commemorated the victory over the infidel Tatars, whose capital, Kazan, had been taken by Ivan IV.[20] Several other monasteries, some as late as 1814, when a Greek monastery called Ierusalimskij was founded near Taganrog, now in Ukraine, continued the tradition until the dawn of the nineteenth century.

These appearances of Jerusalem as a constructed space are interesting for their ideological message, but the ideological message itself is far more fully and clearly expressed in written form than it is perceivable visually. What makes the visual transformation interesting is not that it provides yet another example of something known otherwise, but that it uses in a rather original way a process of visual persuasion known, from its rhetorical origins, as the synecdoche. Normally it means that a part stands for a whole, as when, in the decoration of a medieval church, two or three examples—for instance of the liberal arts or of sins—stand for a complete set, the seven arts or the seven vices.[21] But in the examples given here, this rhetorical procedure is used backwards; it is a case of metonymy, as the whole identifies a part. The whole city, Jerusalem or Zion, is used to designate a church or a monastic establishment, and the use of the name magnifies the glory or the holiness of the patrons or users of a space, because, like David and Solomon or like the masses of people who came to see Christ enter Jerusalem a week before His Passion, these patrons or users do not really deal with a church or with a monastery in the Russian north, but with a city made holy in name as well as in fact and that can be present anywhere.

The souvenirs of today's Jerusalem, which, together with photographs, are the parts of the city carried to the four corners of the earth, perpetuate one aspect of this phenomenon, that of seeing the city exclusively from the point of view of one of the religions claiming rights in it and thereby excluding or diminishing the place of others.[22] Even photography can be and has been manipulated so as to preempt the city for a sacred place, the Western Wall, the Haram al-Sharif, or the Holy Sepulchre. In doing that, the contemporary culture or cultures dealing with Jerusalem simply continue a tradition of seeing and representing the city through its major buildings. Unique historical, emotional, and political reasons made the transfer of these ways of perceiving the city particularly striking in the Muscovite Russia of the sixteenth and seventeenth centuries. But there are traces of comparable transfers in medieval western Europe with considerable variations between the times before and after the Crusades and possibly between different areas.[23]

The originality of the Russian transformation of Jerusalem outside of Jerusalem is, finally, demonstrated by the existence of bronze objects in the shape of domed churches that are called "Zions" or "Jerusalems" (Figure 37).[24] They were known under this name in the fifteenth century, when they became commonly used liturgically in the several entries and processions of the eucharistic service. By the twelfth century, such objects in the shape of buildings, with certain late antique examples if not prototypes, had probably acquired the name of the city of Jerusalem. At that time, the relatively easy access to Jerusalem through the Crusades led, within the many layers of Christian memory associated with the city, to a different kind of awareness than had existed before. This is precisely the time when, like a booster shot for inoculations, the physical and actual Jerusalem affected and modified once again the myths that had developed around it. And the confusion between an imaginary city and a real one led sometimes to unusual results, like, in the seventeenth century, the ordering by a monastery in Russia of a wooden model of the Holy Sepulchre to be copied into a church within the monastery.[25]

Except perhaps in food practices (a "coney island") or in items of exotic clothing (a "fez" or a "bikini"), I do not know of many instances of objects that have acquired the name of a city or even of a concrete geographic space.[26] That this happened with Jerusalem is a testimony to the extraordinary role the city has played in the imagination and practices of believers from three systems of faith who live far away from it. Jerusalem always existed elsewhere than on its own territory. Because of its highly developed iconography of architecture

Figure 37. A "Jerusalem" or
"Zion." Russian Eucharist vessel.

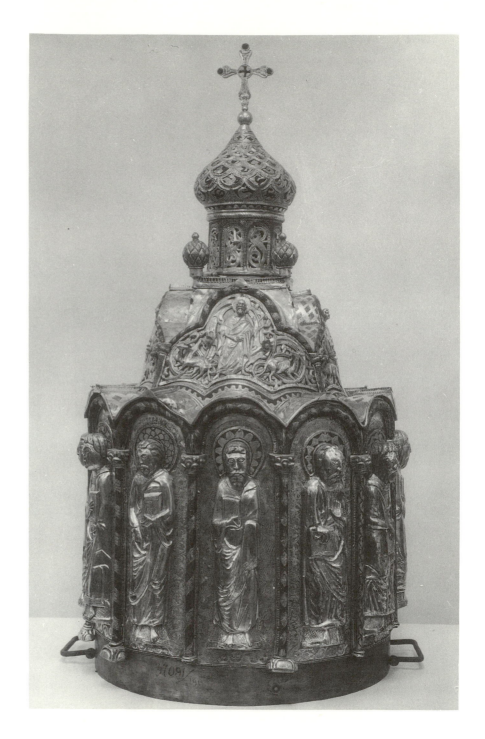

LITERATURE, ART, AND ARCHITECTURE

and representation, and especially because of its highly complex liturgical practices, Christianity has been richer than Islam or Judaism in elaborating other Jerusalems than the Palestinian one and even in making objects of it. It was specific and unusual circumstances of place, as in Indonesia, or of time, as in fourteenth-century painting in Iran, that created Muslim imaginary Jerusalems. For Jews, Jerusalem was stored in memory and ready for the end of time, and it had less need to be expressed visually. What is sure, however, is that, when he built his city and planned its Temple, King David could not have imagined that three thousand years later his city would exist on the edges of the Pacific Ocean or in the monasteries of northeastern Europe. Nor could he have imagined that the search for the many meanings of his city would lead to so many questions of history and of art.

15

The City in Jewish Folk Art

NITZA ROSOVSKY

For nearly six centuries after the Second Temple was destroyed in 70 CE, Jews were forbidden to live in Jerusalem, first by the Romans, then by the Christians. Yet wherever Jews went, they carried the Holy City with them in their memory, in their hearts. To this day, during the Amidah prayer, the observant Jew recites three times a day: "And to Jerusalem, Thy city, return in mercy and dwell therein as Thou hast spoken. And rebuild her soon in our days . . . Blessed art Thou, O Lord, who rebuildest Jerusalem." At home, a bare patch is left on the wall facing Jerusalem, to remember the destroyed Temple, and for the same reason, a glass is broken by the bridegroom at the end of the wedding ceremony.

Jews have always been *am ha'sefer,* "the people of the book," and they have expressed their yearnings for Jerusalem mostly in words. But they have also depicted the city in thousands of images, expressing their longing for Zion and the hope of returning there.

The Second Commandment

Jewish underrepresentation in the visual arts is usually attributed to the Second Commandment: "Thou shalt not make unto thee a graven image, nor any manner of likeness, of any thing that is in heaven above, or that is in the earth beneath, or that is in the water under the earth" (Exodus 20:4). The prohibition is made even more explicit in Deuteronomy (4:16–19), which forbids "even the form of any figure,

344

the likeness of male or female." In the early days of Judaism, when the concept of a one invisible God must have been hard to comprehend, it was crucial to avoid any hint of paganism and to protect the people from anything resembling "graven images." The incident of the Golden Calf, fashioned by Moses' brother, Aaron, at the very moment when Moses was on Mount Sinai receiving the Ten Commandments, shows how close was the danger.

Yet even within the Bible itself there are instances that indicate that the law was not uniformly observed. When God filled the artist Bezalel with His own spirit so that he would create beautiful objects, vessels, even priestly garments, it did not contradict the Second Commandment. The implements were not to be admired for their own beauty, but to be used in the worship and adoration of the Almighty. Moreover, Bezalel did not make any images of animal or human likeness (Exodus 31:2–11). When King Solomon built the Temple in Jerusalem, however, he installed within the Sanctuary two winged "cherubim of olive-wood, each ten cubits high," overlaid with gold (1 Kings 6:23–28); in the Temple's courtyard, twelve oxen supported the molten sea (1 Kings 7:25); and a dozen lions, of which "there was not the likes made in any kingdom," stood on the steps to Solomon's throne (1 Kings 10:18–20). Perhaps Solomon felt secure, certain that his people were no longer in danger of being lured by "graven images," now that his magnificent Temple to the invisible God was completed. Centuries later, when the prophet Ezekiel envisioned the restored Temple, he described not only lions and palm trees decorating it, but also cherubim with human faces.

It is clear that the Second Commandment was interpreted differently over the generations, even within the Bible.[1]

Jerusalem and Synagogue Art

The early history of the synagogue is shrouded in mystery, but many scholars believe that it began sometime after the destruction of the First Temple in 586 BCE. Following the Jews' return from Babylon, synagogues existed for some five centuries, at the same time as the Second Temple, as evidenced by archaeological and literary sources, especially during the last hundred years of the Temple. According to the Mishnah, there was an organic relationship between the Temple and the synagogue in Jerusalem; elsewhere in Eretz Israel and the Diaspora, prayer services at synagogues were a substitute for the sacrifices that could only be offered in Jerusalem. The synagogue was also a place for study, a center for communal meetings, a depository for the Temple dues going to Jerusalem, and a hostel for Jewish travelers. After the destruction of Jerusalem in 70 CE, many of the Temple rituals were transferred to the synagogue, the institution that continued to serve for two millennia as the focus of Jewish life.[2]

There is no evidence of decorative elements in the archaeological ruins of the first century CE synagogues at Gamla, Herodium, or Masada, probably because an aversion to figural representation still lingered after the religious persecutions under Antiochus IV (167–164 BCE), whose placing of pagan deities in the Temple resulted in the Hasmonean revolt.[3] (It is interesting that the first-century historian Josephus found it necessary to blame Solomon's images of bulls and lions on his advanced age and feeble mind.)

After the destruction in the year 70, Jerusalem was often symbolized by the Temple or by the Ark of the Covenant. The earliest such rendition is found on silver coins inscribed "The Third Year of the [Bar Kochba] Revolt" (134/5 CE), which show the facade of the Temple—two pairs of columns on either side of a tall entry. It is possible that sixty-five years after the destruction, some of the community elders still remembered what the Temple looked like. And the memory stayed on, as depictions of the Temple's facade also appear in the wall murals of a mid-third-century synagogue excavated in Dura-Europos, Syria.

In 1932 an archaeological discovery shed a new light on early Jewish art: thirty panels of murals in a synagogue on the Euphrates that was destroyed with the city in 256 were found to contain images of plants, animals, and humans—even a nude female body—many in an excellent state of preservation. Most of the paintings are of biblical scenes: the binding of Isaac, the infant Moses fished out of the reeds by Pharaoh's daughter, Samuel anointing David. In the west wall of the synagogue's prayer room is a niche for keeping the Torah, and above it is a depiction of the Temple facade with two pairs of columns flanking the doorway, topped by a semicircular shell.[4] There is another, more elaborate painting of the Temple on the west wall, the wall oriented toward Jerusalem, but the one over the Torah niche has a striking resemblance to the Bar Kochba coins.

In the Land of Israel itself, synagogues excavated in the past six or seven decades frequently reveal likenesses of birds and animals in stone relief. Later synagogues, from the Byzantine period, feature elaborate mosaic pavements with charming renditions of local flora and fauna. In a sixth-century synagogue discovered in Gaza in 1966, King David himself is depicted, playing his harp to the animals (see Plate 3). In another part of the mosaic is a delightful array of animals: partridges, peacocks, giraffes, a zebra, a leaping tigress, and a lioness suckling her cub.[5]

Some of the most surprising discoveries come from the mosaic pavements of several synagogues dating from the late third to the sixth century; best preserved are the ones at Tiberias and Beit Alpha. The pavements usually consist of three panels, with the zodiac as the theme of the main one. The earliest mosaic zodiac (250–300 CE), which is at Hammath-Tiberias, contains the twelve astrological signs, beautifully executed and each titled in Hebrew. In the center is the sun god Sol, or Helios, riding his chariot through the heavens; four female busts are in the corners, representing the seasons.

In these synagogues, the panel closest to the wall that faced Jerusalem—at times with an enclosure for the Torah shrine—contained similar depictions, of which the one in Tiberias is a fine example: in the large mosaic pavement panel are two lighted seven-branch menorahs, ritual palm branches, incense shovels (with red and black tesserae for the burning coals!), and *shofarim* (ram's horns) flanking an elaborately decorated Holy Ark. Two steps lead to the Ark, whose closed doors are partially covered by a *parochet,* a special curtain. The gabled roof contains a shell design, as did the semicircular roof of the Ark in Dura.[6]

There is no universal explanation for the presence of the zodiac, with its pagan iconography, in the synagogue. Tiberias, where there may have been as many as twelve other contemporary synagogues, was at that time the center of Jewish life in Eretz Israel, so why did the rabbis allow it? Some think that the community felt so secure that the zodiac could be used and was purely a decorative motif. It is also possible that such synagogues represented only one trend within the larger community.

The Palestinian Talmud offers evidence of varying attitudes: "In the days of Rabbi Yohanan they began to paint the walls and he did not prevent them. In the days of Rabbi Abun they began to make designs on mosaics and they did not prevent them" (Avodah Zarah, 4a).

Ancient synagogues in the Roman Empire and elsewhere in Europe contained images of animals and humans, and there is some textual evidence from the eleventh century regarding the admissibility of such images into synagogue decorations. The documents, which show that there was not a uniform attitude toward representational art in the synagogue, are scarce, probably because such art was rare.[7]

In eastern Europe, especially around Poland, the tradition of decorating synagogues was revived and was well established by the seventeenth century. Inside relatively modest wooden synagogues, elaborate pictures were painted directly onto wooden panels covering the walls from top to bottom. The painted synagogues "looked as lively and sumptuous in their way as late baroque churches did."[8] Imaginary depictions of Jerusalem enhanced many synagogues, such as the Isaac Synagogue of Krakow, by 1640, and a century later the synagogue at Khodorov, where the artist Israel ben Mordechai Lisnicki showed Jerusalem framed by a leviathan and a tree.[9] A destroyed city with the Temple in flames could be seen in the synagogue of Kamionka Strumilowa, and in Przedborz a ruined city by a river, with musical instruments hanging in the trees nearby, was painted by Yehuda Leib (1760).[10]

Jews escaping the 1648 Khmelnitzki massacre spread the folk art tradition of synagogue paintings to Hungary, Romania, Moravia, and Bohemia. In those paintings, Jerusalem is an imaginary city with palaces, castles, and turrets surrounded by a wall with many gates and towers.[11] Sometimes a building vaguely similar to the Dome of the Rock could be identified in the center of the city, representing Solomon's Temple. By the eighteenth century, some German village synagogues displayed a similar mode of folk art, perhaps brought there by Polish Jews. Of special interest was the synagogue in Kirchheim (1739–1740), decorated by Eliezer ben Solomon Sussman (Figure 38).[12] Most of these synagogues did not survive World War II.

Other Depictions of the Holy City

After the defeat of the Crusaders, Jewish pilgrims started to frequent tombs of sages, which began to appear in illustrations, in addition to

Figure 38. Jerusalem, depicted on the west wall of the synagogue of Kirchheim. Copied by Max Untermayer Raymer ca. 1935 from the original color painting by Eliezer Sussman, 1739–1740. The synagogue no longer exists.

Jerusalem and other holy sites. The tombs of the Sanhedrin, Rachel, the prophetess Hulda, and Samuel were popular, as were the cities of Hebron, Safed, and Tiberias, which, along with Jerusalem are known as the four Holy Cities. Inscriptions in Hebrew identified the sites in illustrations, and quotes from the Bible and from prayer books, expressing the longing for Jerusalem and forecasting the redemption, became an integral part of the decorations, often forming the borders. The illustrations were divided into four or more tiers, or appeared in concentric circles with Jerusalem in the center, obviously inspired by the round Crusader maps of the city. However, in the center of the Jewish renditions stood the Western Wall, with the Dome of the Rock—usually titled "Solomon's Temple"—above it.[13]

Among the most charming and individualistic representations of Jerusalem—with or without other holy places, and usually enhanced by repetitive flower and tree motifs—were those embroidered by women, in vibrant colors, on Sabbath tablecloths, halah bread covers, and even bags for *tefilim* (phylacteries used in the morning prayer), traditionally decorated by the bride for her intended.

The tradition of illuminated manuscripts began in the East, and some scholars have suggested that the narrative biblical scenes at the Dura-Europos synagogue may have been copied from an illustrated Bible. The earliest extant European illuminated manuscript is a Rashi commentary on the Bible from 1233. The Scrolls of the Book of Esther often contain an image of Jerusalem, as do Haggadot, which contain the saying repeated annually during Passover, at the Seder: "Next year in Jerusalem."[14]

Ketubbot—marriage contracts specifying the rights of the wife and the sums of money she is entitled to receive in case of a divorce or the death of the husband—are often decorated with portraits of Jerusalem. The version of the contract that is still in use is based on a text by Maimonides, although the custom is much older.[15] Many *ketubbot* were highly ornate, with graphics and inscriptions intertwined, the former using floral and other motifs, such pictures of the bride and groom (or occasionally of the naked Adam and Eve in Eden), the latter citing appropriate verses from the Bible celebrating marriage and praising women. Because of Jeremiah's prophecy, "Yet again there shall be heard . . . in the streets of Jerusalem . . . the voice of joy . . . the voice of the bridegroom and the voice of the bride," it was fitting that Jerusalem appeared in marriage contracts; see, for example, the 1732 *ketubbah* from Padua, Italy (Plate 10).

Jerusalem was often depicted on wall decorations used both in the synagogue and in the home, such as the *sheviti,* from "I have set [*sheviti*] the Lord always before me" (Psalms 16:8), and the *mizrah,* meaning east, which indicates the direction of prayer, toward Jerusalem. Among the border inscriptions, always written in Hebrew, the psalmist's words, "If I forget thee, O Jerusalem" (Psalms 137:5) were frequently cited. Other images of Jerusalem within the home mostly enhanced objects related to the observance of the Sabbath and holidays, such as prayer books, Haggadot, embroidered Sabbath tablecloths and halah covers, kiddush cups, Hannukah lamps, and mezuzah (doorpost) cases, but they could also be found on secular objects, such as snuff or jewelry boxes, seals, and amulets.

Emissaries from Eretz Israel, usually traveling to raise money for the city's impoverished Jews, often brought with them as gifts small objects crafted in Jerusalem. Made of local materials such as olive wood or bitumen, later also printed on paper, these tokens were frequently decorated with a likeness of the city.

Realistic representations of Jerusalem began to appear around the middle of the nineteenth century. A favorite view, depicted on hundreds of objects, shows the Western Wall between the Dome of the Rock—standing in for the Temple—and the Aqsa Mosque, with cypresses growing on the platform above the Wall.[16] Interestingly, the Dome of the Rock was often identified correctly or designated "The Mosque of Omar," while at other times it was called "The Temple," "Solomon's Temple," or "The Place of the Temple." Al-Aqsa Mosque was called *"midrash Shelomo,"* or Solomon's study house.

With the rise of Zionism in the late nineteenth century, the traditional, religious symbols of Jerusalem—the Temple and the Western Wall—were replaced by a more secular image—the Tower of David. (The name comes from the Byzantine period, when pilgrims mistook one of the surviving towers that stood near Herod's palace for a remnant from King David's time.) Ironically, in this city of many days, the tower that represents Jerusalem is not the Herodian one but rather a Turkish minaret built in 1655.[17]

16 The Image of the Holy City in Maps and Mapping

MILKA LEVY-RUBIN AND REHAV RUBIN

Jerusalem, the Holy City, the site of many important biblical events, occupied a central place in the hearts and minds of Jews, Christians, and Muslims, in the East and West alike. Both earthly and heavenly Jerusalem were represented in numerous types of compositions that dedicated a special place to the study and the description of the Holy Land and the Holy City.

Often the authors of these compositions were not content with verbal descriptions, and many of them included graphic depictions of the city, usually referred to as "maps" of Jerusalem.[1] Although Jerusalem was indeed holy to Jews and Muslims as well as to Christians, there are almost no such depictions of the city that were drawn by either of the first two groups; it seems that generally this was a Christian genre.

From the Byzantine period until the beginning of the twelfth century and the Crusader conquest, there was only one map of Jerusalem that is known today: the Madaba map, a mosaic that was made in the sixth century. There are about twenty extant medieval maps of the city. After the development of the printing press, from the end of the fifteenth century onward, many new maps were made.

The Madaba Mosaic Map

The earliest surviving map of Jerusalem, the Madaba map, was discovered in 1881 within the ruins of a church in Madaba, an active bishopric at the time and now a small village in Jordan.[2] (See Plate 2.) It is a map of the Holy Land depicting an enlarged image of Jerusalem in the center, a city totally and exclusively Christian. It focuses on the Church of the Holy Sepulchre, whose facade is turned toward the viewer—in spite of the fact that the map faces the east and therefore the eastern facade should have been hidden. Three other central features are the new *cardo,* or colonnaded street; the new complex of the Sancta Maria Nea, built by Justinian; and the Church on Mount Zion, the *mater ecclesiarum.* The color code of the map is also indicative, as all the churches in the city are marked out in red. Another very schematic representation of the city appears in the topographic margins of the mosaic uncovered about a decade ago in Umm al-Rasasin Jordan, under the title "Hagiapolis." (See Figure 17, page 292.)

Not one single map of Jerusalem exists from the Early Islamic period (638 to 1099). But European Christian mapmakers throughout the Middle Ages gave graphic expression to the religious perception of Jerusalem as the center of the world.[3] These maps, called *Orbis Terrarum,* or "T-O" maps, portray the world as a round disk with the oceans and rivers dividing it in a T-shaped fashion, the Mediterranean Sea as its vertical arm, Africa to its right, and Europe to the left. The horizontal bar is formed by the Nile River on the right and the Tannus (Don) River and the Black Sea on the left, while Asia is located on the upper part of the disk, with Jerusalem at its center.[4]

Crusader Maps

The Crusader conquest in 1099 awakened in the West a renewed interest in the Holy Land, and particularly Jerusalem, the site of the redeemed Sepulchre.[5] Sites sanctified by Christian tradition became the targets of renewed interest, and a multitude of reports about the new Crusader Jerusalem, which was being rebuilt, flooded Europe. In addition to the numerous twelfth-century verbal descriptions, many graphic descriptions, especially maps, started making their appearance.[6]

There are fourteen maps, all depicting the twelfth-century Holy City under Crusader rule. These maps continued to be copied until the end of the fourteenth century, even though in 1187, with the collapse of the first Latin Kingdom, Jerusalem fell into Muslim hands and thereafter, excluding a short period from 1229 to 1244, was not a Christian city any more. These fourteen maps include one main group of eleven round maps and three other single exemplars containing three very different maps.

The most important of the three single maps is the well-known Cambrai map (Figure 39), which was drawn in the twelfth century.[7] It faces north, and is rhomboid in shape. Its special importance is that its author knew Crusader Jerusalem well and drew a very detailed, comparatively accurate map of Jerusalem. The Holy Sepulchre in its new Crusader form is correctly depicted, including its new bell tower and the new courtyard facing south. Next to it, the Hospitaler buildings are depicted in a very detailed fashion. On the former Aqsa Mosque the designation "Domus Militum Templi" appears, and in the west the "Curia Regis"—Royal Court—and the "Turris Tancredi"—Tancred's Tower—are depicted. Another element that points to the author's acquaintance with the city is found on the northeastern part of the city wall, where it is written, *"Hic capta est civitas a Francis"*: Here the city was captured by the Franks. A most interesting feature, unique to the Cambrai map, is its familiarity with the Eastern churches in Jerusalem, at least six of which appear on the map. These include the Church of St. Saba;[8] the Church of Kharitun, where the Syrians showed the reliquiae of the saint in a wooden chest; the Jacobite Church of St. Mary Magdalene; the Church of St. George, located in the corn market; the Church of St. Abraham; and the Church of St. Bartholomew. Also unique is the use of the Greek name for the Church of the Holy Sepulchre, Anastasis. The pseudo-topographical lines, another very interesting characteristic of this map, demonstrate well the author's familiarity with the topography of the city and its surroundings.

The second single exemplar is the square map from Montpellier.[9] Its most interesting feature is its attempt to present graphically the battle array of the Crusader forces around Jerusalem. Otherwise, it represents only a few basic traditions, most of which are placed almost arbitrarily on the map and are only remotely related to reality. These include the site of Jesus' disrobing, of his crowning with thorns, his binding, and arrest; the site where Helena found the Cross; and the Navel of the Earth.

The third single exemplar, the round Codex Harleian map,[10] which

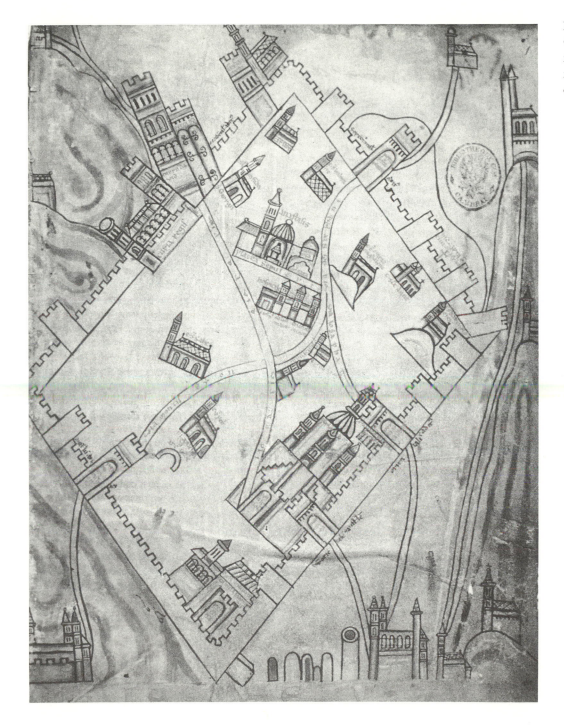

Figure 39.
Cambrai
manuscript
map, twelfth
century.

although round is distinctly different from the other round maps, is actually a map of the Holy Land rather than a map of Jerusalem. This map, which is a graphic presentation of a pilgrim's itinerary, starting at the port towns of Jaffa, Caesarea, Acre, and Ascalon, and reaching the Jordan River in the east and Nazareth and Banias in the north, demonstrates very clearly that its author saw Jerusalem as the highlight of the pilgrimage, while all the other sites were marginal in comparison. It is therefore a good example of a map that clearly has no pretense of accuracy but presents a graphic description of the author's conception of his journey. (See Figure 30, page 318).

The eleven round maps form a large and impressive group whose close resemblance to each other is evident at first sight.[11] Seven of these were drawn in the twelfth century, and four are from the thirteenth and fourteenth centuries. Their common characteristics indicate that this multitude of round maps was not just a product of a certain artistic fashion prevalent in Europe at the time—in which case each of these maps would have been made independently, under the influence of this style—but that there was, indeed, one original round prototype from which the other maps derived, either directly or indirectly.

In all of the round maps, the circle forms the city walls, while the two main streets—which look like the Roman-Byzantine *cardo* and *decumanus*—form a cross in the center. It should be noted that the Harleian map, which is also round, has no element similar to the crossroads that characterizes the round group. The round form may reflect the influence of the T-O world maps or, equally, the common depiction of the Heavenly Jerusalem according to Ezekiel, which was popular even before the time of the Crusades.

The round maps, like the T-O maps, always face eastward, in contrast to the square Montpellier map, which faces north, and the trapezoidal Cambrai map, which faces a general north.

The city plan—including the gates, the main roads and streets, and the main buildings depicted—is identical in all of the round maps; the Harleian map, in contrast, has only four gates, which are symmetrically located. The two main streets that form the crossroads within the city create four quarters, equal in size. The streets cross each other in the middle of the circle, at the marketplace (Forum Rerum Venalium). Apart from these two main streets, an additional street, leading to

Jehoshaphat's Gate, is indicated, and in most of the maps the street starting at St. Stephen's Gate and running under the Temple Mount, in the Tyropeon Valley, is also shown. This plan, although very schematic, is indeed the basic street plan of Jerusalem. In all the round maps, two roads diverge symmetrically from David's Gate in the west: one, leading south to Bethlehem, and the other, north, to Mons Gaudii (Nebi Samwil).

Several structures especially stand out in all of the round maps. The Holy Sepulchre (Sanctum Sepulchrum) and "the Lord's Temple" (Templum Domini, the Dome of the Rock, which was turned into a church by the Crusaders) are often presented as two circles complementing each other. Additional structures that are particularly prominent are David's Tower, the city's citadel, and "Templum Salomonis" (al-Aqsa Mosque on the Temple Mount, which served as the headquarters of the Templar Order).

One of the more notable characteristics of the round maps is the fact that, unlike the Cambrai map, they not only name the sites but also often present many traditions, both biblical and apocryphal, that were attached to certain sites. This element, which will later become very common in maps of Jerusalem, turning them into "condensed" or telescopic visual histories of the city, appears for the first time in the round maps.

A common group of traditions and sites both inside and outside the city appears regularly in all of the round maps and forms their basis.[12] The choice of sites, their location on the map, and the names given to them are identical in almost all cases, emphasizing the strong dependence of these maps on each other, and ultimately on one prototype created somewhere around the middle of the twelfth century. Apart from the monuments already mentioned, the following sites and traditions appear in all of the maps: Porta Speciosa, the Beautiful Gate;[13] Ecclesia S. Anna; the Piscina, the Pool of Bethesda;[14] Forum Rerum Venalium, the marketplace; the Cambium Monete, the money exchange; Lapis Scissus, the rock that split at the Crucifixion;[15] and the so-called Ecclesia Latina, a name that stood for Ecclesia sanctae Mariae Latinae and actually represented the whole complex of the Order of St. John (the Hospitalers), which was in reality located just south of the Holy Sepulchre. The Calvaria and the Golgotha both appear in most of the round maps side by side, the Calvaria being during the Crusader period the name of the site of the Crucifixion, while Golgotha was the name given to the Chapel of Adam, underneath the site of the Crucifixion.[16]

Outside the walls, the main traditions and sites depicted are the Ascensio Domini, the Ascension of the Lord;[17] the Porta Aurea, the Golden Gate through which Jesus entered seated upon the ass;[18] Ecclesia or Sepulchrum S. Mariae[19] and Villa Gethsemani,[20] which were situated in the Kedron or Jehoshaphat Valley; Fons Syloe, the Siloam "Fountain"; and the Cenaculum, located on Mount Zion. Certain sites located further away from the city are also included.

Although all the round maps have a common basis, they nevertheless have individual traits and often present us with unique sites or traditions, from the Old Testament, the New Testament, and the Apocrypha.

The Hague map (Figure 40) is the most famous and most beautiful of the round maps. It is distinguished mostly by its unique graphic features. Especially outstanding is the picture of St. George, in the apparel of a Templar knight, defeating the Muslim foe. To the north of the city there is a group of men with a villainous appearance: these are the Jews, an identification confirmed by the stones in their hands in preparation for stoning St. Stephen, who appears just beneath them.[21] The church dedicated to St. Stephen[22] was pushed all the way down to present this scene, showing us once again that reality and precision were not of considerable importance. The Hague map also mentions one additional tradition connected with the Cenaculum—that is, the Procession of the Holy Ghost, which is noted only here and in the Uppsala map.

The second round map presented here is the Uppsala map (see Plate 11). This map, which was drawn in the twelfth century, is in fact a map whose whereabouts were unknown for more than a hundred years, and it was rediscovered just recently.[23]

The Uppsala map is especially rich in biblical traditions. The author calls Mons Gaudii, the Mount of Joy from which the Crusaders first sighted Jerusalem, Masphat—that is, Mizpah, the place where Samuel congregated the people of Israel and called on them to repent;[24] The Shepherd's Field is named "The place where Jacob grazed his sheep";[25] nearby, the Hay—the second city conquered by Joshua after Jericho—is depicted.[26] Near Bethlehem, the site of the Passio Inno-

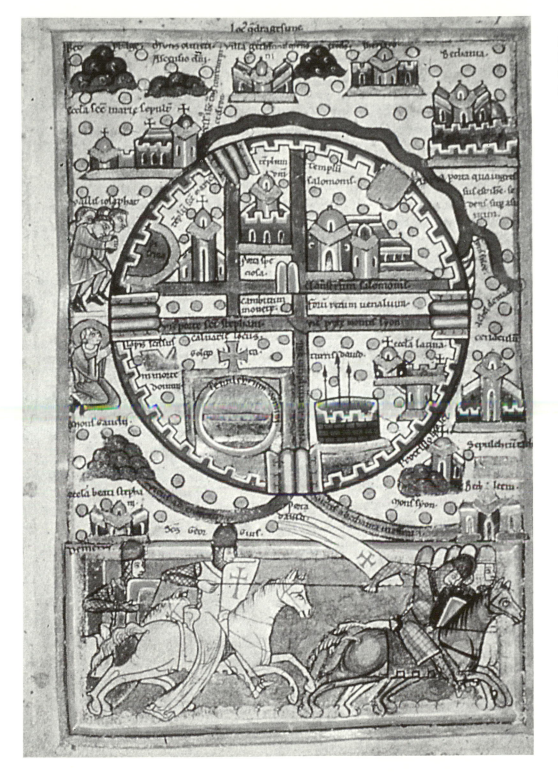

Figure 40. The Hague manuscript map, twelfth century.

centium, the Martyrdom of the Innocents, is shown.[27] An interesting inscription appears by the Sheep's Pool, next to a single column: "Here Jesus was flagellated."[28] The inscription, along with additional sites mentioned in twelfth-century itineraries, may indicate that the tradition of the Via Dolorosa was already formed in the twelfth century.[29] This detail demonstrates that despite the schematic and inaccurate nature of these maps, they may still supply us with information concerning the reality of their time.

What was the object of all of these maps representing Crusader Jerusalem? Were they meant to be realistic maps of the city? Were they meant to serve as a guide for pilgrims, so that they could find their way to the Christian sites or to the hostels of the military orders? Why were the round maps so popular?

The first question that should be raised is whether these maps were indeed attached to any form of guidebook or itinerary describing Crusader Jerusalem. A review of the relevant manuscripts shows that four of the round maps, Brussels A,[30] Brussels B,[31] Uppsala, and St. Omer,[32] all from the twelfth century, illustrate a text describing Crusader Jerusalem, while the London[33] and Paris[34] maps are actually surrounded by such a text on the same page. Since four of the earlier manuscripts are connected with the *Gesta Francorum Expuganantium Hierusalem* (The History of the Franks Who Conquered Jerusalem),[35] it is possible that this was the text that these maps originally illustrated, and that only later were they copied separately without the text.

A short look at the maps themselves will suffice to reject the claim that these are maps that were drawn originally for practical purposes and were meant to be realistic. The argument put forward by some— that the creators of these maps were not technically capable of drawing an accurate, realistic map—is completely unacceptable. The perfect circle symbolizing the walls of Jerusalem in the round maps (as well as the square of the Montpellier map and the trapezoid of the Cambrai map) has no pretensions of representing the actual outline of the city wall. The straight and symmetrical street pattern does not follow the winding streets of Crusader Jerusalem. Often buildings have been moved from one place to another, to make room for others or to present a more aesthetic image. If pilgrims had tried to use these maps, they most likely would have lost their way. It is clear, therefore, that a map, in the modern sense of the word—an accurate and proportional description of the city—was not the object of these artists.

This is definitely true for the round maps, and for the Montpellier map. But even the author of the Cambrai map, who no doubt knew Jerusalem firsthand and was the more realistic of the lot, did not aim to supply the viewer with an accurate map.

The object of these maps was, therefore, different. They were meant to create a certain image of Jerusalem. In the round maps' case, it was an image of a glorious city that combines Christian tradition and Crusader reality; an illustration of the renewed Christian rule in historical Jerusalem; a presentation of the new Christian Jerusalem built by the new David and Solomon, Ezra and Nehemiah, and ruled by them.[36] It was God's new chosen kingdom on earth. To attain this goal, the artists combined in these maps sacred Christian sites and traditions side by side with the important Crusader monuments and buildings. The city they presented was not the one seen by the eyes: among the sites depicted we find places in which biblical events occurred. David's Gate, for example, may be called by its biblical name, "the fish gate" (Nehemiah 3:3); the road to Bethlehem is called "the way to Bethleham Effrata" (Micah 5:1), and Bethlehem is called "Bethlehem of Judah" (Ruth 1:1); southeast of the city, Mons Seir (Edom) is depicted, along with Mons Synai, and the cities of Sodom and Gomorrah.[37]

Jerusalem is presented in these maps as a magnificent city, a mixture of history and reality, a sight that excites the imagination. The viewer of these maps, which are so colorful and ornamental, sees a city full of magnificent buildings and ruled by church spires; a Crusader city shrouded by its past history and glowing with royal splendor. This was the image of Jerusalem that the artists wanted to convey to the Christians in the West, to fill their hearts with pride.

It seems that this special character of the round maps of Jerusalem was the reason for their being so unanimously preferred over the other depictions of the city. The Cambrai map drew a beautiful aesthetic picture of Jerusalem, but it was definitely a contemporaneous one. The Montpellier map mixed tradition with the Crusader reality but did not present a glorious royal city. It was the round maps, laden with both history and royal splendor, with their perfect circle, a symbol of the ideal city, a parallel of the round heavenly Jerusalem, that enraptured the Western Christian.

Post-Crusader Maps

The final collapse of the Latin Kingdom of Jerusalem shattered the image of the rebuilt Christian city, and it could no longer be presented in the West as it had been until then. The few maps we have from the thirteenth to the fifteenth centuries reflect this clearly. The first map that presents Jerusalem under Muslim rule is that of Marino Sanudo, attached to his book *Liber Secretorum Fidelium Crucis super Terrae Sanctae Recuperatione et Conservatione* (Figure 41).[38] (The map was in fact made by Pietro Vesconte, as part of an atlas prepared in 1320.[39]) Sanudo's Jerusalem is presented as a target for reconquest and the reestablishment of a renewed Christian kingdom. In his map, as well as in the rest of the maps from this period, there is none of the splendor of the Crusader maps, and the magnificent churches are gone. Sanudo's is in fact the first map to present a realistic view of the city. It is obvious that the author of this map knew the city well, as can be clearly seen from the accurate outline of the city walls and the locations of the different monuments. That this correct image should not be accepted uncritically, however, is demonstrated by the appearance of the city wall, which is presented as whole and complete. This depiction is very problematic, since there is direct and clear evidence that the Ayyubid ruler al-Malik al-Mu'azzam had purposely destroyed the walls in 1219, when he feared that the city would be reconquered by the Crusaders.[40] There is no evidence that the walls had been rebuilt later. (See Figure 2, page 24.) Sanudo's map, like its followers, is more avid in depicting the important Christian traditions and sites than in depicting the contemporary image of the city.

Another graphic presentation drawn sometime in the fourteenth century is based on the description by Burchard of Mount Zion, written in 1283.[41] Although the description is a realistic one, the map provides a completely imaginary depiction, with no pretense of any acquaintance with the city whatsoever; its author was clearly interested only in the biblical traditions. This type of imaginary depiction would become very popular in printed maps from the sixteenth century onward.

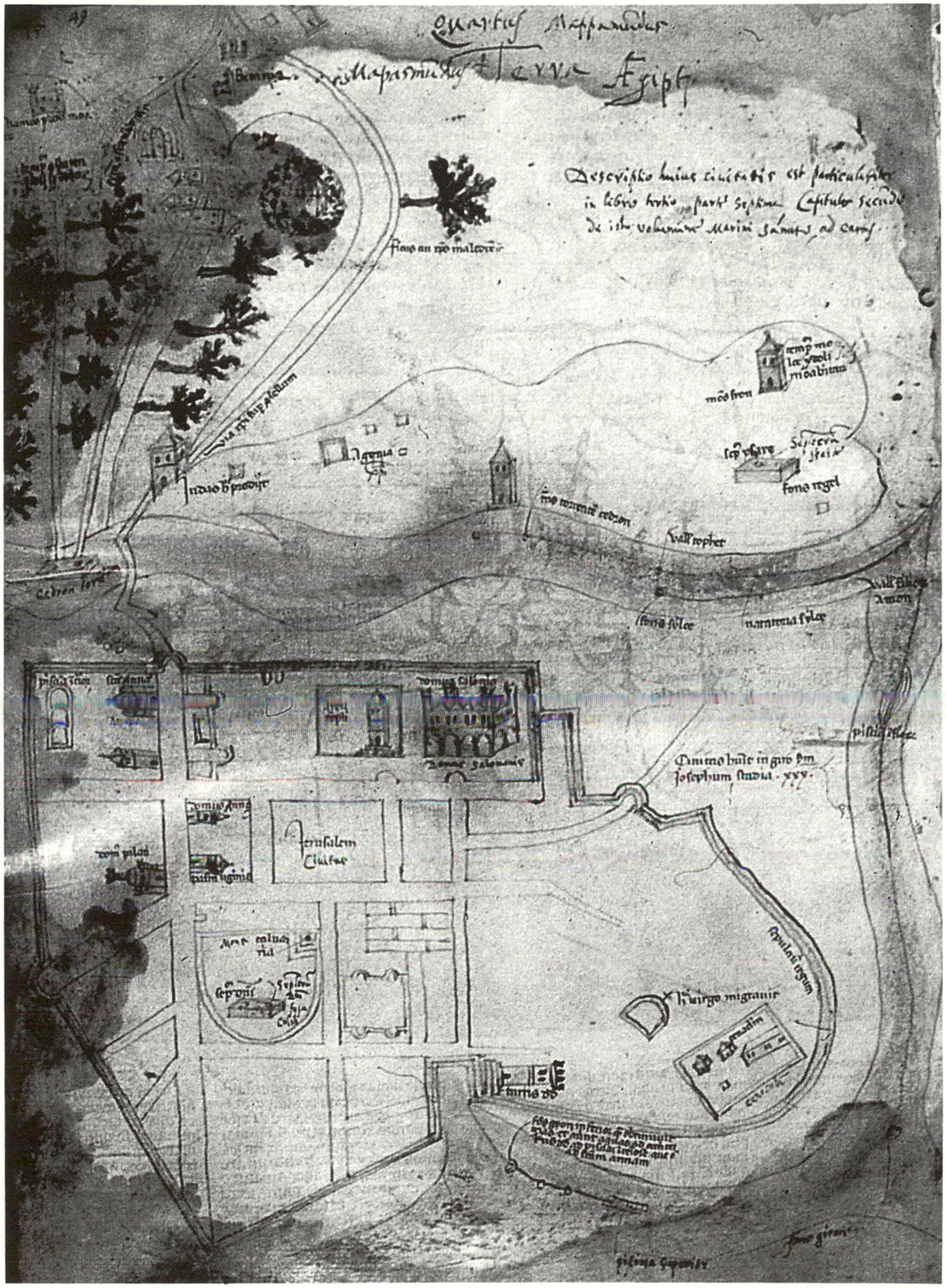

Figure 41. Marino Sanudo's map, 1320.

In the first half of the fourteenth century, a deputation of the Franciscan order was sent to Palestine and was organized as the Custodia Terrae Sanctae, the Guards of the Holy Land. Their task, given by the Pope, was to be the guardians of the holy places, to guide and take care of the pilgrims, and to keep the Catholic interests in the Holy Land, a mission that they have carried out through the centuries since then. The establishment of this mission furthered the revival of European Christian pilgrimage, and the maps that were made by these pilgrims reflect their initial motivation to visit the Holy City and its sites and to walk in the footsteps of Jesus Christ. The two manuscript maps from the last quarter of the fifteenth century, the Sebald Rieter map (Figure 42) and the map attached to a text of Ptolemy,[42] are in fact the heralds of a new genre that was forming under the influence of the Franciscan custody of Jerusalem and later gained widespread influence through the printed maps.

Sebald Rieter's map (ca. 1475) depicted Jerusalem from the top of the Mount of Olives, looking west. This vantage point was chosen for its beauty as well as for its holiness, as the site from where Christ looked over the city. Some of the city's buildings are portrayed schematically, but many of the important buildings are shown in fairly accurate detail. The city is surrounded by a wall in which gates and towers are presented: David's Tower, Samarian Gate (probably Herod's Gate), the gate through which St. Stephen was taken out of the city to be stoned (today's Lions Gate), the Golden Gate through which Jesus entered Jerusalem on Palm Sunday, and Zion Gate. South of the Temple Mount and on Mount Zion, sections of a demolished wall are depicted, as if the mapmaker had seen the remnants of the ancient wall that enclosed the City of David and Mount Zion. North of today's Lions Gate, a section of the wall is drawn broken; evidently this is to be identified with the wall destroyed in 1219 by al-Malik al-Mu'azzam,[43] and it implies, in fact, that the wall was not rebuilt until the time of Suleiman the Magnificent in the sixteenth century. However, Rieter's map evidently testifies to the fact that al-Mu'azzam's destruction of the wall was not systematic, and that parts of the wall remained, broken but still standing, impressing visitors to Jerusalem.

Two large structures are depicted on the Temple Mount: the Dome of the Rock, and al-Aqsa Mosque. Although the former is

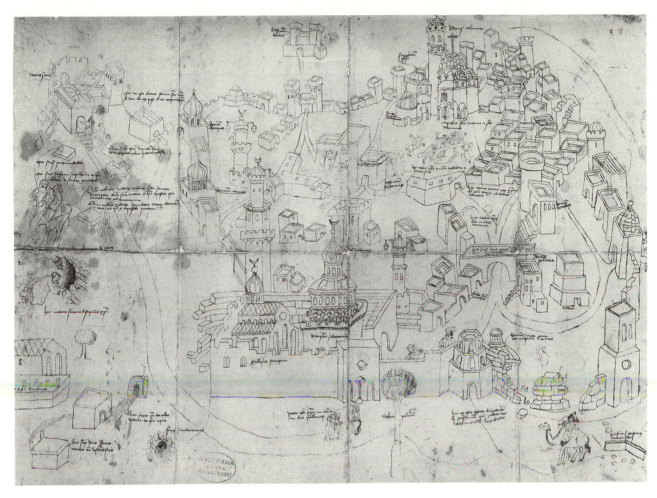

Figure 42. Sebald Rieter's map, ca. 1475.

labeled the Temple of Solomon, a crescent is depicted on its top, as well as on the al-Aqsa and on two of the three other minarets shown on the map, and the area of the Temple Mount itself is called Ecclesie Sarazeni—the Church of the Saracens. Although it was made when Jerusalem was under Muslim Mamluk rule, Rieter's map provides a detailed description of many places in Jerusalem relating to Christian traditions. The Gihon spring is called the Spring of St. Mary, and near the Siloam pool an inscription states that at this spot Jesus miraculously restored the sight of a blind man.[44] In the southern part of the city is "the field of Judas Iscariot" that was bought with Judas's thirty dinar.[45] Several traditions associated with Jesus, his disciples, and Mary are noted on Mount Zion and its slopes, and near St. Stephen's Gate (Lions Gate) note is made of St. Stephen's being taken from the city, and the place where he was stoned to death. The map offers perhaps the earliest graphic depiction of the Via Dolorosa, presenting the House of Pilate, adjacent to which is the arch where Pilate sentenced Jesus; the spot where Jesus met Veronica (today's Sixth Station of the Way of the Cross); and the place where St. Mary saw Jesus on his way to the Crucifixion. (The site where St. Mary fainted is mentioned also in the Sanudo map, today's Fourth Station.) These are followed by the spot where Jesus fell while carrying the cross and, finally, the Church of the Holy Sepulchre, which is depicted as a large structure that includes Golgotha, the tomb of the Savior, a tall bell tower, and the chapels of St. Mary, the Angels, John the Baptist, and Mary Magdalen. The entrance to the church faces south, but the map is oriented to the west, so the artist turned the facade of the church to face east, a distortion that was followed by later mapmakers, so that the viewer is presented with the facade.

Early Printed Maps

In 1450 Gutenberg invented his printing press, and shortly afterward maps were being printed. In 1486 the first edition of Bernhard von Breydenbach's book was printed, describing his pilgrimage to the Holy Land; it included the first printed map of Jerusalem.[46] During the Renaissance and Reformation, various developments and changes in technology, geographical knowledge, scholarship, religious clashes, and politics had immense influence on the proliferation of maps of the Holy Land. Two main trends characterize these printed maps of Jerusalem: on the one hand were maps depicting Jerusalem in a realistic manner, as viewed by Christian-European pilgrims, and on the other were imaginary, historical maps, based mainly on the Scriptures and the work of Josephus Flavius. Some mapmakers and authors put both kinds of maps in their books, sometimes next to each other or even on the same page.[47] However, it seems that the distinction between the imaginary and the realistic, which is so basic in our modern view, was not that sharp at the time, and realistic elements are found alongside imaginary, conceptual, and anachronistic elements in both map groups.

Realistic Maps

The group of maps characterized as "realistic" were claimed by their makers to portray contemporary Jerusalem. Some were drawn by pilgrims and travelers and were based on their own sight and impressions, while others were copies and imitations, drawn in Europe by people who had never seen the city but had used maps by eye witnesses as a basis for their work. The image of Jerusalem as the Holy City where pilgrims walked in the footsteps of Jesus Christ was created and promoted to a large extent by the Franciscan monks of the Custodia Terrae Sanctae, either directly, through maps made by Franciscans who served in Jerusalem—like De Angelis, Amico, and Quaresmius—or indirectly, through maps made by pilgrims who traveled under the auspices of the Custodia, like De Bruyn, who described how the monks helped him conceal from the suspicious Turks and Arabs his intention to draw his panorama, by pretending to have a picnic on the top of the Mount of Olives.

The two best examples of this realistic genre are the maps by Antonio De Angelis, who printed his large map in Rome in 1578 after serving for eight years in Jerusalem,[48] and Francisco Quaresmius (Figure 43), who served for many years in the Levant and was even appointed head of the Franciscans in the Holy Land, and printed his map in his large book in 1639.[49] Thus both maps were based on firsthand information acquired during long years of work in Jerusalem. They depict Jerusalem from the top of the Mount of Olives, looking west. They both cover the area of Jerusalem and its environs, with the Valley of Hinnom to the south (left); Hebron and Bethlehem further south (upper left corner); the Judean Mountains and St. John the Baptist's birthplace to the west (top); the Tomb of Helen Queen of Adiabene—also known as the Tomb of the Kings—to the north (right); and the Mount of Olives itself in the east (lower part). The city itself is in the middle, surrounded by walls, with the Temple Mount, the Church of the Holy Sepulchre, and the Citadel as its most prominent buildings. Many other sites, such as the Via Dolorosa, churches, and monasteries, are marked by numbers explained in the legend. The

Figure 43. Francisco Quaresmius's map, 1639.

central part of the map provides a detailed and reliable depiction of Jerusalem within its walls. The gates are clearly drawn: Herod's Gate and Damascus Gate to the north; Jaffa Gate and the Citadel to the west; Zion Gate and the Dung Gate to the south; and the blocked Golden Gate and St. Stephen's Gate to the east. Within the city, on the eastern side, appears the Temple Mount, with the Dome of the Rock and al-Aqsa Mosque on it. Behind it, within the city, Damascus

Gate with its plaza and the city's two main thoroughfares leading southward from it are clearly depicted. On the main thoroughfare, not far from the Church of the Holy Sepulchre, the three Covered Bazaars appear, identified by the anachronistic Latin term used in the Crusader period, *"forum rerum venalium,"* the marketplace.

Throughout both maps, sites are numbered in reference to the detailed legends. A careful review of these legends reveals that the maps should be regarded as realistic and highly reliable, yet it is clear that, being Franciscan monks, the maps' makers chose to focus mainly on Christian traditions and messages and ignored many of the other sites. Moreover, most sites are arranged in the legends and numbered on the maps, according to various routes leading to holy places in the vicinity of the city—routes that were created by the Franciscans for Christian pilgrims. Series of sequential numbers refer to various routes of this kind, as from Jerusalem, via the Monastery of the Cross, to the spring in which Philip baptized the Ethiopian eunuch (Acts 8),[50] and to the village of Ein Kerem, the birthplace of John the Baptist. A second, longer route led from Jerusalem to Bethlehem and to Hebron, marking the holy places along the way; two other routes led from Mount Zion to Gethsemane and to the Mount of Olives and Bethany.

Other traditions, although of secondary importance and based on the Apocrypha or later writings rather than on the Scriptures, are depicted on the maps, such as the House of the Three Marys; the place where the Jews tried to kidnap the body of St. Mary; the place where the prophet Isaiah was cut up; the pool of Bersabee (*sic!* this should of course be read "Bath-Sheba"); and many more. On the whole, these maps depicted Jerusalem as seen through the eyes of Christian Europeans, and represented the Christian ideology and concept of the city. Realistic and conceptual Jerusalem were, therefore, bound together in these maps. Consequently they are extremely important sources of information about the city as it was perceived by the Christian Catholic pilgrims of the time.

Imaginary Historical Maps

At the same time that "realistic" maps depicting contemporary Jerusalem were being drawn and printed, European scholars were creating maps that were based on the Scriptures and on Josephus, and presenting them as part of their biblical exegeses and other religious literature. This genre of maps has almost no importance as a source on the history of Jerusalem, but it is valuable for the study of the concept of Jerusalem among European scholars of the period.

The best example of this genre is the map of Jerusalem made by Christian van Adrichom (1535–1585), a Dutchman who worked most of his life in Cologne (Figure 44). In 1584 he published a book accompanied by a map, entitled *Jerusalem et Suburbia eius, Sicut Tempore Christi Floruit*.[51] The book and map were published in Latin and later translated into other languages, and they went through many editions. In this map, Jerusalem is depicted facing eastward, surrounded by mountains, with the Kidron Brook lying to its east. The city itself is rectangular and is surrounded by walls. It is depicted as if it were divided into three or even four parts. The southernmost (right) strip is "Mount Zion, the City of David, the Upper City." The central strip—the main part of the city—is larger than the others, and the Temple appears in its eastern (upper) part. In the northern part of the city, two additional strips are separated by inner walls—"The Second City" and "Bezetha—The New City." This image of Jerusalem as a rectangular city divided by walls is a misinterpretation of Josephus's description of the city. Since Josephus's works were well known to European scholars at the time, this graphic concept, which was incorrectly based on them, quickly became very popular and was copied by many later mapmakers.

The city's grounds are filled with buildings and scenes, most of which are mentioned in the Scriptures, in Josephus, and in other historical sources. Each site and tradition is numbered and has a short caption; altogether there are 270 items.[52] There is no differentiation between the various historical periods. Among the many sites, we find the palaces of King David, King Solomon, the Macabeans, Berenice, King Herod, and Pilate; the house of Caiaphas; and the Herodianic amphitheater and hippodrome. Many of them are drawn in the form of European buildings of the sixteenth century. Around the city walls, other scenes are illustrated, among them the anointing of King Solomon, Absalom's monument, the site of the pagan sacrifices to the Molech, and even Solomon's zoo. For many sites, the artist did much more than draw the buildings: he depicted the traditions artistically, as he imagined they had been in reality. Thus we find, for example, the high priest in front of the altar in the Temple, with the menorah (candelabrum) on his left and the table of the shewbread (Exodus 39:36) on his right. The Holy of Holies with the Ark is in front of him, with the Hebrew name of God—Jehovah—between the cherubim on top of it. Next to the Temple and near his palace, Solomon can be seen sitting on his throne. A special group of scenes is the one presenting the Passion of Jesus Christ, from his triumphal entry into the city on Palm Sunday, through the Last Supper, his prayer in Gethsemane, the Judgment, his way along the Via Dolorosa, and the Crucifixion on Mount Calvary. This series continues and depicts his appearance before his disciples on the road to Emmaus (Luke 24:13ff.) and the Ascension from the top of the Mount of Olives. Besides these, there are many other, less important Christian traditions: the cursed fig tree, Judas Iscariot hanging from the tree, and so on.

Adrichom's map is one of the most decorated and famous of the imaginary maps but definitely not the only one. Well known imaginary maps were made by Villalpando, Visscher, and others,[53] and they too were followed by many later editions, copies, and imitations.

From Pictorial Maps to Scientific Maps

The maps that we have discussed thus far were all pictorial, artistic illustrations. Yet at the same time a small but important group of maps that were less pictorial and had a more linear, scientific character, began to appear. Most of these maps, however, still reflected the interest of the Christian pilgrim, who experienced and described the Holy City and its sites from a religious viewpoint and rarely related to the inhabitants of the city or to the realia of its life.

The transition from pictorial to scientific maps is evident in five principal characteristics.[54]

1. The diminishing use of pictorial elements and the increasing use of symbols, letters, and numbers, in particular, to mark buildings, sites, and landscape details. These letters and numbers were identified in the legends on the margin of these maps.
2. The gradual transition from panoramic or oblique birds-eye view

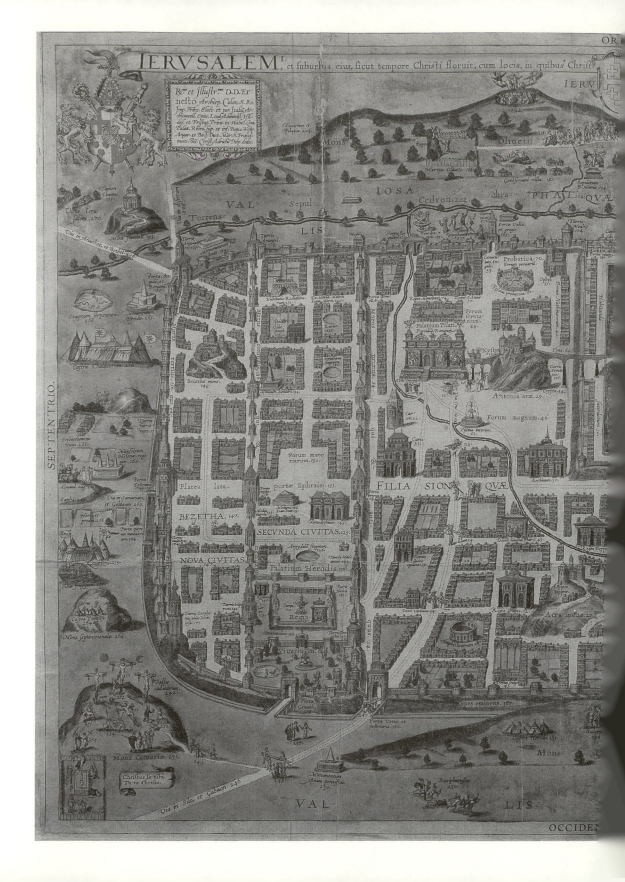

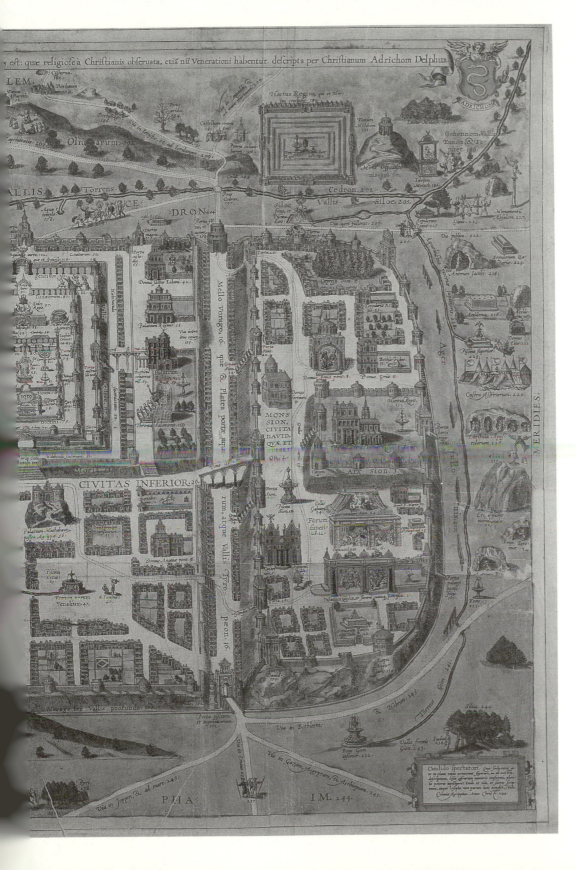

Figure 44. Christian van Adrichom's map of Jerusalem in the time of Jesus, 1584.

drawings that depicted the city from the Mount of Olives to maps that showed the city from a vertical bird's-eye perspective.

3. The development of techniques that enabled the depiction of topographic relief. It was only in the eighteenth century that the techniques of shading and hachuring came into use, and it was only in the second half of the nineteenth century that the first map of Jerusalem with contour lines, which is the accepted technique in modern topographic cartography, was drawn.[55]

4. The tendency to change the orientation of the maps, to the north. The tradition in the Middle Ages was to draw the map facing the east—which is, of course, the origin of the term *orientation*. At the same time, many of the artistic maps viewed the city from the height of the Mount of Olives—that is, from the east, westward. In the course of the development of scientific maps of Jerusalem, an orientation toward the north gradually became more prevalent.

5. Survey maps based on precise measurements began to appear in the nineteenth century. Yet even before their publication, the effort to draw a map of Jerusalem in proper proportion—or at least the pretension to do so—was evident.

These five features did not appear in the maps of Jerusalem simultaneously, but their presence in certain maps testifies to the development of the new "scientific trend"—which will be illustrated through several maps of Jerusalem that best exemplify the process from its beginning, at the close of the sixteenth century, to the first survey map drawn in the early nineteenth century.

The first map in which some of the new characteristics are apparent is that of Zuallardo (Zuallart), a Flemish pilgrim who traveled to the Holy Land, visited Jerusalem in 1586, and included the map in his book that was first printed, in Italian, in 1587 (Figure 45).[56] Zuallardo toned down the artistic component that was so dominant in his time and created the earliest map of Jerusalem in which cleanly drawn lines replaced the more artistic approach. The sites are marked only by letters, which refer to the legend printed below the map.

The second map of this style was that of Baron Louis des Hayes (1592–1632). Des Hayes, a French nobleman who served as a diplomat of the court of King Louis XIII of France, traveled in the Levant in 1621 as part of his diplomatic service, to aid the Franciscans in their

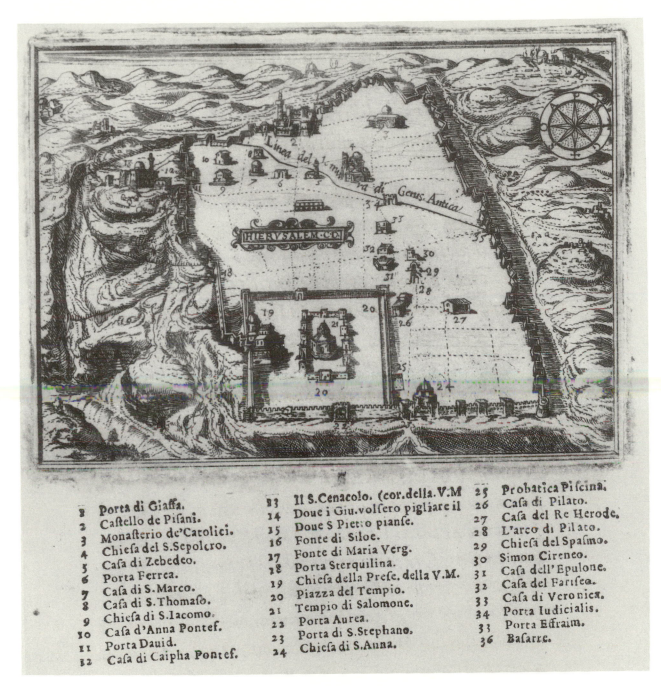

1	Porta di Giaffa.	13	Il S. Cenacolo. (cor. della. V.M	25	Probatica Piscina.
2	Castello de Pisani.	14	Doue i Giu. volsero pigliare il	26	Casa di Pilato.
3	Monasterio de'Catolici.	15	Doue S Pietro pianse.	27	Casa del Re Herode.
4	Chiesa del S. Sepolcro.	16	Fonte di Siloe.	28	L'arco di Pilato.
5	Casa di Zebedeo.	17	Fonte di Maria Verg.	29	Chiesa del Spasmo.
6	Porta Ferrea.	18	Porta Sterquilina.	30	Simon Cireneo.
7	Casa di S. Marco.	19	Chiesa della Prese. della V.M.	31	Casa dell'Epulone.
8	Casa di S. Thomaso.	20	Piazza del Tempio.	32	Casa del Farisea.
9	Chiesa di S. Iacomo.	21	Tempio di Salomone.	33	Casa di Veronica.
10	Casa d'Anna Pontef.	22	Porta Aurea.	34	Porta Iudicialis.
11	Porta Dauid.	23	Porta di S. Stephano.	35	Porta Effraim.
12	Casa di Caipha Pontef.	24	Chiesa di S. Anna.	36	Basarre.

Figure 45. Zuallardo's map
of Jerusalem, 1587.

struggle against the Armenian monks.[57] His book, printed in Paris in 1624, included the earliest map of Jerusalem depicting the city from a bird's-eye view.[58] However, the map did not indicate the scale to which it was drawn, as it did not pretend to provide an exact presentation of the city's appearance.

The maps of Jean Doubdan,[59] Jean-Baptiste Nolin,[60] Richard Pococke,[61] and Thomas Shaw[62] contributed to the development of the scientific trend among the maps of Jerusalem. These maps display the clash between two opposing factors: while the mapmakers were men of learning and their maps were designed in accordance with the most advanced scientific spirit of their time, their visits to Jerusalem were brief and they were not able to become well enough acquainted with the city to map it on the basis of their own observations. When they based their work on earlier sources, they often failed to interpret them correctly, and hence in the eighteenth century, when precise, accurate city maps began to be published in Europe, there appeared a group of Jerusalem maps that were progressive in their form and design but distorted in their content, and they failed to achieve their goal of presenting a realistic image of the city.

Nineteenth-Century Maps of Jerusalem

The first map based on measurement and calculation was prepared in 1818 by W. F. Sieber, a physician and naturalist (Figure 46).[63] He spent six weeks in Jerusalem, where he gathered topographic data and measured 200 different locations in the city. On the basis of these data, Sieber prepared his map, and it met with high praise from geographers and students of Palestine.[64]

Sieber's map is oriented toward the east and shows Jerusalem and its immediate surroundings, from the Mamilla Pool in the west to the top of the Mount of Olives in the east, and from the Hill of Evil Council (Abu-Tor) in the south to the area north of Damascus Gate. The topographic relief around the city is shown through hachuring and shading. Outside the city, particularly to the north, agricultural fields surrounded by stone fences are depicted. The street patterns and houses are shown throughout most of the city, and important buildings, drawn in greater detail, are identified, including the Temple Mount (Haram al-Sharif) with the Dome of the Rock and al-Aqsa

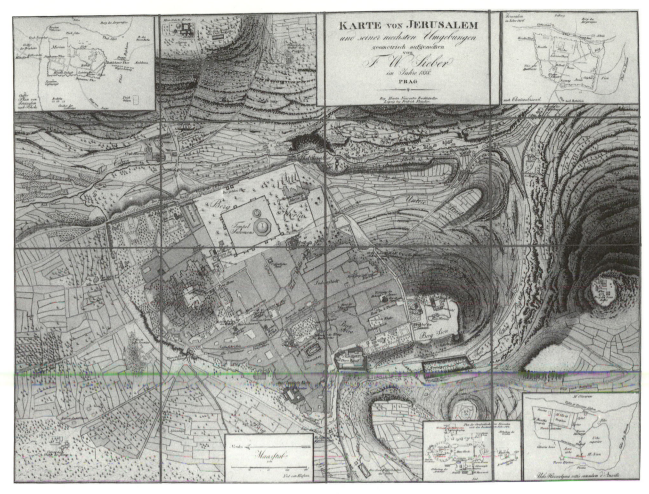

Figure 46. W. F. Sieber's map of Jerusalem, 1818.

Mosque, the Church of the Holy Sepulchre, the Citadel, the Latin monastery, the Armenian Quarter, and the Jewish Quarter and its Sephardic synagogues.

Sieber's map constitutes a turning point in the history of the mapping of Jerusalem. On the one hand, he used maps by three of his predecessors—Pococke, Chateaubriand, and d'Anville—thus aligning himself with older traditions. And on the other hand, his was the first map of Jerusalem to be based on measurements and trigonometric calculations. In that sense it constituted a breakthrough and a significant innovation in the history of the mapping of the city, being the forerunner of the accurate, survey-based maps.

In the nineteenth century, when the Ottoman Empire grew weaker and the European powers became more and more involved in its affairs, Jerusalem and the Holy Land underwent a rapid process of change. The region became more accessible to European travelers as steamships arrived in Acre and Jaffa, and security within the country improved. Many of the travelers were scholars who came to study the landscape, archaeology, geography, and nature of the Holy Land.

This process led naturally to the development of scientific, measurement-based maps, starting with the above-mentioned map of Sieber (1811) and followed by those of F. Catherwood,[65] Aldridge and Simonds,[66] and many others,[67] until the map of Charles Wilson was produced by the British Ordnance Survey in 1864–65.[68] Captain Wilson was an officer of the Royal Engineers and was sent to Jerusalem especially to produce an accurate updated map. Indeed, his map, printed in two scales, 1 : 2,500 and 1 : 10,000, was the first perfectly accurate map, even in the eyes of modern cartography. It was also the first map of any part of the Holy Land that used contour lines to show topography.

The series of maps just mentioned are representative of the new scientific trend, which minimized the illustrative and pictorial elements of the earliest maps. However, at the same time that modern scientific mapping was developing, the traditional artistic mapping style still flourished, and both realistic and imaginary maps were being produced around the world. Several of them, like Eltzner's and Doburg's,[69] were similar to the maps of previous centuries, and if they were not identified by their makers' names and dates, they would be easily regarded, on the basis of style and content, as a continuation of the earlier maps. This trend spread from Europe to the New World, as may be seen in the Doburg map, which was printed in America, illustrating the growing interest in this genre on that side of the Atlantic.

The map in Graf Wartensleben's book about Jerusalem, published as late as 1870, is a combination: it has the style and viewpoint of the old-fashioned artistic maps, presented on a correctly drawn landscape that was so up to date it even showed the newly built Russian compound.

In the second half of the nineteenth century, with the development of archaeological and historical studies, a new type of map of ancient Jerusalem appeared, maps that were based on the actual topography of the city and suggested reconstructions of the Jerusalem of antiquity. Such maps depicted in a rather scientific and critical manner the lines of the three walls described by Josephus, Jerusalem's ancient aqueducts, and the like.

A new medium related to maps also entered the stage at this time: models, or three-dimensional maps.[70] Like the printed maps, some were realistic while others continued the tradition of imaginary historical maps.

The large model made by Stephan Illes in 1873 presented the city in a realistic manner (see Figure 14, page 226). It was a large-scale, fully detailed model that even portrayed consulates' flags, telegraph poles, and some shop signs in the bazaar.[71] Several years later, Illes made two additional models, one of modern Jerusalem (scaled 1:625) and the other of biblical Jerusalem (scaled 1:1,250). The same realistic style was reflected by the models of historical Jerusalem and of the Temple by J. M. Tenz. His models were made in several copies and were sold to schools and churches as educational aids.[72]

Conrad Schick's relief map[73] combines the image of ancient Jerusalem and the depiction of accurate topography. He used a contour, or topographical, map of Jerusalem as a basis, and built on it a three-dimensional map of contemporary Jerusalem; yet at the same time he also drew the outlines of the three walls and other ancient sites. In addition, Schick prepared a model of the Second Temple, which could replace the Dome of the Rock; it was kept in a box on the corner of the map.[74]

Thus we see that in the nineteenth century, when geographical knowledge and cartographic design became accurate, the artistic, subjective, and impressionistic depictions of the Holy City did not disappear. Moreover, even today, when most of the maps are made by modern, partly automated equipment, there is still an ongoing tradition of artistic maps, mainly created for the use of tourists. This represents the perhaps neverending dualism of the realistic image of the city and its historical and imaginary counterpart.

17 Two Islamic Construction Plans for al-Haram al-Sharif

SABRI JARRAR

Like many other cities in Bilad al-Sham (Greater Syria), Jerusalem was captured by the Muslims twice from their Christian adversaries. Both conquests were accomplished without bloodshed, pillage, or destruction of property. The first took place in 638, six years after the death of Prophet Muhammad, when Jerusalem capitulated to the Arabs under the leadership of Umar ibn al-Khattab, the second *Rashid* (rightly guided) caliph, ending three centuries of Byzantine rule. The second conquest was carried out in 1187 by the magnanimous Salah al-Din al-Ayyubi (Saladin), a sultan of Kurdish descent who led the Kurdish, Turkish, and Arab troops that liberated the city from the Franjis, the Crusaders, who in turn had captured it from the Fatimids in 1099.

The Muslim conquests of Greater Syria in the seventh century and again in the twelfth and thirteenth centuries—when the coast and parts of the inland regions were recaptured from the Crusaders—were campaigns launched by a community ideologically committed to the hegemony of Islam. So it was only natural that shortly after these holy wars, Islam's claim to the land was emphasized by the embellishment of its cities with monuments that served as symbols of victory. Both campaigns climaxed in the capture of Jerusalem, the ultimate reward, for apart from becoming the third holiest city of Islam after Mecca and Medina, Jerusalem was Christendom's most dearly held stronghold. The loss to Islam of what Christians believe to be the site of the tomb of Jesus would not only invalidate their claim that God had bequeathed Jerusalem to them but would also deal a final blow to their political unity in Greater Syria, for defending the tomb was the ideological banner under which they rallied whenever that territory came under assault. For the Companions of Muhammad who led the first campaign, such as Abu 'Ubayda and Khalid ibn al-Walid, the capture of Jerusalem must have seemed like part of the fulfillment of the prophetic promise that Islam would prevail.[1] In 1187, Saladin fought not to avenge the massacre of the defenseless population of Jerusalem by the Frankish knights in 1099, but to redeem Islam's dignity, which could not be restored until a final defeat was inflicted on the symbols of infidelity, and Palestine—an Islamic *waqf* (a non-transferable religious endowment)—was returned to the abode of Islam.[2]

After each of their two triumphs over the Christians in Jerusalem, the Muslims' veneration of the city, particularly of al-Masjid al-Aqsa (the Farther, or Distant, Temple) and its vicinity, materialized in a major construction scheme that evolved in unique ways over the ensuing centuries.[3]

Integrating the Israelites' Kibla into That of Abraham and Muhammad: 638–1065

It is believed that Umar built the first congregational mosque in Jerusalem, about 638–643, possibly out of the ruins of the Stoa of Herod at the Temple Mount.[4] The mosque was described in the 670s by the Christian pilgrim Arculf as "a four-sided house of prayer" built of "boards and great beams on some remains of ruins," which could hold 3,000 men.[5] The Herodian platform was identified as the *masjid*, the place of worship or temple, built by the Banu Isra'il, that is, the Israelites, for the worship of the one and true God (Sura 17:1–8), and the direction of prayer—the kibla—that Muhammad faced before the Kaaba in Mecca, the kibla of Abraham (Sura 1:125), was made the final kibla of Islam (Sura 1:144–150).

The orthodox Caliph Umar chose to locate the hypostyle mosque at the very southern end of the Herodian platform, lest it be said that the mosque followed any of the extant structures on the site, particularly the Rock, which was believed to have stood in the Temple of

Banu Isra'il and which the Muslim conquerors may have recognized as the core of the kibla of the Israelites and of nascent Islam. Among the chronicles of the conquest is an account of a Jewish convert to Islam who, after the Temple Mount was cleared of the rubbish accumulated there during centuries of Christian neglect, supposedly tried to convince Umar to pray from behind—or north of—the Rock, so that he would face both the Rock and Mecca, but the caliph accused him of still being inclined toward the Jews and built the mosque south of the Rock.[6] The mosque, which reflected in its modesty the puritanical spirit of the age of the conquests, symbolized a final settlement of the disputes between the Christians and the Jews over the inheritance of the legacy of David and Solomon in Jerusalem. It laid to rest their territorial and political aspirations.

The Rock did not remain long outside the scope of Islamic construction, and by 690, it must have been incorporated into the Muslim liturgical practice in Jerusalem. At the behest of 'Abd al-Malik ibn Marwan, the fifth Umayyad caliph (685–705), the design of the earliest and one of the most spectacular commemorative monuments of Islam was conceived for the enshrinement of the Rock. The design theme—two octagonal ambulatories surrounding a rotunda—was not novel, for it was reminiscent of the Byzantine martyrium.[7]

The construction of the Dome of the Rock (690–692) was supervised by Yazid ibn Salam, a Jerusalemite, and Raja' ibn Hayweh al-Urduni al-Filastini, a theologian who had a strong affiliation with the land of Palestine and its people.[8] To this period belongs the decorative scheme of the interior, which consists of marble paneling and splendid glass mosaics adorning the walls above the capitals and cornices of the piers and columns. (See Plate 7.) Although the scheme recalls the interior of Byzantine martyriums, the mosaics depart from such models in their overall scheme of surface organization as well as in their subject matter.[9] While Byzantine mosaics were executed in sections, each comprising a panel defined by architectonic elements such as pilasters, entablatures, and voussoirs, the mosaics of the Dome of the Rock form continuous representations, possibly because it was deemed more important to unify the different parts of the interior than to emphasize its individual parts. The subject matter of the mosaics adorning the walls as well as the undersides of the arches is nonfigurative, while the mosaics on the inner spandrels of the arches of the octagonal arcade, as well as the inner faces of its piers and the inner wall surface of the circular rotunda, depict imperial jewelry. The provenance of the jewelry motif is the Byzantine and Sassanian (Persian) empires, the two empires that were fighting over the possession of this very spot in Jerusalem seventy-six years before the erection of the monument, and it is probably a reminder of the booty the Muslim armies seized in the territories captured from the two empires.[10]

But the real victory that the Dome of the Rock celebrates is to be found in the koranic inscriptions of the interior, where most of the verses chosen were meant to reintroduce Jesus as a prophet of God—but not his son—to the Christians who, according to the Koran, had gone astray. The truth about Jesus, as revealed by this final message, had triumphed over the doctrines created around his false divinity and crucifixion. When the monument was built, Jerusalem's population and architecture were still predominantly Christian. But the people adopted Arabic, the language of the conqueror, as their official language and therefore could be ideologically challenged by the word of the Koran, transmitted, for the first time, through the medium of monumental architecture. Having firmly established its rule in the Greater Syria, the Islamic state was keen on establishing a dialogue with its Christian subjects. 'Abd al-Malik's affirmation of the triumph of the Islamic faith was communicated to the people of Jerusalem in a language they well understood, namely that of monumental architecture that employs a wide-ranging and rich vocabulary, such as domes, rotundas, ambulatories, mosaics, and inscriptions.

The Dome of the Rock's outer walls were originally built of courses of stone, with seven semicircular arched and recessed panels, both tall and narrow, on each of the eight sides. The lower part of the walls was covered with polished marble slabs, the upper was adorned with gold and polychrome mosaics. The parapet above each of the eight faces housed a row of thirteen semidomed niches, which were also covered with mosaics.[11] Oleg Grabar has suggested that the decoration of whole surfaces of the exterior with mosaics, a feature unknown in the Christian Mediterranean, was due to the patron's desire to give the exterior of the building a colorful impression that would recall the textiles draped over the Kaaba in Mecca.[12]

With the Rock beginning at the same level as its foundation, the whole structure was raised on a platform reached by a series of stairs from the earlier Herodian platform. The elevated edifice with its polychromed exterior and gold-plated dome, surrounded by the vast open space of the Temple Mount, achieved a prominence that outstripped that of the Church of the Anastasis, despite the latter's monumentality and the fact that Golgotha is higher than the top of the Dome of the Rock's platform. This visual domination is especially apparent when one approaches the city from the Mount of Olives, across the steep Kedron Valley.

The octagonal Dome of the Rock is oriented in such a way that one of its eight sides faces Mecca, the direction of prayer. In the center of that wall is the southern door, one of the four axial entrances to the edifice. The monument transformed the Rock—originally an independent point in space—into the focal point of the Temple Mount, and its centrality is emphasized by its position in the center of the impressive domed rotunda. This clearly demonstrates that by the year 690, the Rock must have been perceived by the Muslims as the core of the Temple Mount, the kibla of Banu Isra'il and the abrogated first kibla of Islam. Like the Kaaba, an independent point in space where an infinite number of visual lines converge, the Rock also radiates an infinite number of lines or axes. However, the octagonal monument establishes only four axes, those marked by its four entrances, which extend away from the monument by means of four projecting porticos. Since the southern side of Herod's rectangular platform almost faces Mecca, the four axes generated by the Dome of the Rock are nearly perpendicular to the four sides of the Herodian platform. This new sense of axiality highlighted the central position of the Dome of the Rock and became the major organizational force on the Temple Mount, known in Arabic as al-Haram al-Sharif, the Noble Sanctuary.

Just east of the Dome of the Rock is Qubbat al-Silsila, the Dome of the Chain, whose function is not clear. One explanation is that it served as a model for the Dome of the Rock, another suggests that it was the treasury for the project. Its position at the geometric center of the Haram has led others to believe that its purpose is indeed to mark that very spot.[13]

Al-Aqsa Mosque was built after the Dome of the Rock. From the Aphrodito Papyri, the official correspondence of Qurra ibn Sharik, the governor of Egypt (709–714) and Basilius, the prefect of the District of Aphrodito in Upper Egypt, we learn that the early mosque built by Umar and restored by 'Abd al-Malik was replaced by Umayyad caliph al-Walid ibn 'Abd al-Malik (705–715).[14] Al-Aqsa followed the hypostyle model, with several aisles deployed perpendicularly to the southern, kibla wall, a novel feature in mosque design that allowed for the central, wider aisle to be opposite the southern entrance of the Dome of the Rock. Thus the new Aqsa Mosque established a dialogue with the kibla of Banu Isra'il, which, lest it be forgotten, had been enshrined in a commemorative structure. Yet it was also deemed necessary to remind the visitors that it was the former kibla of Islam, and that the final one is the Kaaba in Mecca, the kibla of Abraham and Muhammad. What could be a more effective way to demonstrate this than making the Rock actually follow the Kaaba? This was made possible by aligning the kibla aisle of al-Aqsa Mosque with that of the kibla axis of the Dome of the Rock, the monument located behind al-Aqsa Mosque which then appeared as if it were leading and directing the Rock toward the Kaaba.

Foundations of six structures that formed one complex immediately below the Herodian platform to the south and southwest of the Aqsa Mosque were revealed during excavations carried out by the Israel Exploration Society and the Institute of Archaeology of the Hebrew University (1968–1970).[15] The size of the walls of the largest structure, just south of the mosque, along with the remains of a bridge on the wall of the Herodian platform facing this structure, make it possible to reconstruct it as a multistory building that was connected to the mosque via a bridge. At this structure, the center of which was dominated by a colonnaded rectangular courtyard, were found fine fragments of Umayyad columns, capitals, lattices, balustrades, and painted plaster with geometric and floral patterns.[16] It was probably a two-story Umayyad palace, unique among similar extant palaces because of the absence of corner towers, perhaps deemed unnecessary for a building within city walls. The Aphrodito Papyri, which date from the time of al-Walid I, mention the construction of a mosque and an administrative palace, *dar al-imara*, in Jerusalem.[17] Also favoring the palace's dating and attribution to al-Walid I is a tenth-century account by al-Muqaddisi, a Jerusalemite historian, of a gate to al-Haram al-Sharif called Bab al-Walid, which may have been the gate where the bridge extending from the palace terminated.[18] This ensemble was built along the streets and stairs that led to the Double, or Huldah, Gate, the Herodian underground entry that led up to the Temple Mount and that was the Muslim's main entrance to the area during this period.[19]

Al-Aqsa was badly damaged by the earthquake of 747, and the aisles to the east and west of the central nave were rebuilt by the Abbasid caliph Abu Ja'far al-Mansur a decade or so later. His expenses were defrayed by the minting of gold dinars and silver dirhams from the plates that covered the Umayyad doors of the ruined mosque.[20] Destroyed later by another earthquake, the mosque was replaced around 780 by the Abbasid caliph al-Mahdi and later restored by 'Abdallah ibn Tahir, governor of Syria (820–822).

The structure was described around 985 by al-Muqaddasi as comprising fifteen aisles with arcades employing both columns and round piers perpendicular to the southern kibla wall. The central aisle or nave was aligned as before with the kibla axis of the Dome of the Rock and was distinguished both in width and height. It was made higher than the other aisles by means of a clerestory, and it was covered by a gable roof terminating at the wooden dome in front of the mihrab, the prayer niche placed in the kibla wall (see Figure 47). Both the raised gable roof and the dome are volumetric accentuations of the Kaaba axis. The side aisles were also covered by gable roofs lower than that of the central one. The northern and southern dome-bearing arches were extended east and west, in order to transfer the thrust through the side walls. The resulting configuration of these arches and the central aisle is a T-plan.[21]

During the first half of the tenth century, the whole platform of al-Haram al-Sharif was transformed into a clearly defined sanctuary when its northern and western sides, the two sides bordering the predominantly Christian parts of the city, were demarcated by porticos. The underground gates to the Haram, facing the Muslim neighborhoods to the south and possibly west, were each provided with a wooden porch at the behest of the mother of the Abbasid caliph al-Muqtadir (908–932), who also ordered the restoration of the dome covering the Rock. According to Ibn 'Abd Rabbihi (913), the sanctuary at that time had four minarets.[22]

Various domes and mihrabs, or prayer niches, within the sanctuary commemorated the Nocturnal Journey of Prophet Muhammad from

Figure 47. Al-Aqsa
Mosque. Interior view
looking toward the
mihrab, the prayer niche,
from the north.

Mecca to Jerusalem, and the lives of several Koranic prophets, most of whom were biblical prophets. By the tenth century a Muslim cemetery with eschatological associations had grown up east of the platform, around the burial site of 'Ubada ibn al-Samit, a companion of Prophet Muhammad. The salience of this cemetery in Islamic funerary cults was attested by the desire of prominent figures from various parts of the Muslim world, such as the Ikshids of Egypt, to be buried there.[23]

After the Fatimids conquered Syria and Palestine in 970, Caliph al-Zahir started the fifth rebuilding of the Aqsa Mosque around 1034, and it was completed by his successor, al-Mustansir, in 1065. The mosque's northern facade remained the same as it was in al-Mahdi's time, since the classic moldings and joggled lintels in two of its three central doorways date no later than the eighth century.[24] Although al-Zahir restored the mosque according to al-Mahdi's plan, it shrank to seven aisles, also perpendicular to the kibla wall.

Among the extant parts of the Fatimid mosque are the arcades of the central aisle, the four dome-bearing arches, the dome's drum, and the dome's zone of transition, comprising spherical-triangular pendentives, the four corners of which rest on squinches.[25] The splendid mosaics, on the north spandrels of the triumphal northern dome-bearing arch, are attributed to al-Zahir, and their designs recall those of 'Abd al-Malik in the Dome of the Rock.[26] Given the sharp ideological and political differences between the Umayyads and the Fatimid Shi'ites, surely there was no desire on al-Zahir's part to associate himself with either 'Abd al-Malik or the glory of the Umayyads. The introduction of the mosaics on the triumphal arch, which serves as a symbolic gate to the Kaaba, was probably a means of visually linking it to the Rock, which is surrounded by similar mosaics. (Visual unification by means of surface decoration was introduced into different parts of the Haram during the Fatimid period.) Nasir-i Khusraw, a Persian traveler who visited Jerusalem in 1047, described splendid mosaics adorning a new gate in the western portico called Bab Dawood (today's Bab al-Silsila) as well as the pillars and arches of the arcade at the top of the stairs known as Maqam al-Nabi and located at the southeastern corner of the platform of the Dome of the Rock, facing al-Aqsa Mosque. Another monumental stairway with a triple flight ascended the platform along the visual Rock-Aqsa axis, thus emphasizing it. At the top of that stairway stood an arcade of green marble columns; each column, like those at Maqam al-Nabi, was "ten cubits tall and so thick that only with difficulty could two men reach around it." The arcade displayed a gold inscription by Prince Layth al-Dawla Nushtakin the Ghorid, who, according to Nasir-i Khusraw, served the sultan of Egypt.[27]

By this time the Muslim population had shifted west and possibly north of al-Haram al-Sharif, as had the city's commercial center. The underground gates south of the platform had been blocked, and access to the sanctuary was through gates in the western and northern porticos.[28] (A recently discovered inscription on a recycled building stone at Bab Hitta, a northern gate rebuilt in 1220, records the endowment of two contiguous houses for pilgrims from Diyarbakir, made in 1053–1054 by Amir Ahmad ibn Marwan, a Kurdish prince.[29]) According to Nasir-i Khusraw, the introduction of gates in the northern portico probably followed the development of Sufi cloisters north of the sanctuary.[30] The Double Gate was superseded by Bab al-Silsila as the main gate to the enclosure, and the *decumanus*—the city's west-to-east axis from the Roman period that begins at Jaffa Gate and terminates at Bab al-Silsila—became the major thoroughfare leading to the Haram. (The earliest Muslim use of the Citadel, which is located next to Jaffa Gate, was during the Fatimid period.[31])

The political and economic role of Jerusalem during the Umayyad and Abbasid periods (750 to 1099) was overshadowed by Ramla, the capital of Palestine founded by Caliph Sulayman ibn 'Abd al-Malik in 716, and later by Tripoli, the seat of the Fatimid governors of Syria and Palestine. The Umayyads might have found Jerusalem too religious or too Christian a place to be a regional capital, a precaution analogous to that taken by the Romans, who made Caesarea their capital because Jerusalem was probably too Jewish a place to be the seat of their government.[32] This may account for the relative harmony in which the Muslims, Christians, and Jews lived in Jerusalem from the early Muslim period until the reign of the Fatimid caliph al-Hakim (996–1021). The Muslims, who from the time of the conquest had allowed Jews to live in the city, also continued to honor the covenant of Umar, which guaranteed the Christian population freedom of worship and the safety of their shrines. But this religious tolerance and cultural assimilation was eclipsed by the religious dogma and zeal of the Fatimids, who, while adorning Muslim religious sites in Palestine with great works of art, such as the mosaics of the Aqsa Mosque, ordered the destruction of the Anastasis in 1009, an act that provoked the belligerency of Europe and eventually led to the Crusades.

The Turkomans, who were called in by the Fatimids to suppress an Arab tribal uprising in Syria, seized Jerusalem in 1071 under the leadership of the warlord Atsiz. In 1078, the Seljuks vanquished Atsiz and bestowed Palestine, including Jerusalem, on Artuq ibn Ekseb, the founder of the Artuqid dynasty in Diyarbakir, Anatolia. His sons, however, were defeated by the Fatimids, who recaptured Jerusalem in 1098 after bombarding it for forty days, only to lose it to the Crusaders in the following year.

The Madrasa Walls of al-Haram al-Sharif: 1260–1517

On October 9, 1187, a week after the liberation of Jerusalem from the Crusaders, Muhyi al-Din ibn al-Zaki, the *qadi* (judge) of Damascus, delivered the Friday sermon from the pulpit of al-Aqsa Mosque. Addressing the sultan, he said: "Glory to God who has bestowed this victory upon Islam and who has returned this city to the fold after a century of perdition! Honor to this army, which He has chosen to complete the reconquest! And may salvation be upon you, Saladin Yusuf, son of Ayyub, you who have restored the spurned dignity of this nation!"[33] But soon the internecine feuds among the Ayyubids proved detrimental to the reconsecration of Jerusalem to Islam after eighty-eight years of European rule. The political upheavals entailed a fifteen-year Crusader interregnum, a considerable hiatus in the systematic effacing of the physical symbols of Crusader rule.[34] With the exception of a few examples dating to the enlightened governorship of al-Mu'azzam 'Isa, Islamic architecture in Jerusalem suffered from stagnation and a lack of inventiveness during the Ayyubid period, a status that contrasted very sharply with the contemporary architecture of Cairo, Damascus, and Aleppo.[35] Nevertheless, the pillage and burning by the Khwarizmians in 1244 destroyed many of the Christian buildings, thus offsetting the interregnum and paving the way for the second stage of the re-Islamization process.

On September 8, 1260, a few days after their victory over the Mongols in the battle of 'Ayn Jalut (Spring of Goliath) south of

Nazareth, the jubilant Mamluks, who put an end to the nominal Ayyubid rule in Egypt in 1252, marched into Damascus amid the cheers of the embattled population. Under this new dynasty, Egypt, Syria, Palestine, and Hijaz (western Arabia) were to enjoy more than two and a half centuries of relative tranquility and prosperity.

Determined to end the reprieve the Crusaders enjoyed due to the internal strife in the house of Saladin, al-Zahir Rukn al-Din Baybars, the fourth Mamluk sultan (1260–1277), launched a punitive campaign against the Crusaders who had sided with the Mongols. Many of the Crusader strongholds once thought impregnable—Antioch, Jaffa, Crac de Chevaliers—were reduced to ruins or evacuated. Having realized that Jerusalem would not be safe so long as the Crusaders maintained a military presence in Greater Syria, Sultan al-Mansur Sayf al-Din Qalawun (1280–1290) launched an offensive against their last strongholds on the coast, where many of those whose lives had been spared by Saladin had settled.[36] In 1291, Sultan al-Ashraf Khalil ibn Qalawun razed the once invincible city of Acre, after which all the remaining Crusader strongholds surrendered. With the Mongols warded off and the last Crusader flung out of the Levant, the Mamluks consolidated Saladin's triumph over the Crusaders a century earlier. They gained uncontested custody over Jerusalem and Hebron, the two Muslim religious centers of Palestine, in addition to the holy cities of Mecca and Medina in the Hijaz.

To demonstrate to the newly repopulated Jerusalem that Muslim sovereignty over the Holy City and its sanctuary was irreversible, the Mamluks sought to transform the environs of al-Haram al-Sharif into a *waqf*, a system of nontransferable religious endowments (see Figure 8, page 113). The perpetual construction campaign during the Mamluk period evolved into a scheme dominated by one theme: namely, fencing the Haram al-Sharif with a wall of madrasas (theological colleges), to form a barrier of intellect and piety that would fend off infidelity and unwholesome ideologies.[37] Six centuries earlier, knowing that the Christians had no attachment to the Temple Mount, 'Abd al-Malik had concentrated on creating there an Islamic monument of great splendor to prevent the city's overwhelming Christian monuments from dazzling the minds of the Muslims. During the Crusader period, the Dome of the Rock, considered to be the site of Solomon's Temple, became a church called Templum Domini, and al-Aqsa

Mosque, regarded as the site of the king's palace, was turned into the Templum Solomonis and served as the headquarters of the order of the Knights Templars. Christians' claim to the Temple Mount—ironic after their centuries of desecration and neglect of the area before the arrival of Islam, in accordance with the prediction of Jesus—was perceived by the Muslims as a sharp shift in Christendom.[38] This prompted a response that would underscore the ideological nature of the contest for Jerusalem, hence the wall of madrasas at the Temple Mount promulgating the Mamluks' Sunni creed.

Two early architectural undertakings by the Bahri Mamluks (1250–1382) illustrate the significant reaction the Dome of the Rock evoked among the Mamluk sultans both in Jerusalem and in Cairo, their capital. To stress that the monument was the epicenter of Mamluk Jerusalem, Sultan Baybars I assembled a special workshop for its restoration, overseen by the *nazir al-haramayn,* the superintendent of the two *harams* (sanctuaries) in Jerusalem and Hebron. The mosaics of the Dome of the Rock were repaired, and the platform around it was repaved.[39] Both the mosaics at Qubbat al-Silsila and the marble inlay of its mihrab were also repaired.

In the center of the mausoleum at Sultan Qalawun's complex in Cairo (1284–1285) is an octagonal structure which is formed by eight arches carried on alternating pairs of square piers and pairs of ancient granite columns—a theme which alludes to the ambulatories of the Dome of the Rock. Moreover, the walls, piers, and mihrab of the mausoleum, as well as the basins of the two fountains *(sabils)* in the complex, are decorated with marble mosaics, a technique which finds its origins in the Umayyad marble paneling of the interior of the Dome of the Rock.

The Earliest Charitable Foundations

The earliest Mamluk charitable foundations near al-Haram al-Sharif were *ribats* or pilgrims' hospices. The first two, Ribat 'Ala' al-Din al-Basir (1267–1268) and Ribat Sultan Qalawun (1282–1283), were built by al-Basir, Sultan Qalawun's superintendent of the Jerusalem and Hebron *harams*. The *ribats* face each other across the street, a few steps away from Bab al-Nazir, the gate in the western wall of the sanctuary, where al-Basir conducted his administrative business. Both

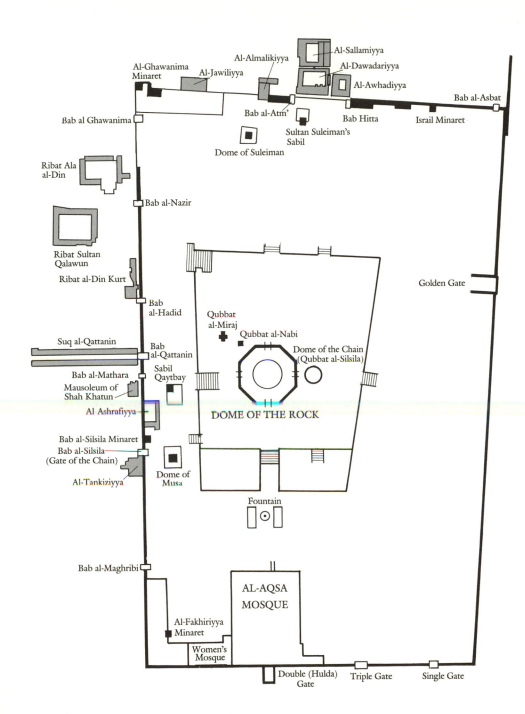

Al-Ghawanima Minaret
Al-Jawiliyya
Al-Almalikiyya
Al-Sallamiyya
Al-Dawadariyya
Al-Awhadiyya
Bab al-Asbat
Bab al-Atm'
Bab Hitta
Israil Minaret
Bab al Ghawanima
Sultan Suleiman's Sabil
Dome of Suleiman
Ribat Ala al-Din
Bab al-Nazir
Ribat Sultan Qalawun
Ribat al-Din Kurt
Golden Gate
Bab al-Hadid
Qubbat al-Miraj
Qubbat al-Nabi
Dome of the Chain (Qubbat al-Silsila)
Suq al-Qattanin
Bab al-Qattanin
Bab al-Mathara
Sabil Qaytbay
Mausoleum of Shah Khatun
Al Ashrafiyya
DOME OF THE ROCK
Bab al-Silsila Minaret
Bab al-Silsila (Gate of the Chain)
Al-Tankiziyya
Dome of Musa
Fountain
Map 4. Al-Haram al-Sharif (Temple Mount), schematic plan.
Bab al-Maghribi
AL-AQSA MOSQUE
Al-Fakhiriyya Minaret
Women's Mosque
Double (Hulda) Gate
Triple Gate
Single Gate

buildings follow the general scheme of an open rectangular court-yard surrounded by cells. Ribat Sultan Qalawun, the first royal Mam-luk charitable foundation in Jerusalem, is not contiguous with the Haram's western wall because the intervening space was occupied by an earlier structure.[40] A third *ribat* was built in 1293–1294 by Sayf al-Din Kurt, a servant of Sultan Qalawun, at Bab al-Hadid, and it adjoins the western wall of the sanctuary. (The lower part of the wall displays Herodian masonry comparable to that seen on its other side, at the Wailing Wall, or Western Wall, which is a segment of the same enclo-sure wall. By the time of the construction of this *ribat,* the landfill on its site had risen to approximately the level of the top of the Herodian platform.[41]) All three *ribats,* which are one story high, are charac-terized by austere architecture that employs stones bearing marks of Crusader masons.[42] The plainness of the street facade of the *ribat* of Sultan Qalawun, except for the alternating red and white voussoirs of the arch of the cross-vaulted entrance porch (which emulates the entrance porch of the *khanakah,* or Sufi lodge, endowed by Saladin in 1189 in the patriarch's former residence in the Christian Quarter), contrasts very sharply with the splendid facade of Qalawun's founda-tion in Cairo.

The portico, a structural element providing shelter around court-yards, was given a new meaning in Mamluk Jerusalem with its incor-poration into the plan of the sanctuary to serve as a datum, or organizer.[43] It acquired unique religious symbolism in addition to generating rhythm and visual unification for the multitude of charita-ble foundations that grew up along the western and northern edges of the Haram (see Figure 48). This is exemplified by the foundation next in chronological sequence, the *khanakah* of the amir 'Alam al-Din Sanjar al-Dawadari, built in 1295 and endowed in 1297, on Bab al-'Atm Road at the northern border of the Haram, a site whose association with Sufism goes back to the eleventh century.

This Sufi *khanakah* has a spatial configuration similar to that of the first two pilgrims' hospices. However, it departs from the early Mamluk development in its frontage on the sanctuary, thenceforth a major factor in the choice of sites as well as in determining the general configuration of the Mamluk religious foundations in Jerusalem. The *khanakah,* like the hospice of Sayf al-Din Kurt, is accessible via an entrance in the main facade, on the street that terminates at one of

Figure 48. Western portico looking south (1437).

the gates of the sanctuary. The novelty of this one-story *khanakah*, however, lies in its projection of a portico of stone piers and cross-vaults onto the Haram's esplanade itself to fill the gap between the portico of al-Mu'azzam 'Isa to the west and the portico built in 1295 by al-Malik al-Awhad, superintendent of the two *harams*, to the east.

By that time, the portico had become an object of strong identification with the sanctuary, and therefore to become symbolically integrated into the blessed precinct of al-Haram al-Sharif, new religious foundations had to be physically attached to this portico. This probably explains al-Dawadari's desire to adjoin the portico, even if it meant building the missing segment. The windows of the *khanakah*'s assembly hall, as well as some of its cells, open onto the portico.[44] This *khanakah* inaugurates a new tradition among Jerusalem's Mamluk foundations of employing decorative schemes on the exterior—the street facade and the frontage on the sanctuary—as well as on the walls of the inner courtyard. Continuing the legacy of numerous similar foundations from Syria and Egypt, the *khanakah* is announced by its tall portal with its virtuoso decoration and the highly stylized calligraphy of its founding inscription. Behind the portico of the Haram, the facade displays alternating red and white masonry in the jambs of the windows pierced in the infill walls blocking the two archways. Examples from the courtyard include the multicolored joggled voussoirs of the oculus, lintels, and a relieving arch in the assembly hall's northern facade.

Al-Jawiliyya

In 1320, Sanjar al-Jawili, superintendent of the two *harams* for Sultan al-Nasir Muhammad ibn Qalawun (1294–1295 and 1299–1340) and one of his most powerful amirs, endowed a madrasa on top of the Antonia Rock, located near the northwestern corner of the sanctuary.[45] It was the location of a massive fortress built by Herod on the site of an earlier fort, named Antonia in honor of Mark Antony. In 1160, to commemorate the incarceration of Jesus on the site, the Crusaders erected the Chapel of Repose, which opened onto the Via Dolorosa in the north—the traditional pilgrimage route that also dates back to the Crusader period. The new Muslim structure was built abutting the ancient Herodian wall.[46]

Sanjar al-Jawili's choice of this prestigious site, from which Christian pilgrims were banned beginning in 1244, the date of the final purging of the Crusaders from the Holy City, until the end of the sixteenth century is indicative of the unique leverage he enjoyed in his positions as superintendent of the *harams* and governor of Gaza, which at that time had jurisdiction over Jerusalem.[47] He was a man with a highly refined appreciation of architecture, reflected by his buildings in Cairo, Gaza, Hebron, and other locations. The layout of the Jerusalem madrasa includes a tripartite kibla unit comprising a monumental *iwan*—a vaulted hall with one of its four sides opening onto a courtyard.[48] Flanked by two cross-vaulted halls, this prayer hall was across the courtyard from the entrance vestibule; the sides of the courtyard were occupied by student cells. This scheme is hitherto unknown in the extant architecture of Jerusalem.[49] The monumental *iwan* also functioned as the lecture hall for the madrasa, which most likely was dedicated to a single rite, that of Imam al-Shafi'i, of which Sanjar was a scholar. Above the facade of the hall, Sanjar's blazon can still be seen.

LITERATURE, ART, AND ARCHITECTURE

This madrasa, the earliest extant Mamluk theological college in Jerusalem, is an intriguing hybrid of contemporary Syrian and Cairene single-rite madrasas. Almost all Syrian ones built approximately between 1150 and 1300 featured a courtyard on the kibla side—the side oriented toward Mecca—off of which a collegiate mosque or a prayer hall opened. Another hall, which doubled as a teaching hall for the rite, opened onto another side of the courtyard. (In madrasas dedicated to two rites, a third hall was introduced on one of the two remaining sides of the courtyard.[50]) The courtyard facades not taken up by a mosque or hall were occupied by recesses and student cells. The exterior of the Syrian madrasas was almost always oriented toward Mecca, instead of following the alignment of the street. In Jerusalem, as in Cairo, the facades are aligned with the street, but since most of the streets run perpendicular to the Haram, there is no divergence between the kibla-oriented interior and the exterior walls. Other differences between Syrian and Egyptian madrasas include the layout of the mosque or hall, which in Syria usually opens onto the courtyard through a triple-arched facade and consists of a central, domed bay in front of the prayer niche, flanked by tunnel-vaulted extensions on the right and left. In Cairo madrasas, the kibla *iwan* serves as a mosque, and is usually shaped as a regular rectangle but with a prayer niche in its kibla wall. In the early madrasas dedicated to one rite only, a second *iwan* faced the kibla *iwan* across the courtyard.[51] Instead of following the spatial hierarchy of the Cairene or Damascene models, the pragmatic Jerusalem architect emulated the abridgement precedent set by the madrasa of Sanjar al-Jawili in his designs for the Jerusalem colleges (generally dedicated to one rite only), especially in urban areas where the density of constructions yielded constricted sites.[52]

Devoid of any signs of Crusader iconography, the Chapel of the Repose was annexed to the Jawaliyya via the western cross-vaulted flank of the prayer hall.[53] The four-meter-thick Herodian wall against which the chapel was built obscured the commanding view of the sanctuary from the site, so the chapel's original architect cut windows into the wall, but due to the wall's unusual thickness the windows appeared as tunnels (see Figure 49). Sanjar's architect, wishing to create a more direct and full visual link between the interior of the madrasa's kibla section and al-Haram al-Sharif, excavated part of the Herodian wall and built the lower section of the foreart of the *iwan*

Figure 49. Madrasa of Sanjar
al-Jawili (1320).

and its flanks.[54] To conceal the brutality of the Herodian masonry of the remaining portion of the wall, now the lower part of the madrasa's south wall, it too was punctuated with windows and cladded on the side facing the Haram with *ablaq*, alternating red and white masonry, which heralds the foundation to the sanctuary. The standard prayer niche in the kibla wall of the hall was replaced by a large window that frames the spectacular view of the Dome of the Rock—the first kibla of Islam—and the Aqsa Mosque, which in turn faces the kibla of Abraham and Muhammad in Mecca. The window itself thus serves as a symbolic mihrab, or prayer niche.

Al-Tankiziyya

A major expansion of the role of the portico of al-Haram al-Sharif was brought about by the foundations of Sayf al-Din Tankiz, the viceroy of all of Syria for Sultan al-Nasir Muhammad ibn Qalawun, a broad authority uncommon in Mamluk bureaucracy.[55] It was during the reign of al-Nasir Muhammad that Jerusalem's status was elevated from a governorship to that of a viceregency, a transformation that involved major public works such as the rebuilding of the citadel, known as the Citadel of David.[56]

Tankiz ordered the construction of a religious complex flanking the small plaza where Bab al-Silsila Road terminates just outside Bab al-Silsila, the sanctuary's most heavily used gate since the mid-eleventh century. The complex, built and endowed between 1328 and 1330, consists of two structures. The larger one, on the southern side of the plaza, includes a cruciform four-*iwan* madrasa, a school of *hadith* (tradition), a *khanakah* (Sufi lodge), and a school for orphans. The other structure, built as a hospice for women, is detached from the rest of the foundation and located on the opposite side of the plaza, in observance of Islam's moral rules regarding the segregation of the sexes. The madrasa's cruciform layout, consisting of a courtyard on each side of which opens an *iwan,* is a novelty in Islamic Syria.[57] It recalls the contemporary cruciform madrasa of al-Nasir Muhammad in Cairo, the first madrasa with four *iwans*—each placed at one of the four arms of the cross and dedicated to the teaching of one of the four rites of Islamic law. Since the two-side *iwans* in the Madrasa of al-Nasir Muhammad are narrower than the kibla *iwan* and the one facing it across the courtyard, vertically stacked living units directly face the courtyard between the lateral *iwans* and the major ones. This four-*iwan* scheme for all four rites of Islamic law has originated in Egypt and is practically unknown anywhere else.[58]

The four-*iwan* madrasa of Tankiz was endowed for the impartation of only one of the four rites of Islamic law. By the time of Tankiz, few large pieces of land were left for new urban construction, especially in the prominent locations near the gates of the Haram. The constricted site of the Tankiziyya Madrasa demanded a modification in the scheme imported from Cairo. The square inner courtyard is roofed by a cross vault with an octagonal skylight in the center, almost certainly a response to climatic considerations (see Figure 50). In the courtyard below the skylight is a fountain fed by the main aqueduct to the Haram, which Tankiz had restored. The courtyard is much smaller than its Cairene rectangular counterpart, and therefore the four *iwans* occupy the whole length of its four sides. Four cells,

Figure 50. The Tankiziyya. Interior view toward mihrab.

LITERATURE, ART, AND ARCHITECTURE

probably for the use of the teachers appointed for this madrasa, are fitted into the four corners between the arms of the cross, and consequently are accessible only from inside the *iwans* instead of from the courtyard.

The resourceful architect overcame the challenge of carrying out a complex plan in this small but highly coveted flank of the plaza by distributing the functions of the foundation building vertically, a scheme without antecedence in Jerusalem's Muslim foundations. Since the school occupies most of the first floor, the cells of its students were constructed on a mezzanine floor in the northeastern corner of the building. The *khanakah*, the Sufi lodge, is on the second floor and is divided into two parts: the Sufis' cells are over the entrance and the northern part of the madrasa, whereas the main unit of the lodge is constructed on top of six bays of the western portico of the Haram, across the whole width of the roof. This "hanging" lodge boldly announces Tankiz's foundation to al-Haram al-Sharif by means of a decorated facade flush with the one of the portico below. The impact of integrating the roof of the portico into the foundation itself was adopted in almost all subsequent foundations built along the western and northern borders of the sanctuary.

The western end of the street facade housed four shops, the revenue from which was used for the upkeep of the Tankiziyya. The eastern section of the facade forms the southern side of the plaza outside the gate (see Figure 51). It displays a splendid portal with a bay that opens onto a vestibule, which in turn opens onto the northern *iwan* of the madrasa. It lies along the north-south axis of the courtyard and ends at an exquisitely decorated prayer niche in the center of the marble-paneled kibla wall of the south *iwan*. All these elements create a strong visual axis commencing in the public urban space outside the portal and terminating at the prayer niche as its focal point, which is uncommon. In Cairene madrasas, the patrons and builders preferred an indirect, sequential approach from the street to the kibla hall, using bent passages which produced a "surprise" effect around each corner. The fitting of the cruciform plan in the small urban site in Jerusalem left little room, if any, for a bent entrance passage. However, the real reason behind this direct, axial, spatial progression to the elaborate prayer niche, made possible by sacrificing the integrity of the north *iwan*,[59] may have been the patron's desire

Figure 51. The portal of
the Tankiziyya.

LITERATURE, ART, AND ARCHITECTURE

to compensate for the awkwardness of a site that did not permit much volumetric articulation of the madrasa's exterior facing the city. This was accomplished with a formal spatial sequence, the ceremonial axis of which extends to the center of the busy plaza, through the monumental portal. This important public space, with its religious associations as the harbinger of the sanctuary to those descending to it from David's Citadel and Jaffa Gate in the west, is further integrated into the spatial hierarchy of the madrasa through the impression of a continuous flow of space between the two, given by means of the concavity of the madrasa's portal, which is highlighted by its large recess and the dripping stalactites carved on its hood. This madrasa must have developed a unique rapport with the city, for by the closing years of the Mamluk period, it became the seat of its judicial tribune.

In 1336–1337, Tankiz transformed the site of a ruined Crusader market perpendicular to al-Wad Street (Tyropeon Valley) into a *waqf*-commercial center that stretched to the sanctuary. It consisted of two rows of shops facing each other across a vaulted thoroughfare, with lodgings above the shops, two bathhouses, and a caravanserai. Called Suq al-Qattanin, Market of the Cotton Merchants, its tax-exempt revenue was allocated for the maintenance of al-Haram al-Sharif and the upkeep of the Tankiziyya.[60] The vaulted commercial street runs at a right angle to the western wall of the sanctuary, where it terminates in a monumental portal incorporated into the Haram's western portico, the Suq al-Qattanin's segment of which was built as part of the new commercial center (see Figure 52). Unlike the other gates to the sanctuary, this portal bears an inscription on its Haram side instead of the side facing the city, which, according to Grabar, signified to the population and pilgrims that it was conceived as a portal heralding the suq from the sanctuary and not the other way around.[61] This may have been seen by the worshippers as presumptuous advertisement, but the suq—albeit a secular establishment—generated income that helped defray the maintenance cost of al-Haram al-Sharif itself.

Al-Ashrafiyya

The evolution in the designing of madrasas surmounting part of the Haram's portico reached its apogee in the Burji Mamluk period (1382–1517), in al-Madrasa al-Ashrafiyya, the only royal foundation from

Figure 52. Bab al-Qattanin, the gate to Suq al-Qattanin.

LITERATURE, ART, AND ARCHITECTURE

that period in Jerusalem, built by Sultan al-Ashraf Qaytbay (1468–1496). The large number of Cairene buildings he commissioned and the refinement and mastery of workmanship displayed in them attest to his position as one of the greatest patrons of Mamluk architecture. During his visit to Jerusalem in 1475, Qaytbay was invited to give a royal appraisal to a madrasa built for Sultan Khushqadum (ca. 1465) that, while still in Cairo, Qaytbay accepted as his own. Located at the western side of the sanctuary, immediately north of Bab al-Silsila and its minaret, the madrasa did not meet the sultan's expectations. It was consequently pulled down and built anew in 1482 by a team of Egyptian craftsmen and a Coptic architect dispatched by the sultan from Cairo. To allow for the construction of a madrasa that conformed to the Cairene formulas and proportions—in its plan as well as the interior and exterior elevations—the architect had to resort to three measures not in concert with the portico codes but sanctioned nevertheless by Qaytbay. First, a ground floor serving as a platform for the madrasa was superimposed on five of the western portico bays, thus appropriating part of the continuous cross-vaulted spine into the madrasa and blocking the pedestrian flow under the vaults of the portico. Second, since the one-bay-deep portico was too narrow for the intended platform, and since it is unlawful to encroach on another endowed foundation—such as al-Madrasa al-Baladiyya directly behind the wall of the sanctuary—a protrusion one bay deep and four bays long was introduced into the Haram's esplanade. This made it possible to build a platform for the madrasa consisting of an assembly hall,[62] and an entrance porch to the madrasa with arched openings on the south and the east. Third, to build a madrasa on the second floor, a portal, vestibule, and staircase were needed behind the bay of the entrance porch, and that made the destruction of some of the piers of the portico unavoidable. Despite these violations, the platform is in harmony with the portico, the datum of the Mamluk madrasas into which it is firmly integrated. The architect's multiplication of the portico's bay or module to produce a layout for the platform makes it appear as a rational outgrowth of the portico.

The architect employed extensive polychromic decoration in the whole entrance area to ensure high visibility for the portal, which is surmounted by a hood decorated with stalactites. In Mamluk religious foundations it is the tall, highly decorated portal, as well as the inscription and royal blazons, that announces the monument. Here the portal is set back from the facade of the assembly hall by the entrance porch's bay. The porch is located in the corner between the assembly hall and the portal opening directly on the vestibule. It is covered with an elaborate folded stone cross vault with diagonal lines that intersect in a recess in the form of a cross, carved with arabesque, a characteristic of fifteenth-century Mamluk architecture, especially at the time of Qaytbay.[63] Alternating red and white courses augment the conspicuousness of this vault; the same colors appear in the carved stone voussoirs of a window and oculus, which, along with the royal cartouches of Sultan Qaytbay on the exterior of the south wall of the assembly hall, draw the gaze of those entering the sanctuary from Bab al-Silsila. To those approaching the foundation from the Dome of the Rock, a striking hallmark of the architecture of the Qaytbay period, a multicolored portal—crowned by a hood with a three-lobed groin vault and set inside a trefoil-arched frame—appears through the eastern arch of the entrance porch. The groin vault terminates in a stone semidome that is adorned with red and black stone inlays of scrolls and palmettes, with highlights of turquoise faience. The contrast between each of the alternating black, red, and white courses of the portal is accentuated by the black color of the lead used here in lieu of mortar (a technique introduced for the first time in Cairo in the entrance portal of the Mosque of Sultan al-Mu'ayyad Shaykh, 1415–1420).

The madrasa on the second floor followed the configuration of a *qa'a,* a tripartite reception hall, with a bent entrance, a scheme hitherto unknown in the extant religious structures of Jerusalem.[64] Representative elements of contemporary Cairene architecture in the interior of the madrasa include the alternating red and white joggled voussoirs, the carving of the stone spandrels of the arches with arabesque patterns, the geometric star-shaped patterns carved on some of the stone lintels above the windows, and the continuous stone cornices carved with intricate calligraphy.

Besides overcoming the scarcity of available land at the borders of the sanctuary, the main advantage of raising the madrasas above the portico, the top of which is slightly higher than the platform of the Dome of the Rock, was the establishment of a direct visual relationship with the monument. This accounts for the elaborate double-arched openings framing the splendid view from the madrasas' loggias, which are enhanced by domes centered above the double arches.[65] The two-*iwan* axis of the Madrasa of Qaytbay is oriented to the south, toward Mecca and consequently the Aqsa Mosque; the eastern-side niche faces the Dome of the Rock. To take full advantage of the unique proximity to the first consciously erected monument of Islam, this niche was transformed into a loggia, from which the view of the monument was framed by a tripartite porch, a novelty in the design of the loggias looking onto the Dome of the Rock. Moreover, the eastern side of the kibla hall and that of the opposite one across the roofed courtyard were pierced with two tiers of windows.[66] Just as the students of al-Ashrafiyya enjoyed the remarkable view of the monument through the lofty arches of their loggia, the worshippers exiting the Dome of the Rock from its western and southern entrances marveled at the madrasa, which was dubbed by historian Mujir al-Din "the third jewel of the Haram."[67] The visual impact of al-Ashrafiyya Madrasa on its beholders on the platform of the Dome of the Rock was amplified by being elevated to their eye level.[68]

Directly facing his madrasa, on the sanctuary's esplanade, Qaytbay erected a *sabil*, a drinking fountain, with arabesque carving on the exterior of the ashlar dome (see Figure 33). It is the only carved stone dome outside Cairo and is characteristic of contemporary Cairene architecture.[69] The composition of this *sabil*—a freestanding square chamber covered by a carved stone dome, with the zone of transition from the square base to the circle expressed on the exterior by multiple tiers of prismatic stone triangles—strongly resembles Cairene detached mausoleums from this period, a resemblance unparalleled by any of the extant Cairene *sabils*, the contemporary ones of which are usually incorporated into the foundation's corner that receives the heaviest traffic and are surmounted by a koranic school for children.[70] While the dearth of space at the site of Qaytbay's madrasa in Jerusalem was not conducive to incorporating the fountain into its structure, it is still possible that the main purpose behind the placement of the fountain on the esplanade of al-Haram al-Sharif, fifteen meters to the northeast of the madrasa, was a symbolic horizontal extension of the charitable foundation into the blessed open space of the Haram. Whereas the religious foundation of Tankiz was the first to expand vertically on the portico of al-Haram al-Sharif, the Madrasa of Qayt-

Figure 53. The *sabil* (fountain) of Sultan Qaytbay (1482).

bay was the first and only one to protrude beyond the portico's line into the esplanade—a detached part that acts as a celebratory pointer to the foundation. The choice of the Cairene mausoleum as a prototype for the *sabil* may be ascribed to Qaytbay's desire to commemorate his charitable deeds at al-Haram al-Sharif in a fashion that emulates the earlier freestanding commemorative structures around the Dome of the Rock, which all belong to the domed-pavilion type.

The Mausoleums in the Vicinity of al-Haram al-Sharif

Although Jerusalem's political status was relegated from that of the capital of the Crusader kingdom to a provincial town under the Mamluks, it became a dignified place of banishment suitable for high-profile political opponents of Cairo's Mamluk community. Many of those who were exiled there sought to perpetuate their name through building and endowing charitable foundations. Some chose to be buried there as well.

A number of foundations at the borders of al-Haram al-Sharif house domed mausoleums that established an audiovisual relationship with the passersby. The earliest one is that of al-Malik al-Awhad, a great-great-nephew of Saladin who was appointed superintendent of the two *harams* in 1295. It is located at the northern border of the sanctuary, between the portico and Bab Hitta Road.[71] From the vestibule and through the sanctuary's portico, koranic recitations poured out onto the stone-paved esplanade, eliciting the blessings of the passersby. Another example, from the western border of the Haram, is the 1437 Isfahan Shah Khatun's madrasa-mausoleum. Its first floor is located between Bab al-Mathara Road and the sanctuary's western wall behind the portico, whereas the second floor sits on top of the portico and comprises a number of vaulted halls and loggias, each consisting of one portico bay. This second floor, like the whole of Madrasa of 'Abd al-Basit built on the roof of the Dawadariyya's portico, is in the form of a narrow strip, maximizing the foundation's frontage facing the Dome of the Rock. The domed, square mausoleum, which is pierced by an opening on each of its four sides, is located at the corner next to the madrasa's portal and vestibule on Bab al-Mathara Road in order to get the maximum exposure to the traffic in and out of the sanctuary.[72]

Other highly desirable sites for burial chambers were the streets leading to the gates of the sanctuary. The Ribat of 'Ala' al-Din, the earliest pilgrim hospice in Jerusalem, includes a burial chamber for the founder, whose grave is located behind a window that opens onto Bab al-Nazir Road. However, it is Bab al-Silsila Road, the main artery leading to al-Haram al-Sharif, that is dominated by seven Mamluk funerary foundations, all of which have burial chambers with windows opening directly on this street.[73] The earliest of these is the mausoleum of Husam al-Din Baraka Khan (the most influential Khwarizmian chief and leader of some of the troops who, along with the Ayyubids, liberated Jerusalem in 1244). It was built between 1265 and 1280 and was incorporated into earlier Crusader shops.[74] This pattern along Bab al-Silsila Road of blessings invoked by koranic recitation from inside the mausoleums corresponds very closely to the funerary character of Shari' al-Mu'izz li Din Allah, the main thoroughfare of Fatimid, Ayyubid, and Mamluk Cairo.

The burial chamber of the madrasa-mausoleum of Sayf al-Din Tashtamur al-'Ala'i (1382–1383), located on the southern side of Bab al-Silsila Road, is the only one among the seven burial chambers with a prayer niche in its southern, kibla wall. The others (except that of Baraka Khan[75]) are situated on the northern side of the street, and a mihrab, a prayer niche, in their southern walls would have left no room for windows on the street, depriving the mausoleums of their crucial visual link with the pedestrians outside. The prayer niche, a highly decorative feature that underscored the religious character of a mausoleum, is replaced here by the blessings of the passersby.[76]

The mausoleum of Sitt Tanshuq al-Muzaffariyya (1398) is a curious small funerary complex situated directly opposite her palace, across the street presently called 'Aqabat al-Takiyya (Khassaki Sultan).[77] Its street facade consists of a portal with the windows of the burial chamber flanking its prayer niche to the right, and a *sabil,* a drinking fountain, to the left. The fountain made up the street section of the small madrasa built as part of this funerary structure. This is the only extant religious foundation from Mamluk Jerusalem that incorporates a *sabil* into its street facade, a popular benevolent practice in the religious complexes of Mamluk Cairo since the addition by Sultan al-Nasir Muhammad ibn Qalawun of a *sabil* at the corner of his father's foundation in 1326.

The Influence of Damascus, Aleppo, and Cairo

By the beginning of the Mamluk period, Cairo, Damascus, and Aleppo, the three most important cities of the sultanate, had each developed a distinctive architectural school that continued to inspire the local builders and craftsmen down to the Ottoman conquest. During the Bahri Mamluk period (1250–1382), the schools of Damascus and Aleppo exerted significant influence on the ateliers of Cairo, as exemplified by the latter's relish for hooded portals with stone stalactites, interlacing inlaid stone patterns, and colored tiers of masonry. Jerusalem was also a recipient of Syrian influence during this period. For example, in the Dawadariyya *khanakah* (1295), the colored stone strings in the sanctuary's north wall window jambs and the polychrome joggled voussoirs of the assembly hall's windows and oculus overlooking the courtyard follow Damascene models.[78] The portal, with its pendent keystone and two shallow stalactite domes, is a direct descendant of the portal of al-Madrasa al-'Adiliyya in Damascus (1171–1222/23).[79] On the other hand, the portal of al-Majd al-Sallami's madrasa north of the Haram (1338) is crowned by a canopy with pendent stalactites that points to the portal of Qawsun's palace in Cairo (1337–1338), and it bears the signature: "Muhammad ibn Ahmad Zaghlish al-Shami" (the Damascene). The same name appears on a cupola with stone stalactites in Jerusalem's Suq al-Qattanin.[80] On the walls of the south *iwan* at al-Tankiziyya is a remaining section of a dado, the marble wall paneling of which is done in a technique seldom encountered in Jerusalem.[81] The stylistic evidence suggests that it was executed by the same team of Damascene craftsmen who, at the behest of Tankiz, produced the paneling of the Aqsa Mosque and the Sanctuary in Hebron in the 1330s.[82] The madrasa's prayer niche, with its blind arcade and the adornment of its hood with glass mosaics forming a vase, green acanthus, and vine scrolls on a gold background, also points to the school of Damascus.[83]

Yet it was the stone workshops of Aleppo that dominated the architectural scene in Syria throughout the Bahri period. Their first large-scale and systematic application, most likely following Crusader antecedents, was in the cross vaults of the Great Mosque of Aleppo (reconstructed in 1285), which became the prototype for those of the porticos of al-Haram al-Sharif (see Figure 54).[84] A strong Aleppo

Figure 54. The western portico of al-Haram al-Sharif, interior.

influence in the architecture of Jerusalem can also be detected, from the fourteenth century onward, in the internal zones of transition from the corners of square burial chambers, loggias, and gateways to the domes covering them, with the exception of Qaytbay's *sabil*.[85] Most minarets in Jerusalem emulated the square Syrian ones, particularly the Aleppo minarets.[86]

The portal of al-Tankiziyya (see Figure 51), which set the tone for many subsequent Jerusalem foundations in both decoration and spatial organization, is crowned by a hood or vault consisting of multiple tiers of niches, with stalactites supporting a small semidome like its prototype, the Tankiz's mosque-mausoleum in Damascus. But the earliest occurrence in Islamic architecture of a stone vault with stalactites surmounting a portal is at the Ayyubid Madrasa of Shadbakht in Aleppo (1193).[87] Another interesting Aleppine feature at al-Tankiziyya is the hood of the prayer niche, which is surrounded by a pattern of interlacing loops executed in a colored stone inlay, a technique that made its first extant appearance in Islamic architecture around the hood of the the prayer niche of Shadbakht's madrasa.[88] The spandrels of the niche are beautifully decorated with a knotted and interlaced marble inlay. The first extant occurrence in the world of Islam of this famous knotted pattern is in Aleppo, at the Mashhad al-Husayn built in 1173–1174.

It was only in the later part of the Bahri period that the strong influence of the Cairo school became apparent. Among the earliest examples of Cairene design are the recessed window panels crowned with cornices (corbeling) with stalactites in the facades, like those at the *khanakah* and madrasa of Majd al-Din al-Is'ardi at the northern portico of al-Haram al-Sharif (1359) (see Figure 55). Other Cairene features at that madrasa include the ribbing of the stone semidome that covers the cantilevered prayer niche in the facade above the portico on the Haram, as well as the use of stone prismatic triangles in the exterior zone of transition between the cylindrical body of the prayer niche and the corbels supporting it.[89]

At the Madrasa of al-Majd al-Sallami (ca. 1338), the tall recessed window panels on the western facade bear a striking resemblance to contemporary window recesses in Cairo, particularly in their sloping sills and the distinctive angular stalactites that crown the middle recess, the only example of this type in Bahri Jerusalem. The facade's entrance

Figure 55. The Madrasa of al-Majd al-Din al-Is'ardi.

portal, with its inscription band with palmette terminals, recessed door lintel with joggled revetment, and roundels flanking the relieving arch over the lintel, finds antecedence only in Bahri Mamluk portals in Cairo. The fact that these powerful signs of Cairene influence on the western facade are to be found nowhere else in this otherwise Syrian-style madrasa has prompted Burgoyne to suggest that a Cairene team was summoned to Jerusalem to build this facade.[90]

Facades showing strong signs of Cairene influence, such as the sta-lactite-crowned recessed panels, are, nevertheless, rarely surmounted by a continuous band of trefoil crenellations, another hallmark of Mamluk facades in Cairo. The only extant example in Jerusalem is the above-mentioned mausoleum of Sitt Tanshuq al-Muzaffariyya, which, like many Mamluk Jerusalem foundations, still exhibits distinctively Syrian elements.

Recalling the Mamluk foundations of the royal Bayn al-Qasrayn area in Cairo, the facades of Jerusalem's foundations on the streets leading to the gates of al-Haram al-Sharif—such as Tariq Bab al-Hadid and Tariq Bab al-Silsila—and above the porticoes of the sanctuary compete for visual dominance with imaginative combinations of elements of virtuoso decoration that have a highly emblematic nature. Perhaps no madrasa facade in the sanctuary dramatizes this competition more perfectly than that of the Madrasa of Al-Malik al-Jukandar, the polo master of al-Nasir Muhammad, built in 1340 at the sanctuary's northern border. Behind this facade is the madrasa's assembly hall, the forepart of which is built on the roof of only two portico bays. This narrow frontage on the sanctuary is compensated for by the articulation of its limited surface area with an assortment of decorative elements, which are organized in a symmetrical fashion that enhances their conspicuousness: the founder flaunts his blazon of polo sticks on the right and left of the foundation inscription in the spandrel between the arches of the portico, above which is a recessed panel displaying alternating red and white stone courses and voussoirs over and around three windows and an oculus and the whole ensemble is crowned by an elaborate cornice with stalactites.

Despite the strong interaction with the architectural schools and workshops of Cairo, Damascus, and Aleppo, the architecture of Mamluk Jerusalem rejected fixed formulas and proportions and instead developed a tradition of pragmatic selectiveness that endured throughout the Mamluk period. New, imaginative configurations of halls, portals, and courtyards were developed in response to the challenges of the limited sites, the functional requirements of the project, and the political agenda of the sultan, amir, or dignitary. Similarly, there were no set patterns for surface decoration, and scattered elements were put together to form an original ensemble for a specific area. In its scope, quantity, original schemes of facades and layouts, maximization of scarce land, and, above all, ingenious response to view as well as to the exigencies of the topography and irregularity of available land, the architecture of Jerusalem outshone that of Aleppo, Damascus, and Gaza—the latter two being the political centers of Mamluk Syria, which had jurisdiction over Jerusalem. Moreover, the concentration of nearly all the foundations of the city in one area, at the borders of the sanctuary, is without analogue in the extant cities of Islam. To this day, these monuments welcome visitors on their way to al-Haram al-Sharif.

Architecture of the City outside the Walls

18

ZIVA STERNHELL

The spiritual splendor of Jerusalem has always far surpassed its physical reality. The place accorded the city in the three monotheistic religions and its influence on the various mystical traditions, and consequently on the development of Western architecture from the Middle Ages until modern times, derive from the rich associations evoked by the "Heavenly Jerusalem." A visit to the Church of the Holy Sepulchre is liable to disappoint anyone who expects to see the ideal structure which served as a model for churches and monasteries.[1] Equally disappointing would be a visit to the Temple Mount in search of the remains of the Temple, which became such an important mystical symbol (a symbol that Joseph Rykwert called "the image of production as path to salvation")[2] that it even influenced the beginning of modern architecture. And indeed, although the small area within the Old City Wall contains some of the world's most historically important religious monuments, Jerusalem is not a monumental city. Historical and political circumstances created its image, and made it a symbol of the gap between the spiritual and the material that always exists in our lives.

During the four hundred years of Turkish rule, which ended with World War I, the material situation of the city declined and the authorities showed little interest in it. In spite of the fact that during the last years of the Ottoman period conditions improved, it was only under the British Mandate that things really changed and the city's status was raised; nevertheless, the period of British rule (1918–1948) was chiefly characterized by a desire to preserve the status quo. Even the new construction undertaken since 1967, such as the restoration of the Jewish Quarter—largely destroyed in the War of Independence (1948)—as part of the State of Israel's endeavor to unite the old and new sections of Jerusalem, did not alter the essential character of the Old City. It remains a provincial oriental city that blends into its rural surroundings, with an urban network dating back to the Middle Ages. Yet at the same time Jerusalem is physically very impressive. Its dominant feature—a harmonious combination of bare hills and low stone buildings, interspersed with sections of wall, minarets, and church steeples—evokes an ancient biblical landscape and stimulates the imagination.

Naturally, it is the historical architecture of the Old City which has always attracted the most attention. For years, the New City outside the Wall remained anonymous, often regarded as no more than a political tool in the struggle for control of the city. And in fact, until recently, modern architecture in Jerusalem received little recognition, although some major figures contributed to it, such as architect Erich Mendelsohn and town planners Patrick Geddes and Charles Robert Ashbee.[3] It was Jerusalem's good fortune that it never became an economic or industrial center, and many projects for the development of the New City that called for the destruction of architecturally valuable buildings remained in the drawer. The perpetual lack of public funds and the limited nature of private business in the city permitted neighborhoods, some of which were built in the nineteenth century, to survive even when people were unaware of their importance. Thus, the evidence of the various layers in the construction of the New City remained intact, permitting us to study a modern chapter in the annals of the Eternal City.

Supposedly, the main thing to be said in favor of the city which has spread west of the Wall since the middle of the nineteenth century is the fact that this new construction did not succeed in swallowing the Old City. The sense of harmony that exists between the two parts of the city is usually ascribed to the British ordinance prohibiting the use of almost any building material except stone and to the general preservation of the low scale of the buildings. A more thorough investigation, however, reveals a remarkable phenomenon—namely, that the harmony between the two sections of the city has been preserved because Jerusalem unintentionally became a laboratory for the Romantic tendencies in the modern movement.

In recent years there has been an increasing recognition of the decisive if not dominant role played since the eighteenth century by these trends in the history of modern Western architecture. Contrary to the accepted myth, the modern movement was not based solely on rational, universal, and objective principles. Today, it is difficult to draw the line between some of the movement's principles and Romantic tenets such as the belief in the power of sentiment, the desire to stress national characteristics, and a definite inclination toward mysticism. The neo-Gothic was not the only style that developed out of the Romantic ideology. Neoclassicism likewise drew upon it, and one finds in the modern movement a tendency to adopt precisely the romantic aspects of the ideas of thinkers such as Goethe and Rousseau. This was very pronounced in German and British architecture,[4] which had a decisive influence on Jerusalem.

The spiritual and mystical significance of Jerusalem, its location in the exotic East, and the ancient untamed landscape that surrounded it fostered the development of an architecture based upon Romantic principles, despite the fact that one of the chief elements of Romantic architecture—the aspiration to the "sublime"—is found in only a few buildings. But the tendency to build modestly may be explained by material conditions—the lack of funds and the primitive materials and technology—as well as by ideological factors: first, by the Protestant belief in the moral value of simplicity and modesty, and later, in the twentieth century, by the dominance of modernist ideology. Undoubtedly a sensitivity to the modest scale of the Old City acted to curb exuberance, but the other characteristics of Romantic architecture are evident throughout.

Buildings during the Ottoman Period

December 9, 1917, the date on which General Allenby conquered Jerusalem, is usually regarded as a turning point. Within two years, the British regime restored normality to the city—whose inhabitants had experienced severe hardship and famine during the war—and began a rapid process of modernization. The establishment of an efficient administration, investment in urban planning, and the spread of the modern architectural idiom gave the impression that a revolution was in progress. But in reality the breakthrough to modernity had occurred much earlier.

Traditional modes of living had changed in the second half of the nineteenth century, when the Ottoman Empire began to open up to the West. The political and economic weakness of the old empire made it dependent on the European powers, whose military assistance in ending the Egyptian occupation of Palestine (1831–1840) and during the Crimean War forced the Ottomans to grant them certain rights, which included ownership of property outside the Old City. Turkish attempts to liberalize their centralized system of government also had some effect, although the reforms were barely felt in Jerusalem. The opening of the Suez Canal in 1869 increased the strategic value of the area as a whole and spurred the European powers to greater rivalry in their efforts to control it.

During that period, Jerusalem began to attract more pilgrims and tourists, as religious revivals in nineteenth-century Europe and Westerners' taste for oriental exotica increased interest in the city. The technological revolution improved communications, bringing Jerusalem closer to Europe and the United States and encouraging an endless stream of writers, painters, and photographers. It turned the city—previously only a symbol or a utopian idea—into a physical reality for millions of people throughout the world.[5]

In addition, there were new populations for whom services and housing had to be provided: a constant influx of Jewish immigrants, as well as many foreign consulates. The involvement of the great powers stimulated economic growth, and the increasing congestion led to higher rents. Moreover, Western culture also fostered Jerusalem's expansion beyond the Old City Wall. Modern ideas about progress and the desire to improve the standard of living percolated into the provincial city and gave its inhabitants the confidence to change their traditional way of life.

Construction outside the Wall began in earnest in the 1860s, immediately after the Crimean War, when the Turks passed new laws permitting the sale of land to foreigners. Members of all three religions took part in a new wave of construction; differences between neighborhoods and buildings reflected not only the economic situations of the various communities, but also their respective social and cultural character.

The majority of the Christian buildings were public, religious, or philanthropic. As might be expected, Jerusalem became a magnet for religious and messianic sects, but in addition to religious activities there were more pragmatic impulses, stemming from the imperialist struggle among the great powers. Behind the founding of religious and philanthropic institutions by the various churches and missionary sects were the parent states with their "earthly" interests. The missionary fervor that combined religious revivalism with an awareness of social problems, a fervor characteristic of the "spirit of the age," was turned into an advantage by the European governments, which hoped thereby to gain power and political influence in the city.[6] Thus, for example, impoverished Russian pilgrims were subsidized by the czarist government.[7]

Rivalries and disputes were rife among the churches. The Catholics preferred to build close to the Church of the Holy Sepulchre, and their buildings were typified by their monumental style. Even when they built outside the Wall, they tried to remain as close to the Old City as possible. Thus, the "French area," which includes the Hospital of Saint Paul, the Hospice of Notre Dame de France, and Saint Vincent de Paul School, sprang up by the northwestern corner of the Old City Wall, along the section that runs from the Damascus Gate to the Jaffa Gate. In contrast, the Protestant Church, which became the dominant factor in the city during the religious struggles of the nineteenth century,[8] was free from any attachment to the holy sites and began to buy land in more distant places. Thus, among the first buildings to be constructed outside the Wall was the Schneller Syrian Orphanage, built a mile or so northwest of the Old City. This charitable and educational institution was founded in 1860 by Johann Ludwig Schneller, a German member of an "Apostle Station" (Apostle Stations were a Swiss-based missionary movement). It eventually included a home for the blind and a vocational school. Six years later the German Protestants established the Talithakumi girls' school, and, in the same period, a lepers' hospital. The Anglicans built, among other things, the Ophthalmic Hospital of the Knights of Saint John in 1882, and the Mission Hospital for Jews in 1897.

This tendency to create self-sufficient compounds, based on European religious traditions, characterized all Christian construction. This was due both to the functional exigencies of running large institutions under an unstable regime and to a desire to create autonomous

Figure 56. The Russian Holy Trinity Cathedral, by architect Milton Ivanovitch Eppinger.

enclaves. One of the most impressive examples of such a compound was built between 1860 and 1884 by the Russian Orthodox Church to cater to the needs of the many Russian pilgrims, most of whom were short of funds (Figure 56). This project extended over eighteen and a half acres, and included a cathedral, a consulate, a hospital, hostels for men and women, shops, cisterns, and gardens, all of which provided accommodations and services for up to two thousand people.[9] The compound was planned by Russian architect Milton Ivanovitch Eppinger as a small independent township surrounded by a wall. The monumental complex with its spacious inner courtyards, white towers, and green onion-domes set a new architectural standard for buildings outside the Old City.

The national character of these religious institutions was clearly reflected in their architectural designs. Protestant architecture was typified at first by modest designs, owing to the limited budgets and perhaps also to missionary ideology, which advocated remaining close to the people.[10] But eventually, when the involvement of the great powers increased, grander monumental buildings created enclaves of richly ornamented architecture stressing unique national traits.

In comparison with the monumental Christian institutions built in a variety of styles, residential buildings in the second half of the nineteenth century were far more homogeneous. Local materials and traditional work methods created a sense of continuity between the Old City and the modern neighborhoods, yet the spread of the city beyond the Wall signified the beginning of a new era. The "spirit of the age" was expressed in more than the adoption of European features such as tiled roofs and the use of "modern" materials such as glass, concrete, and iron, which had already been employed in the Old City. Despite the tranquil rustic appearance of the low stone buildings, with their massive walls (up to three feet thick), arches, and inner courtyards, a revolution was in progress, particularly evident in the town-planning concepts of the various neighborhoods.

Muslim buildings, however, showed no sign of this revolution. Well-to-do Muslims built themselves spacious private villas in order to escape the crowded conditions and poverty of the Old City, though it remained their communal center. They did this in a spontaneous and individualistic fashion, giving no thought to any public considerations; their buildings reflected their lack of concern for the city planning of the Ottoman regime, as well as their desire to maintain the traditional character of the Muslim community.

By contrast, the Jews constructed their buildings so as to emphasize the collective aspect of community life. In fact, the movement beyond the Wall became part of a national saga, adding a unifying element to a phenomenon which until then had been purely religious in character. The dozens of Jewish neighborhoods which were founded from 1860 onward laid the foundations for the New City. There were differences among the many associations, which were generally established along ethnic lines.[11] But with the need to organize the purchase of land and the construction of new buildings, the commitment to the public good became the overriding factor. Detailed and highly regimented plans left no room for any individual expression on the part of the settlers. (One of the few exceptions was the Bukharan Quarter, constructed between 1860 and 1914 by wealthy Bukharan immigrants, many of whom built luxurious villas.) In contrast to the organic architecture of the Old City—a free assemblage of small cubes built one on top of the other in the course of generations—most of the new Jewish neighborhoods were laid out in uniform grids, composed of rows of buildings containing identical apartments.

This uniformity was the result of more than economic considerations, although these were of primary importance to a poor community entirely dependent on charity. A study by Ruth Kark of the bylaws of the various settlers' associations in the New City shows that the process of moving beyond the walls was accompanied by a highly developed social consciousness.[12] In some cases, one can sense the desire to establish a national identity, and also to increase the productivity of the community. A desire for a more productive lifestyle and a change of social structure was already evident in Mishkenot Sha'ananim, the first neighborhood outside the Wall, founded in 1860 by the Anglo-Jewish philanthropist Sir Moses Montefiore through a legacy left by the American benefactor Judah Touro (see Figure 3, page 27).[13] The bylaws, which detailed the rights and duties of each settler, were inspired by the age-old Jewish tradition of close collective living; religious statutes required the individual's total commitment to the community. Yet despite the closed configuration of these neighborhoods, which at times recalls the cramped ghettos of eastern Europe, the utopian ideals that flourished in the West in the nineteenth century among those who were trying to solve the problems of the urban masses probably found their way to the New City as well.

A Jewish neighborhood usually consisted of rows of small two-room apartments that were attached to each other, forming a rectangle or square around an inner courtyard—which could be locked at night—where the common buildings and cisterns were located. The facades of the apartments overlooked the courtyard, while their doorless back walls formed a protective barrier. Financing generally came from external sources, such as Jewish philanthropists or communities abroad. The bylaws were intended to ensure the quality of life through the preservation of moral and religious values, the control of norms of personal conduct, and the maintenance of order and cleanliness. Interestingly, social life in these communities was based on democratic practices, such as the election of officials by secret ballot and the casting of lots for apartments—practices designed to increase the sense of equality among the inhabitants. The idea of building neighborhoods for Jewish workers came at the turn of the century. There were hints of nationalism in the declarations calling for the founding of a modern Jewish city that would renew the connection between the religion and the people.[14]

Christians constructed few residential buildings, but an interesting and important exception was the Templers' neighborhood. The Templers, members of a messianic sect founded in southern Germany in the 1850s, arrived in the country in 1868 and built a number of villages, hoping to hasten the time of the Redemption. In 1873 a group of them reached Jerusalem, intending to create a model neighborhood that would serve as a spiritual center. The group acquired lands in Emek Rephaim (southwest of the Old City) and created an independent entity along the lines of a German village (Figure 57).[15] Although uniformity was a dominant characteristic of this closed sect,[16] which constructed a planned village with public institutions such as a communal center and a school, each family was allowed to build its home separately. The balance between collective order and individual diversity, the combination of German village homes and local materials and work methods, and the care lavished on the large gardens surrounding the houses produced a most attractive mixture which bore witness to economic success. Consequently, the Templer experiment, despite its special character, began in the late nineteenth century to serve as a model for pioneering Jewish village settlements.

Architecture in the Late Ottoman Period

In the period before World War I, the Jewish, Muslim, and Christian areas began to link up with one another. Despite the differences between the various housing blocks and the heterogeneous population of the city, the sense of harmony was preserved. The unifying effect of the local stone and the use of simple fortress-like shapes

Figure 57. Templer house in the
German Colony.

helped blur the differences between the various neighborhoods and
between the Old City and the New.

The Arab neighborhoods, which were based on a clan system,
displayed a marked tendency toward an ornamental eclectic style.
Picturesque influences from European and especially Italian architecture reached Jerusalem at second and third hand (for instance, via
Lebanese architects), as did a number of pattern books imported from
Europe. Turning toward the West was considered part of modernization, but the plan of the buildings remained traditional whereas the
ornamentation was based on a combination of oriental and Western
motifs.[17] Jewish construction, in contrast, was characterized by great
simplicity and a functional approach that were generally due to economic necessity. The uniform, unadorned, fortress-like appearance of

Figure 58. Outer staircase at
Batei Ungarim.

buildings was relieved only by decorated doors and windows, and by
outer stairways, which at times resembled flying buttresses (Figure 58).
Slightly more attention was paid to the design of public buildings,
such as synagogues and yeshivahs. The low quality of construction
and the crowded conditions soon helped turn many of these communal neighborhoods into slums in which numerous additions and
changes concealed the repetitious character and rigid geometry of the
original design.

Christian monumental architecture, which varied owing to the transplantation of so-called national styles, imported both European influence and high professional standards. Within the eclectic architecture of the period, the medieval style was most prominent; it could be justified conceptually and it blended into the local vocabulary.

The return to the Middle Ages and especially to the Gothic style was one of the outstanding characteristics of nineteenth-century architecture in Europe and the United States. The neo-Gothic was not only one of the decorative styles of the eclectic age but the manifestation of a cultural revolt that began with the Romantic movement. It represented a reaction to modernization, and it merged into the Arts and Crafts movement. Nineteenth-century religious architecture turned quite naturally to the Middle Ages, the golden age in which moral and religious values were identical and the "disastrous" secular age had not yet begun. In England and the German states, the interest in medieval architecture—considered the "local" style in both places— had national significance and made a statement against French neo-classicism.

It was to be expected that medieval architecture would influence the style of religious institutions in Jerusalem. The heavy, organic style, especially of the early Middle Ages, blended extremely well with the ancient oriental city and the rustic landscape. It suited the building methods, the roughly hewn stone, and the inhabitants' taste for seclusion. From the Christian point of view, it was ideologically appropriate, since it evoked the times when the Crusaders ruled Jerusalem; it also suited the aims of the missionaries, who were full of socioreligious fervor. The tendency to use the Byzantine, Romanesque, and Gothic styles for Christian religious institutions was apparent both inside and outside the Old City Wall, and was particularly pronounced in buildings designed by professional architects aware of the theoretical aspect of their profession. Most prominent among these were Heinrich Renard, who was sent from Germany in order to build the Dormition Monastery and Abbey on Mount Zion in 1900–1910 (Figure 59), and Robert Leibnitz, likewise a German, who designed the Augusta Victoria Hospice on Mount Scopus in 1906–1910. The English architect George Jeffrey also turned to the Middle Ages when he designed the College and Cathedral of Saint George in 1895–1912, inspired by the Gothic architecture of Oxford University.

Public buildings became grander toward the end of the century,

Figure 59. Dormition Monastery and Abbey on Mount Zion, by architect Heinrich Renard.

when the involvement of the great powers increased and national feeling in Europe intensified. But despite the desire to create specific national monuments in Jerusalem, the sense of continuity remained unbroken. Public buildings reflected the contemporary European fixed formulas for such institutions, influenced by the academic design principles of the Ecole des Beaux Arts. This explains the affinity between buildings such as the Lepers' Hospital, designed by the German-born architect Conrad Schick, and the Ratisbonne Vocational School, built by the French architect M. Doumet.[18] But the rational academic approach was modified by rough stones and primitive construction methods, contributing to the rustic, picturesque character of the architecture. Jerusalem classicism merged into the Romantic classical trend typical of public buildings at the turn of the century—a trend born of the desire to create a nationalistic architectural style that would unite the neoclassical and local idioms. It was difficult to disregard the local context and the oriental character of Jerusalem, and many architects wished to create a synthesis of East and West.

This desire was uniquely expressed by Conrad Schick, who arrived from Basel in 1846 as a member of an Apostle Station and spent the rest of his life (fifty-five years) in Jerusalem. He developed a deep understanding of the city, became involved in archaeology, and designed several of the city's most important Protestant institutions, such as the Talithakumi School and the German Deaconesses Sisters' Hospital.[19] Most of his designs recall provincial German public buildings, but to the formal symmetry of repetitive windows, emphatic portals and quoins, and parallel wings, he often added medieval and oriental decorative motifs, such as flying buttresses and pointed Gothic arches. Schick achieved a genuine synthesis in his private residence, "Thabor," built in 1882–1888 (Figure 60). Here fort-like medieval forms dominate, blending with a structure based on organic local principles of design such as decorative horizontal stringcourses, or bands, between floors. The low, compact building of undressed stone with its two internal courtyards is embellished with local archaeological artifacts.[20] Schick's synthesis of Mediterranean and medieval architecture, plus the tendency to the picturesque which characterizes many Jerusalem buildings, created a precedent for the Mandatory period.

Figure 60. Thabor, the residence of Conrad Schick, which he designed.

Under the British Mandate

At first sight, nothing could be further from Schick's picturesque residence than the white, unadorned, minimalist cube-like buildings which appeared in Jerusalem in the 1930s. This contrast seems to confirm the impression that British rule brought about a revolution. But upon examining the significant architecture of the Mandatory period, one finds that it expresses principles which had begun to emerge under the Ottomans. Although the use of the abstract idiom became increasingly common in the late 1920s, the message it conveyed was similar to that of the preceding era: namely, a search for a local architectural language which would represent the special character of the city, harmonize with the natural surroundings, and provide an organic link between past and present.

As always, it is hard to select the most significant buildings from the mass of different styles. The economic boom that followed the British conquest encouraged construction, carried out mostly by undistinguished architects or even by nonprofessionals. At the same time, Jerusalem did bring together two groups of architects of high caliber—English and central European—who enjoyed the backing of an enlightened administration and broad-minded clients, and it created suitable conditions for the crystallization of a local idiom whose influence is still felt.

British Construction in the 1920s

The emotional approach that the British took to Jerusalem was evident first of all in their decision to make that out-of-the-way, rundown city the capital of Palestine, although as far as the economic and strategic interests of the empire were concerned, Haifa and Jaffa were far better positioned. Establishing the seat of government in Jerusalem gave the city an infusion of new life. A key figure at this period was Sir Ronald Storrs, military governor of Jerusalem from 1918 to 1926. Storrs inherited the spiritual world view of the nineteenth century, and as a believing Christian with a deep attachment to the city, he approached his task as a spiritual mission. The government in London preferred to spend money on other parts of the empire, but in any case Storrs believed that his main purpose was to preserve the status quo. (He regarded all construction around the Wall, even the late nineteenth-century French religious institutions, as detrimental to the city's appearance.) His dedication to the conservation of Jerusalem was manifest in everything he did.

As soon as he took up his position, Storrs founded the Pro-Jerusalem Society, whose main task was to preserve, maintain, and restore the Old City.[21] He invited architect and designer Charles Robert

Ashbee (1863–1942) to serve as secretary of the society and as civic adviser to the governor of Jerusalem out of similar ideological motives. Ashbee had played a central role in the Arts and Crafts movement, which had been regarded as revolutionary in England during the second half of the nineteenth century, but by the 1920s Ashbee's views were in keeping with Storrs' conservative outlook. The ordinance that all buildings must be executed in stone was one outcome of this attitude.

These and other actions by Storrs were decisive in molding the appearance of Jerusalem. When he ended his term of office, a new spirit became manifest in the city, yet some of the early Mandatory principles of planning still survive. The stone-building ordinance came under criticism from modernists, but in retrospect one can see that it gave the city its characteristic, unified appearance and covered up poor architecture and mistakes in urban planning. The focus on the preservation of the Old City may have meant less concern for the new neighborhoods and the pressing needs of their inhabitants, but it prevented numerous "disasters" that would have ruined the small area within the Wall. Thus, for instance, the policy of maintaining open spaces—which allowed the arid mountain landscape to come right up to the Wall—preserved one of the most impressive features of the city.

The chief contribution of the British was their long-range planning. Though they erected few buildings, they created a solid infrastructure based on the British building laws of 1909. (In 1936 local legislation was updated and brought in line with new laws enacted in Britain in 1932.) This planning combined comprehensive vision with professional competence, so that the spontaneous building of the Ottoman period was replaced by an orderly approach which linked up the various neighborhoods, distinguished between areas of different character—residential, commercial, and open spaces—and created a network of roads and services, such as water supply and electricity, which inaugurated the Jerusalem of the modern era.[22] As early as 1918, the authorities invited William McLean, the city engineer of Alexandria and Khartoum, to prepare a plan for future development. In the following year Patrick Geddes, one of the major British planners of the period, was also asked to prepare a new plan. Although this invitation was not officially approved,[23] Geddes, who also participated in the planning of the Hebrew University on Mount Scopus, put forward one plan in 1919 and another (in collaboration with Ashbee) in 1922.

These three conceptual plans, expressive of the thinking that existed at that time in Jerusalem, centered around the authorities' desire to protect the Old City from modernization and to emphasize its importance as a spiritual center. The British, and especially Storrs, were captivated by the romantic images created by painters and photographers who had documented the city before it began to spread outside the Wall. They wished to preserve the "medieval aspect" of the city "in its natural state."[24] McLean's plan reflected this aspiration: it froze construction in the Old City for twenty-five years, created a large space between the Wall and the areas of new construction, and designated territory for a beltway of parks and open spaces. Stringent restrictions on new development prohibited high-rise buildings and the use of artificial materials, and even required roofs to be made of stone so that the general harmony would not be disturbed. Industry was denied a foothold, not only in the vicinity of the Old City but also in the areas set aside for future development.

Geddes and Ashbee likewise made the preservation of the Old City their main goal. They continued in the footsteps of McLean, but modified the tendency to formal design which characterized his plans. Geddes' plan of 1919, in which the axes of movement were adapted to topographic conditions, demonstrated an organic approach, and the plan of 1922 actually grappled with functional issues. Thus, for example, it divided the New City into zones, including industrial and commercial ones, to provide employment for the inhabitants.[25]

The Romantic outlook of Storrs, Ashbee, and Geddes ensured that they agreed on matters of principle, and they were able to put at least some of their ideas into practice. In the years when the rational and futuristic aspects of the modern movement began to prevail in the great cultural centers of Europe, life in Jerusalem still retained the conceptions and rhythms of the nineteenth century. When in 1888 Ashbee founded the Guild and School of Handicrafts in London, believing that one could keep the modern world at bay through a revival of medieval principles, he was considered one of the standard-bearers of progress. Art was regarded as a means of bringing about spiritual renewal and the creation of a society based on classless cooperative communities. Although these ideas provided the basis for the founding of avant-garde schools such as the Bauhaus, the naive forms and ideals of the Arts and Crafts movement could not be expected to survive in the sociopolitical economic realities of the twentieth century. Yet Jerusalem provided Ashbee with a suitable environment for the realization of his ideas, and he enjoyed a period of renewed activity.

Ashbee carried out enthusiastically the tasks with which he had been entrusted. These included preparing a report on the condition of the old buildings in the city, proposing ways of preserving them, and drawing up a program to encourage traditional handicrafts. In this city that served as a spiritual symbol, he found a community untouched by the malaise and alienation of modern industrial societies. In a place where traditional handicrafts constituted an authentic part of life, the ideals of the nineteenth century could be revived. Ashbee soon began to investigate the local creative modes—pottery, printing, weaving, jewelry, and even folk music.[26] Coming from a tradition which combined art with social concern, this British architect and designer sought to improve the quality of life of the citizenry. He had hoped to open schools for handicrafts, but this dream, like most of his architectural projects, never left the planning stage. Nonetheless he succeeded in restoring the traditional markets—including the Cotton Market, with its seventy weavers—and parts of the Old City's Wall and gates. He also made a significant contribution to city planning, and some of his ideas, such as zoning, and the gardens and promenade around the Wall, have survived until today.

Geddes, too, was stimulated by the opportunity to participate in molding the appearance of Jerusalem. The Scottish designer who had a mystical dream of building a "temple of life"—a shrine to the gods and muses in a town resembling a Greek polis[27]—was temperamentally better suited to Jerusalem than to English industrial towns. An erudite man who had formulated a holistic doctrine combining the natural and social sciences, he was invited to the country by Chaim Weizmann on behalf of the Zionist Organization. Geddes was asked to help in planning Haifa and Tel Aviv, and indeed his contributions to the design of the country's major cities can still be felt. He was one of the pioneers of regional urban planning, and, unlike Ebenezer Howard, whose well-known plans for garden cities dictated fixed boundaries, Geddes excelled in open-ended planning that was suited to the landscape, permitting growth and adaptation to changing conditions and developing technology. But in Jerusalem, the mystical-spiritual element was foremost in his plans.

Geddes originally came to the city in order to design the campus of the Hebrew University on Mount Scopus. The ambitious plan he submitted to the leaders of the Zionist Organization far exceeded their budget and was never carried out. It was a formalist plan, based on the shape of a hexagon,[28] with a huge, highly decorated hexagonal building in the center. The structure's vast dome was surrounded by six smaller ones, and it expressed the striving toward a new mystical-spiritual religion typical of turn-of-the-century culture. In planning Jerusalem, Geddes treated the Old City as a spiritual center, and he followed one of his major principles: linking the present to the past and preserving historical buildings as part of a never-ending process.

The collaboration between Geddes and Ashbee was not a matter of chance. Both brought with them the enthusiasm and optimism of people who believed that art and design had the power to change the world. They were not affected by the pessimistic "decadence" of the late nineteenth century which eroded the Arts and Crafts movement, and they found expression in pseudo-picturesque English architecture[29] and in some of the trends of Art Nouveau—styles which never gained a foothold in Jerusalem. Similarly, the "return to order"—expressed in early twentieth-century British architecture and also characteristic of public buildings throughout the world in the interwar years[30]—was hardly represented in the architecture of Mandatory Jerusalem. A monumental bureaucratic style, seen in colonial office buildings in New Delhi and often imitated, was created by Edwin Lutyens, one of the major architects of the period, who began his career under the influence of the Arts and Crafts movement but who switched to neoclassicism at the beginning of the twentieth century.[31] In Jerusalem, however, the neoclassical style always looked like a foreign implant, whereas medieval architecture continued to be a source of inspiration and fused with the local style during the Mandatory period. This fusion is exemplified by the work of two major British architects who were then active in Jerusalem, St. Austen Barbe Harrison and Clifford Holliday. When one looks at the Scottish Hospice and Church of Saint Andrew (1927–1930), which was designed by Holliday and which blends wonderfully into the mountain landscape, one can hardly tell to what period it belongs (Figure 61). The

Figure 61. Scottish Hospice and Church of St. Andrew, by architect Clifford Holliday.

stone mass is divided into small blocks set one above the other according to the principles of organic construction. Holliday wanted to create a building which would spring out of the ground and relate to nature and to history. It was no accident that he chose a porous stone on which moss would quickly grow: the building soon acquired a patina which lent it an aura of antiquity.[32] Only a small tower, a dome, and a half-dome hint at the purpose of the building, outstanding for its simplicity. Holliday succeeded in reviving the ideals of the Arts and Crafts movement. The honesty and modesty that characterized the movement in the beginning reappeared in Jerusalem seventy years later.

A more elaborate and eclectic synthesis is evident in the work of Harrison, who used traces of neoclassical architecture and the principle of design based upon symmetrical elements. But essentially it is the medieval style which gives his buildings their special character. Harrison had lived in Athens and studied Byzantine and early Islamic architecture.[33] As the architect of official buildings for the colonial administration, he continued the nineteenth-century tradition of transferring the medieval style to nonreligious public buildings—a tradition heavily influenced by the American architect H. H. Richardson. It achieved an official monumental idiom that drew inspiration from the simple, massive Byzantine and Romanesque styles which had preceded the Gothic.

In the British High Commissioner's residence (1929–1933) near Talpiot, Harrison, who headed the Mandatory government's Public Works Department, had his first opportunity to design an official building which would be a synthesis of East and West (Figure 62) and based his style on the connection between Mediterranean rural construction and medieval architecture. The link between these two was the principle of organic growth—a revolutionary principle of nineteenth-century British architecture. Although the residence's western facade is composed of various symmetrical blocks—a concept illustrated as well by the sunken garden in front of it—in all the other facades elements develop freely from the center outward. Built of stone quarried on the spot, the building contains public spaces that are vaulted and domed and blends with the surrounding landscape.[34] Its fortress-like appearance, low tower, and arched openings recall both the local oriental architecture and the medieval revival in Western architecture.

LITERATURE, ART, AND ARCHITECTURE

Figure 62. Government House, by architect Austin St. Barbe Harrison.

But the crowning achievement of the work of Harrison and of British Mandatory architecture in general is considered to be the Rockefeller Archaeological Museum (1930–1939). Financed by John D. Rockefeller, Jr., the building faces the northeastern corner of the Old City. Here Harrison created a building that fulfilled the highest possible role of public architecture, namely to express the spiritual ideals that its sponsors and donors wish to represent. Although the structure is not outstandingly innovative or original, there is no doubt that Harrison was able to rise above the usual standard for such buildings.

Its plan consists of a symmetrical arrangement of blocks in the shape of a butterfly (a familiar form in nineteenth-century British architecture), with a central axis that runs from the monumental entrance—surmounted by an octagonal tower—to an old pine tree behind the building.[35] In the center of the structure is a courtyard with a large ornamental pool, flanked by rows of wide arches that form cross-vaulted arcades. The building is divided by three smaller inner courtyards. In his desire to combine the architecture of East and West, Harrison sought out features of Islamic design; he searched through history, going as far back as the Mamluk period and as far afield as the Alhambra in Spain. He probably drew on the knowledge he had gained in Athens, and he was thus able to create a rich and complex synthesis of Islamic and nineteenth-century European architecture.

Despite the eclectic complexity, however, the dominant impression made by the building is that of a revival of the fortified architecture of the Middle Ages. British artist Eric Gill (1882–1940) decorated the museum with ten stone reliefs symbolizing the ancient cultures that had left their imprint on the country,[36] and with inscriptions in Hebrew, Arabic, and English. Gill was a member of a group of artists and craftsmen (which included Ashbee) that set up a rural commune in order to escape industrial towns and exploitative capitalism and revive the spiritual and material values of the Middle Ages, a dominant theme in the British Romantic movement. The technique, style, and symbolism of Gill's stone reliefs were in keeping with Harrison's building, itself an impressive example of the Romantic tendency in modern architecture.

The British artists, architects, and planners invited to Jerusalem were very fortunate. They were not expected to express the grandeur of an imperial power, but represented a regime that respected the spiritual role of the city and that was content to be an example of enlightenment and universality. Some regard the Mandatory architecture of the twenties as behind the times, but one must remember that the white cubic buildings which represented the rational and technological aspect of modern architecture were hardly to be found during that decade outside avant-garde circles. Moreover, Britain, which had been ahead of its time in the nineteenth century, was slow in assimilating the new artistic currents of the early twentieth.[37] Thus, for example, the first International Style building did not appear in England until 1929.

The Romantic outlook reflected in these projects and in the other British enterprises was also in keeping with the culture of Eretz Israel, where in the 1920s the Romantic approach was indisputably dominant. Storrs's dream of an "oriental biblical arcadia" suited the Zionist outlook: at that time, local Jewish art was characterized by images of biblical heroes in exotic landscapes—images that symbolized the return of the people to its roots.[38] The Bezalel School of Art—opened in 1906 by Boris Schatz—was under the influence of the Arts and Crafts movement. It was an attempt to create an oriental "Jewish style" that influenced all areas of art and design (although the prevailing style at the school was closer to the curvilinear decorativeness of Art Nouveau). Though the school gradually declined, and closed in 1929, even its critics among the artists who chose to settle in Tel Aviv continued to seek inspiration in exotic Eastern settings.[39]

The fusion of East and West that first appeared in the Ottoman period became a common characteristic of the architecture of all ethnic communities in Jerusalem in the twenties. Often it was expressed only in decorative elements of domestic construction—Armenian ceramic tiles, corrugated roofs, or "tacked on" domes—by which builders tried to create an architecture suitable to the place. Attempts to combine medieval and Islamic motifs were made by major architects such as Arthur Loomis Harman, who built the YMCA (1926–1933) with an assembly hall resembling a Byzantine church (Harman's next project was the Empire State Building), and Binyamin Checkin, Patrick Geddes, and Frank Mears, who collaborated in planning the National Library on Mount Scopus (1926–1930).

The 1930s

The wave of construction that had begun ten years earlier turned the Jerusalem of the 1930s into a modern city. The rapid growth of the population (from 53,000 people in 1918 to 165,000 in 1948), the construction of Jewish garden suburbs and affluent Arab neighborhoods, and the rise of a crowded urban center full of commercial activity awakened the sleeping city and changed it beyond recognition. The eclectic, nostalgic, rural style was abandoned for the bold, clean lines of modern architecture, giving the impression that Jerusalem had turned its back on the past, alienated itself from the landscape, and begun a new chapter of history.

This new spirit was evident in city planning. In the two plans which became official blueprints—Clifford Holliday's, approved in 1940, and Henry Kendall's plan of 1944—the preservation of the Old City remained a central aim, but they also dealt with the New City and its problems.[40] Kendall's plan actually grappled with the needs of the twentieth century, such as improving the communications system, separating different kinds of residential areas, and recognizing the importance of commercial zones. Both plans showed concern for the aesthetic aspects of modern architecture—creating continuous building areas of a unified character, concealing service accessories such as sewage pipes, and restricting the number and shapes of balconies.[41]

The economic boom that followed the arrival of the British was naturally expressed in architecture. Buildings in the center of the city grew higher (up to eight stories), and new kinds of structures appeared, including luxurious office buildings like the Generali, high-class hotels like the King David and the Palace, cinemas like the Edison, the Rex, and the Eden, and residential neighborhoods for a new bourgeoisie that could afford to live in affluence.

Construction styles reflected a heterogeneous society in the Mandatory period as well, but the clear-cut ethnic differences of the Ottoman period were obscured by the process of modernization that affected the whole society. Picturesque eclecticism continued to be dominant in the new affluent neighborhoods of the Arab bourgeoisie, neighborhoods such as Talbieh and Bak'a, and attractive examples of villas with ornamental gardens prevailed (Figure 63). The desire to give architecture a local Arab flavor was expressed not only in private buildings but in public ones such as the Palace Hotel, which was lavishly decorated with oriental motifs. In the thirties, Art Deco appeared, and curvilinear ornaments were replaced by geometric ones. Eventually, the streamlined International Style influenced Arab architecture, and this helped blur its differences with Jewish architecture, although interior residential design did not change very much.[42] The transition from the twenties to the thirties was reflected in local British architecture, well represented by the work of Harrison and Holliday. A look at two of Harrison's buildings in the twenties—the Central Post Office and the Government Printing Office—shows how the work of this architect moved to an abstract idiom, reflecting a general trend. In the Post Office, the ornaments and historical elements

Figure 63. Arab residence on Hebron Road.

disappeared, and the doorways and windows of the building, which was divided into three blocks, were arranged in repetitive rows. Yet the architect did not lose his sense of place. The large arches of the ground floor's main portal in the central block and the manipulation of stones of various kinds and colors show that Harrison had not broken away from his surroundings but had simply learned to express himself in a more abstract manner. This process was completed in the Printing Office, which was built in concrete and conceived as an entirely modern industrial building.

Jewish Buildings in the 1930s

Although the British and the Arabs were influenced by the modern idiom, in the thirties it was the Jewish architects who took center stage and linked Jerusalem to the great cultural centers of the world. The Zionist enterprise was at that time headed by leaders—such as Chaim Weizmann—who understood the importance and value of architecture. The opening of the Hebrew University and the arrival of large waves of immigration, particularly the one from central Europe, brought to the city people who were architecturally aware of new trends. They provided work for the architects, who in turn applied progressive ideas to their buildings.

In the area of city planning, the Jewish garden suburbs built in the twenties represent a fascinating chapter in the history of modern Jerusalem. As might be expected, the authorities, still favorably disposed toward the Jews, encouraged the creation of these neighborhoods, built far from the Old City and in accordance with British urban policies. The Romantic ideology of a return to nature, which underlay the concept of the garden suburb and which had arisen in nineteenth-century England, suited the Zionist myth, born of a similar outlook. At the same time, the anarchistic aspect of the garden city did not exist in the Jewish national movement. In Eretz Israel the return to nature contained nationalist dimensions—striking new roots and creating a new society, an alternative to the wretchedness of the ghettos and shtetls of Europe. The political factor of "conquering the land" also came into play here. Thus, between 1922 and 1925 six successive neighborhoods appeared, including Talpiot, Beit Hakerem, and Rehavia, on land purchased by the Zionist Organization. The person in charge was Richard Kaufmann, an outstanding architect who headed the planning department of the Jewish National Institutions.

Kaufmann was one of the pioneers of modern architecture in the country. He came from Germany in 1920, and tried to apply the progressive ideas he had brought with him to local conditions.[43] In his work one can see the combination of the academic approach he studied in Germany and the concept of the garden city he gained from his direct contact with Geddes and with Ebenezer Howard, whom he had met in England and who was the founder of the garden city movement. Kaufmann's plans for Jerusalem neighborhoods included a formal distribution of areas according to a symmetrical design, with a main axis leading to public buildings in the center. At the same time, the plans reflected an awareness of the local conditions and landscape, and emphasized setting aside areas for gardens. In time, he moderated his rigid approach to planning and adapted the organic conceptions characteristic of the work of Geddes for his own use.[44]

The sense of euphoria that existed in those days in Israel was very evident in the planning of the Jerusalem garden suburbs. The Balfour Declaration of November 1917, which promised the Jews a national home, followed by the British conquest a month later, created the feeling that redemption was at hand. The first neighborhood, Talpiot, was planned as the basis for an independent Jewish town with its own public institutions, to which Kaufmann tried to give a monumental appearance. In the end, however, these dreams failed to materialize, and in all the neighborhoods only a few of the projected public buildings, such as the Hebrew Gymnasium High School in Rehavia and the Teachers' Seminar in Beit Hakerem, were constructed. But according to the surviving drawings and plans, Kaufmann hoped that the cultural edifices, to which the main axes pointed, would serve as spiritual centers—an intention that suggests the influence of Geddes' "temple of life." Kaufmann was also familiar with urban concepts developed by the German avant-garde at the beginning of the century, concepts that likewise had a clearly mystical goal: creating a "crown" for the city, a monumental spiritual center that would replace the usual center of government.

The connection between the garden city and the Romantic movement is obvious. But the white, cube-like buildings constructed in Jerusalem in the thirties reveal contrasting attitudes on the part of the architects. In some, no stone was used; in others, the stone covering only emphasized the break with traditional architecture. It is easy to regard them as the product of the ideas of the Bauhaus and of architects like Le Corbusier or Gerrit Rietvelt, the figures who brought the modern myth into existence. At first glance it seems that the principles then dominant in Jerusalem architecture constituted a break with the past and with local traditions, a disregard for nature, and a transformation of architecture into a rational mechanical process, producing useful structures that could be erected anywhere regardless of sentiment, the way one might set up a machine.

But as one learns to recognize the Jerusalem buildings and their architects, one discovers a far more complex picture. Since most of the Jewish architects who worked in the Mandatory period came from central Europe and had studied and worked in cities such as Berlin, Munich, and Vienna, one must first examine the context in which their outlook was molded in order to appreciate their local buildings. Knowing their conceptual sources helps one understand their buildings and reveals a variety of relationships linking them with British Mandatory architecture.

At the beginning of the twentieth century, Germany was regarded as the cradle of universalist and rationalist architecture and design. But in the country that had succeeded in combining progressive industrialization with avant-garde aesthetic ideas and revolutionary social theories, the Romantic movement held a dominant position. And although it is usual to place the flowering of the German Romantic movement between 1770 and 1830,[45] and to attribute its theoretical basis to thinkers such as Herder, Fichte, and Schelling, a close look at German architecture from the eighteenth century onward exposes a much wider range of influence. As early as 1772, Goethe, who played a decisive role in the development of all areas of German creativity, declared the Gothic cathedral to be a true expression of the German spirit,[46] and Friedrich Schinkel (1781–1841), the father of modern German architecture and the founder of central European neoclassical architecture, followed in his footsteps. Early on, Schinkel was deeply impressed by the mystical aspects of Gothic architecture, and he also considered neoclassical architecture in Romantic terms: he regarded it as a means of glorifying the king of Prussia and the German nation, as well as an expression of the humanist ideals of the Enlightenment.

These objectives remained unchanged in the twentieth century. The Deutsche Werkband, established in 1907 as an organization of artists and industrialists who sought to combine progressive design with the forces of industry, was primarily intended to promote the aims of the German state.[47] The designers and architects were expected to capture the Zeitgeist, the spirit of the age, in order to modernize German industry. This was also the principle underlying the Bauhaus, founded in 1919 with government backing.

The Bauhaus is usually considered one of the bastions of universalist and rationalist modernism, and Jerusalem architecture of the thirties is often referred to as "Bauhaus architecture." But this term is inaccurate. First of all, the Bauhaus was a far more complex phenomenon than the myth attached to it: in the first three years of its existence it was a workshop for the development of mystical theories and of ideas for escaping from the modern world and returning to the spiritual ideals of the Middle Ages. (At the center of the poster put out for the opening of the school was the image of a cathedral.) In 1922, however, there was a basic change of policy: the irrational tendency was curbed, and the school moved in a more practical and rationalist direction, concentrating on industrial design and on the material problems of mass society.

But the architects of Jerusalem, like culture in the city in the interwar period, were connected with the spiritual world of Germany at the turn of the century, when the second wave of Romanticism swept over that country. This wave found expression in two movements: Jugendstil and Expressionism. The cultural shock of World War I created a feverish spiritual atmosphere that contributed to the development of Expressionism; this was accompanied by a proliferation of mystical sects and associations of artists and architects who wished to take part in a spiritual revolution that would change the face of the planet. This was the atmosphere in which Erich Mendelsohn matured.

One of the major architects of the twentieth century, Mendelsohn burst upon the international scene with a series of Expressionist drawings of futuristic buildings, which he had sketched as a soldier during the war. Immediately after the cessation of hostilities he designed the Einstein Tower in Potsdam, considered one of the main works of Expressionist architecture. Within a short time, Mendelsohn became one of the most successful architects in Germany.

The audacious curving lines that characterized Mendelsohn's early work softened in the course of time. After 1923 he tried to find a way to fuse emotion with logic, and the needs of the industrialized city of the masses with the dynamic spirit of modern life. The Schocken family department store he built in Stuttgart was an example of such a synthesis: situated on a busy crossroads, the building was severe in design with minimalist lines (it had a repetitive grid of huge glass windows), but the inanimate block of concrete was full of vitality and life, its rounded contours protruding forcefully and dominating the entire street-corner.

Mendelsohn's Jerusalem buildings, in contrast, give the impression that his emotional turmoil and dynamism had entirely disappeared, and the quiet, monastic appearance of the stone cubes with their small apertures suggests that the Berlin architect's encounter with the city was a turning-point in his life. This impression, however, is only partly correct. First, the toning-down of the character of his designs was a long process which had already begun in Berlin and which reflected a change in the general atmosphere in Germany. And the restrained design of his Jerusalem buildings concealed great emotional turmoil.

In letters full of lofty sentiments and flowery language, Mendelsohn described his emotional experience during his first visit to Eretz Israel in 1923. As an ardent Zionist he declared his desire to emigrate to the country, yet when he actually left Germany in 1933, he chose to settle in England. "Judea is divine, but too small for me,"[48] he said. Therefore, despite numerous commissions, he lived for less than two years (1939–1941) in Jerusalem, where the greatest concentration of his architecture in the country is to be found: the Hadassah Hospital, the Schocken Residence, the Schocken Library, the Anglo-Palestine Bank (now Bank Le'umi Le'Israel), and others. In these buildings, and especially at Hadassah, Mendelsohn reached one of the peaks of his creativity. His ability to restrain his emotion and to condense his ideas into an abstract form resulted in a strong and convincing statement.

From the street, the Schocken Residence and the Schocken Library, built not far apart in Rehavia, hardly make an impression. Both buildings have plain facades with rows of small windows. The library is characterized by extreme minimalism. Its western and most impressive facade is built of smooth stone, with only a few openings. The windows are arranged in repetitive rows, except for an isolated bay window that breaks the monotony. The rounded line of the huge window—a lattice of glass and steel—erupts suddenly out of the solid fortress-like wall, producing a dramatic effect.

The Schocken Residence has a more dynamic composition, related to the open rocky areas that surrounded the building at the time (Figure 64). It expands into the landscape through a variety of rectangles of different heights, with windows of different sizes, pergolas, and a sunken balcony along the whole building. The interior design, as in all Mendelsohn's buildings, is fastidious and elegant, reflecting his organic Romantic concept that a building in its entirety forms a single

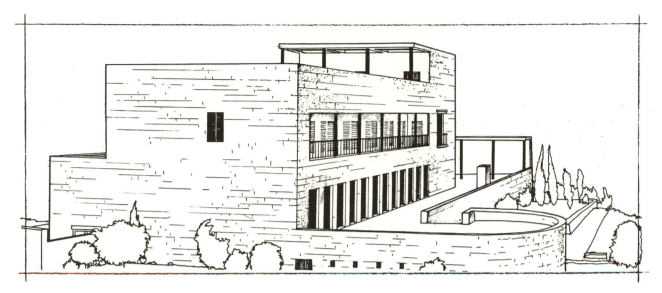

Figure 64. Schocken Residence, by architect Erich Mendelsohn.

work of art. A garden of rounded terraces, planted with olive trees and pines, completes the harmonization of the building with the landscape. The composite nature of the residence suggests many sources of inspiration, including the rustic villas of Schinkel and Le Corbusier.

The synthesis of emotion and logic, and the attempt to create an organic building with the aid of advanced technology—traits that characterized Mendelsohn's work in Germany—received a new interpretation in Eretz Israel. Here the desire to harmonize with nature had nationalist significance as well, since a return to the land of one's forefathers and the fusion of the local idiom with advanced technology symbolized a blend of cultures. Mendelsohn was enchanted by Jerusalem, with its wild, natural landscape and rustic architecture. But in addition to his attraction to archaic cultures (which is characteristic of many modernist artists), he, like many representatives of the British regime, saw the desert landscape as embodying an "eternal biblical purity." And like many others, he saw Jerusalem as a symbol of universal values, although in his case there was a nationalist undertone.

The Hadassah Hospital, as a public building, expresses all the various and sometimes contradictory elements in the architect's makeup (Figure 65). The great mass of the building, on the slopes of Mount

Figure 65. Hadassah Hospital on Mount Scopus, general view, by architect Erich Mendelsohn.

Scopus, is divided into two extended rectangular blocks of different heights, the narrow passageways between them creating two inner courtyards. Endless rows of standardized windows and industrially cut stone attached in a vertical manner emphasize the fact that the building belongs to the modern age in which stone has no constructive function.[49] As a sensitive artist, responsive to the mysteries of the Jerusalem countryside, Mendelsohn succeeded in planting the building within the landscape, linking it up with the local language of Arab architecture, and at the same time making it a powerful expression of his Zionist feelings. The two rectangular blocks are not static, but burst forth toward the Judean desert. They end in two rounded, closed-in balconies, the larger of which forms a broad and dramatic arc, creating a direct connection with what Mendelsohn called the landscape that "leads straight to eternity."

The aspiration to merge with the Orient in both a physical and a spiritual sense without abandoning modern Western culture, and the wish to supply the functional needs of a public building while at the same time making it a symbol, were expressed here in an exemplary manner. The most striking feature of the building—the entrance in the form of a high arcade with three domes—creates a feeling of strength, together with a touch of mysticism. Here one finds an expression of various layers of Jewish existence in Eretz Israel. The desire to blend into the locality is revealed in the three domes, which recall the local architectural idiom. But the pillared arcade is reminiscent of the neoclassical aspect of Mendelsohn's work—an aspect that could be termed Romantic classicism (revealed in a more specific manner in President Chaim Weizmann's home in Rehovot and in the interiors of the Schocken Residence and Library). Mendelsohn was not totally unresponsive to the neoclassical tendencies that appeared in the monumental architecture of the 1930s—tendencies popular throughout the world and not only in Italy and Germany, where they represented the new regimes.

Indeed, one cannot ignore the fact that the architect from Berlin was influenced by the spiritual tendencies prevailing in Germany at the beginning of the century and by the upsurge of nationalism in that period. When he wrote about his visit to Eretz Israel in 1923, he said the experience strengthened "that which has always been strong within me, my blood and therefore race and three-dimensionality." On another occasion he wrote of "the true soil which my blood and my nature desire."[50] But these emotive nationalist sentiments were balanced by rationalist considerations based on humanist values. Mendelsohn recognized that the country was inhabited by another people, whose feelings had to be respected. He advocated avoiding the construction of Western-type buildings, which would constitute "an insensitive provocation of the Arab world."[51]

This famous architect did not find it difficult to fit in to Jerusalem's cultural milieu. From the 1920s onward, a number of thinkers had gathered in the city—renowned academics and artists, most of whom came from the cultural hubs of central Europe and were influenced by the Romantic movement. Gershom Scholem and Martin Buber were concerned with the mystical foundations of Judaism, which they saw as the nation's life force. Elsa Lasker-Schuler brought her Expressionist poetry to Jerusalem. A group of architects and teachers who had fled the Nazis reopened the Bezalel School in 1935 and called for the development of a local idiom that would be based on technology, abstract modernism, and functional requirements. But the final aim of all this, as Mendelsohn himself pointed out, was "to create symbols, which is one of the chief purposes of art in the life of the nation."[52] An analysis of the works produced at Bezalel and of the texts and speeches of its teachers indicates that the Expressionist ideology of the Deutsche Werkbund and the early theories of the Bauhaus had found their way to Jerusalem.

So Mendelsohn's architecture was not created in a vacuum, and its organic principles were not based solely on a desire to blend into the locality. The desire to fuse matter and spirit, the aspiration to uncover the deepest strata of Jewish culture in order to arrive at a new definition of the national identity—an identity not incompatible with universal moral values—were part of the outlook that Mendelsohn and Jerusalem's intellectual circles had in common. In the Jerusalem of that period, this was the basis of design in all fields—from fabrics and household utensils to buildings. Minimalism, geometric patterns, simplicity, and modern materials and labor methods were intended not as a celebration of the machine age but as an expression of deep spiritual principles. Purity—or "biblical simplicity," as Mendelsohn called it—suited both the local conditions and the universal values common to all religions. Just as Ashbee, Holliday, Harrison, and Gill were able to revive the ideals of the Arts and Crafts movement in the Jerusalem of the 1920s, so Mendelsohn and his colleagues succeeded in reviving some of the Romantic spiritual ideals that had existed in Germany at the beginning of the twentieth century.

An examination of buildings by some other architects working in Jerusalem at that period confirms these conclusions. Leopold Krakauer, a Viennese architect who came to the country in 1925, designed only a few buildings in Jerusalem, yet his Bonem residence in Rehavia (1935) is undoubtedly one of the finest examples of modern architecture in Israel (Figure 66). It represented an intelligent interpretation of the principle of organic building. Rising out of the ground, the house is composed of white cubes radiating from a center in a free, yet balanced arrangement based on a harmonious relationship of masses of different heights and sizes. A variety of openings,

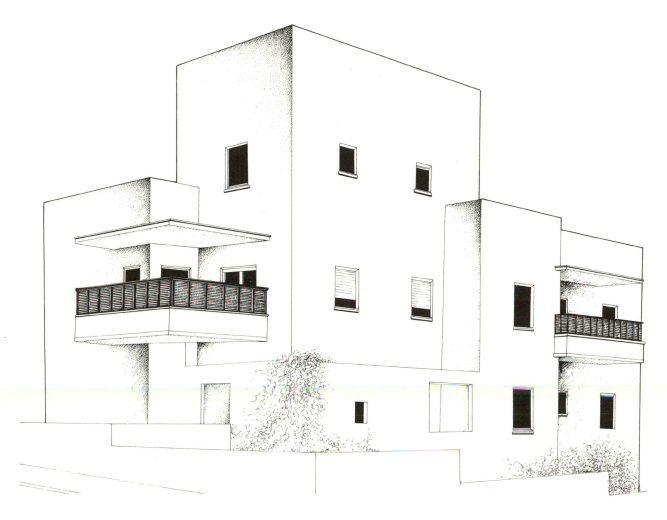

Figure 66. Bonem House, by architect Leopold Krakauer.

balconies covered by thin concrete roofs with balustrades in the form of wooden shutters (a common Muslim motif), and a terraced garden give the building its unique appearance. This is one more example of an interesting fusion of the Arab village with modern principles of organic design, based on breaking up a box-like shape into its component parts in order to create a new body, which in turn blends with its surroundings.

Krakauer did not leave writings that could help us to better understand his work, but his excellent landscape drawings, especially of the desert and of thistles and thorns, impress us with his approach. The Viennese artist brought to this country the central European Expressionist tradition, which attempted to find in nature the deep spiritual principles residing in the human soul and transpose them into the language of art and design.

Another important architect working in Jerusalem in that period was Heinz Rau, who came from Berlin in 1933. His Rosenbaum Building, located at the edge of Rehavia, was the first apartment building in Jerusalem with a terraced form.[53] The minimalist design is very striking: there are few windows, and these are small in size. But here the same principles apply: the house is close to the ground and blends into the steep slope below it. The thin concrete cantilevers that project from the roofs (and that recall the floating roofs of Frank Lloyd Wright) protect the building from the sun and rain and create an interesting play of light and shade. An outside staircase provides a private entrance to each apartment (a local motif), and a rough stone wall contrasts with the white plaster surfaces but links the building with the rocky area surrounding it. (The building was constructed some distance from the Old City, so that it was not subject to the regulation stipulating that surfaces had to be covered with stone.) Even if it is difficult to see the architect's intention at first glance, the structure was an abstract interpretation of the forms of Arab villages, one of which was situated nearby, over the hill.

Mendelsohn, Krakauer, and Rau did not construct many buildings, but they played an important role in creating the forms of the Jerusalem architectural idiom. Although each of them brought with him his own cultural heritage, respect for the city restrained them. They adapted the European idiom to local conditions, building on a modest scale. They became well acquainted with the topography and climate of the mountain city, and they reduced the size of windows in order to prevent the harsh light and hot sun from penetrating the interiors. Mendelsohn abandoned the futuristic elements that remained in his work (and that appeared in his plans for Haifa), and Krakauer toned down the strong emotionality of his drawings. This was regional architecture at its best.

Moreover, in Jerusalem in the thirties there were a number of other fine architects whose work reflected similar principles. Johanan

Rattner, who designed the headquarters of the Zionist Organization, was able to give it a distinguished appearance by using a severe and economical style. Richard Kaufmann built private residences in a massive idiom; his works include the house now used as the prime minister's residence. Dov Kochinsky designed a workers' cooperative neighborhood in Rehavia; it comprises fourteen two-storied buildings built around an internal courtyard and arranged in clusters of broken cubes interspaced with winding external staircases. Abraham and Zippora Cherniak built another workers' complex in the same area and according to the same pattern. Zoltan Harmat, who specialized in designing luxurious villas, was trained in the academic tradition but was influenced by the Jerusalem architects and adopted their styles. Likewise, Alexander Friedman, who had studied in Rome and had brought the neoclassical style to Israel, learned from Mendelsohn and adopted the rounded lines that had typified the latter's work in Germany.

Despite the variations, all these buildings had a common denominator that lent a special character to modern Jerusalem. Although material conditions—building materials, outdated technology, and limited budgets—obviously played a decisive part in creating this unifying factor, an analysis of the special characteristics of the city reveals deeper causes. The continuity in the regional character of the building in Jerusalem from the nineteenth century onward resulted from the fact that the architects restrained their individuality: they were aware that in Jerusalem one cannot escape the collective memory and a heritage going back thousands of years. But this awareness, which greatly increased during the British Mandate and helped crystallize the Jerusalem architectural idiom, was more than the natural reaction of sensitive artists. In modern Jerusalem, a special conjunction of circumstances brought together two Romantic movements, the German and the British.

The interconnection between the two movements had begun in the eighteenth century and had found expression through cross-fertilization in all areas of creativity (for example, the influence of Goethe on English Romantic poetry in the nineteenth century, and the influence of William Blake on German poetry and art). Britain, as a modern and progressive country, served as a model for German architects even in Schinkel's time. Herman Muthesius' study of the architecture of the Arts and Crafts movement, published in 1904, became a catalyst for the modern revolution in architecture and design in Germany. In both countries, architecture was regarded as more than a matter of formal problems alone. Architects and men of ideas ascribed a spiritual, moral, and national significance to architecture. Thus, the English and German opposition to classical architecture stemmed from a wish to be freed from an artificial style representing an outmoded regime, but it was also the expression of a hostility to French cultural preeminence.

Jerusalem created a direct link between these two Romantic movements, which dominated architecture in the city until the end of the Mandatory period. Already in the Ottoman period, there had been an interesting meeting between the German and English branches of the Protestant Church, and they became an important force in public architecture. Influenced by the revival of medieval architecture and aware of indigenous construction in Europe in the nineteenth century, German and British architects left behind a few buildings—the Schick Residence, the Dormition Abbey, and Saint John's Ophthalmic Hospital—representative of the historical phase that constituted the basis for the rise of the Romantic current in modern architecture. The Mandatory regime imported to Israel the ideals of the Arts and Crafts movement (originally rooted in the revival of medieval principles and an interest in local construction), and in the thirties the Jewish architects from central Europe brought the cycle to a close.

Modern Jerusalem architecture did, in fact, reflect the spiritual ferment that had begun in the eighteenth century and that was embodied in the Romantic movement. The city—a symbol of spirituality, universality, and timelessness—represented the deep essence of human existence, and served as a powerful focus of nationalist feelings. It was thus a perfect setting for the expression of Romantic ideas. In the face of the pure, primeval landscape, the individualist and decadent aspects of modern life were forgotten. An enthusiasm for up-to-date technology seemed equally out of place. "Spiritual development is more important than the technological revolution which dominates our lives," said Mendelsohn. Thus, the best Jerusalem architects and designers sought to interpret the secret of the locality: they were not content to understand the physical nature of the landscape, but also wished to express the spiritual values that lay behind it.

This was something that the Romantic movement had always

aspired to. The reaction to the materialist, utilitarian, secular, and rationalist modern world, first expressed in a flight to the Middle Ages, was eventually crystallized in the modern abstract idiom. Despite the cold, mechanical image associated with this idiom, it expresses the same Romantic principles one finds in the nineteenth century. Using this language, the architects and designers who arrived in Jerusalem in the 1930s tried to create a concentrated synthesis of matter and spirit, past and future. They thus attempted to achieve what Buber described as a unique connection between man, nation, and land,[54] and gave rise to the organic Jerusalem architectural language, traces of which survive today.

Bibliography

David Amiran, ed., *Urban Geography of Jerusalem* (New York: W. De Gruyter, 1973)

Nahman Avigad, *Discovering Jerusalem* (Nashville, Tenn.: Thomas Nelson Publishers, 1983)

Michael Avi-Yonah, *The Jews of Palestine: A Political History from the Bar Kokhba War to the Arab Conquest* (Oxford: Basil Blackwell, 1976)

Dan Bahat with Chaim T. Rubinstein, *The Illustrated Atlas of Jerusalem,* trans. Shlomo Ketko (New York: Simon and Schuster, 1990)

Yehoshua Ben-Arieh, *Jerusalem in the Nineteenth Century: The Old City* (New York: St. Martin's Press, 1984)

———, *The Rediscovery of the Holy Land in the Nineteenth Century* (Detroit: Wayne State University Press, 1979)

Meir Ben-Dov, *In the Shadow of the Temple: The Discovery of Ancient Jerusalem* (Jerusalem: Keter Publishing House, 1985)

H. H. Ben-Sasson, ed., *A History of the Jewish People* (Cambridge, Mass.: Harvard University Press, 1976)

Meron Benvenisti, *The Crusaders in the Holy Land* (Jerusalem: Israel Universities Press, 1970)

———, *Jerusalem: The Torn City* (Minneapolis: University of Minnesota Press, 1976)

———, *Conflicts and Contradictions* (New York: Villard, 1986)

Robert Blake, *Disraeli's Grand Tour: Benjamin Disraeli and the Holy Land, 1830–31* (New York: Oxford University Press, 1982)

Michael H. Burgoyne, *Mamluk Jerusalem* (London: World of Islam Festival Trust, 1987)

Henry Cattan, *Jerusalem* (London: Croom Helm, 1981)

Amnon Cohen, *Palestine in the Eighteenth Century: Pattern of Government and Administration* (Jerusalem: Magnes Press, 1973)

Charles Coüasnon, *The Church of the Holy Sepulchre in Jerusalem* (Oxford: Oxford University Press, 1974)

Amikam Elad, *Medieval Jerusalem and Islamic Worship: Holy Places, Ceremonies, Worship* (Leiden: E. J. Brill, 1995)

David Finnie, *Pioneers East: The Early American Experience in the Middle East* (Cambridge, Mass.: Harvard University Press, 1967)

Paula Fredriksen, *From Jesus to Christ: The Origins of Ancient Christianity* (New Haven: Yale University Press, 1988)

Hillel Geva, *Ancient Jerusalem Revealed* (Jerusalem: Israel Exploration Society, 1994)

Moshe A. Gil, *A History of Palestine, 634–1099* (Cambridge: Cambridge University Press, 1992)

Gad G. Gilbar, ed., *Ottoman Palestine 1800–1914: Studies in Economic and Social History* (Leiden: E. J. Brill, 1990)

S. D. Goitein, *A Mediterranean Society* (Berkeley: University of California Press, 1971)

Oleg Grabar, *The Shape of the Holy: Early Medieval Jerusalem* (Princeton, N.J.: Princeton University Press, 1996)

Miron Grindea, ed., *Jerusalem: The Holy City in Literature* (London: Kahn and Averill, 1981)

Menahem Haran, *Temples and Temple-Service in Ancient Israel* (Oxford: Clarendon Press, 1978)

G. R. Hawting and Abdul-Kader A. Shareef, eds., *New Approaches to the Qur'an* (London: Routledge, 1993)

Arthur Hertzberg, ed., *The Zionist Idea* (New York: Doubleday, 1959)

Albert Hourani, *A History of the Arab Peoples* (Cambridge, Mass.: Harvard University Press, 1991)

E. D. Hunt, *Holy Land Pilgrimage in the Later Roman Empire, A.D. 312–460* (Oxford: Clarendon Press, 1982)

Thomas A. Idinopulos, *Jerusalem Blessed, Jerusalem Cursed* (Chicago: Ivan R. Dee, 1991)

Kathleen M. Kenyon, *Digging Up Jerusalem* (London: Ernest Benn Ltd., 1974)

Walid Khalidi, ed., *From Haven to Conquest: Readings in Zionism and the Palestine Problem until 1948* (Washington, D.C.: Institute for Palestine Studies, 1987)

Teddy Kollek with Amos Kollek, *For Jerusalem: A Life* (Jerusalem: Steimatzky, 1978)

David Kroyanker, *Jerusalem Architecture* (New York: The Vendome Press, 1994)

Bianca Kühnel, *From the Earthly to the Heavenly Jerusalem: Representations of the Holy City in Christian Art of the First Millennium* (Rome: Herder, 1987)

Ruth Lapidoth and Moshe Hirsch, *The Jerusalem Question: Selected Documents* (Dordrecht: Martinus Nijhoff Publishers, 1994)

Walter Laqueur, *A History of Zionism* (New York: Holt, Rinehart and Winston, 1972)

Lee I. Levine, ed., *The Jerusalem Cathedra: Studies in the History, Archaeology, Geography, and Ethnography of the Land of Israel,* vols. 2 and 3 (Jerusalem: Yad Izhak Ben-Zvi Institute, 1982, 1983)

Benjamin Mazar, *The Mountain of the Lord* (New York: Doubleday, 1975)

Muhammad Muslih, *The Origins of Palestinian Nationalism* (New York: Columbia University Press, 1988)

———, *Toward Coexistence: An Analysis of the Resolutions of the Palestine National Council* (Washington, D.C.: The Institute for Palestine Studies, 1990)

Amos Oz, *Israel, Palestine and Peace: Essays* (New York: Harcourt Brace, 1995)

F. E. Peters, *Jerusalem: The Holy City in the Eyes of Chroniclers, Visitors, Pilgrims, and Prophets from the Days of Abraham to the Beginnings of Modern Times* (Princeton, N.J.: Princeton University Press, 1985)

———, *The Distant Shrine* (New York: AMS Press, 1993)

Joshua Prawer, *The Latin Kingdom of Jerusalem: European Colonialism in the Middle Ages* (London: Weidenfeld and Nicolson, 1972)

Abraham Rabinovich, *Jerusalem on Earth* (New York: The Free Press, 1988)

Myriam Rosen-Ayalon, *The Early Islamic Monuments of al-Haram al-Sharif,* Qedem 28 (Jerusalem: The Institute of Archaeology, Hebrew University, 1989)

Nitza Rosovsky, *Jerusalemwalks* (New York: Henry Holt, 1992)

Howard M. Sachar, *A History of Israel: From the Rise of Zionism to Our Time* (New York: Alfred A. Knopf, 1982)

E. P. Sanders, *The Historical Figure of Jesus* (London: Penguin Press, 1993)

Uziel Schmeltz, *Modern Jerusalem's Demographic Evolution* (Jerusalem: Institute for Contemporary Jewry, Hebrew University, 1987)

Neil A. Silberman, *Digging for God and Country: Exploration, Archaeology and the Secret Struggle for the Holy Land, 1799–1917* (New York: Alfred A. Knopf, 1982)

Leonard Silk, ed., *Retrievements: A Jerusalem Anthology* (Jerusalem: Keter Publishing House, 1977)

Yigal Shiloh, *Excavations at the City of David, I: 1978–1982,* Qedem 19 (Jerusalem: The Institute of Archaeology, Hebrew University, 1984)

Krister Stendahl, *Paul among Jews and Gentiles* (Philadelphia: Fortress Press, 1976)

Ephraim Stern, ed., *The New Encyclopaedia of Archaeological Excavations in the Holy Land* (London: Simon and Schuster, 1993)

Menahem Stern, ed., *Greek and Latin Writers on Jews and Judaism* (Jerusalem: Israel Academy, 1974–1984)

A. L. Tibawi, *British Interests in Palestine: 1800–1901* (London: Oxford University Press, 1961)

Geza Vermes, *The Religion of Jesus the Jew* (London: SCM Press, 1993)

Franklin Walker, *Irreverent Pilgrims: Melville, Browne, and Mark Twain in the Holy Land* (Seattle: University of Washington Press, 1974)

Robert L. Wilken, *The Land Called Holy* (New Haven: Yale University Press, 1992)

John Wilkinson, *Egeria's Travels* (London: SPCK, 1971)

———, *Jerusalem as Jesus Knew It: Archaeology as Evidence* (London: Thames and Hudson, 1978)

———, *Jerusalem Pilgrims before the Crusades* (Jerusalem: Ariel, 1977)

Yigael Yadin, ed., *Jerusalem Revealed: Archaeology in the Holy City, 1968–1974* (New Haven: Yale University Press, 1976)

Walter Zander, *Israel and the Holy Places of Christendom* (London: Weidenfeld and Nicolson, 1971).

Notes

1. The Inhabitants of Jerusalem

1. See Chapter 16, "The Image of the Holy City in Maps and Mapping." For the account of the Bordeaux pilgrim, see John Wilkinson, *Egeria's Travels in the Holy Land* (London: SPCK), pp. 153–163. For Arculf, as recorded by Adomnan, see John Wilkinson, *Jerusalem Pilgrims before the Crusades* (Warminster, England: Aris and Phillips, 1977), pp. 93–116.

2. Magen Broshi, "The Expansion of Jerusalem in the Reigns of Hezekiah and Manasseh," *Israel Exploration Journal* 24 (1974): 21–26.

3. For Herod's Temple, see Josephus, *Jewish Antiquities* XV, 11, 1–5, and *Jewish War* V, 5, 1.

4. Nahman Avigad, *Discovering Jerusalem* (Nashville: Thomas Nelson Publishers, 1980), pp. 95–120.

5. Magen Broshi, "Methodology of Population Estimates: The Roman Period as a Case Study," in Avraham Biran and Joseph Aviram, eds., *Biblical Archaeology Today, 1990: Proceedings of the Second International Congress on Biblical Archaeology* (Jerusalem: Israel Exploration Society, 1993), pp. 420–425.

6. F. E. Peters, *Jerusalem: The Holy City in the Eyes of Her Chroniclers, Visitors, Pilgrims, and Prophets from the Days of Abraham to the Beginnings of Modern Times* (Princeton, N.J.: Princeton University Press, 1985), p. 176.

7. Nasir-i Khusraw, *Nasir-i Khusraw: Diary of a Journey through Syria and Palestine,* vol. 4, trans. Guy Le Strange (London: Palestine Pilgrims' Text Society, 1893; reprint, New York: AMS Press, 1971), p. 24.

8. *The Itinerary of Benjamin of Tudela: Travels in the Middle Ages* (Malibu, Calif.: Joseph Simon Pangloss Press, 1987), p. 82.

9. John of Würzburg, *Description of the Holy Land (1160–1170)*, vol. 5, trans. Aubrey Stewart (London: Palestine Pilgrims' Text Society, 1896; reprint, New York: AMS Press, 1971), p. 41.

10. Magen Broshi, "Al-Malik Al-Mu'azzam 'Isa: He Who Reconstructed the Walls of Jerusalem Was Also Their Destroyer," in *Eretz Israel,* vol. 19 (Jerusalem: Israel Exploration Society, 1987), pp. 299–302 (in Hebrew).

11. Avraham Ya'ari, *Igrot Eretz Israel* (Ramat Gan: Masada, 1971), p. 85 (in Hebrew).

12. Guy Le Strange, *History of Jerusalem under the Moslems from A.D. 650 to 1500* (Boston: Houghton Mifflin, 1890; reprint, Beirut: Khayat, 1965).

13. Mamluks—literally, slaves—were brought up in special schools where they were trained to serve Egypt's military and political elite.

14. Ya'ari, *Igrot.* Fabri was a Dominican monk from Ulm, Germany, who journeyed to the Holy Land twice, around the years 1480–1483. His extensive descriptions were published in *The Wandering of Felix Fabri* (London: Palestine Pilgrims' Text Society, 1887–1897; reprint, New York: AMS Press, 1971), vols. 7–10.

15. Ya'ari, *Igrot,* p. 127.

16. See Amnon Cohen, "Demographic Changes in the Jewish Community of Jerusalem in the Sixteenth Century on the Basis of Turkish and Arabic Sources," in Amnon Cohen, ed., *Jerusalem in the Early Ottoman Period* (Jerusalem: Yad Izhak Ben-Zvi, 1979), p. 97 (in Hebrew).

17. Uziel Schmelz, "Population Characteristics in the Jerusalem and Hebron Regions at the Beginning of the Twentieth Century," *Cathedra* 36 (1985): 131–132 (in Hebrew).

18. Uziel Schmelz, *Modern Jerusalem's Demographic Evolution* (Jerusalem: Jerusalem Institute for Israel Studies, 1987), p. 28.

19. Ibid., p. 36.

2. The Holy Places

1. If the traditional (cf. Ps. 76:2) though unverifiable identification of Jerusalem with the Salem of Genesis (Gen. 14:18) holds, then the city had not only a king but also a priest of the "God Most High" in Abrahamic days.

2. See 2 Sam. 24:18 and 1 Chron. 21:18–22:1, where the events are spelled out in greater detail and with more sharply etched intent.

3. Joshua ordered that stones be collected and memorials built at the site of the Israelites' Jordan crossing and in the midst of the river itself, "and they

are there today" (Josh. 4:5–9). If that is authentically Jewish, the healing spring in Jerusalem whose waters are mysteriously moved (John 5:1–5) is redolent of a paganism that has an appeal powerful enough to survive into Jesus' day and beyond; A. Duprez, *Jésus et les Dieux Guérisseurs* (Paris: J. Gabalda, 1970), pp. 57–127, and Jack Finegan, *The Archeology of the New Testament,* rev. ed. (Princeton, N.J.: Princeton University Press, 1992), pp. 226–232. For the Christian exegetical debate on both the passage and the event, see W. D. Davies, *The Gospel and the Land: Early Christianity and Jewish Territorial Doctrine* (Berkeley: University of California Press, 1974), pp. 302–313. Siloam, too (cf. John 9:1–12), was likely a Jerusalem holy place associated with cures; Davies, *The Gospel and the Land,* pp. 314–315; Finegan, *Archeology,* pp. 190–192.

4. Still the object of prophetic fulminations as late as Jer. 44:18; Ezek. 20:39.

5. Joachim Jeremias, *Heiligengräber im Jesu Umwelt* (Göttingen: Vanderboeck and Ruprecht, 1958). Num. 19:11–22 appears to be directed against just such cults, and my colleague Baruch Levine finds a good deal of pre-Exilic evidence for grave cults in Israel and is inclined to date this particular piece of legislation to the era of the Return; Baruch Levine, *Numbers 1–20: A New Translation with Introduction and Commentary,* The Anchor Bible (New York: Doubleday, 1993), pp. 468–479.

6. The Pharisees did not surrender the notion of the presence of God, but they could conceive of it apart from the notion of place, a manner of thinking that did not diminish their devotion to the Temple nor, after its destruction, their desire to see it rebuilt; see Davies, *The Gospel and the Land,* pp. 189–190.

7. An early suggestion of the idea is in Ezek. 38:12, which refers, however, to Israel and not Jerusalem. But in Jubilees 8:19 the reference is precisely to Jerusalem (Mount Zion) "in the midst of the navel of the earth"; see Davies, *The Gospel and the Land,* pp. 6–10.

8. There is not a great deal of information on Jewish pilgrimage before the Exile, but the numbers swelled after the Return, and particularly when Herod constructed his magnificent edifice atop the mount. The most complete account of Jewish pilgrimage is found in Shmuel Safrai, *Die Wallfahrt im Zeitalter des Zweiten Tempels* (Neukirchen: Neukirchener Verlag, 1981).

9. There may be an echo of the debate surrounding the relaxation of the eating prescription in m. Pesahim 9:2.

10. M. Pesahim 7:9, 12 suggests that it was the walls of Jerusalem that constituted the legal boundary. However, the walls of the city underwent a number of major modifications between the Hasmoneans and the destruction of the Temple.

11. So, in addition to the other tannaitic evidence (S. Klein, "Das tannaitische Grenzverzichnis Palästinas," *Hebrew Union College Annual* 5 [1928]: 174–259), ll. 13–18 of the Hebrew inscription in the synagogue at Rehob; see J. Sussman, "The Inscription in the Synagogue at Rehob," in Lee I. Levine, ed., *Ancient Synagogues Revealed* (Jerusalem: The Israel Exploration Society, 1981), pp. 149, 152–153. On the full observance of the Law *only* in Eretz Israel, see W. D. Davies, *The Territorial Dimension of Judaism* (Berkeley: University of California Press, 1982), p. 39. Davies points out that fully one-third of the Mishnah is devoted to legislation regarding Eretz Israel (ibid., p. 36). Jerome (ca. 340–420 C.E.), who lived in Palestine and may have had his fill of rabbinic boasting about the Holy Land, *their* Holy Land, has some sarcastic remarks (*Letter* 129:4) about the geographical reality.

12. Jeremias, *Heiligengräber,* pp. 144–145; Georg Kretchmar in *Jerusalem Heiligtumtraditionen in alkirchlicher Zeit und frühislamischer Zeit* (Wiesbaden: Otto Harassowitz, 1987), pp. 67–68. On modern Muslim tomb cults in Palestine and the cult practices attached to them, see Tewfik Canaan, *Mohammedan Saints and Sanctuaries in Palestine* (London: Palestine Exploration Society, 1927), pp. 7–9, 46–53, 186–193.

13. Robert L. Wilken, *The Land Called Holy: Palestine in Christian History and Thought* (New Haven, Conn.: Yale University Press, 1992), pp. 108–109.

14. Ibid., p. 70.

15. Though there was a statue of Hadrian amid the ruins on the Temple Mount, none of the Christian pilgrims notes the existence of a temple there, or the later destruction of such. See F. E. Peters, *Jerusalem: The Holy City in the Eyes of Chroniclers, Visitors, Pilgrims, and Prophets from the Days of Abraham to the Beginning of Modern Times* (Princeton, N.J.: Princeton University Press, 1985), p. 130.

16. Eusebius, *Church History* 3:5–6.

17. There is a detailed discussion of her role in E. D. Hunt, *Holy Land Pilgrimage in the Later Roman Empire, A.D. 312–460* (Oxford: Oxford University Press, 1982), pp. 29–49.

18. For Constantine's work on and at the Jerusalem holy places, see Peters, *Jerusalem,* pp. 131–143, and Wilken, *The Land Called Holy,* pp. 85–100.

19. The open area of the forum covered what is today known as the Muristan, and much of it has reverted to what it was in Hadrian's day, a public marketplace. Hadrian built another forum just to the north of the temple area and covering some of what had formerly been the Fortress Antonia. The pavement of this Hadrianic forum, now under the Sisters of Sion convent, was for a long time erroneously identified as the *lithostratos,* the pavement of Pilate's judgment hall (John 19:13), and so the site of Jesus' scourging before his death; see P. Benoit, "Prétoire, Lithostraton et Gabbatha," *Revue Biblique* 59 (1952): 531–550.

20. It is difficult to imagine how the exact spot was identified, since the immmediate area of Golgotha had been leveled and overbuilt with one of Hadrian's temples. Perhaps local memory recalled where it stood with respect to the tomb, a site which could be *discovered*.

21. This was a current Roman architectural form with no religious associations—it served as royal audience hall and law court—adopted by Christians and Jews alike for their liturgical purposes. The shrine, on the other hand, was generally what it later was in Islam, a domed building, usually circular or octagonal, that surrounded and covered the enshrined site, which was often the grave of a martyr, one who had "witnessed" to the faith by his or her death; Richard Krautheimer, *Early Christian and Byzantine Architecture* (Baltimore: Penguin Books, 1965), pp. 20–21 (basilica), 30–32 (martyrium).

22. C. Coüasnon, *The Church of the Holy Sepulchre in Jerusalem* (Oxford: Oxford University Press, 1974); cf. Krautheimer, *Early Christian Architecture,* pp. 39–41.

23. Wilken, *The Land Called Holy,* pp. 81–82.

24. The swelling flood of Christian pilgrims, and their encouraging accounts of their experiences, can best be traced in John Wilkinson, *Jerusalem Pilgrims before the Crusades* (Jerusalem: Ariel, 1977); cf. John Wilkinson, "Christian Pilgrims in Jerusalem during the Byzantine Period," *Palestine Exploration Quarterly* 108 (1977): 75–101, in which the pilgrims' rituals at the various holy places are sketched.

25. G. T. Armstrong, "Imperial Church Building in the Holy Land in the Fourth Century," *The Biblical Archaeologist* 30 (1967): 90–102; G. T. Armstrong, "Fifth and Sixth Century Church Building in the Holy Land," *Greek Orthodox Theological Review* 14 (1969): 17–30; A. Ovadiah, *Corpus of Byzantine Churches in the Holy Land* (Bonn: Peter Hanstein Verlag, 1970).

26. Constantine had himself built a church at Mamre/Hebron, not to enshrine the patriarchs' graves at Machpelah, which Herod had already done on a grandiose scale, but to commemorate the place where Abraham offered hospitality to three strangers (Gen. 18:1–5), one of whom the Christian tradition was already identifying with the pre-Incarnation Christ. Later, in the sixth century, an anonymous pilgrim from Piacenza reported that Jews and Christians conducted simultaneous rituals there, though they were separated by a partition; Peters, *Jerusalem,* pp. 167–168.

27. Georg Kretschmar, "Festkalender und Memorialstätten in altkirchlicher Zeit," in Heribert Busse and Georg Kretschhmar, eds., *Jerusalem Heiligtumstraditionen in altkirchlicher und frühislamischer Zeit* (Wiesbaden: Otto Harrasowitz, 1987); John Baldovin, *The Urban Character of Christian Worship: The Origins, Development and Meaning of Stational Liturgy* (Rome: Pontificum Instituum Studiorum Orientalium, 1987).

28. Published and authoritatively glossed in M. Avi-Yonah, *The Madaba Mosaic Map with Introduction and Commentary* (Jerusalem: Israel Exploration Fund, 1954). J. T. Milik has supplied further topographical details from the literature of the early seventh century; "La topographie de Jérusalem vers la fin de l'époque byzantine," *Mélanges de l'Université Saint Joseph* 37 (1961): 127–189. The map was clearly intended for pilgrims, and its contemporary literary counterparts are two guidebooks to the Christian Holy Land, the anonymous *Brevarius* and the *Topography of the Holy Land*, attributed to an otherwise unknown Theodosius, the latter accompanied by maps in its original form; Peters, *Jerusalem*, pp. 154–158.

29. The designation "Church of the Holy Sepulchre" is properly Western and became current there only after the Crusades.

30. If we except the two, poorly documented attempts on the part of the Jews to rebuild it—or at least to build an altar on the Temple Mount—during two auspicious but fleeting moments, under the Emperor Julian in 361 CE and under the Persians sometime around 616 CE; see Peters, *Jerusalem*, pp. 145–147, 173.

31. The chief accounts have been edited by Gerard Garitte, *Expugnatio Hierosolymae A.D. 614* (Louvain: Corpus Scriptorum Orientalium Christianorum, 1973), and Frederick Conybeare, "Antiochus Strategus' Account of the Sack of Jerusalem in 614 A.D.," *English Historical Review* 25 (1910): 502–517. There are excerpts in Peters, *Jerusalem*, pp. 170–173.

32. Peters, *Jerusalem*, pp. 137–139.

33. Excerpts from Egeria's account in ibid., pp. 149–150.

34. Ibid., pp. 173–174. Both the chronology and the circumstances of the restoration are confused in the sources; Anatole Frolow, "La Vraie Croix et les Expéditions d'Heraclius en Perse," in *Mélanges Martin Jugie* (Paris: Institut Français des Études Byzantines, 1953), pp. 88–105.

35. On the significance of the event, see Wilken, *The Land Called Holy*, pp. 224–226, and on the legend, see Anatole Frolow, *La Relique de la Vraie Croix: Recherches sur le Développement d'un cult* (Paris: Institut Français des Études Byzantines, 1961).

36. Tabari, *Annals* 1:1279–1280.

37. Ibn Hisham 263–267; excerpts in Peters, *Jerusalem*, pp. 182–185. Cf. F. E. Peters, *Muhammad and the Origins of Islam* (Albany: State University of New York Press, 1994), pp. 144–147, and Heribert Busse, "Jerusalem in the Story of Muhammad's Night Journey and Ascension," *Jerusalem Studies in Arabic and Islam* 14 (1991): 1–40.

38. Heribert Busse, "Omar's Image as the Conqueror of Jerusalem," *Jerusalem Studies in Arabic and Islam* 8 (1986): 149–168.

39. Heribert Busse, "Omar b. al-Khattab in Jerusalem," *Jerusalem Studies in Arabic and Islam* 5 (1984): 93–119, especially 79–86.

40. Busse, "Omar b. Kattab," pp. 86–94. There is an eyewitness testimony to the original mosque from the Christian pilgrim Arculf, who was in the city in 680 CE; Peters, *Jerusalem,* pp. 195–196.

41. For a contemporary view of the Christian holy places in Jerusalem under early Muslim sovereignty, see the documents analyzed by J. T. Milik, "Sanctuaires chrétiens de Jérusalem a l'époque arabe (vii–x s.)," *Revue Biblique* 67 (1960): 354–367, 550–586.

42. J. Mann, *Texts and Studies in Jewish History and Literature,* vol. 1 (Cincinatti: Hebrew Union College Press, 1931), pp. 18, 20.

43. Tabari, *Annals* 1. 2405, for example; cf. Antoine Fattal, *Le Statut Légal des non-Musulmans en Pays de l'Islam* (Beirut: Imprimerie Catholique, 1958), pp. 45–47.

44. It is not impossible that the building was conceived of and planned earlier, perhaps much earlier; see F. E. Peters, "Who Built the Dome of the Rock?" *Graeco-Arabica* 2 (1983): 119–138.

45. The problem and its solutions are reviewed by Heribert Busse, "Tempel, Grabeskirche und *haram as-sharif:* Drei Heiligtümer und ihre gegenseitigen Beziehungen in Legende und Wirklichkeit," in Heribert Busse and Georg Kretschmar, eds., *Jerusalem Heiligtumstraditionen in altkirchlicher und frühislamischer Zeit* (Wiesbaden: Otto Harrasowitz, 1987), pp. 1–6. There are excerpts from the Muslim sources in Peters, *Jerusalem,* pp. 197–199.

46. Ignaz Goldizer, *Muslim Studies,* ed. S. M. Stern, vol. 1 (London: George Allen and Unwin, 1971), pp. 44–45; rebutted by S. D. Goitein, "The Historical Background of the Dome of the Rock," *Journal of the American Oriental Society* 70 (1950): 104–108.

47. Oleg Grabar, "The Omayyad Dome of the Rock in Jerusalem," *Ars Orientalis* 3 (1959): 33–56. So too Busse in "Drei Heilgtümer," who further wishes to link the Dome more closely with Abd al-Malik's son Walid's (r. 705–715) elaborate reconstruction of Umar's prototype of the Aqsa Mosque.

48. Peters, *Jerusalem,* pp. 143.

49. Zev Vilnay, *The Sacred Land,* vol. 1, *Legends of Jerusalem* (Philadelphia: Jewish Publication Society of America, 1973), pp. 5–36; cf. Heribert Busse, "The Sanctity of Jerusalem in Islam," *Judaism* 17 (1968): 455–457.

50. Peters, *Jerusalem,* pp. 217–222.

51. E. Joranson, "The Alleged Frankish Protectorate in Jerusalem," *American Historical Review* 32 (1927): 241–261; S. D. Goitein, "Jerusalem in the Arab Period (638–1099)," in Lee I. Levine, ed., *The Jerusalem Cathedra,* vol. 2 (Jerusalem: Yad Izhak Ben-Zvi; Detroit: Wayne State University Press, 1982), pp. 181–182.

52. Moshe Gil, "Aliya and Pilgrimage in the Early Arab Period (634–1009)," in *The Jerusalem Cathedra,* vol. 3 (1983), 162–191; Avraham Grossman, "Aliya in the Seventh and Eighth Centuries," ibid., pp. 173–187.

53. Gil, "Aliya and Pilgrimage," p. 169, cites a letter referring back to the first Jewish return to the city in the Muslim era and asserting, on the basis of Ezekiel 11:23, that God's presence, the Shechinah, now rested on the Mount of Olives.

54. Ibid., pp. 168–170, with material from the Cairo Geniza.

55. E. Joranson, "The Great German Pilgrimage of 1064–1065," in L. J. Paetow, ed., *The Crusades and Other Essays Presented to Dana C. Monro* (New York: F. S. Crofts, 1928), pp. 3–43.

56. Peters, *Jerusalem*, p. 259.

57. According to Ibn al-Qalanisi, what was attracting so many pilgrims to Jerusalem and what particularly irked al-Hakim was the repetition, on every Holy Saturday, of the "Descent of the Fire," a spectacular display of God's miraculous power before assembled crowds, Christian and Muslim, inside the darkened church. This scheduled miracle, whereby fire descended to within the tomb of Christ, had a long and not always happy history until growing skepticism and a concern for public safety demoted it from a prodigy to a mere occasion late in the nineteenth century; Peters, *Jerusalem*, pp. 261–267, 523–524, 571–578.

58. William of Tyre, *A History of Deeds Done beyond the Sea*, trans. E. A. Babcock and A. C. Krey, vol. 1 (New York: Columbia University Press, 1942), pp. 69–70. Absent the Crusaders' belfry, their new external entry to Golgotha, and some decorative work, it is the same building that stands there today. For a description of it by a Muslim visitor in 1047, see Peters, *Jerusalem*, pp. 267–268, and for one by a Christian pilgrim in 1106, see ibid., pp. 311–314.

59. William of Tyre, *History*, vol. 1, pp. 405–406; on the later history of the quarter, see Peters, *Jerusalem*, pp. 271, 393, 396, 500, 539, 566–567, 586; Yehoshua Ben-Arieh, *Jerusalem in the Nineteenth Century: The Old City* (New York: St. Martin's Press, 1984), pp. 219–238; on the Armenian quarter in the southeast quadrant, ibid., pp. 243–248.

60. William of Tyre, *History*, vol. 1, pp. 79–80.

61. The Byzantines had earlier launched a series of campaigns southward across the Anatolian frontier against the Fatimids in Palestine, and in 975 Emperor John Tzimisces managed to take Damascus and perhaps even parts of Galilee. There was no doubt that this was a holy war, or what Tzimisces's next objective would be, "the Holy City of Jerusalem and the Holy Places of God"; Peters, *Jerusalem*, pp. 242–244.

62. A. C. Krey, *The First Crusade: The Accounts of Eye-Witnesses and Paricipants* (Princeton, N.J.: Princeton University Press, 1921), pp. 30–32.

63. Benjamin of Tudela, a Jewish visitor to Palestine in 1170, makes some interesting remarks about Hebron. "There is a great church called St.

Abram [surely Herod's building], and this was a Jewish place of worship at the time of the Muhammadan rule, but the Gentiles [that is, the Crusaders] have erected there six tombs, respectively those of Abraham and Sarah, Isaac and Rebecca, Jacob and Leah" (Benjamin of Tudela, *Travels* 26).

64. Peters, *Jerusalem,* pp. 316–324.

65. The original Mount Zion was, of course, the southeast spur of Jerusalem's eastern hill, where David's city was, but in the course of time the designation got switched to the *southwestern* spur of the Upper City, and with it, inevitably, some of the Davidic associations, as shall be shown. There had been a Byzantine church there, but it was destroyed in the Persian invasion of 614; rebuilt after Heraclius' reconquest, it was looted and burned by rampaging Beduins in 966. On the reports, chiefly literary, about the Crusader church, see Finegan, *Archeology,* pp. 239–240.

66. Ibid., p. 230. For the effects of the new Christian focus on the Temple Mount, see "Between Mount Moriah and the Holy Sepulchre: The Changing Traditions of the Temple Mount in the Central Middle Ages," *Traditio* 40 (1984): 175–195. For a complete survey of Crusader work on the holy places, see T. S. R. Boase, "Ecclesiastical Art in the Crusader States in Palestine and Syria, Part A: Architecture and Sculpture" in H. W. Hazard, ed., *The Art and Architecture of the Crusader States* (Madison: University of Wisconsin Press, 1977), pp. 69–116; and, more specifically, B. Hamilton, "The Holy Places of Jerusalem in the Twelfth Century," *Studies in Church History* 14 (1977): 105–116.

67. Peters, *Jerusalem,* pp. 342–343, from the Muslim historian Imad al-Din. According to Ibn al-Athir, when Jerusalem was taken and the ransomed Christians were permitted to leave the city, the Patriarch departed "with the treasures from the Dome of the Rock, the Masjid al-Aqsa, and the Church of the Resurrection." The latter presumably included the relics of the True Cross; Peters, *Jerusalem,* p. 346.

68. Emanuel Sivan, "The Beginnings of the Fada'il al-Quds Literature," *Israel Oriental Studies* 1 (1971): 263–271; I. Hasson, "Muslim Literature in Praise of Jerusalem," in *The Jerusalem Cathedra,* vol. 1 (1981), pp. 168–184.

69. Emanuel Sivan, *L'Islam et la Croisade: Idéologie et propagande dans les réactions musulmans aux Croisades* (Paris: Librairie d'Amérique et d'Orient, 1968).

70. M. Kister, "'You shall only set out for three mosques': A Study of an Early Tradition," *Le Museon* 82 (1969): 173–196; cf. Peters, *Jerusalem,* pp. 373–375, and, for one Muslim conservative who would have none of the new exaltation of Jerusalem, ibid., pp. 375–378.

71. Not so completely that the clergy attached to the place could not cut off

pieces and send them to Constantinople and Sicily, or else sell them to pilgrims "for their weight in gold"; Peters, *Jerusalem,* p. 350.

72. On some other of his constructions in Jerusalem, chiefly in the vicinity of the Holy Sepulchre, see Peters, *Jerusalem,* pp. 356–357.

73. In Arabic, *kanisat al-qiyama.* The Muslims, who had theological problems with Jesus' death (Koran 4:157–158), and thus even greater ones with his resurrection, turned *"qiyama"* (resurrection) into *"qumama"* (dung heap), and so it is generally referred to in their sources.

74. Imad al-Din, cited in Peters, *Jerusalem,* p. 352.

75. Excerpts from later Christian visitors' accounts in Peters, *Jerusalem,* 353–356. Nur al-Din had built many more in Damascus, and Saladin did the same in Cairo, the former Fatimid capital.

76. Mecca was one of the less attractive alternatives, but Mecca, too, profited from their pious philanthropy; see David Ayalon, "Discharges from Service, Banishment and Imprisonment in Mamluk Society," *Israel Oriental Studies* 2 (1972): 324–329.

77. On the Mamluk contribution to Jerusalem, see J. Drory, "Jerusalem during the Mamluk Period," in *The Jerusalem Cathedra,* vol. 1 (1981), pp. 190–214, and Michael H. Burgoyne, "The Architectural Developments of the Haram in Jerusalem under the Bahri Mamluks," in *The Third International Conference on Bilad al-Sham, 1980* (Amman: University of Jordan, 1983), pp. 65–102.

78. See Ibn Khaldun's glowing approbation in his *Muqaddimah,* trans. Franz Rozenthal, vol. 2 (Princeton, N.J.: Princeton University Press, 1967), pp. 435–436 and n. 68.

79. On how the *waqfs* functioned in Jerusalem and Hebron, see Peters, *Jerusalem,* pp. 382–388.

80. But one notable instance was in Jerusalem itself, the dwellings of the so-called Moroccan quarter running up to the southwest corner of Herod's platform; Peters, *Jerusalem,* pp. 357–359, 394–396.

81. The Mamluk period is particularly rich in Christian and Jewish pilgrim accounts of the Jerusalem holy places, and for the first time they can be complemented with an equally detailed narrative from a contemporary Muslim historian, Mujir al-Din (d. ca. 1520–21), who was the chief justice of Jerusalem; see the collection of texts in Peters, *Jerusalem,* pp. 388–478, and E. N. Adler, *Jewish Travelers: A Treasury of Travelogues from Nine Centuries,* 2nd ed. (New York: Harmon Books, 1966).

82. See the texts of Felix Fabri amd Ludolph von Suchem cited in Peters, *Jerusalem,* pp. 421–422; and for the papal bull *Gratias agimus,* D. Baldi, *Enchiridion locorum sanctorum,* rev. ed. (Jerusalem: Franciscan Printing Press, 1982), pp. 509–510. Early Protestant reactions to their Franciscan

custodians is recorded in Peters, *Jerusalem,* pp. 509–515. The *Custodia* was eventually moved from the Mount Zion church, which the Mamluks confiscated in 1453, to the Church of St. Savior in the safer confines of the Christian Quarter.

83. Adler, *Travelogues,* pp. 189–199, 239–240; on the Jewish Quarter, see Amnon Cohen, *Jewish Life under Islam: Jerusalem in the Sixteenth Century* (Cambridge, Mass.: Harvard University Press, 1984), pp. 17–20, 206–209, and, for the nineteenth century, Ben-Arieh, *Jerusalem in the Nineteenth Century,* pp. 315–332, 376–389.

84. Between 1630 and 1637, for example, control of the sites inside the Holy Sepulchre changed hands no less than six times; Walter Zander, *Israel and the Holy Places of Christendom* (London: Weidenfeld and Nicolson, 1971), p. 44.

85. For the Greeks, see Speros Vryonis, "The History of the Greek Patriarchate of Jerusalem as Reflected in Codex Patriarchicus No. 428, 1517–1805," in *The Third International Conference on Bilad al-Sham: Palestine 19–24 April 1980* (Amman: University of Jordan, 1983), pp. 155–176; for the Armenians, see Avedis K. Sanjian, "The Armenians and the Holy Places in Jerusalem," ibid., pp. 127–144. The eventual Protestant holy place in Jerusalem is the so-called Garden Tomb, an attractive but not terribly authentic alternative to the Holy Sepulchre north of the city wall, largely the nineteenth-century creation of General Charles George Gordon, the British victim-hero of Khartoum and a not always inspired amateur of *res biblicae;* see Neil Asher Silberman, *Digging for God and Country: Exploration, Archaeology and the Secret Struggle for the Holy Land* (New York: Knopf, 1982), pp. 151–153.

86. Zander, *Holy Places,* pp. 53–54; text, ibid., pp. 178–180. The precise status quo ante in question was that of the decree of 1757.

87. They are enumerated in Elihu Lauterpacht, *Jerusalem and the Holy Places* (London: Anglo-Israel Association, 1968), p. 5 n.1.

88. Benvenisti, *Jerusalem,* p. 75.

89. Ibid., pp. 287–289.

90. Peters, *Jerusalem,* pp. 225–227, citing Lamentations Rabbah 1:31.

91. Moshe Gil, "Aliya and Pilgrimage in the Early Arab Period (634–1009)," in *The Jerusalem Cathedra,* vol. 3 (1983), p. 169.

92. Peters, *Jerusalem,* pp. 527–529.

93. Sir Moses Montefiore offered to buy the place outright; Meir Ben-Dov et al., *The Western Wall* (Jerusalem: The Ministry of Defense Publishing House, 1983), pp. 125–126.

94. Benvenisti, *Jerusalem,* p. 65; for the architecture and contemporary descriptions, see Ben-Dov et al., *The Western Wall,* pp. 39–78.

95. On the Wall controversies in the nineteenth century, see Ben-Dov et al.,

The Western Wall, pp. 121–138, and Ben-Arieh, *Jerusalem in the Nineteenth Century,* pp. 371–375

96. The entire controversy is spelled out in detail in Benvenisti, *Jerusalem,* pp. 305–321.

97. Zander, *Holy Places,* p. 102.

3. Jerusalem in Jewish Spirituality

1. They are called in this ancient treatise *sefirot,* an original term for numerals; this term was used, a thousand years later, by the kabbalists to indicate their system of divine emanations. In the *Sefer Yezira,* however, this term represents mainly cosmological aspects rather than divine powers. In one section it may have been identified with the holy beasts in Ezekiel's vision (1:7).

2. On the *Sefer Yezira,* see G. Scholem, *Origins of the Kabbalah,* trans. A. Arkush, ed. R. J. Zwi Werblowsky (Princeton, N.J.: Princeton University Press, 1986), pp. 24–35; J. Dan, "The Language of Creation and Its Grammar," in *Festschrift für Carsten Colpe* (Berlin: Walter de Gruyter, 1994).

3. See J. Dan, *The Revelation of the Secret of the World and the Beginning of Jewish Mysticism in Late Antiquity* (Providence, R.I.: Brown University Press, 1992).

4. Two general descriptions of this mystical literature have been published recently: P. Schaefer, *The Hidden and Manifest God* (Albany: State University of New York Press, 1992); and J. Dan, *The Ancient Jewish Mysticism* (Tel Aviv: Ministry of Defense, 1993). Both include detailed bibliographies.

5. See Ira Chernus, "The Pilgrimage to the Merkavah: An Interpretation of Early Jewish Mysticism," in J. Dan, ed., *Proceedings of the First International Conference on the History of Jewish Mysticism: Early Jewish Mysticism,* Jerusalem Studies in Jewish Thought 6, no. 1–2 (Jerusalem: n.p., 1987), pp. 1–36 (English section).

6. This has been demonstrated in great detail by Rachel Elior in a series of studies. See, for instance, "Mysticism, Magic and Angelology: The Perception of Angels in Hekhalot Literature," *Jewish Studies Quarterly* 1 (1993–94): 1–53.

7. Compare Ps. 48:3.

8. G. Scholem, in his first study of the subject, emphasized the monarchic aspects of the pictures drawn by the Hekhalot mystics. See his *Major Trends in Jewish Mysticism,* 2nd ed. (New York: Schocken Books, 1954), pp. 40–78. This is contrary to the images governing gnostic mysticism; gnostic myths do not include this element, nor do they emphasize the mystic's position as a servant and slave.

9. Concerning the role of this biblical text in the evolvement of ancient mysticism, see S. Lieberman, "Mishnat Shir ha-Shirim," published as an appendix to G. Scholem, *Jewish Gnosticism, Merkabah Mysticism and Talmudic Tradition*, 2nd ed. (New York: The Jewish Theological Seminary, 1965), pp. 118–126; G. Scholem, *On the Mystical Shape of the Godhead: Basic Concepts of the Kabbalah*, trans. Joachim Neugroschel (New York: Schocken Books, 1992), pp. 20–37. Scholem and Lieberman discuss mainly the image of God in Hekhalot mysticism, the *Shiur Komah*, which is based on the Song of Songs, but the conclusions relate to other aspects as well. Compare B. McGinn, *The Foundations of Mysticism* (New York: Crossroad, 1991), pp. 118–127 and *passim*.

10. The text was often quoted in medieval literature in mystical and utopian contexts. See, for instance, ms. Oxford 1567, the Bodleian Library, pp. 114–116. The fact that the Hekhalot mystics emphasized the Jerusalem-Temple aspect of their experiences is evident from their constant repetition of the formula of the Kedushah, derived from Isaiah's vision (ch. 6) in the Temple in Jerusalem, whereas the formulas of the regular prayer that are not inherently connected to the experience of the Temple are relatively marginal (compare, for instance, their neglect of the Shema Yisrael prayer).

11. Compare also I. Gruenwald, *From Apocalypticism to Gnosticism* (Frankfurt: P. Lang, 1988), pp. 125–144.

12. Bavli Berakhot 7a.

13. See J. Dan, "The Concept of History in Hekhalot Mysticism," in J. Dan, ed., *Binah*, vol. 2, Studies in Jewish History (New York: Praeger, 1989), pp. 47–58.

14. This text is known as the Sar Torah, often appended to Hekhalot Rabbati in manuscripts and printed editions. See J. Dan, "The Theophany of the Prince of the Torah," *Jerusalem Studies in Jewish Folklore* 13–14 (1992): 127–157.

15. Bavli Makot 24a.

16. P. Schaefer, *Synopse zur Hekhalot-Literatur* (Tübingen: Mohr [Siebeck], 1981), pp. 142–158, 172–182, and R. Elior's edition of the text in *Jerusalem Studies in Jewish Thought, Supplement 1* (1982). See below, note 18.

17. Sefer Zerubavel was published in a scholarly edition by Yehudah Even-Samuel Kaufman in his *Midreshey Geulah* (Jerusalem: The Bialik Institute, 1954), pp. 55–88; compare Dan, *Ancient Jewish Mysticism*, pp. 134–143.

18. An unusual structure of this combination is to be found in the Sar Torah narrative, in which individual and communal elements are interwoven together. The divine revelation in the Temple also includes personal advantages to the mystics, and the visionary new era that is beginning with the mystical experience is one in which individual and national aspects are

united. The bizarre element in this picture is that this utopian narrative actually relates to the distant past—the building of the Second Temple by Zerubavel; the story is told several centuries after that Temple has been destroyed. The mystical unification of past, present, and future is clearly evident in this text.

19. Talmudic-midrashic eschatology is almost exclusively national and utopian, relegating salvation to the next world, the world that is to follow after this world has been destroyed. Only in the Middle Ages did the concept of a celestial, parallel world in which the souls of the righteous are rewarded immediately after their death become dominant in Jewish thought, relegating the apocalyptic, messianic salvation to a secondary position. Hebrew mystical speculations during late antiquity served as the main expression of the need for immediate spiritual redemption.

20. A. Aptowitzer, "Beit ha-Mikedash shel Ma'allah al pi ha-Agadah," *Tarbiz* 2 (1931): 137–153, 257–287. The author tried to show that this belief can be found in biblical prophecy, a concept that is very difficult to accept. The detailed study by Avigdor Aptowitzer of this problem, which presented hundreds of Jewish and Christian sources relevant to the development of this idea, has not been updated, and many questions remain unsolved.

21. *Tanhuma,* Buber edition, Nassa par. 19, and see Aptowitzer, "Beit ha-Mikedash," pp. 137–138 and notes there.

22. *De spec. leg. I,* ed. L. Cohen, V 17, par. 66, and see Aptowitzer, "Beit ha-Mikedash," 139–140, n. 1, 6–7.

23. *De somniis,* Cohen III, 251.

24. Several studies have been dedicated to the history and development of this legend in antiquity and in the Middle Ages. See especially Joseph Heinemann and J. Dan, "The Legend of David and the Rock in the Literature of the Ashkenazi Hasidim," *Sinai* 74 (1974): 239–241.

25. The concept of *gilgul mehilot,* belief in which became universal in Judaism, actually indicates the existence of a network of underground caves leading from every place to Jerusalem; these will allow the dead, in messianic times, to reach Jerusalem and be resurrected there.

26. Fourth Ezra, ch. 10, 29–54, and see Aptowitzer, "Beit ha-Mikedash," pp. 267–268.

27. Thus, for instance, the sixteenth-century mystic Rabbi Isaac Luria perceived her in a vision. See M. Benayahu, *Toledot ha-Ari* (Jerusalem: Ben Zui Institute, 1971), pp. 129–136.

28. Despite this, it was Rabbi Judah ha-Levi, a product of Jewish rationalistic culture (though in opposition to various elements in it), who gave the most moving expression of a love of Jerusalem in his poetry, and he died while on his way to the city. See E. Schweid, *Homeland and Promised Land* (Tel Aviv: Am Oved, 1979).

29. This was written following the destruction of the Crusader kingdom of Jerusalem in 1187; the short-lived kingdom remains, to this very day, the only case in three thousand years of history in which Jerusalem served as the capital of a non-Jewish political entity. Nachmanides expressed his attitude by immigrating to Jerusalem. See M. Idel, "Some Conception of the Land of Israel in Medieval Jewish Thought," in R. Link-Salinger, ed., *A Straight Path, Studies in Medieval Philosophy and Culture: Essays in Honor of Arthur Hyman* (Washington, D.C.: Catholic University of America Press, 1988), pp. 129–133.

30. The first kabbalistic messianic treatises were written by Rabbi Isaac ben Jacob ha-Cohen of Castile in the second half of the thirteenth century, and despite the intense mythical nature of his apocalyptic visions, Jerusalem does not play a major part. See J. Dan, "The Beginning of Messianic Myth in Thirteenth-Century Kabbalah," in R. Dán, ed., *Occident and Orient: A Tribute to the Memory of A. Scheiber* (Budapest and Leiden: Brill, 1988), pp. 57–68.

31. Margulioth edition (Jerusalem: Rav Kook Institute, 1953), par. 143. The ancient traditions usually spoke about the celestial city or the celestial temple; the concept of a celestial country is rare in ancient sources, though it is implied in many contexts.

32. On the *Zohar* and its author, see Scholem, *Major Trends in Jewish Mysticism*, pp. 156–204; I. Tishby, *The Wisdom of the Zohar*, trans. D. Goldstein, vol. 1 (Oxford: Oxford University Press, 1989), pp. 1–96; and compare Y. Liebes, *Studies in the Zohar* (Albany: State University of New York Press, 1992).

33. *Zohar* vol. I, folio 186a. Translation in Tishby, *Wisdom of the Zohar*, vol. 1, p. 362. The *Zohar* was written in Aramaic; Tishby translated a large selection of zoharic passages into Hebrew in his monumental *Mishnat ha-Zohar* (Jerusalem: The Bialik Institute, 1949–1961); it was translated into English as *The Wisdom of the Zohar.*

34. Tishby, *Wisdom of the Zohar*, vol. 1, p. 363.

35. I am using here the traditional term "symbolism," which has been central in the scholarly study of the Kabbalah. But the term does not express the true relationship between the symbol and the symbolized. The earthly Jerusalem, in this case, is not the "symbol" and the definition, and the Shechinah the symbolized—nor vice versa. The relationship is one of intrinsic unity between these entities, a mystical metalinguistic concept for which the term "symbolism" is manifestly inadequate. See J. Dan, *The Language of the Mystics* (forthcoming). There may be an interesting parallel between the convergence of the physical and the mystical in the zoharic myth and the convergence of Jerusalem as a geographic-political entity and the spiritual concept of the city in Christianity in the Crusading movement, which emerged as a political force after a millennium in which the spiritual

aspect was dominant. This relationship is the opposite of an allegorical one, in which one level serves as a substitute for another; rather, this kind of symbolism enhances the importance of and the dedication to both levels.

36. The beginning of this process is to be found in *Sefer ha-Bahir*. Several passages are dedicated to the discussion of the sacrifice, which is interpreted as the process of uniting the mystic with God.

37. A comprehensive selection of passages relating to this subject is included in Tishby, *Wisdom of the Zohar*, vol. 3, pp. 867–940. See also R. Patai, *Man and Temple in Ancient Jewish Myth and Ritual* (London: 1947).

38. Zohar Hadash, Midrash Ekhah 92c–92d; Tishby, *Wisdom of the Zohar*, vol. 3, p. 877; and compare Song of Songs 2:6.

39. This is not just a three-way drama but a four-way one, because the evil powers, especially the figure of Samael, the arch-devil in zoharic mythology, takes part in it. The desolation of Jerusalem and the exile of the people of Israel are often attributed to the machinations of the devil, which are symbolically depicted as the erotic designs of Samael concerning the *Shechinah*. Samael is represented in every individual, in his evil drives and material existence.

40. A selection of his apocalyptic treatises has been published by G. Scholem, in *Kiryat Sefer* 2 (1925): 101–141, 269–273; and *Kiryat Sefer* 7 (1931): 149–165, 440–456.

41. This period in the history of Jewish mysticism has been studied intensively. See, for instance, Scholem, *Major Trends in Jewish Mysticism*, pp. 244–286; R. I. Zwi Werblowsky, *Rabbi Joseph Karo: Lawyer and Mystic* (Philadelphia: Jewish Publications Society, 1973); R. Elior and Y. Liebes, eds., *Proceedings of the Fourth International Conference on the History of Jewish Mysticism*, Jerusalem Studies in Jewish Thought, vol. 10 (Jerusalem, 1991).

42. G. Scholem, *Sabbatai Sevi: The Mystical Messiah*, trans. R. J. Zwi Werblowsky (Princeton, N.J.: Princeton University Press, 1973), index s.v.

43. Many of them died in the first few months in a plague; see G. Scholem, *Major Trends in Jewish Mysticism*, p. 331.

44. According to Hasidic legend, the founder of the movement, Rabbi Israel Ba'al Shem Tov (known by the acronym Besht), tried to immigrate to Jerusalem but had to return after reaching Constantinople. Between 1764 and 1777 several groups of his disciples made that journey, and some of them established communities in northern Israel. In 1798 his grandson, Rabbi Nachman of Bratzlav, spent a year in Eretz Yisrael. The Besht's brother-in-law, Rabbi Gershon of Kutow, settled in Jerusalem.

45. R. Shatz, *Hasidism as Mysticism* (Princeton, N.J.: Princeton University Press, 1993; original Hebrew ed., Jerusalem: Magnes Press, 1964), *passim*. Compare also Idel, "The Land of Israel," pp. 136–141.

46. The most paradoxical statement is that which turns upside down the

talmudic statement (Bavli Ketubot 110b), "He who dwells abroad is like one who has no God, and he who dwells in the Land of Israel is like someone who has a God"; the Hasidic text explains (as shown by R. Shatz) that he who dwells abroad looks like someone who has no God, but really he has, while he who dwells in the Land of Israel looks like someone who has a God, but really he has not.

47. This statement has been misunderstood, and was presented as a Zionist slogan in Israel. It was a part of a deliberate attempt carried out by orthodox Zionists in Israel in the middle of this century to portray Hasidism as a Zionist movement.

48. Following the verse *"Zaddik yesod olam"* (the Righteous is an everlasting foundation) in Proverbs 10:25.

49. It should be noted, however, that the messianic enthusiasm that engulfed Habad in the last two decades included a reunification of the spiritual and the earthly Jerusalem; the first event that, according to their belief, should mark the beginning of the messianic era was believed to be the Zaddik's leaving his Brooklyn home and fixing his residence in the Land of Israel. Throughout Jewish history, the bond between Jerusalem and messianic redemption has never been broken.

4. The Holy City in Christian Thought

1. On Jesus of Nazareth in his historical setting, see most recently E. P. Sanders, *The Historical Figure of Jesus* (Harmondsworth, England: 1993); Geza Vermes, *Jesus the Jew* (Philadelphia: 1981) and *The Religion of Jesus the Jew* (Philadelphia: 1993). Arguing for a completely different interpretation than the one advanced here: J. D. Crossan, *Jesus: A Revolutionary Biography* (New York: 1994). On Jesus and the evolution of his movement, see Paula Fredriksen, *From Jesus to Christ: The Origins of the New Testament Images of Jesus* (New Haven, Conn.: 1988).

2. Mark, perhaps the earliest Gospel, never directly attributes the title "christos" (Greek for "messiah") to Jesus until the moment of high drama before the high priest, during the trial that ultimately leads to Pilate, and death (14:61–62; cf. 8:27–30). Paul, some twenty years after the crucifixion, used "christos" virtually as Jesus' last name, but never develops the idea theologically: his chief designations are "lord" and "son." The strongest evidence that *somebody* thought Jesus had made a messianic claim is the way he died.

3. For a reconstruction of this earliest Christian proclamation, see Fredriksen, *From Jesus to Christ,* pp. 133–56.

4. This position was consistent with an articulate tradition within Jewish apocalyptic thought: at the End, when God established his Kingdom, Israel

was to be gathered in from Exile, and the nations would voluntarily aban-
don or destroy their idols; they too would participate in the Kingdom, but
as Gentiles. Cf. Isa 2:2–4; Tobit 13:11; Sibylline Oracle 3:715–724; the second
paragraph of the synagogue prayer the *Alenu,* still part of the modern
service. The original (Jewish-) Christian community's policy of receiving
Gentiles without demanding conversion (and, in the instance of males,
circumcision) is thus a measure of ancient Christianity's roots in Jewish
apocalyptic expectation. For a fuller description of this tradition, and analysis of its role in earliest Christianity, see Fredriksen, *From Jesus to Christ,*
pp. 149–176.

5. On Paul and the later misreadings of him, see esp. Krister Stendahl, *Paul
among the Jews and Gentiles* (Philadelphia: 1976); John Gager, *The Origins
of Anti-Semitism* (New York: 1985).

6. On the composition of the Gospels, and the ways that they relate to
historical traditions from and about Jesus—besides Fredriksen, *From Jesus
to Christ;* Sanders, *The Historical Figure of Jesus;* and Vermes, *Jesus the Jew—*
still valuable is Paul Winter, *On the Trial of Jesus* (Berlin: 1974); also Douglas
Hare, *The Theme of Jewish Persecution in the Gospel of Matthew* (Cambridge:
1967). On the specific effect of the evangelists' postwar perspective, see
Lloyd Gaston, *No Stone upon Another: Studies in the Significance of the Fall
of Jerusalem in the Synoptic Gospels* (Leiden: 1970). These last three are
intended for historians but are clearly written and repay attention.

7. Philo Judaeus of Alexandria, Pilate's contemporary, describes Pilate as a man
whose administration of Judea was marked by "briberies, insults, robberies,
outrages and wanton injuries, ceaseless executions of untried prisoners, and
grievous cruelty," *Embassy to Gaius* 302. According to the Jewish historian
Josephus, Pilate was dismissed from office because of his habit of executing
large numbers of Jews (*Antiquities* 18.88f.). The Roman historian Tacitus,
himself no Judaeophile, also described Pilate and the other procurators of
the period as prone to violent misgovernment, *Histories* V.9–10.

8. Our only historical source for Hadrian's constructing a *naos* to the Capitoline Jupiter is Cassius Dio, *Roman History,* 69.12.1; see the texts collected
in M. Stern, *Greek and Latin Writers on Jews and Judaism,* vol. 2 (Jerusalem:
1980), p. 391. We have no such parallel attestation in Christian historical
sources before the Byzantine period, and the literary reports of a pagan
temple have no archaeological support. Perhaps, then, Hadrian constructed
only an altar, not a building. See B. Isaac, *The Limits of Empire* (rev. ed.,
Oxford: 1992), pp. 353–359. F. E. Peters points out that in 333, the pilgrim
of Bordeaux mentioned seeing two statues of Hadrian but not a temple.
See F. E. Peters, *Jerusalem: The Holy City in the Eyes of Chroniclers, Visitors,
Pilgrims, and Prophets from the Days of Abraham to the Beginnings of Modern
Times* (Princeton, N.J.: 1985), p. 144.

9. Interestingly, he entrusted Romans, not Jews, with this project. According to the contemporary historian Ammianus Marcellinus, Julian appointed Alypius of Antioch to oversee construction; Alypius was aided by the governor of the province. *Res Gestae* 23.1, 2–3; see also Stern, *Greek and Latin Writers,* vol. 2, pp. 607–608.

10. The quotations from *Cività Cattolica* are taken from the recent study by Sergio I. Minerbi, *The Vatican and Zionism: Conflicts in the Holy Land 1895–1925,* trans. Arnold Schwartz (New York: 1990). These ancient theological controversies were determining foreign policy up into our own century.

11. For the pagan cultural context of ancient Christianity, see the excellently written study by Robin Lane Fox, *Pagans and Christians* (New York: 1987); also, with beautiful photographs, Peter Brown, *The World of Late Antiquity* (New York: 1971).

12. These churches took their cue from Paul, who Tertullian complained was the *"apostolus hereticorum."* Seeking to interpret the Pauline epistles in a way that made Paul more consistent than he actually ever was, these Christians saw no continuity between the Law and the Gospel, and thus between the Jewish scriptures and the growing body of Christian ones that first assumed canonical status, as "new" testament, within these heretical groups. On this dualist Christian reading of Paul, see Gager, *Anti-Semitism,* pp. 113–193.

13. On this Christian millenarian tradition, Paula Fredriksen, "Apocalypse and Redemption: From John of Patmos to Augustine of Hippo," *Vigiliae Christianae* 45 (1991): 151–183.

14. On the appeal of classical philosophy to Christian intellectuals, see the elegant book of lectures by Henry Chadwick, *Early Christian Thought and the Classical Tradition* (Oxford: 1966).

15. On the birth and history of Christian Jerusalem, see most recently Robert Wilken, *The Land Called Holy: Palestine in Christian History and Thought* (New Haven, Conn.: 1992).

16. "Behold, from Adam all the years have passed, and behold, the 6000 years are completed, and now comes the Day of Judgment!" Augustine, *Sermo* 113, 8, mocking the response of some Christians to Rome's fall. "The 6000 years" refers to a well-established tradition of Christian chronography which had calculated the end of the world, and thus the second coming of Christ, according to the age of the world: the thousand-year reign of the saints on earth (Rev. 20:4–5) would follow as a millenarian Sabbath after a cosmic "week" of six thousand-year-long "days." These chronographies had variously named the years 400 CE or 500 CE as corresponding to the year 6000. They were not the work of a lunatic fringe: in 397, Augustine's episcopal colleague Hilarianus affirmed these calculations, stating that the End was

scarcely a century off (*de cursu temporum, Chronica Minora*, ed. C. Frick, vol. 1 [Leipzig: 1892]).

17. On traditions of the Antichrist, see the new book by Bernard McGinn, *Antichrist* (San Francisco: 1994).

18. Two outstanding studies in English on Augustine are Peter Brown, *Augustine of Hippo* (Berkeley: 1967) and R. A. Markus, *Saeculum: History and Society in the Thought of St. Augustine* (Cambridge: 1970). The *City of God* is available in many English translations; here I used the Penguin edition translated by Davis Knowles. For Augustine's antimillenarian strategies and arguments, see Fredriksen, "Apocalypse and Redemption," pp. 160–166.

19. On the Persian and Muslim conquest of Christian Jerusalem, see Wilken, *The Land Called Holy*, chaps. 11 and 12; see also the essay by J. Prawer, "Jerusalem in the Christian and Jewish Perspectives of the Early Middle Ages," *Gli Ebrei nell'alto medioevo,* Settimane di studio del Centro Italiano di stud sull'alto medioevo 26 (Spoleto: 1980): 739–813.

20. "A little while after the Temple [the Church of the Holy Sepulchre] had been destroyed it became quite clear that the wickedness of the Jews had brought about this great disaster. Once they knew this, all the Christians throughout the whole world decided unanimously to drive the Jews from their lands and cities. They became the object of universal hatred: they were driven from the cities, some were put to the sword, others were drowned in rivers; some even took their own lives in divers ways. So it was that after this very proper vengeance had been taken, that very few of them were to be found in the Roman world," Radulfus Glaber, *Five Books of the Histories,* III, vii, 24, on the year 1009 (Oxford: 1989).

21. On the pilgrimage of 1033—the millennium since Christ's passion—see, most recently, Richard Landes, *Relics, Apocalypse, and the Deceits of History: Ademar of Chabannes (989–1034)* (Cambridge: 1995), chaps. 14 and 15; on the transmutation from pilgrim to Crusader, see the classic study by Carl Erdmann, *The Origins of the Idea of Crusade* (Princeton, N.J.: 1977; original German published in 1933).

22. Savanarola was evidently influenced by the millenarian speculations of Joachim of Fiore: see Marjorie Reeves, *Joachim and the Prophetic Future* (San Francisco: 1977). Norman Cohn's great classic, *The Pursuit of the Millennium* (New York: 1970), traces the career of late medieval millenarian traditions: see esp. chap. 13 on Muenster as the New Jerusalem. On the scriptural self-consciousness of early English colonists such as Winthrop, see the volume edited by Conrad Cherry, *God's New Israel: The Religious Interpretation of America's Destiny* (Englewood Cliffs, N.J.: 1970).

23. Two of the many excellent recent studies of modern Christian millenarian-

ism are Paul Boyer, *When Time Shall Be No More* (Cambridge, Mass.: 1992), and Stephen D. O'Leary, *Arguing the Apocalypse* (New York: 1994).

5. The Spiritual Meaning of Jerusalem in Islam

1. The thesis developed at the beginning of this essay is presented in more detail in A. Neuwwirth, "Erste Qibla-Fernstes Masgĭd? Jerusalem im Horizont des historischen Muhammad," in F. Hahn, F.-L. Hossfeld, H. Jorissen, and A. Neuwirth, eds., *Zion—Ort der Begegnung: Festschrift für Laurentius Klein* (Bodenheim: 1993), pp. 227–270.

2. For the emergence of particular *epitheta ornantia* for Islamic cities and regions, see E. Gruber, *Verdienst und Rang. Die Fadā'il als literarisches und gesellschaftliches Problem im Islam* (Freiburg: 1975).

3. The triple epitheton can be traced back to the Ayyubid era. It is cited by the preacher Zakiaddin in his sermon in praise of the reconquest of Jerusalem by Saladin. See Ibn Khallikan, *Wafayat al-a'yan*, ed. I. Abbas, vol. 4 (Beirut), p. 232; an English translation is given by De Slane in *Ibn Khallikan*, vol. 2 (Paris: 1843), pp. 636–637.

4. For the complex of the literature on *fada-'il al-Quds* (merits of Jerusalem), see I. Hasson, *Fadā'il al-Bayt al-Muqaddas d'Abu Bakr Muhammad b. Ahmad al-Wasiti*, ed. and annotated by I. Hasson (Jerusalem: 1973), pp. 7–29.

5. See Sura 3:96.

6. The most widespread verbalization of the concept of three Islamic sanctuaries is a tradition ascribed to the Prophet *(hadith):* "You shall only set out for three mosques, the Sacred Mosque [in Mecca], my Mosque [in Medina] and al-Aqsa mosque [in Jerusalem]." The tradition is studied as to its socioreligious context in M. J. Kister, "You Shall Only Set Out for Three Mosques: A Study of an Early Tradition," *Le Muséon* 82 (1969): 173–196, reprinted in M. J. Kister, *Studies in Jahiliyya and Early Islam* (London: 1980), pp. 173–196.

7. Although in the tradition quoted, the sanctuaries are not identified as *haram* (see M. Plessner/E. Graf, "Haram," in Encyclopedia of Islam, vol. III [Leiden: 1980], henceforth EI) but as *masjid* (see J. A. Wensinck, "Masdjid," EI, vol. VI), the term can still be interpreted as referring to places of pilgrimage. The word *masjid* in its koranic usage already covers different types of places of worship, from "temple" to simply "house of prayer." *Masjid* in a broader sense, as "sanctuary" or "destination of pilgrimage," is synonymous with *haram* and is used to designate the real Jerusalem sanctuary, known as al-Haram al-Sharīf as well as al-Masjid al-Aqsa.

8. This attempt at imposing censorship has not been successful; the nearby sanctuary of Abraham at Hebron, al-Haram al-Ibrahimi, already presents an example of a much frequented *masjid,* mostly visited in continuation of a *ziyara,* a pious visit, to Jerusalem. For the social aspects of the custom of pilgrimage to Hebron, see N. Al-Jubeh, "Hebron (al-Halil): Kontinuität und Integrationskraft einer islamisch-arabischen Stadt." Doctoral thesis, Tübingen, 1991.

9. For the development of Medina, see W. M. Watt, "Al-madina," EI, vol. V.

10. Two anthologies of texts compiled and commented on by F. E. Peters— *Jerusalem: The Holy City in the Eyes of Chroniclers, Visitors, Pilgrims and Prophets from the Days of Abraham to the Beginnings of Modern Times* (Princeton, N.J.: 1985) and *Jerusalem and Mecca: The Typology of the Holy City in the Near East* (New York: 1986)—will supply a useful material basis for such a study. The question of the continuity of this kind of pious memory remains unsolved. A study of the sources concerning the Crusades era, by E. Sivan, has shown that the sensibility concerning the religious significance of Jerusalem during that period was weak; see "Le caractère sacré de Jérusalem dans l'islam aux XIIe–XIIIe siècles," *Studia Islamica* 27 (1967): 149–182. Still, as is shown by the collection of *fada'il* compiled by the Iraqi author Al-Wasiti, in the tenth and eleventh centuries pious memory, even outside Syria, had not completely vanished. But the decisive revitalization of a militant awareness of the dignity of the real city of Jerusalem as an Islamic sanctuary is owed largely to the rhetoric appeals made by the Zengids and Ayyubids. See L. Richter-Bernburg, *Der syrische Blitz: Saladins Sekretär zwischen Selbstdarstellung und Geschichtsschreibung* (Stuttgart and Beirut: 1995).

11. The significance of the direction of prayer toward Jerusalem suffers, not only in Islamic tradition but in research as well, from being overshadowed by the prominence of the kibla toward Mecca; thus the question as to its precise role in the development of Islamic worship has never been raised seriously; cf. A. J. Wensinck, "Kibla," in: EI, vol. V; U. Rubin, "The Kaʿba: Aspects of Its Ritual Functions and Position in Pre-Islamic and Early Islamic Times," *Jerusalem Studies in Arabic and Islam* 8 (1986): 97–131 (henceforth JSAI); and H. Busse, "Jerusalem and Mecca, the Temple and the Kaaba: An Account of Their Interrelation in Islamic Times," in M. Sharon, ed., *Pillars of Smoke and Fire: The Holy Land in History and Thought* (Johannesburg: 1986), pp. 236–246.

12. The honorary name itself appears to originate from a local Jerusalemite tradition; still, there are not a few *hadith* utterings with the tendency to recognize Jerusalem as the "natural kibla"; see Al-Wasiti and Kister, "Three Mosques."

13. There is no consensus about the duration of the first kibla. For traditional accounts, see A. Th. Khoury, *Der Koran,* vol. 2, on Sura 2:142; A. Duri goes so far as to accept a tradition that dates the introduction of the Jerusalem kibla immediately after the Hijra that he considers to be the oldest; see "Jerusalem in the Early Islamic Period: 7th–11th Centuries A.D.," K. J. Asali, ed., *Jerusalem in History* (Essex: 1989), pp. 105–128.

14. This becomes clear from the koranic verses about the change of the kibla; see Sura 2:142–145, cf. below.

15. See Wensinck, "Kibla."

16. See At-Tabari, "Jami' al-bayan," in *Bulaq,* vol. 2, pp. 1–16 (on Sura 2:142–145), and also Rubin, "The Ka'ba," p. 29.

17. Rubin holds this opinion, presupposing, however, a very narrow, even mechanical, concept of kibla.

18. The interpretation of al-Masjid al-Aqsa in Sura 17:1 is still subject to controversies in research. The opinions held here are dependent, in the end, on the researcher's position in the debate about the historicity of the basic traditions about the Prophet Muhammad; for possible explanations of al-Masjid al-Aqsa (in the sense of a heavenly sanctuary), see H. Busse, "Jerusalem in the Story of Muhammad's Night Journey and Ascension," JSAI 14 (1991): 1–40, and (in the sense of the Jerusalem Temple Mount) A. Neuwirth, *Zion.*

19. The close relation between "direction of prayer" (kibla) and "nocturnal journey" (Isra) is realized clearly in the Islamic tradition. The causality working between the two, is, however, seen in the sense opposite to our assumption. Tradition holds that it is the experience of the Isra that brought about the introduction of the kibla.

20. The verb *asra* is used in the Koran twice to designate the flight of Lot (Suras 11:81 and 15:65) and appears three times in the context of the exodus account (Suras 20:77, 26:52, and 44:23).

21. This is made plausible by the use of the unspecified word *masjid* to designate the Jerusalem Temple a few verses after the Isra verse itself, 17:7. W. Caskel stresses that there could hardly be another possible sanctuary in the listener's mind; see "Der Felsendom und die Wallfahrt nach Jerusalem," in *Arbeitsgemeinschft für Forschung des Landes Nordrhein-Westfalen* in *Geisteswissenschaften* 114 (Köln: 1963), pp. 9–38.

22. See At-Tabari, "Jami'al-bayan,'" in *Bulaq,* vol. 15, p. 3.

23. See Wensinck, "Isra'."

24. See Wensinck, "Mi'radj," and Busse, "Jerusalem."

25. See Ibn Hisham, "As-sira an-nabawiyya," ed. M. as-Saqqa and others, vol. 1 (Cairo: 1955), p. 39ff.; see below.

26. For the type of prophet gifted with ecstatic capacities, see R. Wilson, *Prophecy and Society in Ancient Israel* (Philadelphia: 1980).

27. The particular diversity of the two images of Muhammad makes up the focus of R. Sellheim's comprehensive "strategraphic" study, "Prophet, Chaliph und Geschichte: Die Muhammed-Biographie des Ibn Ishaq," *Oriens* 18/19 (1967): 33–91.

28. In the framework of an analysis of the entire Sura 17, an attempt has been made to trace the particular significance of the narrative element of "moving out," introduced by the allusion to the exodus, Isra, in the beginning, and taken up anew several times in the sura in the context of descriptions of prayer. See Neuwirth, *Zion*.

29. See I Kings 8:23–53.

30. The worshipper's new situation in space caused by the change of the kibla is characterized in the verses accompanying the change as a "purposeful turning of the face" (Sura 2:144, 149, and 150) after a period of "turning the face around and around without a direction" (2:144).

31. It becomes impressively manifest in the context of the debate around the legitimacy of pilgrimage to sanctuaries other than the Hijazene. See Kister, "Three Mosques."

32. The recognition of such an affinity is demonstrated, for instance, by those prophetical traditions that undertake to quantify the relative value of prayers as performed in the different sanctuaries. See Kister, ibid.

33. The initial attachment of the followers of the Prophet to the Kaaba rites is clearly discernible in the earliest suras. See A. Neuwirth, "Vom Rezitationstext über die Liturgie zum Kanon: Zu Entstehung und Wiederauflösung der Surenkomposition im Verlauf der Entwicklung eines islamischen Kultus" in S. Wild, ed., *Der Koran als Text* (Leiden: 1995), pp. 69–105.

34. In the accounts of the erection (or the reerection) of the Kaaba through Abraham (Suras 2:125 and 22:26–27), those imagined to be the local beneficiaries of the sanctuary are explicitly characterized through their particular ritual gestures, such as standing upright, *qiyam,* prostration, *sajda,* and bowing, *ruku*.

35. Suras 19:11 and 3:39. Here the Temple is described as a mihrab—that is, with a designation that points to a particular architectural image of the place where the biblical figures should have sojourned. Both figures are related to the New Testament, thus their appearance in a mihrab, which in pre-Islamic context means a domed architectural feature, is less surprising: their particular association with this type of architecture should be due less to written than to pictorial sources: both figures appear in Byzantine iconography, as standardized at the latest from the eighth century onward, as

standing in a ciborium, an architectural feature that could have been rendered in Arabic as *mihrab*.

36. Sura 3:37, mihrab.

37. Sura 38:21, mihrab. The singular association of an Old Testament figure with the mihrab requires an explanation. It may be due to the function of a judge, which was carried out by David in this passage, a function that was associated in ancient Arabia with a place so designated.

38. Sura 17:7; the Temple is called here—in accordance with the Meccan sanctuary—*masjid*.

39. At-Tur is mentioned ten times in the Koran, eight times within the story of Moses, and twice (52:1; 95:2), together with the Meccan sanctuary, in allusions to the theophany. See A. Neuwirth, "Images and Metaphors in the Introductory Sections of the Makkan Suras," in G. R. Hawting and A. A. Shareef, eds., *Approaches to the Qur'an* (London and New York: 1993), pp. 3–36.

40. Cf. A. Assmann and J. Assman, "Nachwort," in A. Assmann, J. Assmann, and C. Hardtmeier, eds., *Schrift und Gedächtnis: Beiträge zur Archäologie der literarischen Kommunikation,* vol. 1 (Munich: 1983), p. 272.

41. See J. Assmann, "Das kulturelle Gedächtnis: Schrift, Erinnerung und politische Identität in Frühen Hochkulturen," in ibid., p. 27f.

42. The sanctuary is—with the exception of Sura 90:1—always recalled in the Koran in the contexts of prophetical oaths.

43. For details, see Neuwirth, *Images and Metaphors,* pp. 3–39, and Neuwirth, *Zion.*

44. It is this particular period from which those suras originate that allude in diverse ways to the strong association of the earlier messengers with Scripture. These accounts of earlier prophets are presented, it is true, as revelations to Muhammad, but at the same time they attest to a second function: they are to be transmitted to the listeners as excerpts, as "pericopes" from a heavenly "Scripture"; see Neuwirth, *Rezitationstext.*

45. Besides Mecca, only Mount Sinai and the "collapsed cities," Sodom and Gomorrha, are mentioned (Suras 53:53, 69:9, and 9:70); see J. Horovitz, *Koranische Untersuchungen* (Berlin/Leipzig: 1926), p. 13f.; Palestine is alluded to as the Blessed Land *(al-ard allati barakna fiha)* in Suras 17:1, 21:71, 34:18, and 7:137, or else as the Holy Land *(al-ard al-muqaddasa),* in Sura 5:21.

46. For the introductory sections of these suras, see Neuwirth, "Images and Metaphors."

47. See Horovitz, *Untersuchungen.*

48. For the development of Islamic worship at the time of the *fatiha*'s intro-

duction, see A. and K. Neuwirth, "'Surat al-Fatiha': 'Eröffnung' des Text-Corpus Koran oder 'Introitus' der Gebetsliturgie?'" in W. Groß, H. Irsigler, and Th. Seidl, eds., *Text, Methode und Grammatik: Festschrift für Wolfgang Richter* (St. Ottilien: 1992), pp. 332–357.

49. See A. J. Wensinck and J. Jomier, "Ihram," in EI, vol. III.

50. For particular time periods determining the ancient Arabian worship, see U. Rubin, "Morning and Evening Prayers in Early Islam," JSAI 10 (1987): 40–64.

51. Three from among the five times of prayer are to be presupposed for the Medinan community with certainty; see Wensinck, "Salat," in EI, vol. IV.

52. The sayings of Abraham accompanying the establishment (or the purification) of the Kaaba rites are related in the Koran in different versions. For the entire complex of these texts, see E. Beck, "Die Gestalt Abrahams am Wendepunkt der Entwicklung Muhammads: Analyse von Sure 2.118 (124)–135(141)," *Le Muséon* 65 (1952): 73–94, reprinted in R. Paret, ed., *Der Koran: Wege der Forschung* (Darmstadt: 1975), pp. 11–133.

53. See Busse, "Jerusalem and Mecca," p. 238.

54. As to this concept, which appears to have been developed earlier within the movement of the Hanifiyya, constituted by pre-Islamic Arabian monotheist believers not directly associated with either Christianity or Judaism, see U. Rubin, "Hanifiyya and Ka'ba: An Inquiry into the Arabian pre-Islamic Background of din Ibrahim," paper prepared for the Third International Colloquium, "From Jahiliyya to Islam: Aspects of Social, Cultural, and Religious History in the Period of Transition" (Jerusalem: 1985). Beck, "Die Gestalt Abrahams," dates the koranic testimonies for the association of Abraham with Mecca into the Meccan period of koranic development.

55. See Julius Wellhausen, *Reste arabischen Heidentums* (Berlin: 1889; reprint of 2nd ed., Berlin: 1961).

56. "The abolition of intercalary months is a slight change introduced under Muhammad which has given a definite stamp to Islamic civilization. The pre-Islamic Arabs observed the lunar months, but kept their calendar in line with the solar year by introducing intercalary months where necessary. The matter is referred to in a passage of the Qur'an, 9.36f. Muhammad is said to have made public these verses during the address he gave during the pilgrimage of Farewell." (W. M. Watt, *Muhammad at Medina* [Oxford: 1956], pp. 299–300, with further discussion of calendar reform.)

57. See 1 Kings 8:41–43.

58. See R. Rendtorff, "Die Entwicklung des altisraelitischen Festkalenders," in J. Assmann, ed., *Das Fest und das Heilige: Studien zum Verstehen fremder Religionen* (Gütersloh: 1991), pp. 185–205.

59. The short passage in the Koran presenting Abraham's call to pilgrimage has

inspired a multitude of accounts in the literature of legends of the prophets *(qisas al-anbiya')* about the life of Abraham and his relatives that give a totally novel etiology to the Hajj rites, insofar as these are now interpreted as acts in imitation of particular deeds of those biblical figures. See also Busse, "Geschichte und Bedeutung der Kaaba im Licht der Bibel," in F. Hahn et al., eds., *Zion—Ort der Begegnung,* pp. 169–186.

60. On worshippers standing still *(wuquf)* beneath Mount 'Arafat in expectation of a theophany, which in the original ancient Arabian context marked the climax of the Hajj rites, see Wellhausen, *Reste arabischen Heidentums.* The ceremony is reinterpreted as an anticipation of the assembly of mankind on the Day of Judgment; see, for instance, A. Shari'ati, "Hajj"; also the German translation, "Hadsch," in *Islamische Renaissance,* vol. 9, Botschaft der Islamischen Republik Iran (Bonn: 1983).

61. The awareness of its prosperity, security, and cultic hegemony—in spite of Mecca's geographical situation in the midst of the desert—is often stressed in the Koran as a sign of particular divine mercy.

62. The period of the Hajj already appears as a forceful symbol in an early Meccan sura (89:2), see Neuwirth, "Images and Metaphors," p. 25f.

63. See Busse, "Jerusalem and Mecca."

64. An existentialist testimony about the experience of a *rite de passage* at the entrance point into the haram *(miqat)* is found in A. Shari'ati, "Hajj."

65. Mecca and its haram alone are declared by a koranic commandment as the site where personal presence is indispensable for the fulfillment of a ritual obligation incumbent on every Muslim. In contrast, the Jerusalem sanctuary becomes the focus of a feast only after the koranic development; in addition, the particular feast, *dhikr al-mi'raj,* does not require the presence of the worshippers at the place of its origin.

66. The term *masjid* may, now that all the three places have become real Islamic sanctuaries, be translated rightfully as *mosque.*

67. See Kister, *Studies in Jahiliyya.*

68. Jerusalem has this inferior status in common with Medina; both sanctuaries, however, are in fact mostly visited as part of a common itinerary that culminates in the Hajj; see Wensinck, "Ziyara," in EI, vol. IV.

69. See Busse, "Masdjid," and Busse, "Zur Geschichte und Deutung der frühislamischen Harambauten in Jerusalem," *Zeitschrift des Deutschen Palästina-Voreins* 107 (1991): 144–154 (henceforth ZDPV). He holds the opinion that the erection of the Dome of the Rock is to be considered as an attempt at rebuilding the Temple; it should, however, be stressed that the new sanctuary was destined not to be a Jewish place of worship but more generally a monotheistic one. To ignore the fact that long before the *masjid* of the Banu Isra'il had been physically reached by the Muslims it had already been

recognized as the sole antipode to the Kaaba—as the "further sanctuary," al-Masjid al-Aqsa—and as such had played a significant role in the emerging Islamic worship, would be to underestimate the factor of continuity. The Islamization of the sanctuary is part of the genesis of the structure of Islam.

70. The most suggestive Islamic testimony for the thesis that the building activities of 'Abd al-Malik were inspired by the *'qubbat al-qiyama'*, the Church of Anastasis or the Church of Resurrection, as the Holy Sepulchre is called in the Byzantine tradition, as well as by other Jerusalem churches, is given by al-Muqaddasi, *Ahsan at-taqasim fi ma'rifat al-aqalim,* ed. M. De Goeje (Leiden: 1877), p. 159. The most frequently quoted passage is from *Al-Muqaddasi: Description of Syria, including Palestine,* trans. and annotated by G. Le Strange (London: Palestine Pilgrims' Text Society, 1896; reprint, New York: 1971), vol. 3, pp. 22–23.

71. For the relation between the Church of Anastasis and the Dome of the Rock, see K. Bieberstein and H. Bloedhorn, "Jerusalem: Grundzüge der Baugeschichte vom Chalkolithikum bis zur Frühzeit der osmanischen Herrschaft," in *Beihefte zum Tübinger Atlas des Vorderen Orients* Reihe B, N (Wiesbaden: 1994), vol. 3, pp. 72–92.

72. For the ensemble of buildings on the Temple Mount, see ibid. and, particularly, M. Rosen-Ayalon, *The Early Islamic Monuments of Al-Haram al-Sharif: An Iconographic Study* (Jerusalem: 1989), and also Busse's diligent review presenting a survey on the research carried out until now, "Zur Geschichte." For the influence the Dome of the Rock still exerts on Islamic architecture, see R. Hillenbrand, "Das Vermächtnis des Felsendoms," in *Forschungsforum,* Berichte aus der Otto-Friedrich-Universität, vol. 2 (Bamberg: 1990), pp. 64–71.

73. See Busse, "Jerusalem and Mecca."

74. For the notion of the Haram as the center of the world, see the testimonies adduced by J. van Ess, "Abd al-Malik and the Dome of the Rock: An Analysis of Some Texts," in J. Raby and J. Johns, eds., *Bayt al-Maqdis: 'Abd al-Malik's Jerusalem,* vol. 1 (Oxford: 1992), p. 89. On the account of al-Muqaddasi, see also A. Miquel, "L'Organisation de l'espace dans la presentation de la Palestine par le géographe Al-Mukaddasi (IVe/Xe siècle)," in *Geography and Civilization of Palestine,* vol. 2, Third International Conference on Bilad al-Sham, Palestine, April 19–24, 1980 (Amman: 1984), pp. 27–135.

75. See van Ess, ibid., pp. 89–104, and also J. van Ess, "The Youthful God: Anthropomorphism in Early Islam," University Lecture in Religion, Department of Religious Studies, Arizona State University, 1988.

76. The building inscription is presented in M. van Berchem, *Matériaux pour un Corpus Inscriptionum Arabicarum II: Jerusalem Haram,* Mémoires de

l'Institut Français d'Archéologie Orientale du Caire, vol. 44 (Cairo: 1925–1927), Nr. 215–217; translated into German by H. Busse, "Die arabischen Inschriften im und am Felsendom in Jerusalem," in *Das Heilige Land* 109.1–2 (1977), 8–24.

77. The initial colon of the Throne verse taken alone could be interpreted as an allusion to the debate on whether Jerusalem's Temple Mount could be considered God's worldly throne that took place—according to Islamic tradition—in the presence of the caliph 'Abd al-Malik. See the testimonies adduced by van Ess, "Abd al-Malik," and Ibn Taymiyya, "Iqtidl a'-sirat al-mustaqim fi mukhalafat ashab al-jahim," ed. M. H. al-Fiqi (Cairo: 1950), p. 445. An English translation of the passage is in M. U. Memon, *Ibn Taimiya's Struggle against Popular Religion* (Paris: 1976). The entire Throne verse is reproduced in the Ottoman Inscription placed in the cupola; it is possible that this is no more than the restoration of the former epigraphic decoration of the cupola, about whose Umayyad shape we know nothing.

78. Polemical statements against Christianity are to be found in the inner ambulatorium: Suras 4:171–172, 19:34–36, and in the outer ambulatorium, 17.III. On these texts in detail, see H. Busse, "Monotheismus und islamische Christologie in der Bauinschrift des Felsendoms in Jerusalem," in *Theologische Quartalschrift* 161 (181): 168–178. For the entire inscription, see also J. van Ess, *Theologie und Gesellschaft im 2. und 3. Jahrhundert Hidschra: Eine Geschichte des religiösen Denkens im frühen Islam,* vol. 1 (Berlin: 1991), p. 10f.

79. The first part of the Islamic confession of God's unity and Muhammad's dignity as a messenger, *shahada,* appears nine times. In addition, the idea of unity is taken up often in the context of koranic quotations.

80. Muhammad's distinguished position is mentioned five times through the quotation of the second part of the *shahada,* and often in other contexts as well; twice his elevation into the rank even above that of the angels—who utter their benedictions on him—is recalled through the verse 33:26.

81. The identity of the formulas used in the inscription and in the coinage contemporary to it are stressed again by van Ess, "Abd al-Malik," 10f. Anthony Welch underlines the paradigmatic character of the forms created by 'Abd al-Malik in coinage and epigraphy, which were to become prototypes for the later development of Islamic epigraphy and numismatics. See "Epigraphs as Icons: The Role of the Written Word in Islamic Art," in J. Gutmann, ed., *The Image and the Word: Confrontations in Judaism, Christianity and Islam* (Montana: 1977), pp. 63–74.

82. The problem of a secondary intention for the building aimed at the legitimation of the new dynasty—which was at the time in question, confronted with an anticaliphate established at Mecca—is discussed anew in van Ess, *Theologie und Gesellschaft,* vol. 1.

83. The formula that reappears stereotypically in the inscription, "May God bless Muhammad, His servant and prophet," is echoed in the formula found in the inner ambulatorium: "Oh God, bless Your messenger and Your servant, Jesus."

84. Sura 33:56 is to be found in both the outer and the inner ambulatorium. It reads: "God and His angels bless the Prophet. O believers, do you also bless him, and pray him peace."

85. The full text of the inscription reads: "Oh God, we pray to You, grant us—through Your celebrated names [al-asma' al-husna], Your noble face, Your elevated majesty, and Your perfect word by which You preserve heaven and earth, through Your mercy which shelters us from Satan and saves us from Your punishment at the Day of Resurrection, through Your overflowing generosity, through Your kindness, through Your gentleness and Your omnipotence, through Your forgiveness and Your magnanimity, that You might utter Your blessing over Muhammad, Your servant and prophet, and that You might accept his intercession for his community—may God bless him and grant him mercy."

86. See Ibn Hisham, "As-sira," vol. 1, pp. 397ff. An English translation is given by A. Guillaume in his *The Life of Muhammad: A Translation of ibn Ishaq's Sirat Rasul Allah* (Oxford: 1955; reprinted in Pakistan, 1974), p. 186f.

87. The heavenly world as reflected in the iconography of the Dome of the Rock could well be associated by later visitors with the Miraj experience of the Prophet: angels appear iconographically most prominent in the mosaic of the Dome of the Rock. This is one of the most interesting conclusions reached by Rosen-Ayalon in *Early Islamic Monuments*. She presents a most convincing reinterpetation of the rather cryptic amphora-like shapes that dominate the mosaic decoration of the drum of the Dome, and that had hitherto—following the interpretation presented by A. Creswell and O. Grabar—been understood to be stylized images of the precious spolia brought home by the victorious Islamic rulers from their expeditions against the neighboring empires. According to the inscription, it is the angels who—even before man—utter the blessings over the Prophet (Sura 33:56) and who testify together with God Himself to the divine unity.

88. Thus Rosen-Ayalon's interpretation of the building is affirmed by Busse in "Jerusalem and Mecca."

89. The part of the inscription above the eastern gate culminates in the long prayer that Muhammad's intercession on the Day of Judgment, *yawm al-qiyama,* might be accepted; a shorter version of this prayer is found in the outer ambulatorium. Similarly, Jesus is placed in an eschatological context through the quotation of Sura 19:34. God appears as He who gives life and takes it again *(yuyhi wa-yumit).* The twice-appearing term *resurrec-*

tion (qiyama) evokes—at least for the local reader—the official name of the Holy Sepulchre Church of Jerusalem—the Church of Resurrection, or Anastasis, kanisat al-Qiyama.

90. It is well known that the four gates of the Dome of the Rock face the cardinal points. For further symbols with cosmic significance, see Rosen-Ayalon, *Early Islamic Monuments,* affirmed by Busse in "Zur Geschichte."

91. For the interpretation of the Qubbat as-Silsila as the *omphalos mundi,* see Rosen-Ayalon, *Early Islamic Monuments.* There is unequivocal testimony as to this interpretation available for the period shortly after the erection of the building. See the sources adduced by van Ess in "Abd' al-Malik." The idea is evolved in detail by al-Muqaddasi. See Miquel, "L'Organisation de l'espace."

92. Sura 19:35 is quoted in the inner ambulatorium.

93. In the prayer for the intercession of the Prophet (over the eastern gate) there is explicit recourse to the "perfect word," *al-kalima at-tamma.*

94. On the Haram gates in general, see M. H. Burgoyne, "The Gates of the Haram al-Sharif," in Raby, ed., *Bayt al-Maqdis,* pp. 125–140. The southern gate called Bab ar-Rahma—whose name was, however, sometimes applied to another gate—goes back to the original building complex of 'Abd al-Malik. The Gate of Darkness, Bab al-'Atm, originally a double gate like the Bab ar-Rahma, also belongs to the original building complex. See Burgoyne, "Gates of the Haram."

95. The Valley of Hinnom, *gehenna,* is located southwest of Jerusalem's Old City. On the traditions that "migrated" there see Peters, *Jerusalem,* pp. 455–458.

96. The place name *as-sahira* seems to go back to a rather daring interpretation given to a somewhat unusually phrased koranic passage. The verse, 79:14f., speaks about resurrection: "But it shall be only a single scare, and behold, they are awakened," meaning in the state of being awake, *fi as-sahira.* The last word was reinterpreted as a toponym covering the place with which, in Jerusalem, the assembly of the resurrected was traditionally associated.

97. See Hasson, *Fada'il.*

98. A most significant anthology of relevant travel accounts is to be found in Kamil Jamil al-'Asali, *Bayt al-Maqdis fi kutub ar-rahhalat 'inda l-'arab wa-muslimin* (Amman: 1992). The Haram as the site of the eschatological scenario was described by writers of the tenth and eleventh centuries; see Al-Muqaddasi, *Ahsan at-taqasim,* and Nasir-e Khusrow, *Sefer Nameh,* ed. M. D. Siyaqi (Tehran: n.d.), pp. 25ff.

99. The inscription of Saladin—published in van Berchem, *Matériaux pour un Corpus Inscriptionum Arabicarum II*—cites the beginning of Sura Ta Ha, 20:1–21, where the event of the Burning Bush is associated typologically with

the reconsecration of the sanctuary: Moses is made aware that he treads on holy ground; so should be the visitor to the reconsecrated Dome of the Rock. In a similar way, the event of the recommuting of the Rod of Moses should be interpreted—in accordance with Rosen-Ayalon—as prototypical of the recommuting of the Dome of the Rock to its original status as an Islamic sanctuary. The Koran quotation ends with the words: "We will restore it to its first state" (20:21).

100. As is pointed out by Busse in "Die arabischen Inschriften," p. 23f., and "Jerusalem and Mecca." Sura 32 (Ya Sin) plays a particularly important role among the koranic quotations of the Ottoman inscription.

101. See also Miquel, "L'Organisation de l'espace," p. 135, on Al-Muqaddasi's account of Jerusalem.

102. M. H. Burgoyne, *Mamluk Jerusalem: An Architectural Study* (London: 1987), pp. 84–85, adduces at least seven mausoleums located in Bab al-Silsila Road.

103. R. S. Humphreys, "The Expressive Intent of the Mamluk Architecture of Cairo: A Preliminary Essay," *Studia Islamica* 35 (1972): 69–119, stresses the importance of realizing—in addition to the function of the building as its primary intention—the effectiveness of the structure's secondary intention in communicating a particular consciousness or ideology.

104. See Burgoyne, *Mamluk Jerusalem,* p. 84f.

105. See L. A. Mayer, *Saracenic Heraldry: A Survey* (Oxford: 1933), and M. Meinecke, "Zur Mamlukischen Heraldik," *Mitteilungen des DAI Abteilung Kairo* 28 (1972): 213–287 (I owe this reference to the kindness of my collegue Ulrich Haarmann).

106. See D. Little, "Jerusalem and Egypt during the Mamluk Period According to Literary and Documentary Sources," in G. Cohen and G. Baer, eds., *Egypt and Palestine: A Millennium of Association* (Jerusalem: 1984). The texts were presented by Little in his *Documents of the Haram ash-Sharif in Jerusalem,* Beiruter Texte und Studien 29 (Wiesbaden and Beirut: 1984) and by al-'Asali, *Waitha'iq maqdisiyya ta'rikhiyya* I-III (Amman: 1983–1989).

107. Burgoyne, in *Mamluk Jerusalem,* shows that those structures whose main tracts open up to the street through extended windows were constructed in this particular fashion to allow the koran recitation conducted inside, near the tomb of the founder or within one of the lecture halls, to be heard outside in the street itself. That certain places in Jerusalem were resounding with koran recitation is attested by Muslim pilgrims coming from far countries, as in the account left by Abu Bakr Ibn al-'Arabi, who sojourned in Jerusalem in 1093 and 1095. See Al-Maqarri, *Nafh al-tib,* ed. I. Abbas (Beirut: 1968), vol. 2, p. 42.

108. Accounts about pious visitors, *jiran,* who had come to Jerusalem to seek

spiritual experience through meditation on the Temple Mount, are to be found in the *fada'il* literature (see Hasson, "Fada'il") as well as in the vitae of mystics, Sufis; they are particularly numerous in Mujiraddin al-'Ulaymi (fifteenth century), "Al-uns al-jalil fi ta'rikh al-Quds wa-l-Khalil," vols. 1 and 2 (Amman: 1976), and Burhanaddin ibn al-Firkah, "Ba'ith an-nufus ila ziyarat al-Quds al-mahrus" (written in 1350), ed. C. D. Matthews, *Journal of the Palestine Oriental Society* 14, 15 (1935–1936), and translated by him under the title *Palestine: Mohammedan Holy Land* (New Haven, Conn.: 1949).

6. Christian Pilgrimage to the Holy Land

1. Gregory of Nyssa, *epistola* 2.
2. Hugeburc, "Life of St. Willibald," in John Wilkinson, *Jerusalem Pilgrims before the Crusades* (Jerusalem: 1977), p. 126.
3. The literature on Christian pilgrimage is large, and in recent years there have been a number of fine studies on early Christian pilgrimage to Jerusalem and the Holy Land. Among the more recent studies, see E. D. Hunt, *Holy Land Pilgrimage in the Later Roman Empire A.D. 312–460* (Oxford: 1982); Pierre Maraval, *Lieux saints et pèlerinages d'Orient: Histoire et géographie: Des origines à la conquête arabe* (Paris: 1985); Robert L. Wilken, *The Land Called Holy: Palestine in Christian History and Thought* (New Haven, Conn.: 1992).
4. *Institutes* 4.13.7. For other criticisms of the practice of pilgrimage, see Sabine MacCormack, "Loca Sancta," in R. Ousterhout, ed., *Blessings of Pilgrimage* (Urbana, Ill.: 1990), p. 9ff.
5. On pilgrimage in the ancient world, see B. J. Koetting, *Peregrinatio Religiosa* (Muenster: 1950), and M. Philonenko and M. Simon, *Les Pèlerinage de l'antiquité biblique et classique à l'occident médiéval,* Université de Science Humaine de Strasbourg, Centre de Recherches d'Histoire des Religions, Études d'histoire des Religions, no. 1 (Paris: 1973). There is useful material in Ramsay MacMullen, *Paganism in the Roman Empire* (New Haven, Conn.: 1981), pp. 17ff., 41ff. For Muslims, pilgrimage means pilgrimage to Mecca (the Hajj) (Koran 2.196; 3.97). It was, however, considered meritorious to make the trip to Jerusalem and Hebron, the site of Abraham's tomb. On Muslim attitudes toward Jerusalem, see the article "al-Kuds" in *The Encyclopedia of Islam,* vol. 5, pp. 322–344, by S. D. Goitein (history) and Oleg Grabar (monuments). See also F. E. Peters, *The Distant Shrine: The Islamic Centuries in Jerusalem* (New York: 1993), pp. 104, 165–166, 195. For translations of Muslim accounts of visits to Jerusalem, see Guy Le Strange, *Palestine under the Moslems* (Boston: 1890), pp. 139–142.

6. *De Dea Syria* 10.

7. *De Dea Syria* 55–56.

8. *De Dea Syria* 10.

9. Walter Burkert, *Greek Religion* (Cambridge: 1985), p. 84.

10. "All Greek sacred architecture explores and praises the character of a god or a group of gods in a specific place. That place is itself holy and, before the temple was built upon it, embodied the whole of the deity as recognized actual force" (V. Scully, *The Earth, the Temple and the Gods* [New Haven, Conn.: 1979], p. 1). See also R. A. Tomlinson, *Greek Sanctuaries* (London: 1976), p. 226. "As for this place, it is clearly a holy one" (Sophocles, *Oedipus at Colonus,* ln. 16). On the distinction between "chosen" and "discovered," see Mircea Eliade, *Patterns in Comparative Religion* (New York: 1974), p. 369, and the useful article by Shigeru Matsumoto, "The Meaning of Sacred Places, as Phenomenologists of Religion Understand It," *Tenri Journal of Religion* 10 (1969): 46–56.

11. Pausanias, *Description of Greece,* 1.16–17.

12. Tadeusz Zawakzki, "Quelques remarques sur l'entendue et l'accroissement des domaines des grands temples en Asia Mineure," *Eos* 46 (1953–54): 83–96. In Japan the territory around the residence of the divinity came to be viewed as a sacred area; in time this was extended to the nation as a whole. Allan G. Grapard, "Flying Mountains and Walkers of Emptiness: Toward a Definition of Sacred Space in Japanese Religions," *History of Religions* 21 (1982): 195–221.

13. *De Dea Syria* 1.

14. *De Dea Syria* 56.

15. *Dio Cassius* 36.11.

16. Pausanias, *Description of Greece* 1.13.8, 1.31.5, 1.35.8, 1.41.2, etc., and Lucian, *De Dea Syria* 55; on collective memory in Greco-Roman religions, see Jean Rudhardt, "Mnémosyne et les Muses," in Philippe Borgeaud, ed., *La Mémoire des Religions* (Geneva: 1988), pp. 37–62.

17. Philo, *Spec.* 1.69. Some of the hymns sung by pilgrims are preserved in the pilgrim songs, or "songs of ascents," in the book of Psalms (Ps. 24, 84, 118, 120–134). On Jewish pilgrimage during the period of the Second Temple, see Shmuel Safrai, *Die Wallfahrt im Zeitalter des Zweiten Tempels* (Neukirchen-Vluyn: 1981); see also Shmuel Safrai, "Relations between the Diaspora and the Land of Israel," in Shmuel Safrai and Menachem Stern, eds., *The Jewish People in the First Century* (Philadelphia: 1974), pp. 184–215.

18. Josephus, *Antiquities* 4.203–4.

19. Victor and Edith Turner, *Image and Pilgrimage in Christian Culture* (New York: 1978), p. 7.

20. *Corpus Inscriptionum Iudaicarum* 2, no. 1404. On this inscription, see M. Schwabe in *Sefer Yerushalayim* 2 (1956): 362–365 (in Hebrew).

21. Jerome, *Commentarius in Sophoniam* 114–116; *Corpus Christanorum* 76a, 673.

22. Text in M. Margolioth, *Halakhoth on the Land of Israel from the Genizah* (Jerusalem: 1974), pp. 139–141 (in Hebrew). Compare this description of a Jewish pilgrim to Jerusalem with the sixth-century account of a Christian pilgrim sighting the Holy City for the first time. "When they had reached the outskirts of the holy city of Jerusalem which they loved, they saw from a high place five stades away the lofty roof of the Holy Church of the Resurrection, shining like the morning sun, and cried aloud: 'See that is Sion, the city of our deliverance!' They fell down upon their faces, and from there onwards they crept upon their knees, frequently kissing the soil with their lips and eyes, until they were within the holy walls and had embraced the site of the sacred Cross on Golgotha." "Life of Peter the Iberian," by Mayuma of Gaza, in Marshall Lang, ed., *Lives and Legends of the Georgian Saints* (Crestwood, N.Y.: 1956), p. 64. For rituals associated with pilgrimage to Jerusalem among Syriac-speaking Christians, see J. M. Fiey, "Le pèlerinage des Nestoriens et Jacobites à Jérusalem," *Cahiers de civilisation médiévale* 12 (1969): 117ff.

23. b. Moed Katan 26a.

24. Marcel Proust, *Remembrance of Things Past*, vol. 1 (New York: 1934), p. 34.

25. *In Joannem* 1:28 (6.204–207); *Sources Chrétiennes* 157, 284ff.

26. Fragment no. 3 in Eusebius, *Historia Ecclesiastica* 4.26.3–4.

27. Eusebius, *Historia Ecclesiastica* 6.11.2.

28. Text of *Itinerarium Burdigalense* edited by P. Geyer and O. Cuntz in *Corpus Christianorum* 175. Translation in John Wilkinson, *Egeria's Travels to the Holy Land* (Jerusalem: 1981), pp. 153–163. For discussion, see H. Windisch, "Die ältesten christlichen Palästinapilger," *Zeitschrift des deutschen Palestina-Vereins* 48 (1925): 145–148.

29. Wilkinson, *Egeria's Travels*, p. 155, par. 588.

30. Ibid., pp. 595–599.

31. Job's dung heap was in Arabia. John Chrysostom writes: "Many undertake the long and arduous journey traveling from the ends of the earth to Arabia to see that dung heap, and when they behold it they kiss the earth which received that wrestling place of that victor" (*Homilies on the Statues* 5.1; *Patrologia Graeca* 49.69a). Only two water pots remained at Cana, according to the Piacenza Pilgrim, 161 (Wilkinson, *Jerusalem Pilgrims*, p. 79).

32. Cynthia Ozick, "Toward a New Yiddish," in Cynthia Ozick, ed., *Art and Ardor* (New York: 1983), p. 154.

33. Pilgrim of Bordeaux, *Itinerary*, p. 595.

34. Text edited by Pierre Maraval in *Sources Chrétiennes* (Paris: 1982), p. 296; translated into English by John Wilkinson (1981). For recent discussion of the identity of Egeria, see Hagith Sivan, "Who Was Egeria? Piety and Pilgrimage in the Age of Gratian," *Harvard Theological Review* 81 (1988): 57–72.

35. *Itinerarium Burdigalense*, 2.2, 7; 3.7; 5.1, 5, 8, 9, *passim*. The impact of actually "seeing" the holy places is vividly described by Asterius, bishop of Amasea, a city in Cappadocia, in the late fourth century. Asterius is comparing the experience of visiting the tomb of a martyr (Phocas) in his native country to visiting the Oak of Mamre in Hebron, the shrine of the patriarchs. "When one comes into the precious tomb of this one [Phocas] and touches the holy tomb of the body, the place fills me with a remembrance of all the stories that were told of him here." In Hebron the "sight of the holy places" renews the "image" so that one "sees in one's mind the faithful patriarch" and becomes a "spectator of their whole history" (*homilia* 9.2; ed. *Datema* 116–117). See Jerome, *epistola* 46.13 and Gregory of Nyssa, *epistola* 2.2. On this point see Maraval, *Lieux saints et pèlerinages d'Orient*, pp. 138–139.

36. Wilkinson, *Egeria's Travels*, p. 94.

37. Maurice Halbwachs, *La Topographie légendaire des évangiles en terre sainte* (Paris: 1971), p. 126.

38. Myst. catech. 5.22; see also John Chrysostom, *Patrologia Graeca* 63.898a.

39. *Patrologia Graeca* 30.112c.

40. Ibid. 46.739a–b.

41. Jerome, *epistola* 114; *Vigil.* 4. On the *"praesentia"* of the saint at the tombs, see P. Brown, *The Cult of the Saints* (Chicago: 1981), p. 109. On veneration of the tombs of the faithful departed martyrs, see Brown, ibid.; H. Delehaye, *Les Origines du culte des martyrs* (Brussels: 1933); and H. J. W. Drijvers, "Spätantike Parallelen zur altchristlichen Heiligenverehrung unter besonderer Berücksichtigung des syrischen Styliten-Kultes," *Erkentnisse und Meinungen* 2 (1978): 77–113.

42. Gary Vikan, *Byzantine Pilgrimage Art* (Washington: 1982), p. 13; see also the essays in Ousterhout, *The Blessings of Pilgrimage*.

43. *Itinerarium Burdigalense*, p. 37 (Wilkinson, *Egeria's Travels*, p. 137).

44. *Hist. Relig.* 9.2. Inscription at the tomb of St. Martin of Tours reads: "Here lies Martin the bishop, of holy memory, whose soul is in the hand of god; but he is *fully here*, present and made plain in miracles of every kind." E. Le Blant, *Les inscriptions chrétiennes de la Gaule*, vol. 1 (Paris: 1856), p. 240. Seeing is a form of touching. Augustine: "Quia radios qui per eos emicant et quidquid *cernimus tangunt*" (*De trinitate* 9.3.3); also 9.6.11. On this point, see Margaret Miles, "Vision: The Eye of the Body and the Eye of the Mind in Saint Augustine's *De trinitate* and *Confessions*," *Journal of Religion* 63 (1983): 127.

45. Jerome, *epistola* 109.1.

46. *Vita Macrinae*, preface (*Patrologia Graeca* 46, 960a); *epistola* 3 (G. Pasquali, ed., *Gregori Nysenni Opera*, vol. 8, part 2, *Epistulae* [Leiden: 1925], p. 20).

47. *Contra Eunomium* 3.9.54–60 (W. Jaeger, ed., *Gregori Nysenni Opera,* vol. 2, *Contra Eunomium Libri* [Leiden: 1960], pp. 284–288).

48. *Epistola* 3.4 (Pasquali, p. 21).

49. In the Pasquali edition, the argument about whether pilgrimage is commanded occurs in paragraphs 3–4 (14); about place, in paragraphs 8–9 (15–16) and 16 (18); about morals, in paragraphs 6–8 (15). Basil also discouraged travel by monks (*regulae fusius tractatae* 39). Similar sentiments appear in a letter attributed to Athanasius (preserved in Syriac), written to a group of nuns who had gone to Jerusalem on pilgrimage. The letter commends them for their devotion but goes on to spiritualize the holy places: "You have seen the place at the Nativity; let your souls be reborn. You have seen the place of the Cross: let the world be crucified to you and you to the world." J. Lebon, "Athanasiana Syriaca II: Une lettre attribuée à Saint Athanase d'Alexandrie," *Le Museon* 41 (1927): 169–216. On this point, see Joseph T. Rivers, "Pattern and Process in Early Christian Pilgrimage," Ph.D. diss., Duke University, 1983. Vigilantius objected to the veneration of the tombs of the martyrs (*Contra Vigil.* 1). For criticism of pilgrimage among Syriac-speaking Christians, see Fiey, *Le pèlerinage,* pp. 115–117.

50. Chrysanthus Notaras's *History and Description of the Holy Land* (Vienna: 1728) (in Greek) is a defense of Christian pilgrimage to the Holy Land and of Gregory of Nyssa's letter on pilgrimage. See p. 141.

51. *Imag.* 3.34.

52. Samuel Johnson, *Rasselas, Poems and Selected Prose,* ed. Bertrand H. Bronson (New York: 1971), p. 631.

53. Stephen Graham, *With the Russian Pilgrims to Jerusalem* (London: 1914).

7. Jewish Pilgrimage after the Destruction of the Second Temple

I would like to thank Nitza Rosovsky for her help in preparing this chapter. My special thanks go to my teacher, Professor Arthur Hertzberg, for his continuing friendship and encouragement.

1. Michael Avi-Yonah, *Be-Yemei Roma u-Byzantium* (In the Days of Rome and Byzantium) (Jerusalem: Bialik Institute, 1970), pp. 40–41 (in Hebrew). Elhanan Reiner, *Aliyah ve-Aliyah le-Eretz Yisrael, 1099–1517* (Pilgrims and Pilgrimages to the Land of Israel, 1099–1517), Ph.D. dissertation, Hebrew University, Jerusalem, p. 81 (in Hebrew). Maimonides, *Mishneh Torah,* Book of Judges, ch. 5.

2. F. E. Peters, *Jerusalem: The Holy City in the Eyes of Chroniclers, Visitors, Pilgrims, and Prophets from the Days of Abraham to the Beginnings of Modern*

Times (Princeton, N.J.: Princeton University Press, 1985), pp. 124–125. See also Avi-Yonah, *Roma u-Byzantium*, p. 19.

3. Shmuel Safrai, "The Era of the Mishnah and Talmud (70–640)," in H. H. Ben-Sasson, ed., *A History of the Jewish People* (Cambridge, Mass.: Harvard University Press, 1976), pp. 333–335.

4. Avi-Yonah, *Roma u-Byzantium*, pp. 70–71.

5. The ban began in the Roman period with an edict from Emperor Hadrian. Ibid., p. 142.

6. The Bordeaux Pilgrim, *Itinerary from Bordeaux to Jerusalem,* vol. 1 (London: Palestine Pilgrims' Text Society, 1887–1897), p. 22. The statues were on the Temple Mount, according to Jerome, and the perforated, or pierced, stone probably refers to *even ha-sheteya,* the Foundation Stone, over which the Dome of the Rock was built. Others believe that the stone may have been on the Mount of Olives, the same stone that became the focal point of a communal event under the Muslims. See the section on the Early Arab period in this chapter.

7. Avi-Yonah, *Roma u-Byzantium,* pp. 141–143. Safrai, "Mishnah and Talmud," pp. 349, 354.

8. Babylonian Talmud, Tractate Moed Katan 26a. See also Shmuel Safrai, "Talmudic Sources on Aliya and Pilgrimage," in Lee I. Levine, ed., *The Jerusalem Cathedra,* vol. 3 (Jerusalem: Yad Izhak Ben-Zvi; Detroit: Wayne State University Press, 1983), p. 188.

9. S. D. Goitein, "Jerusalem in the Arab Period (638–1099)," in *The Jerusalem Cathedra,* vol. 2, (1982), p. 170.

10. Avraham Ya'ari, *Igrot Eretz Yisrael* (Letters of Eretz Israel) (Ramat Gan: Masada, 1971), pp. 47–48, 51 (in Hebrew).

11. See S. D. Goitein's introduction to Jacob Mann's *The Jews in Egypt and in Palestine under the Fatimid Caliphs* (1920–1922; reprint, New York: Ktav Publishing House, 1970), p. xix. See also Peters, *Jerusalem,* p. 232, and Avraham Grossman, "Aliya in the Seventh and Eighth Centuries," *The Jerusalem Cathedra,* vol. 3, pp. 174–180.

12. Moshe Gil, "Aliya and Pilgrimage in the Early Arab Period (634–1009)," *The Jerusalem Cathedra,* vol. 3, pp. 163–168. Zvi Ankori, *Karaites in Byzantium: The Formative Years, 970–1100* (New York: Columbia University Press, 1959), p. 22. Yaari, *Igrot,* pp. 56–59. Avraham Ya'ari, *Masa'ot Eretz Yisrael* (Travels in Eretz Israel) (Tel Aviv: Department of Youth Affairs of the Zionist Organization, 1945), pp. 221–223 (in Hebrew).

13. Yaari, *Igrot,* p. 54; also Gil, *Aliyah,* p. 164.

14. Yaari, *Igrot,* p. 60.

15. Ankori, *Karaites,* pp. 186–188. Zvi Ankori, "The Correspondence of Tobias ben Moses the Karaite of Constantinople," in Joseph L. Blau et al., eds.,

Essays on Jewish Life and Thought Presented in Honor of Professor Salo Wittmayer Baron (New York: Columbia University Press, 1959), pp. 1–38.

16. This custom seems to have originated in an earlier period. See Safrai, *Talmudic Sources,* pp. 188–189.

17. S. D. Goitein, *A Mediterranean Society: The Community,* vol. 2 (Berkeley: University of California Press, 1971), pp. 284–285.

18. Ibid., p. 201.

19. Abraham ibn Daud, *Sefer ha-Qabbalah: The Book of Tradition,* ed. Gerson D. Cohen (Philadelphia: Jewish Publication Society, 1967), p. 94.

20. Reiner, *Aliyah,* pp. 183–187.

21. Ibn Daud, *Sefer ha-Qabbalah,* p. 94.

22. Gil, "Aliya and Pilgrimage," p. 167. Yaari, *Igrot,* pp. 47–68.

23. Reiner, *Aliyah,* p. 187.

24. S. D. Goitein, "Genizah Sources for the Crusader Period," in B. Z. Kedar et al., eds., *Outremer: Studies in the History of the Crusading Kingdom of Jerusalem* (Jerusalem: Yad Izhak Ben-Zvi, 1982), pp. 306–311. The volume honored Joshua Prawer.

25. Goitein, "Genizah Sources," pp. 311–312.

26. Reiner, *Aliyah,* p. 26.

27. Joshua Prawer, "The Hebrew Itineraries of the Crusader Period," *Cathedra* 40 (1986): 32–35 (in Hebrew). The city was considered "ruined" even when it flourished, because it was held by non-Jews.

28. See Benjamin of Tudela, *The Itinerary of Benjamin of Tudela: Travels in the Middle Ages* (Malibu, Calif.: Joseph Simon/Pangloss Press, 1987), pp. 82–86, and Yaari, *Masa'ot,* pp. 31–55.

29. Yaari, ibid., pp. 64, 70–71.

30. The arrival of Jews from England and France in 1211 is known from a late literary source, which gave their number as 300. But based on a letter from the Genizah, Goitein believed the number was closer to 100. Goitein, "Genizah Sources," pp. 319–320.

31. Joshua Prawer, "Jerusalem in Jewish and Christian Thought of the Early Middle Ages," *Cathedra* 17 (1980): 72 (in Hebrew).

32. At least until 1236, when pilgrimages were again permitted. Goitein, "Genizah Sources," pp. 320–321.

33. Yaari, *Masa'ot,* pp. 71–80. Yaari, *Igrot,* pp. 83–86.

34. Reiner, *Aliyah,* pp. 88–105.

35. Reuben Levy, *The Social Structure of Islam* (Cambridge: Cambridge University Press, 1969), p. 250. Levy quotes a tenth-century source as claiming that a *ziyara* to a certain shrine was considered equivalent to going on Hajj to Mecca.

36. Reiner, *Aliyah,* pp. 124–125, 217–228.

37. Yaari, *Masa'ot*, p. 41, and Reiner, *Aliyah*, pp. 160–161.

38. Minna Rozen, "The Position of the Musta'rabs in the Inter-Community Relationships in Eretz Israel from the 15th to the End of the 17th Century," *Cathedra* 17 (1980): 73–82 (in Hebrew).

39. Yaari, *Igrot*, pp. 100, 127–130. Ovadiah's letters constitute an excellent source for Jewish life in the city.

40. Rozen, "The Position of the Musta'rabs," p. 83; Yaari, *Masa'ot*, pp. 148–149.

41. Yaari, *Igrot*, p. 85.

8. Jerusalem and Zionism

1. Musaf service for festivals, e.g., *The Complete Art Scroll Siddur* (Nusah Sefarad), ed. Nosson Sherman (New York: Mesorah Publications, 1989), p. 725.

2. Isaiah 10:5.

3. Leon Pinsker, "Auto-Emancipation," excerpt in Arthur Hertzberg, ed., *The Zionist Idea* (New York: Doubleday, 1959), pp. 183, 197.

4. Theodor Herzl, "The Jewish State," excerpt in Hertzberg, *The Zionist Idea*, p. 222.

5. Theodor Herzl, *The Jewish State*, 50th anniversary ed. (New York: American Zionist Emergency Council, 1946), p. 146.

6. Ibid.

7. Theodor Herzl, *Tagebücher 1895–1904*, 3 vols. (Berlin: Jüdischer Verlag, 1922), see vol. 1, p. 426; vol. 2, pp. 207, 221, 602; vol. 3, pp. 556–557; see also Chaya Harel, "Yahaso shel Herzl le-Yerushalayim," in Hagit Lavsky, ed., *Yerushalayim ba-Todaah u'ba-Asiyah ha-Zionit* (Jerusalem: Merkaz Zalman Shazar, 1989), pp. 75–90. Herzl did imagine creating a modern Jewish city in Jerusalem outside the enclave that included the great shrines of all three monotheistic religions, but even at his most expansive, he accepted the probability that the Old City would have a separate status.

8. Ber Borochov, "The National Question and the Class Struggle," excerpt in Hertzberg, *The Zionist Idea*, pp. 355–360.

9. A. D. Gordon, "Logic for the Future," excerpt in Hertzberg, *The Zionist Idea*, pp. 371–372; A. D. Gordon, "Some Observations," excerpt in ibid., p. 376.

10. Ahad Ha'am, *Al Parashat Derachim*, vol. 1 (Berlin: Judischer Verlag, 1921), p. 43.

11. Leon Simon, *Ahad Ha'am: A Biography* (Philadelphia: Jewish Publications Society, 1960), p. 266.

12. On the first stirrings toward the creation of a Jewish university, see Yosef

Gorni, "Yerushalayim shel Ma'alah ve-Yerushalayim shel Matah ba-Mediniyut ha-Leumit," in Avi Bareli, ed., *Yerushalayim ha-Hetsuyah, 1948–1967* (Jerusalem: Yad Izhak Ben-Zvi, 1994), p. 12; H. N. Bialik, "On the Hebrew University," excerpt in Hertzberg, *The Zionist Idea*, pp. 281–288.

13. Jerusalem was the capital of an independent *sanjak,* ruled by a governor directly responsible to Constantinople. The administration of Palestine was divided between the *vilayet* of Beirut, whose authority extended from the sea to the river Jordan as far south as Jaffa, including the districts of Nablus and Acre, and the district of Jerusalem, which had authority over the rest of the area between the river and the sea.

14. For population figures on Jerusalem, see Yehoshua Ben-Arieh, *Ir be-Re'i Tekufah* (Jerusalem: Yad Izhak Ben Zvi, 1977), pp. 318, 403; for the population after 1922, when the British Mandate government was formally established, see "Jerusalem" in the *Encyclopaedia Judaica,* vol. 9 (Jerusalem: Keter Publishing House, 1972), columns 1471 and 1478.

15. On August 28, 1929, five days after the outbreak of rioting in Jerusalem, an emergency conference of Zionist leaders was convoked in Marienbad, Czechoslovakia, under the chairmanship of Chaim Nachman Bialik, to frame a memorandum that Weizmann was asked to present to the British government. In a set of demands about British policy in Palestine, this group included as a matter of course the issue of the status of the Western Wall. Weizmann, as president of the World Zionist Organization, took the lead in this negotiation during the next two years. See Meyer W. Weisgal and Joel Carmichael, eds., *Chaim Weizmann: A Biography by Several Hands* (London: Weidenfeld and Nicolson, 1962), pp. 225–228.

16. Yehuda Alkalai, "Minchat Yehudah," excerpt in Hertzberg, *The Zionist Idea,* pp. 105–107.

17. Abraham Isaac Kook, "Orot," excerpt in Hertzberg, *The Zionist Idea,* pp. 419–431.

18. See the summary of Weizmann's appearances, both formal and informal, before the Peel Commission, in Weisgal and Carmichael, *Chaim Weizmann,* pp. 236–241. He knew, early in the deliberations, that the Peel Commission was moving to suggest the partition of Palestine. Weizmann encouraged that outcome, as it would be a historic breakthrough. Despite likely unsatisfactory boundaries, it would be the first time in nineteen centuries that a Jewish state was proposed by the government that ruled Palestine.

19. Vladimir Jabotinsky, "Evidence Submitted to the Palestine Royal Commission," excerpt in Hertzberg, *The Zionist Idea,* pp. 559–570.

20. Walter Laqueur, *A History of Zionism* (New York: 1972), pp. 517–520. See also Moti Golani, "Zionut le-lo Zion?" in Bareli, *Yerushalayim ha-Hetsuyah,* pp. 32–36.

21. Laqueur, *A History of Zionism,* pp. 580, 587.

22. See their essays in Hebrew describing their feelings about Jerusalem: Amos Oz, "Ir Zarah?" in Bareli, *Yerushalayim ha-Hetsuyah,* pp. 294–297; Hayim Guri, "Beyn Tel Aviv le-Yerushalayim," in Lavsky, *Yerushalayim ba-Todaah u'ba-Asiyah ha-Zionit,* pp. 451–455.

9. Palestinian Images of Jerusalem

1. Quotation from a work by Burhan al-Din al-Fazari, lecturer and preacher at the Umayyad Mosque in Damascus and the leading Arab geographer of his time; he died in 1329. The quotation is cited by Walid Khalidi in *Before Their Diaspora: A Photographic History of the Palestinians 1876–1948.* (Washington, D.C.: Institute for Palestine Studies, 1984), p. 21.

2. Koran, Sura 17, "al-Isra'," verse 1.

3. *Hadith* (narrative relating deeds and utterances of the Prophet Muhammad and his Companions).

4. Abdul Aziz Duri, "Jerusalem in the Early Islamic Period, 7th–11th Centuries AD," in K. J. Asali, ed., *Jerusalem in History* (New York: Olive Branch Press, 1990), p. 115.

5. Ibid., pp. 115–120; S. D. Goitein, "The Sanctity of Jerusalem and Palestine in Early Islam," in his *Studies in Islamic History and Institutions* (Leiden: 1966), pp. 134–148.

6. Quoted by Donald P. Little, "Jerusalem under the Ayyubids and Mamluks 1187–1516 AD," in Asali, *Jerusalem in History,* p. 179.

7. Mujir al-Din al-Ulaymi, *Al-Uns al-Jalil Fi Tarikh al-Quds wal-Khalil,* vol. 1 (Amman: 1973), pp. 335–339; K. J. Asali, *Watha'iq Maqdisiyya Tarikhiyya,* vol. 1 (Amman: 1983), pp. 85–99; K. J. Asali, *Ma'ahid al-'Ilm fi Bayt al-Maqdis* (Amman: 1981), pp. 60–65.

8. Little, "Jerusalem under the Ayyubids and Mamluks," pp. 188–196.

9. K. J. Asali, "Jerusalem under the Ottomans, 1516–1831 AD," in Asali, *Jerusalem in History,* pp. 200–213.

10. Asali, ibid., pp. 214–222.

11. Alexander Scholch, "Jerusalem in the 19th Century (1831–1917 AD)," in Asali, *Jerusalem in History,* pp. 228–239; Haim Gerber, *Ottoman Rule in Jerusalem, 1890–1914* (Berlin: Klaus Schwarz Verlag, 1985).

12. Muhammad Muslih, *Origins of Palestinian Nationalism* (New York: Columbia University Press, 1988), pp. 19–21.

13. Yehoshua Porath, *The Emergence of the Palestinian-Arab National Movement, 1918–1929* (London: Frank Cass, 1974), p. 6.

14. See Khalidi, *Before Their Diaspora,* p. 41.

15. Muslih, *Origins,* pp. 218–219.

16. Gabriel Baer, "Village and City in Egypt and Syria: 1500–1914," in A. L. Udovitch, ed., *The Islamic Middle East, 700–1900: Studies in Economic and Social History* (Princeton, N.J.: Darwin Press, 1981), p. 638.

17. For details on the life of al-Hajj Amin, see Philip Mattar, *The Mufti of Jerusalem: Al-Hajj Amin Al-Husayni and the Palestinian National Movement* (New York: Columbia University Press, 1988).

18. Porath, *Emergence;* Muslih, *Origins.*

19. Porath, *Emergence,* pp. 41–42.

20. See "Al-Quds," in *al-Mawsu'a al-Filastiniyya* (The Palestinian Encyclopedia), vol. 3 (Damascus: Hay'at al-Mawsu'a al-Filastiniyya, 1984); Michael C. Hudson, "The Transformation of Jerusalem, 1917–1987 AD," in Asali, *Jerusalem in History,* pp. 260–267; Daphne Tsimhoni, "Demographic Trends of the Christian Population in Jerusalem and the West Bank, 1948–1978," *Middle East Journal* 37, no. 1 (Winter 1983): 54–64.

21. *Tarikh al-Haram al-Qudsi* (Jerusalem: n.p., 1947).

22. *Tarikh al-Quds* (Jerusalem: n.p., 1922).

23. *Muthir al Gharam bi fada'il al-Quds wal-Sham* (Jaffa: Maktabat al-Tahir, 1945).

24. *Buldaniyat Filastin al-'Arabiyya* (Beirut: Jeanne d'Arc Press, 1948).

25. For a detailed discussion of this subject, see Tarif Khalidi, "Palestinian Historiography: 1900–1948," *Journal of Palestine Studies* 10, no. 3 (Spring 1981): 59–76.

26. This image can be found in numerous memoranda submitted by Palestinian leaders to the British government, the Allied powers, and the League of Nations. See Akram Zu'aytir, *Watha'iq al-Haraka al-Wataniyya al-Filastiniyya 1918–1939* (Beirut: Institute for Palestine Studies, 1979), particularly documents 1, 11, 12, 39, and 44.

27. 'Arif al-'Arif, *al-Mufassal fi Tarikh al-Quds,* vol. 1 (Jerusalem: Maktab al-Andalus Matba'af Dar al-Ma'arif, 1961).

28. A detailed treatment of this topic can also be found in al-Asali, *Ma'ahid al-'Ilm fi Bayt al-Maqdis.*

29. *'Urubat Bayt al-Maqdis* (Beirut: PLO Research Center, 1969).

30. Beirut: Institute for Palestine Studies, 1969.

31. *Al-Quds,* Aug. 12, 1993, p. 1.

32. Walid A. Khalidi, "Perspectives for an Israeli-Palestinian Peace," in William G. Miller and Philip H. Stoddard, eds., *Perspectives on the Middle East 1983: Proceedings of a Conference* (Washington, D.C.: Middle East Institute, and the Fletcher School of Law and Diplomacy, 1983), pp. 22–23.

33. Ibid., pp. 24–25.

34. Ibrahim Dakkak, "The Meaning of Jerusalem," in *Jerusalem: A Special*

Report (Washington, D.C.: The Center for Policy Analysis on Palestine, 1993), pp. 3–6.

35. Adnan Abu Odeh, "Two Capitals in an Undivided Jerusalem," *Foreign Affairs* (Spring 1992): 183–188.

36. Bernard Sabella, "Sovereignty Sharing Is the Key to Equality," in *Jerusalem: Perspectives towards a Political Settlement* (Tel Aviv: Middle East Magazine Project, July 1993), pp. 39–41.

37. Hanna Siniora, "The Solution Is the One Which Is Acceptable to Both Sides," in ibid., pp. 28–32. Similar ideas were also expressed by Sali Nusseibeh, who endorsed the idea of sharing the city and dividing sovereignty over it with the redrawing of physical, tangible borders. Nusseibeh's ideas can be found in *Jerusalem: Visions of Reconciliation, an Israeli-Palestinian Dialogue* (New York: United Nations Department of Public Information, 1993), pp. 49–53.

38. For details on the "scattered sovereignty" model, see *A Model for the Future of Jerusalem, Working Draft No. 2, Feb. 1993,* created by the Israeli-Palestinian Roundtable Discussion on the Future of Jerusalem, under the auspices of the Israel/Palestine Center for Research and Information (IPCRI).

39. Albert Aghazarian, "Growing Up in Jerusalem: City of Mirrors," *Middle East Report* 23, no. 182 (May/June 1993): 13–15.

40. See, for example, Azmi Bishara, "The Myth of Jerusalem," in *Jerusalem: Perspectives Towards a Political Settlement,* pp. 22–26.

41. Aghazarian, "City of Mirrors."

42. Tibawi, *Jerusalem: Its Place in Islam and Arab History,* pp. 42–44.

43. Henry Cattan, *Jerusalem* (New York: St. Martin's Press, 1981).

44. *Al-Quds al-'Arabiyya* (Amman: Dar al-Tiba'a wal-Nashr, 1971).

45. *Al-Mu'amarat al-Isra'iliyya 'ala al-Quds ma Bayna 1965–1975* (Amman: Municipality of Jerusalem, 1975).

46. *Mudhakkira Hawla Muhawalat Sulutat al-Ihtilal al-'Askari al-Isra'ili Itida'atiha li-Taghyir Awda' Madinat al-Quds* (Amman: Municipality of Jerusalem, 1977).

47. Washington, D.C.: Institute for Palestine Studies, 1985.

48. Quoted in Abdel Wahab M. El-Messiri, "The Palestinian Wedding, Major Themes of Contemporary Palestinian Resistance Poetry," *Journal for Palestine Studies* 10, no. 39 (Spring 1981): 89.

49. See, for example, Yusuf Qutteineh, "Al-Quds Awwalan" (Jerusalem First), *Al-Quds,* Aug. 18, 1993, p. 10; see also references cited in notes 51 and 52.

50. Daoud Kuttab, "Occupied Territories: Frustration and Anger," *Middle East International,* no. 464, Dec. 3, 1993, pp. 5–6.

51. For more details on how the Palestinian opposition dealt with the Jerusalem question and other related issues, see Riyad al-Malki, *al-Mu'arada al-*

Wataniyya, Tahlil al-Bada'il (The Nationalist Opposition: An Analysis of the Alternatives) (Nablus: Center for Palestine Research and Studies, Aug. 1993); Ziyad Abu 'Amr, Ali al-Jarbawi, and Khalil al-Shiqaqi, *Qira' Tahlili-yya lil-Ittifaq al-Filastini al-Isra'ili "Ghazza wa-Ariha awwalan"* (An Analytic Study of the Israeli-Palestinian "Gaza-Jericho First" Agreement) (Nablus: Center for Palestine Research and Studies, Sept. 1993).

52. Ibrahim Matar, "To Whom Does Jerusalem Belong?" *Jerusalem* (Washington, D.C.: The Center for Policy Analysis on Palestine, 1993), pp. 7–17; Henry Cattan, "Chronology of Jerusalem," in *The Palestine Question* (London: Croom Helm, 1988). A treatment of this subject can be found in Meron Benvenesti, *Jerusalem: The Torn City* (Minneapolis: University of Minnesota Press, 1976) and in his *The West Bank Data Project: The Shepherd's War, Collected Essays (1981–1989)* (Jerusalem: The Jerusalem Post, 1989), pp. 35–51.

53. Ibrahim Matar, "From Palestinian to Israeli: Jerusalem 1948–1982," *Journal of Palestine Studies* 12, no. 4 (Summer 1983): 57–64; Soraya Antonious's review of Teddy Kollek's book *For Jerusalem: A Life*, in *Journal of Palestine Studies* 8, no. 4 (Summer 1979): 105–108; Azmy Bishara, "Jerusalem Voices," *Middle East Report* 23, no. 182 (May–June 1993): 28.

54. Ziyad Abu Zayyad, "The Historical, Cultural, Religious and National Significance of Jerusalem," in *Jerusalem: Perspectives towards a Political Settlement*, pp. 6–9.

55. Ibrahim Dakkak, "Jerusalem's Via Dolorosa," *Journal of Palestine Studies* 11, no. 1 (Autumn 1981): 148–149. A general discussion of some of these problems can be found in Naomi Chazan, *Negotiating the Non-Negotiable: Jerusalem in the Framework of an Israeli-Palestinian Settlement*, Occasional Paper no. 7, March 1991, International Security Studies Program, American Academy of Arts and Sciences, Cambridge, Mass.

56. Quoted by Nafez Nazzal, "The Significance of Jerusalem for Moslems," in *Jerusalem: Perspectives towards a Political Settlement*, p. 20.

10. Jerusalem in Medieval Islamic Literature

1. See S. D. Goitein, "al-Kuds" (Jerusalem), in *The Encyclopaedia of Islam*, 2nd ed. (Leiden: E. J. Brill, 1954–); hereafter cited as *EI/2*. The first verse was associated with the following verses, since the present order of the Koran was fixed during the caliphate of 'Uthman (r. 644–656).

2. F. E. Peters, *Jerusalem: The Holy City in the Eyes of Chroniclers, Visitors, Pilgrims, and Prophets from the Days of Abraham to the Beginnings of Modern Times* (Princeton, N.J.: Princeton University Press, 1985), p. 176; most of

the travelers' accounts referred to in this chapter are quoted in Peters's book.

3. Peters, *Jerusalem,* pp. 196–197.

4. On these works, see the essays in Julian Raby and Jeremy Johns, eds., *Bayt al-Maqdis: 'Abd al-Malik's Jerusalem,* Oxford Studies in Islamic Art, 9 (Oxford: Oxford University Press for the Board of Faculty of Oriental Studies, University of Oxford, 1992).

5. Nasser Rabbat, "The Dome of the Rock Revisited: Some Remarks on al-Wasiti's Accounts," *Muqarnas* 10 (1993): 67–75.

6. On Ramla, see *EI/2,* s.v. "Ramla."

7. Goitein, p. 326a.

8. *EI/2,* s.v. "Fadila."

9. I. Hasson, "The Muslim View of Jerusalem—The Qur'an and Hadith," typescript, p. 43. The typescript translation of this chapter from Hasson's *Sefer Yerushalayim* (forthcoming) was generously made available to me by the author.

10. M. J. Kister, "You Shall Only Set Out for Three Mosques: A Study of an Early Tradition," *Le Muséon* 82 (1969): 173–196.

11. Abu Bakr Muhammad b. Ahmad al-Wasiti, *Fada'il al-Bayt al-Muqaddas* (Praises of Jerusalem), ed. Isaac Hasson, Max Schloessinger Memorial Series Texts, 3 (Jerusalem: The Magnes Press/Hebrew University, 1979). For Jerusalem in the *fada'il* literature, see Hasson, typescript.

12. *EI/2,* s.v. "Mi'radj."

13. Hasson, typescript, pp. 14–15.

14. Hasson, typescript, pp. 19–20.

15. *EI/2,* s.v. "Ibn al-Fakih."

16. Eva Baer, "The Mihrab in the Cave of the Dome of the Rock," *Muqarnas* 3 (1985): 8–29.

17. *EI/2,* s.v. "Mukaddasi."

18. The others were al-Mutahhar b. Tahir, a student of religion, and Abu Sulayman Muhammad b. Ma'shar al-Qudsi, credited with being one of the authors of the *Rasa'il ikhwan al-safa'* (Epistles of the Sincere Brethren), an Isma'ili compendium of Hellenic lore and science.

19. Much of al-Muqaddasi's account is translated in Peters, *Jerusalem.* See also Guy Le Strange, *Palestine under the Moslems* (reprint, Beirut: Khayat, 1965).

20. W. M. Thackston, Jr., *Naser'e Khosraw's Book of Travels (Safarnama),* Persian Heritage Series, 36 (New York: Bibliotheca Persica, 1986), pp. 21–38.

21. Peters, *Jerusalem,* p. 280, and *EI/2,* s.v. "Ghazali."

22. *The Autobiography of Ousâma,* trans. George Richard Potter (London: George Routledge and Sons, Ltd., 1929), pp. 176–177.

23. *EI/2,* s.v. "Harawi al-Mawsili," and *Guide des lieux de pèlerinage,* ed. with French trans. by J. Sourdel-Thomine (Damascus: 1952–1957).

24. Michael Hamilton Burgoyne, *Mamluk Jerusalem, an Architectural Study,* with additional historical research by D. S. Richards (London: World of Islam Festival Trust, 1987).

25. *EI/2,* s.v. "Mudjir al-Din al-'Ulaymi."

26. The text of this chapter was complete before the publication of Amikam Elad, *Medieval Jerusalem and Islamic Worship: Holy Places, Ceremonies, Pilgrimage* (Leiden: E. J. Brill, 1995).

11. Nineteenth-Century Portraits through Western Eyes

1. Yehoshua Ben-Arieh, *The Rediscovery of the Holy Land in the Nineteenth Century* (Detroit: Wayne State University Press, 1979), pp. 15, 118, 235.

2. Only fifty-one Americans, for example, registered with the first U.S. consul in Cairo between 1832 and 1842. Eight other travelers are known from other sources. See David Finnie, *Pioneers East: The Early American Experience in the Middle East* (Cambridge, Mass.: Harvard University Press, 1967), pp. 281–286.

3. Serious investigators who contributed greatly to the understanding of the country and the city are beyond the scope of this essay. For the contributions of Edward Robinson, Carl Ritter, Titus Tobler, H. B. Tristram, Félicien de Saulcy, Charles Warren, Charles Wilson, the Palestine Exploration Fund, and others, see Ben-Arieh, *Rediscovery.* Works by novelists not discussed in this essay are Gustave Flaubert's *Notes de Voyages,* Pierre Loti's *Jerusalem,* and Selma Lagerlöf's *Jerusalem.*

4. Laurie Magnus, "The Legacy in Modern Literature," citing historian J. R. Green, in E. R. Bevan and Charles Singer, eds., *The Legacy of Israel* (Oxford: Oxford University Press, 1927), pp. 499–500.

5. H. M. Jones, "The Legacy of Israel in the Anglo-Saxon Tradition," in Moshe Davis, ed., *Israel: Its Role in Civilization* (New York: Jewish Theological Seminary, 1956), p. 242.

6. Moshe Davis, "The Holy Land Idea in American History," in Moshe Davis, ed., *With Eyes toward Zion: Scholars Colloquium on America–Holy Land Studies* (New York: Arno Press, 1977), pp. 3–4.

7. Lottie Davis, "Biblical Place Names," in ibid., pp. 246–252.

8. William Blake, *Milton* (c. 1808), prefatory poem. "Blake's 'Jerusalem' was to be built by strenuous intellectual, imaginative and artistic labors: 'to Labour in Knowledge is to Build up Jerusalem,'" writes E. P. Thompson

in *Witness against the Beast: William Blake and the Moral Law* (New York: The New Press, 1993), p. 227. See also M. D. Paley, *The Continuing City: William Blake's Jerusalem* (Oxford: Clarendon Press, 1983), pp. 178–184, and S. F. Damon, *A Blake Dictionary: The Ideas and Symbols of William Blake* (Hanover, N.H.: The University Press of New England, 1988), pp. 206–213.

9. Jones, "Legacy of Israel," p. 247.

10. Finnie, *Pioneers East*, p. 5.

11. David Klatzker, "Teaching the America–Holy Land Experience in the Context of American Culture and Religious Thought," in Moshe Davis, ed., *With Eyes toward Zion-II: Themes and Sources in the Archives of the United States, Great Britain, Turkey and Israel* (New York: Praeger, 1986), p. 376.

12. Alphonse de Lamartine, *A Pilgrimage to the Holy Land Comprising Recollections, Sketches, and Reflections, Made during a Tour in the East,* vol. 1 (1835; reprint, New York: D. Appleton and Co., 1846), pp. 9–10.

13. Harriet Martineau, *Eastern Life: Present and Past* (Philadelphia: Lea and Blanchard, 1848), pp. 389, 372. Martineau had spent several months on camelback touring Egypt, the Sinai, and Transjordan before arriving in Palestine.

14. Mark Twain, *The Innocents Abroad* (1869; reprint, New York: New American Library, 1966), pp. 349–350, 403.

15. W. M. Thackeray, *Notes of a Journey from Cornhill to Cairo; by Way of Lisbon, Athens, Constantinople, and Jerusalem: Performed in the Steamers of the Peninsular and Oriental Company* (1846; reprint, London: J. M. Benet and Co., 1903), p. 115.

16. R. Browne, *Yusef; or, The Journey of the Frangi: A Crusade in the East* (New York: Harper and Bros., 1853), pp. 177–179. Not all dragomans were as superior as Yusef.

17. Lamartine, *Pilgrimage,* vol. 1, p. 307. Other travelers to the East, such as Seetzen and Burckhardt, donned Arab garb, a practice that survived well into the twentieth century, best demonstrated by Lawrence of Arabia.

18. W. C. Prime, *Tent Life in the Holy Land* (New York: Harper and Bros., 1858), p. 243.

19. Vivien Noakes, ed., *Edward Lear: Selected Letters* (Oxford: Clarendon Press, 1988), pp. 153–154.

20. Lamartine, *Pilgrimage,* vol. 1, pp. 249, 271.

21. Eliot Warburton, *The Crescent and the Cross; or, Romance and Realities of Eastern Travel,* vol. 2 (New York: George P. Putnam, 1848), pp. 52–53.

22. H. C. Horsford, ed., *Journal of a Visit to Europe and the Levant, Oct. 11, 1856–May 6, 1857, by Herman Melville* (Princeton, N.J.: Princeton University Press, 1955), pp. 124–125.

23. J. W. DeForest, *Oriental Acquaintance; or, Letters from Syria* (1846; reprint, New York: Edwards, 1856), pp. 65–66.

24. Franklin Walker, *Irreverent Pilgrims: Melville, Browne, and Mark Twain in the Holy Land* (Seattle: University of Washington Press, 1974), p. 39.

25. François-René Chateaubriand, *Travels to Jerusalem and the Holy Land through Egypt,* trans. Frederic Shoberl (London: Henry Colburn, 1835), vol. 1, p. 321.

26. Lamartine, *Pilgrimage,* vol. 1, p. 260.

27. J. L. Stephens, *Incidents of Travel in Egypt, Arabia Petraea, and the Holy Land,* vol. 2 (New York: Harper and Bros., 1837), pp. 195–196. The book was extremely successful—a tenth edition had been printed by 1839.

28. Thackeray, *Cornhill to Cairo,* p. 133.

29. Finnie, *Pioneers East,* p. 174.

30. Chateaubriand, *Travels,* vol. 2, p. 19; vol. 1, p. 10.

31. Lamartine, *Pilgrimage,* vol. 1, p. 260.

32. W. H. Bartlett, *Walks about the City and Environs of Jerusalem* (London: Hall, Virtue and Co., 1844?), p. 174. The question of whether the Church stood on the actual site of Golgotha was fiercely debated throughout the nineteenth century. In 1883, General Charles Gordon identified another tomb with a rolling stone at the foot of a hill that resembled a skull (*gulgolet,* in Hebrew) as the possible location of Golgotha. Situated outside the Old City Wall north of Damascus Gate, it is now known as the Garden Tomb.

33. Stephens, *Incidents of Travel,* vol. 2, pp. 205–207, 215.

34. Martineau, *Eastern Life,* pp. 385, 430.

35. Thackeray, *Cornhill to Cairo,* pp. 144–145.

36. Bartlett, *Walks,* p. 176.

37. Twain, *Innocents,* pp. 405, 415. Twain wrote that he copied the description of Helena discovering Calvary from "Grime's *Tent Life.*" Grime was a fictional character he based on William Prime, author of *Tent Life in the Holy Land,* whom Twain mocked for his naïveté and enthusiasm. Twain neglected to mention one book from which he himself copied shamelessly: J. L. Porter's *Handbook for Travellers in Syria and Palestine* (London: John Murray, 1858), generally known as Murray's *Handbook.*

38. Browne, *Yusef,* p. 361.

39. Warburton, *Crescent,* vol. 2, p. 67.

40. Thackeray, *Cornhill to Cairo,* p. 148.

41. Lamartine, *Pilgrimage,* vol. 1, p. 215.

42. Martineau, *Eastern Life,* p. 384.

43. Stephens, *Incidents of Travel,* vol. 2, p. 205.

44. Prime, *Tent Life,* p. 84.

45. Twain, *Innocents,* p. 404.

46. Prime, *Tent Life,* pp. 179–194. His description contained many common errors, such as the Mosque of al-Aqsa being a former church built by Emperor Justinian and taken over by the Muslims, a misconception that also appeared in Murray's *Handbook.*

47. Twain, *Innocents,* pp. 419, 421.

48. Chateaubriand, *Travels,* vol. 2, pp. 70.

49. Judith Montefiore, *Private Journal of a Visit to Egypt and Palestine, 1827,* photocopy ed. from a private printing (Jerusalem: Yad Izhak Ben-Zvi, 1975; London: Joseph Rickerby, 1836), pp. 81, 87.

50. Stephens, *Incidents of Travel,* vol. 2, pp. 237–238.

51. Thackeray, *Cornhill to Cairo,* p. 138.

52. Interestingly, when Bartlett drew a picture of the Wall ("Jews Place of Wailing—Temple Wall") in 1842, he stressed that he "saw no weeping or outward signs of sorrow" but that he had heard from others that Jews "wail over the desolation of Judah and implore the mercy and forgiveness of their God" (Bartlett, *Walks,* p. 141).

53. Martineau, *Eastern Life,* p. 405. Muslims, by law, were forbidden to convert.

54. Horsford, *Journal,* pp. 157–160. Had Melville returned to Palestine two decades after his 1857 visit, he would have encountered the Orthodox Jewish pioneers who set out from Jerusalem to found Petah Tikva, the first Jewish agricultural settlement that preceded Zionism.

55. Noakes, *Edward Lear,* pp. 155–156. After the death of Anglican Bishop Alexander (ironically, a converted Jew), it was the Prussians' turn to appoint a successor, and they chose Samuel Gobat, a Swiss who did not get along with James Finn, the long-term British consul in Jerusalem.

56. Chateaubriand, *Travels,* vol. 2, pp. 160–161.

57. A. W. Kinglake, *Eöthen* (Edinburgh: William Blackwood and Sons, 1904), p. 203. First published in 1844, nine years after his journey, the book was an immediate success.

58. Twain, *Innocents,* p. 365.

59. Thackeray, *Cornhill to Cairo,* pp. 137–140. In more than a dozen generally favorable reviews of *Cornhill to Cairo,* only one mentioned that the book presented a spirit "occasionally of spleen, sometimes of prejudice and bigotry." See Dudley Flamm, *Thackeray's Critics: An Annotated Bibliography of British and American Criticism, 1836–1901* (Chapel Hill: University of North Carolina Press, 1967), pp. 50–51.

60. Jones, "The Legacy of Israel," p. 234.

61. Warburton, *Crescent,* p. 134.

62. Twain, *Innocents,* p. 442.

63. Benjamin Disraeli, *Contarini Fleming, A Psychological Autobiography,* Col-

lection of British Authors, vol. 93 (1832; reprint, Leipzig: Bernhard Tauch-nutz, 1846), p. 319.

64. Benjamin Disraeli, *The Wonderous Tale of Alroy: A Romance*, Collection of British Authors, vol. 101 (1833; reprint, Leipzig: Bernhard Tauchnutz, 1846), p. 86.

65. Robert Blake, *Disraeli's Grand Tour: Benjamin Disraeli and the Holy Land 1830–31* (Oxford: Oxford University Press, 1982), p. 131. Blake cited Disraeli discussing with Lord Stanley the possibility of the Jews' returning to Palestine, buying land, and developing the country's natural resources. Disraeli thought that the man who would lead the Jews "would be the next Messiah, the true Saviour of his people."

66. Benjamin Disraeli, *Tancred, or the New Crusade* (1847; reprint, London: Peter Davies, 1927), p. 56.

67. She listed the Latins, Armenians, Greeks, Abyssinians, Maronites, and Copts, in addition to the English (Protestant) church.

68. Disraeli, *Tancred*, pp. 195–202.

69. Blake, *Disraeli's Grand Tour*, p. 123.

70. Disraeli, *Tancred*, p. 489.

71. Sarah Bradford, *Disraeli* (London: Weidenfeld and Nicolson, 1982), pp. 179, 34. In December 1847, the same year *Tancred* was published, Disraeli made his great speech in the House of Commons pleading the cause of Jewish emancipation, reminding the British people of their—and the whole human family's—debt to the Hebrew people for the knowledge of the true God.

72. Horsford, *Journal*, p. 4.

73. Letter from Melville to James Billson, New York, Oct. 10, 1884, Martin Collection of H. B. Martin, Jr., New York, N.Y., in Jay Leyda, *The Melville Log: A Documentary Life of Herman Melville 1819–1891*, vol. 2 (New York: Harcourt Brace, 1951), p. 786.

74. Horsford, *Journal*, p. 125. See also Raymond Weaver, ed., *Herman Melville: Journal up the Straits, October 11, 1856–May 5, 1857* (New York: Cooper Square Publishers, 1971).

75. Weaver, *Herman Melville*, p. 127.

76. *Clarel* is based on entries in Melville's diary plus at least a hundred images, facts, and fiction from the Bible as well as from sources that had become available between 1857 and 1876, such as Murray's *Handbook* and A. P. Stanley's *Sinai and Palestine*. Melville was familiar with, among others, Chateaubriand, Lamartine, Disraeli, Bartlett, Warburton, Scott's *Talisman*, and Kinglake's *Eöthen*. See Walter Bezanson, ed., *Herman Melville's Clarel: A Poem and a Pilgrimage in the Holy Land* (New York: Hendricks House, 1960), pp. xxxiv–xxxv.

77. Ibid., p. xxxiv.

78. Horsford, *Journal,* p. 144.

79. Ibid., pp. 149–150.

80. Bezanson, *Melville's Clarel,* p. liii, citing *Clarel,* I.xxxvi.29. The City of Dis is Dante's Nether Hell in *The Inferno,* Canto IX—a city of sorrow, a grieving city, the city of the dead.

81. Horsford, *Journal,* p. 24. In Egypt, on his way to the Holy Land, Melville wrote: "It was in these pyramids that was conceived the idea of Jehovah . . . Moses learned in all the lore of the Egyptians. The idea of Jehovah born here.—" (p. 118). Bezanson wondered: "Was it really the Jehovah concept that made Melville shudder, or was it the remembered Calvin-God, known to a child chiefly through the image of his own father? That father had died raving when Melville was twelve" (*Melville's Clarel,* p. xvii).

82. Browne, *Yusef,* p. 321.

83. Judith Montefiore, *Private Journal of a Visit to Egypt and Palestine by way of Italy and the Mediterranean* (privately printed, London, 1885). The entry, dated June 12, 1830, was made during the Montefiores' second visit. Quoted in Miron Grindea, ed., *Jerusalem: The Holy City in Literature* (London: Kahn and Averill, 1981), p. 190.

84. Blake, *Disraeli's Grand Tour,* p. 71. The city was cleaner in winter, after it rained, and Disraeli was there in January.

85. Ben-Arieh, *Rediscovery,* p. 70.

86. Lamartine, *Pilgrimage,* vol. 2, pp. 267–268.

87. Randall Stewart, ed., *The English Notebooks of Nathaniel Hawthorne* (New York: Modern Languages Association of America, 1941), pp. 432–433.

88. Horsford, *Journal,* p. 154.

89. On Twain's plagiarism, see Dewey Ganzel, *Mark Twain Abroad: The Cruise of the "Quaker City"* (Chicago: University of Chicago Press, 1968); Justin Kaplan, *Mr. Clemens and Mark Twain* (New York: Simon and Schuster, 1966); Walker, *Irreverent Pilgrims;* and Nitza Rosovsky, "Mark Twain's Visit to the Holy Land," in Ely Schiller, ed., *Zev Vilnay's Jubilee Volume,* vol. 2 (Jerusalem: Ariel, 1987), pp. 358–364 (in Hebrew).

90. Ganzel, *Mark Twain Abroad,* pp. 261–273.

91. Martineau, *Eastern Life,* p. 404.

92. MaryAnne Stevens, ed., *The Orientalists: Delacroix to Matisse: European Painters in North Africa and the Near East* (London: Royal Academy of Arts, 1984), p. 21.

93. Letter dated "Damascus. 27th May. 1858," in Noakes, *Edward Lear,* p. 156.

94. Ganzel, *Mark Twain Abroad,* p. 251, quoting from "Unpublished Notebook n. 8" (Typescript p. 50), Mark Twain Papers, the University of California Library, Berkeley, Calif.

95. Dated "Cairo, 30 March 1831," in J. A. W. Gunn, ed., *Benjamin Disraeli's Letters, 1815–1834* (Toronto: University of Toronto Press, 1982), p. 188.

96. A. P. Stanley, *Sinai and Palestine in Connection with Their History* (New York: W. J. Widdleton, 1865), p. 165 (first ed. 1856).

97. For population numbers, see Yehoshua Ben-Arieh, *Jerusalem in the Nineteenth Century: The Old City* (New York: St. Martin's Press, 1984), pp. 279, 358.

12. Depictions in Modern Hebrew Literature

1. Mendele Mocher Sefarim, *Kol Kitvey Mokher Sefarim* (Tel Aviv: 1947), pp. 148–149.

2. Chaim Nachman Bialik, *Devarim she'Ba'al Pe,* vol. 2 (Tel Aviv: 1935), p. 30. Translations into English are my own unless otherwise indicated.

3. See, for instance, Bialik's poignant, albeit indirect, reference to the desecration of the Temple of Jerusalem and to the undermining of its ritual in his autobiographical poem "Shirati." *Kol Shirey Ch. N. Bialik* (Tel Aviv: 1966), pp. 110–113.

4. Adam Hakohen Lebenzon, *Shirey Sefat Kodesh,* vol. 1 (Vilna: 1842–1870), pp. 201–205.

5. Shmuel Yoseph Agnon, *Kol Sipurav shel Sh. Y. Agnon,* vol. 5: *Temol Shilshom* (Jerusalem and Tel Aviv: 1960), p. 190.

6. Yoseph Chaim Brenner, *Ketavim,* vol. 2 (Tel Aviv: 1978), p. 1267.

7. Nathan Alterman, *Rega'im,* vol. 1 (Tel Aviv: 1974), p. 172.

8. Nathan Alterman, *Pizmonim ve'Shirey-zemer,* vol. 1 (Tel Aviv: 1976), p. 269.

9. Ahad Ha'am, *Kol Kitvey Ahad Ha'am* (Tel Aviv and Jerusalem: 1947), p. 30.

10. See Dan Miron, *Imahot-Meyasdot, Ahayot Horgot* (Tel Aviv: 1991), p. 219.

11. Alterman, *Rega'im,* vol. 1, p. 173.

12. Ibid., vol. 3.

13. Alexander Pen, *Le'orech ha-Derech* (Tel Aviv: 1956), pp. 45–53.

14. Nissim Kalderon, "Kol ha-Inyan ha-Yerushalmi ha-Matok ha-Ze," *Siman Kri'a* 5 (Feb. 1976): 460.

15. Agnon, *Temol Shilshom,* pp. 258, 263.

16. Ibid., p. 351.

17. Ibid., p. 490.

18. Ezra Zusman, *Shirim* (Tel Aviv: 1968), p. 46.

19. Ibid., p. 27.

20. Avigdor Hame'iri, *Sefer ha-Shirim* (Tel Aviv: 1932), p. 365.

21. Yehuda Karni, *Shirim,* vol. 2 (Jerusalem: 1992), p. 221.

22. Ibid., p. 245.

23. Ibid., p. 229.

24. Ibid., p. 222–223.

25. Uri Tsvi Greenberg, *Kol Kitvey Uri Tsvi Greenberg,* vol. 2 (Jerusalem: 1990–1995), p. 54.

26. Ibid., vol. 1, p. 90.

27. Ibid., p. 85.

28. Ibid., p. 83.

29. Ibid., vol. 4, p. 29.

30. Ibid., vol. 1, pp. 63–64.

31. Ibid., vol. 2, p. 26.

32. Translated from its original version, which is collected in Dan Pagis, *She'on ha-Tsel* (Tel Aviv: 1959), pp. 40–41. In his *Kol ha-Shirim* (Jerusalem: 1991), a somewhat contracted version appears on page 35.

33. Yehuda Amichai, *Hazman* (Jerusalem and Tel Aviv: 1957), p. 32.

34. See his "El Maleh Rahamim," Yehuda Amichai, *Shirim 1948–1962* (Jerusalem and Tel Aviv: 1962), p. 70.

35. Ibid., p. 35.

36. Ibid., p. 20.

37. Ibid., p. 16. See also *Selected Poetry of Yechuda Amichai,* ed. and trans. Chana Bloch and Stephen Mitchell (New York: 1986), p. 1.

38. Amichai, *Shirim 1948–1962,* p. 57.

39. Ibid., p. 78.

40. Ibid., p. 85.

41. Ibid., p. 185; *Selected Poetry,* p. 35.

42. *Shirim,* p. 220; *Selected Poetry,* p. 39.

43. Yehuda Amichai, *Achshav ba'Ra'ash* (Jerusalem and Tel Aviv: 1968), p. 11; *Selected Poetry,* p. 49.

44. Amichai, *Achshav,* p. 9; *Selected Poetry,* p. 48.

45. Amichai, *Achshav,* pp. 15–16; *Selected Poetry,* p. 52.

46. Amichai, *Achshav,* p. 10; *Selected Poetry,* p. 48.

47. Amichai, *Achshav,* p. 19; *Selected Poetry,* p. 54.

48. Amichai, *Achshav,* p. 18; *Selected Poetry,* p. 53.

49. Yehuda Amichai, *Shalva Gedola: She'elot u'Teshuvot* (Jerusalem and Tel Aviv: 1980), p. 78; *Selected Poetry,* p. 136.

50. Amichai, *Shalva,* p. 56; *Selected Poetry,* p. 135.

51. Amichai, *Hazman,* p. 52.

13. Geography and Geometry of Jerusalem

1. Bianca Kühnel, *From the Earthly to the Heavenly Jerusalem: Representations of the Holy City in Christian Art of the First Millennium* (Freiburg: 1987), esp. pp. 17–112 (hereafter cited as Kühnel).

2. Peter and Paul flank an Etimasia representation and are accompanied by an

explicatory papal inscription: "Xystus Episcopus Plebi Dei." See J. Wilpert and W. Schumacher, *Die römischen Mosaiken der kirchlichen Bauten vom IV.–XIII. Jahrhundert* (Freiburg: 1916; reprint, 1976), pls. 68–70, 71 (Bethleem), 72 (Hierusalem); B. Brenk, *Die frühchristlichen Mosaiken in S. Maria Maggiore zu Rom* (Wiesbaden: 1975), pp. 9–52.

3. Two recent publications devoted to a Roman church where the motif is represented, with parallel examples and exhaustive bibliographies, are by Rotraut Wisskirchen: *Das Mosaikprogramm von S. Prassede in Rom: Ikonographie und Ikonologie, Jahrbuch für Antike und Christentum,* Ergänzungsband 17 (Münster: 1990); and *Die Mosaiken der Kirche Santa Prassede in Rom,* Zaberns Bildbände zur Archäologie 5 (Mainz: 1992).

4. The motif also appears in sixth- and seventh-century Ravenna, on the triumphal arches of St. Vitale and St. Apollinare in Classe, probably as an outcome of the rivalry between the church of Ravenna and that of Rome. Otto G. von Simson, *Sacred Fortress: Byzantine Art and Statecraft in Ravenna* (reprint, Princeton, N.J.: 1987), p. 62, pls. 4, 21.

5. Mark R. Petersen, "*In cor descendit:* The Motif of the Heavenly Jerusalem at San Giovanni in Laterano in Rome," *Source* 11 (1991): 1–6.

6. Michael Avi-Yonah, *The Madaba Mosaic Map* (Jerusalem: 1954); H. Donner and H. Cuppers, *Die Mosaikkarte von Madaba,* Part I (Tafelband), Abhandlungen des Deutschen Palästinavereins (Wiesbaden: 1977); P. Donceel-Voute, "La carte de Madaba: cosmographie, anachronisme et propagande," *Revue Biblique* (1988): 519–542.

7. Kühnel, pp. 89ff.

8. Michele Piccirillo, *The Mosaics of Jordan,* American Center of Oriental Research Publications 1 (Amman: 1993), pp. 218ff, figs. 344–358.

9. John Williams, *The Illustrated Beatus: A Corpus of the Illustrations of the Commentary on the Apocalypse,* vol. 1: *Introduction* (London: 1994).

10. Wilhelm Neuss, *Die Apokalypse des hl. Johannes an der altspanischen und christlichen Bibel-Illustration* (Münster: 1931); Peter Klein, *Trierer Apokalypse, Vollständige Faksimile-Ausgabe im Originalformat des Codex 31 der Stadtbibliothek Trier,* 2 vols., Codices Selecti 48 (Graz: 1973), esp. pp. 52–56, with earlier bibliography; R. K. Emmerson and S. Lewis, "Census and Bibliography of Medieval Manuscripts Containing Apocalypse Illustrations, ca. 800–1500," *Traditio* 40 (1984): 337–379; R. K. Emmerson and B. McGinn, *The Apocalypse in the Middle Ages* (New York: 1992), esp. pp. 159–289, "The Apocalypse in Medieval Art."

11. Klein, *Trierer Apokalypse.*

12. F. von Juraschek, *Die Apokalypse von Valenciennes,* Veröffentlichungen der Gesellschaft für österreichische Frühmittelalter Forschung, Heft 1 (Linz: 1954); Kühnel, pp. 129ff, fig. 78.

13. Klein, *Trierer Apokalypse,* facsimile vol.; Kühnel, figs. 56–58.

14. Bibliothèque Nationale, nouv. acq. lat. 1132, fol. 33; H. Omont, "Un nouveau manuscrit illustré de l'apocalypse au XIe siècle: notice du ms. lat. nouv. acq. 1132 de la Bibliothèque Nationale," *Bibliothèque de l'École des Chartes* 83 (1922): 1–24; Kühnel, pp. 128ff, fig. 79.

15. Williams, *The Illustrated Beatus,* vol. 2: *The Ninth and Tenth Centuries,* pp. 21–33, fig. 97.

16. Henk van Os, *The Art of Devotion in the Late Middle Ages in Europe, 1300–1500,* exhibition catalogue (Amsterdam: Rijksmuseum, 1994), p. 54, fig. 14.

17. Ibid., p. 55.

18. Kühnel, pp. 128ff, 141ff, with earlier bibliography; Bianca Kühnel, "Likeness and Vision: *Loca Sancta* Tradition and Apocalyptic Inspiration in Christian Medieval Imagery," *The Israel Museum Journal* 5 (1986): 57–66.

19. Ellen J. Beer, *Die Rose der Kathedrale von Lausanne und der kosmologische Bilderkreis des Mittelalters* (Bern: 1952); Anton von Euw, "Imago mundi," in *Monumenta Annonis, Cologne and Siegburg: Weltbild und Kunst im hohen Mittelalter: Eine Ausstellung des Schnütgen-Museums der Stadt Köln in der Cäcilienkirche vom 30. April bis zum 27. Juli 1975* (Cologne: 1975), pp. 89ff; Anna-Dorothee v. den Brincken, "Mappa mundi," in ibid., pp. 118ff; Rudolf Simek, *Erde und Kosmos im Mittelater: Das Weltbild vor Kolumbus* (Munich: 1992).

20. "Cologne, Dombibliothek, Codex 83 II," in *Monumenta Annonis,* A35, pp. 92–95, 102.

21. G. B. Ladner, "St. Gregory of Nyssa and St. Augustine on the Symbolism of the Cross," in *Late Classical and Medieval Studies in Honor of A. Mathias Friend Jr.* (Princeton: 1955), pp. 88–95; Ellen J. Beer, "Nouvelles réflexions sur l'image du monde dans la cathédrale de Lausanne," *Revue de l'art* 10 (1970): 57–62; Barbara Bronder, "Das Bild der Schöpfung und Neuschöpfung der Welt als *orbis quadratus,*" *Frühmittelalterliche Studien* 6 (1972): 188–210, esp. pp. 200ff, with sources.

22. *Elucidarium, Patrologia Latina* 172, col. 1125D. On the German and Flemish textual reception of the *Elucidarium,* see Dagmar Gottschall, *Das "Elucidarium" des Honorius Augustodunensis* (Tübingen: 1992). Cassiodorus already proposed correlating circle and square: the square earth should be represented in the middle of the round cosmos. See Beer, "Nouvelles réflexions," p. 62.

23. Martin Werner, "On the Origin of the Form of the Irish High Cross," *Gesta* 29 (1990): 98–110.

24. Munich, Bayerische Staatsbibliothek, Clm. 210; J. B. Harley, D. Woodward, eds., *The History of Cartography,* vol. 1 (Chicago: 1987), p. 335, fig. 18.38.

25. The Christian symbolism of the number four has roots in Aristotelian

thought. See John Emery Murdoch, *Antiquity and the Middle Ages: Album of Science* (New York: 1984), pp. 346–359; Harley and Woodward, *The History of Cartography,* vol. 1, p. 335.

26. Wilhelm Bousset, "Platons Weltseele und das Kreuz Christi," *Zeitschrift für neutestamentliche Wissenschaft und die Kunde des Urchristentums* 14 (1913): 273–285; Hugo Rahner, *Griechische Mythen in christlicher Deutung* (Darmstadt: 1966), esp. p. 78 (Das Mysterium des Kreuzes).

27. Bousset, "Platon's Weltseele," p. 273.

28. University Library of Prague, fol. 168v; Karel Stejskal, ed., *The Welislaw Bible,* facsimile, *Cimelia Bohemica* 12 (Prague: 1970).

29. Colleen McDannell and Bernhard Lang, *Heaven: A History* (New Haven: 1988), esp. chap. 4, pp. 69ff.

30. F. van der Meer, *Maiestas Domini: Théophanies de l'Apocalypse dans l'art chrétien,* Studi di antichità cristiana 13 (Vatican City: 1938). *Maiestas* comes from the Italian word for "majesty."

31. Florence, Laurentian Library, cod. Amiatinus 1; K. Weitzmann, *Late Antique and Early Christian Book Illumination* (London: 1977), fig. XVII.

32. Paris, Bibliothèque Nationale, ms. lat. 1, fol. 329v; F. Mütherich and J. E. Gaehde, *Carolingian Painting* (London: 1977), pl. 23; Herbert L. Kessler, *The Illustrated Bibles from Tours* (Princeton: 1977), fig. 49; id., "'Facies bibliothecae revelata': Carolingian Art as Spiritual Seeing," in *Testo e immagine nell'alto medioevo,* Settimane di studio del Centro Italiano di studi sull'alto medioevo 41 (Spoleto: 1994), p. 546, fig. 5.

33. Otto-Karl Werckmeister, *Der Deckel des Codex Aureus von St. Emmeram: Ein Goldschmiedewerk des 9. Jahrhunderts* (Baden-Baden/Strasbourg: 1963), esp. pp. 47ff; id., *Irisch-northumbrische Buchmalerei des 8. Jahrhunderts und monastische Spiritualität* (Berlin: 1967).

34. Kessler, *The Illustrated Bibles from Tours,* p. 51, fig. 75.

35. Munich, Bayerische Staatsbibliothek, Cod. lat. 30111, *olim,* Pommersfelden, Gräflich Schönborn'sche Schlossbibliothek, cod. 347 (2940), fol. 21r; P. E. Schramm and F. Mütherich, *Denkmale der deutschen Kaiser und Könige* (Munich: 1962), cat. no. 80; R. Lauer, in *Vor dem Jahr 1000: Abendländische Buchkunst zur Zeit der Kaiserin Theophanu . . .* (Cologne: 1991), cat. no. 21 (with exhaustive earlier literature on the school of Mainz, p. 96).

36. Berlin, Staatsbibliothek Preussischer Kulturbesitz, ms. theol. lat. fol. 283, fol. 11r; Anton von Euw in *Vor dem Jahr 1000,* cat. no. 39 (with earlier bibliography on p. 146).

37. Cologne, Erzbischöfliche Diözesan- und Dombibliothek, ms. 1a, fol. 1v; Anton von Euw in *Vor dem Jahr 1000,* cat. no. 6 (previous bibliography on p. 48). See also id., "Die Maiestas-Domini-Bilder der ottonischen Kölner Malerschule im Licht des platonischen Weltbildes," in Anton von

Euw and Peter Schreiner, eds., *Kaiserin Theophanu, Begegnung des Ostens und Westens um die Wende des ersten Jahrtausends,* vol. 1 (Cologne: 1991), pp. 379–400, fig. 2.

38. Cologne, Erzbischöfliche Diözesan- und Dombibliothek, cod. 192, fols. 36r and 37v; von Euw, "Die Maiestas-Domini-Bilder," pp. 379ff, figs. 8, 9.

39. Wolfenbüttel, Herzog August Bibliothek, cod. Guelf. 1 Gud. lat., fol. 64v, dated between 1150 and 1170; A. Derolez, ed., *Liber Floridus Colloquium: Papers Read at the International Meeting Held in the University Library Ghent . . . 1967* (Ghent: 1973); von Euw, "Imago mundi," p. 102, fig. p. 96; von Euw, "Die Maiestas-Domini-Bilder," p. 384f, fig. 5.

40. *Visio 6, Patrologia Latina* 180, col. 182D, in P. Dinzelbacher, *Vision und Visionsliteratur im Mittelater* (Stuttgart: 1981), p. 109.

41. London, The British Library, cod. Royal 19.A.IX, fol. 149r; R. Simek, *Erde und Kosmos im Mittelater: Das Weltbild vor Kolumbus* (Munich: 1992), fig. 2 and cover.

42. Manuscript illuminations directly related to John 1:1–5 also belong to the category of representations that document the strong influence of scientific depictions of the cosmos on Gospel illustration. See Anton von Euw, "Creatio mundi," in *Monumenta Annonis,* pp. 89ff and 152ff; id., "Die Maiestas-Domini-Bilder," pp. 379ff.

43. Koninklijke Bibliotheek, The Hague, hs. 76 F 1, fol. 215r; von Euw, in *Vor dem Jahr 1000,* no. 49, pp. 165ff, fig. 128.

44. Von Euw, *Vor dem Jahr 1000,* p. 168.

45. H. Wölfflin, *Die Bamberger Apokalypse* (Munich: 1921); A. Fauser, *Die Bamberger Apokalypse,* facsimile ed. (Wiesbaden: 1958); E. Harnischfeger, *Die Bamberger Apokalypse* (Stuttgart: 1981).

46. Walafrid Strabo, "The Geography 3.4.4," in H. L. Jones, ed. and trans., *The Geography of Strabo,* vol. 2, (Cambridge, Mass.: 1969), pp. 67–69.

47. P. R. Hardie, "Imago Mundi: Cosmological and Ideological Aspects of the Shield of Achilles," *Journal of Hellenic Studies* 105 (1985): 11–31.

48. Malcolm M. Willcock, *A Companion to the Iliad* (Chicago: 1976), p. 210; Harley and Woodward, eds., *The History of Cartography,* vol. 1, p. 131, fig. 8.1.

49. British Museum, London, BM 92687. Wayne Horowitz, "The Babylonian Map of the World," *Iraq* 50 (1988): 147–165, fig. 2 and pl. X.

50. Metropolitan Museum of Art, New York, inv. no. 14.7.1. C. L. Ranson, "A Late Egyptian Sarcophagus," *Bulletin of the Metropolitan Museum of Art* 9 (1914): 112–120; Harley and Woodward, *The History of Cartography,* vol. 1, p. 120f, fig. 7.5.

51. British Library, London. Add. 28681, fol. 9. See P. D. A. Harvey, *Medieval Maps* (London: 1991), p. 25, no. 20.

52. This map, 1.3 meters across, was drawn by Richard of Holdingham, probably at Lincoln in the 1280s. Harvey, *Medieval Maps,* p. 28, n. 22.

53. Harvey, *Medieval Maps,* p. 28, n. 21.

54. Kühnel, pp. 145–149, fig. 109.

55. Ibid., pp. 128ff, fig. 79.

56. Bianca Kühnel, "Das Jerusalem-Bild Bischofs Bernward," in Shmuel Bahagon, ed., *Recht und Wahrheit bringen Frieden, Festschrift für Niels Hansen* (Gerlingen: 1994), pp. 162–169, fig. p. 167.

57. Royal ms. 14 C.IX, fols. 1v–2. Harvey, *Medieval Maps,* p. 35, no.26. Other copies of the Chester monk's universal history show a circular world (British Library, Harley ms. 3673, fol. 84r, in Harley and Woodward, *The History of Cartography,* vol. 1, fig. 18.68) or a pointed oval, like a mandorla (British Library, Royal ms. 14.C.xii, fol. 9v, in ibid., fig. 18.69).

58. Bronder, "Das Bild der Schöpfung," p. 192 and fig. 30.

59. F. Saxl and H. Meier, *Verzeichnis der astrologischen und mythologischen Handschriften des lateinischen Mittelalters,* vol. 3: *Englische Bibliotheken* (London: 1953), p. 422f; Konrad Hoffmann, "Sugers 'Anagogisches Fenster' in St. Denis," *Wallraf-Richartz-Jahrbuch* 30 (1968): 70, fig. 55, n. 101.

60. Metropolitan Museum of Art, New York, inv. no. 17.190.185. Manufactured in Cologne, ca. 1300. See van Os, *The Art of Devotion,* pp. 55, 178f, pl. 16.

61. H. Swarzenski, *Monuments of Romanesque Art: The Arts of Church Treasures in Northwestern Europe,* 2nd ed. (London: 1967), pl. 207, fig. 479; Hoffmann, "Sugers 'Anagogisches Fenster' in St. Denis," p. 72, fig. 57, n. 100; Bronder, "Das Bild der Schöpfung," fig. 32.

62. Rainer Haussherr, "Templum Salomonis und Ecclesia Christi: Zu einem Bildvergleich der Bible moralisée," *Zeitschrift für Kunstgeschichte* 31 (1968): 101–121.

63. See, for example, the illustration in the Vienna manuscript, Österreichische Nationalbibliothek (cod. 1179, fol. 1v), in Simek, *Erde und Kosmos,* fig. 4, or that in the Oxford manuscript, Bodleian Library (ms. 270b, fol. 1r), in Stanislaw Kobielus, "Deus ut Artifex," *Biuletyn Historii Sztuki* 55 (1993): 401–417, fig. 10. Measure, number, and weight are the prerogatives of the Creator, according to the Old Testament (Isa. 40:12; Prov. 8:27; Sap. 11:21) and the Christian exegeses (Augustine, *In Ioannis Evang.* 1, 13, in *Patrologia Latina* 35, col. 1386). Hrabanus Maurus even identifies number, measure, and weight with God: *"Numerus, et mensura, et pondus, ipse est Deus. Ipse est enim numerus sine numero, a quo est omnis numerus, ipse est mensura sine mensura, a quo est omnis mensura; ipse est pondus sine pondere, a quo est omne pondus." Quaestiones super Genes.,* in *Patrologia Latina* 93, col. 238D.

64. Augustinus, *Epistola* 205, 17, in *Patrologia Latina* 33, col. 948.

65. See sources in Bronder, "Das Bild der Schöpfung," p. 205, n. 76.

66. *"Omnia per cruce esse recuperata, et per Christi passionem renata et melio-rata."* Hrabanus Maurus, *De laudibus crucis,* in *Patrologia Latina* 107, col. 177A–D.

67. T. Tobler, *Planographie von Jerusalem* (Gotha: 1858); R. Röhricht, "Karten und Pläne zur Palästinakunde aus dem 7. bis 16. Jahrhundert," *Zeitschrift des Deutschen Palästinavereins (ZDPV)* 14 (1891): 8–11, 87–92, 137–141, *ZDPV* 15 (1892): 34–39, *ZDPV* 18 (1895): 173–182; Konrad Miller, *Die ältesten Welt-karten,* vol. 3 (Stuttgart: 1895), pp. 61ff. See also Rehav Rubin, *Jerusalem through Maps and Views* (Tel-Aviv: 1987), in Hebrew; Milka Levy, "Medieval Maps of Jerusalem," in Joshua Prawer and Haggai Ben-Shammai, eds., *The History of Jerusalem: Crusaders and Ayyubids (1099–1250)* (Jerusalem: 1991), pp. 418–507 (in Hebrew, with good color reproductions). And see Milka Levy-Rubin and Rehav Rubin in this volume.

68. British Library, London, add. 32343, fol. 15r (ca. 1150); Württembergische Landesbibliothek, Stuttgart, cod. bibl.2.56, fol. 135r (before 1150); Bib-liothèque municipale, St. Omer, Codex Aldomarensi, fol. 15v (ca. 1150); Bibliothèque Royale, Brussels, no. 9823–9824, fol. 157r (ca. 1150); ibid., ms. II-2208, fol. 93r (twelfth century); Koninklije Bibliotheek, The Hague, ms. 76 F 5, fol. 1r (ca. 1170); Bibliothèque nationale, Paris, lat. 8865 *(Liber Floridus),* fol. 133r (ca. 1260); Det Armamagnaenske Institut, Copenhagen, AM 736, I, 4* (ca. 1300); ibid., AM 544, 4*, fol. 19r (fourteenth century); ibid., AM 732b, 4*, fol. 8v (fourteenth century); British Library, London, Harley 658, fol. 39v (thirteenth century); Florence, lost, publ. by Röhricht, p. 35 (fourteenth century). All these maps, with the exception of the two fourteenth-century Copenhagen maps, are illustrated in Levy, "Medieval Maps."

69. Bibliothèque interuniversitaire, Montpellier, Section médecine, H. 142, fol. 67v. Levy, "Medieval Maps," p. 480.

70. Bibliothèque municipale, Cambrai, ms. 466, fol. 1r. Levy, "Medieval Maps," p. 426.

71. Levy, "Medieval Maps," p. 420, n. 8; Michael Avi-Yonah et al., *Jerusalem: The Saga of the Holy City* (Jerusalem: 1954), p. 61; R. S. Lopez, "The Crossroads within the Walls," in O. Handlin and J. Burchard, eds., *The Historian and the City* (Cambridge, Mass.: 1962), pp. 27–43; L. Mumford, *The City in History* (Harmondsworth: n.d.), pp. 346–351. See also Joseph Rykwert, *The Idea of a Town: The Anthropology of Urban Form in Rome, Italy and the Ancient World* (London: n.d.).

72. Staatsbibliothek Preußischer Kulturbesitz, Berlin, ms. lat. 2* 902, fol. 14r. *Reisen nach Jerusalem: Das Heilige Land in Karten und Ansichten aus fünf Jahrhunderten: Sammlung Loewenhardt.* Cat. Jüdisches Museum (Berlin Museum), ed. A. Bekemeier (Wiesbaden: 1993), fig. 4.

73. Lucas Brandis de Schass, *Rudimentum novitiorum sive chronicarum histo-riarum epitome* (Lübeck: 1475); E. Laor, *Maps of the Holy Land: Cartobib-liography of Printed Maps, 1475–1900* (New York: 1986), no. 128. See also *Reisen nach Jerusalem*, no. 21, pl. 1.

74. Laor, *Maps*, no. 1123; *Reisen nach Jerusalem*, no. 197, pl. 3.

75. Heinrich Bünting (1545–1606), *Itinerarium Sacrae Scripturae* (Magdeburg: Andreas Duncker, 1600), part I, pp. 37–38; Laor, *Maps*, no. 968B; *Reisen nach Jerusalem*, no. 176, pl. 24.

76. Rubin, *Jerusalem*, p. 62.

77. Frans Hogenberg and Georg Braun, *Ciritates Orbis Terrarum*, vol. 2 (Co-logne: 1576), no. 54; Laor, *Maps*, no. 1040A; *Reisen nach Jerusalem*, no. 181, pl. 21.

78. Laor, *Maps*, no. 1077; Rubin, *Jerusalem*, p. 74.

79. Laor, *Maps*, no. 987; Rubin, *Jerusalem*, p. 134.

80. Cornelius de Bruyn (1652–1726), *Reizen* . . . (Delft: 1698); Kaplan Collection, in Rubin, *Jerusalem*, p. 44.

81. Collection of the Jewish and National Library, Jerusalem; Rubin, *Jerusalem*, p. 146.

82. Matthäus Merian, *Biblia dt. Das ist die ganze Heilige Schrift* . . . (Frankfurt-am-Main: 1704), The Jewish and National Library, Jerusalem. See also *Apokalypse: Ein Prinzip Hoffnung? Ernst Bloch zum 100. Geburtstag*, exhi-bition catalogue (Heidelberg: 1985), p. 120, no. 52.2.

83. Compare this Apocalypse illustration with Merian's own 1647 map of Jeru-salem, drawn after Reuwich-Breidenbach. Laor, *Maps*, no. 1082; Rubin, *Jerusalem*, p. 122.

84. High Altar of Xanten, olim Stiftskirche St. Victor, 1529–1534; see M. Feltes, *Architektur und Landschaft als Orte christlicher Ikonographie: eine Unter-suchung zur niederrheinischen Tafelmalerei des 15.Jh.* (diss., Aix-la-Chapelle: 1987), esp. pp. 205–218 with other examples, fig. 97b.

85. R. Haussherr, "Spätgotische Ansichten der Stadt Jerusalem (oder: War der Hausbuchmeister in Jerusalem?)," *Jahrbuch der Berliner Museen* 29/30 (1987/88): 47–70, figs. 7 and 11. For parallels in Italian Renaissance art, see David R. Marshall, "Carpaccio, St. Stephen, and the Topography of Jeru-salem," *Art Bulletin* 66 (1984): 610–620, and Chiara Frugoni, *A Distant City: Images of Urban Experience in the Medieval World* (Princeton, N.J.: 1991). For the development of city views and plans in the fifteenth and sixteenth centuries, see the basic study by Wolfgang Braunfels, "Anton Woensams Kölnprospekt in der Geschichte des Sehens," *Wallraf-Richartz-Jahrbuch* 22 (1960): 115–136. See also Jürgen Schulz, "Jacopo de' Barbari's View of Venice: Map Making, City Views and Moralized Geography before the Year 1500," *Art Bulletin* 60 (1978): 425–474.

86. To the examples of Genoa and Venice in the focus of a cosmographical diagram, one can add the view of Dresden by C. A. Richter, 1824, now in Berlin, which shows the round Church of Notre Dame as the nucleus of a circular, linearly circumscribed, flattened city landscape surrounded by water: Kartenabteilung, Staatsbibliothek, Berlin, Kart.Y 18216.

87. F.-D. Jacob, "Prolegomena zu einer quellenkundlichen Betrachtung historischer Stadtansichten," *Jahrbuch für Regionalgeschichte* 6 (1978): 133; id., *Historische Stadtansichten* (Leipzig: 1982).

88. F. E. Peters, *Jerusalem and Mecca* (New York: 1986). For a common basis shared by the three monotheistic religions, see also id., *Judaism, Christianity, and Islam* (Princeton, N.J.: 1990).

89. British Library, London, Add. ms. 27566, in H. Ettinghausen, *Die bildliche Darstellung der Ka'ba im islamischen Kulturkreis, Zeitschrift der Deutschen Morgenländischen Gesellschaft,* NF, 12, 3/4, 1934, 111–137; H. Rosenau, *Vision of the Temple: The Image of the Temple of Jerusalem in Judaism and Christianity* (London: 1979), fig. 80.

90. Peter Bloch, "Nachwirkungen des Alten Bundes in der christlichen Kunst," in *Monumenta Judaica: 2000 Jahre Geschichte und Kultur der Juden am Rhein* (Cologne: 1963), pp. 735–781; Paul von Naredi-Rainer, *Salomos Tempel und das Abendland: Monumentale Folgen Historischer Irrtümer* (Cologne: 1994). See also Heribert Busse, "Geschichte und Bedeutung der Kaaba im Licht der Bibel," in *Zion—Ort der Begegnung, Festschrift für Laurentius Klein,* Bonner Biblische Beiträge 90 (Bodenheim: 1990), pp. 169–185.

91. Berlin, Museum für Völkerkunde, Indische Sammlung, IC 24341. Ettinghausen, *Die Darstellung der Ka'ba,* fig. 17.

92. Haussherr, "Spätgotische Ansichten," pp. 47–70. For Italy, see Marshall, "Carpaccio."

93. Centraal Museum, Utrecht. Joanna Woodall, "Painted Immortality: Portraits of Jerusalem Pilgrims by Antonis Mor and Jan van Scorel," *Jahrbuch der Berliner Museen* 31 (1989): 149–165, fig. 10; Haussherr, "Spätgotische Ansichten," p. 54, figs. 13, 14.

94. Epitaph of Adelheid Tucher, Stadtgeschichtliche Museen, Tucherschloß, Nuremberg. *Der Traum von Raum, Gemalte Architektur aus 7 Jahrhunderten: Eine Austellung . . .* (Nuremberg, Marburg: 1986), no. 14.

95. Bayerische Staatsbibliothek, Munich, Cod.iconogr.172. Tobler, *Planographie,* p. 7; Röhricht, pl. 7; Rubin, *Jerusalem,* p. 35.

96. Haussherr, "Spätgotische Ansichten," pp. 64ff.

97. Five copies of Israel Zifroni's Haggadah were printed between the years 1609 and 1740, accompanied by wood engravings. The illustration shown here belongs to the 1740 Venice edition, now in the Gross family collection.

See Nitza Behrouzi, *Jerusalem: Spirit and Matter,* exhibition catalogue (Tel Aviv: Eretz Israel Museum, 1993), no. 37.

98. Behrouzi, *Jerusalem,* nos. 41, 42; Rosenau, *Vision of the Temple,* fig. 67.

99. Kühnel, esp. pp. 17–62.

100. Morris Rosenfeld, *Lieder des Ghetto* (Berlin: 1902); Milly Heyd, "Lilien and Beardsley, 'To the pure all things are pure,'" *Journal of Jewish Art* 7 (1980): 58–69, fig. 8.

101. Behrouzi, *Jerusalem,* no. 67.

102. Zeev Raban, title page illustration in Boris Schatz, *Built Jerusalem: A Dream with Open Eyes* (Jerusalem: 1924), in Hebrew.

103. Günther Anders, *Die atomare Drohung* (Munich: 1981).

104. Ibid., p. 224f.

105. For example, in the works of Jan Koblassa, in *Apokalypse, Ein Prinzip Hoffnung?* p. 178f.

106. Richard W. Gassen: "Apokalypse-Bilder sind Bilder aus Krisenzeiten," in *Apokalypse, Ein Prinzip Hoffnung?* p. 228.

107. *Apocalypse,* fig. 65, p. 246.

108. Ibid., Kat. 176.3, p. 241.

109. Ibid., Kat. 183, p. 353; for Peter Apian's map, see ibid., fig. 75.

110. *A Bitter Truth: Avant-Garde Art and the Great War,* exhibition catalogue (London: 1994), p. 52, fig. 45.

111. In the collection of Mitchell Wolfson Junior College, Miami Beach and Genoa. The original title is in German: *Der Krieg. A Bitter Truth,* p. 193, fig. 527.

112. S. A. Shuster and Ye. V. Ktyukova Collection, in *A Bitter Truth,* p. 176, fig. 234.

113. Gouache on paper, Städtische Galerie, Albstadt-Ebingen, in ibid., p. 205, fig. 277.

114. Ludwig Meidner, *Apokalyptische Landschaften,* ed. C. S. Eliel, exhibition catalogue (Munich: 1990), figs. 35, 37, 34, and 58, respectively.

115. Ziva Amishai-Maisels, *Tapestries and Mosaics of Marc Chagall at the Knesset* (New York: 1973), color plate of the cartoon on pp. 60–61.

116. Ibid., p. 62.

117. Gannit Ankori, "The Other Jerusalem: Images of the Holy City in Contemporary Palestinian Painting," *Jewish Art* 14 (1988): 74–92, fig. 13.

118. On parallels between Palestinian Arab and Jewish contemporary art, see Heyd, "Lilien and Beardsley."

119. I would like to thank Gannit Ankori for bringing this work by Nabil Anani to my attention and providing a slide of it.

120. Kühnel, fig. 106; *Trierer Apokalypse,* vol. 1, fig. 59.

121. The explanation and interpretation of the three compositions follows the artist's own depictions, as he kindly formulated them for me in a letter dated Feb. 5, 1994. I would like to thank him again for sending me the photos of his work and for his valuable comments.
122. Letter of July 5, 1994.

14. Jerusalem Elsewhere

1. There is no single introduction to the history of the city of Jerusalem that is consistently accurate and up-to-date, inasmuch as every year brings a new crop of contributions and subdivisions to established chronological periods (prehistory, Israelite, Post-Exilic to Roman, Christian, Arab Muslim, Ottoman, twentieth century) or to common analytical or synthetic competencies (linguistic, archaeological, historical, national, archival, visual). As a result, parallel accounts are constantly created that rarely meet, if ever. Instead of providing a long list of complementary references, many of which are bound to be out of date, I would argue that the best "introduction" to the history of the city lies in the articles on Jerusalem found in the *Encyclopedia Britannica, The Jewish Encyclopedia, The Encyclopedia of Islam* (under "al-Kuds"), *The Dictionary of the Bible*, the *Reallexikon der byzantinische Kunst*, and so on. In fact, a slightly updated and well-illustrated selection of all these encyclopedia entries would make a useful introductory anthology of a type apparently favored by book publishers. Although all the entries are out of date and often inaccurate in many details, the overall information they provide corresponds more or less to what a reader wishes and needs to know. Furthermore, the errors often cancel each other out.
2. For the Jewish example, see Raphael Patai, *The Messiah Texts* (New York: Scribner, 1979), pp. 224ff. Otherwise the most recent discussions of visionary Jerusalem are Werner Müller, *Die Heilige Stadt* (Stuttgart: W. Kohlhammer, 1966); Marie-Thérèse Gousset, "Iconographie de la Jérusalem Céleste: IX–XII siècles" (thesis, University of Paris, 1978); Bianca Kühnel, *From the Earthly to the Heavenly Jerusalem* (Rome: Herder, 1987); M. L. Gatti-Ferrer, *La Gerusalemme Celeste* (Milan: n.p., 1983), a catalogue of an important exhibition that seems to have escaped notice in most scholarly literature.
3. The notion of "another" Jerusalem arose while I was completing a lengthy study of the city between ca. 600 and 1000 CE, the time when the Christian city became a Muslim one. For this study, see Oleg Grabar, *The Shape of the Holy: Early Medieval Jerusalem* (Princeton, N.J.: Princeton University Press, 1996).
4. Naser-e Khosraw, *Safernama (The Book of Travels)*, trans. Wheeler M.

Thackston, Jr. (New York: Bibliotheca Persica, 1986), p. 21. The whole issue of local or even pan-Islamic uses of Jerusalem's holiness, especially during the Ottoman centuries, deserves a fuller investigation than it has received on the part of cultural historians and, particularly, ethnographers.

5. For some vivid examples of this interaction, the best book is still Norman Cohn, *The Pursuit of the Millennium* (London: Secker and Warburg, 1957), pp. 10, 44–45, 127, and elsewhere.

6. For preliminary and, on the whole, still very simple-minded attempts in this direction, see Gatti-Ferrer, *La Gerusalemme Celeste,* and Françoise Robin, "Jérusalem dans la Peinture franco-flamande," in Daniel Poiron, ed., *Jérusalem, Rome, Constantinople* (Paris: Presses de l'Université de Paris-Sorbonne, 1986). The latter volume also contains an interesting study by Mireille Mentré on illustrations of celestial Jerusalem in manuscripts and so far the only existing study of the Haram in the context of Muslim holy places, presented and discussed by Janine Sourdel. Both of these topics are, however, outside the concerns of this chapter.

7. Much has been written on these topics. For a basic introduction to all of them, see, in *The Encyclopedia of Islam,* the entries "al-Aksa," "isra'," and "mi'radj" (Leiden: E. J. Brill, 1954–).

8. For the latest references, see Martin Frishman and Hasan-uddin Khan, *The Mosque* (London: Thames and Hudson, 1994), pp. 235–236.

9. The Madaba map (see Chapter 16 and Plate 2) has often been published and discussed; the latest statements on it are Herbert Donner and Heinz Cuppers, *Die Mosaikkarte von Madeba* (Wiesbaden: O. Harrassowitz, 1977), and in a more summary form, Michele Piccirillo, *The Mosaics of Transjordan* (Amman: American Center of Oriental Research, 1993). For other maps and drawings in general, the most accessible survey with the best pictures is Kenneth Nebenzahl, *Maps of the Holy Land* (New York: Abbeville Press, 1986). Unfortunately, the number of beautifully illustrated books has not been matched by intelligent discussions of the meaning of their illustrations.

10. I owe my knowledge of this painting to an old family friend, M. Boris Lossky, for many years director of the museum of Tours and now long retired. To my knowledge, it has never been published. Further studies should be able to identify other buildings as well as many of the sanctuaries near Jerusalem or in the rest of the strictly Christian Palestine.

11. I owe my knowledge of this painting to a postcard received from Garth and Elizabeth Fowden.

12. Richard Ettinghausen, "Persian Ascension Miniatures of the Fourteenth Century," in his collected essays, *Islamic Art and Archaeology,* ed. Miryam Rosen-Ayalon (Berlin: G. Mann Verlag, 1984), first published in 1957. The picture itself has often been reproduced and appears in color in M. S.

Ipsiroglu, *Masterpieces from the Topkapi Museum* (London: Thames and Hudson, 1980), fig. 10.

13. Jamel Eddine Bencheikh, *Le Voyage Nocturne de Mahomet* (Paris: Imprimerie Nationale, 1988), pp. 174–176.

14. It is worth noting that the image of the city in this miniature was used to illustrate a "typical" city by Paolo Cuneo, *Storia dell'Urbanistica, Il Mondo Islamico* (Laterza, Rome: Roma-Bari, 1986), pp. 18–19.

15. T. B. Virsaladze, *Rospis Ierusalimskogo Krestnogo Monastyra* (Paintings in the Monastery of the Holy Cross in Jerusalem) (Tblissi: n.p., 1973).

16. Further information on this and other related issues was passed on to me by my friend and colleague Professor Ihor Sevcenko.

17. This statement and most of the information that follows has been inspired by A. Batalov and A. Lidov, eds., *Ierusalim v Russkoi Kultury* (Jerusalem in Russian Culture) (Moscow: Ed. Nauka, 1994), a very remarkable compendium of articles on the subject.

18. Severus ibn al-Muqaffa, *History of the Patriarchs of Egypt,* vol. 2 (Cairo: Le Caire, 1948), pp. 151ff. It should be added that, according to the same source, a monastery of New Jerusalem existed in the Egyptian wilderness, vol. 1, p. 60.

19. M. V. Roshdestvenskaia, "Obraz Cviatoi Zemli v drevnerusskoi literatury" (The Image of the Holy Land in Old Russian Literature), in Batalov and Lidov, eds., *Ierusalim.*

20. William C. Brumfield, *A History of Russian Architecture* (Cambridge: Cambridge University Press, 1993), pp. 122–129, 165–167; André Grabar, *L'Art du Moyen Age en Europe Orientale* (Paris: A. Michel, 1968), p. 192; Batalov and Lidov, *Ierusalim.*

21. Although he did not use the term *synecdoche,* André Grabar described the procedure in his *Les Voies de la Création en Iconographie Chrétienne* (Paris: Flammarion, 1979), pp. 169–170. The earlier English edition of this book does not contain this section.

22. There probably are ecumenical souvenirs, but I do not recall any.

23. Here are a few randomly assembled examples of studies that have dealt with the subject or alluded to it: Robert Konrad, "Das himmlische und das irdlische Jerusalem im mittelalterichen Denken," in C. Brauer et al., eds., *Speculum Historiale* (Munich: n.p., 1965), pp. 527–540; Linda Seidel, *Songs of Glory* (Chicago: University of Chicago Press, 1981), pp. 12 and 53 (esp. n. 61); Robert G. Ousterhout, "The Church of Santo Stefano, a 'Jerusalem' in Bologna," *Gesta* 20 (Fort Tryon Park, New York: International Center of Medieval Art, 1981).

24. André Grabar, "Reliquaire d'Aix-la-Chapelle," in A. Grabar, *L'Art de la Fin de l'Antiquité et du Moyen Age* (Paris: Collège de France, 1968), pp. 427ff.,

with important corrections to the translation of one of the basic Russian texts for the interpretation of these objects; W. B. R. Saunders "The Aachen Reliquary," *Dumbarton Oaks Papers* 36 (1982), with the identification of the sponsor of the object and its place of manufacture; I. A. Sterligova in Batalov and Lidov, *Ierusalim,* pp. 46–48, with a major and, I believe, justified disagreement with Grabar's original explanation. What makes the whole problem of these small objects in the shape of domical buildings even more interesting and more complicated is that such objects exist in the secular art of the Muslim world as well, and there is little doubt of an ultimate formal relationship, a point that probably had an impact on Grabar's interpretation when he had put it together (1957). On this score, however, we are escaping from our original topic. For examples and a very provocative as well as thoughtful discussion, see Souren Melikian-Chirvani, "State Inkwells in Islamic Iran," *The Journal of the Walters Art Gallery* 44 (1986).

25. N. Brunov, "Model Ierusalimskogo Hrama" (A Model for the Holy Sepulchre in Jerusalem), *Soobcheniya Rossiiskogo Palestinskogo Obchestva* 29 (1926): 139–148. I owe this reference to my erstwhile colleague Professor E. T. Keenan of Harvard University.

26. Names of cities are used for rugs and porcelain, but in all cases the name is a modifier for an omitted term. Even the instance of *fez* is uncertain, because the etymology of the Turkish word from which the English comes is dubious.

15. The City in Jewish Folk Art

1. For additional information about Jewish art and the Second Commandment, see Joy Ungerleider-Mayerson, *Jewish Folk Art from Biblical Days to Modern Times* (New York: Summit Books, 1986), pp. 13–23.

2. Lee E. Levine, "Ancient Synagogues—A Historical Introduction," in Lee E. Levin, ed., *Ancient Synagogues Revealed* (Jerusalem: Israel Exploration Society, 1981), pp. 6–18; "Synagogue," in *Encyclopaedia Judaica,* vol. 15 (Jerusalem: Keter, 1972), pp. 579–620. See also I. Levy, *The Synagogue: Its History and Function* (London: n.p., 1963).

3. Levine, "Ancient Synagogues," p. 7.

4. Joseph Gutmann, ed., *The Dura-Europos Synagogue* (New York: American Academy of Religion and Society of Biblical Literature, 1973). The synagogue in the remote town of Dura sheds a totally new light on early Jewish art, and it leaves one wondering about the lost art from larger major synagogues, now gone.

5. A. Ovadiah, "The Synagogue at Gaza," in Levine, *Ancient Synagogues,* pp. 129–132.

6. The Tiberias site was excavated by Moshe Dothan, author of *Hammath-Tiberias* (Jerusalem: Israel Exploration Society, 1983). See also his article, "The Synagogue at Hammath-Tiberias," in Levine, *Ancient Synagogues,* pp. 63–69.

7. Carol Herselle Krinsky, *Synagogues of Europe: Architecture, History, Meaning* (Cambridge, Mass.: MIT Press, 1985), pp. 45–46.

8. Ibid., p. 56.

9. Ibid., pp. 56–58. The image of Jerusalem within a leviathan's tail appeared in other synagogues. A reminder of days to come when the righteous will feast on the meat of the leviathan?

10. Zusia Ephron, "Descriptions of Jerusalem in the Wall Painting of East European Synagogues," in Nitza Behrouzi, *Jerusalem—Spirit and Matter* (Tel Aviv: Eretz Israel Museum, 1993), p. 90 (in Hebrew). The Przedbroz painting was based on Psalms 137:1–2: "By the rivers of Babylon there we set down, yea, and we wept when we remembered Zion. Upon the willows in the midst thereof we hung up our harps."

11. Ephron, "Descriptions of Jerusalem," pp. 90–91.

12. Sussman came from Brody, Galicia. Krinsky, *Synagogues,* p. 58, and Behrouzi, *Jerusalem—Spirit and Matter,* p. 10.

13. Behrouzi, *Jerusalem—Spirit and Matter,* pp. 54–55.

14. Ibid., p. 49.

15. Ungerlieder-Mayerson, *Jewish Folk Art,* pp. 41–59. See also Iris Fishof, "Jerusalem above My Chief Joy: Depictions of Jerusalem in Italian Ketubot," *Journal of Jewish Art* 9 (1982): 61–75.

16. The first such dated depiction is an 1837 lithograph, drawn in Jerusalem by a well-known local author, Yehoseph Schwartz, and printed and distributed in Europe. See Naomi Feuchtwanger-Sarig, "Fischach and Jerusalem: The Story of a Painted Sukkah," *Jewish Art* 19/20 (1994).

17. Renee Sivan, ed., *David's Tower Rediscovered* (Jerusalem: Hamakor Press Ltd., 1983), p. 37.

16. The Image of the Holy City in Maps and Mapping

1. We will follow here the broad definition of maps suggested by Tony Campbell, demanding only two minimum requirements for identifying a document as a map: "a. It must attempt to convey, in a graphic form, information about the real world or some part of it; b. It would be concerned—however inaccurately or schematically—with direction and relative

distance of one place or feature from another." Tony Campbell, *The Earliest Printed Maps, 1472–1500* (London: The British Library, 1987), p. 17.

2. P. Palmer and Hermann Guthe, *Die Mosaikkarte von Madeba* (Leipzig: Verlag des Deutschen Vereins zur Erforschung Palaestinas, 1906); Michael Avi-Yonah, *The Madaba Mosaic Map* (Jerusalem: Israel Exploration Society, 1954); Herbert Donner and Heinz Cüppers, *Die Mosaikkarte von Madeba* (Wiesbaden: O. Harrassowitz, 1977); Pauline Donceel-Voute, "La Carte de Madaba: Cosmographie, anachronisme et propaganda," *Revue Biblique* 95, no. 4 (1988): 519–542; Herbert Donner, *The Mosaic Map of Madaba: An Introductory Guide* (Kampen: Kok-Pharos, 1992).

3. This view was based on an interpretation of verses in Ezekiel: "I set this Jerusalem in the midst of nations, with countries round about her" (5:5), and ". . . living at the center of the earth" (38:12). This concept already existed earlier in the Jewish tradition in Midrash Tanhuma (Kedoshim 10), which holds that Eretz Israel sits in the center of the world, and Jerusalem in the center of Eretz Israel, and the Temple in the center of Jerusalem, and the Holy of Holies in the center of the Temple.

4. Vicomte de Santarem, *Atlas Composé des Mappemondes, des Portulans, et des Cartes Hydrographiques et Historiques depuis le VIIe Siècle* (Paris, 1842–1853); Konrad Miller, *Mappae Mundi: Die Altesten Weltkarten* (Stuttgart, 1895–1898); Marcel Destombes, ed., *Mappemondes, AD 1200–1500* (Amsterdam: N. Israel 1964); David Woodward, "Reality, Symbolism, Time and Space in Medieval World Maps," *Annals of American Association of Geographers* 75, no. 4 (1985): 510–521; David Woodward, "Medieval Mappaemundi," in David Woodward and B. J. Harley, *History of Cartography*, vol. 1 (Chicago: Chicago University Press, 1987), pp. 286–370.

5. For a general survey of the Crusader period in Palestine, see Joshua Prawer, *The Latin Kingdom of Jerusalem* (London: Weidenfeld and Nicolson, 1973).

6. The medieval maps of Jerusalem were presented at the end of the last century by Reinhold Röhricht, "Karten und Pläne zur Palästinakunde aus dem 7. bis 16. Jahrhundert," *Zeitschrift des Deutschen Palästina-Vereins* 14 (1891): 8–11, 87–92, 137–141; ibid., 15 (1892): 34–39; ibid., 18 (1895): 173–182. For a recent detailed account of the medieval maps, see Milka Levy, "The Medieval Maps of Jerusalem," in Joshua Prawer and Haggai Ben Shammai, eds., *Sefer Yerushalayim: The Crusader and Ayyubid Period: 1099–1250* (Jerusalem: Yad Ben-Zvi, 1991), pp. 418–506 (in Hebrew).

7. Bibliothèque de Cambrai, ms. 466, fol. 1r. On this map, see L. H. Heydenreich, "Ein Jerusalem-Plan aus der Zeit der Kreuzfahrer," *Miscellanea pro Arte, H. Schnizller zur Vollendung des 60 Lebensjahres,* Schriften des pro Arte Medii Aevi, vol. 1 (Düsseldorf, 1965); Levy, "The Medieval Maps of Jerusalem," 425–433.

8. Probably part of the Metochion of the monastery of Mar Saba, which existed in Jerusalem.

9. The map appears in *Recueil des Historiens des Croisades, Historiens Occidentaux,* vol. 3 (Paris: Imprimerie impériale, 1866), p. 102. Levy, "The Medieval Maps of Jerusalem," 479–482.

10. British Library, Codex Harleian, 658, fol. 39v; Reinhold Röhricht, "Karten und Pläne" (1891), 141; Levy, "The Medieval Maps of Jerusalem," pp. 475–478. See also pp. 318–319 in this volume.

11. Seven of these were presented in Reinhold Röhricht, "Karten und Pläne." Since then, four more have been located.

12. For a description of Jerusalem during the Crusader period, see Joshua Prawer, "Jerusalem in the Crusader Days," in Yigael Yadin, ed., *Jerusalem Revealed* (Jerusalem: Israel Exploration Society, 1976), pp. 102–108; Dan Bahat, *The Illustrated Atlas of Jerusalem* (Jerusalem: Carta, 1989).

13. Acts 3:2, 10.

14. John 5:2–15.

15. Matthew, 27:51.

16. See John Wilkinson, *Jerusalem Pilgrims before the Crusades* (Jerusalem: Ariel, 1977), p. 177.

17. Luke 24:50–51; Mark 16:19.

18. Matthew 21:7–11; Mark 11:7–10; Luke 19:36–40.

19. This is an apocryphal tradition. See Wilkinson, *Jerusalem Pilgrims,* p. 158.

20. Matthew 26:36.

21. Acts 7:54–60.

22. This church was built by Eudokia in 460 to accommodate Stephen's bones, which had been found in 415. On this matter, see *Dictionnaire d'Archéologie et de Liturgie,* vol. 1 (Paris, 1922), Paul Peeters, "Le Sanctuaire de la lapidation de Saint Etienne, à propos d'une controverse," *Analecta Bollandiana* 27 (1906): 359–368.

23. See Milka Levy-Rubin, "The Rediscovery of the Uppsala Map of Crusader Jerusalem," *Zeitschrift des Deutschen Palästina-Vereins* (forthcoming).

24. I Samuel 7:5.

25. Luke 2:8–20; this site was already identified in the Byzantine period. See Erich Klostermann, ed., *Eusebius Werke,* vol. 3: *Das Onomastikon der biblischen Ortsnamen* (Leipzig: J. C. Hinrichs, 1904), p. 42.

26. Joshua 8:1ff.

27. Matthew 2:16–19.

28. In the Brussels B map, which is very similar to the Uppsala map graphically, there are two such columns, but no inscription.

29. See Levy-Rubin, "The Rediscovery of the Uppsala Map."

30. Brussels, Bibliothèque Royale, no. 9823–9824, fol. 157r; printed in Zev Vilnay, *The Holy Land in Old Prints and Maps* (Jerusalem: R. Mass, 1963), p. 50; Levy, "The Medieval Maps of Jerusalem," p. 455.

31. Brussels, Bibliothèque Royale, ms. II-2208, fol. 93r; Levy, "The Medieval Maps of Jerusalem," p. 459.

32. St. Omer, Bibliothèque municipale, Codex Aldomarensi, fol. 15b. The map appears in *Recueil des Historiens des Croisades, Historiens Occidentaux,* vol. 3, p. 510; Levy, "The Medieval Maps of Jerusalem," p. 472.

33. British Library, ms. add. 32343, fol. 15r. Printed in Levy, "The Medieval Maps of Jerusalem," p. 434.

34. Biblithèque Nationale, Fonds latins, no. 8865, fol. 133. Printed in Vilnay, *The Holy Land . . .* , p. 58; Levy, "The Medieval Maps of Jerusalem," p. 438.

35. *Recueil des Historiens des Croisades, Historiens Occidentaux,* vol. 3, pp. 487–543.

36. The connection between David, Solomon, Ezra, and Nehemiah and the Crusaders is made explicitly in the text surrounding the London and Paris maps.

37. These are called here Regio Penthapolis, a name emanating from an apocryphal tradition about the cities destroyed by God in Genesis (14:2, 19:13–29). See The Wisdom of Solomon 10:6.

38. Edited by Bongars, published in 1611 (reprint, Jerusalem: Massada Press, 1972).

39. Konrad Kretschmer, "Marino Sanudo der Ältere und die Karten des Petrus Vesconte," *Zeitschrift der Gesellschaft der Erdekunde* 26 (1891): 352–370; B. Degenhart and A. Schmitt, *Corpus der italienischen Zeichnungen 1300–1450,* part 2 (Berlin, 1980), pp. 3ff.

40. The destroyed wall, which the inscription proclaims was rebuilt only a short time before by al-Malik al-Mu'azzam himself, was found in excavations along the southern part of the city wall. See Magen Broshi, "Al-Malik Al-Mu'azzam 'Isa: Evidence in a New Inscription," *Eretz Israel* 19 (M. Avi-Yonah Memorial volume, 1987): 299–302 (in Hebrew). See Chapter 1, Figure 2.

41. Florence, Bibliotheca Laurentiana, Plut. LXXXVI, no. 56, fol. 97r; Vilnay, *The Holy Land,* p. 59; Levy, "The Medieval Maps of Jerusalem," p. 484.

42. Reinhold Röhricht and H. Meisner, eds., "Das Reisbuch der Familie Rieter," *Bibliothek des Litterarischen Vereins in Stuttgart,* vol. 168 (Tübingen, 1884); see München, Bayer. Staatbibliothek, Cod. iconog. 172.

A second map of the same period was preserved in a manuscript of the Latin version of Ptolemy by Hugo Comminelli in 1473. See Bibliothèque Nationale, Fonds latins, no. 4802, fol. 133.

43. See Broshi, "Al-Malik Al-Mu'azzam 'Isa."

44. John 9:1–14.

45. Matthew 27:7.

46. Bernhard von Breydenbach, *Peregrinatio in Terram Sanctam* (Mainz, 1486).

47. This is the case, for example, with the Jerusalem maps in George Braun and Franz Hogenberg, *Civitates Orbis Terrarum*, six vols. (Cologne, printed between 1572 and 1617); for a reprint edition, see R. A. Skelton and A. O. Vietor, eds., *Mirror of the World* (Cleveland and New York, 1976). Electus Zwinner, *Blumen Buch, Dess Heiligen Lands Palestinae* (Munich, 1661), maps facing p. 70, and p. 80. Alain Manesson Malet, "Ancienne Jerusalem" and "Ierusalem Moderne," in *Description de l'Universe* (Frankfurt-am-Main, 1685), vol. 2, fig. CIX–CX. Eran Laor, *Maps of the Holy Land: A Cartobibliography of Printed Maps 1475–1800* (New York and Amsterdam: A. R. Liss, 1986), no. 1076–1077, p. 156. Franciscus Halma, *Kannan en d'omleggende Landen* (Leeuwarden, 1717).

48. Alfred Moldovan, "The Lost De Angelis Map of Jerusalem, 1578," *The Map Collector* 24 (1983): 17–24. Rehav Rubin, "The De Angelis Map of Jerusalem (1578) and Its Copies," *Cathedra* 52 (1989): 100–111 (in Hebrew).

49. Francisco Quaresmius, *Historica theologica et moralis Terrae Sanctae Elucidatio* (Antwerp, 1639).

50. This tradition was linked with a fountain on the way from Jerusalem to Hebron during the Byzantine period, but during this later period it was associated with another site—Ain Haniya—southwest of the city.

51. Christian Adrichomios, *Jerusalem et Suburbia eius, Sicut Tempore Christi Floruit* (Cologne, 1584). For other editions see Reinhold Röhricht, *Bibliotheca Geographica Palaestinae* (Berlin, 1890), pp. 209–211.

52. The first English edition, Christian Adrichom, *A Brief Description of Hierusalem and of the Suburbs Therof, as It Flourished in the Time of Christ*, trans. T. Tymme (London, 1595), counted only 268 items.

53. On imaginary maps in general, see Rehav Rubin, *Jerusalem in Maps and Views, from the Sixth to the Nineteenth Century* (Tel-Aviv: Nahar and Kinnereth, 1987), in Hebrew. For Villalpando's map see J. B. Villalpando, "Vera Hierosolymae veteris imago," in H. Pradus and J. B. Villalpando, *Ezechielem explanationes et Apparatuss urbis, ac templi Hierosolimitani*, vol. 3 (Rome, 1604), following fol. 68. On the Visscher family and its maps, see Laor, *Maps of the Holy Land*, pp. 168, 187; I. C. Koeman, *Atlantes Neerlandici*, vol. 3 (Amsterdam: Theatrum Orbis Theatrum, 1969), pp. 150–184.

54. Rehav Rubin, "From the Artistic to the Scientific Map: A Chapter in the History of the Cartography of Jerusalem," *Cathedra*, forthcoming (in Hebrew).

55. The first contour map of Jerusalem, drawn 1 : 2500, was by Charles Wilson,

Ordnance Survey of Jerusalem (Southampton: Ordnance Survey Office, 1864–65).

56. Giovanni Zuallardo, *Il Devotissimo Viaggio di Gerusalemme* (Rome: F. Zanetti and G. Ruffinelli, 1587), see the map of Jerualem on p. 131.

57. See "Hayes, Louis," in *Nouvelle Biographie Générale,* vol. 23 (Paris, 1858), pp. 661–662.

58. Louis des Hayes, *Voiage de Levant, Fait par le commandement Du Roy en l'année 1621,* 2nd ed. (Paris: Adrian Tavpinart, 1629 [*sic!*]).

59. M. I. Doubdan, *Le Voyage de la Terre Sainte,* 3rd ed. (Paris, 1666), see the map of Jerualem between pp. 172 and 173. See also "Doubdan, Jean," in *Nouvelle Biographie Générale,* vol. 14 (Paris, 1858), p. 671.

60. J.-B. Nolin, *La Terre Sainte, Autrefois terre de Chanaan et de Promission* . . . (Paris, 1700). See also "Nolin, Jean-Baptiste," in *Nouvelle Biographie Générale,* vol. 38 (Paris, 1858), pp. 212–213.

61. Richard Pococke, *A Description of the East and Some Other Countries,* 2 vols. (London, 1743–1745). See also "Pococke, R.," in Leslie Stephen and Sidney Lee, eds., *The Dictionary of National Biography,* vol. 16 (Oxford: Oxford University Press), pp. 12–14.

62. Thomas Shaw, *Travels, or Geographical, Physical and Miscellaneous Observations Relating to Several Parts of Barbary and the Levant* (London, 1757; first ed., 1738).

63. F. W. Sieber, *Travels in the Island of Crete* . . . (London, 1823).

64. F. W. Sieber, *Karte von Jerusalem, und seiner naechsten Umgebungen, geometrisch aufgenomen* (Prague, 1818). His travels were also described in a book; see F. W. Sieber, *Reise von Cairo nach Jerusalem und wieder zurück* (Prague, 1823).

65. Yehoshua Ben-Arieh, "The First Survey Maps of Jerusalem," *Eretz Israel* 11 (1973): 64–74 (in Hebrew); Yehoshua Ben-Arieh, "The Catherwood Map of Jerusalem," *The Quarterly Journal of the Library of Congress* 31, no. 3 (1974): 150–160.

66. Yolande Jones, "British Military Surveys of Palestine and Syria, 1840–41," *The Cartographic Journal* 10, no. 1 (June 1973): 29–41.

67. Yehoshua Ben-Arieh, *The Re-Discovery of the Holy Land in the Nineteenth Century* (Jerusalem: Carta, 1979).

68. Wilson, *Ordnance Survey of Jerusalem.*

69. Adolph Eltzner was a printer who worked in Hamburg in the 1850s. One of his famous works is *Hambourg from a Bird Eye's View,* and its relation to the same kind of depiction of Jerusalem is obvious. See Emmanuel Benezit, *Dictionnaire critique et documentaire des peintres, sculpteurs, dessinateurs et graveurs* . . . , vol. 3 (Paris: Librairie Gründ, 1966), p. 573. "Doburg's Original View of Ancient Jerusalem A.D. 65," Boston, ca. 1844.

70. There is a problem of terminology here, as these kinds of three-dimensional maps are called in English both maps and models while they are often described in French as *maqouets,* and in German as *reliefplans.*

71. Rehav Rubin and Motti Yair, "The Maps of Stephan Illes: A Cartographer of Jerusalem in the 19th Century," *Cathedra* 36 (1985): 63–72 (in Hebrew). Rehav Rubin, "The Search for Stephan Illes," *Eretz Magazine* (1985): 44–48.

72. J. M. Tenz, *Authorities and Brief Descriptive Notices of the Model of Ancient Jerusalem* (London, 1883). A model of the Temple is now in the collection of the Palestine Exploration Fund in London, and a model of Jerusalem is in the Bible Museum in Amsterdam.

73. August Ströbel, *Conrad Schick: Ein Leben für Jerusalem* (Fürth: Bay, 1988).

74. This map is part of the collection of the German Lutheran Institute for the Study of the Holy Land, in Jerusalem.

17. Two Islamic Construction Plans for al-Haram al-Sharif

1. 'Awf ibn Malik, a companion of Muhammad, recounted: "During the battle of Tabuk, and while sitting under a dome of animal skin, the Prophet, peace be upon him, told me: 'Count six signs before the day of judgment: My death, the conquest of Bayt al-Maqdis [Jerusalem], a plague that claims the lives of many of you, the abundance of wealth . . . , a *fitna* [schism], of which every Arab house will be a part, and a truce between you and the Byzantines which will be broken by them." From Mujir al-Din al-Hanbali, *al-'Uns al-Jalil bi Tarikh al-Quds wa al-Khalil,* vol. 1 (Amman: Maktabat al-Muhtasib, 1973), p. 244 (in Arabic).

2. According to Muslim jurists, al-Masjid al-Aqsa and its environs—that is, Palestine—are a divine Islamic endowment, the deed of which is the Koran itself.

3. Al-Masjid al-Aqsa has been known since the Ottoman period as al-Haram al-Sharif, meaning the Noble Sanctuary, an appellation rejected by Salafi (Orthodox) Muslims as an innovation. According to them, the term *haram* may be used for Mecca and Medina only. See Ibn Taymiyyah, *Risalah fi Ziyarat Bayt al-Maqdis,* ed. A. Shanuhah (Jedda: Dar al-Matbu'at al-Haditha, 1987), pp. 24–25.

4. Extant large beam sockets carved in the Antonia rock scarp in the north-western corner of the Haram corroborate the account by Josephus Flavius, the first-century historian, of a Herodian monumental portico that ran along three sides of the Temple Mount; the southern side was distinguished by Herod's Royal Stoa.

5. *The Pilgrimage of Arculfus in the Holy Land,* trans. J. R. MacPherson, vol.

3 (London: Palestine Pilgrims' Text Society, 1895), pp. 4–5. See also K. A. C. Creswell, *Early Muslim Architecture,* vol. 1, part 1 (New York: Oxford University Press; reprint, New York: Hacker Art Books, 1979). For the pagan temple which may have stood on the Temple Mount, see Cyril Mango, "The Temple Mount, A.D. 614–638," in Julian Raby and Jeremy Jones, eds., *Bayt al-Maqdis: ʿAbd al-Malik's Jerusalem,* part 1, Oxford Studies in Islamic Art IX (New York: Oxford University Press, 1992), pp. 1–16.

6. For this account from Muthir al-Gharam, see F. E. Peters, *The Distant Shrine* (New York: AMS Press, 1993), pp. 51–52.

7. The prototype seems to be the Roman mausoleums that were built to house the remains of an emperor, such as the Mausoleum of Diocletian in Split. Palestinian examples of an ambulatory surrounding a rotunda include the Holy Sepulchre in Jerusalem, the church at Capernaum, and the no-longer extant timber-roofed rotunda or octagon said to have been constructed over the Tomb of the Virgin in Gethsemane by Emperor Maurice. The Byzantine structure with a rotunda enshrining a sacred rock that could have served as its prototype, both in form and function, is the late fifth-century church on top of Mount Gerizim, a site near Nablus sacred to the Samaritans. See John Wilkinson, "Architectural Procedures in Byzantine Palestine," *Levant* 8 (1981): 156–172.

8. Nasser Rabbat, "The Dome of the Rock Revisited: Some Remarks on al-Wasiti's Accounts," *Muqarnas* 10 (1993): 70–71.

9. Oleg Grabar, "Al-Kuds," in *Encyclopaedia of Islam,* 2nd ed., vol. 5 (Leiden: E. J. Brill, 1980), p. 340.

10. Oleg Grabar, "The Umayyad Dome of the Rock in Jerusalem," *Ars Orientalis* 3 (1959): 33–62, and id., "The Meaning of the Dome of the Rock," in M. J. Chiat and K. L. Reyerson, eds., *The Medieval Mediterranean: Cross-Cultural Contacts* (St. Cloud, Minn.: North Star Press, 1988), pp. 1–10.

11. The restoration by Ottoman Sultan Suleiman from 1545 to 1566 included the replacement of the mosaics on the drum with faience, or glazed tiles. Later, the parapets were also covered with faience tiles, which totally concealed the semidomed niches. The mosaics on the upper part of the walls were similarly covered, and the semicircular arches were given a slightly pointed outline. The description of these hidden forms in the chronicles was confirmed when parts of the parapet and the outer walls were exposed for a short period during the Ottoman restorations of 1873–1874. The original structure's windows displayed double grilles, the inner ones made of pierced marble, their openings filled with stained glass. The outer grilles were made of iron. Suleiman also introduced double grilles, with stained glass inner ones and the outer ones forming part of the faience scheme. See Beatrice St. Laurent and András Riedlmayer, "Restorations of Jerusalem and the

Dome of the Rock and Their Political Significance, 1537–1928," *Muqarnas* 10 (1993): 76–84.

12. Grabar, "The Meaning of the Dome of the Rock," pp. 1–10.

13. Miryam Rosen-Ayalon, "The Early Islamic Monuments of Al-Haram al-Sharif: An Iconongraphic Study," *Qedem* 28 (Jerusalem: Institute of Archaeology, Hebrew University, 1989): 25–29. See also Chapter 4 in this publication.

14. Some suggest that ʿAbd-al-Malik began the construction of al-Aqsa and his son al-Walid completed it. See Rosen-Ayalon, "Early Islamic Monuments," pp. 4–7, and Michael Burgoyne, *Mamluk Jerusalem* (London: World of Islam Festival Trust on behalf of the British School of Archaeology in Jerusalem, 1987), p. 45.

15. James Allan, *A Short Account of Early Muslim Architecture* (Aldershot: Scholar Press, 1989). Benjamin Mazar and Meir Ben-Dov, *The Excavations in the Old City of Jerusalem* (Jerusalem: 1971). Meir Ben-Dov, *In the Shadow of the Temple Mount: The Discovery of Ancient Jerusalem* (Jerusalem: Keter Publishing House, 1985), pp. 293–321.

16. This feature is to be seen in other early eighth-century palaces, such as Qasr Jabal, Qasr al-Minya, Qasr al-Hayr al-Gharbi, and the lesser enclosure of Qasr al-Hayr al-Sharqi.

17. Building an administrative palace next to the congregational mosque is an early Muslim practice that was inaugurated in Kufa, Iraq, in 638.

18. James Allan, *A Short Account,* p. 96.

19. S. Corbett, "Some Observations," *Palestine Exploration Quarterly* (1952–53).

20. Mujir al-Din, *al-ʾUns al-Jalil,* vol. 1, p. 282.

21. This can be detected on paper only, for in reality the arcades of the other aisles are carried through these arches to the southern, kibla wall. This plan is the precursor of the famous T-plan (both on paper and in reality) of the Great Mosque of Qairawan, as rebuilt by Aghlabid Ziyadat Allah in 836.

22. Ibn ʿAbd Rabbihi, *Al-ʿIqd al-Farid;* trans. A. Marmardji as *Textes géographique arabes sur la Palestine* (Paris: n.p., 1951), pp. 212–213.

23. Grabar, "Al-Kuds," p. 342.

24. Terry Allen, *A Classical Revival in Islamic Architecture* (Wiesbaden: Ludwig Reichert, 1986).

25. This combination of pendentive and squinch is preceded only by that in the Tetrapylon of Korykos, possibly dating from the end of the sixth century.

26. Plaster concealing the Fatimid mosaics was stripped away during the restoration undertaken by the Turkish architect Kemal-al-Din in 1924 to 1927. During the 1937 to 1942 restorations, many late Ottoman decorations of dubious quality were removed. On the design motifs, see H. Stern, "Recherches sur la Mosquée al-Aqsa," in *Ars Orientalis* 5 (1963).

27. Naser-e Khosraw, *Safarnama (Book of Travels)*, ed. Ehsan Yarshater, trans. Wheeler Thackston, Jr. (New York: Bibliotheca Persica, 1986), p. 34.

28. Ibid., pp. 24–25.

29. Michael Burgoyne, "A Recently Discovered Marwanid Inscription in Jerusalem," *Levant* 14 (1982): 118–121.

30. Khosraw, *Safarnama*, p. 25.

31. C. H. Johns, "The Citadel," *Quarterly of the Department of Antiquities of Palestine (QDAP)* 14 (1950). It was in the so-called Citadel of David that Iftikhar al-Dawla, the commander of the Egyptian garrison, was ensconced with his men when the Crusaders stormed the city walls in 1099, and it was from there that the Crusaders, under the agreement negotiated with Saint-Gilles, departed safely to Ascalon.

32. Peters, *The Distant Shrine*, p. 68.

33. Amin Maalouf, *The Crusades through Arab Eyes*, trans. Jon Rothschild (New York: Schocken Books, 1989), p. 200.

34. During the Ayyubid period, and in order to reassert the Muslim identity of the city, many Crusader buildings, especially churches, were converted into Muslim religious institutions or dismantled for recycling. Among them were the palace of the patriarch, turned by Saladin into a Sufi lodge; the Church of St. Anne, where he established a college of theology, al-Madrasa al-Salahiyya; and part of the hospital ascribed to Charlemagne, which became al-Bimaristan al-Salahi, the Hospital of Saladin. The dining halls of the Knights Templars, adjoining al-Aqsa to the west, became the Women's Mosque in 1194. See also Meron Benvenisti, *The Crusaders in the Holy Land* (Jerusalem: Israel Universities Press, 1970).

35. Al-Mu'azzam 'Isa served as governor of Damascus and Jerusalem (1200–1218) for his father, al-Malik al-'Adil I Sayf al-Din, sultan of Egypt and Syria. He was sultan of Damascus and Jerusalem from 1218 until 1227.

36. By sparing the lives and property of the Crusaders, Saladin set an example for magnanimity to the enemy as well as to his own soldiers. "We must apply the letter of the accords we have signed, so that no one will be able to accuse the believers of having violated their treaties. On the contrary, Christians everywhere will remember the kindness we have bestowed upon them," he is reported to have said. (See Maalouf, *The Crusades*, p. 200.) He may have also wanted to show the Crusaders that his true veneration of Jerusalem compelled him to extend peace not only to the shrines of the city but to its Christian population as well. This unique concept of veneration contrasts sharply with that of the Crusaders, who inaugurated their prayers in the Holy City with a bloodbath.

37. A madrasa is a college of Islamic theology and jurisprudence, usually including *hadith* (tradition) and koranic exegesis. The first madrasas were

private, established at Nishapur during the reign of Mahmud of Ghazna. Realizing the crucial role this institution could play in disseminating the Sunni doctrine and opposing Shiʻi propaganda, the Seljuk vizier Nizam al-Mulk elevated the madrasa's status to that of a state-sponsored college around the middle of the eleventh century. It was from Syria that the madrasa was introduced into Egypt by Saladin, after he had extinguished the Shiʻi Fatimid rule there. In Jerusalem, in addition to al-Madrasa al-Sala-hiyya, the Ayyubid sultans and princes sponsored the construction of new buildings dedicated to the teaching of the Ashʻari doctrine of theology and Shafiʻi law, the two most important constituents of the Sunni rite they espoused. The sultans constructed madrasas for other rites as well, such as the Maliki, Hanafi, and Hanbali rites.

38. At al-Aqsa, parts to the east and west of the nave, much of the mosque's eastern, western, and northern facades, and the first version of its porch in front of the main (northern) facade are attributed to the Crusaders (1099–1187). Just as after the first conquest of Jerusalem, Saladin, too, initiated his sovereignty by paying homage to al-Haram al-Sharif. Having reconsecrated al-Aqsa Mosque to Islam, he redid the decoration of the whole kibla wall, including the mihrab, and in 1169 installed the minbar, the pulpit made in Aleppo at the order of Nur al-Din Zengi, the saint-king under whose tutelage Saladin's military career commenced. (Tragically, this masterpiece was burned in a fire started by a deranged Australian tourist in 1969.) Qubbat al-Silsila, which had been dedicated as a chapel to St. James, the Dome of the Rock, and several Crusader structures were stripped of any remaining crucifixes and icons. Beneath the marble that covered the Rock, the Muslims found the marks from the chips the monks had carved out and sold in Constantinople and Sicily as relics from the Temple. The Rock was encircled by an iron screen, a masterpiece of Frankish hammered ironwork, which the Muslims left in place. The Rock was washed, in a special cere-mony, with rose water. To complete the reassertion of the Islamic character of the sanctuary, an inscription was introduced above one of its entrances declaring the premises forbidden to Christians.

39. The Dome of the Rock's mosaics were restored again in 1295–96 by Sultan Kitbugha.

40. Burgoyne, *Mamluk Jerusalem*, p. 456.

41. Possibly due to wars and destruction, a great deal of landfill accumulated in the area bordering the western side of the Herodian platform (the end of the Tyropeon Valley or al-Wad Street, which starts at Damascus Gate), for instead of the underground gates of the Fatimid period, by the time of the Ayyubids the streets leading to the sanctuary terminated at new gates

built on the same level as the top of the Herodian platform. See R. W. Hamilton, "Street Levels in the Tyropœon Valley," *QDAP* 1–2 (1932).

42. Except for a small room over the prayer hall at the northern end of the Ribat of Kurt, the structures over the ground floor of all three buildings are Ottoman additions.

43. Part of the western section of the northern portico of the sanctuary dates to 1213–1214, to the reign of al-Mu'azzam 'Isa. See Max van Berchem, *Matériaux pour un Corpus Inscriptionum Arabicarum, Deuxième partie: Syrie du Sud II, Jérusalem 'Haram'* (Cairo, 1925–27), pp. 82–97. He also ordered wooden doors for the gates of the Haram and rebuilt the Crusader portico in front of al-Aqsa. His reconstruction of the two porticoes may have been conceived as part of a grand scheme to transform the open space of the Haram into a congregational mosque's courtyard surrounded by porticos on its four sides, like the Umayyad Mosque of Damascus or the Fatimid al-Hakim Mosque in Cairo.

44. These openings were made in the preexisting wall of the sanctuary. This adjoining segment of the wall is thought to date from the days of Nasir-i Khusraw or earlier, since the two westernmost windows pierce infill walls that seal two round-headed archways, each replicating the adjacent Bab al-'Atm archway. The three archways must have comprised a triple gate, most probably that referred to by Nasir-i Khusraw as leading to the cloisters of the Sufis. See Khosraw, *Safarnama*, p. 25. The sealing of its two eastern bays dates from the time of the construction of the *khanakah*. See Burgoyne, *Mamluk Jerusalem*, p. 156.

45. On the western border of the sanctuary, the rock scarp rises northward from about Bab al-Ghawanimah. The rock's northern edge rises westward from about Bab al-'Atm. See Burgoyne, *Mamluk Jerusalem*, p. 204.

46. Frescoes and mosaics, the media of figurative representation used during the early Christian and Byzantine periods to emphasize the sanctity of a place, were here replaced by sculpture—the vogue in the realm of figurative representation in Europe since the eleventh century. The sculptures of this Crusader *locus sanctus* were carved on column capitals, a technique also favored by contemporary Romanesque architects, especially in France. These sculptures, which depicted Jesus reposing for the night and watched over by the angels, were decapitated, probably when the domed porch of this chapel—now gone—was turned into a mausoleum for Ibn Darbas, ca. 1200, in compliance with Islam's prohibition against figurative representation, particularly heads and faces. In their new innocuous state, these capitals, a rare example of Crusader sculpture from the Holy Land, were removed in 1300 to decorate the muezzin's balcony of the Minaret of

al-Ghawanimah, at the northwestern corner of the sanctuary. For an account of the three extant capitals, see Jaroslav Folda, "Three Crusader Capitals in Jerusalem," *Levant* 10 (1978): 139–155.

47. A sketch of the interior of the madrasa was produced by Bernardino Amico, who visited the site between 1594 and 1597; see Bernardino Amico, "Plans of the Sacred Edifices of the Holy Land," trans. T. Bellorini and E. Hoade, *Publications of the Studium Biblicum Franciscanum* 10 (1953): 78.

48. The *iwan* is a tunnel-vaulted square or rectangular space with one of its two opposite sides perpendicular to the axis of the vault, totally opening on a courtyard.

49. The only extant part is the kibla section; the rest was destroyed in 1923–24. Fortunately, the madrasa was carefully described by Elzear Horn, "Ichnographiae Monumentorum Terrae Sanctae (1724–1744)," ed. and trans. Eugene Hoade, *Publications of the Studium Biblicum Franciscanum* 15 (1962): 148. The scheme is reminiscent of Shaykh Yusuf al-'Ajami al-'Adawi's *ribat*-mausoleum (the so-called Mausoleum of Mustafa Pasha) built by the Mamluk Amir Azdamir al-Salihi around 1267–1273 in Cairo's Southern Cemetery, a layout unique among extant Egyptian religious foundations in Egypt.

50. The only exception is the Hanafite Madrasa of Abu Mansur Kumushtakin at Bosra, from 1136, where the two *iwans* of the madrasa are both employed by the same rite.

51. The teaching unit of the funerary foundation of Amir Sanjar al-Jawili in Cairo (1303–1304), which very likely served as a Sufi lodge whose curriculum included courses in theology and Shafi'i law, consists of a large *iwan* that opens on a rectangular courtyard surrounded on the other sides by cells. Facing the large *iwan* across the courtyard is a smaller one. Creswell has suggested that the origin of the two-*iwan* madrasas in Egypt is the domestic tripartite reception hall from the twelfth century known as a *qa'a*, which consists of two *iwans* on the opposite sides of a square space covered by a skylight. Many of the early two-*iwan* madrasas were originally professors' houses where teaching took place and which were turned into madrasas on the death of their owners. See K. A. C. Creswell, "Origin of the Architectural Form of the Two-Liwan Madrasa," *The Muslim Architecture of Egypt*, vol. 2 (Oxford: Clarendon Press, 1959; reprint, New York: Hacker Art Books, 1978), pp. 129–131. Cairene madrasas also depart from their Syrian counterparts in the invariable incorporation of a minaret into their scheme. The Jerusalem madrasas built on or near al-Haram al-Sharif do not have minarets, due to their proximity to the minarets of the sanctuary, which are located near the gates and were all rebuilt during the Mamluk period. Minarets built at some distance from the Haram, especially near Jewish or Christian places of worship, serve as symbolic reminders of the hegemony

of Islam, such as the minaret of al-Malik al-Qahir at al-Mu'azzamiyya on the Via Dolorosa (1274–1275), the minaret at al-Khanqah al-Salahiyya in the Christian Quarter (before 1417–1418), and the minaret at the so-called Jami' Sidi Umar in the Jewish Quarter (1397). According to Mujir al-Din, this third minaret rose from a mosque adjoining the south side of a synagogue. The synagogue is named after its founder, the Ramban, or Nachmanides, the famous scholar who came to Jerusalem from Spain in 1267. For the history of this synagogue, see Shimon Ben-Eliezer, *Destruction and Renewal: The Synagogues of the Jewish Quarter* (Jerusalem, 1973), pp. 11–13.

52. Representatives of this adaptation include the Bahri Mamluk Madrasa of Baydamur al-Khawarizmi, which he built in 1379–80, during his exile in Jerusalem, for the Hanbali rite; the two Burji Mamluk Shafi'i rite madrasas; the Khanakah-Madrasa of Jawhar al-Qunqubay (endowed in 1440); and the Madrasa of Abu Bakr ibn Muzhir (1481). All three madrasas are located on the street leading to Bab al-Hadid, one of the sanctuary's gates in the western portico.

53. Ironically, this madrasa, like the Crusader associations with its site, became the praetorium or seat of government (*majlis* or *iwan al-hukm*) of Jerusalem during the governorship of Shuja' al-Din Shahin (known as al-Dhabbah, meaning "the slaughterer"), who restored the building around 1427. See van Berchem, *Corpus Inscriptionum, Deuxième partie,* pp. 230–233. This transformation was probably due to its commanding view of the Haram and the monumentality of its *iwan*. The governor sat at the kibla side of the *iwan* until a loggia with a ceiling of painted wood, like those of the houses of justice in Egypt, was built in 1486–87 by the governor Khidrbak, next to the north side of the *iwan*. See Mujir al-Din, *al-'Uns al-Jalil*, vol. 2, p. 337. The madrasa continued to serve as the house of government during the Ottoman period, until the occupation of Ibrahim Pasha (1831–1840), when it was turned into a barracks, a conversion that involved a major restoration of the whole structure. The second floor above the kibla section, which overlooks the city and its environs like a watchtower, probably dates from this period. It continued to be the barracks of the Ottoman garrison until the surrender of the city to the British in 1917. Interestingly, many Europeans who visited the building from the end of the sixteenth century until the middle of the nineteenth referred to its *iwan* as the Praetorium in which Jesus was sentenced to death. In 1923–24, the Supreme Islamic Council of Jerusalem ordered the demolition of many of its parts and built modern classrooms there, known today as the Umariyya School.

54. The Herodian wall, a vestige of the Antonia Fort, is believed to have extended from the site of the madrasa to the east, since traces of it can be seen in the Is'ardiyya Madrasa approximately twenty-five meters to the east.

55. The governorship of Damascus was bestowed on Tankiz in 1312. He was removed from office in 1340 and put to death in Alexandria, and was interred in the burial chamber of his mosque in Damascus in 1343.

56. Huda Lutfi, *Al-Quds al-Mamlukiyya: A History of Mamluk Jerusalem Based on the Haram Documents* (Berlin: Klaus Schwarz Verlag, 1985), p. 155.

57. None of the extant Syrian madrasas from the twelfth and thirteenth centuries adopts the cruciform, four-*iwan* configuration. However, cruciform axial planning, which is believed to be of Persian origin, is not unknown in Syrian architecture, for the sixth-century praetorium outside the north gate of Rusafa and the Umayyad Palace at the Citadel of Amman both follow a cruciform layout.

58. It was preceded by only one cruciform, four-*iwan* Cairene example, at the no-longer-extant Madrasa of Baybars I, which was dedicated to the Hanafi and Shafi'i rites. See K. A. C. Creswell, "The Origin of the Cruciform Plan of Cairene Madrasas," *The Muslim Architecture of Egypt,* vol. 2, pp. 104–134.

59. Only three of the four halls of the Madrasa of Tankiz were used as lecture halls, for since the vestibule opens directly on the north *iwan* through a doorway in the center of its back wall, the entry axis goes straight through the *iwan,* thus appropriating it for the circulation system, and, consequently, rendering it unsuitable for teaching. In most Cairene cruciform madrasas, the four *iwans* are accessible only from the courtyard, which is reached from the entrance corridor through a doorway in one of its sides between the *iwans.*

60. Suq al-Qattanin, and the Caravanserai of Sultan Barquq (1386–1387) are the only extant commercial establishments from the Mamluk period. Almost all the other markets, such as the three covered bazaars, date from the Crusader period.

61. Oleg Grabar, "A New Inscription from the Haram al-Sharif in Jerusalem," *Studies in Honour of Professor K. A. C. Creswell* (Cairo, 1965), pp. 72–83.

62. Employed for convening public inquiries toward the end of the Burji period.

63. M. Amin and Laila Ibrahim, *Architectural Terms in Mamluk Documents* (Cairo: The American University in Cairo Press, 1990), p. 108.

64. The second floor was destroyed by an earthquake in 1545. For descriptions and reconstructions, see Mujir al-Din, *al-'Uns al-Jalil,* vol. 2, pp. 328–329; Robert Hillenbrand, *Islamic Architecture* (New York: Columbia University Press, 1994), pp. 202–206; Michael Meinecke, *Die Mamlukische Architektur in Ägypten und Syrien* (Glückstadt: Augustin, 1992); Shlomo Tamari, "Al-Ashrafiyya: An Imperial Madrasa in Jerusalem," *Atti della Accademia Nazionale dei Lincei,* series 8, vol. 19 (1976); A. G. Walls and D. A. King, "The Sundial on the West Wall of the Madrasa of Sultan Qaytbay in Jerusalem,"

Art and Archaeology Research Papers 15, 16–21 (1979): A. G. Walls, *An Attempted Reconstruction of the Design Procedures and Concepts during the Reign of Sultan Qaytbay (872/1468–901/1496) in Jerusalem and Cairo* (Ph.D. diss., Edinburgh College of Art, Heriot-Watt University, 1979); A. G. Walls, *Geometry and Architecture in Islamic Jerusalem: A Study of the Ashrafiyya* (London: Scorpion, for World of Islam Festival Trust, 1990); A. G. Walls, "Ottoman Restorations to the Sabil and to the Madrasa of Qaytbay in Jerusalem," *Muqarnas* 10 (1993): 85–97. The *qaʿa* layout originates in the houses and palaces of Cairo, where it is usually a lofty tripartite reception hall consisting of a square hall with a central fountain lit and ventilated by a wooden skylight in the roof and flanked by two opposing *iwans* whose floors are elevated above that of the central one by one or two steps. The two other sides of the central square hall display opposing rectangular alcoves that look like miniature *iwans*. The *qaʿa* layout was originally borrowed from Cairene domestic architecture by the builders of the Burji Mamluk period in adapting the cruciform four-*iwan* layout to narrow or irregular sites. The Madrasa of Qaytbay finds a much closer parallel in the cruciform Cairene Bahri Madrasa of Amir Mithqal al-Anuki (1361–1363), whose attenuated plan was caused by the imposition of a formal architectural scheme on a constricted exigent site, and where another unusual engineering challenge was the suspension of the whole structure over a vaulted alley. It produced, like at the foundation of Qaytbay, a "hanging madrasa." The courtyard of Qaytbay's madrasa was covered by a flat wooden roof with gilded decorations on its ceiling and a central wooden skylight, an indication that the design was not the only element that was imported for this madrasa. See Mujir al-Din, *Al-ʾUns al-Jalil*, vol. 2, p. 329, and Walls, *Geometry and Architecture*. The only extant *qaʿa* in Jerusalem is that on the upper floor of the Palace of Lady Tanshuq al-Muzaffariyya (1388).

65. Other examples of such domed loggias, which were introduced at the foundation of Majd al-Din al-Isʿardi (1359) at the northern border, are the madrasas of ʿAbd al-Basit (1431, dome no longer extant), and Manjak al-Yusufi (1361). The various elements of their facades above the porticoes of the sanctuary—windows set in recessed panels and double arches with alternating red and white voussoirs below stone domes—are generally centered above either a portico arch or pier so that the constellations they form, symmetric or asymmetric, are governed by the modularity of the portico's plan and elevation.

66. Mujir al-Din's description of the loggia, along with Edward Reuwich of Utrechti's 1486 illustration from Bernhard of Breydenbach, *Peregrinationes in Terram Sanctum* (at the Bodleian Library, Oxford) makes the evidence

for its existence unimpeachable. See Walls, *Geometry and Architecture,* for the illustration and for the madrasa's windows.

67. Mujir al-Din, *al-'Uns al-Jalil,* vol. 2, p. 329.

68. As the only structure projecting with a monumental loggia into a rectangular open space surrounded by a portico, the foundation of Qaytbay finds a striking analogue in the 'Ali Qapu built by the Safavid Shah 'Abbas I (early seventeenth century, on fifteenth-century Timurid foundations) in Isfahan.

69. Christel Kessler, *The Carved Masonry Domes of Mediaeval Cairo* (Cairo: The American University in Cairo Press, 1976), p. 4. Mayer shed light on a small dome carved with an arabesque design over the marble minbar, or pulpit, at the Mosque of Ibn 'Uthman in Gaza (1431). See L. A. Mayer, "Arabic Inscriptions of Gaza," *Journal of the Palestinian Oriental Society* 10 (1930): 59–62.

70. The earliest Cairene example of a children's school surmounting a *sabil* to form a unified composition is at the madrasa-mausoleum of Amir Iljay al-Yusufi (1373). In 1479 Qaytbay's architects introduced the first detached children's school fountain in Cairo; it still shared many of the compositional aspects of an attached one.

71. The Bahri Mamluks continued the practice of attaching a mausoleum to the religious foundation of the departed, which was introduced in Cairo by Shajarat al-Durr in 1250, when she had her late husband, Sultan al-Salih Najm al-Din Ayyub, the master of the Bahri Mamluks, interred in a domed burial chamber that she had built adjoining his school. This practice was a Syrian influence, initiated in Damascus by Nur al-Din Zengi in 1172, when he, emulating his Seljuk overlords, built his mausoleum contiguous with his madrasa. See Christel Kessler, "Funerary Architecture within the City," *Colloque international sur l'histoire du Caire* (Cairo: Ministry of Culture of the Arab Republic of Egypt), p. 259.

72. Other burial chambers with windows opening directly on the western portico include the madrasas of Manklibugha al-Ahmadi (1380) and Oghul Khatun (1354–1380).

73. Another example of a funerary foundation on a street leading to a sanctuary gate is the Madrasa of Arghun al-Kamili (1358). The mausoleum, with a window that opens on Bab al-Hadid Road, is located in the corner between two of the four *iwans* of the cruciform madrasa, as in several earlier foundations in Cairo.

74. Burgoyne, *Mamluk Jerusalem,* p. 111.

75. The other funerary structures on Bab al-Silsila Road belong to Baybars al-Jaliq (1307), Sa'd al-Din Mas'ud (1311), Turkan Khatun (1352–1353), Jamal al-Din Pahlavan (1352), and Sayf al-Din Taz (1361).

76. A similar sacrifice of a prayer niche for the sake of receiving such blessings

is found at the burial chamber of the foundation of Sultan Barsbay, on Shari'
al-Mu'izz in Mamluk Cairo.

77. Van Berchem suggested that she was a Muzaffarid princess who fled Timur's invasion of Iran. His theory is fostered by the Iranian influence on the decoration: the star inlay bordering the window in the west portal of the palace, the stucco decoration of the hood of the prayer niche of her mausolem, and the square Kufic inscription at the entrance to the tomb antechamber, all of which are unparalleled by any other Mamluk foundation in Jerusalem (Burgoyne, *Mamluk Jerusalem,* p. 509).

78. The earliest use of *ablaq,* or different-colored stones, coursing in post-Umayyad Syrian architecture can be found on the exterior of the burial chamber of Nur al-Din Zengi attached to his madrasa in Damascus (1172). See Terry Allen, "The Concept of Regional Style," *Five Essays in Islamic Art* (Solipsist Press, 1988), p. 101. The first Cairene monument to incorporate *ablaq* treatment into its decorative program was the Mosque of Baybars I (1267–1269, northeastern gateway). Two of Baybars's buildings in Syria also exhibit this Damascene technique, the no-longer-extant palace of al-Ablaq in Damascus, and the fort of ibn Ma'n.

79. The portal of al-Dawadariyya bears the signature of master engineer or architect 'Ali ibn Salama. The prototype of al-'Adiliyya's suspended keystone and domes is the portal of Nur al-Din's madrasa in Damascus (1172), followed, also in Damascus, by the portal of the Qillijiyya Madrasa (1253–54), which had four instead of two bays (domes).

80. See Allen, "The Concept of Regional Style," pp. 91–111. Besides the portal of al-Dawadariyya and the cupola at Suq al-Qattanin, another example of the signature of a craftsman, this one of Muhammad ibn al-Zayn, can be read on a fine iron grille in the burial chamber of the Is'ardiyya foundation.

81. Burgoyne, *Mamluk Jerusalem,* p. 235.

82. That this team came from Damascus is strongly suggested by the tantalizing accounts of the marble paneling ordered for the Great Mosque of Damascus and completed in 1328 during the viceregency of Tankiz, only to be destroyed by fire in 1401. The provenance of marble wall mosaics or paneling in medieval Islamic architecture is to be found in Damascus in the Maristan of Nur al-Din (1154) and the Mausoleum of Baybars I (1281), representing a revival of Umayyad marble paneling such as is in the interior of the Dome of the Rock and the Mosque at Medina (707–709, no longer extant). See also Burgoyne, *Mamluk Jerusalem,* p. 235.

83. The earliest recorded example of an arcaded prayer niche was part of Seljuq Malik Shah's works at the Great Mosque of Damascus in 1082–83, built after the fire of 1069 and destroyed by the fire of 1401, as described by Ibn Jubayr in 1184; see Creswell, *The Muslim Architecture of Egypt,* vol. 2, p. 202. Similar

arcades and mosaics are to be seen in the mihrab of Tankiz in the sanctuary of Hebron (1331–32), in the no-longer-extant mihrab of the Mosque of Tankiz in Damascus (1317–18), and in the Madrasa of Sultan Qalawun in Cairo (1284–1285). Glass mosaics, the resurgence of which was expanded by Sultan al-Zahir Baybars in his restoration of the Dome of the Rock and the Dome of the Chain, are on the walls of the interior of his mausoleum in the madrasa he built in Damascus in 1277. Upon Tankiz's request, the dome of the Dome of the Rock was restored and regilded in 1318–19, and the dome of the Aqsa Mosque was restored in 1327–28. Glass mosaics, which form an integral part of the decorative schemes of both of these monuments, were among Tankiz's restorations at the Great Mosque of Damascus, which were completed in 1328. However, they must have commenced during the opening years of Tankiz's appointment in Damascus, for according to al-'Umari, the kibla wall of the Mosque of Tankiz (1317–1318) was decorated with some of the mosaics amassed for the restoration workshop of the Great Mosque of Damascus. Ibn Fadl Allah al-'Umari, *Masalik al-Absar fi Mamalik al-Amsar*, ed. Ahmad Zaki Pasha (Cairo, 1924), p. 193. Analogous to the restoration of mosaics by Baybars, the Damascene restoration workshop was enlisted by Tankiz to decorate his new structures with the same technique, as is shown by the mihrabs of his mosque in Damascus, his madrasa in Jerusalem, and that at the sanctuary in Hebron (1331–1332).

84. Other examples of cross vaults include the Great Mosque of Tripoli (1293), the Mosque of Sanjar al-Jawili added to the sanctuary in Hebron (1318–1820), and the Great Mosque of Abu al-Fida' in Hama (1326–1327).

85. The square burial chambers of Mamluk Jerusalem were almost invariably covered by domes. According to Burgoyne (*Mamluk Jerusalem*, p. 92), several of them, like that of the Sa'diyya, Arghuniyya, and Baladiyya (Manklibugha al-Ahmadi) foundations, which now have cross-vaulted ceilings, were originally domed. In addition to mausoleums, gateways, and loggias, domes appear in the two bathhouses at Suq al-Qattanin. Like many features from the Madrasa of Qaytbay—the folded cross vault over the entrance porch and vestibule and the trilobed groin vault crowning the portal—the arabesque carving of the exterior of the dome was executed by a foreign craftsman and remained an isolated example. Its uniqueness in Jerusalem also stems from having its transitional zone expressed externally in the typical Cairene stepped fashion, which here consists of two tiers of prismatic triangles. On the inside, the transition is effected by several tiers of *muqarnas,* or stalactites, niches that form a triangular spherical pendentive at each of the four corners. The niches exhibit low-relief arabesque carving.

86. A major exception is the minaret of Bab al-Asbat (1367–68), which has a circular shaft.

87. Creswell (*The Muslim Architecture of Egypt,* vol. 2, p. 147) suggested that the provenance of this Aleppine feature is the Abbasid portal, like that of the Bayt al-Khalifa at Samarra, Iraq, where a deep entrance bay is covered by a semidome on a pair of squinches.

88. The technique is also to be seen in Palestine in the mihrab of the sanctuary at Hebron decorated for Tankiz in 1331–32. The interlacing-loops pattern was introduced in Cairo on the voussoirs around the entrance of the so-called Mausoleum of Mustafa Pasha, built around 1270, and in Damascus on the south facade of the madrasa-mausoleum of Sultan Baybars I, finished in 1281.

89. Stone prismatic triangles, which appear for the first time in Islamic architecture as a form of transition from the square base to the octagonal shaft of the minaret of the mosque-mausoleum of Shaykhu al-'Imari in Cairo in 1349, were also employed in the transitional zones of the minarets of Jerusalem, represented by the minaret built at Bab al-Asbat (between the square base and the intermediate polygonal shaft) and the minaret of al-Fakhriyya at the southwestern corner of the sanctuary, rebuilt after 1672 (between the top of the square shaft and the octagonal base of the domed finial).

90. Burgoyne, *Mamluk Jerusalem,* p. 307.

18. Architecture of the City outside the Walls

1. From a lecture by Stanford Anderson presented at the Jerusalem Seminar in 1994.

2. Joseph Rykwert, *The First Moderns: The Architects of the Eighteenth Century* (Cambridge, Mass.: MIT Press, 1980).

3. No one has played a more important role in raising the public's awareness of modern architecture in Jerusalem than architect David Kroyanker. His monumental work, published in six volumes (by Keter of Jerusalem, in Hebrew), documents the city's architecture inside and outside the Old City Wall. It has established the basis for further research, including this article. See also his book *Jerusalem Architecture* (New York: Vendome, 1994).

4. Robert Rosenblum, *Modern Paintings and the Northern Romantic Tradition* (London: Thames and Hudson, 1975).

5. Yehoshua Ben-Arieh, *Painting Palestine in the Nineteenth Century* (Jerusalem: Yad Izhak Ben-Zvi, 1992), pp. 9–11 (in Hebrew).

6. Yehoshua Ben Arieh, *A City Reflected in Its Time: Jerusalem in the Nine-

teenth Century (Jerusalem: Yad Izhak Ben-Zvi, 1977), pp. 219–221 (in Hebrew).

7. Ely Schiller, "A Rare Photographic Collection from the Russian Compound," *Kardom* 21–23 (July 1982): 165–171 (in Hebrew).

8. Ben Arieh, *A City Reflected in Its Time,* pp. 286–302.

9. Schiller, "Rare Photographic Collection," p. 20.

10. Alex Carmel, "Conrad Schick's Road to Jerusalem," in Ely Schiller, ed., *Sefer Zev Vilnay,* vol. 1 (Jerusalem: Ariel, 1984), pp. 115–126 (in Hebrew).

11. Closed communities, segregated according to country of origin, had been common among Jews in the Old City for generations.

12. Ruth Kark, *Jerusalem Neighborhoods: Planning and By-laws* (Jerusalem: Mount Scopus, 1991).

13. Montefiore first visited Eretz Israel in 1827, and tried throughout the nineteenth century to improve the quality of life for the impoverished Jewish community.

14. Kark, *Neighborhoods,* pp. 44, 84–87.

15. David Kroyanker, *Architecture in Jerusalem: European-Christian Building outside the Walls, 1855–1918* (Jerusalem: Keter, 1987), pp. 67–78 (in Hebrew).

16. Alex Carmel, *German Settlement in Eretz Israel at the End of the Ottoman Period* (Jerusalem: Hebrew University, 1973).

17. R. Kark and S. Lanman, "The Establishment of Muslim Neighbourhoods in Jerusalem outside the Old City during the Late Ottoman Period," *Palestine Exploration Quarterly* 122 (July 1980): 113–135.

18. For the connection between French and German building, see D. Watkin, *German Architecture and the Classical Ideal* (Cambridge, Mass.: MIT Press, 1987).

19. Carmel, *Conrad Schick,* p. 125.

20. Kroyanker, *European-Christian Building,* pp. 193–202.

21. Ely Schiller, "The Pro-Jerusalem Society and Its Contribution to the Preservation and Rehabilitation of the Old City," *Kardom* 21–23 (July 1982): 127–135 (in Hebrew).

22. Sarah Markovitz, "The Development of Modern Jerusalem" (senior thesis, School of Architecture, Princeton University, 1982).

23. G. Herbert and S. Sosnovsky, *Bauhaus on the Carmel* (Jerusalem: Yad Izhak Ben-Zvi, 1993), p. 76 (in Hebrew).

24. Henry Kendall, *Jerusalem, the City Plan: Preservation and Development during the British Mandate, 1918–48* (London: H. M. Stationery Office, 1948), p. 6.

25. Markovitz, "Modern Jerusalem."

26. Menachem Levin, "Ashbee's Projects in Jerusalem," in Ely Schiller, ed., *Sefer Zev Vilnay,* vol. 2 (Jerusalem: Ariel, 1987), pp. 76–83 (in Hebrew).

27. Volker Welter, "The Republic of Patrick Geddes," in Clarence Epstein and Volker Welter, eds., *Edinburgh Architecture Research* (Edinburgh: University of Edinburgh, 1994).

28. David Kroyanker, *Architecture in Jerusalem: Building during the Period of the British Mandate* (Jerusalem: Keter, 1989), pp. 101–102 (in Hebrew).

29. Mark Girouard, *Sweetness and Light: The Queen Ann Move, 1860–1900* (New Haven, Conn.: Yale University Press, 1977).

30. Franco Brosi, *The Monumental Era* (New York: Rizzoli, 1986).

31. It should be noted that even after he turned toward neoclassicism, Lutyens persisted in his efforts to blend in with the local idiom.

32. Micha Levin, *The Twenties in Art in Israel*, exhibit catalog (Tel Aviv: Tel Aviv Museum, 1982) (in Hebrew).

33. Herbert and Sosnovsky, *Bauhaus on the Carmel*, p. 113.

34. Kroyanker, *Building during the British Mandate*, p. 84.

35. One can compare the building with Draogo Castle, which Edwin Lutyens built in Devon, England (1910–1930), and which also has a butterfly shape.

36. Ayala Zussman and Ronnie Reich, "The History of the Rockefeller Museum in Jerusalem," in Ely Schiller, ed., *Sefer Zev Vilnay*, vol. 2 (Jerusalem: Ariel, 1987), pp. 83–93 (in Hebrew).

37. It is customary to attribute the beginning of modern art in Britain to the post-Impressionism exhibition that Roger Fry organized in 1910.

38. Nurit Shiloh Cohen, ed., *The Bezalel of Boris Schatz, 1906–1929*, exhibit catalog (Jerusalem: Israel Museum, 1983), in Hebrew.

39. Yigal Zalmona, "The Orient in Israel; Art in the Nineteen Twenties," in Micha Levin, *The Twenties in Art in Israel*, exhibit catalog (Tel Aviv: Tel Aviv Museum, 1982), in Hebrew.

40. Kroyanker, *Building during the British Mandate*, p. 30.

41. Kendall, *Jerusalem, the City Plan*, p. 28.

42. Kroyanker, *Building during the British Mandate*, pp. 378–387.

43. Levin, *The Twenties in Art in Israel*.

44. Herbert and Sosnovsky, *Bauhaus on the Carmel*, pp. 85–98.

45. Gordon A. Craig, *The Germans* (London: Penguin Books, 1991).

46. J. Gearey, ed., *Goethe: Essays on Art and Literature* (Princeton: Princeton University Press, 1994), p. 8.

47. Joan Campbell, *The German Werkbund* (Princeton: Princeton University Press, 1978).

48. The quotes are from letters by Mendelsohn that appeared in Oskar Beyer, ed., *The Letters of an Architect* (London: Abelrad-Schuman, 1967).

49. Micha Levin, *White City: The Architecture of the International Style in Israel*, exhibit catalog (Tel Aviv: Tel Aviv Museum, 1984), p. 16.

50. Herbert Gilbert and Ita Heinze Greenberg, eds., *Erich Mendelsohn in Israel* (Haifa: Technion-Israel Institute of Technology, 1987).
51. Ibid.
52. Gideon Efrat, *The New Bezalel* (Jerusalem: Bezalel Academy of Art and Design, 1987), in Hebrew.
53. Levin, *White City,* p. 54.
54. For the connection between Buber and Mendelsohn, see Ziva Sternhell, "From Berlin to Jerusalem: Erich Mendelsohn's Architecture in Eretz Israel," *Prose* (May–June 1988): 101–102 (in Hebrew).

Contributors

JONATHAN M. BLOOM, an independent scholar, lives in Richmond, New Hampshire. He is coauthor of *The Art and Architecture of Islam: 1250–1800* (New Haven, Conn.: Yale University Press, 1994).

MAGEN BROSHI, an archaeologist and historian, has dug extensively in Jerusalem, both inside and outside the Old City walls. He served as curator of the Shrine of the Book (where the Dead Sea Scrolls are housed) at the Israel Museum in Jerusalem, from 1964 to 1994.

JOSEPH DAN is the Gershom Scholem Professor of Kabbalah at the Hebrew University of Jerusalem. Among his many books are *Jewish Mysticism and Jewish Ethics* (Seattle: University of Washington Press, 1986), and *Jewish Intellectual History in the Middle Ages* (Westport, Conn.: Praeger, 1994).

PAULA FREDRIKSEN is the Aurelio Professor of the Appreciation of Scripture at Boston University and a 1994–95 Lady Davis Visiting Professor at the Hebrew University of Jerusalem. She is the author of *From Jesus to Christ: The Origins of Ancient Christianity* (New Haven, Conn.: Yale University Press, 1988).

MARK FRIEDMAN is a historian who lives in Englewood, New Jersey.

OLEG GRABAR is a professor at the School of Historical Studies, Institute for Advanced Study, at Princeton and the Aga Khan Professor, Emeritus, of Islamic Art at Harvard University. The latest of his many books is *The Shape of the Holy: Early Medieval Jerusalem* (Princeton, N.J.: Princeton University Press, 1996).

SABRI JARRAR was born to Palestinian parents. He studied architecture at the University of Amman and the Massachusetts Institute of Technology. As a research associate at MIT and Harvard University, he wrote a compendium and source book for the monuments of the Islamic world (in electronic and printed form).

ARTHUR HERTZBERG is Visiting Professor of the Humanities at New York University, Professor of Religion, Emeritus, at Dartmouth College, and Rabbi Emeritus of Temple Emanu-El in Englewood Cliffs, New Jersey. He is the author of many books and editor of *The Zionist Idea*.

ANGELIKA NEUWIRTH has taught at the universities of Munich, Amman, Cairo, Bamberg, and Berlin. Currently she is the Director of the Orient-Institute in Beirut and Istanbul. Among her many publications is "Images and Metaphors in the Introductory Sections of the Mekkan Suras," in G. R. Hawting and Abdul-Kader A. Shareef, eds., *New Approaches to the Qur'an* (London: Routledge, 1993).

BIANCA KÜHNEL is Professor of Medieval Art History at the Hebrew University, Jerusalem, and author of *From the Earthly to the Heavenly Jerusalem: Representations of the Holy City in Christian Art of the First Millennium* (Rome: Herder, 1987), and *Crusader Art in the Twelfth Century: A Geographical, an Historical, or an Art Historical Notion* (Berlin: Gebr. Mann Verlag, 1984).

MILKA LEVY-RUBIN, born and brought up in Jerusalem, received her doctorate at the Hebrew University in Jerusalem (1994). She is a lecturer in the Department of History at Ben Gurion University of the Negev, Beer Sheba.

DAN MIRON teaches Hebrew literature at the Hebrew University, Jerusalem, and at Columbia University, New York. The author of many books and other publications, mostly in Hebrew, he was the recipient of the Israel Prize in 1994.

MUHAMMAD MUSLIH, who grew up in Jerusalem, is Associate Professor of Political Science and Director of the International Studies Program at C. W. Post College, Long Island University. Among his publications are *The Origins of Palestinian Nationalism* (New York: Columbia University Press, 1988) and *Political Tides in the Arab World,* coauthored with A. R. Norton (New York: Foreign Policy Association, 1991).

F. E. PETERS is Professor of History and Near Eastern Languages and Literature at New York University. He is author of *Jerusalem: The Holy City in the Eyes of*

Chroniclers, Visitors, Pilgrims, and Prophets from the Days of Abraham to the Beginnings of Modern Times (Princeton, N.J.: Princeton University Press, 1985). His most recent works are *Muhammad and the Origins of Islam* (Albany, N.Y.: State University of New York Press, 1994), *Mecca*, and *The Hajj* (both at Princeton, N.J.: Princeton University Press, 1994).

NITZA ROSOVSKY was born and brought up in Jerusalem. She is the author of *Jerusalemwalks* (New York: Henry Holt, 1992) and coauthor of *The Museums of Israel* (New York: Harry N. Abrams, 1989).

REHAV RUBIN, born and raised in Jerusalem, received his doctorate at the Hebrew University in Jerusalem (1986). He is Senior Lecturer in the Department of Geography at the Hebrew University and the author of *Jerusalem in Maps and Views from the Byzantine Period to the Nineteenth Century* (Tel Aviv: Kineret, 1987; in Hebrew).

ZIVA STERNHELL teaches the theory of modern architecture at the Bezalel Academy of Arts and Design in Jerusalem. She frequently writes about architecture and design for *Ha'aretz*, Israel's main daily newspaper, and for professional periodicals.

ROBERT L. WILKEN is the William R. Kenan, Jr., Professor of the History of Christianity at the University of Virginia in Charlottesville, and author of *The Land Called Holy* (New Haven, Conn.: Yale University Press, 1992).

Illustration Credits

Page ii: Inside Jaffa Gate, ca. 1890, photograph by Bonfils. Courtesy of Daniel Tassel.

Page iii: Inside Jaffa Gate, 1985, photograph by Daniel Tassel.

Page 35: The Tower of David, photograph by Nitza Rosovsky.

Page 147: A street in the Old City, photograph by Nitza Rosovsky.

Page 203: Damascus Gate, photograph by Daniel Tassel.

Maps 1 through 4 drawn by Robert Forget.

COLOR PLATES

1. Courtesy of the Jewish National and Hebrew University Library, Jerusalem.
2. Photograph by Bouky Boaz.
3. Courtesy of the Israel Antiquities Authority, Jerusalem.
4. Courtesy of the Israel Museum, Jerusalem.
5. Laurentian Library, Florence, cod. Amiatinus 1, fol. 796v. Courtesy of the Laurentian Library, Florence.
6. Topkapi Seray Museum, Istanbul, Hazine 2154, fol. 107a. Courtesy of the collection of Oleg Grabar.
7. Photograph by Saïd Nuseibeh. © 1992 Saïd Nuseibeh Photography.
8. Courtesy of Nabil Anani.
9. Collection Lair, Musée du Château de Saumur. Courtesy of Musée du Château de Saumur. Cliché B. Renoux.
10. Photograph by Nahum Slapak. Courtesy of the Israel Museum, Jerusalem.

11. Uppsala University Library, C 691, fol. 39. Courtesy of the Uppsala University Library, Sweden.

FIGURES

1. Courtesy of Tel Dan Excavations, Israel.
2. Photograph by Ze'ev Radovan.
3. Photograph by Mendel John Diness (1856–1860). Courtesy of the John Barnier Collection, Archives for Historical Documentation, Brighton, Mass.
4. Photograph by Eli Ne'eman. Courtesy of the Tower of David, Museum of the History of Jerusalem, Jaffa Gate.
5. Courtesy of the Jewish National and Hebrew University Library, Jerusalem.
6. Photograph by Bonfils. Courtesy of the Ralph Marcove Collection, Archives for Historical Documentation, Brighton, Mass.
7. Photograph by Bonfils. Courtesy of the Fouad C. Debbas Collection, Archives for Historical Documentation, Brighton, Mass.
8. Photograph by Bonfils. Courtesy of the Fouad C. Debbas Collection, Archives for Historical Documentation, Brighton, Mass.
9. Bayerische Staatsbibliothek, Munich, cod. Lat. 30111, fol. 21r. Courtesy of the Bayerische Staatsbibliothek, Munich.
10. Photograph by Nitza Rosovsky.
11. Photograph by Bonfils. Courtesy of the Fouad C. Debbas Collection, Archives for Historical Documentation, Brighton, Mass.
12. Photograph by Nitza Rosovsky.
13. Photograph by Daniel Tassel.
14. Photograph by David Harris. Courtesy of Tower of David, Museum of the History of Jerusalem, Jaffa Gate.
15. Photograph by Bonfils. Courtesy of Daniel Tassel.
16. Photograph by Daniel Tassel.
17. Courtesy of Michele Piccirillo, Studium Biblicum Franciscanum, Jerusalem.
18. Municipal Library, Valenciennes, cod. 99, fol. 38r. Courtesy of the Municipal Library, Valenciennes.
19. The Pierpont Morgan Library, New York, ms. 644, fol. 222v. Courtesy of The Pierpont Morgan Library, New York.
20. Rijksmuseum-Stichting, RBK-17205. Courtesy of the Rijksmuseum-Stichting, Amsterdam.
21. The Cathedral Library, Cologne, cod. 83, II. Courtesy of the Cathedral Library, Cologne.
22. The Cathedral Library, Cologne, cod. 83, II. Courtesy of the Cathedral Library, Cologne.

23. Bayerische Staatsbibliothek, Munich, clm. 210, fol. 132. Courtesy of the Bayerische Staatsbibliothek, Munich.

24. Staatsbibliothek zu Berlin, ms. theol. lat. fol. 283, fol. 11r. Courtesy of Bildarchiv Foto, Marburg.

25. Herzog August Bibliothek, Wolfenbüttel, cod. Guelf. 1 Gud. lat., fol. 64v. Courtesy of the Herzog August Bibliothek, Wolfenbüttel.

26. Koninklijke Bibliotheek, The Hague, ms. 76 F 1, fol. 215r. Courtesy of the Koninklijke Bibliotheek, The Hague.

27. Staatsbibliothek, Bamberg, msc. Bibl. 140, fol. 55r. Courtesy of the Staatsbibliothek, Bamberg.

28. Metropolitan Museum of Art, New York, Gift of Edward S. Harkness, 1914 (14.7.1). Courtesy of the Metropolitan Museum of Art, New York.

29. The British Library, London, Add. 28681, fol. 9. By permission of the British Library, London.

30. The British Library, London, Harley 658, fol. 39v. By permission of the British Library, London.

31. Preusischer Kulturbesitz, Staatsbibliothek, Berlin, ms. Lat. fol. 2. 902, Bl. 14 r. Courtesy of the Staatsbibliothek, Berlin.

32. Courtesy of the Jewish National and Hebrew University Library, Jerusalem.

33. Courtesy of the Jewish National and Hebrew University Library, Jerusalem.

34. Courtesy of Centraal Museum, Utrecht.

35. Courtesy of the Gross family collection, Tel Aviv.

36. Museum of Popular Traditions, Aleppo. Courtesy of the collection of Oleg Grabar.

37. Copy of object in the Cathedral of the Dormition, Historical Museum, Moscow. Courtesy of the collection of Oleg Grabar.

38. Courtesy of Eretz Israel Museum, Tel Aviv.

39. Bibliothèque Municipale ms. 466, fol. 1. Courtesy of the Mediathèque Municipale de Cambri.

40. Koninklijke Bibliotheek, The Hague, 76 F 5, fol. 1r. Courtesy of the Koninklijke Biblioteek, The Hague.

41. The British Library, London, Add. 27376 fol. 189v. By permission of the British Library, London.

42. Bayerische Staatsbibliothek, Munich Cod. Iconog. 172. Courtesy of the Bayerische Staatsbibliothek, Munich.

43. Photograph by Y. Leehman. Courtesy of the Jewish National and Hebrew University Library, Jerusalem.

44. Photograph by Y. Leehman. Courtesy of the Jewish National and Hebrew University Library, Jerusalem.
45. Courtesy of the Jewish National and Hebrew University Library, Jerusalem.
46. Photograph by Y. Leehman. Courtesy of the Jewish National and Hebrew University Library, Jerusalem.
47. Fine Arts Library, Harvard College Library, 158. J 489 2A(i)1a 2. Courtesy of the Fine Arts Library, Harvard College Library.
48. Photograph by Sabri Jarrar.
49. Photograph by Sabri Jarrar.
50. Fine Arts Library, Harvard College Library, 158. J 489 5(Te (i) 1. Courtesy of the Fine Arts Library, Harvard College Library.
51. Photograph by Nitza Rosovsky.
52. Fine Arts Library, Harvard College Library, 158. J 489 13 HBQ 1b. Courtesy of the Fine Arts Library, Harvard College Library.
53. Fine Arts Library, Harvard College Library, 158. J 489 13 HSQ 1a. Courtesy of the Fine Arts Library, Harvard College Library.
54. Photograph by Sabri Jarrar.
55. Photograph by Sabri Jarrar.
56. From David Kroyanker, *Jerusalem Architecture* (New York: The Vendome Press, 1994). Courtesy of David Kroyanker.
57. Courtesy of David Kroyanker.
58. Courtesy of David Kroyanker.
59. Photograph by Nitza Rosovsky.
60. Photograph by Nitza Rosovsky.
61. Photograph by Nitza Rosovsky.
62. Courtesy of David Kroyanker.
63. From David Kroyanker, *Jerusalem Architecture* (New York: The Vendome Press, 1994). Courtesy of David Kroyanker.
64. Courtesy of David Kroyanker.
65. Photograph by A. Bernhein. Courtesy of the Israel Museum, Jerusalem.
66. From David Kroyanker, *Jerusalem Architecture* (New York: The Vendome Press, 1994). Courtesy of David Kroyanker.

Acknowledgments

The idea for this book came from Aida D. Donald, Assistant Director and Editor-in-Chief of Harvard University Press, who invited me to edit it two years ago.

In trying to decide which topics to include in a book that was to mark three thousand years in the history of a most complicated city—and who should be asked to write about such topics—I sought the advice of many. For their help, I am grateful to Fouad Ajami, Shalom Eilati, Shula and Shmuel Eisenstadt, Carney E. S. Gavin, Ben Zion Gold, James Kugel, Roy Muttahedeh, Martin Peretz, Ruth and Michael Rabin, Moshe Safdie, Irvin Scheiner, Ruth and Eytan Sheshinski, Krister Stendahl, and Yosef Yerushalmi. I wish to thank all the authors who participated in this volume, especially Magen Broshi, Joseph Dan, Oleg Grabar, Arthur Hertzberg, and F. E. Peters, who suggested the names of other participants. Special thanks are due to Elizabeth C. Carella, Herbert C. Kelman, Hava Lazarus-Yafeh, Naomi Miller, Judy Rosovsky, Danny Rubinstein, Jeffrey Spurr, Daniel Tassel, and Wheeler M. Thackston, Jr. I sorely miss the advice and enthusiasm of my late friend and coauthor, Joy Ungerleider-Mayerson, a lover of Jerusalem.

Isaac Hasson kindly allowed us to quote from an upcoming article. David Kroyanker generously shared with us his own photographs and illustrations, some of which appear in his book *Jerusalem Architecture* (New York: The Vendome Press, 1994). Permission has been granted by the following publishers to reprint selections of poetry: HarperCollins Publishers, Inc., for "Mayor" and "Too

Many" from *The Selected Poetry of Yehuda Amichai* by Yehuda Amichai, edited and translated by Chana Bloch and Stephen Mitchell, English translation copyright © 1986 by Chana Bloch and Stephen Mitchell, and Poem 52 from *Time* by Yehuda Amichai, copyright © 1979 by Yehuda Amichai; The Bialik Institute for a poem in *Be'livnat Ha'saphir—Shirim* by Avigdor Ha'meiri (1932); Ha'Kibbutz Ha'Meuhad Publishers for "Ir Ha'Tamid" in *Kol ha'Shirim* by Dan Pagis (1991); Am Oved Publishers for a poem in *Shirim* by Erza Zusman (1968); and Schocken Publishing House for "In Yemin Moshe" and "Poems for Rosh Hashana" in *Poems 1948–1962* by Yehuda Amichai, world copyrights © Schocken Publishing House Ltd.

Everyone I worked with at Harvard University Press was always helpful. I wish to thank Gail Graves for her good work, Marianne Perlak for the design of the book, Julie Hagen for her capable editing, and Susan Wallace Boehmer, who shepherded this project calmly and efficiently. Most of all I am grateful to Aida Donald, who, like a good godmother, was there when the book and I needed her.

My husband, Henry Rosovsky, has always been generous with both criticism and support, and I am most grateful to him for his patience and his help. And finally I wish to thank Teddy Kollek, who had nothing to do with this book but who nurtured Jerusalem wisely and lovingly through many difficult years. Along with King David, Mayor Kollek deserves praise and gratitude from all those who care about the city.

It is almost impossible to be consistent in the transliteration of Arabic and Hebrew. We generally preferred to use traditional spellings for words that have become part of the English language—for example, "Koran" rather than "Qur'an." *Revolt in the Desert* opens with a "Publisher's Note" in which two pages of correspondence between an exasperated proofreader and T. E. Lawrence are reproduced: "Q. 'Jedha, the camel, was Jedhah on slip 40.' A. 'She was a splendid beast.'" Lawrence went on to say that while there are some "scientific systems" of transliteration, they are "helpful to people who know enough Arabic not to need helping, but a washout for the world. I spell my names anyhow, to show what rot the systems are."